CW01637445

hugo

ENGLISH DICTIONARY

HUGO'S LANGUAGE BOOKS LTD
LONDON

FIRST PUBLISHED 1973

This impression 1987

© 1973 Hugo's Language Books Ltd
ISBN 0 85285 063 8

Compiled and edited by
D. M. Caswell and R. Batchelor-Smith

Printed in Great Britain

PREFACE

This English Dictionary has been produced in reply to the great demand for a really compact edition similar to Hugo's world-famous range of foreign language dictionaries, and has our many years of experience in this field behind it.

Every effort has been made to include most important words in use today, and in order to accommodate these many have been 'hung on' to a headword from which their meaning may be deduced. Hence, 'attract' is fully explained; 'attraction', 'attractive', 'attractively' and 'attractiveness' follow this verb. Alphabetical order is sometimes sacrificed here: 'reputable' and 'reputation' follow the headword 'repute'. To save space, we do not give pronunciation and use common abbreviations. Thus, *pt* & *pp* indicate the past tense and past participle—given for all truly irregular verbs.

Inevitably, some words have been left out; we hope none is too serious an omission. The English language's vocabulary is expanding rapidly and careful thought must be given to those 'vogue' words which may never stay in permanent use. We trust this dictionary will be found helpful by all—students both young and old, English and foreign; businessmen and office secretaries, and as a handy book in the home.

ABBREVIATIONS USED IN THIS DICTIONARY

a, as adjective(s)
abbrev abbreviation
adv, advs adverb(s)
anat anatomical
ar archaic
archi architecture
Aust Australian
biol biological
bot botanical
cap capital initial
chem chemical
coll colloquial
collect collective
comp comparative
conj cunjunction
dem demonstrative
eccles ecclesiastic
elect electrical
esp especially
fem feminine
fig figuratively
geog geography
geom geometry
geol geology
her heraldry
hist historical
hort horticulture
interj interjection
interrog interrogative
leg legal
lit literally
masc masculine
mech mechanics
med medical
mil military
mus music
myth mythology
n, ns noun(s)
naut nautical
obs obsolete
[**P**] proprietary name
pass passive
photo photography
pl plural
poet poetical
poss possessive
pp past participle
prep preposition
print printing
pron, prons pronoun(s)
pr p present participle
psyc psychology
rad radio
RC Roman Catholic
reflex reflexive
rel relative
Scot Scottish
sing singular
sl slang
specif specifically
sup superlative
theo theological
usu usually
v, vs verb(s)
v aux auxiliary verb
vul vulgar

ENGLISH DICTIONARY

a, an *a* indefinite article meaning one.
aardvark *n* S. African ant-eating mammal.
aback *a & adv* backwards, back; **taken—**, startled.
abacus *n* counting-frame with beads strung on parallel wires; *pl* **abacuses.**
abaft *adv & prep* towards the stern of ship; behind.
abalone *n* mollusc, shell lined with mother-of-pearl.
abandon *v* give up, forsake, desert; *a* **abandoned** unrestrained, profligate; *ns* **abandonment, abandon.**
abase *v* humble, humiliate; *n* **abasement.**
abash *v* embarrass, cause to feel shy; *n* **abashment.**
abate *v* become less or lower; *n* **abatement.**
abattoir *n* slaughter-house.
abbey *n* religious house of priests or nuns; building occupied by such a community.
abbot *n* head of abbey or monastery; *fem* **abbess.**
abbreviate *v* shorten; *n* **abbreviation.**
abdicate *v* relinquish power, surrender a throne; *n* **abdication.**
abdomen *n* belly; *a* **abdominal.**
abduct *v* carry off unlawfully, kidnap; *n* **abduction.**
abeam *adv* at right angles to a ship's keel.
abed *adv* in bed.
abele *n* white poplar.
aberration *n* wandering from natural or fixed course; mental disorder; *a* **aberrant.**
abet *v* help or take part in (offence); *n* **abettor.**
abeyance *n* state of ineffectiveness, suspension.
abhor *v* detest, loathe; *a* **abhorrent**; *n* **abhorrence.**
abide *v* dwell, remain at a place; endure; *pt & pp* **abode; abide by** be faithful to; *a* **abiding** lasting.
ability *n* power to do something; cleverness.
abject *a* miserable, cast down, servile; *adv* **abjectly**; *n* **abjectness.**
abjure *v* renounce on oath; *ns* **abjurer, abjuration.**
ablative *n* Latin case of nouns expressing origin, direction from, cause.

ablaut *n* gradation of vowel sounds, indicating changes of tense or meaning.
ablaze *a* & *adv* on fire, blazing.
able *a* having the power or skill to do a thing; clever, talented; *adv* **ably**; *n* **ability**.
ablution *n* act of washing *esp* of person; ceremonial act of cleansing; *a* **ablutionary**.
abnegate *v* deny oneself, renounce; *n* **abnegation**.
abnormal *a* out of ordinary, deviating from normal; *adv* **abnormally**; *n* **abnormality**.
aboard *adv* in or on a ship, train, aeroplane etc.
abode *n* home, dwelling place; *pt* & *pp* of **abide**.
abolish *v* do away with, wipe out; *ns* **abolition**; **abolitionist** one who favours abolition.
abominate *v* detest, loathe; *a* **abominable**; *adv* **abominably**; *n* **abomination** object of disgust.
aborigines *n pl* primitive natives; *a* **aboriginal** existing from beginning *esp* races, flora & fauna.
abortion *n* natural or induced miscarriage of foetus; something misshapen, unnatural; *v* **abort** to miscarry; to cause this; stop (space flight) prematurely; *a* **abortive** futile, incomplete.
abound *v* be plentiful, well-supplied; *a* **abounding**.
about *prep* concerning, on the subject of; around; nearly; *adv* in the opposite direction.
above *prep* over, higher than, more than; *adv* & *a* overhead; *n* **the above**, something mentioned before (in business letters).
abracadabra *n* magic formula; spell; gibberish.
abrade *v* rub or wear off; *n* & *a* **abrasive**; *n* **abrasion** place where skin is scraped off, sore so caused.
abreast *adv* & *a* side by side; on a line with.
abridge *v* shorten, condense; *n* **abridg(e)ment**.
abroad *adv* in another country; outdoors, at large.
abrogate *v* repeal, annul; *n* **abrogation**.
abrupt *a* gruff, sudden; *adv* **abruptly**; *n* **abruptness**.
abscess *n* inflamed swelling containing pus.
abscond *v* run away secretly, *esp* to escape law.
absent *a* not present, inattentive; *v* stay away; *adv* **absently**; *ns* **absence**; **absentee** one who is not present, habitually absent; **absenteeism**.
absinthe *n* wormwood; liqueur flavoured with this.

absolute *a* unlimited; independent of other factors; undiluted, pure; *adv* **absolutely**; *n* **absoluteness.**
absolve *v* pronounce free from sin; release from obligation; pardon; *n* **absolution.**
absorb *v* take in, soak up, swallow up; *adj* **absorbing** engrossing; *ns* **absorbent, absorption.**
abstain *v* keep from, refrain from (*esp* alcohol); *ns* **abstainer; abstinence;** *a* **abstinent.**
abstemious *a* temperate; not given to excess, *esp* in food and drink; *adv* **abstemiously;** *n* **abstemiousness.**
abstract *a* withdrawn from reality; *n* summary; *v* steal; take away; *a* **abstracted** absent-minded; *n* **abstraction;** *advs* **abstractedly, abstractly.**
abstruse *a* difficult to understand; obscure; *adv* **abstrusely ;** *n* **abstruseness.**
absurd *a* unreasonable; ridiculous; *adv* **absurdly;** *ns* **absurdity, absurdness.**
abundance *n* plenty; *a* **abundant;** *adv* **abundantly.**
abuse *v* misuse; betray trust; insult; *ns* **abuse; abusiveness;** *a* **abusive;** *adv* **abusively.**
abut *v* border on; *n* **abutment** support of arch.
abysm *n* abyss; *a* **abysmal;** *adv* **abysmally.**
abyss *n* bottomless pit; *a* **abyssal.**
acacia *n* genus of thorny trees.
academy *n* place of higher education; society for advancement of learning; *n* **academician;** *a* **academic** pedantic; *adv* **academically.**
acanthus *n* genus of prickly leaved plants; leaf shape used in architectural decorations.
acaudal, acaudate *a* tailless.
accede *v* succeed to; give consent or support; comply with; *n* **accedence.**
accelerate *v* increase speed; *ns* **accelerator** device for increasing speed in machines etc; **acceleration.**
accent *n* stress or emphasis; mark used to indicate sound of vowel; manner of pronunciation; *v* stress, accentuate; *n* **accentuation.**
accept *v* receive; take; admit; believe in; agree to; *a* **acceptable;** *ns* **acceptability, acceptance.**
access *n* means of approach; right of entry;

a **accessible** easy to reach, approach; *ns* **accessibility; accession** coming to throne, office.
accessary *n* helper *esp* in crime (*a* also).
accessory *a* contributing; *n* additional equipment.
accidence *n* part of grammar dealing with the variable forms of words.
accident *n* unexpected event; mishap; *a* **accidental** *adv* **accidentally.**
acclaim *n* loud applause; welcome; approval; *v* **applaud;** *n* **acclamation;** *a* **acclamatory.**
acclimatize *v* adapt to new climate; *n* **acclimatization.**
acclivity *n* upward slope of a hill.
accolade *n* light stroke with sword used in bestowing knighthood; any supreme reward.
accommodate *v* fit; lodge; help by act of kindness; *a* **accommodating** obliging; *n* **accommodation** lodgings.
accompany *v* go with; escort; play music supporting (a soloist); *ns* **accompanist, accompaniment.**
accomplice *n* partner in crime; confederate.
accomplish *v* finish; bring to successful conclusion; *a* **accomplished** finished; talented; *n* **accomplishment.**
accord *v* be in harmony; agree; bestow; *a* **according;** *n* **accordance** agreement; *adv* **accordingly** therefore.
accordion *n* musical instrument with bellows, keys & metal reeds.
accost *v* speak first to; solicit (of prostitute).
account *v* estimate; explain; give statement (money); *n* record of money transactions; description; *n* **accountant** one who keeps or audits accounts; *a* **accountable** answerable; *adv* **accountably.**
accredit *v* appoint with credentials; recognize.
accrue *v* increase, *esp* interest on invested money.
accumulate *v* amass; increase in mass or number; *ns* **accumulation; accumulator** apparatus for storing electrical or hydraulic energy; *a* **accumulative.**
accurate *a* exact in detail; precise; *ns* **accuracy, accurateness;** *adv* **accurately.**
accurse *v* curse; *a* **accursed (accurst)** under a

curse; ill-fated; detestable; *adv* **accursedly.**
accuse *v* bring charge against; blame; *ns* **accuser, accusation**; *as* **accusative** grammatical case expressing direct object of a verb.
accustom *v* make familiar; get used to; *a* **accustomed.**
ace *n* single spot on dice or cards; highest; best.
acerbate *v* make sour or bitter; irritate; *n* **acerbity.**
acetate *n* salt of acetic acid.
acetic *a* pertaining to vinegar; *(specif)* **acetic acid** organic acid giving vinegar characteristic taste.
acetone *n* inflammable liquid used as a solvent.
acetylene *n* inflammable gas formed by the action of water on calcium carbonate.
ache *v* suffer dull, continuous pain, physically or emotionally; *n* dull, continuous pain.
achieve *v* finish; gain; win; *n* **achievement.**
achromatic *a* colourless.
acid *n* sour substance as vinegar, usually having corrosive effect; *a* sour & sharp to taste; sharp-tempered; *ns* **acidity, acidness**; *adv* **acidly.**
acidosis *n* an acid condition of the blood.
aciform *a* sharp, fine, like needle or bristle.
acknowledge *v* admit; recognize as true; indicate receipt of; *n* **acknowledg(e)ment** recognition of; *a* **acknowledgeable.**
acme *n* highest point; summit; perfection.
acne *n* pimples; common skin disease.
acolyte *n* one holding minor orders in Church; priest's attendant; any devoted assistant.
aconite *n* poisonous plants Monkshood & Wolf's Bane; a drug obtained from such plants.
acorn *n* the fruit of the oak tree.
acoustic *a* connected with hearing or sound; *adv* **acoustically**; *n* **acoustics** theory of sound.
acquaint *v* inform; make aware of; *ns* **acquaintance** person slightly known; **acquaintanceship.**
acquiesce *v* agree passively or tacitly; *n* **acquiescence**; *a* **acquiescent.**
acquire *v* get or gain possession of; *n* **acquisition** act of gaining; object gained; *a* **acquisitive** desirous of gain; *n* **acquisitiveness.**

acquit *v* declare not guilty (of offence); cancel debt; behave oneself; *ns* **acquittal** release by court; **acquittance** release from debt, *esp* written evidence.
acre *n* measure of land (4840 sq. yds); *n* **acreage** acres collectively.
acrid *a* bitter; caustic; *n* **acridity**; *adv* **acridly**.
acrimony *n* severity, asperity of manner or speech; *a* **acrimonious**; *adv* **acrimoniously**.
acrobat *n* highly skilled gymnast; *n* **acrobatics**; *a* **acrobatic**; *adv* **acrobatically**.
acropolis *n* high fortified part of Greek city.
across *prep* & *adv* on other side; from side to side; to the other side; crosswise.
acrostic *n* verse or puzzle in which first and/or last letters, reading across and down, make words.
act *n* thing done; division of play or opera; legislative measure; *v* perform on stage; carry out duties; influence; behave; *ns* **actor, actress**; *a* **acting** performing another's duties.
actinium *n* a radio-active element.
action *n* act; influence; movement of working parts of machine; lawsuit; battle; events of play or novel; *a* **actionable** giving cause for lawsuit.
active *a* in action; quick; lively; *adv* **actively**; *v* **activate** make active; set in motion.
activity *n* agility; liveliness; motion; pursuit.
actual *a* really existing now; *v* **actualize** make actual; *adv* **actually**.
actuary *n* expert who calculates insurance risks; *a* **actuarial**.
actuate *v* stir up; put in action; cause to work.
acumen *n* sharpness of wit or intelligence.
acute *a* sharp; keenly intelligent; shrill; critical; *n* **acuteness**; *adv* **acutely**.
adage *n* an old saying; a popular proverb.
adagio *n* a slow movement in music.
adamant *n* hard, unyielding substance; *a* stubborn; *a* **adamantine** extremely hard.
adapt *v* modify; make fit for new use; conform to changed circumstances; *a* **adaptable**; *ns* **adaptability**; **adaptation**; **adapter** one who adapts; **adaptor** thing which adapts.

add *v* join; say further; *ns* **addition**; **additive** something added; *a* **additional**; *adv* **additionally**.
addendum *n* a thing to be added; *pl* **addenda**.
adder *n* small venomous snake of viper family.
addict *v* give (oneself) up to; habituate; *n* one so addicted (to drugs, drink); *n* **addiction**; *a* **addicted**
addle *v* make confused; go bad.
address *v* to speak to; write destination on; apply (oneself to); call by conventional title; *n* formal speech; place where one lives; bearing; promptness; *ns* **addressee**; person addressed; **addresser**.
adduce *v* cite as proof; *as* **adduceable, adducible**.
adenoids *npl* growths at back of nose, near throat.
adept *a* expert; *n* skilled person; expert; *adv* **adeptly**.
adequate *a* equal to; competent for; sufficient; *adv* **adequately**; *ns* **adequateness, adequacy**.
adhere *v* stick to; give allegiance to; *n* **adherence** state of adhering; *n* & *a* **adherent**.
adhesion *n* act of adhering; *n* & *a* **adhesive**; *adv* **adhesively**; *n* **adhesiveness**.
adieu *interj* & *n* goodbye; *pl* **adieus** or **adieux**.
adipose *a* fatty; *n* **adiposity**.
adjacent *a* lying near to; adjoining; *adv* **adjacently**.
adjective *n* word used to qualify a noun; *a* **adjectival**
adjoin *v* be next to; *a* **adjoining** neighbouring.
adjourn *v* put off, postpone; *n* **adjournment**.
adjudge *v* judge according to law; grant or award.
adjudicate *v* judge; pronounce judgment on; act as a judge; *ns* **adjudicator, adjudication**.
adjunct *n* subordinate thing added to another.
adjure *v* charge under solemn oath; *n* **adjuration**.
adjust *v* fit; arrange; *a* **adjustable**; *n* **adjustment**.
adjutant *n* officer assisting C.O. administratively.
administer *v* manage; dispense (justice); give (aid) to *ns* **administrator, administration**; *a* **administrative**.
admiral *n* naval officer commanding fleet; *n* **admiralty** board that controls naval affairs.
admire *v* regard with pleasure or esteem; *a* **admirable** worthy of esteem; *adv* **admirably**; *ns* **admiration, admirer**.
admit *v* give access to; confess; *ns* **admittance**;

admission fact conceded as true; entrance fee; *a* **admissible**; *adv* **admissibly, admittedly.**
admix *v* mix with something else; *n* **admixture.**
admonish *v* warn; reprove; *n* **admonition**; *a* **admonitory.**
ado *n* fuss; pother; trouble; bustle.
adobe *n* clay brick dried in the sun.
adolescence *n* state of growing up; *a* & *n* **adolescent** boy, girl growing up.
adopt *v* take and bring up as one's own child; accept formally; *n* **adoption**; *a* **adopted**; *n* **adoptability.**
adore *v* worship; regard with lavish affection, love; *n* **adoration**; *a* **adorable**; *adv* **adorably.**
adorn *v* beautify; embellish; *n* **adornment** decoration.
adrenal *a* near kidney; *n* **adrenalin** hormone produced in adrenal glands.
adrift *a* & *adv* loose on water; without purpose.
adroit *a* dexterous; *adv* **adroitly**; *n* **adroitnes.**
adulate *v* flatter servilely; *ns* **adulation**; *a* **adulatory**
adult *a* & *n* grown-up; mature.
adulterate *v* corrupt; make impure; *n* **adulteration.**
adultery *n* sexual infidelity in marriage; *n* **adulterer, adulteress** (fem); *a* **adulterous.**
advance *v* move forward; lend money; promote; *a* **advanced** in front rank; elderly; having ultra-modern ideas etc; *n* **advancement** promotion.
advantage *n* favourable condition; *a* **advantageous**; *adv* **advantageously.**
advent *n* coming, *esp* of Christ; four weeks preceding Christmas; *n* **Adventism** belief in Millennium.
adventitious *a* accidental; casual.
adventure *n* exciting incident; hazardous exploit; *n* **adventurer** one who lives by his wits; *a* **adventurous**; *adv* **adventurously.**
adverb *n* word qualifying verb, adjective or another adverb; *a* **adverbial.**
adversary *n* enemy; opponent; *a* **adverse** unfavourable; *adv* **adversely**; *n* **adversity** misfortune, affliction.
advertise *v* give public notice of; inform; *ns* **advertisement, advertiser, advertising.**

advice *n* counsel; guidance; information.
advise *v* give advice to; inform of; *n* **adviser**; *adv* **advisedly** expedient; *as* **advisable, advisory.**
advocate *v* plead on behalf of cause etc; recommend; *n* one who pleads in court of law, *specif* Scottish.
adze *n* curved bladed tool for cutting wood surface.
aegis *n* patronage; protection; auspices.
aeon *n* a great age of time; eternity.
aerate *v* expose to air; charge with gas; *n* **aeration.**
aerial *a* of, in, like air; *n* antenna, rod or wire for receiving or sending electromagnetic waves.
aerie *n* nest of eagle or other bird of prey.
aerobatics *n* spectacular flying display.
aerodrome *n* area of level ground for aircraft.
aerodynamics *n* branch of physics dealing with forces exerted by moving air or gases; science of flight; *a* **aerodynamic**; *adv* **aerodynamically.**
aerofoil *n* aeroplane wing.
aeronaut *n* flyer of balloon or aircraft; *n* **aeronautics** science of air navigation; *as* **aeronautic, aeronautical.**
aeroplane *n* heavier-than-air flying machine driven by high-powered engine(s).
aerosol *n* spray of suspension of particles in gas.
aesthete *n* one who appreciates beauty, *esp* art; *a* **aesthetic**, *adv* **aesthetically**, *n* **aesthetics.**
afar *adv* at, to or from a distance.
affable *a* friendly; polite; *adv* **affably**; *n* **affability.**
affair *n* social event; irregular sexual relationship; *pl* business of any kind; transactions.
affect *v* act upon; influence; work on feelings; *ns* **affectation** show; **affection** love; *a* **affectionate**; *adv* **affectionately**; *n* **affectionateness.**
affiance *v* betroth; *a* & *n* **affianced** become engaged.
affidavit *n* written statement made under oath.
affiliate *v* accept persons, societies as members of institution; determine paternity; *n* **affiliation.**
affinity *n* kinship (by marriage); chemical attraction; relationship between, implying common origin.
affirm *v* declare positively; confirm; *n* **affirmation**; *n* & *a* **affirmative**; *adv* **affirmatively.**
affix *v* fix; fasten; *n* addition *esp* to word; to modify.

afflict *v* cause to suffer; *a* **afflicted**; *n* **affliction.**
affluence *n* wealth; *n* **affluent**, tributary stream; *a* **affluent**; *adv* **affluently.**
afford *v* have means for; supply; furnish; yield.
afforest *v* plant trees on; *n* **afforestation.**
affray *n* a public fight; quarrel; riot.
affright *n* sudden terror; alarm; *v* to frighten.
affront *v* insult; offend; *n* impudent or defiant act.
afield *adv* to, in or on the field; astray.
afire *a* & *adv* on fire; burning.
aflame *a* & *adv* in flames; on fire.
afloat *a* & *adv* floating; in circulation.
afraid *a* frightened; timid; feeling fear.
afresh *adv* again; anew; once more.
aft *adv* at, toward or near stern of vessel.
after *adv* later; behind; *prep* imitating; *ns* **aftermath** result; **afternoon, afterthought**; *adv* **afterwards.**
again *adv* once more; return back.
against *prep* close to: opposite; in anticipation of.
agape *a* & *adv* gaping.
agate *n* a semiprecious stone.
age *n* length of time, thing or person has existed; historical period; closing years of life; *v* grow old; *a* **aged**; **ageless** timeless.
agenda *a* list of things to be discussed at meeting.
agent *n* one who acts for person or company; natural force; *n* **agency** occupation or place of business of an agent; activity.
agglutinate *v* glue together; *n* **agglutination.**
aggrandize *v* make greater in power, rank or wealth; *n* **aggrandizement.**
aggravate *v* make worse; annoy; *a* **aggravating.**
aggregate *n* entire sum; *v* collect; *n* **aggregation.**
aggress *v* begin a quarrel; *a* **aggressive** rude.
agress *v* begin a quarrel; *a* **aggressive**, rude, offensive; *adv* **aggressively**; *ns* **aggression**; **aggressor.**
aggrieve *v* hurt; cause distress to; **aggrieved.**
aghast *a* struck with horror or amazement.
agile *a* active; nimble; *adv* **agilely**; *n* **agility.**
agitate *v* disturb; shake violently; stir up unrest; *ns* **agitation, agitator.**

aglow *a* & *adv* glowing; in a glow.
agnostic *n* one believing that nothing can be known concerning God; *n* **agnosticism** theory of this belief.
ago *adv* gone by; in the past.
agog *a* & *adv* excited; eagerly anticipating.
agony *n* anguish of mind or body; *v* **agonize**; *a* **agonizingly**.
agoraphobia *n* morbid fear of open spaces.
agrarian *a* relating or belonging to land.
agree *v* consent (to); settle; concede (that) *as* **agreed**; **agreeable** pleasant; *adv* **agreeably**; *n* **agreement**.
agriculture *n* art and theory of farming.
aground *a* & *adv* grounded; beached; stranded (on shore).
ague *n* fever accompanied by shivering fits.
ahead *adv* in front; in advance; forward.
ahoy *interj* a call used in hailing (a ship).
aid *v* help in any way; *n* support; money loan.
aide-de-camp *n* officer assisting a general.
ail *v* be out of health; *a* **ailing**; *n* **ailment**.
aim *v* point weapon; direct energy towards; *n*; *a* **aimless**; *adv* **aimlessly**; *n* **aimlessness**.
air *n* gaseous substance around the earth; manner; tune; *pl* affected manner; *as* **airy, airless**; *adv* **airily**; *n* **airing** exposure to air; outing in open air.
air-brake *n* brake worked by compressed air.
air-brush *n* device used for spraying paint or ink.
air-condition *v* treat air to ensure purity and even temperature; *n* **air-conditioning**.
air-cooled *a* cooled, *esp* engines, by currents of air.
aircraft *n* any kind of flying machine.
aircraft-carrier *n* ship designed to carry aircraft.
Airedale *n* large kind of terrier.
airfield *n* place where aircraft land or take off.
air-gun *n* gun discharged by compressed air.
airline *n* company operating aircraft on regular route; **air-liner** aircraft used by airline.
airmail *n* mail carried by aircraft.
airman *n* a member of the crew of an aircraft.
air-pocket *n* current causing aircraft to drop suddenly.

airport *n* aerodrome for transport of passengers etc.
air raid *n* raid by aircraft dropping bombs.
airscrew *n* aircraft propeller.
airship *n* flying machine supported by gas bags.
air-strip *n* narrow runway for use by aircraft.
airtight *a* impermeable to air.
airworthy *a* fit or safe to fly; *n* **airworthiness.**
aisle *n* passageway between seats or pews.
aitch-bone *n* rump bone; cut of meat from this.
ajar *a* & *adv* partly open.
akimbo *adv* with hands on hip and elbows bent.
akin *a* related by blood; alike; similar.
alabaster *n* smooth, white; opaque form of gypsum.
alack *interj* expressing dismay, regret, sorrow.
alacrity *n* speed; briskness; eagerness.
alarm *n* call to arms; warning of danger; *v* fill with fear; *a* **alarming**; *adv* **alarmingly**; *n* **alarmist.**
alas *interj* expressing dismay, grief, sorrow.
alb *n* long, white linen robe worn by priests.
albatross *n* large seabird of the petrel type.
albeit *conj* even though; notwithstanding.
albino *n* man or animal with white skin and hair, and pink eyes due to lack of pigment; *pl* **albinos.**
album *n* book of blank pages for stamps, photographs etc.
albumen *n* white of a bird's egg.
alchemy *n* mediaeval chemistry; *n* **alchemist.**
alcohol *n* pure spirit of wine; intoxicating liquor; *a* **alcoholic**; *ns* **alcoholism** disease due to excessive drinking of alcohol; **alcoholic** one so addicted.
alcove *n* recess in room or garden; artificial bower.
alder *n* tree of the birch family.
alderman *n* senior councillor in borough or city.
ale *n* kind of beer.
alert *a* ready in body or mind; *n* **alertness.**
alfresco *adv* & *a* in the open air.
alga *n* lowly organized plant, as seaweed etc; *pl* **algae.**
algebra *n* branch of mathematics using symbols for number & quantity; *a* **algebraic**; *adv* **algebraically**
alias *adv* otherwise; *n* false name; *pl* **aliases.**
alibi *n* proof of being elsewhere when crime was

committed; *pl* **alibis.**
alien *a* foreign; repugnant; *n*; *v* **alienate** estrange; *ns* **alienation**; **alienist** specialist in mental disease.
alight *a* lit; *v* dismount; come to rest.
align *v* bring into line; *n* **alignment.**
alike *a* similar; *adv* to same degree.
aliment *n* food; *a* **alimentary** of food channel in body.
alimony *n* allowance to wife after legal separation.
aliquant *a* not dividing without remainder.
aliquot *a* dividing exactly without remainder.
alive *a* living; aware; alert; sensitive; swarming.
alizarin *n* synthetic red dye.
alkali *n* potash; substance neutralizing acid; *a* **alkaline.**
all *a* whole of; full number of; total; *n* everything, everyone; one's whole property; *adv* entirely.
allay *v* ease; soothe; make more bearable.
allege *v* state as fact; *a* **alleged**; *n* **allegation.**
allegiance *n* loyalty.
allegory *n* story with moral; *a* **allegoric.**
allegretto *n* & *a* fast musical movement, rather slower than **allegro.**
allergy *n* abnormal sensitiveness to any substance; *a* **allergic.**
alleviate *v* lighten; relieve (pain); *a* **alleviation.**
alley *n* narrow passage between houses; *pl* **alleys.**
alliance *n* treaty between States.
alligator *n* reptile of crocodile family.
alliteration *n* recurrence of same stressed sounds in verse or prose; *a* **alliterative.**
allocate *v* grant; assign (to); *n* **allocation.**
allot *v* assign as lot; *n* **allotment** share; plot of land.
allow *v* permit; grant; *n* **allowance.**
alloy *n* mixture of two or more metals.
allspice *n* pungent W. Indian spice.
allude *v* refer to; *n* **allusion**; *a* **allusive.**
allure *v* attract; *a* **alluring**; *ns* **allure, allurement.**
alluvium *n* soil deposited by water; *a* **alluvial.**
ally *v* combined, joined by treaty; *n* States associated by treaty; *pl* **allies.**
almanac, almanack *n* calendar of months and days.

almighty *a* omnipotent; *n* **the Almighty** God.
almond *n* kernel of fruit of almond-tree.
almoner *n* official distributor of alms.
almost *adv* very nearly; not quite.
alms *n* money given in charity to poor; **almshouse** endowed home for poor and aged people.
aloe *n* genus of plant, leaves yielding bitter juice.
aloft *adv* on high; overhead.
alone *a* & *adv* single; apart from others; unsupported.
along *prep* beside whole or part of length of; *adv* lengthwise; **alongside** at side of.
aloof *adv* apart from; *a* haughty; *n* **aloofness**.
alopecia *n* baldness.
aloud *adv* in an audible voice; loudly.
alp *n* mountain pasture; *a* **alpine**; *n* **alpinist** climber.
alpaca *n* kind of llama; fabric made from its wool.
alphabet *n* letters used in a language; the A.B.C.; *a* **alphabetical**; *adv* **alphabetically**.
already *adv* before this; by this time.
also *adv* & *conj* besides; in addition; as well.
altar *n* Communion table; slab used for sacrifices.
alter *v* change; *a* **alterable**; *n* **alteration**.
altercate *v* dispute angrily (with); *n* **altercation**.
alternate *a* occurring by turns; *v*; *n* **alternative** choice; *adv* **alternately**; *n* **alternating current** electricity reversing direction of flow regularly.
although *conj* even though; notwithstanding.
altimeter *n* instrument measuring height above sea.
altitude *n* height above sea level.
alto *n* highest male or lowest female voice.
altogether *adv* completely; wholly; in the main.
altruism *n* unselfishness; *a* **altruistic**; *n* **altruist**.
alum *n* mineral salt; crystalline substance used as astringent.
aluminium *n* white metal of remarkable lightness.
alumnus *n* graduate of university; *pl* **alumni**.
alveolus *n* small cavity; *a* **alveolate**; *pl* **alveoli**.
always *adv* at all times; invariably.
amalgam *n* mixture; *v* **amalgamate** unite; *n* **amalgamation**.
amanuensis *n* literary assistant; secretary.
amaryllis *n* bulbous plant with lily-like flowers.

amass *v* heap together; pile up.
amateur *n* person following pursuit for love of it, not to make money; *a* **amateurish** not well done.
amatory *a* relating to love.
amaze *v* astound; *a* **amazing**; *n* **amazement.**
Amazon *n* legendary female warrior.
ambassador *n* diplomat representing his country at foreign court; *fem* **ambassadress.**
amber *n* hard yellow fossil resin.
ambergris *n* secretion of sperm-whale used in perfume.
ambidextrous *a* able to use both hands equally.
ambient *a* entirely surrounding.
ambiguous *a* not clear in meaning; *n* **ambiguity.**
ambit *n* full scope; compass; extent.
ambition *n* strong desire for success; *a* **ambitious.**
amble *v* move at easy pace, *esp* horse; walk easily.
ambrosia *n* food of gods; *a* **ambrosial** tasting delicious.
ambulance *n* vehicle for carrying sick and wounded.
ambulatory *a* connected with walking; *v* **ambulate** walk.
ambush *n* surprise attack; *v* waylay.
ameliorate *v* improve; *n* **amelioration**; *a* **ameliorative.**
amen *interj* 'So be it'; *n* word of assent.
amenable *a* tractable; submissive; *n* **amenability**; *adv* **amenably.**
amend *v* improve; correct; *ns* **amendment, amends,** reparation.
amenity *n* desirable feature; pleasantness.
amethyst *n* purple kind of quartz; its colour.
amiable *a* kindly; lovable; *adv* **amiably**; *n* **amiability.**
amicable *a* friendly; *adv* **amicably**; *n* **amicability.**
amid(st) *prep* in middle of; among.
amidships *adv* in middle of ship.
amir, emir *n* title of Mohammedan ruler.
amiss *adv* wrongly; *a* faulty.
amity *n* friendship; good relations.
ammeter *n* meter for measuring ampere units.
ammonia *n* pungent, colourless gas; *a* **ammoniac.**

ammonite *n* fossil shell like ram's horn.
ammunition *n* gunpowder, bullets, shells, etc.
amnesia *n* loss of memory.
amnesty *n* pardon given to offenders against State.
amoeba *n* microscopic one-celled animal.
amok, amuck *adv* in a frenzy; *v* **run amok** get out of control.
among, amongst *prep* in midst of; by joint or mutual action of.
amoral *a* without morals; *n* **amorality.**
amorous *a* prone to love; *adv* **amorously.**
amorphous *a* formless.
amortize *v* pay off a debt gradually.
amount *v* add up to; *n* sum total; quantity.
amour *n* a love affair (usually illicit).
ampere *n* electric unit of force; *n* **amperage.**
ampersand *n* the sign & (meaning 'and').
amphetamine *n* inhalant or stimulant drug.
amphibian *n* animal or vehicle able to live or operate on land or in water; *a* **amphibious.**
amphitheatre *n* arena surrounded by tiered seats.
amphora *n* Greek or Roman jar; *pl* **amphorae.**
ample *a* plenty; large; *adv* **amply**; *n* **ampleness**; *v* **amplify** make louder; *ns* **amplifier, amplification.**
ampoule *n* glass tube holding dose of drug.
amputate *v* cut off part of body; *n* **amputation.**
amulet *n* talisman; charm *esp* hung round neck.
amuse *v* provoke mirth or interest; divert; *a* **amusing**; *adv* **amusingly**; *n* **amusement.**
anabolism *n* building up process of metabolism.
anachronism *n* event or thing incongruous to period at which it happens or exists.
anaconda *n* large S. American snake of boa family.
anaemia *n* lack of red corpuscles in blood; *a* **anaemic**
anaesthesia *n* insensibility caused by drugs or disease; *ns* **anaesthetic**; **anaesthetist** one who gives anaesthetic.
anagram *n* word made by re-arranging letters in another word; *a* **anagrammatic**; *adv* **anagrammatically.**
analgesia *n* absence of pain; *a* **analgesic** pain killing.

analogy *n* similarity; *a* **analogous**; *adv* **analogically**.
analyse *v* (*gram*) examine minutely structure of sentence; break down into smallest parts; *a* **analytic**; *adv* **analytically**; *ns* **analysis, analyst.**
anarchy *n* no supreme power in State; lawlessness; *n* **anarchism** practice of anarchy; *n* **anarchist.**
anathema *n* curse; hateful thing; *v* **anathematize.**
anatomy *n* science of structure of body; *a* **anatomical**; *v* **anatomize** dissect; *n* **anatomist.**
ancestor *n* forebear; *a* **ancestral**; *n* **ancestry** lineage.
anchor *n* mass of iron, securing ships to sea-bed; *v* fasten by anchor; *n* **anchorage**, place for anchoring.
anchorite *n* a hermit; recluse; *fem* **anchoress.**
anchovy *n* small fish of the herring type.
ancient *a* belonging to distant past; very old.
ancillary *a* subordinate; auxiliary.
and *conj* word joining words, phrases; also; as well as.
andante *adv* (play music) slowly.
andiron *n* iron bracket for supporting burning logs.
anecdote *n* trivial story of isolated event.
anele, aneal *v* annoint; give extreme unction to.
anemometer *n* gauge for speed and force of wind.
anemone *n* wind-flower; **sea-anemone** small sea creature.
anent *prep* about; concerning.
aneroid *a* dry; containing no fluid.
aneurism *n* abnormal distension of an artery.
anew *adv* again; afresh.
angel *n* celestial being; old gold coin; *a* **angelic.**
angelica *n* herb used in medicine; its candied stalk.
angelus *n* devotion of R.C. church commemorating Incarnation; bell rung to call to this rite.
anger *n* wrath; rage; *v* provoke to anger; *a* **angry** showing anger; inflamed.
angina *n* heart spasm; quinsy.
angle *v* to fish; *ns* **angling, angler.**
angle space between two lines that meet; corner; *a* **angular.**
Anglican *n* member of the Church of England.
anglicize *v* give English form to (a foreign word).

angora *n* type of rabbit, cat or goat; fabric made from this goat's wool.
angostura *n* bitter aromatic bark used as tonic.
anguish *n* acute pain of body or mind.
aniline *n* chemical product used in dye manufacture.
animadversion *n* depreciatory reference to.
animal *n* living creature with power of voluntary motion; *a* of animal nature; sensual.
animate *v* give life to; *a* living; *n* **animation**; *a* **animated** lively; gay.
animosity *n* enmity; hatred.
aniseed *n* aromatic seed used for flavouring.
ankle *n* the joint between foot and leg.
anklet *n* ornament or support for the ankle.
ankylosis *n* stiffening of a joint; *v* **ankylose.**
anna *n* Indian coin.
annals *n* yearly chronicle of events.
anneal *v* temper (metal, glass) by gradual cooling.
annex *v* join to; steal; *n* **annexation.**
annexe *n* supplementary building.
annihilate *v* destroy utterly; *n* **annihilation.**
anniversary *n* yearly celebration of an event.
annotate *v* make explanatory notes on; *n* **annotation.**
announce *v* declare; *ns* **announcement, announcer.**
annoy *v* vex; irritate; *a* **annoying**; *n* **annoyance.**
annual *a* yearly; *n* plant living for year only; yearly publication of book; *adv* **annually.**
annuity *n* fixed sum paid yearly; *n* **annuitant.**
annul *v* cancel; do away with; nullify; *n* **annulment.**
annular *a* ring-shaped.
annunciation *n* announcement, *esp* of Incarnation made to Virgin Mary; *v* **annunciate.**
anode *n* positive electric pole.
anodyne *n* drug which relieves or soothes pain.
anoint *v* pour oil upon; *esp* by use of consecrated oil in religious ceremony; *a* **anointed**; *n* **anointment.**
anomaly *n* irregularity; *a* **anomalous.**
anon *adv* soon; presently.
anonymous *a* not named; *abbrev* **anon**; *adv* **anonymously**; *n* **anonymity.**
anopheles *n* malaria-carrying mosquito.

anorak *n* warm, hooded jacket (rain- & wind-proof).
another *a* additional; different; *pron* one more.
answer *v* give reply to; *a* **answerable** responsible.
ant *n* any of a group of small insects (social).
antacid *n* substance that counteracts acid.
antagonist *n* adversary; opponent; *v* **antagonize** render hostile; *n* **antagonism**; *a* **antagonistic**.
antarctic *a* belonging to south polar regions.
antecedent *a* prior to; *n pl* line of descent.
antechamber *n* waiting-room outside main room.
antediluvian *a* age before the Flood; old-fashioned.
antelope *n* deer-like animal allied to goat.
antenatal *a* occurring before birth.
antenna *n* feeler of insect; radio aerial; *pl* **antennae**.
anterior *a* before; earlier; more to the front.
anthem *n* sacred words set to music; song of praise.
anther *n* part of stamen containing pollen.
anthology *n* collection of poems, stories, etc.
anthracite *n* hard slow-burning smokeless coal.
anthrax *n* pustular disease attacking animals & man.
anthropoid *n* like a man; *n* man-like creature.
anthropology *n* science of man; *a* **anthropological**.
anti- *prefix* against (**ant-** before vowel).
antibiotic *a* destroying growth, *esp* of bacteria; *n* such a substance.
antibody *n* natural antidote to infection produced in blood.
antic *n* playful, comic gesture; *a* fantastic.
Antichrist *n* one hostile to Christ & His teaching.
anticipate *v* take action in advance; *n* **anticipation**; *a* **anticipatory**.
anticlerical *a* opposed to influence of clergy, *esp* in political affairs.
anticlimax *n* drop from important to trivial.
anticyclone *n* state of high atmospheric pressure, tending to produce fine weather; *a* **anticyclonic**.
antidote *n* specific against poison.
antimacassar *n* protective chair-back.
antimony *n* brittle silver-white metallic element.
antipathy *n* dislike; repugnance; *a* **antipathetic**.
antipodes *n* places on opposite side of earth.
antiquary, antiquarian *n* one who collect antiques;

a **antiquated** old-fashioned.
antique *a* old; *n* relic of past age; *ns* **antiquity** remote past; **antiquities** ancient museum pieces.
antirrhinum *n* the snapdragon plant.
anti-Semite *n* hater of Jews; *n* **anti-Semitism.**
antiseptic *n* substance for preventing infection; *n* **antisepsis** method of preventing infection.
antithesis *n* contrast (of ideas); *pl* **antitheses.**
antler *n* a branched horn of deer.
antonym *n* word of opposite meaning to another.
anus *n* opening at lower end of alimentary canal.
anvil *n* block of iron on which blacksmith works.
anxious *a* worried; eager to do (something); *adv* **anxiously;** *n* **anxiety.**
any *a* & *pron* some; every; *prons* **anybody, anyone, anyway, anywhere.**
Anzac *n* Australian or New Zealand soldier.
aorta *n* main artery of human body; *a* **aortic.**
apace *adv* at a quick pace; swiftly.
Apache *n* N. American Indian.
apart *adv* separately; aside; *a* separate.
apartheid *n* segregation of races.
apartment *n* a room; flat; set of rooms.
apathy *n* indifference; *a* **apathetic.**
ape *n* monkey *esp* tailless kind; *v* mimic; *n* **aping.**
aperient *a* laxative; *n* such a substance.
aperitif *n* drink taken as an appetizer.
aperture *n* hole; opening, *esp* that into a camera.
apex *n* tip; top; peak; *pl* **apexes, apices.**
aphasia *n* loss of power of speech.
aphis *n* green-fly; *pl* **aphides.**
aphorism *n* maxim; short pithy saying.
aphrodisiac *a* exciting sexual desire; *n* such a drug.
apiarist *n* bee-keeper; **apiary** bee-hive; **apiculture.**
apiece *adv* to or for each; each by itself.
aplomb *n* self-possession.
Apocalypse *n* Book of Revelation; prophetic vision.
apocryphal *a* not genuine; fictitious.
apogee *n* point in heavenly body's orbit farthest from earth; culmination.
apology *n* expression of regret; *v* **apologize;** *a* **apologetic;** *adv* **apologetically.**

apoplexy *n* sudden loss of consciousness, usually caused by brain haemorrhage; *a* **apoplectic.**
apostasy *n* defection from one's faith; *n* **apostate.**
apostle *n* one sent out to preach; reformer; *a* **apostolic.**
apostrophe *n* exclamatory address to person present or absent; a mark (') showing omission of letter(s).
apothecary *n* old name for druggist, pharmacist.
apotheosis *n* deification of human being.
appal *v* horrify; *a* **appalling**; *adv* **appallingly.**
apparatus *n* equipment; instruments for specific use.
apparel *n* dress; clothing; *v* dress.
apparent *a* visible; *adv* **apparently** seemingly.
apparition *n* supernatural visual impression; ghost.
appeal *v* seek higher judgment; ask earnestly; attract; *n* act of appealing; *a* **appealing** attractive.
appear *v* become visible; present oneself; seem; *n* **appearance** bearing; look.
appease *v* soothe; pacify; satisfy; *n* **appeasement.**
appellant *n* one appealing to higher court; *n* **appellation** a name or title.
append *v* add; attach; *n* **appendage.**
appendix *n* addition to book; (*anat*) **vermiform appendix** tube leading out of caecum; *pl* **appendixes, appendices.**
appendicitis *n* inflammation of vermiform appendix.
apperception *n* self-consciousness.
appertain *v* be appropriate or relate (to).
appetite *n* enjoyment of food; desire; *n* **appetizer** anything giving relish for a meal.
applaud *v* express approval by clapping of hands; *n* **applause.**
apple *n* firm, fleshy fruit with pips.
appliance *n* a device; gadget; machine.
applique *n* one material cut out & applied to surface of another, as in embroidery etc.
apply *v* put on; bring into contact; administer; devote; request; have relevance; *a* **applied** put to practical use; *n* **application** act of applying; something applied; close attention; **applicant** person applying; *a* **applicable** relevant, suitable.

appoint *v* fix; ordain; select for office; equip; *n* **appointment** act of appointing; assignation.
apportion *v* share out; allot; *n* **apportionment.**
apposite *a* apt; pointed; *n* **apposition.**
appraise *v* assess price; *ns* **appraisal, appraisement.**
appreciate *v* estimate highly; be sensible of; increase value; *n* **appreciation**; *a* **appreciative** grateful; *adv* **appreciatively**; *a* **appreciable** noticeable; *adv* **appreciably.**
apprehend *v* arrest; understand; dread; *n* **apprehension**; *a* **apprehensive**; *adv* **apprehensively.**
apprentice *n* one learning a trade or craft & bound by indentures; *n* **apprenticeship.**
apprise *v* inform.
approach *v* come near; make advances to; *n* drawing near; *a* **approachable** willing to be consulted.
approbation *n* commendation; approval; *a* **approbatory.**
appropriate *v* take for oneself; filch; *a* suitable to; *adv* **appropriately**; *n* **appropriation** funds granted for special purpose.
approve *v* sanction; commend; *n* **approval**; *as* **approved, approving**; *adv* **approvingly.**
approximate *a* very near; about correct; *v* make or come close to; *adv* **approximately**; *n* **approximation.**
appurtenance *n* adjunct; an accessory.
apricot *n* orange-red fruit allied to peach; colour.
April *n* 4th month of year.
a priori *adv* deductive reasoning.
apron *n* garment worn to protect clothes; part of a theatre stage, in front of curtain.
apropos *a* appropriate; *adv* with reference to.
apse *n* domed recess at end of church; *a* **apsidal.**
apt *a* fit; likely; skilled; *adv* **aptly**; *ns* **aptness, aptitude** fitness; capacity.
aquamarine *n* bluish-green stone; colour.
aquaplane *v* ride on board towed by motorboat; *n* such a board.
aquarium *n* tank where water plants & fish are kept; *pl* **aquaria, aquariums.**

aquatic *a* living in water; taking place in or on water.
aquatint *n* etching process producing print like water-colour; print made by this process.
aqueduct *n* artificial conduit for water; bridge-like part of a structure supporting conduit.
aqueous *a* watery.
aquiline *a* eagle-like; (nose) curved as an eagle's beak.
Arab *n* native of Arabia; horse; **street Arab** homeless urchin; *a* **Arabian**; *n* **Arabic** language of the Arabs.
arabesque *n* fanciful pattern of leaves, scrolls etc. in Arabian decoration; posture in ballet.
arable *a* suitable for tilling, cultivation.
arachnid *n* one of the genus including spiders.
arbitrate *v* decide; dispute; *ns* **arbiter, arbitrament, arbitration, arbitrator**; *a* **arbitrary** offhand.
arbor *n* main support or spindle of machine.
arboreal *a* living in, resembling trees; *n* **arboretum** collection of rare shrubs and trees.
arbour *n* shady retreat in garden.
arc *n* part of curved line; luminous glow produced in certain electric lamps; *ns* **arc lamp, arc light.**
arcade *n* passage with arched roof, lined with shops.
arch *a* coy; *prep* chief; *adv* **archly**; *n* **archness.**
arch *n* curved structure acting as support; curve itself; *v* build arch over; form an arch.
archaeology *n* study of prehistoric cultures; *a* **archaeological**; *n* **archaeologist.**
archaic *a* out of date; *adv* **archaically.**
archangel *n* chief angel.
archbishop *n* chief bishop; *n* **archbishopric** office of archbishop.
archer *n* one shooting with bow and arrows; *n* **archery.**
archetype *n* prototype; *a* **archetypal.**
archiepiscopal *a* relating to archbishop or his office.
archipelago *n* sea containing many islands; group of such islands; *pl* **archipelagoes.**
architecture *n* art and science of building; *a* **architectural**; *adv* **architecturally**; *n* **architect** one who designs buildings.

architrave *n* beam resting on top of supporting columns; moulding around door, window or arch.
archives *n* place where records are kept; records themselves; *n* **archivist** keeper of archives.
archway *n* way or passage under an arch.
arctic *a* of or near region of the N. Pole.
ardent *a* fiery; eager; *adv* **ardently**; *n* **ardour.**
arduous *a* difficult; strenuous; *adv* **arduously.**
are *n* 100 square metres.
area *n* region; surface measured in sq. units; scope.
arena *n* place of combat or conflict; *pl* **arenas.**
argent *n* silver; white colour in heraldry.
argil *n* kind of clay used by potters.
argosy *n* large, richly-laden merchant vessel(s).
argot *n* slang.
argue *v* dispute; prove; debate; *ns* **argument** discussion in which reasons are given; *as* **arguable, argumentative.**
aria *n* vocal solo in operas and oratorios.
arid *a* dry; parched; barren; *adv* **aridly**; *n* **aridity.**
aright *adv* rightly; without error.
arise *v* ascend; occur; *p t* **arose**; *p p* **arisen.**
aristocracy *n* ruling class; nobility; *n* **aristocrat**; *a* **aristocratic**; *adv* **aristocratically.**
arithmetic *n* science of numbers; *n* **arithmetician.** *a* **arithmetical**; *adv* **arithmetically.**
ark *n* flat bottomed boat; Jewish chest containing Tablets of the Law; coffer.
arm *n* upper limb of human body; anything extending from main body (arm of tree, chair etc.).
arm *n* weapon; branch of military forces; *pl* heraldic symbols; *v* supply with weapons; prepare for battle.
armada *n* fleet of warships, *specif* Spanish.
armadillo *n* S. American burrowing mammal.
armament *n* force equipped for war; war equipment.
armature *n* part of dynamo rotating in magnetic field.
armchair *n* chair with armrests.
armistice *n* truce pending a formal peace treaty.
armlet *n* cloth band for the arm.
armorial *a* relating to heraldic arms.
armour *n* protective covering for the body in battle; protective plating of ship or vehicle; *a* **armoured**;

ns **armoury**; **armourer** one who makes or repairs armour.
army *n* organised body of trained men or women for service in war; any great number.
arnica *n* genus of plants; drug used for sprains etc.
aroma *n* pleasant smell; *a* **aromatic** fragrant, spicy.
around *adv* on all sides; in a circle; *prep* about.
arouse *v* stir up; awaken.
arpeggio *n* rapid playing of notes of chord.
arraign *v* accuse; indict on criminal charge; *n* **arraignment** act of indictment.
arrange *v* put in order; fix; adapt (novel, music); *n* **arrangement.**
arrant *a* unmitigated; out-and-out; *adv* **arrantly.**
arras *n* tapestry used as wall hanging.
array *v* dress; draw up; *n* troops; impressive display.
arrears *n* debt not paid; work not done.
arrest *v* seize by legal authority; gain attention; stop; stay (judgment); *a* **arresting** striking; *n* **arrest.**
arrive *v* reach destination; achieve fame; *n* **arrival.**
arrogate *v* claim as one's own; *n* **arrogation**; *a* **arrogant** haughty; proud; *n* **arrogance**; *adv* **arrogantly.**
arrow *n* feathered rod with sharp point shot from bow.
arrowroot *n* W. Indian plant with starchy roots.
arse *n* (*vul*) the buttocks.
arsenal *n* place where weapons and ammunition are made or stored.
arsenic *n* metallic poison; *as* **arsenical, arsenous.**
arson *n* deliberate setting on fire of property.
art *n* creative skill and its application; craft or trade; cunning; *pl* humanities as opposed to sciences; *ns* **artist, artistry; artiste** professional entertainer.
artery *n* blood-vessel conveying blood from heart; main line of communication; *a* **arterial.**
artesian well *n* well sending up constant supply of water under pressure.
artful *a* cunning; crafty.
arthritis *n* painful inflammation of joints; *a* **arthritic.**
artichoke *n* plant with edible roots or flower base.
article *n* item; short piece of writing; clause in legal

document; in grammar, words *the, a, an*; *v* bind to trade or profession; *a* **articled.**

articulate *a* formed with joints; expressive; having the power of speech; *v* join; utter distinctly; *adv* **articulately**; *ns* **articulation, articulateness.**

artifact, artefact *n* any object made by human skill.

artifice *n* ingenuity; trickery; *a* **artificial** not natural; *n* **artificiality** insincerity; *adv* **artificially.**

artificer *n* skilled craftsman, *esp* in armed forces.

artillery *n* guns of various types; branch of army which uses heavy guns.

artisan *n* skilled manual worker.

artless *a* naive; sincere; simple.

arum *n* kind of lily; wild lily or 'Lord & Ladies'.

Aryan *n* descendant of people who spoke original Indo-Iranian language; this language; *a* relating to Aryan people or language.

as *adv* & *conj* at time that; because; equal to; e.g.; while; so far; in capacity of.

asafoetida *n* gum resin with nauseous smell.

asbestos *n* fibrous fireproof mineral substance.

ascend *v* go up; rise to higher rank; slope upwards; climb; *ns* **ascent**; **ascendancy** domination; **ascension.**

ascertain *v* find out; get to know for certain.

ascetic *a* self-denying; austere; *n* hermit; *adv* **ascetically**; *n* **asceticism.**

ascribe *v* attribute (to); *a* **ascribable.**

aseptic *a* free from pus-forming bacteria; *n* **asepsis.**

ash *n* grey powdery residue of anything burnt; *pl* **ashes** cremated human remains; **the Ashes** symbol of victory in cricket series between Australia & England; *n* tree of olive family; *as* **ashen, ashy.**

ashamed *a* troubled by sense of guilt or shame.

ashlar *n* square-hewn building stone.

ashore *a* & *adv* on shore; to shore; on land.

Asian *a* & *n* native of Asia; *a* **Asiatic.**

aside *adv* on, to or at one side; apart; *n* phrase spoken in an undertone.

asinine *a* like an ass; stupid; *n* **asininity.**

ask *v* seek answer to; request; invite.

askance *adv* with sideways glance, with suspicion.

askew *a* & *adv* sideways; out of the straight.
aslant *adv* on the slant; obliquely.
asleep *adv* & *a* into or in a state of sleep; numb.
asp *n* a small poisonous snake.
asparagus *n* plant whose shoots are eaten as veg.
aspect *n* appearance; expression; view; look.
aspen *n* poplar tree with tremulous leaves.
asperity *n* harshness; severity; roughness.
asperse *v* besmirch; slander; *n* **aspersion.**
asphalt *n* bituminous substance for surfacing roads.
asphyxiate *v* cause or undergo suffocation; *ns* **asphyxia, asphyxiation.**
aspic *n* savoury jelly.
aspidistra *n* indoor plant with green glossy leaves.
aspirate *n* breathed sound, usually expressed by letter h; *v* pronounce with breath; draw off (fluid etc) from cavity, by means of **aspirator**; *a* **aspirated.**
aspire *v* seek eagerly; *a* **aspiring**; *n* **aspiration** strong desire; act of breathing; pronunciation of an aspirate.
aspirin *n* drug used for relief of pain.
ass *n* member of horse family; stupid person.
assail *v* attack; *a* **assailable**; *n* **assailant.**
assassin *n* treacherous (*usu* political) murderer; *v* **assassinate**; *n* **assassination.**
assault *n* sudden attack; make an assault.
assay *n* testing purity of metals; *v* test or analyse (metals); *n* **assayer.**
assegai *n* light spear used by S. African tribes.
assemble *v* collect; fit together; *ns* **assembler**; **assembly** gathering of persons; collection of parts.
assent *v* agree; concur; *n* compliance, agreement.
assert *v* state strongly; declare; *n* **assertion**; *a* **assertive** aggressively confident; *adv* **assertively.**
ssess *v* estimate & fix amount of (fine or tax); estimate value; *a* **assessable**; *ns* **assessment, assessor.**
asset *n* thing of value belonging to person, business etc; *pl* all such property.
asseverate *v* state emphatically; *n* **asseveration.**
assiduity *n* diligence; perseverance; *a* **assiduous**;

adv **assiduously;** *n* **assiduousness.**

assign *v* make over; allot; fix; ascribe; *a* **assignable;** *ns* **assignment** allotted task; **assignee; assignation** secret meeting.

assimilate *v* absorb physically or mentally, make similar; *a* **assimilable;** *n* **assimilation.**

assist *v* help; aid; attend; *ns* **assistant, assistance**

assizes *n* periodical sessions of judges held to try criminal and civil cases.

associate *v* join; connect; combine; *n* partner; member of a society; *a* linked in function; *n* **association,** union of persons for common purposes.

assonance *n* rhyming of vowel sounds; *a* **assonant.**

assort *v* separate into sorts or classes; *a* **assorted;** *n* **assortment** mixed kinds.

assuage *v* soothe; quench; *n* **assuagement.**

assume *v* put on; take upon oneself; adopt; *n* **assumption.**

assure *v* make sure; state positively; *a* **assured** confident; *adv* **assuredly** certainly; *n* **assurance** pledge; confidence; insurance.

aster *n* genus of daisy-like plants.

asterisk *n* symbol (*) used by printers.

astern *adv* towards rear of ship; aft; backwards.

asteroid *n* small planet; *a* star-shaped.

asthma *n* chronic or acute affection of organs of respiration; *as* **asthmatic, asthmatical.**

astigmatism *n* defect in eye causing faulty vision; *as* **astigmatic;** *adv* **astigmatically.**

astir *a* & *adv* in motion; in state of excitement.

astonish *v* fill with wonder; amaze; *a* **astonishing;** *adv* **astonishingly;** *n* **astonishment.**

astound *v* strike with amazement or alarm; *a* **astounding;** *adv* **astoundingly,**

astraddle *a* & *adv* straddling; astride.

astrakhan *n* curly pelt of unborn Astrakhan lamb.

astral *a* of stars; **astral body** a ghost.

astray *a* & *adv* off right path; of mental error; of moral lapse.

astride *adv* with one leg on each side.

astringent *n* drug or other agent causing contraction (of tissues, cut blood vessels); *n* **astringency.**

astrology *n* pseudo-science of prediction of events by stars; *n* **astrologer;** *a* **astrological.**
astronaut *n* traveller in space.
astronomy *n* science of heavenly bodies; *n* **astronomer;** *a* **astronomical.**
astute *a* shrewd; wily; *adv* **astutely;** *n* **astuteness.**
asunder *adv* apart; into parts; *a* separated.
asylum *n* sanctuary; place for care of insane.
asymmetry *n* irregularity; absence of symmetry; *adv* **asymmetrically.**
at *prep* expressing general position in space or time.
atavism *n* resemblance to remote ancestor; reversion to earlier type; *a* **atavistic.**
atelier *n* artist's studio or workshop.
atheism *n* belief that there is no God; *n* **atheist;** *a* **atheistic.**
athirst *a* thirsty; eagerly desiring.
athlete *n* one skilled in physical exercises; *a* **athletic;** *adv* **athletically;** *n* **athletics.**
athwart *prep* across; against; *adv* crosswise.
Atlantic *a* relating to the Atlantic Ocean.
atlas *n* book of maps; top vertebra of neck.
atmosphere *n* gaseous envelope surrounding earth or any heavenly body; any moral or mental influence; *a* **atmospheric;** *adv* **atmospherically;** *n* **atmospherics** disturbances in radio reception.
atoll *n* coral island; belt of coral reefs surrounding lagoon.
atom *n* smallest particle of an element; *v* **atomize** reduce to atoms; *ns* **atomization; atomizer** device for changing liquids into fine spray.
atomic *a* pertaining to atoms. Hence: **a. bomb; a. energy; a. number; a. reactor; a. warfare; a. weight.**
atone *v* make amends; expiate; *n* **atonement.**
atop *a* & *adv* & *prep* on the top; over; above.
atrocious *a* abominable; wicked; evil; *adv* **atrociously;** *ns* **atrociousness; atrocity** brutal deed.
atrophy *n* wasting away of body; weakening of mental or moral power; *v*; *a* **atrophied.**
atropine *n* poison obtained from belladonna.

attach *v* fasten, affix; seize legally; *a* **attached**; *n* **attachment.**
attache *n* member of diplomatic staff; **attache-case** small case for carrying documents.
attack *v* assault; assail; work upon; *n* **attacker.**
attain *v* accomplish; achieve; *a* **attainable**; *ns* **attainment, attainability.**
attainder *n* loss of civil rights through judicial sentence; disgrace; dishonour.
attaint *n* disgrace; stain; *v* dishonour.
attar *n* perfume distilled from flower petals.
attempt *v* try; endeavour; *n* an effort, try.
attend *v* give heed (to); be present; escort; *n* **attendance** those present; *a* & *n* **attendant**; *a* **attentive**; *adv* **attentively**; *ns* **attentiveness, attention.**
attenuate *v* make thin; *a* **attenuated**; *n* **attenuation.**
attest *v* testify; put (someone) on oath; *n* **attestation.**
attic *n* small room under roof of house; a garret.
attire *v* dress; put robes on; *n* dress; clothing.
attitude *n* posture; disposition; *v* **attitudinize** adopt affected gestures.
attorney *n* lawyer; one acting for another in legal matters; **Attorney General** chief legal officer.
attract *v* draw towards; allure; *n* **attraction**; *a* **attractive**; *adv* **attractively**; *n* **attractiveness.**
attribute *n* characteristic quality of thing or person; *v* ascribe (to); *a* **attributable**; *n* **attribution.**
attrition *n* act of wearing away by friction.
attune *v* bring into harmony, tune.
aubergine *n* fruit of egg-plant; deep purple colour.
auburn *a* reddish- or golden-brown.
auction *n* public sale in which articles are sold to highest bidder; *v* sell by auction; *n* **auctioneer.**
audacious *a* bold; impudent; *adv* **audaciously**; *ns* **audaciousness, audacity.**
audible *a* able to be heard; *adv* **audibly**; *n* **audibility**
audience *n* assemblage of persons present or looking on; interview or formal hearing.
audiometer *n* instrument measuring power of hearing.
audit *v* official scrutinizing of accounts; *n* **auditor.**

audition *n* sense of hearing; test-hearing for singer, actor, etc; *v* conduct such a test.
auditorium *n* building in which an audience gathers.
auditory *a* of the sense of hearing.
auger *n* tool for boring holes in wood.
aught *n* anything; anything at all; any part.
augment *v* cause to increase; *n* **augmentation.**
augur *n* soothsayer; *v* predict; *n* **augury** an omen.
august *a* imposing; awe-inspiring; *n* **August** the eighth month of the year.
auk *n* web-footed sea-bird resembling puffin.
aunt *n* mother's or father's sister; uncle's wife.
aura *n* mysterious emanation surrounding living things; phase in the onset of epilepsy etc.
aural *a* of the ear; *adv* **aurally.**
aureola, aureole *n* sun's corona; celestial crown or halo.
aureomycin *n* antibiotic penicillin-like drug.
auricle *n* external ear of animals; upper chamber of the heart; *a* **auricular.**
auricula *n* primrose-like flower.
aurora *n* the dawn; **a. borealis** Northern Lights; **a. australis** similar lights in S. Polar sky.
auspices *npl* omens; patronage; *a* **auspicious** favourable; *adv* **auspiciously.**
austere *a* stern; ascetic; *adv* **austerely**; *n* **austerity.**
austral *a* of or coming from the south; southerly.
Australasian *a* of Australia, N. Zealand & adjacent islands; native of Australasia.
Australian *a* of Australia, its people, their culture, etc; *n* native of Australia.
authentic *a* genuine; reliable; *adv* **authentically**; *n* **authenticity**; *v* **authenticate** prove real or genuine.
author *n* writer of book, play, poem, etc; originator; *fem* **authoress**; *n* **authorship.**
authority *n* right to command; natural power; expert; controlling body; *a* **authoritative**, *adv* **authoritatively**; *v* **authorize** give authority or approval to.
auto- *prefix: forms compounds meaning* self-.
autobiography *n* life of person written by himself;

a **autobiographic (al)**; *n* **autobiographer.**
autoclave *n* pressure-cooker.
autocrat *n* absolute monarch; *n* **autocracy**; *a* **autocratic**; *adv* **autocratically.**
autograph *n* person's own signature; *v* write one's signature (in); *a* **autographic.**
autogyro *n* aircraft designed for vertical ascent and descent by means of horizontal propeller.
automat *n* food-dispenser operated by coins in slots.
automatic *a* working by itself; behaving mechanically; *adv* **automatically.**
automation *n* control of industrial processes by electronic and other means.
automaton *n* machine that performs human actions; *pl* **automatons**; *n* **automatism** mechanical action.
automobile *n* a motor-car.
autonomy *n* self-government; *as* **autonomic, autonomous**; *n* **autonomist** one who supports autonomy.
autopsy *n* examination of dead body by dissection.
auto-suggestion *n* suggestion coming from within oneself.
autumn *n* third season of the year; *a* **autumnal.**
auxiliary *a* helping; additional; supplementary; *n* verb helping to make up tense, mood etc of another.
avail *v* be of use; benefit; *a* **available** at hand; capable of being used; *n* **availability.**
avalanche *n* mass of snow, ice rushing down a mountain.
avarice *n* greed; cupidity; *a* **avaricious**; *adv* **avariciously.**
avast *interj* stop!
avaunt *interj* begone!
avenge *v* inflict retribution for a wrong; take revenge for injury on behalf of someone; *n* **avenger.**
avenue *n* way of approach; roadway bordered by trees; wide street in a town.
aver *v* affirm positively; *n* **averment.**
average *n* mean proportion; *a* mean, ordinary; *v* estimate average of; rate of.
averse *a* opposed; unwilling; *n* **aversion** antipathy; dislike; thing or person disliked.

avert *v* turn aside; prevent.
aviary *n* large cage for keeping birds; *n* **aviarist, aviculture.**
aviation *n* art of flying aircraft; everything connected with flying; *v* **aviate** fly an aircraft; *n* **aviator** a pilot.
avid *a* eager; greedy; *adv* **avidly**; *n* **avidity.**
avocado *n* pear-shaped tropical fruit; alligator-pear.
avocation *n* occupation; minor pursuit; hobby.
avocet *n* wading bird of the snipe family.
avoid *v* shun; keep away from; refrain from; *a* **avoidable**; *adv* **avoidably**; *n* **avoidance.**
avoirdupois *n* system of weights used in U.K. & U.S.A.; (*colloq*) excessive weight of person.
avouch *v* guarantee; maintain truth of; vouch for.
avow *v* own publicly to; admit openly; *a* **avowed**; *adv* **avowedly** admittedly; *n* **avowal** confession.
avuncular *a* of or like an uncle.
await *v* wait for; expect; be ready for.
awake, *v* rouse from sleep or inaction; *pt* **awoke**; *pp* **awaked, awoke**; *a* no longer sleeping; vigilant.
award *v* grant after due judgment; *n* something awarded after judgment; a prize.
aware *a* conscious; cognizant; knowing; *n* **awareness.**
awash *a* just above or level with surface of water.
away *adv* at or to a distance; absent.
awe *n* fear with respect; solemn wonder; *v* fill with awe; *a* **awesome** causing awe; *n* **awesomeness.**
awe-struck *a* filled with awe
awful *a* appalling; very bad; *adv* **awfully** very.
awhile *adv* for a short time.
awkward *a* clumsy; ungainly; difficult to manage; disconcerting; ill at ease; embarrassed; *adv* **awkwardly**; *n* **awkwardness.**
awl *n* small pointed tool for piercing holes.
awn *n* beard on a head of barley etc.
awning *n* canvas sheet stretched on frame-work used as protection from sun.
awry *a* crooked; twisted; *adv* wrong; askew.
axe *n* chopping tool with wooden handle & iron head.
axiom *n* obvious truth; principle accepted without question; *a* **axiomatic**; *adv* **axiomatically.**

axis *n* imaginary line about which a body may rotate; real or imaginary line dividing figure into two equal parts; *pl* **axes**; *a* **axial**; *adv* **axially**.
axle, axle tree *n* rod or bar connecting two wheels and on which wheel revolves.
ay, aye *adv* & *n* always; yes.
azalea *n* flowering shrub of rhododendron family.
azimuth *n* distance of a star in angular degrees from N or S point of meridian; *a* **azimuthal**.
Aztec *n* American Indian race ruling Mexico before Spanish conquest.
azure *a* blue like the sky; *n* the colour sky-blue.

baa *n* the bleat of a sheep; *v* bleat.
babble *v* talk indistinctly; reveal (secrets); *n* foolish talk; murmur of stream; *n* **babbler**; *a* **babbling**.
babe *n* baby; inexperienced person.
babel *n* confused chattering; uproar.
baboon *n* kind of large ape.
baby *n* young child or animal; infant; *a* **babyish** childish; *ns* **babyhood**; **baby-sitter** one minding children when parents are out.
baccarat *n* gambling card game.
bacchanal *a* of Bacchus; riotous; *n* drunken reveller; drinking orgy; *a* & *n* **bacchanalian**.
bachelor *n* unmarried man; holder of junior degree at university; *ns* **bachelorhood, bachelor-girl**.
bacillus *n* minute plant organism either harmful or harmless; bacterium; *pl* **bacilli**; *a* **bacilliform**.
back *n* rear part of human body; corresponding part in animals; part opposite front; *v* move (something) backwards; support; gamble on; *a* situated at rear; behind in time; *adv* towards rear; in return; in reserve; in or to a former condition, time or place.
backbite *v* speak maliciously of someone absent; *n* **backbiting**.
backbone *n* spine, vertebrae; courage, firmness.
backchat *n* answering back in a cheeky manner.
back-drop *n* scenic curtain hung at back of a stage.
backer *n* one who supports another, *esp* with money; one who bets on a horse, or sporting event.

backfire *n* premature explosion of gas in an internal combustion engine; *v* bring results opposite to those planned.
backgammon *n* a board game played with draughtsmen and dice.
background *n* hinder part of picture behind chief figures; a person's past history; place of obscurity.
backhanded *a* done with back of hand; sloped backwards (of writing); ambiguous; *a* & *n* **backhand**.
backing *n* anything used to cover back of object; support, aid; act of one who backs.
backlash *n* sudden sharp recoil; play in badly fitted or worn parts of machinery.
backlog *n* accumulation of unfinished business.
backside *n* rear part of person or animal, rump.
backslide *v* relapse into bad habits: *n* **backslider**.
backstay *n* rope from masthead to ship's side.
backstroke *n* swimming on the back.
backward, backwards *adv* towards rear; with back first; *a* turned back; retarded mentally; shy.
backwash *n* waves caused by passage of vessel.
backwater *n* small creek containing stagnant water.
backwoods *n* wild forest region beyond cleared land.
bacon *n* back and sides of pig, salted and smoked.
bacterium *n* one-celled plant organism; *pl* **bacteria**; *a* **bacterial**; *n* **bacteriology** study of bacteria; *a* **bacteriological**; *n* **bacteriologist**.
bad *a* evil; faulty; rotten; ill; *adv* **badly**; *n* **badness**.
bade *v pt* of verb BID.
badge *n* emblem of office, token of membership.
badger *n* nocturnal burrowing animal; *v* bait, tease.
badinage *n* teasing; banter.
badminton *n* game played with shuttlecock and racquets.
baffle *v* confuse, puzzle; *n* plate to divert flow of liquid, gas, or sound waves; *n* **bafflement**; *a* **baffling**.
bag *n* pouch, sack; day's take of game; *v* capture, acquire; *n* **bagful**; *a* **baggy** loosely hanging; *n* **bagginess**.
bagatelle *n* trifle; inferior kind of billiards.
baggage *n* army equipment; luggage; hussy or worthless girl.

bagpipe *n* musical wind instrument *esp* Scottish.
bail *n* sum paid as security for person's reappearance in court; in cricket, one of two small sticks laid across top of wicket; *v* release on bail; scoop water out; **bail out** jump with parachute from aircraft.
bailey *n* outer wall of castle; court enclosed by it.
bailiff *n* sheriff's officer; land agent or steward.
bairn *n* a child, baby.
bait *n* anything used to lure prey; *v* put bait on; torment; give food to (*esp* horses); *n* **baiting**.
baize *n* coarse woollen cloth, usually green.
bake *v* cook or harden by means of heat; *ns* **baker**; **bakery**; **baking powder** powder used instead of yeast.
Bakelite *n* [P] non-inflammable synthetic resin.
baksheesh, bakshish *n* a tip, gratuity.
balalaika *n* kind of guitar played *esp* in Russia.
balance *n* weighing instrument; equilibrium; remainder; difference between credit and debit sides of an account; regulating mechanism in clock or watch; *v* weigh; be equal in weight to; adjust; be in state of equilibrium; *n* **balance-sheet** statement of accounts.
balcony *n* projecting platform outside window, protected by railing; tier of seats above circle (theatre).
bald *a* having no natural covering *esp* of hair; bare; plain; *adv* **baldly**; *n* **baldness**.
balderdash *n* rubbish, nonsense.
baldric *n* ornamented belt worn over shoulder to carry sword, bugle, *etc*.
bale *n* bundle of goods, hay etc. bound with cord or wire; *v* make into a bale.
baleful *a* evil, malicious; *adv* **balefully**; *n* **balefulness**.
balk, baulk *n* hindrance; heavy, squared beam; division on billiard table; *v* avoid; hinder; jib *esp* of horse.
ball *n* roundish body of any size; bullet or shot; *v* form into a ball.
ball *n* social gathering for dancing; *n* **ballroom**.
ballad *n* traditional story in song; simple song.
ballade *n* poem with three eight-lined verses and four-line envoy.

ballast *n* heavy material placed in ship's hold or balloon, to steady it; *v* steady with ballast.
ball-bearings *n* steel balls used to relieve friction on bearings.
ball-cock *n* device for regulating level of liquid.
ballerina *n* a female ballet dancer.
ballet *n* action or story expressed by dancing, miming etc; *n* **balletomane** ballet lover.
ballistics *n* theory, science of projectiles & means of their propulsion; *a* **ballistic**.
balloon *n* gas- or hot air-filled bag that rises in air; inflatable rubber bag; *v* inflate; billow out in wind; *n* **balloonist**.
ballot *n* printed sheet used in voting; act of voting, secret or not; *v* vote by ballot.
ballyhoo *n* vulgar, showy publicity; loud empty talk.
balm *n* aromatic resin; fragrant garden herb; healing ointment; *a* **balmy**; *adv* **balmily**; *n* **balminess**.
baloney *n* stupid talk, nonsense. Also **boloney**.
balsa *n* tropical American tree whose wood is extremely light.
balsam *n* aromatic resin; anything healing, soothing or restorative (*lit* & *fig*).
baluster *n* small post supporting a hand-rail; *n* **balustrade** set of balusters.
bamboo *n* giant grass with hard, hollow, jointed stem.
bamboozle *v* mystify, trick, confuse, puzzle.
ban *n* prohibition; denunciation; *v* forbid, exclude.
banal *a* trite, trivial, ordinary; *n* **banality**.
banana *n* tropical fruit tree; its fruit.
band *n* tie, ligament of any material; flat strip applied on another object; body of persons united for common purpose, *esp* company of musicians; *v* unite; gather together; tie, fasten with a band.
bandage *n* strip of cloth etc. used to bind up wounds; *v* apply a bandage to.
banda(n)na *n* large brightly coloured handkerchief.
bandbox *n* light-weight box for hats.
bandeau *n* band or ribbon keeping hair in place; band inside a hat.
banderilla *n* barbed dart stuck into bull's neck by the banderillo in bull-fighting.

bandit *n* an outlaw, robber, brigand.
bandolier, bandoleer *n* shoulder-belt with pockets for cartridges.
band-saw *n* endless steel saw running over wheels.
bandy *v* pass to and fro; *a* **bandy-legged** bow-legged.
bane *n* source of evil; curse; ruin; *a* **baneful**; *adv* **banefully**; *n* **banefulness**.
bang *n* sudden loud noise; sharp blow; *v* thump; beat, shut noisily; explode.
bang *n* hair cut to form fringe.
bangle *n* ornamental bracelet for arm or ankle.
banish *v* drive into exile; (of mental action) dismiss; *n* **banishment**.
banister *n* rail and supports along a stairway.
banjo *n* musical instrument of guitar family.
bank *n* heap or mound of earth; edge of river etc; *v* pile up; put aircraft at angle when turning.
bank *n* commercial concern engaged in keeping, lending & exchanging money; *v* deposit money in bank; have an account with bank; depend (on); *ns* **banker, banking**.
bankrupt *n* & *a* an insolvent person; *v* make bankrupt; *n* **bankruptcy**.
banner *n* flag as symbol of country, regiment etc.
bannock *n* flat cake made of oatmeal or barley meal.
banns *n* announcement in church of intended marriage.
banquet *n* ceremonial or official feast; *n* **banqueter**.
banshee *n* fairy whose wail supposedly warns of death.
bantam *n* breed of small fowl; light-weight boxer.
banter *n* good-natured chaff; *v*; *a* **bantering**.
baptism *n* ceremony of admitting person to Christian church by immersing in or sprinkling with water; *v* **baptize** name; *a* **baptismal**; *n* **baptist(e)ry** part of church where baptism is administered.
bar *n* rod of solid material; sandbank at mouth of river; rail in courtroom; legal profession; counter in public house; obstruction; musical unit; non-material obstacle; *v* fasten with (bar); rule out.
barb *n* backward-curving point on arrow, fish-hook, harpoon, etc; *as* **barbed, barbate**.

barbarian *n* uncivilized person; *ns* **barbarism, barbarity, barbarousness**; *a* **barbaric**; *adv* **barbarously.**
barbecue *n* outdoor feast; grid for roasting meat over charcoal fire; *v* cook in such manner.
barbel *n* large European freshwater fish.
barber *n* one who cuts hair, shaves or trims beards.
barbican *n* outer defence of castle or fortress.
barbiturates *n pl* group of drugs used to induce sleep or ease pain; *a* **barbituric.**
bard *n* Celtic poet or minstrel; *a* **bardic.**
bare *a* naked; simple; empty; scanty; *v* reveal; *n* **bareness**; *a* **bare-faced** shameless; *adv* **barely.**
bargain *n* agreement; pact; something obtained at small price; *v* make agreement; discuss or argue about terms.
barge *n* broad flat-bottomed boat; state or pleasure boat; *n* **bargee**; *v* force way clumsily.
baritone *n* & *a* voice ranging between tenor & bass.
barium *n* heavy, white metallic element.
bark *n* outside covering of trees; *v* strip bark from; scrape skin off (*colloq*).
bark, barque *n* three-masted sailing ship; small ship; *ns* **barkentine, barquentine** small bark.
bark *n* sharp cry or noise made by dog or fox; *v* speak sharply; *n* **barker** tout who induces people at a fair or circus to see show.
barley *n* cereal plant; its seed or grain.
barm *n* yeast; leaven; *a* **barmy** frothy; dimwitted (*sl*).
barn *n* building for storing hay, grain etc; *ns* **barn-dance** lively rustic dance; **barn-yard; barn-owl.**
barnacle *n* species of goose; type of shell-fish that cling to rocks, ship's bottom, etc.
barnstormer *n* strolling player, ranting actor.
baro- *prefix* weight, pressure, *esp* of atmosphere.
barometer *n* instrument for recording atmospheric pressure; *a* **barometric**; *adv* **barometrically**; *ns* **barograph** type of barometer.
baron *n* lowest rank in peerage; *fem* **baroness**; *n* **barony**; *a* **baronial**; *n* **b. of beef** double sirloin.
baronet *n* lowest hereditary title; *n* **baronetcy.**

baroque *a* grotesque, fantastical; *n* style of music, architecture & art.
barouche *n* four-wheeled carriage with folding hood.
barrack *n* (usually *pl*) building in which soldiers live; *v* jeer derisively at in public; *n* **barracking.**
barracuda *n* large edible fierce fish.
barrage *n* barrier placed in river; continuous gunfire to cover movement of troops.
barrel *n* cylindrical vessel or cask with bulging sides; measure of capacity; metal tube of gun; *v* pack, stow in barrel.
barren *a* sterile; bare & bleak; *n* **barrennes.**
barricade *n* makeshift barrier; *v* block with barricade.
barrier *n* anything obstructing passage or advance.
barrister *n* advocate in higher courts of law.
barrow *n* burial mound of earth or stones; a tumulus.
barrow *n* a small wheeled handcart.
barter *n* trading by exchange of goods; *v*.
basalt *n* dark-coloured volcanic rock; *a* **basaltic.**
bascule *n* mechanism working on see-saw principle.
base *n* bottom; starting point; word-stem; main ingredient; *v* make base on; *as* **basal, basic, baseless**; *n* **basement** floor below ground level.
base *a* low, mean; vicious; vile; (of metal) counterfeit; *n* **baseness**; *adv* **basely.**
baseball *n* American ball-game similar to rounders.
bash *n* a heavy blow; *v* strike violently.
bashful *a* shy, modest; *adv* **bashfully**; *n* **bashfulness.**
basil *n* aromatic plant of mint family.
basilica *n* church with double colonnade & apse.
basilisk *n* fabulous lizard whose breath & glance were fatal; kind of crested lizard.
basin *n* hollow vessel; region drained by river; dock; land-locked harbour.
basis *n* base, foundation, principle; *pl* **bases.**
bask *v* luxuriate in (sun etc).
basket *n* container made of woven rushes or canes; *ns* **basket-work**; **basket-ball** kind of ball game.
Basque *n* member of race living in W. Pyrenees.
bas-relief *n* sculpture with design standing away slightly from background.

bass *n* voice of deep quality; lower part of musical register; *a* low in tone.
bass *n* common perch; **sea-bass** fish like salmon.
basset *n* type of hound with short legs.
bassinet *n* hooded wicker-work cradle or pram.
bassoon *n* woodwind instrument with bass tone.
bast *n* fibrous strips from trees used for mats, ropes.
bastard *n* illegitimate child; *a* spurious.
baste *v* moisten (roasting meat) with melted fat, etc; tack loosely; thrash; *pr p* **basting**.
bastion *n* projecting part of fortification; bulwark.
bat *n* small nocturnal mammal which flits about.
bat *n* wooden implement used in ball-games; blow; *v* strike with bat; *ns* **batsman**; **batting**.
batch *n* whole product of one baking; set of things of the same kind.
bate *v* diminish, abate, moderate.
bath *n* act of washing; vessel to wash in; *pl* place where baths may be taken.
bathe *v* apply water to; swim; *ns* **bather, bathing**.
bathos *n* fall from sublime to ridiculous; *a* **bathetic**.
bathysphere *n* large metal sphere used for deep-sea observation.
batiste *n* a fine cotton muslin.
batman *n* servant to an officer.
baton *n* a staff, *esp* of orchestral conductor.
battalion *n* Army unit of about 1000 men.
batten *n* narrow strip of wood; *v* secure with battens.
batten *v* grow fat; feed greedily on.
batter *v* beat heavily with repeated violent blows; *n* mixture of flour, milk & eggs beaten together.
battery *n* physical assault; artillery unit; group of cells for storing electrical energy.
battle *n* fight between armies, fleets or aircraft; *v* fight, struggle; *ns* **battlefield** place of battle; **battleship** heavily armed & armoured warship.
battledore *n* small bat used to strike shuttlecock.
battlement *n* low wall on top of fort, castle, etc, with openings or embrasures.
bauble *n* flashy jewellery; gewgaw; trifle.
bauxite *n* clay from which aluminium is obtained.

bawd *n* prostitute; procuress; *a* **bawdy** lewd; *n* **bawdiness**.
bawl *v* shout, cry loudly; *n* loud cry.
bay *n* kind of laurel.
bay *n* inlet of sea; division of building; recess in a room; **sick-bay** sick quarters.
bay *n* deep bark of hound *esp* in pursuit; *v* howl.
bay *a* of a reddish-brown colour, chestnut.
bayonet *n* dagger-like blade fixed to rifle; *v* wound with bayonet.
bazaar *n* Oriental market; sale in aid of charity.
bazooka *n* portable anti-tank gun.
be *v* exist; have quality, feeling or state; *pt* **was, were**; *pp* **been**; *pr p* **being**.
beach *n* sea-shore *esp* if sand; *v* run (a boat) on shore; *n* **beachcomber** beach-haunting tramp; *n* **beach-head** position established by invading troops.
beacon *n* signal light or fire on hill, tower, etc.
bead *n* small ball of glass, wood, etc. with hole through it, used to form necklace, rosary; small drop of moisture; *as* **beaded**; **beady** round, bright; *n* **beading**.
beadle *n* mace-bearer; minor parish or church officer.
beagle *n* small hound used in hunting.
beak *n* bill of bird; (*sl*) magistrate, headmaster.
beaker *n* large cup or mug; glass vessel used by chemists.
beam *n* thick piece of timber; bar of balance; shaft of light; radio waves; extreme breadth of ship; *v* shine, emit, radiate.
bean *n* leguminous plant; its kidney-shaped seed.
beano *n* a feast, jollification.
bear *n* heavy, clumsy, fur-clad mammal; rude, bad-tempered person; *a* **bearish**; *n* **bearishness**.
bear *v* support, carry; endure; bring forth, give birth to; *pt* **bore**; *pp* **borne** (**born** in most contexts relating to birth, bring forth); *n* **bearer** carrier; *adv* **bearable**.
beard *n* growth of hair on man's cheeks and chin; awn; gills of oyster; *v* oppose, confront face to face; *as* **bearded, beardless**.
bearing *n* behaviour; meaning; direction; heraldic

emblem; part of machine where moving parts revolve.

beast *n* four-footed animal; a brutal person; *a* **beastly** brutal; *n* **beastliness.**

beat *v* hit repeatedly; conquer; mark (time) by strokes; pulsate; *pt* **beat;** *pp* **beaten;** *n* blow; throb; regular route; *a* **beaten** shaped by beating; defeated; mixed by beating; *n* **beater** one who rouses game.

beatify *v* make happy, blessed; *a* **beatific**; *adv* **beatifically**; *n* **beatitude** supreme bliss.

beau *n* dandy; boyfriend; *pl* **beaux.**

Beaufort Scale *n* number scale indicating wind speeds.

beauty *n* loveliness, charm, grace; a lovely woman; *a* **beautiful**; *v* **beautify** make beautiful.

beaver *n* water-loving rodent; its fur.

becalm *v* make calm; *a* **becalmed** (ship) deprived of wind.

because *conj* & *adv* for reason that, on account of.

beck *n* small stream; a nod, sign of command.

beckon *v* signal or call by a gesture.

become *v* come to be; suit; *pt* **became**; *a* **becoming** proper, enhancing appearance of; *adv* **becomingly.**

bed *n* thing to sleep on; piece of ground; foundation; mineral stratum; bottom of sea or river; *v* plant out; place on foundations; *ns* **bedrock** solid rock base; **bedstead** framework of bed; *a* **bedridden** kept in bed by illness; *pl* **bedding, bedclothes.**

bedeck *v* decorate, adorn.

bedevil *v* confuse, harass, bewitch; *n* **bedevilment.**

bedizen *v* dress in a cheap, gaudy way.

bedlam *n* lunatic asylum; noisy scene or uproar.

Bedouin *n sing* & *pl* nomadic Arab.

bedraggle *v* drag through mire; *a* **bedraggled.**

bee *n* four-winged insect, producing honey; *ns* **bee eater** small brightly coloured bird; **bee hive**; **bee-line** shortest way; **beeswax.**

beech *n* tree with smooth grey bark; its wood; **beech-mast** beech nuts.

beef *n* flesh of ox, cow, considered as food; *pl* **beeves**; *a* **beefy** sturdy; *n* **Beefeater** Yeoman of the Guard.

beer *n* alcoholic drink made from malted hops, yeast, etc; *a* **beery**.
beet *n* red succulent, edible root; white root used in sugar manufacture.
beetle *n* insect with biting mouth parts; heavy wooden mallet.
beetle *v* overhang; *a* **beetling**; *n* **beetle-brow** heavy projecting brow.
befall *v* happen to; *pt* **befell**; *pp* **befallen**.
befit *v* be worthy of; fitting; *a* **befitting**; *adv* **befittingly**.
befog *v* obscure; confuse.
before *prep* in front of; preceding in time, rank; *adv* in front; sooner; *conj* rather than; *adv* & *a* **beforehand** in advance, ahead of time.
befoul *v* foul, make dirty.
befriend *v* be a friend to, help.
befuddle *v* confuse, make hazy.
beg *v* entreat; live by receiving alms; plead; *n* **beggar** person who begs; *a* **beggarly**.
beget *v* produce; father; *pt* **begot, begat**; *pp* **begotten**; *n* **begetter**.
begin *v* commence, start; originate; *pt* **began**; *pp* **begun**; *ns* **beginner** novice; **beginning**.
begone *interj* be off! go away!
begonia *n* colourful tropical plant.
begrime *v* soil with dirt, *esp* from soot, smoke.
begrudge *v* envy (a person something); be stingy in giving.
beguile *v* deceive, cheat; amuse, charm; *ns* **beguiler** deceiver, seducer; **beguilement**.
begum *n* high-ranking Moslem woman, princess.
behalf *n* in name of; for sake of.
behave *v* conduct (oneself); act with decorum; *n* **behaviour** conduct, manners.
behead *v* cut the head off.
behest *n* an order; command.
behind *prep* at back of; with, in support; inferior to; *adv* in arrears; *a* & *adv* **behindhand** late, slow.
behold *v* to look at, see; *pt* & *pp* **beheld**; *n* **beholder**; *adj* **beholden** under an obligation.

beige *n* undyed or unbleached woollen fabric; greyish-brown colour.
being *n* existence; human creature; essence, nature.
belabour *v* beat heartily, thrash.
belated *a* unduly deferred; *adv* **belatedly.**
belay *v* make fast or secure (a rope).
belch *v* release wind through mouth; pour out under force; *n* release of wind; spurt of flame, smoke etc.
beleaguer *v* besiege.
belfry *n* bell-tower.
belie *v* give lie to, misrepresent.
believe *v* accept as true, place trust in; have faith; *ns* **believer, belief;** *as* **believable, believing.**
belittle *v* make little of; disparage; *n* **belittlement.**
bell *n* hollow cup-shaped object giving musical sound when struck; cry of stag in rut; *v* roar, bellow.
belladonna *n* deadly nightshade; poisonous drug.
belle *n* beautiful young woman.
belles-lettres *n* essays which are purely literary.
bellicose *a* war-like, quarrelsome; *n* **bellicosity.**
belligerent *a* waging war; aggressive; *adv* **belligerently;** *n* **belligerence.**
bellow *v* roar, cry out; *n* roar of a bull etc.
bellows *n* apparatus for producing draughts of air.
belly *n* lower part of body beneath diaphragm, abdomen; *v* swell out, bulge.
belong *v* be owned by; be part or member (of); *n* **belongings** possessions.
beloved *a* greatly loved; *n* one who is greatly loved.
below *prep* lower than; *a* & *adv* beneath.
belt *n* band of leather or other fabric worn round waist; zone; endless band used in driving machinery; *v* encircle; (*sl*) thrash; *a* **belted.**
bemoan *v* lament; sorrow for.
bemuse *v* daze, confuse, stupefy.
bench *n* long seat, work-table; judge's, magistrates' seat in court; *coll* of magistrates, judges.
bend *n* curve; type of knot; *v* twist; turn, curve; submit; *p t* & *p p* **bent.**
beneath *adv* below; *prep* underneath.
benediction *n* blessing; blessing at end of church service.

benefit *n* favour; profit; *v* do *or* receive good; *p t* & *p p* **benefited**; *ns* **benefaction** good deed; **benefactor**; *a* **beneficial** useful, improving; *adv* **beneficially**; *ns* **benefice** church living; **beneficiary** one benefiting from will, etc.
benevolence *n* kindliness, generosity; *a* **benevolent**.
benighted *a* overtaken by darkness; ignorant.
benign *a* kindly, gentle, gracious; (of diseases) not malignant; *n* **benignity**; *adv* **benignly**.
benison *n* a benediction, blessing.
bent *n* inclination, aptitude; stiff coarse grass.
benumb *v* make numb, deprive of sensation.
benzedrine *n* drug used as stimulant and nasal spray.
benzene *n* aromatic liquid obtained from coal-tar.
benzine *n* colourless inflammable solvent obtained from petroleum.
benzoin *n* fragrant resin used in medicine.
bequeath *v* give or leave by will; *n* **bequest**.
berate *v* scold, rebuke.
bereave *v* to deprive by death; rob (*fig* of immaterial things); *p p* & *p t* **bereaved** (but *p p* **bereft** in *fig* sense); *n* **bereavement**.
beret, biretta *n* small, soft, flat cap.
beri-beri *n* disease caused by lack of vitamin B.
berry *n* small fleshy fruit containing seeds but no stone; *a* **berried**.
berserk *a* mad, wild, frenzied.
berth *n* space for anchoring ship in dock; sleeping-place on ship or train; *v* moor a ship.
beryl *n* mineral group including emerald, aquamarine.
beseech *v* implore, beg; *a* **beseeching**; *adv* **beseechingly**; *p t* & *p p* **besought**.
beseem *v* be suitable to.
beset *v* surround; assail; *a* **besetting**.
beside *prep* at side of; *adv* & *prep* **besides** other than; in addition to.
besiege *v* beset with armed forces; *n* **besieger**.
besmirch *v* soil, smear.
besom *n* rough broom made of twigs.
besot *v* make dull; mentally; *a* **besotted** foolish.

bespeak *v* arrange in advance; claim; *p t* **bespoke**; *p p* **bespoken**; made to order.
best *a* & *adv* (*superl* of GOOD, WELL) supreme excellence; *v* beat (someone): get the better of.
bestial *a* coarse, brutish; *n* **bestiality.**
bestir *v* stir up, rouse to action.
bestow *v* give, stow away; *n* **bestowal.**
bestride *v* put one's legs on each side of (something); *p t* **bestrode**; *p p* **bestridden.**
bet *v* wager; *n* stake given; *n* **better** one who bets.
betel *n* kind of pepper plant.
betide *v* happen to, befall.
betimes *adv* in good time, early.
betoken *v* presage.
betray *v* act falsely towards; reveal secret improperly; *ns* **betrayal, betrayer.**
betroth *v* promise, engage in marriage; *ns* **betrothal, betrothed.**
better *a* & *adv* (comp. of GOOD, WELL) expressing superiority to; improvement to; *v*; *n* **betterment.**
between *prep* & *adv* separated by; union; reciprocity.
betwixt *prep* & *adv* between.
bevel *n* sloping edge; joiner's tool; *v* form angle.
beverage *n* a drink.
bevy *n* group of girls or women; flock of larks, quails.
bewail *v* mourn over, lament; complain over.
beware *v* be on one's guard, take heed.
bewilder *v* perplex, confuse; *as* **bewildered, bewildering**; *n* **bewilderment**; *adv* **bewilderingly.**
bewitch *v* cast a spell over; fascinate; *a* **bewitching.**
bey *n* Turkish district governor.
beyond *prep* on farther side of; in addition; *adv* farther along; out of reach.
bezique *n* card-game for two or four players.
bias *n* slant, prejudice; tendency; *v* influence unfairly; *p t* & *p p* **bias(s)ed**; *pr p* **bias(s)ing**; *a* **biased** prejudiced.
bib *n* garment placed under child's chin to protect its clothes; *v* tipple; *n* **bibber** tippler.
Bible *n* sacred writings of Christian Church; *a* **biblical**; *adv* **biblically.**
bibliography *n* study of books; list of books on a

particular subject; *a* **bibliographical**; *n* **bibliographer.**

bibulous *a* given to drinking alcoholic drinks.

bice *n* blue or green pigment.

biceps *n* muscle with double attachment, *esp* of upper arm.

bicker *v* quarrel, wrangle; *n* **bickering.**

bicycle *n* two-wheeled vehicle propelled by foot pedals; *v* ride this vehicle; *n* **bicyclist.**

bid *v* command, invite; *p t* **bade**; *p p* **bidden**; offer, try; *p t* & *p p* **bid**; *n* offer to give certain price; attempt; (in card-games) a call; *ns* **bidder, bidding.**

bide *v* wait, remain, dwell.

biennial *a* happening every two years; *n* plant lasting two years; *adv* **biennially.**

bier *n* wooden frame on which a coffin is carried.

biff *n* sharp blow with fist; *v* strike such a blow.

big *a* possessing great size, bulk etc.

bigamist *n* one who marries another whilst still married; *n* **bigamy**; *a* **bigamous**; *adv* **bigamously**.

bight *n* loop in rope; a wide bay.

bigot *n* narrow-minded, intolerant person; *a* **bigoted**; *n* **bigotry.**

bijou *n* (of house, flat etc.) small, elegant.

bilateral *a* having two sides; *adv* **bilaterally.**

bilberry *n* moorland shrub, or its bluish berries.

bile *n* secretion of liver, aiding digestion; ill-humour; *a* **bilious**; *n* **biliousness.**

bilge *n* space in ship's bottom into which filth & seawater drain; foul dirt collecting there; *colloq* stupid talk or writing.

bilingual *a* of or using two languages.

bilk *v* cheat, defraud, elude payment of (debt).

bill, billhook *n* curved chopping tool for cutting brushwood, hedges etc.

bill *n* a bird's beak; point of anchor.

bill *n* draft of proposed legislation; statement of money due; written programme of events; poster; bank-note.

billet *n* soldier's quarters; *v* provide lodgings.

billet *n* faggot; block of wood.

billiards *n* game played with cue and balls on cloth-covered table with pockets.
billion *n* a million millions; (U.S.A.) a thousand millions.
billow *n* large swelling wave; *v* swell out; *a* **billowy, billowing**.
billy, billy-can *n* can used as camp kettle.
bin *n* container for corn, coal, waste etc; rack for storing wine bottles.
binary *a* dual, involving two.
bind *v* tie round; make fast; pledge (oneself); fasten sheets of book into cover; *p t* & *p p* **bound**; *ns* **binder** bookbinder; thing that binds; **binding** book-covering.
bindweed *n* climbing plant; convolvulus.
binge *n* a spree, drinking bout.
bingo *n* gambling game involving random numbers.
binnacle *n* box for compass in ship.
binocular *a* using both eyes at once; *n* **binoculars** field or opera glasses.
binomial *n* algebraic expression having two terms.
bio- *prefix*=life; *forms compound words as* **biography** written life-story; **biology** science of life; etc. *Where the meaning may be deduced easily from the simple word, the compounds are not given here.*
bioscope *n* apparatus for projecting motion pictures.
bipartite *a* having two parts; shared by two parties.
biped *n* a two-footed animal.
biplane *n* aircraft with two planes.
birch *n* tree with thin, smooth bark; wood of this tree; birch rod used for caning; *v* to flog.
bird *n* feathered biped which lays eggs.
birdlime *n* sticky material spread to snare birds.
birth *n* bearing of offspring; act of being born; parentage, descent; *n* **birthright** patrimony.
biscuit *n* thin crisp cake made of eggs, flour etc.
bisect *v* divide into two parts; *a* **bisectional**; *ns* **bisection**; **bisector** divider of angle into two equal parts.
bisexual *a* pertaining to both sexes; hermaphrodite.
bishop *n* clergyman of high rank in Christian Church; *n* **bishopric** his diocese or office.

bismuth *n* metallic element used as medical drug.
bison *n* large wild ox, American buffalo.
bissextile *a* pertaining to leap year.
bistro *n* small wine shop or restaurant.
bit *n* small portion, fragment; tool for boring; metal mouth-piece of bridle; *v* fit bit in (horse's mouth).
bitch *n* female dog or wolf, vixen.
bite *v* use teeth upon; act on by friction; pierce; *p t* **bit**; *p p* **bitten**; *pr p* **biting**; *a* **biting**; *adv* **bitingly** scathingly; *n* **bite** nip with teeth; wound (by teeth); sting; taking of bait.
bitter *a* of sharp taste; opposite of sweet; rankling; piercing; *adv* **bitterly**; *n* **bitter** light beer.
bittern *n* marsh bird noted for deep, booming cry.
bittersweet *n* woody nightshade.
bitumen *n* asphalt; natural mineral pitch; *a* **bituminous.**
bivalve *n* mollusc with double-hinged shell, as oyster.
bivouac *n* temporary camp in open air; *v* camp temporarily without tents.
bizarre *a* unusual, odd, fantastic.
blab *v* reveal secrets; *n* **blabber** tale-teller.
black *n* darkest colour; negro; darkness; *a* sombre; wicked; sullen; *v* **black, blacken** make black; denigrate; *n* **blackness**; *v* **blackball** vote against; *ns* **blackberry** bramble; **blackbird** song-bird; **blacking** black polish; **blackleg** one who works during strike; **blackmail** extortion of money under threat; **black Maria** police van.
blackguard *n* scoundrel, worthless person; *v* revile; *a* **blackguardly.**
blackout *n* failure of electricity; temporary loss of consciousness.
blacksmith *n* a smith who forges iron.
blackthorn *n* thorntree, which bears sloes.
bladder *n* sac in body for holding secreted liquids; any tough, inflated, membraneous bag.
blade *n* cutting edge of knife etc; flat of oar; bat, propeller, etc; long thin leaf of grass, corn etc; gay young fellow; *a* **bladed.**
blame *v* censure; find fault with; hold responsible;

n culpability; *as* **blameless, blameworthy**; *adv* **blamelessly.**
blanch *v* make white; scald; grow pale.
blancmange *n* sweet dish based on cornflour.
bland *a* gentle, mild; urbane; *n* **blandness.**
blandish *v* flatter, coax; *n* **blandishment.**
blank *n* empty space; cartridge without shot; *a* without writing, print, expression or features; (of verse) unrhymed; *adv* **blankly**; *n* **blankness.**
blanket *n* soft woollen cloth used for bedcover, horse-rug etc; *v* cover with (as with blanket).
blare *v* utter loudly, like a trumpet; *n* harsh noise.
blarney *n* flattery; *v* cajole, speak coaxingly.
blasé *a* dulled by pleasure, bored, cynical.
blaspheme *v* speak profanely of, talk irreverently; *ns* **blasphemer, blasphemy**; *a* **blasphemous.**
blast *n* sudden strong gust of wind; explosion; *v* scorch; shatter by explosion.
blatant *a* noisy, vulgarly obvious; *adv* **blatantly** *n* **blatancy.**
blather *v* talk foolishly; *n* stupid; foolish talk.
blaze *n* burst of flame or intense light; outburst of rage etc; *v* burst into flame; shine brilliantly.
blaze *n* mark tree by cutting bark; white mark on face of animal; *v* mark (tree or trail) by cutting bark.
blazer *n* light flannel sports jacket.
blazon *n* coat of arms; *v* paint shield with arms; proclaim widely.
bleach *v* whiten, *esp* of cloth; *n* **bleaching.**
bleak *a* bare, desolate; cheerless; *n* **bleakness.**
blear *a* watery, dim; *v* dim, blur; *a* **bleary.**
bleat *n* cry of sheep, goat; *v* cry so; *n* & *a* **bleating.**
bleed *v* draw blood from; extort money from; lose blood; *p t* & *p p* **bled**; *ns* **bleeder, bleeding.**
blemish *n* physical, moral defect, flaw; *v* mar, deface.
blench *v* flinch, quail, grow pale.
blend *v* mix together; *n* mixture, mingling; *p t* & *p p* **blended.**
bless *v* pronounce benediction; make holy; make happy; *a* **bless**; *n* **blessing**; *adv* **blessedly**; *n* **blessedness.**

blight *n* disease or insect pest attacking plants; *v* spoil, exercise an evil influence on.
blimp *n* small non-rigid airship.
blind *a* sightless; lacking foresight; reckless; closed at one end; *n* window shade; artifice; *v* make blind; *a* **blinding**; *adv* **blindly**; *n* **blindness**; *v* **blindfold** put something over the eyes of.
blindworm *n* legless lizard, a slow-worm.
blink *v* flap eyelids rapidly; flicker; (*fig*) attempt to evade; *n* wink, twinkle.
blinkers *n pl* small flaps preventing horse from seeing sideways.
bliss *n* perfect enjoyment, happiness; *a* **blissful**; *adv* **blissfully**; *n* **blissfulness.**
blister *n* swelling containing fluid, on skin; *v* raise a blister; *a* **blistered.**
blithe *a* gay, carefree; *adv* **blithely**; *a* **blithesome.**
blitz *n* sudden attack.
blizzard *n* blinding snowstorm with high wind.
bloat *v* swell; cure by salting & smoking; *a* **bloated**; *n* **bloater** smoked herring.
blob *n* spot, drop of liquid.
bloc *n* political or national alliance of interests.
block *n* lump of wood; mould; plate used in letter-press printing; group of buildings; obstruction; large quantity; *v* stop; shape, *esp* hats; *n* **blockead**; stupid person.
blockade *v* stop access by siege; *n* closure of port etc.
bloke *n* (*sl*) man, chap, fellow.
blond(e) *a* fair-coloured; *n* person with fair hair and complexion.
blood *n* red fluid circulating through body; kinship; life itself; dashing fellow; *adv* **bloodily**; *n* **bloodiness**; *as* **bloodless**; **bloodshot** suffused with blood; **bloody** blood-stained; murderous; (*vulg*) = damned or similar meaningless intensive.
bloodhound *n* a hunting dog; detective.
bloodshed *n* the shedding of blood.
blood-stone *n* opaque green stone with red flecks.
bloodthirsty *a* ferocious, savage, cruel.
bloom *n* blossom; prime of life; thin film on certain fruits; *v* flower, prosper; *n* **bloomer** mistake; *a*

blooming flowering; euphemism for (*vulg*) bloody.
blossom *n* flower; *v* come into bloom.
blot *n* spot; disgrace; *v* stain, smudge, obliterate; *n* **blotting paper** absorbent paper to dry up ink.
blotch *n* discoloured patch on skin, etc; *a* **blotchy.**
blouse *n* loose kind of shirt.
blow *v* produce current or gust of air; expel air from lungs into trumpet etc; *p t* **blew**; *p p* **blown**; *n* blast; hard knock; sudden set-back; *a* **blown** winded; putrefying; *ns* **blow-fly** meat fly; **blow-hole** nostril of whale; breathing hole in ice; **blow-out** tyre-burst; feast; **blow-pipe** through which air is used to increase intensity of flame; *v* **blow up** explode; enlarge; inflate.
blowzy *a* coarse; slovenly, dishevelled.
blubber *n* fat of whales; *v* weep.
bludgeon *n* short heavy club; *v* strike with this.
blue *n* colour of unclouded sky; pigment; University sportsman; unhappy; indecent; *v* make or treat with blue; *pl* sad kind of Negro jazz; depression; *a* **bluish**; *ns* **bluebell** wild hyacinth; **blueberry** bilberry; **bluebottle** meat-fly; **bluejacket** sailor; **blueprint** copy of plan; **bluestocking** pedantic woman.
bluff *n* steep headland, bank; *a* having steep perpendicular front; hearty; outspoken; *adv* **bluffly.**
bluff *v* deceive; *n* deception, hoax, fraud.
blunder *n* mistake; *v* make such; stumble, flounder; *n* **blunderer**; *a* **blundering**; *adv* **blunderingly.**
blunderbuss *n* short large-bored gun with wide muzzle.
blunt *a* having dull edge or point; outspoken; *v* dull edge of; *adv* **bluntly**; *n* **bluntness.**
blur *n* & *v* smear; blot.
blurt *v* utter hastily or indiscreetly.
blurb *n* laudatory announcement on book jacket, etc.
blush *v* grow red; *n* flush; *n* & *a* **blushing.**
bluster *v* (wind) blow boisterously; rage; scold; *n* noise; empty threats; *n* **blusterer**; *a* **blustery.**
boa *n* non-poisonous snake that kills by crushing; fur or feather neck wrap.
boar *n* male pig; wild hog.
board *n* plank; thick, stiff, compressed paper; table;

official body; thin slab of covered wood or cardboard on which games (chess, etc.) are played; *pl* the stage; *v* provide with meals; *n* **boarder** one who pays for food, lodging; child living at school in term.
boast *v* praise oneself; claim proudly; *ns* **boaster, boastfulness**; *a* **boastful**; *adv* **boastfully.**
boat *n* generic term for all water-craft; *v* sail in boat; *ns* **boathouse**; **boatswain, bosun** ship's officer.
bob *n* quick up-and-down movement; clumsy curtsey; short haircut; *v* move jerkily up and down.
bobbin *n* spool or reel on which thread is wound.
bobby *n* (*sl*) policeman.
bobcat *n* American lynx, wild cat.
bobsled *n* sledge steered by wheel on movable front portion, also **bobsleigh.**
bode *v* portend; be an omen of; *a* **boding** foretelling.
bodice *n* part of woman's dress above the waist.
bodkin *n* large-eyed blunt needle.
body *n* physical organism of living creatures; corpse; main part; mass of matter; trunk exclusive of head & limbs; substance; group of people; *v* give shape to; *a* **bodiless**; *a* & *adv* **bodily.**
bodyguard *n* person or persons guarding someone.
bog *n* marsh; swamp; (*sl*) latrine; *v* become stuck in bog etc; *a* **boggy.**
bogey *n* goblin; standard score for golf course.
boggle *v* bungle; shrink from; *n* **boggler.**
bogie *n* wheeled frame-work beneath front of locomotive or railway coach.
bogus *a* not genuine, sham.
boil *v* bubble with heat; cook in boiling water; *n* **boiler** vessel or tank for heating, also boiling (*esp* water to make steam power).
boil *n* inflamed swelling, filled with pus.
boisterous *a* rough, turbulent; *adv* **boisterously**; *n* **boisterousness.**
bold *a* daring; shameless; clear, prominent; *adv* **boldly**; *n* **boldness.**
bole *n* trunk or stem of a tree.
bolero *n* lively Spanish dance; loose short jacket.
bollard *n* mooring post for ship on dockside.
Bolshevik *n* Russian communist; revolutionary.

bolster *n* long cushion; *v* support; *a* **bolstered.**
bolt *n* metal rod used to bar door etc; thunderbolt; heavy arrow; *v* secure with bolt; gulp food; run away.
bomb *n* metal shell filled with explosive, etc; *v* attack with bombs; *n* **bomber** bomb-carrying aircraft.
bombard *v* attack with shells, missiles, words; direct rays from radio-active substance at; *ns* **bombardment; bombardier** artillery N.C.O.
bombast *n* pompous, empty, insincere talk; *a* **bombastic;** *adv* **bombastically.**
bona fide *a* in good faith.
bonanza *n* rich vein of ore; unexpected wealth.
bonbon *n* sweetmeat.
bond *n* shackle; link; covenant; *v* bind; store goods until payment of duty; *a* **bonded** held in bond.
bondage *n* servitude, slavery; *n* **bondsman** slave.
bone *n* substance of which skeleton of vertebrates is made; any bone of skeleton; *v* take out bones; *as* **bony, boneless, bone-dry.**
bonfire *n* open-air fire lighted on festive occasions, or to burn rubbish.
bonnet *n* head covering; covering over motor engine.
bonny *a* handsome, comely; *adv* **bonnily.**
bonus *n* sum paid beyond what is due; premium; *pl* **bonuses.**
boo *interj* exclamation used to indicate disapproval, to startle; *v* make this sound.
boob *n* (*coll*) stupid error; dunce; (*v*) make mistake; *n* (*sl*) woman's breast.
booby *n* dunce; seabird; *ns* **booby prize** award for lowest score; **booby trap** device to catch the unwary; practical joke.
book *n* sheets of paper bound together in cover to form a volume; literary composition; list of bets in race; *v* reserve in advance; enter in book; *a* **bookish;** scholarly; *ns* **booklet** small book; **bookkeeper, bookkeeping** keeping of accounts; **bookshelf** shelving for books.
bookmaker *n* professional betting man, a bookie.
bookworm *n* one devoted to study of reading.
boom *n* long pole keeping bottom of sail extended;

barrier across harbour; hollow roar; *v* make such a sound; *n* sudden prosperity; *v* rise in prices.
boomerang *n* wooden missile returning to thrower.
boon *n* petition; blessing; favour.
boor *n* peasant, lout, ill-bred person; *a* **boorish**; *adv* **boorishly**; *n* **boorishness**.
boost *v* raise; augment; praise; *n* **booster** device for raising power or voltage.
boot *n* foot and ankle covering; space for luggage in car (in U.S.A.=trunk); *v* kick.
boot *n* benefit; profit; *v* avail; *a* **bootless**; *adv* **to boot** in addition.
booth *n* temporary stall in market etc.
bootlegger *n* one engaged in traffic in illicit liquor; *v* & *a* **bootleg**; *n* **bootlegging**.
booty *n* spoils of war, plunder.
borage *n* plant used for flavouring.
borax *n* white crystalline salt used as antiseptic, etc, *a* **boracic**.
border *n* edge; frontier; flower bed; *v* line; verg (on).
bore *v* make hole in; weary by being dull; *n* hole bored; dull person; high tidal wave in river; *a* & *pr p* **boring**; *n* **boredom** state of being bored.
borough *n* town or city with municipal corporation; one with privileges granted by royal charter.
borrow *v* obtain on loan; adopt; use another's material; *ns* **borrower; borrowing**.
borzoi *n* large Russian wolfhound.
bosh *n* empty talk; rubbish.
bosom *n* human breast; seat of affection or emotions.
boss *n* head man; overseer; *v* direct; *a* **bossy** arrogant; *a* **bossiness**; *n* any projecting part; ornamental stud.
botany *n* science of plant life; *n* **botanist**; *as* **botanic, botanical**; *adv* **botanically**; *v* **botanize**.
botch *v* patch roughly; bungle; *n* clumsy piece of work.
botfly *n* parasitic fly affecting horses etc.
both *a* & *pron* the two; *conj* & *adv* as well.
bother *v* worry; feel anxiety; *n* fuss.
bottle *n* glass container for liquids; its contents; *v* put into bottles; *n* **bottler**.

bottleneck *n* narrow passageway; condition hindering free circulation.
bottom *n* lowest part of anything; bed of sea, river, lake etc; human rump; *a* lowest; *a* **bottomless.**
botulism *n* form of food poisoning.
boudoir *n* lady's small private sitting-room.
bough *n* limb of tree.
bouillon *n* a clear soup.
boulder *n* large rounded mass of rock or stone.
boulevard *n* broad avenue.
bounce *v* rebound, as ball, on striking anything; *n* spring; *n* **bouncer** chucker-out; *a* **bouncing** robust.
bound *v* move with sudden spring; *n* leap, spring.
bound *v* set limit to, restrict; **bound to** *v* obliged to, certain to; *n* that which limits, confines; **out of bounds** beyond permitted area; *a* **boundless**; *adv* **boundlessly**; *n* **boundary** something fixing limit, area etc.
bound *a* intending to go; on the way to.
bounder *n* vulgar, overbearing fellow.
bounty *n* generous gift; *as* **bountiful; bounteous** liberal; *advs* **bountifully, bounteously** plentiful.
bouquet *n* bunch of flowers; aroma of wine.
bourgeois *n* & *a* middle-class; *n* **bourgeoisie.**
bourn(e) *n* rivulet; limit; realm.
bout *n* spell; turn; trial, contest; space of time.
bovine *a* pertaining to ox or cow; patient, stolid.
bow *n* inclination of head or body in respect; *v* make bow; submit, yield; defeat.
bow *n* weapon for shooting arrows; implement for playing violin etc; bend; curve; *v* use bow; *n* front part of ship, *a* **bowlegged** bandy-legged.
bowdlerize *v* expurgate (a book).
bowels *n* the intestines.
bower *n* leafy grove; *n* **bower bird** Australian bird.
bowl *n* hollow dish; drinking cup.
bowl *n* wooden ball; *v* roll ball; *ns* **bowls** game played on **bowling green; bowling alley** indoor area for bowls etc; **bowler** one who bowls; hard round felt hat.
bowsprit *n* spar projecting from bow of ship.
box *n* hardwood tree; case; private compartment in

theatre; sentry's shelter; carriage driver's seat; ruled-off space; *v* put in box.

box *v* strike with fist or hand; *n* such a blow to head; *n* **boxer** one who fights with fists as sport **(boxing)**.

boy *n* male child, youth; *a* **boyish**; *n* **boyhood**.

boycott *v* ban, stop dealing with.

brace *n* support; pair; device for holding bit; *pl* support for trousers; *v* support; *a* **bracing** invigorating.

bracelet *n* wrist band or ornament.

bracken *n* coarse common fern.

bracket *n* projecting support; *pl* symbols [ ], (), enclosing word, etc; *v* join; associate.

brackish *a* (of water) salty; *n* **brackishness**.

bract *n* small leaf at base of flower.

brad *n* thin flat nail; **bradawl** boring tool.

brag *v* boast; *n* boast; card-game; *n* **braggart** boaster.

braid *n* plait of hair; band of fabric; *v* plait.

braille *n* system of printing for use by the blind.

brain *n* soft mass of nervous substance within skull; *pl* intelligence; *v* dash out brains of; hit on head; *as* **brainy, brainless**; *n* **brainwave** sudden bright idea; *v* **brain-wash** indoctrinate.

braise *v* cook by simmering in closed pan.

brake *n* device for checking wheel's motion; thicket; kind of waggon; *v* apply brake to, slow down.

bramble *n* prickly shrub, blackberry.

bran *n* husks remaining after grain is ground.

branch *n* limb of tree; any offshoot from main stem; *a* secondary; *v* produce branches; *n* & *a* **branching**.

brand *n* trade-mark; identifying mark; particular type of goods; burning stick; *v* mark with brand.

brandish *v* flourish, wave.

brandy *n* strong spirit distilled from wine.

brash *a* forward, loud, tactless, impudent.

brass *n* alloy of copper & zinc; (*sl*) money; effrontery; *as* of brass; **brassy** strident; *n* **brass-hat** high ranking officer.

brassard *n* arm-band.

brassiere *n* undergarment supporting woman's breasts.

brat *n* uncomplimentary name for a child.
bravado *n* show of boldness or bluster.
brave *a* courageous; fine; *n* N. American Indian warrior; *v* face with courage; *adv* **bravely**; *n* **bravery.**
bravo *interj* well done!
brawl *n* & *v* noisy, quarrel, fight.
brawn *n* muscle, strength; pickled cut-up pork; *a* **brawny** strong.
bray *v* cry, as donkey; shout harshly; crush.
braze *v* cover with brass; join with solder; *a* **brazen** shameless; *v* adopt defiant manner; *adv* **brazenly.**
brazier *n* iron basket for holding hot coals; brass-worker.
breach *n* break; violation of law, contract; *v* make an opening in.
bread *n* food made from flour, water, yeast and baked; food in general; livelihood; (*sl*) money; *n* **bread-fruit** fruit resembling bread when roasted.
breadth *n* distance across, width.
break *v* smash; destroy; tame; make bankrupt; interrupt; snap; crack; *p t* **broke;** *p p* **broken;** *n* breach; fracture; interruption; lucky change; *as* **breakable, breakneck** reckless; *ns* **breakdown** accidental stoppage; collapse; analysis; **breaker** large wave; **breakwater** structure breaking force of waves; **breakfast** first meal of day.
bream *n* fish of carp family.
breast *n* bosom; mammary gland; *v* face boldly; *ns* **breastplate** armour to cover breast; **breastwork** defensive wall.
breath *n* air drawn into or expelled from lungs; slight breeze; fragrance; *v* **breathe** inhale & exhale air; live; utter gently; blow lightly; *ns* **breathing, breathlessness, breather** pause; *as* **breathless.**
breech *n* hind end of anything; buttocks; *pl* **breeches** trousers; *n* **breeches buoy** device for rescuing at sea.
breed *v* bear offspring; rear; nourish; give rise to; *p t* & *p p* **bred;** *n* strain; kind; *ns* **breeder; breeding** manners.
breeze *n* gentle wind; *a* **breezy** airy; jolly; *adv* **breezily.**

breeze *n* cinders, coal-dust mixed with cement; **breeze blocks** bricks made of this.
bren gun *n* light machine gun.
brethren *pl* of brother.
breviary *n* book of daily prayers used by R. Catholics
brevity *n* briefness, conciseness.
brew *v* make beer, tea etc; contrive; be afoot; *n* act or product of brewing; *ns* **brewing, brewer, brewery.**
briar, brier *n* thorny shrub, wild rose, bramble.
bribe *n* money, favour given to influence person; *v* influence thus; *n* **bribery.**
bric-a-brac *n* curios, knick-knacks.
brick *n* oblong block of baked clay used in building; *v* build with bricks; **drop a brick** make a gaffe; *ns* **bricklayer; brickbat** broken piece of brick.
bride *n* newly-married woman; **bridegroom** newly-married man; **bridesmaid** girl attendant on bride.
bridge *n* a card-game.
bridge *n* structure allowing access over river, railway, etc; part of ship used by captain & navigating officer; wooden strut under strings of violin etc; upper part of nose; *v* build bridge over; *n* **bridging** loan of credit for business.
bridle *n* head harness of horse; curb; *v* fit with bridle; check; show disdain etc.
brief *a* lasting short time; concise; *n* synopsis of law case; *v* give final instructions to; *adv* **briefly.**
brig *n* two-masted, square-rigged vessel.
brigade *n* military unit; organised body of people.
brigadier *n* officer commanding a brigade.
brigand *n* bandit, robber, outlaw.
bright *a* shining; lively; vivid; intelligent; *v* **brighten** make bright; become fine; *n* **brightness.**
brill *n* flat sea-fish similar to turbot.
brilliance *n* splendour, radiance; outstanding talent; *a* **brilliant**; *adv* **brilliantly**; *n* **brilliant** diamond cut in particular way.
brim *n* rim, edge (of cup, hat, etc.); *v* be full to rim; *as* **brimming, brimful, brimless.**
brimstone *n* sulphur.
brindled *a* light brown colour with darker streaks.
brine *n* salt water used for pickling meat; *a* **briny.**

bring *v* cause to come, fetch; carry; cause; **bring about** cause to happen; **bring forth** give birth; **bring to** revive; **bring up** rear; *p t* & *p p* **brought.**

brink *n* edge (of chasm, precipice etc.).

briquette *n* block of compressed coal dust.

brisk *a* lively, energetic, bracing; *adv* **briskly.**

brisket *n* joint of beef cut from breast.

brisling *n* small sardine-like fish.

bristle *n* short, stiff hair; *v* stand on end, as bristles; show indignation; *a* **bristly.**

brittle *a* easily broken; *n* **brittleness.**

broach *n* boring tool; roasting spit; *v* pierce (cask); open, begin (a subject).

broad *a* wide, large; general; coarse; of marked accent; *v* **broaden** make wider; *a* **broad-minded** tolerant; *adv* **broadly**; *n pl* the **Broads** stretches of water in Norfolk; *ns* **broadcloth** woollen cloth; **broadside** simultaneous discharge of all guns on one side (of ship).

broadcast *v* scatter (seed) widely; spread abroad; transmit (radio, television); *pt* & *pp* **broadcast;** *n* such a transmission.

brocade *n* stiff silk fabric with raised design.

broccoli *n* hardy type of cauliflower.

brochure *n* pamphlet, printed folder.

brogue *n* stout rough shoe; accent *esp* Irish.

broil *n* noisy quarrel; *v* grill on open fire; *n* **broiler** quickly-reared chicken sold ready for broiling; *a* **broiling** very hot (*colloq*).

broker *n* one buying for another on commission; *n* **brokerage** his commission or business.

bromide *n* a sedative drug.

bronchitis *n* inflammation of bronchial tubes; *a* **bronchial.**

bronco *n* half-tamed horse.

bronze *n* alloy of copper and tin; its colour; *v* make or become bronze; *a* **bronzed** sun-tanned; covered with bronze.

brooch *n* ornamental clasp or pin.

brood *n* young of animals *esp* birds; *v* sit on eggs; ponder anxiously; *a* **broody** inclined to brood.

brook *n* small stream; *v* endure, tolerate.

broom *n* flowering shrub; sweeping brush; *n* **broomstick.**
broth *n* thin meat soup.
brother *n* son of same parents; member of religious order, trade union etc; *pl* **brothers, brethren;** *a* **brotherly;** *ns* **brotherhood** group united by common interest; **brother-in-law** brother of husband/wife.
brow *n* eyebrow; forehead; top of hill etc.
browbeat *v* bully, cow.
brown *n* colour made by mixing black, red & yellow; *a* tanned; *v* make or become brown; **brown study;** reverie.
brownie *n* fairy, elf; junior Girl Guide.
browse *v* feed (as animal) on grass, leaves etc; glance through book.
bruise *n* injury that discolours flesh; contusion; *v* inflict thus; *n* **bruiser** prizefighter.
brunch *n* breakfast and lunch combined.
brunette *n* woman with dark hair and complexion.
brunt *n* chief stress, strain of attack.
brush *n* implement ior sweeping, painting, dressing hair etc; tail of fox; skirmish; small shrubs; electrical device; light touch; *v* sweep, use brush; touch lightly; *ns* **brush-off** snub; **brushwood** broken or cut branches.
brusque *a* abrupt, curt; *n* **brusqueness.**
brute *n* lower animal; cruel person; *as* **brutal, brutish** cruel, sensual; *adv* **brutally;** *ns* **brutality, brutishness.**
bubble *n* globule of gas, air; plan lacking solidity; *v* form bubbles; make bubbling sound.
bubo *n* suppurating swelling of gland in armpit, groin; *a* **bubonic (plague).**
buccaneer *n* pirate; *n* **buccaneering.**
buck *n* male deer, rabbit etc; dandy; sudden spring; (*sl*) dollar; *v* leap suddenly; *n* **buckskin** soft leather.
bucket *n* vessel for carring water etc; pail; scoop in dredger; *n* **bucketful.**
buckle *n* clasp with catch for fastening; bulge, warp; *v* fasten with buckle; warp; **buckle to** begin work.
buckram *n* coarse stiff fabric.

bucolic *a* countrified, rustic, pastoral.
bud *n* new growth from stem, whence leaf or flower will develop; *v* put forth buds; graft.
buddy *n* friend, chum.
budge *v* move position.
budgerigar *n* small parakeet, love-bird.
budget *n* estimated financial schedule; *v* plan spending.
buff *n* soft leather; pale yellow colour; bare skin; *v* polish; *n* **buffer** polisher; device to absorb shock.
buffalo *n* kind of ox; American bison; *pl* **buffaloes.**
buffet *n* & *v* slap; cuff.
buffet *n* side-board; refreshment bar.
buffoon *n* clown; *n* **buffoonery.**
bug *n* small parasitic insect; *v* install hidden device for spying; *a* **bugged.**
bugbear *n* source of real or fancied fear.
bugle *n* kind of small trumpet; glass bead; *ns* **bugler, bugle-call.**
build *v* construct; *p t* **built**; *n* form; *ns* **builder, building.**
bulb *n* globular, modified leaf-bud, usually underground; electric lamp; *a* **bulbous.**
bulge *n* rounded outward swelling; *v* swell outward; *as* **bulgy, bulging.**
bulk *n* size, volume; larger part; cargo; *v* be of large size; *n* **bulkiness**; *a* **bulky.**
bulkhead *n* partition dividing ship into compartments.
bull *n* male of ox family etc; speculator in rising stock values; *ns* **bullock** castrated bull; **bull's-eye** centre of target.
bull *n* official Papal enactment.
bulldog *n* powerful dog with protruding lower jaw; University proctor's attendant.
bulldozer *n* powerful tractor-type of machine for earth moving; *v* **bulldoze** overcome opposition by brute force.
bullet *n* metal ball or missile fired from gun.
bulletin *n* brief official statement.
bullion *n* gold or silver before being coined.

bully *n* overbearing, cruel ruffian; *v* cow, frighten, intimidate.
bulrush *n* large rush of sedge family.
bulwark *n* rampart; any form of defence; ship's side above deck; breakwater.
bum *n* buttocks; tramp, loafer.
bumble-bee *n* large wild humming bee.
bumbledom *n* fussy officialdom.
bump *n* blow, collision; swelling due to blow; protuberance; *v* collide with, strike; jolt; *n* **bumper** motor-car fender; full glass; *a* plentiful.
bumpkin *n* country yokel, rustic.
bumptious *a* arrogant; offensively self-assertive; *adv* **bumptiously**; *n* **bumptiousness**.
bun *n* small cake; small round bunch of hair.
bunch *n* cluster of things growing, or tied together.
bundle *n* number of things tied or rolled together; *v* tie in a bundle; hustle (someone) away.
bung *n* cork, wooden stopper *esp* for cask; *v* insert bung; (*colloq*) throw away.
bungalow *n* one-storied house.
bungle *v* botch; blunder; *n* something botched; confusion; *n* **bungler**; *a* **bungling**.
bunion *n* inflamed swelling, *esp* on big toe.
bunk *n* sleeping-berth; (*colloq*) escape.
bunk, bunkum *n* empty talk, nonsense.
bunker *n* large bin, *esp* for fuel; military dugout; hazard on golf course.
bunsen-burner *n* type of gas burner.
bunting *n* small bird allied to finch; coloured flags used for decoration *esp* of streets, ships etc.
buoy *n* floating object anchored in water to mark channel, rocks etc; a life-buoy; *v* mark with buoy; keep afloat; sustain morally; *a* **buoyant**; *adv* **buoyantly**; *n* **buoyancy**.
bur, burr *n* seed-case covered with hooked spines.
burble *v* make gentle gurgling sound; babble.
burden *n* load; something difficult to bear; *v* load, encumber; *a* **burdensome**.
bureau *n* writing table; information office; government department; *pl* **bureaux**.

bureaucracy *n* government by state officials; *n* **bureaucrat**; *a* **bureaucratic**.
burgee *n* flag or pennant with swallow-tail.
burgeon *v* to bud.
burgess *n* dweller in borough, with full municipal rights.
burgh *n* Scottish variant spelling of borough.
burglar *n* one who breaks into house etc. by night; *n* **burglary**; *v* **burgle**.
burlesque *n* derisive imitation; *v* ridicule; *a* mocking.
burly *a* of sturdy build; *n* **burliness**.
burn *v* injure or destroy by fire; cause to flame, shine; be on fire; be consumed by fire; yearn; *p t* & *p p* **burnt, burned**; *n* mark caused by heat; *a* **burning**; *n* **burner**.
burn *n* brook, stream.
burnish *v* & *a* polish; *n* **burnisher**.
burr *n* hard stone; rough edge or line made by etching-tool on metal.
burrow *n* hole scooped in ground by animal *esp* rabbit, fox etc; *v* make hole; dig, search.
bursar *n* treasurer, *esp* of college; *n* **bursary** grant.
burst *v* explode; open out; erupt; puncture; *p t* & *p p* burst; *n* explosion; sudden spurt.
bury *v* inter; conceal; *p t* & *p p* **buried**; *n* & *a* **burial**.
bus *n* omnibus.
busby *n* fur hat worn by certain British regiments.
bush *n* shrub; thicket; wild country; *a* **bushy**; *n* **bushiness**.
bush *n* metal lining for circular hole; *v* fit bush.
bushel *n* dry measure equal to eight gallons.
business *n* occupation, profession, trade etc; affair; *a* **businesslike** efficient, practical.
bust *n* upper part of human body; sculpture of such part.
bustard *n* large, swift-running bird.
bustle *n* noisy movement; *v* move quickly, fussily.
busy *a* at work; fully occupied; *v* occupy (oneself); *adv* **busily**; *ns* **busyness**; **busybody** meddling officious person.
but *adv* only just; without; *prep* except; *conj* on the contrary; yet; unless; **all but** almost.

butane *n* inflammable gaseous compound.
butcher *n* tradesman dealing in meat; brutal murderer; *v* kill for food, or indiscriminately.
butler *n* head man-servant of a household.
butt *n* large cask; thick blunt end (of gun etc). target; *pl* shooting range; *v* abut; push violently with head *esp* of animal; **butt in** interfere.
butter *n* solidified fat obtained from cream by churning; *v* spread with butter; flatter; *n* **buttermilk** liquid remaining after churning.
buttercup *n* yellow cup-shaped wild flower.
butterfly *n* four-winged insect, usually brightly coloured; flighty person.
butterscotch *n* kind of toffee.
buttery *n* place for storing wines, liquors etc.
buttocks *n* the rump.
button *n* small flat disc for fastening clothing etc; small knob; *v* fasten with button.
buttress *n* support giving extra strength to anything; *v* support, prop.
buxom *a* robust, plump, rosy, comely; *n* **buxomness**
buy *v* obtain by paying; bribe; *p t* & *p p* **bought**; *n* **buyer.**
buzz *n* low humming noise, as of bee; *v* make such sound; murmur; *n* **buzzer** mechanical device making such sound.
buzzard *n* large bird of prey.
by *prep* near; close to; through, over; not later than; expressing agency; *adv* at hand; aside; past; **by & by** after a while.
by-*prefix* near; secondary; indirect; subsidiary; apart from. *Where the meaning may be deduced easily from the simple word, the compounds are not given here.*
bye *n* something out of regular course; *a* incidental.
by-election *n* election held by itself, not during General Election.
bygone *a* past, gone by; *n pl* **bygones** the past.
by-law *n* local law or regulation.
by-pass *n* alternative road, avoiding traffic; side-passage in pipe etc; controlling circulation of gas, air, etc.
by-product *n* subsidiary product or result.

byre *n* cowshed.
bystander *n* one standing near, an onlooker.
byway *n* a quiet road or path.
byword *n* typical example; object of contempt; proverb.

cab *n* taxi; driver's shelter on engine, lorry or bus; *n* **cabby**, taxi driver.
cabal *n* intrigue; secret plot.
cabbage *n* green edible vegetable.
caber *n* pole tossed in contest in Highland games.
cabin *n* small room on ship, *esp* for sleeping; hut.
cabinet, *n* case or set of drawers; body of ministers governing country.
cable *n* thick strong rope or line; telephone, telegraph line; message sent by cable; *v* send cable.
cacao *n* plant from seeds of which cocoa & chocolate are made.
cache *n* secret store or hiding place.
cachet *n* mark of excellence, authenticity.
cackle *n* noise made by hen, goose; shrill chatter; *v* make such noise.
cacophony *n* harsh discordant sound.
cactus *n* prickly plant with fleshy stem.
cad *n* ill-bred vulgar person.
cadaverous *a* looking like corpse; pale, gaunt.
caddie, caddy *n* golfer's attendant.
caddy *n* small box for tea.
cadence *n* rhythm in poetry; rise and fall of voice in speaking.
cadet *n* younger son; student training for commissioned rank.
cadge *v* beg; sponge on others; *n* **cadger**.
cadre *n* permanent nucleus of military unit.
caecum *v* vermiform appendix.
cafe *n* restaurant serving light meals; *n* **cafeteria** self-service cafe.
caffeine *n* alkaloid stimulant, obtained from coffee and tea plants.
cage *n* structure for confining animals, etc; *v* to confine to cage; *a* **cagey** wary.

cairn *n* pile of stones built as monument etc; small terrier.
caisson *n* ammunition cart; box in which men work under water.
cajole *v* flatter with ulterior motive; *n* **cajolery**.
cake *n* kind of sweet dough, baked in tin; hard mass; *v* to form hard mass, as of clay etc.
calamity *n* terrible, disastrous event; *a* **calamitous**.
calcareous *a* made of lime.
calcium *n* metallic element, base of lime.
calculate *v* reckon *esp* by arithmetic; fit for particular purpose; *a* **calculating** able to make calculations; scheming; *ns* **calculation, calculator**; **calculus** mode of calculation.
calendar *n* almanac; system for fixing beginning and end of year; list of official documents.
calender *n* rolling machine for smoothing, polishing paper etc; *v* smooth so.
calf *n* young of cow & various other mammals; its leather; *pl* **calves**; *v* **calve** give birth to calf.
calf *n* fleshy back of leg below knee; *pl* **calves**.
calibre *n* diameter of bore of gun; quality of mind or character; *v* **calibrate**; *n* **calibration**.
calico *n* cloth made of cotton.
caliph *n* descendant of Mahomet.
call *v* shout; pay visit; summon; give name to; *n* shout; short visit; player's bid (cards); speak on telephone; *ns* **caller**; **calling** occupation; vocation; **call up** conscription.
calligraphy *n* handwriting; beautiful writing; *n* **calligrapher**.
cal(l)iper *n* instrument for measuring; leg brace.
callous *a* hard-hearted; unfeeling; hardened (of skin); *n* **callousness**; *adv* **callously**.
callow *a* undeveloped; inexperienced.
calm *n* windlessness; stillness; *a* quiet; peaceful; *v* become still, tranquil; *adv* **calmly**; *n* **calmness**.
calorie *n* unit of heat; *esp* in relation to value of food; *a* **calorific** heat making.
calumny *n* false accusation; slander.
calyx *n* cup of leaves surrounding flower petals.
cam *n* projection on shaft controlling desired move-

ment; *n* **camshaft** device in engine to lift valves.
camber *n* slight convexity on road, ship's deck, etc; curvature of aircraft wing.
cambric *n* fine white linen cloth.
camel *n* large, ruminant, humped animal.
cameo *n* gem carved in relief on contrasting background.
camera *n* photographic apparatus; *legal* privately; *n* **cameraman.**
camomile *n* plant with aromatic flowers, used medicinally.
camouflage *v* disguise appearance of objects *esp* from enemy; *n* deception.
camp *n* temporary shelter for travellers; place where tents or huts are erected for troops; faction or party; *a* (*sl*) effeminate; too ornate; dandified; *v* build, lodge in camp; *ns* **camping, camper**; **camp-bed** narrow folding bed; **camp-chair** portable folding chair; **camp-follower** civilian hanger-on of troops etc.
campaign *n* series of military operations; action to achieve particular purpose; *v* serve in, organize campaign.
campanile *n* lofty detached tower in which bells are rung.
campanologist *n* one who studies or peals bells; *n* **campanology**.
camphor *n* aromatic volatile white substance; *a* **camphorated** impregnated with camphor.
campus *n* chief grounds of American school, etc.
can *v aux* be able; be allowed to; *pt* **could**; *pp* been able.
can *n* tin vessel used for holding food for preserving; *v* preserve in can; *n* **cannery** place where canning is done.
canal *n* artificial waterway; duct in living body.
canary *n* yellow song-bird; sweet wine.
canasta *n* card game similar to rummy.
cancel *v* delete, cross out; abolish; suppress; *n* **cancellation.**
cancer *n* malignant tumour or growth in body; *a* **cancerous.**

candid *a* frank, honest, outspoken; *adv* **candidly**; *ns* **candidness, candour.**

candidate *n* one seeking appointment, office, election to parliament etc.

candle *n* stick of wax with wick, for giving light; *ns* **candle-light**; **candle-power** unit of measure of light; **candlestick** candle holder.

candy *n* crystallized sugar; *v* preserve, become encrusted with sugar; *a* **candied.**

cane *n* hard stem of bamboo etc; walking stick; *v* beat with stick; *n* **caning.**

canine *a* of, related to dog.

canister *n* box, usually of tin.

canker *n* ulcerous sore; disease in trees; (*fig*) moral corruption; *a* **cankered** spiteful.

cannibal *n* human who eats human flesh; *n* **cannibalism.**

cannon *n* large mounted gun; stroke in billiards; *pl* **cannon, cannons**; *v* make cannon in billiards collide; *n* **cannonade** discharge of; artillery.

cannot *v* can not.

canny *a* cautious, shrew, wary.

canoe *n* light boat propelled by paddling; *pl* **canoes**; *n* **canoeist.**

canon *n* rule, law *esp* of church; ecclesiastical dignitary; list of saints; *v* **canonize** declare officially to have been a saint.

cant *n* insincere speech; whining; *v* use cant; *adv* **canting.**

cant *v* slope, lean to one side; slant; *adj* **canted.**

cantaloup(e) *n* type of melon.

cantankerous *a* ill-natured, touchy, quarrelsome.

cantata *n* choral composition.

canter *n* easy hand-gallop; *v* ride at such pace.

cantilever *n* girder etc securely fixed at one end, free hanging at other; *n* **cantilever bridge** centre part supported by cantilever arms.

canto *n* chief division of long poem.

canton *n* state in Swiss Republic.

canvas *n* strong coarse hempen cloth used for sails or painting pictures on.

canvass *v* solicit votes; discuss; *n* **canvasser** one soliciting votes.
canyon *n* deep gorge between cliffs.
cap *n* brimless head-covering; military headdress; cap. as sign of membership of sports team; lid; *v* put cap on; confer University degree on.
capable *a* able; competent; having capacity, power; *n* **capability**; *adv* **capably**.
capacity *n* power of holding, absorbing (material or non-material things); *a* **capacious** spacious, receptive; *n* **capacitor** condenser (elect).
cape *n* sleeveless cloak; headland, promontory.
caper *v* skip about, frisk; *n* leaping about; *pl* silly pranks.
capillary *a* hair-like; *n* very narrow blood vessel.
capital *n* chief city; large-sized letter; head of column; accumulated wealth; *a* punishable by death; vital; excellent; leading; *adv* **capitally**; *ns* **capitalism** system of individual ownership of wealth; **capitalist**.
capitation *n* tax payable by or on each person.
capitulate *v* surrender, cease to contend; *n* **capitulation**.
capon *n* castrated fowl, *esp* when prepared for table.
caprice *n* whim, sudden fancy; *a* **capricious**; *n* **capriciousness**.
capsize *v* upset, overturn; *esp* of boats.
capsule *n* seed-container (of plant); part of spaceship in which astronaut travels; small, thin gelatine case containing drug or medicine.
captain *n* naval or military officer; leader of team or side; *v* act as leader of side or team.
caption *n* title of picture, etc; heading.
captious *a* fond of finding fault; critical.
captivate *n* enchant, fascinate, charm; *prp* & *a* **captivating** delightful, alluring.
capture *v* take prisoner; catch; *n* act of taking; *ns* **captive** prisoner; **captivity, captor**.
car *n* motor-car; railway carriage; wheeled vehicle.
carafe *n* bottle, usually glass, for water, wine.
caramel *n* sweetmeat; burnt sugar for flavouring.

carat *n* measure (of weight of diamonds, etc; of purity of gold).
caravan *n* covered vehicle, used as home, by gipsies, holiday-makers; party of merchants, etc crossing desert; *n* **caravanserai** Eastern inn accommodating caravans.
caraway *n* aromatic seed used for flavouring.
carbide *n* compound of calcium, producing acetylene gas.
carbine *n* short rifle used by mounted troops.
carbolic *a* derived from carbon; *n* **carbolic acid** used as disinfectant.
carbon *n* non-metallic element occurring as graphite, diamond etc; *as* **carbonic, carbonaceous** like coal. **carboniferous** coal-producing; *v* **carbonize** impregnate with carbon; *n* **carbon paper** coated one side with carbon, for duplicating typed or written matter.
carborundum *n* compound of carbon & silicon, used as abrasive.
carboy *n* large glass vessel covered by wicker-work.
carbuncle *n* inflamed boil, tumour; deep-red gem.
carburettor *n* device for mixing petrol vapour & air, forming explosive mixture, in internal combustion engines.
carcass, carcase *n* dead body; skeleton or framework (of ship, building).
carcinoma *n* type of cancer.
card *v* comb wool or cotton; *n* comb for cleansing wool etc.
card *n* thin pasteboard; visiting-card; playing-card; post-card.
cardiac *a* concerning heart; *n* **cardiograph** record of heart action.
cardigan *n* knitted woollen or cotton jacket.
cardinal *a* of chief importance; *n* prince of R.C. Church, next in rank to Pope; *ns* **cardinal numbers** 1, 2, 3, etc; **cardinal points** N. S. E. and W.
care *n* grief; concern; caution, charge; *v* feel anxiety; look after; have affection for; *as* **carefree, careful, careless**; *ns* **carefulness, carelessness**; **caretaker** one who looks after, cleans a building.

careen *v* expose keel of ship for cleaning or repair.
career *n* rapid course; mode of living; occupation; rush wildly.
caress *n* mark of affection, as kiss, embrace etc; *v* fondle, embrace.
caret *n* mark (∧) used to show insertion of letter, word.
cargo *n* freight or load of ship etc.
caricature *n* grotesque, laughable drawing or imitation of person; *v* represent in caricature.
caries *n* decay, *esp* of bones, teeth.
carillon *n* peal or chime of bells; melody played thereon.
carmine *n* crimson-red colour, obtained from cochineal.
carnage *n* severe slaughter, massacre.
carnal *a* pertaining to flesh; sensual; *adv* **carnally**; *n* **carnality**.
carnation *n* cultivated variety of clove pink.
carnival *n* organized festivities; revelry.
carnivore *n* flesh-eating mammal; *pl* **carnivora**; *a* **carnivorous** of animals & also some plants.
carol *n* joyful song *esp* Christmas hymn; *v* sing.
carouse *n* drinking bout; *v* drink deeply; *n* **carousal** noisy drinking bout.
carp *n* fresh-water fish.
carp *v* find fault unreasonably; *a* **carping** captious.
carpenter *n* wood worker in house-building, etc; *n* **carpentry** craft of carpenter.
carpet *n* fabric for covering floor etc; *v* cover with carpet.
carriage *n* railway coach; transportation of anything; cost of carriage; deportment, bearing; vehicle.
carrion *n* rotten flesh; putrefying animal carcass.
carrot *n* edible reddish-orange root; *a* **carroty** reddish *esp* of hair.
carry *v* transport; bear, support weight of anything; (*mil*) capture; retain (in memory); *n* range of projectile from gun; *n* **carrier** one carrying goods; kind of pigeon.
cart *n* two- or four-wheeled vehicle, usually horse-

drawn; *v* carry; *ns* **carter**; **carthorse** strong horse **cart-track** rough road.

cartel *n* written agreement for exchange of prisoners-of-war; agreement between manufacturers, fixing prices etc.

cartilage *n* strong, elastic tissue; gristle.

cartography *n* art of making maps, charts; *n* **cartographer.**

carton *n* box made of cardboard, corrugated board.

cartoon *n* sketch or design for work of art; topical drawing in newspaper etc; *n* **cartoonist.**

cartridge *n* metal case containing charge for gun; *n* **cartridge paper** strong drawing-paper.

carve *v* cut and shape wood, stone, etc; engrave; cut in slices or pieces (meat); *ns* **carving** piece of carved work; **carver, carving-knife** long knife for carving meat.

cascade *n* small waterfall; something resembling this; *v* **fall in cascades.**

case *n* condition; state of affairs; grammatical relationship; instance; law-suit; patient (*med*).

case *n* box; chest; protective covering, wrapping; *v* put in case.

casein *n* main protein of milk; basis of cheese.

casement *n* window side-hung on hinges.

cash *n* money, coin or notes; *v* give, receive cash in exchange for cheque etc; *ns* **cashier** one in charge of cash; **cash-register** till.

cashier *v* dismiss from the service; deprive of rank.

cashmere *n* soft material woven from goat's hair.

casino *n* public room with gambling facilities.

cask *n* barrel, mainly used for liquids.

casket *n* small box, plain or ornamented, for jewels, trinkets etc; coffin (U.S.A.).

casserole *n* fireproof dish for cooking & serving food; food cooked in this way.

cassock *n* long vestment, usually black, worn by clergy etc.

cast *v* throw down, off; shed (snake-skin); reckon up (accounts); mould (metal etc); hurl; assign parts in a play; *pt* & *pp* **cast**; *n* throw; impression taken of something; actors in a play; *adj* formed by moulding

metal; *ns* **casting** piece of metal shaped by casting; **castaway** ship-wrecked person.
caste *n* division of Indian society; exclusive social class.
castigate *v* chastise; punish severely; scold bitterly; *n* **castigation.**
castle *n* fortress; stronghold; piece in chess (rook); *a* **castellated** like a castle, having turrets etc.
castor, caster *n* vessel with perforated top for sprinkling pepper, sugar etc; small wheel on swivel fixed to leg of chair etc.
castor-oil *n* laxative oil made from seeds of castor-oil plant.
castrate *v* remove testicles; geld; emasculate; expurgate (book etc); *n* **castration.**
casual *a* accidental; careless; occasional; *adv* **casually**; *n* **casualty** victim of accident, battle; *pl* **casualties** number killed, wounded in war.
casuistry *n* specious reasoning; application of ethical rules & principles; *n* **casuist.**
cat *n* small, domesticated, carnivorous quadruped; any animal of genus *Felix*; spiteful woman; whip with nine lashes; *ns* **catgut** cord made from animal intestines; **catkin** flower of certain trees; **cat's-eye** semi-precious stone; reflective glass in roadway; **cat's-paw** dupe.
catabolism *n* destructive metabolism.
cataclysm *n* violent upheaval, social or physical; *as* **cataclysmal, cataclysmic.**
catacomb *n* subterranean cemetery.
catalogue *n* list of objects, names etc arranged in order; *v* make such list.
catamaran *n* raft of logs lashed together; twin-hulled sailing boat.
catapult *n* elastic sling fixed on forked stick for shooting pellets, stones; apparatus assisting aircraft to take-off *esp* from ship.
cataract *n* large, high waterfall; disease of eye.
catarrh *n* inflammation of mucous membrane, *esp* of nose; *a* **catarrhal.**
catastrophe *n* disaster; sudden irrevocable calamity; *a* **catastrophic.**

catch *v* get hold of; seize; grasp (of mind); be infected by (disease); become entangled; be in time for; overtake; *pt* & *pp* **caught** *n* act of catching, *esp* ball; something caught; mechanical device to secure lock; **catcher** one who catches; **catchment** drainage area of river; **catchword** temporary popular phrase; *as* **catchpenny** worthless; showy; **catchy** attractive; easy to remember (of tune).

catechize *v* teach by question & answer; examine by searching questions; *n* **catechism** form of instruction *esp* religious.

category *n* class, division, mode of grouping; *a* **categorical** absolute, positive.

catenate *v* link together; *n* **catenation**; chain, series of links.

cater *v* provide food, pleasure for; *n* **caterer.**

caterpillar *n* larva of butterfly, moth; endless belt of plates, on vehicle, used instead of wheels.

cathedral *n* chief church of diocese; *a* belonging to, containing such.

catheter *n* tube introduced into one of passages of body, to draw off fluid, or to dilate.

cathode *n* negative electrode; **cathode rays** negative discharge.

catholic *a* universal; *specif* whole body of Christians; Roman Catholic Church; *ns* **Catholic** a Roman Catholic; **Catholicism.**

cattle *n* bovine animals; human beings (disparaging).

Caucasian *n* & *a* (member) of the white races of mankind.

caucus *n* inner group of people controlling political policy.

cauldron, caldron *n* large metal pot or boiler.

cauliflower *n* white, fleshy, edible flower-head, variety of cabbage.

caulk, calk *v* make seam (of ship) watertight, by packing in oakum, tow & pitch; *n* **caulking, calking.**

cause *n* force producing effect; motive; reason; lawsuit; *v* bring about; effect.

causeway *n* raised path across wet, marshy ground.

caustic *a* corrosive; burning; satirical; *n* corrosive substance; *adv* **caustically.**

cauterize *v* sear, burn with hot iron or caustic; *ns* **cautery, cauterization.**
caution *n* carefulness; warning; *v* warn; *as* **cautious;** **cautionary** serving as warning; *n* **cautiousness.**
cavalcade *n* procession of riders, carriages etc.
cavalier *n* horseman; adherent of Charles I in Civil War; *a* careless, thoughtless; *n* **cavalry** horse soldiers.
cave *n* hollow in earth with lateral extension; den; *n* **cavern** deep cave; *a* **cavernous;** *n* **cavity** hole; *v* **cave in** collapse; give up; *n* **cave-man** primitive man.
caviar (e) *n* delicacy of salted sturgeon roe.
cavil *v* quibble; raise frivolous objections to.
cavort *v* frisk, prance about noisily.
cavy *n* small rodent, as guinea-pig.
caw *n* call of rook, crow; *v* utter such cry.
cayenne *n* ground red pepper.
cayman *n* variety of alligator.
cease *v* desist from; discontinue; *a* **ceaseless.**
cedar *n* large coniferous evergreen tree.
cede *v* yield, surrender; grant, admit.
ceiling *n* lining of upper surface of room; extreme height attainable by aircraft; upper limit of prices, wages etc.
celandine *n* wild flower, resembling buttercup.
celebrate *v* observe with proper rites; do honour to (by ceremony); (*colloq*) have good time; *ns* **celebrant** priest; **celebration; celebrity** famous person; fame; *a* **celebrated** well-known.
celerity *n* swiftness, rapidity.
celery *n* vegetable with long, juicy edible stalks.
celestial *a* pertaining to sky; divine, heavenly.
celibacy *n* unmarried state *esp* of one under a vow; *n* **celibate.**
cell *n* small room, in monastery, prison etc; biological basic unit; compartment in honeycomb; component of galvanic battery; *a* **cellular** of open texture; of cells.
cellar *n* underground part of house; stock of wine; *ns* **coal-cellar, wine cellar.**
Cellophane *n*[**P**] transparent foil for wrapping.

celluloid *n* inflammable plastic material.
cellulose *n* carbohydrate cell-walls of plants; raw material used in plastics; *v* varnish with nitro-cellulose lacquer.
cement *n* powdery substance which, mixed with water, sets hard; liquid adhesive; *v* cover with, join by cement; *fig* unite closely.
cemetery *n* burial-ground, other than churchyard.
cenotaph *n* monument raised in memory of one whose body is not therein.
censor *n* one authorized to prevent publication of books, plays etc; official, *esp* in wartime, empowered to open all written communications and suppress any harmful to safety of nation; *v* subject to censorship; *n* **censorship**; *a* **censorious** disapproving; severely critical.
censure *v* criticize adversely; blame; *n* reproof.
census *n* official periodic counting of population of a state.
cent *n* hundredth part of dollar; **per cent** in every hundred.
centenary *n* hundredth anniversary; *a* celebration of this; *n* **centenarian** one who is 100 years old; **centennial** occurring every 100 years.
centigrade *a* having 100 equal parts; *esp* **c. thermometer** freezing point 0° & boiling point 100°.
centigramme *n* measure of weight, hundredth part of a gramme.
centimetre *n* measure of length, hundredth part of metre.
centipede *n* long, crawling insect with many feet.
centre *n* middle point; axis; point in body on which certain activity depends; *a* **central**; *adv* **centrally**; *v* **centralize** bring under one control; *as* **centrifugal** tending away from centre; **centripetal** tending towards centre; *n* **central heating**.
centurian *n* officer in Roman army commanding 100 men.
century *n* 100 years; 100 things of same kind, collectively.
ceramic *a* pertaining to pottery; *npl* **ceramics** art of making pottery etc. of clay.

cereal *a* pertaining to edible grain; *n* grain itself.
cerebral *a* pertaining to brain; *n* **cerebration** working of brain.
ceremony *n* act of reverence; public observance of solemn event; *n* & *a* **ceremonial**; *a* **ceremonious.**
certain *a* definite; inevitable; of some amount; unerring; *adv* **certainly**; *ns* **certainty, certitude** mental conviction.
certify *v* assure; attest in written document; *a* **certifiable** *esp* of insanity; *n* **certificate** written declaration.
cessation *n* stopping; pause; ceasing.
cess-pit *n* cavity in ground, used for draining sewage from house etc.
chafe *v* rub against; become sore from friction; become restive; *n* **chafing dish** dish for keeping food hot.
chaff *n* husk of grain; chopped straw; teasing.
chaffinch *n* small wild bird.
chagrin *n* mortification; disappointment.
chain *n* series of connected metal links; connected series of things, visible or non-material; confine; restrain. *Makes many compounds e.g.* **chain-drive, chain-letter, chain-reaction, chain-smoker, chain-stores** etc.
chair *n* single seat with back & four legs; professorship; seat of authority etc; *v* carry person in triumph; *n* **chairman** one presiding at meeting; chief director of firm.
chalet *n* small wooden Swiss house; wooden cabin.
chalice *n* drinking cup; *specif* Communion-cup.
chalk *n* soft limestone; crayon; *v* mark with chalk; *a* **chalky.**
challenge *n* summons to fight; dispute; objection taken; *v* call in question; summon to fight; *n* **challenger.**
chamber *n* room; apartment; body of persons composing legislative assembly; *npl* lawyer's office; lodgings; *ns* **chamberlain** court official; **chambermaid** housemaid at hotel; **chamber-music** music suitable for room, or small hall, with few instruments.

chameleon *n* small lizard able to change colour; *a* inconstant.
chamfer *n* bevel; groove; *v* make bevel, groove.
chamois *n* goat-like animal; *n* **chamois-leather** soft pliable leather.
champagne *n* French white sparkling wine.
champion *n* upholder of cause; one who excels (in sport, shows or exhibitions); *v* act as champion.
chance *n* course of events; opportunity; possibility; unforseen fortune; risk; *a* accidental, fortuitous; *v* happen; risk; *a* **chancy** hazardous.
chancel *n* east part of Christian church, where altar stands.
chancellor *n* chief judge; head of University; chief finance minister.
chancery *n* division of High Court of Justice.
chandelier *n* branched support for lights, hanging from ceiling.
chandler *n* one making, dealing in candles; *n* **ships' chandler** dealer in stores & provisions for ships.
change *v* exchange; alter; substitute; interchange (train etc); put on different clothes; *n* alteration; small money; *as* **changeable** variable, fickle; **changeless** constant; *n* **changeling** child secretly substituted for another.
channel *n* river bed; body of water joining two seas; deep passage in shallow water; groove; that through which liquid flows; (*fig*) means of communication; frequency band for transmission of TV, radio; *v* form, supply through channel.
chant *n* song; sacred hymn; *v* sing; utter in musical monotone; *ns* **chanter** singer; pipe of bagpipes, producing notes; **chanty, shanty** sailor's song.
chaos *n* confusion, utter disorder; muddle; *a* **chaotic**.
chap *v* split, become sore from exposure to cold etc; *n* crack in skin; man, boy (*coll*); *a* **chapped** sore.
chapel *n* private church; place of worship for non-conformists to C. of E.; cathedral antechamber with small altar; association of journeymen printers.
chaperon *n* older lady accompanying younger one in public or on social occasions; *v* act in this way.

chaplain *n* clergyman attached to institution, armed forces, or private household.
chapter *n* main division of book; stage in history; governing body of cathedral; fraternity; **chapter house** room where chapter meets, attached to cathedral.
char *v* scorch, burn; *a* **charred.**
char *v* do housework for hourly, daily payment; *n* **charwoman.**
char *n* small fish of salmon or trout family.
char-a-banc *n* motor-coach.
character *n* mark; symbol; letter; essential nature; personality (in play, book etc); testimonial of ability, habits; *a* **characteristic**; *v* **characterize** describe; *n* **characterisation**; *a* **characterless.**
charade *n* form of riddle, when each syllable of word is acted.
charcoal *n* form of carbon, made from charred wood.
charge *v* load; restore electricity to battery; cost; attack; accuse; entrust; *n* cost; accusation; command; amount of electricity in battery; *a* **chargeable.**
chariot *n* ancient two-wheeled car for fighting, state occasions, racing; *n* **charioteer.**
charity *n* love; benevolence (of mind); liberality; *a* **charitable.**
charlatan *n* imposter; quack.
charm *n* magic spell; fascination; small object worn on person; *v* attract; bewitch; enchant; *n* **charmer** fascinating person; *a* **charming.**
charnel-house *n* vault where bodies or bones are stored.
chart *n* map *esp* for navigational use; graph; *v* make map, graph.
charter *n* document granting rights etc; *v* let or hire; *a* **chartered** licensed, privileged; *n* **charter-party** contract made between ship owner & skipper.
chary *a* careful; parsimonious; *n* **chariness**; *adv* **charily.**
chase *v* pursue; drive away; *n* hunting; pursuit; *n* **chaser** drink taken after stronger one.
chase *v* engrave ornamentally.

chasm *n* deep abyss; fissure.
chassis *n* framework, wheels & machinery of motor vehicle; undercarriage of aircraft.
chaste *a* pure; continent; *adv* **chastely**; *n* **chastity.**
chasten *v* punish in order to correct; *a* **chastened** subdued.
chastise *v* punish by beating; *n* **chastisement.**
chat *n* easy, informal talk; *v* talk idly; *a* **chatty**; *n* **chatter** rapid, trivial talk; *v* talk idly; rattle teeth; *ns* **chatterer, chattering, chatterbox** incessant chatterer.
chattel *n* movable property; *pl* goods, possessions.
chauffeur *n* driver of motor-car, usually paid; *fem* **chauffeuse.**
chauvinism *n* perverted, blind patriotism.
cheap *a* of low price, relative to value; inferior; *v* **cheapen**; *adv* **cheaply**; *n* **cheapness.**
cheat *v* swindle; defraud; practise trickery; *n* swindler; trickster.
check *v* retard; restrain; stop; verify; *n* call in chess; control; ticket (cloakroom); pattern in squares; *ns* **checkmate** final winning move in chess; defeat; **checkout** pay desk in supermarket; **checkpoint** place where traffic is checked.
cheek *n* side of face below eye; impudence; pertness; *v* address rudely; *a* **cheeky.**
cheer *n* state of mind; rich food and drink; applause; *v* applaud vocally; encourage; *a* **cheerful**; *n* **cheerfulness**; *a* **cheery**; *adv* **cheerily**; *a* **cheerless**; *n* **cheerlessness.**
cheese *n* consolidated milk curd used as food; *n* **cheesecake** sweet cake; *a* **cheeseparing** miserly, stingy.
chef *n* head cook in hotel, restaurant etc.
chemistry *n* natural science dealing with composition, reaction of substances; *n* **chemist**; *n* & *a* **chemical.**
chenille *n* tufted cord of silk or worsted.
cheque *n* paper form for withdrawing money from bank; *n* **cheque book.**
chequer *n* pattern of squares, as chess board; *v* mark in squares; *a* **chequered.**

cherish *v* hold dear; take care of; keep in mind.
cheroot *n* kind of cigar, open at both ends.
cherry *n* edible small-stoned fruit either red, black, or white; tree bearing this fruit; *a* red.
cherub *n* heavenly being, rosy-faced child; beautiful, innocent child; *pl* **cherubim, cherubs**; *a* **cherubic**.
chess *n* game of skill, played with 32 chessmen, on chequered board; *ns* **chessmen, chess-board**.
chest *n* coffer; larger box; upper front part of body.
chestnut *n* tree bearing nuts; (**sweet c.** edible; **horse c.** inedible); *n* reddish-brown colour; hoary joke.
chevron *n* V-shaped stripe(s) indicating rank, worn on uniform.
chew *v* masticate; *n* **chewing-gum**.
chic *n* smartness; style; elegance; *a* smart, elegant.
chicane *n* trick; (bridge) hand with no trumps; obstacle in motor race; *v* quibble; *n* **chicanery** verbal trickery.
chick *n* newly hatched bird; affectionate name for child; *n* **chicken** young bird, *esp* hen; *a* **chicken-hearted** timid; *n* **chicken-pox** mild contagious disease, chiefly of children.
chicory *n* blanched salad vegetable.
chide *v* reprove, scold; *pt* **chid**; *pp* **chidden**; *a* & *n* **chiding**.
chief *n* leader; head; *a* principal; foremost; *adv* **chiefly**; *n* **chieftain** head *esp* of Highland Clan.
chiff-chaff *n* bird of warbler species.
chiffon *n* thin gauze-like material.
chilblain *n* painful swelling on feet, hands, or ears, due to cold.
child *n* young human being; *pl* **children**; *a* **childish**; pertaining to child; foolish; silly; *ns* **childhood** period of life to puberty; **childbirth**; **childbed** state of giving birth to child; *as* **childless, childlike**; *n* **child's play** simple task.
chill *n* coldness; illness due to cold; *a* frigid (of manner); discouraging; *v* make or become cold; *as* **chilled, chilly** unwelcoming; *n* **chilliness** coldness of sensation or manner.
chime *n* set of bells; musical sequence produced by

such; *v* ring chime on bells; *v* **chime in** break into a conversation.
chimera *n* fabulous monster; bogey, fancied horror.
chimney *n* outlet for smoke; narrow cleft in rock.
chimpanzee *n* arboreal ape, related to gorilla.
chin *n* part of jaw below mouth.
china *n* fine porcelain ware; *a* made of this.
chine *n* narrow ravine; backbone; *v* to chop backbone (joint of meat).
chink *n* slit; cleft.
chink *n* tinkling, metallic sound; *v* make such sound.
chintz *n* printed cotton fabric; used in upholstery.
chip *n* small piece of substance cut, broken off; *v* cut chips off; *v* **chip in** interrupt.
chiropody *n* care of feet; *n* **chiropodist**.
chirp, chirrup *v* utter short piping note (of birds); *n* this sound.
chisel *n* cutting tool, for stone, wood etc; *v* to use chisel.
chit *n* short note; memo; *n* **chit-chat** gossip.
chivalry *n* body of knights; courtesy, courage; *a* **chivalrous** having knightly qualities.
chive *n* plant of onion tribe; usually *pl* **chives**.
chlorine *n* non-metallic element; poison gas; *ns* **chloral** hypnotic; **chloride** bleaching agent; *v* **chlorinate** purify water.
chloroform *n* volatile liquid used as anaesthetic; *v* to make insensible with this.
chlorophyll *n* green colouring matter in plants.
chock *n* wooden wedge; *v* make secure, prevent rolling; *a* & *adv* **chockfull, chock-a-block** packed tight.
chocolate *n* sweetmeat made from ground cacao beans; drink; *a* dark brown colour.
choice *n* act of choosing; something specially selected; *a* of high excellence.
choir *n* group of singers *esp* in church; chancel; *n* **chorister** singer; *a* **choral**.
choke *v* smother; obstruct; throttle; stifle; *n* act of choking; device to reduce air supply to carburettor; *a* **choked**.
choler *n* anger; wrath; *a* **choleric** irascible.
cholera *n* infectious disease of bile, often fatal.

choose *v* select; prefer; *pt* **chose**; *pp* **chosen.**
chop *v* cut with knife etc; make quick blow; *n* piece of lamb, pork with rib-bone; *n* **chopper** axe; *a* **choppy** rough (sea).
chord *n* blending of notes in harmony.
choreography *n* art of ballet dancing, or arranging dances; *n* **choreographer.**
chorus *n* group of singers; refrain of song; *n* **chorale** hymn for congregational use.
Christian *n* followers of Christ; *a* pertaining to Christians; **C. name** baptismal name; **C. Science** belief in healing by prayers; *ns* **Christianity** teaching of Christ.
chromatic *a* relating to colour; (*mus*) scale ascending or descending by semitones.
chromium *n* brittle metallic element, used for plating.
chronic *a* long-lasting (of disease); *sl* tedious, bad.
chronicle *n* record of events in order of time; *v* register (events, dates); *n* **chronicler.**
chronology *n* table or list of dates; *a* **chronological** in order of time.
chronometer *n* watch for measuring time exactly.
chrysalis *n* sheath enclosing insect larva during resting stage.
chub *n* river fish of carp family.
chubby *a* fat, stumpy; plump; *n* **chubbiness.**
chuck *v* throw; **c. out** eject forcibly; **c. up** give up; *n* tap; throw.
chuckle *v* laugh softly; *n* low laugh of satisfaction.
chukker *n* period of play in polo.
chum *n* close friend.
church *n* place of Christian worship; whole body of Christians; clergy; *ns* **churchwarden** officer representing parish; long clay pipe; **churchyard.**
churlish *a* boorish, ungracious; selfish, mean.
churn *n* vessel for making butter; *v* shake liquid violently.
chute *n* inclined slope for sending down logs, water, any heavy thing.
chutney *n* hot sweet-tasting pickle or relish.
cider *n* drink made of fermented apple juice.

cigar *n* solid roll of tobacco leaves for smoking.
cigarette *n* finely cut tobacco, rolled in thin paper.
cinder *n* remains of burnt-out coal; *a* **cindery.**
cine- *prefix* indicating a relationship to cinematography, e.g. **c.-camera, c.-film, c.-projector,** etc.
cinema *n* place where cine-films are shown.
cinematography *n* art of producing moving pictures on film; *a* **cinematographic** projecting film.
cinnamon *n* bark of Ceylon laurel, used as spice; *a* of yellowish-brown colour.
cipher, cypher *n* symbol 0; zero; person of no importance; monogram; secret way of writing.
circle *n* perfectly round plane figure; group of people united by common interest; ring; *v* move round; surround; *a* **circular** round; moving around; *n* notice sent to many people; *v* **circulate** pass from hand to hand, move freely; *n* **circulation** flow of blood round body; number of newspapers sold; act of moving around.
circuit *n* distance round; series of places where Assizes are held; path of electric current; *a* **circuitous** indirect.
circumcise *v* cut off foreskin; *n* **circumcision.**
circumference *n* boundary of a circle.
circumnavigate *v* sail round.
circumscribe *v* limit; restrict.
circumspect *a* decorous; prudent; cautious.
circumstance *n* event; fact; *pl* financial condition; pomp; *a* **circumstantial** accidental; incidental; indirect.
circumvent *v* outwit; frustrate; *n* **circumvention.**
circus *n* entertainment with, clowns, animals etc; round open space in city.
cirrhosis *n* disease of liver.
cirrus *n* high fleecy cloud.
cistern *n* water-tank; natural reservoir.
citadel *n* fortress protecting a town.
cite summon; quote an authority; *n* **citation.**
citizen *n* one living in city or town; *n* **citizenship**; *a* **civic** pertaining to city or citizen.
citron *n* fruit like lemon or lime, less acid; *a* **citric** of acid of lemon etc.

citrus fruit *n pl* citrons, lemons, oranges etc.
city *n* large-sized town.
civil *a* relating to citizens of same State; non-military; affable; polite, (law) not criminal; *ns* **civility** politeness; **civilian** non-military person; *v* **civilize** bring from barbarism; *n* **civilization**; *a* **civilized**.
claim *v* assert; apply for as right; *n* demand for, assertion of just title to something; *n* **claimant**.
clairvoyant *n* person having second sight; *n* **clairvoyance**.
clamber *v* climb clumsily or laboriously.
clammy *a* moist and cold to touch; sticky; *n* **clamminess**.
clamour *n* loud outcry; noise; *n* **clamourous**.
clamp *n* tool for holding things together; heap of potatoes, etc straw covered for winter storage; *v* fasten with clamp; **~down on** suppress.
clan *n* tribe; group of families under chief, having common ancestor; *a* **clannish**; *ns* **clannishness, clansman**.
clandestine *a* guiltily secret; surreptitious.
clang *n* loud, metallic ring; *v* make such sound; *n* **clangour** repeated ringing.
clank *n* sharp metallic sound; *v* to make such sound.
clap *v* strike together, with noise; applaud with hands; *n* sharp noise; sudden burst of thunder; *ns* **clapper** tongue of bell; **clap-trap** empty talk.
claret *n* red wines of Bordeaux.
clarify *v* purify; make clear; *ns* **clarification, clarity**.
clarion *n* kind of trumpet; *a* ringing; *ns* **clarionet, clarinet** wood-wind instrument.
clash *v* come together suddenly; disagree; *n* metallic sound; conflict.
clasp *n* hook, bolt for fastening; *v* fasten; embrace; grasp; *n* **clasp-knife**.
class *n* any division, kind, sort; rank; category; *v* **classify** arrange methodically in classes; *n* **classification**; *a* **classifiable**.
classic *a* of highest merit; of ancient Greek & Roman culture; *n* work of art or literature, regarded as

model of excellence; *pl* Greek or Latin language; *a* **classical** possessing excellence *esp* of music.
clatter *n* series of dull, hard noises; rattle; noisy talk; *v* make clatter.
clause *n* short sentence, part of main one; article in treaty, will, contract, etc.
claustrophobia *n* morbid fear of enclosed spaces.
clavichord *n* early predecessor of piano.
clavicle *n* collar-bone; *a* **clavicular.**
claw *n* sharp nails or talons of animals & birds; *v* seize, scratch with claws.
clay *n* sticky earth; human body; *a* **clayey**; *n* **clay-pigeon** clay disc used in shooting contest.
clean *a* free from dirt; pure; shapely; neat; *v* render clean; *adv* **cleanly**; *ns* **cleaner, cleanness, cleanliness**; *v* **cleanse** remove impurity from.
clear *a* audible; bright; distinct; unimpeded; free from doubt; transparent; net profit; *adv* **clearly**; *v* make, become clear; acquit; disentangle; *ns* **clearance** act of clearing; riddance of surplus stock; certificate that ship has discharged port dues; clear space between two objects; **clearness**; **clearing** land cleared of trees; **clearing-house,** where documents, etc are sorted; *as* **clear-headed, clear-sighted** discerning.
cleat *n* wedge, of wood or iron, for securing ropes.
cleave *v* split; divide by force; *pt* **clove, cleft**; *pp* **cloven, cleft**; *ns* **cleft** split, fissure; **cleavage** (*coll*) hollow between woman's breasts; **cleaver** chopper.
clef *n* sign of pitch of stave in music.
clematis *n* climbing, flowering plant.
clemency *n* (of weather) mildness, warmth; *fig* gentleness, leniency; *a* **clement.**
clench *v* make firm; close (fist); set closely together.
clerestory *n* upper rows of windows in church.
clergy *n* body of ordained ministers in Christian Church; *ns* **clergyman**; **cleric** any person in Holy Orders; *a* **clerical** of clergy.
clerk *n* official in Government, Corporation service; office subordinate; *a* **clerical** pertaining to office work.

clever *a* intelligent; adroit; dexterous; *adv* **cleverly**; *n* **cleverness**.
cliché *n* hackneyed phrase; catch-word.
click *v* make slight, sharp sound; have luck; *n* thin, rapid, sharp sound.
client *n* customer of professional man or tradesman; *n* **clientele**; whole body of clients.
cliff *n* steep rock-face *esp* facing sea.
climacteric *n* critical phase in human life; menopause.
climate *n* weather conditions of a country etc; *a* **climatic**.
climax *n* culminating point; point of greatest tension in film, story etc.
climb *v* ascend by effort; creep up; *n* **climber**.
clinch *v* make fast; decide; *n* grip, lock (boxing); *n* **clincher** decisive argument.
cling *v* stick to; remain near to; *pt* & *pp* **clung**.
clinic *n* practical teaching of medicine, surgery; place for medical examination, treatment; *a* **clinical** of sick bed; *adv* **clinically**; *n* **clinical thermometer** used to take temperature of patient.
clink *n* slight tinkling sound; *v* make or cause this sound; *n* (*sl*) prison.
clinker *n* refuse of coal or coke.
clip *v* grip; hold together; cut hair, twigs etc; *n* all wool from one shearing.
clipper *n* fast sailing ship; air-liner; *pl* small shears.
clique *n* exclusive set; select and snobbish group.
cloak *n* outer sleeveless garment; disguise; *v* cover; hide; *n* **cloak-room** place where coats, hats, luggage etc may be left.
cloche *n* bell-shaped protective glass for plants.
clock *n* device for measuring time, not intended for wearing; embroidery on side of sock; *v* **clock in, out** record automatically arrival, departure from work.
clod *n* lump of earth; (*fig*) stupid person; *n* **clodhopper** oaf.
clog *n* impediment; hindrance; wooden-soled shoe; *v* hinder, cause to jam.
cloister *n* covered arcade, *esp* in monastery, college; *v* confine, seclude; *a* **cloistered**.

close *a* shut up; reticent; near; dense; careful; sultry, heavy (of weather); *n* precinct of cathedral; *adv* **closely**; *n* **closeness**; *a* **close-fisted** mean; *n* **close-up** film shot taken near subject.
close *v* shut; conclude; come together; *n* end.
closet *n* small, private room; cupboard; *adj* **closeted** private.
clot *n* coagulated, partially solidified mass, *esp* of blood; *v* coagulate; cause to clot.
cloth *n* woven fabric; *pl* **clothes** garments; bed-coverings; *n* **clothing**; *v* **clothe** to dress; *pt* & *pp* **clothed, clad**; *n* **clothier**.
cloud *n* mass of condensed water vapour in sky; mass of smoke; dust in air; *v* make dark; dim; become cloudy; as **cloudy, cloudless, clouded.**
clout *n* piece of rough cloth; blow, *esp* on head.
clove *n* dried flower bud, used for flavouring.
clover *n* plant, trefoil grown as fodder.
clown *n* jester; buffoon in circus or pantomime; *v* play the fool; *n* **clowning**.
cloy *n* satiate, glut with sweetness or pleasure.
club *n* thick wooden stick; stick for golf; group of people associated for benefit or pleasure; black trefoil on playing card; *v* beat with club; unite for common purpose.
cluck *n* noise made by hen; *v* make such noise.
clue *n* guide to solution of mystery, crime; *a* **clueless** utterly helpless, stupid.
clump *n* compact mass; group of trees, plants; clout; *v* mass together; strike.
clumsy *a* ungainly; unwieldy; *adv* **clumsily**; *n* **clumsiness**.
cluster *n* bunch; group; *v* come together; grow in clusters.
clutch *v* grasp suddenly; *n* set of eggs hatched at one time; device permitting gradual engagement of mechanism.
coach *n* railway carriage; passenger bus; horse-drawn carriage; instructor; tutor; *v* tutor; *n* **coachman**.
coagulate *v* clot; form moss; curdle; *n* **coagulation**.
coal *n* combustible carbonised vegetable matter, used as fuel; *v* take in, supply with coal; *n* **coal-field**.

coalesce *v* unite; intermingle; *ns* **coalescence, coalition** alliance, *esp* political.
coarse *a* rough; common; crude; gross; *adv* **coarsely**; *n* **coarseness.**
coast *n* edge of land at seashore; *v* sail along coast; slide down; free wheel; *n* **c.-guard** official employed to prevent smuggling, man light-houses etc.
coat *n* outer garment with sleeves; natural covering of animals; layer of paint, etc applied to surface; *v* cover with coat; *n* **coat of arms** heraldic device.
coax *v* persuade by flattery; wheedle; cajole.
co-axial *a* having common axis.
cob *n* thick-set, stocky horse; male swan; building material; cobnut; head of maize.
cobalt *n* metallic element; dark blue colour.
cobble *n* round stone; *v* pave with cobbles; mend roughly; repair shoes; *n* **cobbler** shoe mender.
cobra *n* venomous snake, with erectile hood.
cobweb *n* spider's web, single thread of this.
cocaine *n* drug used as local anaesthetic, or taken as stimulant.
cochineal *n* red dye made from dried insects.
cock *n* male bird; leader; stop valve to regulate flow of liquids; hammer of gun; *v* set cock of gun; set, turn up jauntily; *n* **cockerel** young cock.
cock *n* pile of hay; *v* put hay into cocks.
cockade *n* hat badge, rosette of ribbon.
cockatoo *n* crested parrot.
cockchafer *n* large, nocturnal winged beetle.
cockle *n* edible bivalve; weed; small boat.
cockle *v* wrinkle, pucker up.
Cockney *n* native of London.
cockpit *n* small space in aircraft for pilot.
cockroach *n* insect, blackbeetle.
cocksure, cocky *a* conceitedly self-confident.
coco, coconut *n* tropical palm, with edible nut.
cocoa *n* fine powder made from cacao beans; drink.
cocoon *n* sheath of silk, silk-like thread enclosing chrysalis.
cod *n* large edible sea fish; *n* **codling** young cod.
coddle *v* pamper, cosset.
code *n* cypher used in sending (secret) messages;

symbols used in computers; accepted social customs; set of laws; *ns* **codification**; **coding** translation into code; *v* **codify** put into code or systematic form.
codeine *n* alkaloid narcotic derived from opium.
codicil *n* addition to will.
co-education *n* education of boys & girls together.
coefficient *n* joint agent or factor.
coerce *v* constrain; force; *a* **coercive**; *n* **coercion** forcible compulsion.
co-exist *v* exist, live together; *n* **co-existence**
coffee *n* evergreen shrub; ground & roasted coffee-beans; drink made from this; light brown colour.
coffer *n* chest; money-box.
coffin *n* case for dead body.
cog *n* tooth-like projection on wheel; *n* **cog-wheel**.
cogent *a* impelling; urgent; clear, forceful; *n* **cogency**
cogitate *v* ponder; think deeply; *n* **cogitation**.
cognac *n* high quality French brandy.
cognate *n* related; from common stock; origin.
cognizant *n* knowledge; fact of being aware; *a* **cognizant**.
cognomen *n* appellation; surname.
cohabit *n* live together, *esp* as man & wife.
cohere *v* stick together; be consistent; *a* **coherent** intelligible; sticking together; *n* **cohesion** state of union.
cohort *n* body of troops, army.
coiffeur *n* hair-dresser.
coil *n* series of spiral loops; *v* wind in rings, spiral folds.
coin *n* piece of money; *v* mint; invent new word etc; *ns* **coinage** money of country; **coiner** maker of counterfeit coins.
coincide *v* happen at same time; correspond exactly; *a* **coinciding**; *n* **coincidence**.
coition, coitus *n* sexual intercourse.
coke *n* fuel obtained after heating of coal to extract gas.
colander *n* strainer used in cooking.
cold *a* without heat; unmoved; frigid; *n* lack of heat; acute nasal catarrh; *n* **coldness**; *ns* **c. feet** fear (*sl*); **c. shoulder** rebuff; **c. storage** refrigeration.

colic *n* acute pain in bowls.
collaborate *v* work together; *esp* in literature, art; *ns* **collaborator, collaboration.**
collapse *v* fall down in; fail; *n* break down (of health) falling away; *a* **collapsible** capable of being folded, packed up.
collar *n* band on garment, round neck; *v* capture; seize hold of (*sl*); *n* **collar-bone** clavicle.
collate *v* compare critically; place printed sheets in order; *n* **collation** light repast.
collateral *a* accompanying; from common ancestor; *n* additional security for loan.
colleague *n* associate in work or profession.
collect *v* gather, come together; accumulate; *as* **collected** not distracted; gathered; **collective** viewed as whole; *ns* **collection** group of articles of same nature; **collector.**
college *n* institution of higher learning; self governing body of persons; *a* **collegiate.**
collide *v* crash into; strike forcefully together; *n* **collision.**
collier *n* coal-miner; coaling ship; *n* **colliery** coal-mine.
colloquial *a* used in common speech; *n* **colloquy** conference.
collusion *n* conspiracy (to deceive) *esp* in legal matters; *a* **collusive.**
colon *n* part of large intestine; punctuation mark (:).
colonel *n* commander of regiment.
colonnade *n* row of columns.
colony *n* body of people in new country, who remain subject to fatherland; area so settled; group of aliens in city, town etc; *ns* **colonist, colonial**; *v* **colonize**; *n* **colonization.**
colophon *n* publisher's device, imprint.
colossus *n* huge statue; strikingly large person or thing; *a* **colossal.**
colour *n* hue, tint; paint; pigment; (*fig*) pretext; semblance; *pl* badge, ribbons symbolic of party, school etc; flag of ship, regiment; *v* paint; exaggerate; influence; blush; *a* **coloured** non-white.
colt *n* young male horse.

column *n* vertical pillar or support; vertical division of page; military formation; *a* **columnar.**
coma *n* deep unconsciousness *a* **comatose.**
comb *n* toothed instrument for dressing hair, cleaning wool; cock's crest; *v* apply comb to.
combat *v* oppose; fight; *n* **combatant.**
combine *v* join together; mix; *ns* **combination** union; **combine** syndicate.
combustion *n* process of burning; *a* **combustible.**
come *v* move towards; arrive; occur; happen; be derived from; *pt* **came**; *pp* **come**; *prp* **coming.**
comedy *n* gay, amusing play; *n* **comedian** comic actor.
comely *a* attractive; handsome; *n* **comeliness.**
comet *n* luminous heavenly body, with gaseous tail.
comfort *v* reassure; console; *n* well-being; bodily ease; consolation; *a* **comfortable.**
comic *a* laughable; funny; *n* comedian; comic paper; *a* **comical.**
comity *n* courtesy, urbanity of manners.
comma *a* punctuation mark (,), separating words, phrases etc.
command *v* order; be in authority; *n* peremptory order; power to control, govern, dominate; *ns* **commandant, commander, commandment**; *v* **commandeer**; *v* appropriate.
commando *n* unit of shock troops; member of such unit.
commemorate *v* celebrate solemnly; *n* **commemoration**; *a* **commemorative.**
commence *v* begin; start; *n* **commencement.**
commend *v* entrust; praise; *a* **commendable**; *n* **commendation.**
commensurate *a* proportionate; in accordance.
comment *n* remark; annotation; *v* explain; express view; *ns* **commentary** series of critical remarks; **commentator** radio or TV reporter.
commerce *n* dealings; business trading; *a* **commercial**; *v* **commercialize** make business of.
commiserate *v* express sympathy; condole; *n* **commiseration.**

commissar *n* head of a Soviet government department.

commissariat *n* department for supplies of food and transport (*mil*).

commission *n* warrant giving authority *esp* to officer in armed forces; body appointed to hold enquiry; authority to act as agent, agent's percentage; *v* authorize; give order for; *ns* **commissioner** member of commission; one empowered to act by warrant; **commissionaire** uniformed door-keeper (*usu* retired N.C.O.); messenger.

commit *v* entrust; send for trial; perpetrate (crime); *ns* **committal, commitment.**

committee *n* group appointed to consider particular activity.

commodious *a* spacious, roomy.

commodity *n* article of commerce; useful object.

commodore *n* naval officer; courtesy title; *eg* president of yacht club, etc.

common *n* tract of public land; *a* shared by two or more; usual; ordinary; vulgar; *npl* common people of realm; *adv* **commonly**; *n* **commoner** person not of nobility; *a* **commonplace** ordinary; trite; *n* **commonwealth** democratic state.

commotion *n* agitation; tumult; upset.

commune *v* hold intimate conversation; *n* small political unit; *a* **communal** for common use; *n* **Holy Communion** sacrament of Eucharist.

communicate *v* impart; transmit; exchange information; receive Holy Communion; *a* **communicable**; *n* **communication**; *a* **communicative** talkative.

communique *n* official communication.

communism *n* extreme form of Socialism; *a* & *n* **communist.**

community *n* body of people sharing locality, religion etc; fellowship.

commutator *n* device for altering direction of electric current; *v* **commutate** alter so.

commute *v* exchange; travel daily by season ticket; *n* **commuter** daily traveller to work.

compact *n* agreement; contract.

compact *a* neatly packed into small space; *n* small case holding face powder.
companion *n* comrade, associate; one of matching pair; *a* **companionable**; *n* **companionship.**
company *n* gathering of guests; companionship; group of business associates; group of actors; unit of regiment; ship's crew.
compare *v* observe similarity of one thing with another; be like; *as* **comparable, comparative** relative; *n* **comparison.**
compartment *n* part divided off by partition, *esp* in railway carriage.
compass *n* boundary; extent; range; instrument showing N; *pl* instrument drawing circles.
compassion *n* sympathy; pity; *a* **compassionate.**
compatible *a* able to co-exist; agreeing; *n* **compatibility.**
compatriot *n* fellow-countryman.
compel *v* enforce; bring about by force; *n* **compulsion.**
compensate *v* make amends; reward; make up for; *n* **compensation.**
compete *v* contend with; vie with; *a* **competitive**; *ns* **competition, competitor.**
competence, competency *n* ability; efficiency; sufficiency; *esp* of money; *a* **competent.**
compile *v* collect together from various sources; eg as a book; *n* **compilation.**
complacent *a* self-satisfied; *ns* **complacence, complacency.**
complain *v* grumble; find fault with; bring charge; *ns* **complaint** expression of discontent; ailment; **complainant** (*law*) plaintiff.
complaisant *a* obliging; compliant; *n* **complaisance.**
complement *n* that which completes; full allowance; *a* **complementary.**
complete *a* entire; finished; *v* make whole; *n* **completion.**
complex *a* complicated; involved; *n* psychological obsession; *n* **complexity.**
complexion *n* colour, texture of face; disposition.

complicate *v* make difficult, involved; *n* **complication.**
complicity *n* partnership in crime etc.
compliment *n* expression of esteem, praise, regard; *v* pay compliment to; *a* **complimentary.**
comply *v* agree; consent, yield; *a* **compliant**; *n* **compliance.**
component *n* constituent part; *a* forming part.
compose *v* create musical form, literary work; set up type; settle; make up; *a* **composed** calm; *ns* **composer** one who composes *esp* music; **composition**; **compositor** typesetter; **composure** calmness; *a* **composite** of distinct parts.
compost *n* mixture of manure, soil, rotten vegetable matter.
compote *n* fruit in syrup.
compound *v* mix together; compromise; condone (an offence); *a* not simple; composite; *n* mixture; compound substance; enclosure.
comprehend *v* take in; comprise; understand; *n* **comprehension**; *a* **comprehensive** taking in wide range of objects; *a* **comprehensible.**
compress *v* press together; concentrate; make smaller; *n* wet pad put on inflamed part; *n* **compression.**
comprise *v* include; contain; *prp* **comprising.**
compromise *v* make concession; incur risk, suspicion; *n* middle course.
compunction *n* regret for wrong done; remorse.
compute *v* calculate, reckon; *ns* **computer** mechanical calculator; **computation.**
comrade *n* friend, companion, associate; *n* **comradeship.**
con *v* examine carefully; learn by heart; swindle (*sl*).
concave *n* hollow, curved inwardly; *n* **concavity.**
conceal *v* keep secret, hide; *n* **concealment.**
concede *v* surrender; admit truth of; allow; *n* **concession** that which is conceded.
conceit *n* vanity; *a* **conceited** holding exaggerated opinion of one's own importance.
conceive *v* think of; imagine; become pregnant; *a* **conceivable**; *ns* **conception, concept** idea.

concentrate *v* direct to single centre; increase strength; fix efforts on one point, object; *n* **concentration.**
concentric *a* having common centre.
concern *v* relate to; be worried; affect; *n* business; affair; *a* **concerned** interested; anxious; connected with; *prep* **concerning** regarding, about.
concert *n* harmony; agreement; (*mus*) entertainment; *a* **concerted** planned in common; *ns* **concerto** musical composition for solo instrument with orchestra; **concertina** musical instrument.
conciliate *v* pacify; win over; *ns* **conciliation, conciliator**; *a* **conciliatory.**
concise *a* brief, terse; *n* **conciseness.**
conclave *n* secret, private assembly, *esp* for election of Pope.
conclude *v* end, finish; arrange; infer; *n* **conclusion**; *a* **conclusive** decisive.
concoct, *v* invent; make up story; new dish etc; *n* **concoction.**
concord *n* agreement, harmony; *n* **concordance** index (words).
concourse *n* crowd; broad open space *esp* in airport buildings.
concrete *n* mixture of sand & cement; *a* of concrete; actual; *v* cover with concrete; *adv* **concretely.**
concubine *n* woman living with man, outside lawful wedlock.
concupiscence *n* sexual desire; lust.
concur *v* agree; coincide; *a* **concurrent.**
concuss *v* shake violently; injure brain by blow on head; *n* **concussion.**
condemn *v* censure; declare unfit for use; find guilty; *n* **condemnation.**
condense *v* abridge; concentrate; reduce gas etc to liquid; *ns* **condensation, condenser** device for storing electricity.
condescend *v* deign; patronise; be affable; *a* **condescending**; *n* **condescension.**
condiment *n* spicy, pungent seasoning for food.
condition *n* state of being; rank; stipulation; *n* determine state or condition; train; make

healthy; *a* **conditional** subject to conditions.

condole *v* offer sympathy; grieve with; *n* **condolence.**

condone *v* overlook; find excuses for; *n* **condonation.**

condor *n* large S. American vulture.

conduce *v* help; tend to produce; *a* **conducive.**

conduct *v* lead; manage; behave; direct; transmit (heat, electricity); *n* behaviour; *ns* **conductor** guide; fare-collector on bus etc; director of orchestra; substance capable of transmitting (electricity etc); **conductivity.**

conduit *n* channel or pipe for conveying fluids, or protecting electric cables.

cone *n* solid body with circular base & tapering to apex; fruit of conifers; storm warning; *a* **conic, conical.**

confection *n* sweetmeat, preserve; *ns* **confectioner** dealer in sweets, cakes, etc; **confectionery** sweetmeats.

confederate *n* accomplice; *v* ally with; *ns* **confederacy, confederation.**

confer *v* grant; discuss; *ns* **conferment** act of bestowing; **conference** meeting to discuss.

confess *v* admit; declare sins orally; *ns* **confession; confessional** priest's box; **confessor** priest hearing confession.

confetti *n* small pieces of coloured paper thrown at weddings etc.

confide *v* trust in; tell, as secret; *ns* **confidant** one entrusted with secret; **confidence** trust, self-reliance; *as* **confident, confidential, confiding** trusting.

configuration *n* figure, form; relative aspect of planets.

confine *v* imprison; limit; keep in (bed, house); *npl* **confines** boundaries; *n* **confinement** imprisonment; child-birth.

confirm *v* make firm; ratify; administer Confirmation; *n* **Confirmation** rite to confirm vows made at baptism; corroboration; *a* **confirmed** habitual.

confiscate *v* seize, appropriate *esp* by authority; *n* **confiscation.**

conflagration *n* a great fire.

conflict *n* fight; variance; clash (of opinion); *v* contend; be incompatible.
confluence *n* uniting of streams etc; crowd; *a* **confluent.**
conform *v* comply; submit; be in agreement; *ns* **conformation** adaptation; formation; **conformity.**
confound *v* confuse; perplex; puzzle; dismay.
confront *v* bring face to face; meet boldly, in opposition; *n* **confrontation.**
confuse *v* mix up; bewilder; *n* **confusion.**
confute *v* disprove; convict of error; *n* **confutation.**
congeal *v* freeze; solidify.
congenial *a* having same nature, tastes etc; suited to.
congenital *a* born with, *esp* defects, diseases etc.
conger *n* large salt-water eel.
congest *v* overcrowd; impede flow of; fill to excess; *a* **congested** overcharged (with blood); *n* **congestion.**
conglomerate *v* gather, collect into mass; *n* **conglomeration** jumble of things.
congratulate *v* wish joy; express pleasure at; *n* **congratulation;** *a* **congratulatory.**
congregate *v* assemble; *n* **congregation** gathering of persons, *esp* for worship; *a* **congregational.**
congress *n* formal assembly; legislative body; *a* **congressional;** *n* **Congressman** member of U.S. Congress.
conifer *n* cone-bearing tree, shrub, as pine, fir etc; *a* **coniferous.**
conjecture *v* guess; surmise; *n* guess-work; *a* **conjectural.**
conjoin *v* unite; combine; *a* **conjoint.**
conjugal *a* pertaining to marriage; between husband and wife.
conjugate *v* inflect verb in various moods, tenses etc; *n* **conjugation.**
conjunction *n* part of speech, as *and*, *but*; simultaneous occurrence; *a* **conjunctive** done jointly.
conjure *v* ask earnestly; perform tricks by sleight-of-hand; cast spells; *ns* **conjuration** solemn spell; **conjurer, -or, conjuring.**
connect *v* unite with; join together; associate

(mentally); *n* **connection, connexion** relation to; *as* **connective, connected.**
conning-tower *n* armoured control station on warship, submarine etc.
connive *v* acquiesce in wrong-doing of another; *n* **connivance** tacit agreement.
connoisseur *n* expert in artistic matters.
connote *v* imply in addition to primary meaning; *n* **connotation.**
connubial *a* of married state, conjugal.
conquer *v* overpower; subjugate; prevail; *ns* **conqueror, conquest.**
consanguinity *n* relationship by blood; kinship.
conscience *n* sense of right and wrong; *a* **conscientious** thorough; *n* **conscientiousness.**
conscious *a* in possession of one's senses; awake; *n* **consciousness** awareness.
conscript *v* enrol by compulsion for military service; *n* one so enrolled; *n* **conscription.**
consecrate *v* render holy; set apart as sacred; *n* **consecration.**
consecutive *a* following in regular order; expressing consequence.
consensus *n* general agreement.
consent *v* agree to; permit; *n* acquiescence; permission; *a* **consentient.**
consequence *n* outcome; logical result; importance; *as* **consequent, consequential** pompous; *adv* **consequently** therefore.
conserve *v* protect; preserve *esp* from change, waste, etc; *ns* **conservancy** board responsible for preservation of nature, rivers, trees, etc; **conservation**; **conservative** moderate political party; **conservatory** greenhouse; *a* **conservative** opposed to change.
consider *v* reflect on; pay regard to ; allow for; hold opinion; *a* **considerable** noteworthy; rather large; *n* **consideration** meditation; solicitude; payment; *a* **considerate** thoughtful for others; careful.
consign *v* commit; entrust; send goods; *ns* **consignor, consignee, consignment** goods consigned.
consist *v* be made up of; be compatible; *a* **consistent**

agreeing with; *n* **consistence, consistency** degree of density; relevance.

console *v* comfort; make up for; *as* **consolable, consolatory**; *n* **consolation.**

console *n* ornamental bracket supporting shelf etc; large cabinet for radio, TV etc; control panel (*usu* for electrical machinery); organ keydesk.

consolidate *v* make, become solid, firm; combine; *n* **consolidation**; *npl* **consols** *abbrev* Consolidated Annuities, British Government securities.

consomme *n* clear meat soup.

consonant *n* letter other than vowel; *a* agreeing, consistent; *n* **consonance** harmony *esp* of sounds.

consort *n* husband, wife *esp* of monarch; ship accompanying another; *v* associate with; be in harmony with.

conspicuous *a* outstanding; remarkable; plainly visible; *n* **conspicuousness.**

conspire *v* plot; join another in secret, *usu* for unlawful purpose; *ns* **conspiracy, conspirator**; *a* **conspiratorial.**

constable *n* policeman; warden of fortress; high officer of State; **Chief C.** head of police in city or county; *n* **constabulary** police force.

constant *a* continuous; unvarying; steadfast; faithful; *n* (math) unvarying term, factor; *n* **constancy** steadfastness.

constellation *n* group of fixed stars.

consternation *n* surprise and alarm, dismay.

constipation *n* inactivity of bowls; *v* **constipate** make bowels sluggish.

constituent *a* component; entitled to elect; *n* essential part; voter in constituency; *n* **constituency** place represented in Parliament; body of voters.

constitute *v* make into; set up; give form to; *n* **constitution** structure; natural state of body, mind etc; principles of government; *a* **constitutional** pertaining to constitution; *n* walk taken for the health; *adv* **constitutionally.**

constrain *v* bring force to bear on person; *n* **constraint** compulsion; embarrassment.

constrict *v* contract; compress; cramp; *ns* **constrictor, constriction**; *a* **constrictive.**
construct *v* build; form; put together; *ns* **constructor, construction**; *a* **constructive.**
construe *v* translate; analyse grammatically; deduce.
consul *n* official appointed by State, living in foreign country & protecting nationals & business interests there; *a* **consular**; *ns* **consulate, consulship.**
consult *v* seek advice from; confer with; *ns* **consultant, consultation**; *a* **consultative** advisory.
consume *v* destroy by fire, waste, etc; use up, devour, drink up; *ns* **consumer** buyer, user of commodity; **consumption** using up; tubercular disease, *esp* phthisis; *a* **consumptive** destructive; *n* sufferer from T.B.
consummate *v* complete; finish; *a* complete, of greatest perfection; *n* **consummation** completion, *specif* physical, of marriage.
contact *n* being in touch; close proximity; *v* get in touch with; *n* **c. lens** lens resting directly on eyeball.
contagion *n* spreading of disease by contact; disease, physical or moral, spread so; *a* **contagious.**
contain *v* hold; compromise; enclose; restrain (oneself); *n* **container** box, jar, etc holding something.
contaminate *v* pollute; defile; make impure; *n* **contamination** pollution.
contemplate *v* gaze on; consider; intend; meditate; *n* **contemplation**; *a* **contemplative.**
contemporary *a* living; existing, made at same time; *n* one having same age, or living during same age as another; *a* **contemporaneous.**
contempt *n* act of despising, scorn; **c of court** disregard for, disobedience to court of law; *as* **contemptible, contemptuous.**
contend *v* struggle; fight; assert; *n* **contention** controversy; disputed point; *a* **contentious** quarrelsome.
content *a* satisfied; *n* holding capacity; real meaning; *pl* that which is inside; list of topics in book; *v* satisfy; *n* **contentment** satisfaction.

contest *v* dispute; fight for; *n* strife; competition; *n* **contestant.**
context *n* parts of book, speech, etc, which come immediately before & after passage, words, etc and which fix meaning.
contiguous *a* touching; adjoining; *n* **contiguity.**
continence *n* self-restraint, *esp* sexually; *a* **continent.**
continent *n* one of the great unbroken land areas of earth; *a* **continental**; *n* inhabitant of Europe.
contingency *n* possibility, chance occurrence; *a* **contingent** possible, dependent on; *n* quota *esp* of troops.
continue *v* go on; persist; prolong; resume; remain; *a* **continual**; *ns* **continuance, continuation** resumption; sequel; *a* **continuous** unceasing; *n* **continuity** unbroken succession.
contort *v* distort; twist out of shape; *ns* **contortion, contortionist** acrobat.
contour *n* outline, shape of figure, mountain, etc.
contraband *n* smuggled goods; illicit trading.
contraception *n* birth-control; *n* **contraceptive** that which prevents conception.
contract *n* solemn, binding agreement; *v* enter into agreement; become smaller; incur; catch (disease); *a* **contracted** shortened; drawn together; *ns* **contraction, contractor** one making contract *esp* builder.
contradict *v* deny; be opposed to; argue; *a* **contradictory**; *n* **contradiction.**
contralto *n* female voice of deep tone; singer with such a voice.
contraption *n* contrivance; eccentric device.
contrary *n* exact opposite, of object, fact, quality; *a* different; against; perverse; *advs* **contrarily, contrariwise** conversely; **contrariness** perversity.
contrast *v* compare, show difference; *n* striking difference.
contravene *v* infringe; disobey (law); *n* **contravention.**
contretemps *n* unlucky, embarrassing incident, mishap.

contribute *v* give to common fund; write for the press; have share in producing result; *ns* **contributor contribution** donation; *a* **contributory**.
contrite *a* penitent; sorrowful for sin; *n* **contrition** remorse.
contrive *v* invent, devise; scheme; manage; *n* **contrivance** device; artful scheme.
control *v* restrain; regulate; test; command; *n* restraint; domination; standard for testing; *npl* instruments guiding machine; *a* **controllable**; *n* **controller** *specif* person regulating expenditure.
controversy *n* dispute; argument; debate; *a* **controversial** liable to provoke controversy.
contumacy *n* stubborn, perverse resistance; *a* **contumacious**.
contumely *n* contemptuous insolence of speech or manner; disgrace.
contuse *v* bruise without breaking skin; *n* **contusion**.
conundrum *n* riddle; problem.
convalesce *v* regain health gradually; *ns* **convalescence** state of recovering health; **convalescent** person recovering from illness; *a* **convalescing**.
convection *n* transference of heat by liquids or gases; *n* **convector** circulator of warm air.
convene *v* summon; convoke; *ns* **convener** official, *esp* of Trade Union, who convenes meeting; **convention** formal assembly; custom, usage; *a* **conventional** dictated by convention.
convenient *a* suitable; handy; *n* **convenience** personal comfort; ease; lavatory.
convent *n* community of monks or nuns; building occupied by community.
converge *v* meet at given point; *a* **convergent**; *n* **convergence, convergency**.
converse *v* talk with someone; *n* **conversation**; *as* **conversational** ready to talk; **conversant** familiar with, informed concerning.
converse *a* contrary, opposite, reversed; *n* the opposite.
convert *v* change, transmute a thing; cause to alter religious, moral beliefs; *ns* **convert** one who is

converted; **conversion** change of state; misappropriation of property; *a* **convertible** capable of being converted.

convex *a* curving outwards; reverse of concave; *n* **convexity.**

convey *v* carry; impart; transmit; (*leg*) make over by deed; *ns* **conveyance** deed by which title to property is transferred; **conveyancer** lawyer dealing with conveyance of property; **conveyancing** his business.

convict *v* prove, find guilty of crime; *ns* **convict** criminal serving sentence of imprisonment; **conviction** act of convicting; assured belief.

convince *v* persuade, arouse belief in, by argument or proof; *a* **convincing** compelling belief.

convivial *a* festive; sociable; *n* **conviviality.**

convoke *v* call together; summon to assemble; *n* **convocation** assembly, *esp* of clergy, university graduates.

convolution *n* spiral fold, coil, whorl; *a* **convoluted.**

convolvulus *n* genus of plants with twining, climbing stems; bindweed.

convoy *v* escort & protect; *n* **convoy** group of ships, vehicles etc being convoyed; protecting force.

convulse *v* agitate violently; cause sudden violent muscular spasms; *a* **convulsive**; *npl* **convulsions** hysterical fits of emotion; spasms.

cony, coney *n* rabbit; fur made of rabbit skins.

coo *v* utter soft murmuring sound (of doves); speak softly & caressingly; *n* such sound.

cook *n* one who prepares food for eating; *v* prepare food for tables; *esp* by heat; (*fig*) fake, tamper with; *ns* **cooker** stove for cooking; fruit suitable for cooking; **cookery** art of cooking; **cook-house** camp kitchen.

cool *a* pleasantly cold; (*fig*) calm; casual; not ardent; *v* make, become cool; *ns* **coolness** state of being cool; absence of cordiality; **cooler** vessel in which anything is made or kept cool; *adv* **coolly.**

coolie *n* hired native labourer in India or China.

coomb, combe *n* deep, narrow valley.

coon *n* Negro (*sl*).

coop *n* wooden cage or pen for hens; *v* shut up in coop; confine.

cooper *n* one who makes barrels and casks; *n* **cooperage** work, workshop of cooper.

co-operate *v* act together for common aim; *ns* **co-operation** working together; **co-operative** profit sharing concern; *a* **co-operative** working together, helpful.

co-ordinate *a* having equal rank, order etc; *v* adjust, cause to harmonize; *n* **co-ordination**.

coot *n* small black water bird of rail family.

cop *n* mass of thread on spindle; hillock.

cop *v* catch (*sl*); be punished; *n* (*sl*) policeman, a catching.

cope *n* ceremonial clerical vestment; covering; *n* **coping** protective covering course of wall.

cope *v* handle successfully, contend with efficiently.

copious *a* plentiful, abundant, profuse, full; *adv* **copiously**.

copper *n* reddish, ductile, malleable metal; washing vessel for clothes; (*sl*) policeman; *v* cover with copper; *ns* **copper plate** one used for etching, print from this; copybook style of writing.

coppice, copse *n* thicket, wood of small trees.

copra *n* dried coconut kernels.

copulate *v* join, unite sexually; *n* **copulation**; *a* **copulative**.

copy *n* imitation, reproduction; single specimen of book etc; written material for press; example to be copied; *v* imitate; follow pattern; *ns* **copyhold** (*leg*) form of land tenure; **copyright** legal exclusive right to reproduce book, music, work of art etc; **copywriter** one who writes text of advertisements.

coquette *n* female flirt; *a* **coquettish** engagingly enticing; *n* **coquetry**.

coracle *n* light boat made of wicker covered with hide etc.

coral *n* hard red or white substance made by marine polyps & which forms reefs etc; *a* made of coral; *a* **coralline** coral (red) in colour.

corbel *n* stone or wood support projecting from wall.

cord *n* stout string or thin rope; ribbed cloth; *v* bind

with cord; *n* **cordage** cords or ropes, *esp* rigging of ship.
cordial *a* hearty, friendly, sincere; *n* stimulating, warming drink; *n* **cordiality**.
cordite *n* smokeless explosive.
cordon *n* line of troops or police; ribbon of an Order; fruit tree pruned to single stem.
corduroy *n* ribbed cotton stuff, with pile like velvet.
cordwainer *n* shoemaker, worker in leather.
core *n* innermost, central part; seed-case of some fruits; *v* take out core; *n* **corer** implement for removing cores.
co-respondent *n* person charged with adultery with petitioner's husband/wife in divorce case.
corgi *n* breed of small Welsh dog.
coriander *n* plant with aromatic seeds used as flavouring.
Corinthian *a* of Corinth; *specif* ornate type of Greek column.
cork *n* bark of cork oak; piece used as stopper for bottle etc; *v* stop up with a cork; *a* **corked** (of wine) tasting of decayed cork; *ns* **corkscrew** tool for extracting corks; **corkage** charge made by innkeepers for serving wine not bought in the house.
corm *n* solid fleshy underground stem.
cormorant *n* large seabird.
corn *n* grain; seed of cereals; *ns* **corn-chandler** retailer of corn; **corn-crake** landrail; **cornflour** finely ground maize, rice flour; **cornflower** blue-flowered wild plant of cornfields.
corn *n* hardened, thickened skin causing pain, usually on toe.
cornea *n* transparent protective membrane over front of eyeball; *a* **corneal**.
cornelian *n* reddish or white semi-precious stone.
corner *n* meeting place of two converging lines; hidden remote place; angle formed by meeting walls, sides (of box etc); *v* force into difficult position; buy up all available stocks of; *a* **cornered**; *n* **cornerstone** (*fig*) something indispensable, basis.
cornet *n* trumpet having valves; cone shaped wafer holding ice-cream.

cornice *n* carved moulding round top of building or room.
cornucopia *n* symbolic horn of plenty; (*fig*) abundance, overflowing supply.
corolla *n* cup-like form made by petals of flowers.
corollary *n* additional inference; result.
corona *n* luminous circle around heavenly body.
coronary *a* like a crown; (*anat*) relating to arteries supplying heart muscle; **c. thrombosis** formation of clot in coronary artery.
coronation *n* act or ceremony of crowning a sovereign.
coroner *n* (*leg*) officer holding inquiry as to cause of any unnatural death, or into ownership of treasure-trove.
coronet *n* small crown.
corporal *n* N.C.O. ranking below sergeant.
corporal *a* of the human body.
corporation *n* group of persons regarded as a unit; legally formed business company; civic or municipal authority; (*sl*) large protruding stomach.
corporeal *n* bodily, physical; tangible.
corps *n* largest tactical military unit; any organised group of persons.
corpse *n* dead body, usually human.
corpulent *a* stout, obese, fat; *n* **corpulence.**
corpus *n* body; principal of estate, fund; all extant writings on a subject.
corpuscle *n* minute body, organism, *esp* red & white constituent particles of blood.
corral *n* enclosure for horses, cattle; *v* drive into corral.
correct *v* put right; punish; adjust; neutralize; *ns* **correction, correctness**; *a* **corrective.**
correlate *v* bring into mutual relation; *n* either of two reciprocally related things; *n* **correlation**; *a* **correlative.**
correspond *v* agree with; be equal to; write letters to; *ns* **correspondent, correspondence** similarity; exchange of letters; *a* **corresponding.**
corridor *n* passage in building, railway coach, etc; strip of land (or air route) passing through state to which it does not belong.

corroborate *v* confirm; make more certain; *n* **corroboration**; *a* **corroborative.**
corrode *v* eat into; wear away gradually, *esp* by chemical action; *a* **corrosive**; *n* **corrosion.**
corrugate *v* form wrinkles or folds; bend into ridges; *a* **corrugated**; *n* **corrugation.**
corrupt *a* rotten, putrid; depraved; bribable; (of texts) not genuine; *v* make corrupt; pervert; *a* **corruptible**; *n* **corruption.**
corsage *n* bodice of woman's dress; spray of flowers worn thereon.
corsair *n* pirate; pirate ship.
corset *n* close-fitting undergarment worn for support; stays.
corslet, corselet *n* body armour.
cortege *n* ceremonial procession *esp* funeral cortege.
cortex *n* bark; outer covering; *pl* **cortices.**
cortisone *n* drug used in treatment of rheumatoid arthritis.
corundum *n* hard mineral used in grinding & polishing.
coruscate *v* sparkle, scintillate; *n* **coruscation.**
corvette *n* fast naval escort vessel.
coryza *n* nasal catarrh.
cos *n* long-leaved lettuce.
cosh *n* small bludgeon; *v* strike with cosh.
cosine *n* sine of complement of angle.
cosmetic *n* preparation for beautifying hair, complexion, skin; *a* **cosmetic.**
cosmic *a* relating to universe & laws governing it; *ns* **cosmogony** theory of universe & its creation; **cosmography** mapping of universe; **cosmology** science of universe; **cosmos** the universe; **cosmic rays** shortest electro-magnetic rays from outer space.
cosmonaut *n* astronaut, space traveller.
cosmopolitan *n* citizen of the world; *a* of all parts of world; free from national prejudice.
Cossack *n* member of S. Russian tribe of horsemen.
cosset *v* pamper, fondle, pet.
cost *n* price of purchase; expenditure of time, energy, labour; *pl* **costs** expenses of law suit; *v* cause expenditure of; cause loss of; estimate cost of pro-

duction; *pt* & *pp* **cost**; *a* **costly** expensive; valuable; *n* **costliness.**
costal *a* pertaining to ribs or side of body.
costard *n* large kind of apple.
coster, coster monger *n* seller of fruit & vegetables from a barrow.
costive *a* constipated; (*fig*) sluggish.
costume *n* mode of dress; *esp* if peculiar to nation, period etc; theatrical clothes; *n* **costumier** dress-maker; *n* **costume jewellery** artificial jewellery.
cosy *a* warm, snug, comfortable; *adv* **cosily**; *n* **cosiness.**
cot *n* small, humble cottage.
cot *n* light bed; swing bed on ship; child's bed.
cote *n* shed, shelter for domestic animals, birds.
coterie *n* set, group of people with similar tastes etc; social clique.
cotillion *n* lively dance; music for this.
cottage *n* small house, *esp* in the country; *n* **cottager** dweller in cottage.
cotton *n* plant; downy covering of its seeds; thread, fabric made from this down; *a* made of cotton; *v* (of persons) like; (of ideas etc) accept.
cotyledon *n* primary leaf of seed embryo.
couch *n* sofa, long seat for reclining on; *v* express (in words); crouch; lie down.
couch-grass *n* coarse grass, with creeping roots.
cougar *n* puma.
cough *v* expel air noisily & violently from lungs; *n* act of coughing, usually caused by irritation of lungs or throat.
coulomb *n* unit of measure for electricity.
council *n* deliberative or executive assembly; *n* **councillor** member of council.
counsel *n* guidance, advice; barrister; *v* advise; recommend; *n* **counsellor** adviser; barrister.
count *v* enumerate; reckon total number; include; possess value; depend on; *n* (*leg*) each charge in indictment; act of reckoning; *a* **countless**; *n* **count-down** counting down to zero in timing firing of missile; **counting-house** office where accounts are kept.

count *n* foreign title corresponding to British Earl; *n fem* **countess** wife, widow of count, earl.
countenance *n* facial expression; favour; *v* approve; tolerate.
counter *n* table in bank, shop across which money is paid, goods sold; small disc used in scoring in card or other games.
counter *a* & *adv* opposite; contrary; *v* oppose; (*boxing, fencing*) parry; *n* parry.
counter- *prefix makes compounds meaning* opposite, retaliatory, neutralizing. *Such compounds are not given, where the meaning may be deduced from the simple word.*
counterfeit *a* forged, spurious; *v* imitate with intent to deceive; *n* **counterfeiter**.
counterfoil *n* part of cheque, receipt etc, kept by issuer as record.
counterpane *n* bedspread, quilt.
counterpart *n* person or thing exactly resembling another; duplicate.
counterpoint *n* harmonious, simultaneous combination of two or more melodies.
counterpoise *n* weight balancing another, equilibrium.
countersign *n* password given in reply to another; *v* (*fig*) ratify.
countersink *v* sink head of screw, etc level with surface of material being used.
country *n* land with definite boundaries, distinctive name, occupied by one nation; land of birth; rural areas; *a* **countrified** rustic in appearance and manners; *n* **countryman** one living in country; compatriot.
county *n* division of a country; a shire.
coup *n* successful move or gamble.
coupé *n* closed two-seater motor car.
couple *n* two objects or persons; leash for two hounds; pair; brace; *v* join; unite; link together; (of animals) mate; associate (in mind); *ns* **coupling** link connecting railway carriages; **couplet** two lines of rhyming verse.
coupon *n* negotiable ticket, voucher, etc, entry form

for pools, competitions etc; voucher exchangeable for goods.

courage *n* bravery; ability to face danger, pain etc. without fear; *a* **courageous.**

courier *n* express messenger; person conducting travellers on tour.

course *n* line followed by moving object; passage of time; mode of action; part of meal served at one time; area of land used for racing, golf etc; channel (water); series of lectures, lessons; continuous layer of bricks, etc at same level in building; *v* hunt; *esp* with greyhounds; *n* **courser** swift horse.

court *n* open space, paved yard enclosed by buildings or walls; space marked out, for playing games like tennis; household of sovereign; place of justice where trials are held; body with judicial powers; *v* woo; seek favour of; *n* **courtier** attendant at royal court; *a* **courtly** elegant, refined; *n* **courtliness;** *ns* **court-card** king, queen or knave in cards; **court-martial,** *pl* **courts-martial** court of officers trying military or naval offences; **courtroom, court-house** room, place where courts of law are held; **courtship** wooing.

courtesan *n* prostitute.

courtesy *n* politeness, considerateness, civility; *a* **courteous** polite, urbane; *n* **courtesy title** one held by favour, not by right.

cousin *n* son or daughter of uncle or aunt; any kinsman.

cove *n* small sheltered bay, or inlet.

covenant *n* formal agreement, contract; *v* grant, promise by covenant.

cover *v* place, spread over; include; shield; report on; point gun at; protect financially, by insurance; conceal; *n* anything which covers; individual table setting; *n* **coverlet** counterpane.

covert *n* place, *esp* thicket sheltering game; *a* veiled, implied.

covet *v* desire ardently, *esp* property of another; *a* **covetous;** *n* **covetousness.**

covey *n* brood of partridges; set.

cow *n* adult female of bovine & various other

animals; *ns* **cowboy** mounted cattle herdsman; **cow-pox** disease of cows, source of vaccine immunizing from small-pox.

cow *v* frighten, overawe, intimidate.

coward *n* one lacking courage; *a* **cowardly** fearful; *n* **cowardice.**

cower *v* shrink fearfully from; cringe; crouch.

cowl *n* hooded cloak worn by monk; hood-shaped top for chimney or ventilator; *n* **cowling** casing round aero-engine.

cowrie *n* small shell used as money in parts of S. Asia and Africa.

cowslip *n* wild plant of primrose family.

cox, coxswain *n* one steering boat; (naval) petty officer in charge of ship's boat; *v* **cox** act as cox.

coy *a* affecting shyness; demure; *n* **coyness.**

coyote *n* N. American prairie wolf.

coypu *n* large water rodent, with fur known as nutria.

cozen *v* act deceitfully; beguile.

crab *n* edible shell-fish, with 8 legs & two pincers; *v* find fault with; *a* **crabbed** bitter; bad-tempered; cramped (handwriting); *n* **crab** small sour wild apple.

crack *v* break with sharp noise; split partially; make sharp noise, (whip etc); (of voice) become hoarse; make (joke); *n* fissure; sharp blow; report of gun; *ns* **cracker** firework; brittle biscuit; **crackle** sound of small cracks; **crackling** crisp, browned skin of roast pork; **cracksman** burglar.

cradle *n* baby's bed or cot; supporting framework; *v* rock, lay to rest as in cradle; nurse.

craft *n* cunning; manual dexterity; members of skilled trade, guild; boat; *ns* **craftsman, craftsmanship**; *a* **crafty** subtly cunning; *adv* **craftily.**

crag *n* rough, steep mass of rock; *a* **craggy** rugged.

cram *v* stuff, pack tightly into; eat greedily; coach intensively for exams; *n* **crammer** tutor who crams pupils for exams.

cramp *n* sudden painful muscular spasm; tool with tightening screw to hold wood, masonry together; *v* hamper, confine, restrict.

crampon *n* iron spike on climbing boots.
cran *n* measure for herrings, 37½ gallons.
cranberry *n* small red berry, used in cooking.
crane *n* slender wading bird with long neck; machine for raising heavy weights; *v* stretch out one's neck.
cranium *n* skull; *a* **cranial.**
crank *n* bar with right angle bend for turning things; eccentricity of manner or thought; fad; *v* wind, turn; start up engine by hand; *a* **cranky** shaky; cross; crazy; *n* **crankshaft** main shaft of engine.
cranny *n* chink, narrow opening; *a* **crannied.**
crape *n* thin wrinkled black material used for mourning.
crash *v* fall violently with loud noise; (*fig*) collapse; be ruined; (of vehicles) to have collision, smash; *n* loud noise caused by impact or fall; (*fig*) ruin.
crash *n* coarse linen cloth.
crass *a* grossly obtuse, stupid.
crate *n* wooden or wicker packing case; *v* pack in crate.
crater *n* bowl-shaped hole in ground; mouth of volcano.
cravat *n* necktie.
crave *v* beg, entreat; have strong desire for; *n* **craving** longing.
craven *a* cowardly; faint-hearted; *n* coward.
craw *n* bird's crop.
crawl *n* creeping movement; stroke in swimming; *v* advance on hands & knees; creep; (*fig*) abase oneself.
crayfish, crawfish *n* fresh water edible shell-fish like lobster.
crayon *n* stick of charcoal or coloured chalk; drawing made with crayons.
craze *n* popular fashion; exaggerated fondness; *v* become mad; *as* **crazed** insane; marked with surface cracks; **crazy** mentally deranged; rickety, shaky (of structure); madly eager for.
creak *n* grating, squeaking noise; *v* make such sound.
cream *n* fat part of milk; best of anything; *v* skim cream from milk; form into a cream; take best of;

a **creamy** like cream; *n* **creamery** place where milk is bottled, butter & cheese are made, or dairy produce sold.

crease *n* wrinkle; ridge made by folding; line marking position of batsman or bowler in cricket; *v* make creases; become wrinkled.

create *v* make; bring into existence; (*sl*) make a fuss; *ns* **creator**; **creature** a living being; servile dependant; **creation**; *a* **creative.**

crêche *n* public day nursery.

credence *n* belief.

credentials *npl* letters of introduction; *esp* of ambassador; testimonials.

credible *a* trustworthy; worthy of belief; *n* **credibility.**

credit *n* belief; integrity; prestige gained by merit; sum in person's bank account; allowing person to have goods for later payment; *v* believe; attribute; place on credit side of account; *a* **creditable** adding honour to; *n* **creditor** one to whom money is due.

credulous *a* easily deceived; gullible; *n* **credulity.**

creed *n* set of principles; formally phrased confession of faith.

creek *n* narrow inlet on sea coast; arm of river.

creel *n* angler's wicker basket.

creep *v* move stealthily, slowly; crawl; (*bot*) grow along ground or wall; (*fig*) squirm with fear; cringe; *pt* & *pp* **crept**; *n* **creeper** creeping or climbing plant; *a* **creepy** eerie; feeling fear.

cremation *n* burning (corpse) to ashes; *v* **cremate**; *n* **crematorium** place where cremation takes place.

crenellated *a* having battlements; *n* **crenellation.**

creosote *n* oily antiseptic distilled from wood- or coal-tar, used for preserving wood.

crêpe *n* fabric resembling crape; *n* **crêpe-de-chine** fine silk; *n* **crêpe rubber** washed rubber.

crepitate *v* crackle, creak, rattle; *n* **crepitation.**

crescendo *a, adv* & *n* gradual increase in loudness, *esp* of music.

crescent *n* shape of new moon; curved row of houses.

cress *n* various edible pungent leaved plants.

cresset *n* fire-basket slung as beacon.
crest *n* tuft or ridge on animal's head; top of mountain, wave etc; device on coat of arms; *a* **crestfallen** dejected, disappointed.
cretaceous *a* chalky.
cretin *n* idiot, often deformed.
cretonne *n* strong cotton cloth, printed with design.
crevasse *n* deep cleft in glacier.
crevice *n* small chink, fissure.
crew *n* ship's, aircraft's company; gang (of workmen, people).
crib *n* fodder-rack, manger; child's bed; copy; plagiarism; *v* copy closely; confine closely.
cribbage *n* card game for two, three or four players.
crick *n* painful spasm of back or neck muscles.
cricket *n* chirping insect.
cricket *n* game played by teams of eleven a side, with wickets, bats & ball.
crime *n* grave violation of law; any evil act; (*mil*) offence against regulations; *a* & *n* **criminal**; *n* **criminology** study of crime & criminals.
crimp *v* press into tiny pleats; curl (hair); *n* **crimping-iron** implement for crimping hair, or fabric.
crimson *n* deep, slightly bluish red colour; *a* of this colour; *v* turn crimson; *specif* blush.
cringe *v* cower; fawn; shrink from.
crinkle *v* wrinkle; rumple; *n* undulation.
crinoline *n* hooped skirt.
cripple *n* lame, disabled or maimed person; *v* maim; impair.
crisis *n* decisive movement; turning-point, *esp* in illness; time of acute danger; *pl* **crises.**
crisp *a* dry, brittle; curly *esp* hair; (*fig*) brisk; bracing.
criterion *n* standard of judgment; test; *pl* **criteria.**
critic *n* professional reviewer of plays, books, art etc; fault-finder; *a* **critical** relating to crisis; crucial; discerning; censorious; *v* **criticize** pass judgment on; censure; *ns* **criticism, critique** art of criticism.
croak *v* emit hoarse, dismal cry, as frog, raven; grumble; (*sl*) die; *n* sound itself; *a* & *n* **croaking.**

crochet *n* kind of fancy-work done with small hooked needle; *v* make such work.
crock *n* earthenware pot; brokenpiece of this; old worn-out person, horse; *n* **crockery** domestic china and earthenware articles.
crocodile *n* large amphibious reptile.
crocus *n* small spring-flowering plant.
croft *n* small farm or piece of arable land; *n* **crofter** one who owns and works croft.
cromlech *n* prehistoric structure of flat stone resting on two upright ones.
crone *n* hideous, withered old woman.
crony *n* old friend, close companion.
crook *n* shepherd's staff; long hooked stick; (*coll*) criminal; bend; sharp turn; *v* bend sharply; *a* **crooked** bent; winding; dishonest; deformed.
croon *v* sing softly, sentimentally; *ns* **crooner**; **crooning**.
crop *n* season's produce or yield of any cultivated plant; pouch in gullet of birds; stock of whip; closely cut hair; *v* reap, gather; clip hair; graze; *n* **cropper** heavy fall (*colloq*).
croquet *n* game played on lawn, with mallets, balls and hoops.
croquette *n* fried ball of meat, fish potato etc.
crosier, crozier *n* pastoral staff of bishop.
cross *n* upright stake with transverse bar, used for execution; *specif* the Cross, on which Christ died; symbol of Christian faith; mark made by intersecting lines; mixture of breeds; mongrel, hybrid etc; affliction; *v* place or lay across; traverse; make sign of cross on or over; interbreed; thwart; obstruct; *a* transverse; contrary; bad-tempered; intersecting; *advs* **crossways, crosswise, crossly**.
cross- *prefix: makes compounds meaning* opposing; crossing; transverse, across. *Such compounds are not given where the meaning may be deduced from the simple word.*
crossbill *n* bird with crossed mandibles.
cross-eyed *a* squinting.
cross-grained *a* perverse.
crosspatch *n* cross, peevish person.

crossword *n* puzzle built up of intersecting words, in numbered squares, with some letters in common.
crotch *n* forked stick; fork of tree or branch; where legs fork from body.
crotchet *n* note in music, half time value of minim, fad, whim; **crotchety** faddy, peevish.
crouch *v* stoop low; cringe; lie close to ground.
croup *n* childish disease of throat; hind-quarters of horse.
croupier *n* one presiding at gaming table, who rakes in & pays out money.
crow *n* large black bird of raven family.
crow *v* utter cry of cock; triumph (vocally); *pt* **crowed, crew** (of birds only); *pp* **crowed.**
crowbar *n* heavy iron bar for levering.
crowd *n* large number of people or things close together; throng; *v* cram into small place; press forward in mass; **c.-out** exclude for lack of time, space; *a* **crowded** filled by crowd; too full.
crown *n* royal head-dress; wreath worn on head; sovereignity; supreme power; summit; head; top of hat; (*fig*) highest achievement; various foreign coins; *v* place crown on; make king.
crucial *a* critical; decisive; severe.
crucible *n* melting-pot, for use in great heat.
crucify *v* put to death by nailing or binding to cross; *ns* **crucifixion; crucifix** figure of Christ on the Cross.
crude *a* raw; not prepared for use; in natural state; blunt, rude; *n* **crudity.**
cruel *a* willing to cause physical or mental pain; pitiless; painful; *n* **cruelty.**
cruet *n* stand holding containers for condiments.
cruise *v* travel at leisurely speed, *esp* ship, car etc; *n* sea voyage for pleasure; *n* **cruiser** ship that cruises; fast warship.
crumb *n* very small particle, scrap, *esp* of bread or cake; *v* cover with crumbs.
crumble *v* break into crumbs; decay; disintegrate.
crumpet *n* thin, unsweetened doughy cake, usually toasted; (*sl*) a girl.
crumple *v* make creases or folds; fall into wrinkles; *a* **crumpled.**

crunch *v* chew, crush noisily with teeth; tread heavily on gravel etc; *n* sound made by crunching.
crupper *n* hind quarters of horse; strap passing under tail, holding saddle in place.
crusade *n* holy war with religious object *esp* to free Holy Land; campaign against social abuse or evil; *n* **crusader**.
cruse *n* small pot or jar for liquids.
crush *v* compress violently; squeeze, press out of shape; pulverize; (*fig*) subdue forcibly; *n* act of crushing.
crust *n* hard outer part; dry piece of bread; hard covering of anything; *v* form crust; *a* **crusty** crust-like; (*fig*) harsh, irritable.
crustacean *n* animal having hard crust-like shell, *eg* lobster, crab, etc.
crutch *n* staff with cross piece to go under arm, to help lame to walk; support; crotch.
crux *n* knotty point; important or critical point; puzzle.
cry *n* loud call; weep; slogan; characteristic call of animal; *v* make such sound; announce; weep; *pt* & *pp* **cried**; *prp* **crying**.
crypt *n* underground vault, *esp* of church; *a* **cryptic** secret, mystic; *ns* **cryptogram** written cypher; **cryptography** art of cypher writing, decoding.
crystal *n* clear transparent quartz; solidified inorganic substance of geometrical form; fine, hard glassware; *as* **crystalline, crystalloid**; *v* **crystallize** form crystals; become clear; *ns* **crystallization**; **crystallography** science of structure & formation of crystals.
cub *n* young fox, bear, etc; *v* bring forth cubs; *n* **cubbing** hunting of foxcubs.
cubby, cubby-hole *n* snug place; small storage place.
cube *n* regular geometric solid with six equal square faces; anything cube shaped; (*maths*) 3rd power; *v* calculate cube of; *as* **cubic, cubical**; *n* **cubism** abstract form of art.
cubicle *n* small, enclosed part in larger room, sleeping car, etc.
cubit *n* ancient measure of length.

cuckold *n* man whose wife is unfaithful.
cuckoo *n* migratory bird, with characteristic call, which lays eggs in another bird's nest.
cucumber *n* long fleshy green fruit of plant of gourd family, used in salads.
cud *n* partially digested food brought up by ruminants, to chew at leisure; *v* (*fig*) **chew the cud** ponder, reflect on.
cuddle *v* hug; nestle; be close to; *n* a hug.
cudgel *n* stout, short thick stick; *v* beat with cudgel.
cue *n* word serving as signal to another to act or speak; (*fig*) hint, lead.
cue *n* long tapering rod used in billiards.
cuff *n* wrist-band of garment; end of sleeve.
cuff *v* hit with fist or hand; *n* such a blow.
cuirass *n* piece of body-armour; *n* **cuirassier** mounted soldier wearing cuirass.
cuisine *n* quality, style of cooking; organization of kitchen.
cul-de-sac *n* blind alley; passage with one open end.
culinary *a* connected with cooking or the kitchen.
cull *v* gather; pluck (flowers); select; *n* something picked out.
culminate *v* reach climax, highest point; come to a head; *n* **culmination**.
culpable *a* worthy of blame; guilty; *n* **culpability**.
culprit *n* one guilty of crime, offender.
cult *n* system of religious belief; devotion to person or cause; a fashion.
cultivate *v* till, work land; grow (crops); improve; seek acquaintance of; *ns* **cultivation, cultivator**.
culture *n* rearing of animals, plants; high intellectual development; artificial rearing *esp* of bacteria; elegance of manners; *as* **cultured** refined; **cultural** pertaining to culture.
culvert *n* channel carrying water under road etc.
cumber *v* hinder, hamper; *as* **cumbersome** clumsy, unwieldy; **cumbrous**.
cummerbund *n* broad sash round waist.
cumulative *a* increasing in force, value etc. by successive additions.

cumulus *n* cloud formation of rounded, heaped up masses.
cunning *n* skill, dexterity; (of mental qualities) slyness; *a* having such qualities; wily; artful.
cup *n* small drinking vessel with handle; contents of cup; trophy in shape of cup, usually silver; drink made of wine mixed with other ingredients; *v* bleed surgically; *ns* **cupful, cupboard** small closet with shelves for china, etc.
cupidity *n* avarice; greed; covetousness.
cupola *n* small dome.
cupreous, cupric, cuprous *a* of, containing or like copper.
cur *n* mongrel dog; *esp* snappy one; low ill-bred fellow.
curacao *n* orange-flavoured liqueur.
curate *n* rector's or vicar's assistant; *v* act as curator; *n* **curacy** his office.
curator *n* keeper; *esp* of art gallery, museum etc.
curb *n* restraining chain, strap fastened to horse's bit; (*fig*) check, restraint; edging of pavement; kerb; *v* restrain, subdue.
curd *n* thick substance separated from milk by acid action; *c* **curdle** turn into curd; coagulate; (*fig*) **c. the blood** terrify; *a* **curdy.**
cure *v* restore to health; heal; preserve (food) by salting; *n* remedy, treatment restoring health; *as* **curable, curative** tending to cure disease.
curfew *n* regulation requiring all persons to be indoors by stated hour.
curiosity *n* inquisitiveness; strange, interesting object; *a* **curious** eager to know; prying; puzzling; rare; *n* **curio** rare object of art.
curl *n* coiled lock of hair; ringlet; spiral or similar shape; *a* **curly**; *v* twist, roll or press into spirals; play at curling; *n* **curling** game like bowls, played on ice.
curlew *n* wading bird of snipe family.
curmudgeon *n* surly, miserly fellow.
currant *n* small dried grape; edible fruit of various shrubs.
current *a* in general use; up-to-date; generally

known; *n* flow of body of water, air; movement of electricity; *n* **currency** state of being current; money in circulation.

curry *v* rub down (horse) with comb; dress (leather).

curry *n* highly spiced, hot flavoured dish of meat, fish etc; *v* make into a curry; *n* **curry powder** mixture of turmeric & other spices.

curse *v* call down divine wrath or vengeance; swear (at); afflict; *n* words used to curse; profane oath, imprecation; bane; (*coll*) menstrual period; *a* **cursed** wicked; afflicted by a curse; *n* **cursedness** perversity.

cursive *a* in a flowing style (of hand writing).

cursory *a* rapid, superficial.

curt *a* short, abrupt, rudely brief; *n* **curtness**; *v* **curtail** cut short; reduce; *n* **curtailment**.

curtain *n* sheet of material hung to screen window, door etc; screen separating stage & audience; anything which screens, covers; *v* cover with a curtain.

curtsey, curtsy *n* movement of respect, bending, of knees made by women; *v* make such gesture.

curve *n* line of which no part is straight, rounded bend; *v* impart a curve to; *n* **curvature** act of curving, being curved.

cushion *n* pillow, soft pad to lie, sit or rest upon; any resilient support; lining round inner side of billiard table; *v* protect with cushion.

cushy *a* (*sl*) easy, light, profitable.

cusp *n* horn of crescent; *a* **cuspidal** ending in point.

cuspidor *n* spittoon.

custard *n* dessert made of milk, eggs, sugar, baked or boiled.

custody *n* safe-keeping; guardianship; imprisonment; *n* **custodian** keeper, curator.

custom *n* habit; business patronage; practice; *pl* duties on imports; *a* **customary** usual; *ns* **customer** buyer; **custom house** place where custom duties are collected.

cut *v* wound, separate, gash with sharp instrument; shape, trim, carve by cutting; mow, reap; abridge; ignore (person); strike sharply; intersect; *pt* & *pp* **cut**; *n* **cutting** act of cutting; thing cut off, *esp* excavation through high ground, for railway, road etc; slip cut from plant; *a* sarcastic, bitter; *a* **cut-throat** merciless; *n* type of razor; fierce ruffian; *n* **cutter** small vessel sloop-rigged; person, thing that cuts.

cutaneous *a* of skin.

cute *a* sharp, quick-witted, clever.

cuticle *n* outer layer of skin; skin at base of nails.

cutlass *n* short, broad-bladed sword.

cutler *n* one who makes, mends, sells knives and cutting instruments; *n* **cutlery** such implements.

cutlet *n* small meat chop.

cuttle, cuttle-fish *n* marine mollusc which squirts out inky fluid.

cyanide *n* prussic acid.

cyanosis *n* blueness of skin.

cybernetics *n* study of automatic communication and control *esp* in relation to computers.

cycle *n* period of time during which there is regular, orderly series of events; great period of time; group of poems, connected with central theme; (*coll*) bicycle; *v* recur in cycles; ride bicycle; *a* **cyclic, cyclical**; *ns* **cyclist** bicycle rider; **cyclometer** device for measuring distance travelled by wheel.

cyclone *n* rotating winds surrounding regions of low pressure; *a* **cyclonic.**

cygnet *n* young swan.

cylinder *n* solid or hollow roller-shaped body; piston chamber of engine; *a* **cylindrical.**

cymbal *n* musical percussion instrument, one of two brass plates struck to make clashing sound.

cynic *n* sceptical, mocking person; *a* **cynical** sneering; thinking worst of people; *n* **cynicism** being a cynic.

cynosure *n* centre of attraction.

cypress *n* dark evergreen coniferous tree.

cyst *n* (*med*) abnormal sac containing pus, fluid; *a* **cystic** of bladder; *n* **cystitis** inflammation of the bladder.

czar *n* emperor (*usu* Russian); *ns* **czarevitch** eldest son of reigning czar; **czarina** title of czar's wife.

dab *v* touch lightly; *n* slight tap; small flat fish.
dabble *v* dip in & out of water; engage in half-heartedly (study, etc.); *n* **dabbler.**
dabchick *n* small water-bird.
dace *n* small river-fish.
dachshund *n* type of long-bodied, short-legged dog.
dad, daddy *n* childish word for father.
daddy-long-legs *n* crane-fly.
dado *n* border or panelling on wall of room.
daffodil *n* spring-flowering bulb; narcissus.
daft *n* foolish, feeble-minded.
dagger *n* short two-edged blade for stabbing.
dahlia *n* type of autumn-flowering plant.
dainty *a* delicate; elegant; refined; *n* a delicacy (food); *n* **daintiness.**
dairy *n* place where milk & its products are dealt with or sold.
dais *n* raised platform.
daisy *n* type of common wild flower.
dale *n* valley *esp* in N. England; *n* **dalesman.**
dally *v* linger; trifle with; delay; *pt* & *pp* **dallied;** *pr p* **dallying;** *n* **dalliance.**
Dalmatian *n* large white dog, with black spots.
dam *n* barrier arresting water flow; water so obstructed; *v* hold back by dam.
dam *n* mother, usually of animals.
damage *n* harm, injury, hurt to persons, property etc.; *pl* money claimed, or paid as compensation for injury libel etc; *v* harm, injure.
damask *n* silk, linen material with pattern woven into it; colour of damask rose; rosy-pink; *v* **damascene** decorate metal with inlaid gold or silver.
dame *n* lady; (*cap*) title of lady member of Order of British Empire.
damn *v* condemn to eternal punishment; curse; *interj* oath; *a* **damnable;** *n* **damnation.**
damp *n* moisture; noxious gas in coal-mines; *a* slightly wet; *v* make damp; (*fig*) discourage; (of plants) to wither off from mildew; *v* **dampen** become damp; depress; *n* **damper** anything which discourages; plate in flue to regulate draught.
damsel *n* young girl.

damson *n* small, purple, very sour plum.
dance *v* move, leap with rhythmic sequence of steps, usually to music; *n* social gathering organized for dancing; form of dance; *ns* **dancer**; **dancing** art and practice of the dance.
dandelion *n* common yellow wild flower.
dandruff *n* small scales of dead skin on scalp, scurf.
dandy *n* a fop; extravagantly fashionable man.
danger *n* menace; exposure to peril, risk of death; *a* **dangerous.**
dangle *v* hang, sway loosely; show as enticement.
dank *a* disagreeably damp; *n* **dankness.**
daphne *a* flowering shrub.
dapper *a* neat and smart in appearance; trim.
dapple *v* mark with spots of different colour; *a* **dappled**, variegated.
dare *v* have courage for; venture to; challenge; *pt* **dared, durst**; *pp* **dared**; *prp* **daring.**
daring *a* bold; *n* audacity.
dark *a* without light; (of colour, complexion) deep in shade; secret; evil; *v* **darken** make, or become darker; *as* **darkish**; **darkling** growing dim; *n* **darkness**, absence of light.
darling *n* dearly loved person; term of endearment.
darn *v* repair hole with interlacing stitches; *n* part so mended; *n* **darning.**
darn *interj* milder form of damn.
dart *n* light pointed missile; sudden rapid forward movement; tapering seam in garment; *pl* indoor game played with target & small darts; *v* shot out or forward quickly, swiftly.
dash *v* fling with violence; rush furiously; sprinkle; *n* rush; small quantity (of liquid); short line (–) used to denote a pause; *a* **dashing** spirited, eager.
dashboard *n* instrument panel inside car, in front of driver.
dastard *n* despicable coward; *a* **dastardly** mean.
data *n pl* known facts from which conclusion can be drawn; *sing* **datum.**
date *n* given point of time, day, month or year when event occurred; indication of day, month or year on any document written or printed; *v* affix or assign

date to, make appointment to meet; *a* **dateless,** immemorial.
date *n* sweet, single stoned fruit of date palm.
dative *n* case of noun or pronoun expressing indirect object.
daub *v* smear, coat, plaster, paint roughly; *n* unskilful painting; smear.
daughter *n* female child or offspring; *a* **daughterly;** *n* **daughter-in-law** son's wife.
daunt *v* inspire with fear, dismay; discourage; *a* **dauntless** intrepid, fearless.
dauphin *n* former title of eldest son of French king.
daw *n* kind of crow; jackdaw.
dawdle *v* linger, loiter, waste time; *n* **dawdler.**
dawn *v* begin to grow light; (*fig*) begin to realize; *n* daybreak; *n* **dawning** the dawn; (*fig*) beginning.
day *n* period between sunrise & sunset; 24 hours; specified day; *pl* epoch, period of time; *a* **daily** happening each day; *ns* **day-book** for recording daily sales; **day-break** dawn; **day-dream** reverie; **daylight** natural light; **daytime** hours between sunrise and sunset.
daze *v* stupefy, confuse, usually by blow, shock; *a* **dazed.**
dazzle *v* confuse vision; blind by brilliant light; daze by hope of success.
de- *prefix*: *forms compounds expressing* down, off, away, deficiency, negation. *Where the meaning may be deduced from the simple word, the compounds are not given here.*
deacon *n* ordained person, lower order than priest; (*fem*) **deaconess** woman appointed to help in church work.
dead *a* no longer living; obsolete (of language); complete; lifeless; extinguished; numbed; *n* (*coll*) dead persons; *v* **deaden** reduce force of; muffle; benumb; *a* **deadly** fatal; implacable; *ns* **deadliness; dead letter** undeliverable letter; **dead line** time limit; **dead lock** standstill, impasse.
deaf *a* without whole or partial hearing; inattentive; *v* **deafen** make deaf; *n pl* deaf persons; *n* **deafness;** *a* **deafening;** *n* **deaf-mute** deaf & dumb person.

deal *v* give, hand out; distribute, *specif* playing cards; trade in; manage (affairs); *pt* & *pp* **dealt**; *n* business transaction; act of dealing cards etc; *ns* **dealer**; **dealing** trading; *pl* behaviour to others.
dean *n* head of chapter of cathedral; head of university faculty; *ns* **rural dean** one with powers over group of parishes; **deanery** office or house of dean.
dear *a* precious, beloved; costly; expensive; polite form of address in letter; *n* lovable person; *adv* **dear, dearly,** at high price; *n* **dearness.**
dearth *n* scarcity, want; (*esp* of food) famine.
death *n* end of life; annihilation; state of being dead; *n* **d. duty** tax due on estate of person at death *a* **deathless,** immortal; *a* & *adv* **deathly,** like death;
debacle *n* rout; sudden & overwhelming disaster.
debar *v* prevent; exclude; prohibit.
debark *v* disembark, put, go ashore.
debase *v* lower in value, *esp* of coinage; render base (dignity, morals); *n* **debasement.**
debate *v* discuss; argue; consider; *n* formal public discussion; *a* **debatable** questionable; *n* **debater.**
debauch *v* corrupt; lead astray; seduce; *n* orgy; licentious bout; *ns* **debauchee, debauchery.**
debenture *n* certificate of stock held, bond of company or corporation.
debility *n* weakness, feebleness of health; *v* **debilitate** make weak.
debit *n* entry in account, of sum owing; *v* charge as due.
debonair *a* genial, affable, cheerful, sprightly.
debris *n* broken remains; rubbish; loose rock fragments.
debt *n* something owed; liability; *n* **debtor.**
debut *n* first appearance in public; *n fem* **debutante** girl making her debut in Society.
dec-, deca- *prefix,* ten, tenfold; *e.g.* **decametre** 10 metres. *Where the meaning may be deduced from the simple word the compounds are not given here.*
decade *n* group, series of ten, *specif* period of ten years.
decadent *a* deteriorating; declining in morals; *n* **decadence.**

decagon *n* plane figure with 10 sides.
decahedron *n* solid with 10 faces.
decalcify *v* remove lime from, as teeth, bones etc.
Decalogue *n* 10 Commandments.
decamp *v* break camp; run away, abscond.
decant *v* pour off gently, leaving sediment; *n* **decanter** stoppered glass vessel for decanted wine.
decapitate *v* cut off head, behead; *n* **decapitation.**
decarbonize *v* deprive of, remove carbon from; *n* **decarbonization.**
decay *v* rot, lose vigour, power etc.; decline; *n* decomposition; rotting; gradual breaking up; *a* **decayed.**
decease *v* die; *n* death; *n* deceased the dead person.
deceive *v* mislead; delude oneself; cheat; *ns* **deceiver; deceit, deception** act of deceiving; fraud; sham; *as* **deceitful, deceptive** misleading, giving false idea.
decelerate *v* decrease speed; (motoring).
December *n* twelfth month of year.
decent *a* seemly; respectable; modest; *n* **decency.**
decibel *n* unit of measure of loudness of sounds.
decide *v* determine; settle; make up one's mind; *a* **decided** determined; definite; *n* **decision;** *a* **decisive.**
deciduous *a* (of trees, shrubs etc.) shedding leaves annually.
decimal *a* based on number ten; *n* decimal fraction; **decimalize** reduce to decimal fractions or system; *n* **decimalization** process of converting to decimals.
decimate *v* kill every tenth man, or large proportion of anything; *n* **decimation.**
decipher *v* decode; make out meaning of; *a* **decipherable.**
deck *n* horizontal flooring of ship, bus, etc.; pack of cards; *v* cover with deck; adorn, decorate.
declaim *v* utter rhetorically, dramatically; *n* **declamation.**
declare *v* proclaim in words; state formally; give list of goods liable for Customs duty; name trump suit in bridge; close cricket innings before fall of last wicket; *n* **declaration.**
decline *v* slope downwards; deteriorate; refuse; give

inflexions of nouns etc; *n* gradual loss of vigour; wasting disease; *ns* **declination** deviation; **declension** act of declining; inflexion of nouns etc.
declivity *n* downward slope.
declutch *v* (of engine etc) disengage clutch.
decoct *v* boil down, extract essence by boiling, *n* **decoction.**
decode *v* translate from cipher or code.
decollete *a* low necked dress.
decompose *v* rot, decay; break into constituent parts; *n* **decomposition** state of being decomposed.
decor *n* decorative scheme of room, stage set, etc.
decorate *v* adorn by additions; paint, paper a room; invest with badge, medal etc., showing honour to; *ns* **decoration**; **decorator** tradesman who paints and papers rooms etc.; *a* **decorative.**
decorous *a* seemly, sober, decent; *n* **decorum** propriety.
decoy *v* lure into danger; *n* thing or person used as lure or bait.
decrease *v* lessen; grow, make smaller; *n* lessening.
decree *n* decision; formal order; edict; *v* order, command by decree.
decrepit *a* old, feeble, tottery; *n* **decrepitude.**
decry *v* disparage, cry down; *pt* & *pp* **decried**; *pr p* **decrying.**
dedicate *v* devote solemnly; inscribe (book etc.) to a person; *n* **dedication.**
deduce *v* infer; draw as conclusion from given facts; *n* **deduction** conclusion reached; *a* **deductive** by deduction.
deduct *v* subtract, take away; *n* **deduction** amount subtracted.
deed *n* action; reality; legal document.
deem *v* believe; consider; regard; *n* **deemster** a justice of Isle of Man.
deep *a* extending far down, in; of, at given depth; hard to fathom; engrossed (in study etc.); dark, rich (of colour); low-pitched (of sound etc.); cunning; *n* deep water, sea; *v* **deepen**; *ns* **deepness** quality of being deep; *as* **deep-rooted** firmly fixed; **deep-seated** not superficial.

deer *n* family of ruminants, with deciduous antlers; *pl* **deer**; *ns* **deer-hound**; **deer-stalker**, one who hunts deer; kind of hat.
deface *v* disfigure; mar; obliterate; *n* **defacement**.
defalcation *n* misappropriation of property, funds etc.; embezzlement.
defame *v* speak evil of; calumniate; *n* **defamation**; *a* **defamatory**.
default *v* fail to appear (*leg*); fail to pay, or act; *n* **absence** deficiency; *n* **defaulter**; **in default of** in absence of.
defeat *v* conquer; frustrate; *n* conquest; frustration; *n* **defeatism** acceptance of defeat; pessimism.
defecate *v* remove impurities; void excrement; *n* **defecation**.
defect *n* fault; blemish; shortcoming; *v* desert ones country, duty; *ns* **defector** one who defects; **defection**; *a* **defective** faulty, imperfect.
defend *v* guard; ward off attack; (*leg.*) oppose, fight case; uphold; *ns* **defence**; **defender**; *a* **defensive** protecting; *n* attitude of defence; *a* **defensible** justified; *n* **defensibility**.
defer *v* delay, put off; *n* **deferment**.
defer *v* yield to another's wishes; *n* **deference** respect, consideration for; *a* **deferential**.
deficiency *n* shortage; lack; *a* **deficient** lacking, incomplete in something; *n* **deficit** excess of liabilities over assets.
defile *v* pollute; corrupt; desecrate; *n* **defilement**.
defile *v* march in file; *n* narrow valley or pass.
define *v* show clearly; fix limits of; state meaning; *as* **definable**; **definite** exact; clear; certain; **definitive** decisive; *n* **definition** exact description.
deflate *v* let out air, gas from; reduce inflated currency; *n* **deflation**.
deflect *v* change course of; deviate; *ns* **deflection** **deflexion**; **deflector** device causing deflection.
deforest *v* clear land of trees; *n* **deforestation.**
deform *v* spoil shape, beauty of; disfigure; *ns* **deformation**; **deformity**.
defraud *v* cheat; swindle; deprive of lawful rights.
defray *v* bear cost of.

defrost *v* remove frost or ice from; unfreeze.
deft *a* skilful, neat; competent; *n* **deftness.**
defunct *a* dead, deceased.
defy *v* challenge; resist; flout; disobey openly; *a* **defiant**; insolently disobedient; *n* **defiance.**
degenerate *v* decline from higher to lower state or condition; *a* lower in quality; depraved; *n* degenerate person, thing; *ns* **degeneration**; **degeneracy.**
degrade *v* reduce in rank, status, quality; debase; humiliate; *a* **degraded**; *n* **degradation** act of degrading; state of misery, squalor.
degree *n* unit of measurement; grade in any series; extent of progress, skill; amount; university rank; station in life.
dehydrate *v* remove water from; *n* **dehydration.**
deify *v* look on, worship as god; *n* **deification.**
deign *v* condescend to do; think fit.
deity *n* a god, divinity; **the Deity** God.
deject *v* depress, dispirit; *a* **dejected**; *n* **dejection.**
delay *v* retard; keep back; linger, *n* act of delaying; tardiness.
delectable *a* delightful, enjoyable; *n* **delectation** pleasure.
delegate *v* send as representative; entrust with duties etc.; *n* representative; *ns* **delegation**; **delegacy** body of delegates.
delete *v* erase, remove, obliterate; *n* **deletion.**
deleterious *a* harmful, injurious.
deliberate *v* discuss; study closely; *a* studied; intentional; unhurried; *n* **deliberation** careful reflection on.
delicate *a* sensitive; pleasing; dainty; not robust; finely made; easily injured; *n* **delicacy** fineness; refinement; weakness (of health); tasty food.
delicious *a* agreeable to senses *esp* taste; delightful.
delight *n* great pleasure; *v* charm; give, take great pleasure; *a* **delightful** pleasing; fascinating.
delimitation *n* fixing of boundaries; *v* **delimit** define limits.
delineate *v* depict; describe; *ns* **delineator, delineation.**

delinquent *n* offender; *a* failing in duty; *n* **delinquency** offence, fault.
delirium *n* mental disorder; *a* **delirious** incoherent; light-headed.
deliver *v* set free; hand over; utter (sermon etc.); aim (blow etc.); assist at childbirth; *ns* **delivery**; **deliverer**; **deliverance** rescue.
dell *n* small wooded hollow.
delphinium *n* genus of plants, including larkspur.
delta *n* alluvial land at river mouth; Greek letter.
delude *v* deceive; mislead; *n* **delusion**; *a* **delusive**.
deluge *v* inundate; flood; overwhelm; *n* flood; torrent (of words etc.); downpour.
delve *v* dig, burrow; (*fig*) look deeply into.
demagogue *n* political agitator.
demand *v* require; ask as by right; question; *n* urgent claim; need; call for specific commodity.
demarcation *n* boundary line; limit; distinction.
demean *v* behave, conduct oneself; *n* **demeanour** bearing, deportment.
demean *v* lower, degrade oneself.
demented *a* insane, crazy, wild; *n* **dementia** form of insanity.
demerara *n* kind of brown sugar.
demesne *n* landed property, estate.
demi- *prefix*: *forms compounds with meaning* half, partial. *Where the meaning may be deduced from the simple word, the compounds are not given here.*
demigod *n* heroic character.
demijohn *n* large narrow-necked bottle with wicker covering.
demi-monde *n* woman of dubious social standing and reputation.
demise *v* convey by lease; leave as legacy; *n* conveyance by will etc; death.
demobilize *v* disband, discharge forces; *n* **demobilization**.
democracy *n* rule by the people; state so governed; *a* **democratic**; *n* **democrat** supporter of democracy.
demolish *v* pull down; destroy; break up; *n* **demolition**.

demon *n* devil; evil spirit; wicked, cruel person; *as* **demoniac** possessed by demon; **demonic** inspired by demon.
demonetize *v* deprive currency of value; *n* **demonetization.**
demonstrate *v* prove by reasoning; show by example; show feelings; *as* **demonstrable** proved; **demonstrative** conclusive; showing clearly; *ns* **demonstration** proof; exhibition of method; expression of force, public feeling; **demonstrator** one who demonstrates.
demoralize *v* lower morale of; dishearten, discourage; *n* **demoralization.**
demote *v* reduce in order, rank, etc.; *n* **demotion.**
demur *v* hesitate; raise objections to; *n* (*leg*) **demurrer** exception taken against point.
demure *a* modest; affecting coyness, gravity.
demurrage *n* undue delay in unloading ship, rail wagon etc.; charge made for this.
den *n* lair of wild animal; cage; small room, study.
denature *v* alter natural quality of; adulterate.
dene *n* small valley.
denier *n* unit of weight showing fineness of silk; nylon yarn.
denigrate *v* sneer at; defame; *n* **denigration.**
denim *n* coarse cotton, cloth.
denizen *n* inhabitant.
denominate *v* name, designate; *ns* **denomination** name of particular class, religion etc. **denominator** divisor in vulgar fractions.
denote *v* mark, indicate by sign, symbol; mean.
denouement *n* final situation (in play, book etc.); climax.
denounce *v* accuse publicly; repudiate (treaty); *n* **denunciation**; *a* **denunciatory.**
dense *a* crowded; thick; compact; (*fig*) stupid; *ns* **denseness, density,** specific gravity; (*fig*) stupidity.
dent *n* slight hollow made by blow etc.; *v* make, mark with dent.
dental *a* pertaining to teeth or dentistry; *a* **dentate** toothed.
dentist *n* surgeon who cares for teeth; **dentistry** art

of dentist; **dentifrice** paste, powder for cleaning teeth; **dentine** hard part of tooth; **dentition** teething; **denture(s)** set of false teeth.

denude *v* make bare; strip; *n* **denudation** erosion of soil by natural forces.

deny *v* declare untrue; refuse (request); disown; abstain from; *n* **denial**.

deodorize *v* remove smell from; *ns* **deodorization**; **deodorizer**; **deodorant**.

deoxidize *v* remove oxygen from; *n* **deoxidization**.

depart *v* go away; leave; die; deviate; *ns* **department** branch; part; division; **d. store** large shop selling variety of goods; **departure** starting out, leaving; *a* **departmental**.

depend *v* hang; rely on; be contingent on; *a* **dependable** reliable; *ns* **dependant** person relying on another for support; *a* **dependent**; *ns* **dependence**; **dependency** subordinate territory.

depict *v* describe verbally; represent pictorially.

depilatory *n* substance able to remove hair; *n* **depilation** act of removing hair.

deplete *v* empty out; exhaust; *n* **depletion**.

deplore *v* lament; regret; disapprove; *a* **deplorable** lamentable; disastrous.

deploy *v* extend, open out (troops etc.); *n* **deployment**.

deponent *n* one who makes statement on oath; *v* **depone**.

depopulate *v* drive out, destroy population; *n* **depopulation** decline in population.

deport *v* banish; expel; behave oneself; *ns* **deportation** expulsion from state; **deportment** carriage, behaviour.

depose *v* remove from office, dethrone; testify, *n* **deposition**.

deposit *v* entrust for safe keeping; leave (as sediment) set down; *n* sediment; money deposited at bank or given as pledge of good faith; *ns* **depositor**; **depository** place where things are deposited; storehouse.

depot *n* storehouse; regimental H.Q.; bus garage.

deprave *v* pervert, corrupt; *n* **depravity** viciousness, moral corruption.

deprecate *v* express disapproval of; *a* **deprecative; deprecatory** *n* **deprecation.**
depreciate *v* lower value of; (*fig*) disparage; lose quality (by wear); *n* **depreciation** reduction in value (by wear & tear); allowance made for this in valuations; *a* **depreciatory.**
depredation *n* plundering; laying waste; *n* **depredator** one who robs, despoils.
depress *n* press down; make dejected; weaken; *n* **depression** concavity; despondence; low atmospheric pressure; slump in trade; *a* & *n* **depressant** sedative.
deprive *v* take away from; dispossess; *n* **deprivation.**
depth *n* degree of deepness.
depute *v* appoint as agent, substitute; delegate; *ns* **deputy** substitute, delegate; **deputation** body of persons acting as deputies; *v* **deputize** act for another.
derail *v* leave or cause to leave rails; *n* **derailment.**
derange *v* upset; disturb; drive mad; *n* **derangement** mental disorder.
derelict *a* deserted; worthless; neglected; *n* thing forsaken *esp* ship; *n* **dereliction** neglect of duty.
deride *v* mock at; ridicule; *n* **derision**; *a* **derisive derisory** mocking, ironical.
derive *v* get from; trace origin of; spring from; *ns* **derivation; derivative**; *a* **derivative.**
derm, derma *n* inner layer of skin; *as* **dermal**; *ns* **dermatitis** inflammation of skin; **dermatology** study of skin & its diseases; **dermatologist.**
derogate *v* detract (from); disparage; *n* **derogation**; *a* **derogatory** disparaging, taking away merit.
derrick *n* crane, stationary or movable; latticed tower over oil well.
dervish *n* Mohammedan monk vowed to poverty.
descant *n* song accompanying plainsong; talk at length.
descend *v* move, come down; stoop; lower oneself; be derived; pass by inheritance; *ns* **descendant** offspring; **descent** act of coming down, slope.
describe *v* give account of; depict in words; mark out, trace form or line of; *a* **descriptive**; *n* **description** account; kind, species.

descry *v* make out, discern.
desecrate *v* profane; *ns* **desecration, desecrator.**
desert *v* forsake, abandon; (*mil*) abscond from service; *ns* **deserter, desertion.**
desert *n* barren, uninhabited tract; *a* uninhabited, lonely.
deserve *v* be worthy of; merit; *a* **deserved, deserving** worthy of.
desiccate *v* dry completely; *a* **desiccated**; *n* **desiccation.**
desideratum *n* acknowledged want.
design *v* plan out; intend; make, invent pattern; *n* purpose, intention; decorative pattern; *n* **designer** one who makes artistic designs; *a* **designing** artful, scheming.
designate *v* indicate; nominate for office; specify; *a* nominated but not installed; *n* **designation** distinctive name.
desire long for; yearn for; request; *n* strong longing; wish, hope; something desired; *a* **desirable** worth having; *n* **desirability**; *a* **desirous** wishful.
desist *v* stop, cease.
desk *n* table or other piece of furniture used for reading or writing on.
desolate *a* waste, dismal; forsaken; lonely, forlorn; *v* lay waste; make lonely, sad.
despair *v* lose hope; *n* hopelessness.
despatch, dispatch *v* send off; kill; finish off speedily; *n* sending off; official report, message; speed.
desperate *a* beyond hope; driven to extremity; frantic; *ns* **desperation, desperado** adventurer; violent ruffian.
despise *v* look down on; feel contempt; *a* **despicable** contemptible, mean.
despite *n* spite, hatred, malice; *prep* in spite of.
despoil *v* plunder; strip of; *n* **despoliation.**
despond *v* lose hope, courage; be dejected *a* **despondent**; *n* **despondency.**
despot *n* tyrant, oppressor; *n* **despotism** tyranny.
dessert *n* fruit, sweet served at end of meal.
destine *v* determine future of; intend; *ns* **destiny**

pre-ordained fate; **destination** place where person is going.

destitute *a* extremely poor; lacking in; penniless; *n* **destitution.**

destroy *v* ruin; demolish; *n* **destroyer** one that destroys; type of fast warship; *as* **destructible**; **destructive** ruinous; mischievous; *n* **destruction.**

desuetude *n* state of disuse.

desultory *a* rambling, aimless, disconnected.

detach *v* unfasten; disconnect; *a* **detached**; separate; impartial; aloof; *n* **detachment** separation; unconcern; number of troops etc. detached for special duty; *a* **detachable.**

detail *v* deal with item by item; select for duty; *n* small part; item.

detain *v* hinder; withold; retain in custody; *n* **detention** forced delay, keeping in custody.

detect *v* discover, find out; *ns* **detection**; **detective** police investigator of crime; **detector** one who detects; (radio) frequency changer.

detent *n* checking device; catch regulating striking of clock.

deter *v* hinder; discourage from; *a* & *n* **deterrent.**

detergent *a* cleansing; *n* cleansing, purifying substance.

deteriorate *v* become worse; depreciate; *n* **deterioration.**

determine *v* decide; resolve; set limit to, fix; *as* **determined** resolute; **determinate** fixed; *n* **determination** resolution.

detest *v* hate, abhor, loathe; *a* **detestable**; *n* **detestation.**

dethrone *v* remove from throne, depose; *n* **dethronement.**

detonate *v* explode (bomb etc.) *ns* **detonator** **detonation**, violent explosion.

detour *n* a going round; alternative route.

detract *v* take away from; disparage; *n* **detraction.**

detrain *v* set down, alight from train.

detriment *n* harm, loss, injury; *a* **detrimental** damaging.

detritus *n* rock debris; *n* **detrition** wearing down by friction.
deuce *n* die or playing card with two spots; score 40-all, in tennis; *a* **deuced** excessive.
devastate *v* lay waste, make desolate; *n* **devastation.**
develop *v* grow; unfold; elaborate; cause to appear *esp* image on photographic plate; exploit building site; *ns* **developer**; **development.**
deviate *v* turn aside, diverge; *ns* **deviator**; **deviation** *a* **devious** rambling, crooked; (*fig*) shifty.
device *n* plan, trick; invention, mechanical contrivance; artistic or heraldic design.
devil *n* Spirit of evil, Satan; wicked, evil person; *a* **devilish**, (*sl*) very; *ns* **devilry** cruel behaviour; **devilment** mischievous prank; *v* **devil** grill with hot spices; do hack work for another.
devise *v* invent, contrive, plan; leave by will.
devoid *a* lacking, without.
devolve *v* transfer, delegate; fall upon; (*leg*) pass by succession.
devote *v* set apart, dedicate; addict oneself to; *a* **devoted** given up (to); loyal; fond of; *ns* **devotee** one fervidly devoted; **devotion** strong affection; adherence; *pl* religious observances; *a* **devotional.**
devour *v* eat voraciously; consume; (*fig*) read eagerly, absorb; *n* **devourer.**
devout *a* pious; devoted, earnest.
dew *n* condensed moisture from air, falling on earth; *v* wet with, or as dew; *n* **dewiness**; *a* **dewy**; *n* **dew-pond** ancient artificial pond.
dewlap *n* thick fold of skin under neck of cattle.
dexterity *n* adroitness, manual & mental; deftness; manual skill; *a* **dexterous** skilful; quick; *a* **dexter** on right-hand side; (*her*) on spectator's left.
dextrose *n* starch sugar, glucose.
dhow *n* Arab sailing vessel.
dia- *prefix forms compounds with meaning* through, across, apart. *Where the meaning may be deduced from the simple word, the compounds are not given here.*
diabetes *n* disease characterised by excess sugar in urine; *a* & *n* **diabetic.**

diabolic (*al*) *a* devilish, fiendish; (*sl*) very bad, unpleasant.
diacritic *a* distinctive; *n* mark showing phonetic value.
diadem *n* fillet, crown.
diaeresis *n* sign (¨) placed over second vowel of two, to indicate separate pronunciation.
diagnose *v* identify disease from symptons; *n* **diagnosis**; *a* **diagnostic**.
diagonal *a* oblique; *n* line from corner to corner.
diagram *n* plan, chart; geometric illustration of theorem; *a* **diagrammatic**.
dial *n* face of clock; graduated face of gauge, meter, compass etc.; disc on automatic telephone; (*sl*) human face; *v* use telephone.
dialect *n* regional form of language.
dialecties *n pl* art of logical discussion and disputation.
dialogue *n* conversation; its representation in writing, in drama, books etc.
diameter *n* straight line passing from side to side, through centre of solid or geometric figure; length of such line; unit of magnifying power of lenses; *a* **diametrical** opposite.
diamond *n* hard, brilliant precious stone of crystalized carbon; suit at cards; rhombus; *a* made of, set with diamonds.
dianthus *n* genus of plants, including pinks, etc.
diapason *n* range, compass of voice, instrument; organ stop.
diaper *n* linen cloth woven with diamond pattern; baby's napkin.
diaphanous *a* transparent, translucent.
diaphragm *n* muscular wall between thorax & abdomen; device controlling transmission of light, sound etc.; vibrating disc producing sound waves.
diarrhoea *n* excessive, irritable laxity of bowels.
diary *n* daily record, *esp* of personal events or thoughts; book used for keeping such record; *n* **diarist**.
diastole *n* dilation of heart muscle.

diathermy *n* electro-medical treatment with high frequency current.
diatribe *n* vituperative attack; abusive criticism.
dibber, dibble *n* pointed tool for making holes in ground, for seeds or plants; *v* **dibble** use a dibble.
dice *n pl* (*sing* **die**) cubes marked on each side (1-6 spots), used in game of chance; small cubes of meat, vegetables etc.; *v* to gamble with dice; cut into small cubes; *n* **dicer.**
dicephalous *a* two-headed.
dichotomy *n* division into two parts.
dicker *v* haggle, bargain, chaffer.
dicky *n* open seat at back of car; (*sl*) false shirt-front.
dictate *v* speak or read aloud for another to transcribe; command; prescribe; impose arbitrarily; *n* order, command; *ns* **dictation**; **dictator** despot, absolute ruler; **dictatorship**; *a* **dictatorial** overbearing, imperious.
diction *n* choice and use of words.
dictionary *n* book listing words alphabetically, with their meanings etc.; reference book with details of subject arranged alphabetically.
dictum *n* formal statement; maxim; *pl* **dicta.**
didactic *a* intended to instruct; dictatorial.
diddle *v* cheat, swindle.
die *v* expire; cease; grow weaker; long for; wither; *n* **diehard** one who resists change to the end.
diesel *a* of oil-burning internal combustion engine.
diet *n* usual food; planned feeding, for medical reasons; *v* follow prescribed diet, *esp* to lose weight; *a* **dietary**; *n pl* **dietetics** science of diet; *n* **dietician** one who plans diets.
diet *n* international or parliamentary assembly, conference.
differ *v* disagree; be unlike; quarrel; *n* **difference** disagreement; dissimilarity; remainder left after subtraction *a* **different** unlike; separate, distinct; *a* **differential** relating to, showing difference in outward circumstances; *n* (*math*) having small quantitative differences; **d.gear** one enabling rear wheels to revolve at different speeds, when cornering; *v* **differentiate** discriminate; become different.

difficult *a* not easy; needing great physical or mental effort; hard to please; *n* **difficulty** obstacle; objection; *pl* **difficulties** in trouble *esp* financial.
diffident *a* shy; self-effacing; timid; *n* **diffidence**.
diffuse *v* scatter, spread around; radiate; *a* not localized; verbose; *ns* **diffusion**; act of diffusing; dissemination; **diffuser**; *a* **diffusive** tending to diffuse.
dig *v* work, turn over earth with spade; excavate; form hole etc; (*fig*) discover; prod; (*sl*) taunt, jeer; *pt* & *pp* **dug**; *n* archaeological excavation; nudge; *pl* (*sl*) **digs, diggings** lodgings.
digest *v* convert food in digestive tract for assimilation into blood; summarize, condense; absorb mentally; *n* classified summary; magazine containing condensed versions of books, etc.; *as* **digestive**; **digestible**; *n* **digestion**.
digit *n* single figure or numeral; finger or toe; *as* **digital** pertaining to digits or fingers; **digitate** having separate fingers, toes.
digitalis *n* genus of plants including foxglove; drug made from foxglove.
dignify *v* do honour to; exalt; ennoble; *n* **dignity** stateliness; serenity; high office, rank; *a* **dignified** stately; serene; *n* **dignitary** holder of high office *esp* in church.
digress *v* depart from main subject *esp* in talking, writing, etc.; wander, ramble; **digression**.
dihedral *a* having two plane faces.
dike, dyke *n* ditch; embankment or causeway to prevent flooding.
dilapidate *v* fall or allow to fall into disrepair; deteriorate; *a* **dilapidated** fallen into disrepair; (*of persons*) shabby, down-at-heel; *n* **dilapidation**.
dilate *v* expand; swell; write, speak at length; *n* **dil(at)ation.**
dilatory *a* causing delay; slow; belated; *n* **dilatoriness.**
dilemma *n* choice of evils; quandary.
dilettante *n* one with superficial knowledge of fine arts; *a* unprofessional.
diligent *a* pains taking; industrious; *n* **diligence.**

dill *n* herb of carrot family, used medicinally and for flavouring.
dilute *v* weaken, thin down fluid by adding another fluid; *a* **diluted**; *n* & *a* **diluent**; *n* **dilution**.
diluvium *n* deposit left by flood or glacier; *as* **diluvial**; **diluvian**.
dim *a* faint; not bright; indistinct; *v* make or become less bright; *n* **dimness**.
dime *n* (in U.S.A.) 10-cent coin.
dimension *n* length, breadth, thickness; extent; size; (*algebra*) number of factors in a term; *a* **dimensional**.
diminish *v* lessen; reduce; *n* **diminution**; *a* **diminutive** tiny.
diminuendo *n* (*mus*) gradual decrease in loudness.
dimity *n* corded cotton fabric.
dimple *n* small depression in surface of skin, *esp* of cheek; *v* make dimples.
din *n* loud continuous noise; clamour; *v* make din; repeat insistently.
dine *v* take, give dinner to; *ns* **dining-room**; **diner** one who dines; dining-car on train; **dinner** chief meal of day; formal banquet.
ding *v* make ringing sound; *n* **ding-dong** sound of bell; (*coll*) equally balanced, hard-fought fight.
dinghy *n* small boat (*usu* with sails).
dingle *n* dell, small valley.
dingo *n* Australian wild dog.
dingy *a* dull; dirty; shabby; *n* **dinginess**.
dinosaur *n* gigantic, extinct reptile.
dint *n* dent, mark; **by dint of** by force of.
diocese *n* district under jurisdiction of bishop; *a* **diocesan**.
dioxide *n* oxide having two parts of oxygen to one of metal.
dip *v* put, plunge quickly into liquid; lower and raise rapidly; sink, drop suddenly; (*geol*) slope down; *v* (*fig*) **dip into** glance at briefly; *n* act of dipping; hollow; *n* **dipper** ladle, etc.; kind of bird.
diphtheria *n* serious, infectious disease of throat.
diphthong *n* two vowel sounds pronounced as one syllable.
diploma *n* document attesting holder's proficiency;

one granting honour, privilege; state documents.
diplomacy *n* art of management of international relations; tactful skill in dealing with people, situations etc.; *n* **diplomat** professional employed in diplomacy; **diplomatist** tactful person; *a* **diplomatic.**
dipolar *a* having two poles; *n* **dipole** type of aerial.
dipsomania *n* morbid & irresistible craving for alcohol.
dire *a* dreadful, terrible.
direct *v* guide, control; address (letter); show way; focus, aim; order with authority; *a* straight; frank; without intermediary; (*speech*) exact; *n* **direction**; guiding; command; course taken by moving object; (*pl*) instruction; *ns* **directness**; **director** one who controls; member of board managing company; **directorate** board of directors; **directory** book listing names & addresses, telephone numbers etc.
dirge *n* lament for dead; mournful song.
dirigible *n* airship capable of being steered; *a* steerable.
dirk *n* short dagger.
dirty *a* soiled; not clean; indecent; (*of weather*) stormy, rough; mean; *ns* **dirt** filth; dust; soil; obscenity; **dirtiness** state of being dirty; *v* **dirty** soil, make dirty.
dis- *prefix expressing* separation; negation *or* reversal; deprivation; *e.g.* **disable** make unfit, **disorder** lack of order **dispossess** deprive of possession. *Where the meaning may be deduced from the simple word, the compounds are not given here.*
disability *n* handicap; incapacity.
disabuse *v* undeceive, free from illusion.
disaffection *n* disloyalty; *a* **disaffected** discontented, seditious.
disagree *v* differ; quarrel; **d.with** (of health) not to suit; *n* **disagreement** difference of opinion, dispute; *a* **disagreeable** bad-tempered; distasteful.
disallow *v* refuse to sanction; prohibit.
disappear *v* vanish; *n* **disappearance.**
disappoint *v* fail to fulfil the desires or hopes of; *n* **disappointment**; *a* **disappointed.**

disarm *v* deprive of weapons; conciliate; reduce armaments; *n* **disarmament.**
disarray *v* throw into confusion; disturb.
disaster *n* sudden great misfortune; calamity; *a* **disastrous.**
disavow *v* repudiate; deny belief in; *n* **disavowal.**
disband *v* scatter, disperse; break up (organized body, etc.).
disbar *v* expel from the Bar (of barristers).
disburse *v* give, pay out, spend money; *n* **disbursement.**
disc, disk *n* round, flat thin object; gramophone record; *n* **disc jockey** (*sl*) radio announcer of programme of recorded popular music.
discard *v* throw aside as valueless; reject; cast off.
discern *v* make out; distinguish (by senses or with mind); *as* **discerning**, shrewd; discriminating; **discernible** that can be clearly seen; *n* **discernment**, insight; keen judgment.
discharge *v* fire (gun etc.); emit; unload (ship); dismiss; release; *n* act of discharging; release; matter discharged or emitted; payment.
disciple *n* follower, one who learns from another *esp* one of the twelve Apostles.
discipline *n* systematic training in obedience, self-control & orderliness; maintenance of order and control; *v* control; train mentally, morally, physically; *n* **disciplinarian** one who enforces strict discipline; *a* **disciplinary.**
disclaim *v* repudiate, disown; *n* **disclaimer**; (*leg*) renunciation of right, title etc.
disclose *v* reveal, bring to light; make known; *n* **disclosure**, revelation.
discolour *v* alter, change colour of; stain; *n* **discoloration.**
discomfit *v* disconcert; defeat; *n* **discomfiture.**
discommode *v* trouble, inconvenience, disturb.
discompose *v* disturb calmness of, agitate; *n* **discomposure.**
disconcert *v* discompose, embarrass.
disconsolate *a* forlorn, sad, unhappy.

discord *n* disagreement; strife; harsh sound; *a* **discordant**; *n* **discordance.**
discount *n* sum deducted from debt, for prompt or cash settlement; *v* pay or receive money in advance in payment (for bill of exchange etc. not yet due); depreciate; allow for exaggeration.
discountenance *v* disapprove, discourage.
discourage *v* dishearten; advise against; try to prevent; *n* **discouragement.**
discourse *n* speech, lecture; conversation; *v* lecture, preach; converse.
discover *v* find out *esp* something unknown before; *ns* **discovery**; **discoverer.**
discreet *a* careful, prudent, circumspect, *ns* **discreetness**; **discretion** prudence; freedom of choice; *a* **discretionary.**
discrepancy *n* inconsistency; contradiction; *a* **discrepant.**
discriminate *v* distinguish (between); treat differently; *n* **discrimination.**
discursive *a* dealing with wide range of subjects, rambling.
discus *n* heavy disc thrown in contest of strength.
discuss *v* debate fully; argue in detail, *n* **discussion.**
disdain *v* treat with contempt, scorn; *n* hauteur, aloofness; *a* **disdainful.**
disease *n* illness; ailment; *a* **diseased** suffering from or impaired by disease.
disembark *v* go, put ashore from ship; *n* **disembarkation.**
disenchant *v* disillusion; *n* **disenchantment.**
disengage *v* release, set free; *a* **disengaged** free, at leisure.
disfigure *v* mar, render unsightly; *ns* **disfigurement** defect, blemish; **disfiguration.**
disfranchise *v* deprive of rights of citizenship; *specif* of right to vote.
disfrock *v* unfrock, expel from clergy.
disgorge *v* give up; eject from throat.
disgrace *v* bring shame on; dismiss from favour; *n* shame, disrepute; dishonour; *a* **disgraceful,** shameful.

disgruntled *a* displeased; sulky; in bad temper.
disguise *v* change appearance of; conceal identity of; *n* deceptive appearance; misrepresentation.
disgust *n* strong aversion; repugnance; *v* fill with loathing; nauseate; *a* **disgusting**, repulsive, sickening.
dish *n* shallow vessel with rim, for holding, cooking food; contents of dish; (*sl*) attractive person; *v* serve in dish; (*sl*) upset, spoil; **dish out** (*sl*) share out.
dishearten *v* make despondent, depress; *a* **disheartening.**
dishevelled *a* (of hair) ruffled, untidy; unkempt in appearance.
disillusion *v* reveal truth; undeceive.
disinfect *v* destroy infection; remove harmful germs etc.; *n* **disinfectant** substance that disinfects.
disinherit *v* deprive of right to inherit.
disintegrate *v* split up, resolve into parts, elements; fall to pieces.
disinterested *a* without selfish motives; impartial.
disjoint *v* dismember; separate at joints; *a* **disjointed** dismembered; (of speech, thought) incoherent; disconnected.
dislocate *v* put out of joint; displace; (*fig*) disorganize, confuse; *n* **dislocation.**
dislodge *v* remove from resting-place; drive out (enemy); *n* **dislodgement.**
dismal *a* depressing; gloomy, cheerless.
dismantle *v* strip of equipment, furnishings etc.; remove defences; *n* **dismantling.**
dismay *v* alarm, frighten; *n* apprehension, consternation.
dismember *v* tear limb from limb; divide up; *n* **dismemberment.**
dismiss *v* send away; expel from office; disperse; banish from mind; *n* **dismissal.**
disparage *v* belittle; throw doubt upon; *n* **disparagement.**
disparate *a* essentially different; unequal; *n* **disparity** inequality; incongruity.
dispassionate *a* calm; unbiassed.
dispatch *see* **despatch.**

dispel *v* drive away; disperse, cause to vanish.
dispense *v* give out; make up medicine; grant exemption (from rule etc.); do without; *ns* **dispenser**; **dispensary** place where medicine is made up; **dispensation** divine decree; (*eccles.*) relaxation of law; *a* **dispensable**.
disperse *v* drive away; scatter; *a* **dispersed**; *ns* **dispersion**; **dispersal**.
dispirit *v* deject, cast down; discourage; *a* **dispirited**
displace *v* move out of place; oust; *a* **displaced** out of place; *n* **displacement** displacing; volume of liquid or gas displaced by solid in it.
display *v* show; exhibit; make obvious; *n* parade; showing off; exhibition.
displease *v* annoy; offend; cause dissatisfaction; *n* **displeasure**; anger, indignation.
disport *v* play; amuse oneself; frolic.
dispose *v* arrange; make willing; adjust; determine; **dispose of** get rid of; sell; consume; *ns* **disposal**; **disposition** plan; temperament; ordering.
disproportionate *a* out of proportion; excessive; *n* **disproportion**.
disprove *v* refute, show to be false.
dispute *v* discuss; question validity; oppose; wrangle; *n* argument; controversy; **beyond d.** finally decided; *n* **disputation** verbal argument.
disqualify *v* make ineligible, debar; incapacitate; *n* **disqualification**.
disquiet *v* make anxious, apprehensive, restless; *n* **disquietude**.
disrobe *v* undress; take off official robes.
disrupt *v* break up, shatter; *n* **disruption**.
dissect *v* (*anat* & *bot*) cut up for examination; divide in pieces; criticize in detail; *ns* **dissection**; **dissector**.
dissemble *v* conceal feelings, motives etc.; deceive; act hypocritically.
disseminate *v* spread abroad; scatter as seed; *ns* **dissemination**; **disseminator**.
dissent *v* disagree; withold assent; *ns* **dissention**; **Dissenter** Nonconformist, person disagreeing with views of established C. of E.

dissertation *n* formal discourse or treatise.
dissident *a* not in agreement; *n* **dissidence** disagreement.
dissimulate *v* conceal one's feelings; dissemble; *n* **dissimulation.**
dissipate *v* scatter; dispel; squander; engage in dissolute occupations; *n* **dissipation** dispersion; intemperance; extravagance; *a* **dissipated** dispelled; debauched.
dissociate *v* separate; sever, repudiate connection with; *n* **dissociation.**
dissolute *a* lax in morals, conduct; debauched.
dissolve *v* liquefy; melt; become faint; break up; terminate; annul; *a* **dissoluble** capable of being dissolved; *ns* **dissolvent** that which dissolves; **dissolution** act or process of dissolving; breaking up (*esp* of Parliament).
dissonant *a* discordant; at variance; *n* **dissonance.**
dissuade *v* persuade against; advise against; *n* **dissuasion.**
dissymmetry *n* lack of symmetry; symmetry in reverse; *a* **dissymmetrical.**
distaff *n* stick on which wool was wound for spinning; **d.side** female line, maternal side.
distance *n* space between two things; remoteness; aloofness; *v* put, keep far away; outstrip; *a* **distant** far off; faint; haughty, reserved.
distaste *n* aversion; dislike; *a* **distasteful** unpleasant; repellent.
distemper *n* contagious disease of dogs; thick paint used for internal walls; *v* paint with distemper.
distend *v* inflate; become blown out.
distil *v* evaporate liquid & condense it again; refine by this method; trickle; *ns* **distillation**; **distiller** one who distils, *esp* alcoholic spirit; **distillery** place where distillation is carried on.
distinct *a* separate; easily seen; definite; *ns* **distinctness**; **distinction** difference; high standing or special quality; mark of favour; *a* **distinctive** characteristic.
distinguish *v* discern; mark difference in; make, become honoured; *a* **distinguished** famous, celebrated.

distort *v* spoil shape of; misrepresent; *n* **distortion.**
distract *v* divert (thoughts); perplex; drive mad; *n* **distraction** amusement; madness; *a* **distraught** agitated; driven mad.
distrain *v* (*leg*) seize goods to enforce payments; *n* **distraint** legal seizure.
distrait *a* absent-minded; preoccupied.
distress *n* grief; physical exhaustion; danger; extreme poverty; *v* afflict, cause mental or bodily pain to; *as* **distressed** poor; **distressing** painful.
distribute *v* deal, share out; disperse; *a* **distributive** involving distribution; *ns* **distribution; distributer distributor** switch distributing electricity in motor-car engine.
district *n* region; area; locality.
distrust *n* doubt; suspicion; lack of confidence in; *v* feel distrust.
disturb *v* alter normal state, position of; unsettle; disorder; alarm; *ns* **disturbance; disturber.**
disunite *v* become, cause to separate; *n* **disunion.**
disyllabic *a* having two syllables.
ditch *n* narrow trench cut in earth, used for drainage or defence; *v* make, repair ditches; (*sl*) drive car into ditch; throw away.
dither *v* waver; tremble; hesitate nervously.
ditto *n* the same, as already said or written.
ditty *n* short simple song.
diurnal *a* daily; lasting a day; of the day.
divan *n* low backless couch, bed; oriental council.
dive *v* plunge *esp* head first into water; descend suddenly; *n* act of diving; (*sl*) low resort, club *esp* in basement; *n* **diver** one who dives; water bird of diving habits.
diverge *v* branch off set course; separate; *n* **divergence; diversion** turning aside or away; alternative route; *a* **divergent.**
diversify *v* make different; give variety to; *a* **diverse** dissimilar; varied; *ns* **diversification; diversity.**
divert *v* turn aside; distract; amuse; *n* **diversion** entertainment; *a* **diverting.**
divest *v* strip, undress; deprive of, dispossess.
divide *v* split into two or more parts; share out;

separate for voting (of Parliament); find out number of times one number is contained in another; *ns* **dividend** number divided by another; profit on money invested; share of profits etc.; *pl* **dividers** measuring compasses; **division** act of dividing; barrier; political, or administrative section of country; army unit; separation; (*math*) process of dividing; **divisor** number dividing dividend; *as* **divisible** capable of division; **divisional** pertaining to a division.

divine *a* pertaining to God; godlike; sacred; *n* theologian, priest; *n* **divinity** god; theology; quality of being divine; *v* predict; discover by intuition; *ns* **diviner** soothsayer; one who finds hidden water, metal; **divining rod** twig used in discovering water.

divorce *v* disolve marriage; separate; *n* legal dissolution of marriage; separation; *n* **divorcee** divorced spouse.

divot *n* small piece of turf.

divulge *v* make known, reveal (secret etc.); *ns* **divulgement**; **divulgence**.

dizzy *a* giddy; suffering from vertigo; confused; *v* make dizzy; *n* **dizziness**.

do *v* perform; bestow; work at; afflict with; cook food; suffice; act (role etc.); (*colloq*) cheat, swindle; visit (as sightseer); behave; *pt* **did**; *pp* **done**; *v/aux* for emphasis, interrogation & negative; *n* (*sl*) party; *v* **do for** ruin, kill; **do with** make use of.

docile *a* tractable; amenable to training & discipline; *n* **docility**.

dock *n* coarse, large-leaved weed.

dock *n* artificial basin where ships are loaded, repaired; *v* enter, put into dock; *ns* **dockyard**, series of docks, warehouses etc.; **docker** dock labourer.

dock *n* enclosure in court, for accused.

dock *v* cut short, *esp* animal's tail; deduct part of.

docket *n* label, ticket; list of contents, cases for trial.

doctor *n* holder of highest degree in any faculty of University; medical practitioner, *v* give medical treatment to; repair; falsify; *n* **doctorate** degree of doctor.

doctrine *n* accepted belief; dogma *esp* of sect; *n* **doctrinaire** narrow-minded, obstinate person seeking to apply theory, regardless of consequences.
document *n* written information, evidence; *v* bring written evidence; *ns* **documentary** factual report, film; **documentation** documentary proof, evidence.
dodder *v* move shakily, feebly; totter; *n* **dodderer**; *a* **doddering** infirm, senile.
dodge *v* swerve from, *esp* pursuit; evade by tricking; shirk; *n* act of dodging; (*coll*) trick; ingenious plan; device; *n* **dodger** trickster; shirker.
dodo *n* extinct bird, with useless wings.
doe *n* female of deer, rabbit, hare etc.
doff *v* take off *esp* hat etc.; abandon.
dog *n* domestic quadruped, related to wolf; male wolf, fox etc.; andiron; toothed grip; *v* follow closely; *as* **dogged** obstinate; **doggy** pertaining to dogs; *n* **dog-rose,** wild rose; *v* **go to the dogs** (*coll*) degenerate; attend greyhound racing.
doggerel *n* rough, worthless verse.
dogma *n* article of belief; body of such theories etc.; *a* **dogmatic** relating to dogma; dictatorial; *n* **dogmatism.**
doily, doyley *n* small mat placed on, under dish.
doldrums *n pl* low spirits; calm seas near Equator.
dole *n* charitable gift; unemployment benefit; *v* give out sparingly.
doleful *a* woeful, sad, lugubrious.
doll *n* child's toy, like human figure; (*sl*) any girl; *n* **dolly** child's name for doll.
dollar *n* unit of coinage in U.S.A., Canada etc.
dollop *n* big shapeless lump.
dolmen *n* prehistoric stone chamber, cromlech.
dolour *n* grief, sorrow, distress; *a* **dolorous.**
dolphin *n* sea-mammal akin to whale, but smaller.
dolt *n* slow witted, stupid person; *a* **doltish** stupid.
domain *n* land, realm held, ruled over; (*fig*) sphere of activity or influence.
dome *n* convex curved roof; cupola; *a* **domed.**
Domesday (Book) *n* record made in 1086, of lands, owners, extent, value.
domestic *a* pertaining to home or family; not

foreign; (*of animals*) kept by man; *n* household servant; *v* **domesticate** tame animals; *ns* **domestication**; **domesticity.**

domicile *n* usual dwelling-place; *as* **domiciliary** of dwelling-place; **domiciled** residing.

dominate *v* control; prevail; tower over; *a* **dominant** *ns* **domination**; **dominance.**

domineer *v* act harshly, arrogantly; tyrannise; bully; *a* **domineering.**

dominion *n* supremacy, sovereignty; self-governing territory of British Commonwealth.

domino *n* loose cloak with mask; small oblong piece of bone etc. marked with 1-6 dots; *pl* **dominoes** game using 28 such pieces.

don *v* put on, assume.

don *n* Spanish title; fellow, tutor of college.

donate *v* give; *ns* **donation** gift; **donor.**

donkey *n* ass; (*fig*) stupid person.

doodle *v* draw, scribble idly; *n* design so made.

doom *n* fate, evil destiny; formal judgement; *v.* condemn; destine to ruin; *n* **Doomsday** Day of Judgement.

door *n* hinged, sliding, revolving structure for closing an entrance; *n* **doorway** opening so closed.

dope *n* kind of lacquer; drug *esp* narcotic; (*sl*) foolish person; *v* treat with dope; drug; *a* **dopey** drugged.

Doric *a* simplest style of Greek architecture.

dormant *a* inactive; sleeping; hibernating; *n* **dormancy.**

dormer *n* vertical window in sloping roof.

dormitory *n* sleeping room with several beds.

dormouse *n* small hibernating rodent, like mouse.

dormy *a* (*golf*) leading by as many holes as are left to play.

dorsal *a* pertaining to, on, near the back.

dose *a* amount of drug etc. taken at one time; *v* give medicine to; *n* **dosage.**

doss *n* (*sl*) cheap bed; *v* (*sl*) sleep; *n* **doss-house**, cheap lodging house.

dossier *n* set of documents etc., concerning particular person or subject.

dot *n* small round mark or spot; *v* mark with dot; scatter; *a* **dotty** (*sl*) silly.
dot *n* dowry.
dotage *n* senility.
dote *v* love blindly, be foolish over.
dotterel *n* kind of plover.
double *a* twice as much; ambiguous; twofold; *n* thing or person exactly like another; running; twice the amount; *v* make, become double; fold in two; run, turn sharply; act as substitute; *v* **double-cross** betray; *a* **double-dyed** (*fig*) iniquitous; *a* **double-jointed** joints that bend at abnormal angles; *adv* **doubly** in two ways; twice over.
doubloon *n* obsolete Spanish gold coin.
doubt *v* be uncertain; waver; suspect; *n* uncertainty; misgiving; lack of belief; *as* **doubtful**; **doubting**; *adv* **doubtless** assuredly; probably.
douche *n* jet of liquid sprayed on to, into, the body; *v* apply douche to; (*fig*) damp enthusiasm.
dough *n* flour moistened and kneaded; (*sl*) money; *a* **doughy**.
doughty *a* bold, valliant; *n* **doughtiness** valour.
dour *a* stern, grim, obstinate.
douse *v* dip in water; extinguish (light).
dove *n* bird of pigeon family; symbol of peace; *n* **dovetail** joints made with fan-shaped tenons; *v* **dovetail** join by dovetails; (*fig*) fit facts etc. together neatly.
dowager *n* widow whose title derives from deceased husband.
dowdy *a* unfashionable; ill-dressed, shabby.
dower *n* widow's share of husband's property; dowry; *v* endow.
down *n* fine soft feathers; any fine fluffy substance; *a* **downy** like down; (*sl*) astute; *n* **down** bare open uplands; *a* **downy** undulating.
down *adv* towards lower position, size, quality etc.; *prep* from higher to lower position; along; *v* (*sl*) **down tools** strike; *a* **downcast** dejected; *n* **downpour** heavy rain; *a* **downright** emphatic; *a* & *adv* **downward** descending.
dowry *n* woman's marriage portion.

dowse *v* seek water with divining-rod; *n* **dowser.**
doxology *n* short hymn of praise to God.
doyen *n* senior member of body or profession.
doze *v* sleep lightly; be half asleep; *n* light sleep.
dozen *n* set of twelve; **baker's d.** thirteen.
drab *a* mud-coloured; (*fig*) monotonous.
drab *n* slattern; prostitute.
drachm *n* unit of weight, dram.
draft *n* body of troops for special duty; rough sketch, scheme; order for payment; *v* send on special duty; make draft; *n* **draftsman, draughtsman** one who makes drawings etc.
drag *v* pull along; sweep with nets, grappling irons etc.; lag behind; move slowly; *n* dredge; delayed motion; strong smelling lure, in hunting; *v* **draggle** soil by trailing in mud etc.
dragon *n* fabulous winged reptile, breathing out fire.
dragon-fly *n* iridescent long bodied insect.
dragoon *n* mounted infantryman; *v* enforce rigidly.
drain *v* draw off (liquid) gradually; exhaust gradually; *n* pipe, ditch, sewer; (*fig*) constant strain (on strength, time etc); *ns* **drainage; drainer.**
drake *n* male duck.
dram *n* unit of weight; drachm; small drink of liquor.
drama *n* play for stage, radio, TV. etc.; *a* **dramatic** pertaining to drama; thrilling, exciting; *n* **dramatist** playwright; *v* **dramatize** make into play, drama; exaggerate; *n* **dramatization.**
drape *v* arrange in folds; cover loosely; *ns* **draper** dealer in cloth etc.; **drapery** draper's business, goods etc.; hangings.
drastic *a* having powerful effect; violent; severe.
draught *n* act of hauling; drink; depth of water displaced by ship; current of air; *pl* game played on chess board; *v* to draft; *n* **draughtsman** one who makes plans etc.; piece used in draughts; **draughtsmanship; draught-horse** strong horse; *a* **draughty** exposed to currents of air.
draw *v* drag; haul; pull; extract (liquid); inhale; obtain (salary etc.); extend; attract; sketch with pencil etc.; *pt* **drew**; *pp* **drawn**; *n* act of drawing;

tie at end of game; *ns* **drawing** art of depicting in pencil etc; **drawback** disadvantage; **drawer** one who draws; lidless, sliding box in table etc.

drawl *v* speak slowly & affectedly; *n* such manner of speech.

dray *n* low sideless cart used for heavy loads.

dread *v* feel, fear, misgiving; *n* anxiety, fear; *a* awesome; **dreadful** terrible; *n* **dreadnought** battleship.

dream *v* illusion of senses occurring in sleep; fantasy; *v* have dreams; *pt* & *pp* **dreamed, dreamt**; *ns* **dreamer, dreaminess,** *as* **dreamy** vague; **dreamless.**

dreary *a* gloomy; tedious; dismal; *n* **dreariness.**

dredge *v* bring up (mud etc.) from under water; *n* type of net, scoop etc.; *n* **dredger** ship used for dredging.

dredge *v* sprinkle with flour, sugar etc.; *n* **dredger.**

dregs *n pl* sediment; (*fig*) lowest, worthless part.

drench *v* soak thoroughly; give dose of medicine (to animal); *n* large dose; *a* & *n* **drenching** soaking.

dress *v* put clothes on; arrange for display; prepare (food); align (troops); apply dressing to (soil, wound etc.); *n* frock; formal clothes; *ns* **dresser** one who dresses (actors etc.); assistant to surgeon; kitchen sideboard; **dressing** thing applied (fertilizer, bandage etc.); *a* **dressy** smart; *n* **dress-circle** first tier of seats in theatre.

dribble *v* trickle; *n* drop; *ns* **driblet** small amount;

drift *n* deviation from course; something driven by wind, water; general meaning; *v* move aimlessly; *n* **drifter** fishing vessel using drift-net; **drift-net** one allowed to float with the tide.

drill *n* instrument for boring holes; narrow furrow for seeds; *v* bore hole; sow seed in rows.

drill *n* regular physical, mental exercise; military training; *v* perform, cause to perform drill.

drill *n* coarse, cotton twill.

drink *v* swallow liquid; (*fig*) absorb eagerly; take alcoholic liquor; *pt* **drank**; *pp* **drunken, drunk**; *n* liquid swallowed; beverage *esp* alcoholic; *n* **drinker** *a* **drinkable** fit for drinking.

drip *v* trickle, let fall drop by drop; *n* act of dripping;

n **dripping** falling in drops; fat dripping from roast meat; *a* **dripping** very wet.
drive *v* force into movement; set in motion & control (vehicle); go, travel in vehicle; advance strongly; hit with force (ball etc.); *pt* **drove**; *pp* **driven**; *n* strong impulse; energy; private road to house; ride in vehicle; *n* **driver** one who drives; golf-club; *a* **driving** transmitting force, movement.
drivel *v* talk foolishly; *n* nonsense.
drizzle *v* rain finely; *n* very fine rain.
drogue *n* sea-anchor; wind-indicator.
droll *a* funny, quaint; queer; *n* **drollery**.
dromedary *n* riding camel, having one hump.
drone *n* male honey bee; (*fig*) idler; low humming sound; *v* hum, speak monotonously.
drool *v* slaver over.
droop *v* sink, hang down limply; wilt; *a* **drooping**.
drop *n* small globule of liquid; minute quantity; descent; decrease in amount etc; *v* let fall in drops; let fall; release; utter casually; reduce force, pitch of (voice etc.); *n* **droplet** little drop.
dropsy *n* abnormal collection of fluid in tissues, cavities of body; *a* **dropsical**.
dross *n* scum of molten metal; waste matter; (*fig*) anything worthless.
drought *n* lack of rain; long period without rain.
drove *n* moving herd of cattle; *n* **drover** driver of, dealer in cattle.
drown *v* die, kill by suffocation in water; (*fig*) overwhelm; muffle (sound).
drowsy *a* sleepy, lethargic; *adv* **drowsily**; *n* **drowsiness**; *v* **drowse** doze, be half asleep.
drub *v* belabour, beat violently; *n* **drubbing**.
drudge *n* overworked servant; *v* work like drudge; *n* **drudgery** hard, wearisome toil.
drug *n* any vegetable, mineral substance used in medicine; *v* give drug (*esp* narcotic) to; habitually take drugs; *n* **druggist** pharmaceutical chemist.
drugget *n* coarse, woollen floor-covering.
Druid *n* ancient Celtic priest; official of Welsh Eisteddfod.
drum *n* percussion instrument; various hollow

cylindrical objects; part of ear; *v* play drum; rap continuously; *ns* **drummer**; **drum-major** commander of regimental band.
drunk *a* intoxicated; *pp* of drink; *n* **drunkard** habitual heavy drinker.
dry *v* be without, remove or lose moisture; *a* without moisture; having low rainfall; (*of wine*) not sweet; *adv* **drily**, **dryly** without emotion; *ns* **dryness**; **dry-dock**; **dry rot** fungoid decay of timber; *a* **dryshod** with dry feet.
dryad *n* wood nymph.
dual *a* of two; double; twofold; *n* **duality**.
dub *v* confer knighthood on; (*of films etc.*) re-record sound track, with additions etc.; *n* **dubbing**, **dubbin** grease for water-proofing leather.
dubiety *n* doubt, hesitancy; *a* **dubious** doubtful.
ducat *n* medieval gold or silver coin.
duck *n* flat-billed water bird; female duck; score of nought in cricket; *ns* **duckling** young duck; **ducky** (*coll*) darling.
duck *v* plunge person, thing into liquid; bob down (to avoid blow); *n* **ducking**.
duct *n* tube for conveying liquid; ventilating flue; *as* **ductile** malleable; **ductless.**
dud *n* unsuccessful person, thing; bad coin, note; *a* useless.
dudgeon *n* state of sullen resentment, anger.
due *a* (*of money*) owing; adequate; scheduled to arrive; caused by; *adv* (*of direction*) exactly; *n* something owed, deserved; (*pl*) regular fee, levy; *adv* fitly; at proper time.
duel *n* contest (physical or intellectual) between two persons; *v* fight duel; *n* **duellist**.
duenna *n* elderly Spanish lady; chaperon.
duet *n* musical work for two performers.
duffel, **duffle** *n* thick woollen cloth; **d.coat** coat made of this fabric.
duffer *n* stupid, clumsy person.
dugout *n* hollowed out canoe; underground shelter.
duke *n* holder of highest hereditary rank of peerage; (*fem*) **duchess**; *ns* **dukedom**; **duchy** small state.
dulcet *a* melodious; sweet-sounding; pleasing.

dulcimer *n* old, harp-like instrument.
dull *a* stupid; tedious; lacking clearness, brightness; blunted; overcast; *v* make, become dull; *ns* **dullard** oaf; **dullness**; *adv* **dully.**
dumb *a* incapable of speech; silent; (*sl*) unintelligent; *n* **dumbness**; *n pl* **dumbbells** weights used for exercise; *v* **dumbfound** strike dumb with amazement.
dumdum *n* soft-nosed expanding bullet.
dummy *n* sham object; tailor's model; (*bridge*) hand exposed on table; *a* sham; used in pretence.
dump *v* unload roughly (refuse etc.); *n* rubbish heap; place for depositing refuse; depot for ammunition, stores etc.; *pl* depression, low spirits.
dumpling *n* small piece of boiled suet dough; *a* **dumpy** squat, short.
dun *a* of dull grey brown colour.
dun *v* demand persistently for payment of debt.
dunce *n* dullard; pupil slow to learn.
dune *n* wind-driven sand hill.
dung *n* excrement of animals; manure.
dungarees *n pl* overalls of coarse cotton fabric.
dungeon *n* dark, underground prison cell.
dunk *v* dip bread etc. in liquid before eating it.
dunnage *n* wood, other material protecting, steadying cargo in hold of ship.
duodecimal *a* twelfth; reckoned by twelves.
duodenum *n* upper part of small intestine; *a* **duodenal.**
dupe *v* deceive, trick; *n* victim of duping.
duplex *a* double, twofold; *v* **duplicate** make double; make exact copy; *n* replica; *ns* **duplication**; **duplicator** copying machine; **duplicity** double dealing, deception.
durable *a* long-lasting; *ns* **durability**; **duration** length of existence; *prep* **during** throughout; in course of.
duress *n* imprisonment; restraint; compulsion.
dusk *n* late twilight; *a* **dusky** dark; swarthy.
dust *n* powdery particles (of earth etc.) suspended in air; *v* remove dust; sprinkle with powder etc.; *ns* **duster** cloth for wiping away dust; **dust-bin** receptacle for household refuse; *a* **dusty.**

Dutch *a* & *n* pertaining to Holland, its people and language.
duty *n* legal or moral obligation; proper expression of respect; tax on goods; *as* **dutiful** showing respect; **dutiable** liable to customs or other duty.
dwarf *n* person, animal or plant much below usuals ize; *pl* **dwarfs**; *v* make look small, overshadow.
dwell *v* live, reside; ponder; speak at length on; *pt* & *pp* **dwelt, dwelled**; *ns* **dweller** inhabitant; **dwelling** abode.
dwindle *v* become smaller, waste away, diminish.
dyad *n* two units considered as one.
dye *v* impart colour to; tint; change colour; *n* substance, colouring matter used for dyeing; *n* **dyer** one whose trade is dyeing.
dynamics *n pl* branch of physics dealing with force as producing changes of motion; *a* **dynamic** pertaining to force in motion; forceful, vigorous; opposed to static.
dynamite *n* high explosive made with nitroglycerine; *v* blow up with dynamite.
dynamo *n* machine for converting mechanical energy into electrical energy.
dynasty *n* succession of rulers of same family; *n* **dynast** hereditary ruler; *a* **dynastic**.
dyne *n* unit of force.
dysentery *n* disease of large intestine, akin to diarrhoea.
dyslexia *n* pathological inability to spell or read; word-blindness; *as* **dyslectic, dyslexic**.
dyspepsia *n* indigestion; *a* **dyspeptic**.

each *a* & *pron* everyone considered separately.
eager *a* keen, impatient to act; *n* **eagerness** keenness.
eagle *n* large bird of prey; *n* **eaglet** young eagle.
ear *n* organ of hearing; sense of tune; attention; *n* **earmark** owner's mark on cattle ear; *v* mark so; assign for specific purpose; *ns* **earring** ornament; **ear-shot** hearing distance.

ear *n* spike, cluster of seeds of cereal.
earl *n* rank in peerage below marquis; *n* **earldom** title or territory of earl.
earn *v* gain by labour, merit etc.; deserve; *n pl* **earnings**.
earnest *a* sincere; serious; *n* sincerity; seriousness.
earnest *n* pledge, token of future payment; *fig* foretaste.
earth *n* planet inhabited by man; dry land; soil, mould; lair of fox etc.; conductor of electricity to earth; *v* cover with earth; connect electric wire with earth; *as* **earthen** made of baked clay; **earthly** belonging to earth; **earthy** like earth; *ns* **earthenware** coarse pottery; **earthquake** tremor of earth's surface.
ease *n* comfort; freedom from pain, trouble, exertion, poverty etc.; absence of difficulty; *v* relieve pain, anxiety, strain; *as* **easy** not difficult; **easy-going** casual; *n* **easement**, (*leg*) right or privilege to use another's land (right of way etc.).
easel *n* frame to hold paintings, blackboard etc.
east *n* one of four cardinal points; part of horizon where sun rises; eastern countries; *a* situated in, coming from east; *as* **easterly** from, to east; **eastern** of living in the east; *a* & *adv* **eastward** towards east.
Easter *n* annual festival commemorating Resurrection.
eat *v* partake of food; consume; corrode; *pt* **ate**; *pp* **eaten**; *a* **eatable** fit, suitable to eat.
eaves *n pl* projecting edge of roof; *v* **eavesdrop** listen secretly; *n* **eavesdropper**.
ebb *n* going out of tide; (*fig*) decline; *v* flow back; diminish; *n* **ebb-tide**.
ebony *n* hard, black wood; jet black colour.
ebullient *a* boiling; exuberant; *ns* **ebullience** act of boiling over; exuberance; **ebullition**, (*fig*) sudden outburst.
eccentric *a* odd, unconventional, slightly crazy; (*geom*) not having same centre; *n* odd, slightly mad person; device for converting rotary into to-and-fro movement.

ecclesiastic(al) *a* pertaining to Church or clergy; *n* clergyman.
echelon *n* arrangement of troops, planes etc., in steplike formation.
echo *n* sounds reflected back from solid surface; imitation; *pl* **echoes**; *v* reverberate; imitate closely.
eclair *n* finger-shaped iced cake, filled with cream.
eclat *n* applause; striking success.
eclectic *a* selecting from various sources; not exclusive; *n* philosopher who selects doctrines.
eclipse *n* obscuration of light of sun, moon by another heavenly body; (*fig*) obscurity; *a* **ecliptic**.
ecology *n* science dealing with living organisms in relation to their environment.
economy *n* management of affairs of household or State; avoidance of waste; *a* **economic(al)** relating to economics; cheap; *n pl* **economics** scientific study of production and distribution of wealth; *n* **economist** student of economics; *v* **economize** cut down expenses.
ecstasy *n* rapture; intense exaltation; *a* **ecstatic**.
eczema *n* inflammatory disease of skin.
eddy *n* small whirlpool; spiral current of air etc.; *v* move in whirls.
edelweiss *n* white flowered Alpine plant.
edge *n* boundary, extreme border; cutting side of knife etc.; (*fig*) acrimony; *v* sharpen; give edge to; sidle away; *a* **edgy** irritable; **on edge** excitable.
edible *a* suitable, wholesome to eat; *n* **edibility**.
edict *n* formal order, decree issued by authority.
edifice *n* large building; *v* **edify** benefit morally; *n* **edification** improvement of mind.
edit *v* prepare for publication, broadcasting; direct policies of editing; *ns* **editor**; **edition** one of several forms in which a book etc. is published; total number of copies published at one time; **editorial** leading article; *a* **editorial** of editor; *n* **editorship** position of editor.
educate *v* train, cultivate mind of; instruct; pay for education of; *n* **education**; *as* **educational**; **educative**; *n* **educator** teacher; **educationalist** expert in educational theory, methods.

eel *n* long snake-like fish.
eerie, eery *a* strange, uncanny, causing fear; *n* **eeriness.**
efface *v* erase; (*reflex*) keep oneself in background; *n* **effacement**; *a* **effaceable.**
effect *v* cause, bring about; *n* result; impression (mental or physical); *pl* property, goods; *as* **effectual** producing intended effect; **effective** producing result; competent; *n* **effectiveness.**
effeminate *a* unmanly; weak, womanish; *n* **effeminacy.**
effervesce *v* bubble up; (*fig*) be excited; *n* **effervescence**; *a* **effervescent.**
effete *a* worn out; sterile.
efficacy *n* power; effectiveness; *a* **efficacious** having desired effect; *n* **efficiency** confidence; *a* **efficient.**
effigy *n* image, representation.
efflorescent *a* blossoming; *n* **efflorescence**; *v* **effloresce.**
effluent *a* flowing out; *n* stream flowing out of lake etc.; liquid sewage; *ns* **effluvium** exhalation, smell *esp* tainted; **efflux(ion)** act of flowing out.
effort *n* mental, physical exertion; attempt; *a* **effortless.**
effrontery *n* impudence, audacity.
effulgent *a* shining, radiant; *n* **effulgence.**
effusion *n* profuse, gushing speech, writing; *a* **effusive** profuse, gushing; *v* **effuse** pour, gush out.
eft *n* newt.
egg *n* oval body, containing embryo bird; ovum.
egg *v* incite, urge.
ego *n* conscious awareness of self; *ns* **egoism** selfishness; **egoist**; *a* **egoistic(al)**; *ns* **egotism** self-conceit; **egotist**; *a* **egotistical** conceited.
egregious *a* remarkable, in bad sense; *n* **egregiousness.**
egress *n* way out; departure.
egret *n* lesser white heron.
eider *n* arctic sea-duck; *n* **eiderdown** soft down of eider; quilt stuffed with this.
eight *a* & *n* cardinal number, one above seven; *n* crew of 8-orr boat; *as* & *ns* **eighth** ordinal number;

eighth part; **eighteen** eight plus ten; **eighteenth**; **eighty** eight tens; **eightieth.**
eisteddfod *n* assembly of Welsh bards.
either *a* & *pron* one of two; *adv*, *conj* choice of.
ejaculate *v* exclaim; eject suddenly; *n* **ejaculation.**
eject *v* fling out; dispossess; emit; *ns* **ejection**; **ejector.**
eke *v* add to; spin out; lengthen.
elaborate *v* work out in detail; *a* complicated; highly ornamented; *ns* **elaboration, elaborator.**
eland *n* large S. African antelope.
elapse *v* (*of time*) pass, slip past.
elastic *a* resuming normal shape after distension; (*fig*) adaptable; *n* fabric having rubber woven in it; *n* **elasticity** resilience.
elation *n* exaltation; high spirits; *v* **elate** make proud.
elbow *n* joint between forearm & upper arm; *v* push, jostle with elbows.
elder *a* (*comp* of OLD) older, senior; *as* **elderly** growing old; (*sup* of OLD) **eldest** oldest.
elder *n* tree having white flowers and black fruit.
elect *v* choose, select by vote; *a* selected, but not yet in office; *ns* **election**; **elector**; **electorate** body of voters; *a* **electoral**; *v* **electioneer** canvass for votes.
electricity *n* form of energy, produced by friction, magnetism etc; supply of electrical current, for lighting etc.; *a* **electric(al)**; *v* **electrify** charge with electricity; *fig* startle; *ns* **electrification**; **electrician** mechanic who works with electricity.
electro- *prefix makes compounds with meaning* by (*or* caused by) electricity, *e.g.* **electrocute** *v* kill by electricity; *ns* **electrolysis** decomposition by electricity; **electroplate** metal articles coated with silver etc., by electrolysis. *Where the meaning may be deduced from the simple word, the compounds are not given here.*
electron *n* particle of matter bearing negative charge, revolving round atom; *a* **electronic**; *n pl* science concerned with action of electrons.
elegant *a* refined; graceful, tasteful; *n* **elegance.**
elegy *n* song of mourning; sad poem; *a* **elegiac** mournful.

element *n* basic constituent; natural, suitable environment; *pl* atmospheric powers, storm etc.; *as* **elemental** relating to elements; **elementary** simple.
elephant *n* very large mammal with trunk & ivory tusks; *a* **elephantine** huge; *n* **elephantiasis** skin & limb disease.
elevate *v* lift, raise up (physically or morally); exalt; *ns* **elevation**; **elevator** person, thing which elevates; grain storehouse; lift.
eleven *a* & *n* cardinal number one above ten; team of eleven players; *a* **eleventh** ordinal number.
elf *n* small woodland sprite; (*fig*) mischievous child; (*pl*) **elves**; *a* **elfin** fairy like; roguish.
elicit *v* bring, draw out (information); obtain.
eligible *a* fit, qualified to be chosen; suitable.
eliminate *v* remove; get rid of; exclude; *n* **elimination**.
elite *n* select body of persons; aristocracy.
elixir *n* powerful invigorating remedy.
elk *n* large deer.
ell *n* measure of length, 1¼ yds.
ellipse *n* oval; *a* **elliptic** having shape of ellipse.
ellipsis *n* omission of word, usually understood, from sentence.
elm *n* kind of deciduous tree; its wood.
elocution *n* art & manner of speaking; voice management; *a* **elocutionary**; *n* **elocutionist** teacher of elocution.
elongate *v* extend; prolong; *n* **elongation**.
elope *v* run away secretly, with lover; *n* **elopement**.
eloquence *n* fluency; persuasiveness in speech; *a* **eloquent**.
else *adv* besides; instead; otherwise; *adv* **elsewhere** in, to, another place.
elucidate *v* explain, make clear; *n* **elucidation**.
elude *v* dodge; baffle; *n* **elusion**; *a* **elusive** evasive; difficult to catch, to remember.
em- *prefix* (*see* **en-**).
em *n* unit of measure of type (printing).
emaciate *v* make, become very thin; *n* **emaciation** abnormal thinness.
emanate *v* issue forth; originate from; *n* **emanation**.

emancipate *v* set free; *n* **emancipation** freedom.
emasculate *v* castrate; weaken; *n* **emasculation.**
embalm *v* preserve corpse from decay, by use of preservatives; *n* **embalmment.**
embankment *n* artificial bank carrying road, railway etc., or damming water.
embargo *n* order prohibiting movement of ships; official ban on trade etc.
embark *v* put, go on board ship; (*fig*) start, engage in; *n* **embarkation.**
embarrass *v* hinder; perplex; abash; *n* **embarrassment.**
embassy *n* staff, official residence, of ambassador; deputation; mission.
embed, imbed *v* implant deeply, firmly; (*fig*) fix deeply.
embellish *v* adorn; improve; *n* **embellishment.**
ember *n* (*usu pl*) glowing, smouldering ashes, cinders.
embezzle *v* misappropriate money in trust; *ns* **embezzlement, embezzler.**
embitter *v* make bitter, worse, discontented.
emblazon *v* adorn with coat-of-arms; extol.
emblem *n* concrete symbol of idea, quality etc; badge; *a* **emblematic.**
embody *v* give form to; represent; include, *n* **embodiment.**
emboss *v* cover with design in relief.
embrace *v* hug, clasp in arms; include; *n* such action.
embrasure *n* recess for door, window; opening in wall for cannon etc.
embrocation *n* pain-relieving lotion.
embroider *v* ornament with needlework; (*fig*) add fanciful details (to story etc.) *n* **embroidery.**
embroil *v* involve in quarrel, confusion; *n* **embroilment.**
embryo *n* unborn, not fully developed animal; any rudimentary object, idea etc; *a* **embryonic.**
emend *v* correct mistake; improve (text); *n* **emendation.**
emerald *n* bright green precious stone; this colour.
emerge *v* come out; appear; rise to view; become

known, apparent; *n* **emergence**; *a* **emergent**.
emergency *n* unexpected happening, requiring swift action; crisis.
emeritus *n* title given to retired professor etc.
emery *n* hard variety of corundum, used for grinding etc. *n* **emery cloth, -paper** cloth, paper coated with ground emery.
emetic *n* & *a* (*medicine*) causing vomiting.
emigrate *v* leave one's country to live in another; *ns* **emigration**; **emigrant**.
eminence *n* distinction, fame; height, high ground; title of cardinal; *a* **eminent** outstanding; famous.
emir *n* title of Mohammedan prince.
emit *v* give out; send out; *ns* **emission**; **emissary** one sent on mission.
emmet *n* ant.
emollient *a* softening, soothing; *n* soothing medicinal substance.
emolument *n* salary, profit from employment.
emotion *n* agitation of feelings (joy, fear, hatred etc.) *a* **emotional** given to, appealing to, the emotions.
emperor *n* ruler of an empire; (*fem*) **empress**.
emphasis *n* stress; emphatic assertion; special importance; *v* **emphasize**; *a* **emphatic** positive; stressed.
empire *n* supreme power; large group of States under supreme rule of an emperor.
empiric *a* relying on experience, not theory; *n* quack doctor.
emplacement *n* position, site *esp* for mounting guns.
employ *v* use; give work to; occupy (time); *n* **employment** work, occupation; use of, **employee**; **employer**.
emporium *n* large general store; trading centre.
empower *v* authorize; enable.
empty *a* containing nothing; unoccupied; pointless, stupid; *v* make, become, devoid of contents; *n* **emptiness**.
empyrean *n* highest heaven; the sky; *a* **empyreal**.
emu *n* large Australian bird, resembling ostrich.
emulate *v* try to equal; imitate; *n* **emulation** rivalry; *as* **emulative, emulous** eager to imitate.

emulsion *n* globules of one liquid suspended in another; *v* **emulsify.**
en- *prefix* (**em-***before labials b, m, p) forms verbs with sense of* on, into, put into, *e.g.* **encash** turn into cash. *Where the meaning may be deduced from the simple word, the compounds are not given here.*
en *n* unit measure of type, half an em (printing).
enable *v* make able; empower; give means to.
enact *v* make into law; act a part.
enamel *n* hard, glossy coating, paint, used to preserve surface; outer coating of tooth; *v* coat with enamel.
enamour *v* inspire love in; be fond of.
encamp *v* settle in camp; pitch tents; *n* **encampment.**
enceinte *a* with child, pregnant.
enchant *v* charm; delight; captivate; *ns* **enchantment; enchanter;** *fem* **enchantress.**
encircle *v* surround; form circle round.
enclave *n* district surrounded by foreign territory.
enclose *v* surround completely; insert; *n* **enclosure** object enclosed.
encompass *v* surround, encircle (*fig* & *lit*).
encore *n* call for repetition (of song etc); repetition; *v* ask for encore.
encounter *v* meet face to face, in hostility; *n* meeting.
encourage *v* inspire with courage, hope; further a cause; *n* **encouragement.**
encroach *v* usurp (rights etc.); (of sea) advance on; trespass; *n* **encroachment.**
encrust *v* form, cover with crust; stud thickly with.
encumber *v* burden; hinder; *n* **encumbrance.**
encyclical *n* Papal letter sent to whole R.C. Church.
encyclopaedia *n* book, set of books, of classified information on one or all subjects.
end *n* final limit; conclusion; cessation; death; purpose; result; *v* finish; complete; cease; *n* **ending;** *a* **endless** eternal.
endear *v* make, cause to be, dear; *a* **endearing;** *n* **endearment** affectionate term or word.
endeavour *v* strive, try hard; *n* vigorous effort.

endemic *a* (*of disease*) regularly occurring in an area.
endive *n* kind of chicory, used in salads.
endocrine *a* & *n* hormone, or secretion produced by ductless glands.
endorse *v* sanction; ratify; write (name) on back of (document etc.); *n* **endorsement**.
endow *v* bestow, provide permanent income for; *n* **endowment**.
endure *v* last; remain staunch; tolerate; *a* **endurable** bearable; *n* **endurance**.
enema *n* injection, injector, of fluid into rectum.
enemy *n* opponment; hostile person, factor; *a* **pertaining** to enemy.
energy *n* power, force, vigour; *a* **energetic**; *v* **energize** stimulate.
enervate *v* weaken; *n* **enervation** weakness.
enfeeble *v* make feeble, weak.
enfilade *v* raking fire from artillery.
enforce *v* demand, insist on; compel by force; *n* **enforcement**; *a* **enforceable**.
enfranchise *v* grant right to vote; set free; *n* **enfranchisement**.
engage *v* bind by promise, contract; hire; interlock; occupy; join in battle; *n* **engagement** *esp* betrothal; *a* **engaged**.
engender *v* cause; arouse, stir up.
engine *n* any machine converting physical force into mechanical energy; *n* **engineer** one skilled in mechanical science; one in charge of engine.
English *a* & *n* relating to England; language, people of England.
engrain *v* dye thoroughly; implant (habits etc.) firmly; *a* **engrained** deeply-rooted.
engrave *v* cut (lines etc.) deeply; (*fig*) fix firmly; *ns* **engraving** print taken from engraved plate; **engraver**.
engross *v* write out in legal form, or in clear formal manner; absorb attention; *n* **engrossment**.
enhance *v* add to, heighten; intensify.
enigma *n* riddle; puzzle; baffling person; *a* **enigmatic(al)**.
enjoin *v* insist on; order; give directions to.

enjoy *v* take joy, pleasure in; have benefit of; *a* **enjoyable**; *n* **enjoyment.**
enlarge *v* make, grow, larger; **enlarge upon** explain in detail; *n* **enlargement.**
enlighten *v* free from ignorance, bias etc.; make meaning clear; *n* **enlightenment.**
enlist *v* enrol in services; obtain (help, sympathy in a cause etc.) *n* **enlistment** enrolment *esp* in services.
enliven *v* add liveliness to; cheer up; make brisker.
enmity *n* hatred; animosity; hostility.
ennui *n* boredom, lack of interest.
enormity *n* atrocious crime; gross offence; *a* **enormous** huge, vast; *n* **enormousness.**
enough *a* as much as necessary; sufficient; *n* sufficiency; required amount.
enquire *see* **inquire.**
enrage *v* infuriate; provoke to rage.
enrapture *v* delight, entrance with joy.
enrich *v* make rich; add to; *n* **enrichment.**
enrol *v* record, register (name) on list etc., *esp* as member; *n* **enrolment.**
ensconce *v* place, conceal safely, snugly.
ensemble *n* parts considered as whole; (music) combination of soloists & chorus.
enshrine *v* place in shrine; (*fig*) cherish memory of.
ensign *n* badge of office etc.; naval, military, flag.
ensilage *n* green fodder stored in silo.
enslave *v* reduce to slavery; deprive of liberty; *n* **enslavement.**
ensnare *v* entangle; catch in trap.
ensue *v* follow; be consequent on.
ensure *v* make safe, secure; guarantee.
entail *v* (*leg*) restrict succession (of estate etc.) to certain person, & his heirs; *n* such settlement; *v* necessitate.
entangle *v* involve; catch (as in net); entrap; *n* **entanglement.**
entente *n* friendly understanding, *esp* between nations.
enter *v* come, go into; put in writing; enrol; pierce; join; *n* **entrance** going, coming in; opening, door;

ns **entrant** one who enters esp. contest; **entry** way in; item noted down (in book etc.).
enteric *a* of, relating to intestines; *n* typhoid fever; *n* **enteritis** imflamation of intestines.
enterprise *n* plan, project *esp* daring, difficult venture; ability to take initiative; *a* **enterprising**.
entertain *v* give, show hospitality to; amuse; foster (an idea etc.); *ns* **entertainer**; **entertainment** amusement.
enthral(l) *v* captivate, absorb, hold spellbound.
enthusiasm *n* zeal; intense admiration; *n* **enthusiast** one animated by intense zeal; *a* **enthusiastic**; *v* **enthuse** express enthusiasm.
entice *v* attract, allure, tempt; *n* **enticement**; *a* **enticing**.
entire *a* whole, complete; perfect; *n* **entirety**.
entitle *v* give title to; give right, claim to.
entity *n* real thing in itself; being, existence.
entomology *n* study of insects; *n* **entomologist**; *a* **entomological**.
entourage *n* surroundings; retainers, associates.
entracte *n* interval, music played between acts of play.
entrails *n pl* internal organs; intestines; viscera.
entrance *v* enrapture; carry away with delight.
entreat *v* beg earnestly; beseech; implore; *n* **entreaty** urgent request.
entrée *n* privilege, right of entering; dish served between fish and meat.
entrench *v* establish firmly in position; *n* **entrenchment**.
entrust *v* give into care of; charge with.
enumerate *v* count; *ns* **enumeration**; **enumerator**.
enunciate *v* utter distincly; proclaim; state formally *n* **enunciation**.
envelop *v* wrap round; (*fig*) obscure, conceal; *ns* **envelopment**; **envelope** outer covering, *esp* of paper for enclosing letters etc; wrapper.
environ *v* surround; *ns* **environment** surroundings; external conditions of living etc.; *pl* **environs** immediate surroundings.
envisage *v* visualize; contemplate.

envoy *n* agent; diplomatic representative.
envy *v* begrudge another's success, possessions etc.; feel jealous of; *n* covetousness; jealousy; *as* **envious** feeling envy; **enviable** exciting envy.
enzyme *n* chemical ferment.
ep-, eph-, epi-, *prefix: forms compounds with meaning* upon, during; *e.g.* **ephemeral** of short duration; **epicarp** outer skin of fruits; **epitaph** memorial inscription upon tomb. *Where the meaning may be deduced from the simple word, the compounds are not given here.*
epaulette *n* ornamental shoulder piece on uniform.
epic *n* long, narrative poem.
epicene *a* having characteristics of both sexes.
epicentre *n* area immediately above origin of earthquake.
epicure *n* person who enjoys good food and drink, & has fastidious taste; *a* **epicurean.**
epidemic *a* (of disease) prevalent in one community; *n* such disease.
epidermis *n* outer skin.
epiglottis *n* cartilage at entrance to larynx.
epigram *n* brief, pointed, witty saying, or poem; *a* **epigrammatic.**
epigraph *n* inscription on stone etc.
epilepsy *n* nervous disease, attended by fits and unconsciousness; *a* & *n* **epileptic** arising from, or sufferer from epilepsy.
epilogue *n* concluding lines of play; short speech at end of day.
Epiphany *n* festival of the manifestation of Christ to the Magi.
episcopal *a* pertaining to bishop; *n* **episcopacy** government by body of bishops; *n* **episcopalian** member of episcopal church.
episode *n* one of series of events; incident in story etc.; *a* **episodic.**
epistle *n* letter *esp* apostolic.
epitaph *n* memorial inscribed on tomb.
epithet *n* descriptive adjective, name or phrase.
epitome *n* concise statement; summary; *v* **epitomize** abridge.

epoch *n* period of time, era *esp* of great events; *a* **epochal.**
equable *a* steady, uniform; unvarying; *n* **equability.**
equal *a* of like amount, degree, value, merit; equable; *n* one having same rank, qualities etc. as another; *v* be equal to; *n* **equality** condition of being equal; *v* **equalize** make, become equal; *n* **equalization.**
equanimity *n* tranquillity, calmness of mind; composure.
equate *v* consider as equal; reduce to common standard; *n* **equation,** (*math*) statement of equality between known and unknown quantities.
equator *n* imaginary circle dividing earth into two equal parts; *a* **equatorial.**
equerry *n* officer in attendance on prince.
equestrian *a* pertaining to horses, horse-riding; *n* horseman; *fem* **equestrienne.**
equidistant *a* equally distant.
equilateral *a* having equal sides.
equilibrium *n* state of perfect balance; *n* **equilibrist** performer of balancing tricks.
equine *a* of or like a horse.
equinox *n* time of year when day & night are of equal length; *a* **equinoctial.**
equip *v* fit out; provide, supply; *ns* **equipment; equipage** retinue; carriage & horses; requisites.
equity *n* fairness, justice; correction of severe, unfair law; *n pl* **equities** Ordinary shares; *a* **equitable** just, reasonable.
equivalent *a* equal in value, amount, meaning etc.
equivocal *a* ambiguous; doubtful; *v* **equivocate** use words of doubtful meaning to mislead.
era *n* period of time dating from particular point; epoch.
eradicate *v* root out; destroy; abolish; *ns* **eradication eradicator.**
erase *v* rub out; expunge; *ns* **eraser; erasure.**
ere *prep* & *conj* before; sooner than.
erect *v* set upright; raise; build; *a* upright; *ns* **erection; erector.**
erg *n* unit of work, energy.
ergot *n* fungus disease in cereals; drug from this.

ermine *n* common stoat, in winter coat; such fur.
erode *v* eat into; corrode; *n* **erosion**; *a* **erosive.**
ero(to)genous *a* producing sexual desire.
erotic *a* pertaining to sexual desire, love; *n* **eroticism** sexual excitement.
err *v* go astray; make mistakes; be wrong; *as* **erratic** irregular; wandering; **erroneous** wrong, mistaken; *ns* **erratum**, *pl* **errata** mistake in printing etc; **error** mistake.
errand *n* short journey with definite purpose; *n* **errand-boy** messenger.
errant *a* wandering; roving.
ersatz *a* artificial; substitute.
erst, **erstwhile** *adv* formerly.
eructate *v* belch; *n* **eructation.**
erudite *a* well-read, learned; *n* **erudition** learning.
erupt *v* burst out; become active; *n* **eruption** bursting out, *esp* of volcano.
escalate *v* increase by stages; *n* **escalation.**
escalator *n* moving stairway.
escallop *n* scallop; edible bi-valve.
escape *v* get free; issue out; avoid; elude; *n* evasion; leakage (of gas, etc.); *ns* **escapement** mechanical device; balance wheel of watch etc.; **escapade,** wild, mischievous prank; **escapism** avoidance of realities, by indulging in fantasy.
escarpment *n* steep hillside, inland cliff.
escheat *n* reversion of property to State, in absence of heirs.
eschew *v* shun, avoid.
escort *v* go with, as protector, or as sign of courtesy; *n* person, persons escorting another.
escritoire *n* writing desk or table.
escutcheon *n* (*her*) shield bearing coat of arms.
Eskimo *n* member of N. American Indian race living in Arctic.
esoteric *a* secret; for initiated only.
esparto *n* Spanish, Algerian grass, used in paper-making etc.
especial *a* remarkable; principial, particular.
Esperanto *n* artificial, universal language.
espionage *n* spying; use of spies.

esplanade *n* levelled terrace *esp* promenade along sea-front.
espouse *v* marry; support (a cause etc.) *n* **espousal**.
espy *v* perceive; catch sight of.
esquire *n* title of respect used on letter, abbreviated to Esq.; formerly knight's attendant.
essay *v* try, attempt; *n* short treatise; attempt; *n* **esssayist**.
essence *n* intrinsic nature of anything; existence; distilled extract; *a* **essential** indispensable; characteristic; pertaining to essence; *ns* **essential** essential quality, factor; **essentiality**.
establish *v* set up; give firm basis to; prove; *n* **establishment** establishing; household; permanent civil, military force; business; Established Church.
estate *n* stage, condition of life; landed property; (*leg*) possessions.
esteem *v* respect, consider highly; *n* respect.
estimate *v* appraise, calculate value of; form opinion of; *n* computation, in advance, of approx. cost; *n* **estimation** opinion; esteem; *a* **estimable** worthy of respect.
estrange *v* alienate; hurt feelings of; *n* **estrangement** decrease in affection.
estuary *n* mouth of river, where tide enters.
etch v make designs on metal, by eating away by acid; *ns* **etcher**; **etching**.
eternal *a* everlasting; increasing; *n* **eternity**.
ether *n* highly volatile liquid, used as anaesthetic; the upper air; hypothetical medium supposed to fill all space; *a* **ethereal** light, airy; spiritual.
ethical *a* moral; *n pl* **ethics** system of morally correct conduct.
ethnic *a* of race; *n* **ethnography** study of races of men; *a* **ethnographic**; *n* **ethnology** science of racial characteristics; *a* **ethnological**.
etiquette *n* polite conventional procedure, manners.
etymology *n* branch of philology dealing with derivation of words; *a* **etymological**; *ns* **etymologist**, **etymon** primitive word form.
eucalyptus *n* genus of Australasian trees, yielding pungent, volatile oil.

Eucharist *n* Holy Communion; consecrated elements
eugenic *a* promoting breeding of fine, healthy stock; *n pl* **eugenics** this science.
eulogy *n* praise, written or spoken; *v* **eulogize** praise, extol; *a* **eulogistic.**
eunuch *n* castrated man.
euphemism *n* mild word used in place of unpleasant one; *a* **euphemistic.**
euphony *n* pleasing sound; *as* **euphonic; euphonious** harmonious; *n* **euphonium** bass saxhorn.
euphoria *n* sense of well-being; *a* **euphoric.**
euphuism *n* artificial, affected literary style.
Eurasian *n* person of mixed European & Asiatic blood.
eurhythmics *n pl* art of rhythmical free movement.
eustachian tube *n* duct leading from pharynx to middle ear.
euthanasia *n* painless death, such as is administered to avoid suffering by incurable illness.
evacuate *v* make empty; withdraw from; discharge (contents); *ns* **evacuation; evacuee** person removed from danger zone.
evade *v* escape; avoid; shirk; *n* **evasion** excuse; subterfuge; *a* **evasive** ambiguous; elusive.
evaluate *v* find value of; appraise; *n* **evaluation.**
evanesce *v* fade away; vanish; *a* **evanescent** transient; *n* **evanescence.**
evangelic, evangelical *a* of, based on the Gospels; *ns* **evangelism** spreading of the Gospel; **evangelist** one of four writers of Gospels; travelling preacher; *v* **evangelize** preach Gospel to.
evaporate *v* turn into vapour; expel moisture, by heating; *n* **evaporation.**
eve *n* evening or day before festival or event; *ns* **even** evening; **evensong** evening prayer.
even *a* flat; uniform; equal; balanced; divisible by two; *v* make even; equalize.
evening *n* early part of night; end, decline.
event *n* happening; outcome; item in series of games; noteworthy occurrence; *as* **eventful** momentous; **eventual** in course of time; final; *n* **eventuality** possible event.

ever *adv* at any time; in any degree; *adv* **evermore** always.
every *a* each one of all; *ns* **everybody; everyone; everything;** *a* **everyday** usual; *adv* **everywhere** in all places.
evict *v* put out; expel by legal process; *n* **eviction.**
evidence *n* testimony; providing of proof; ground for belief.
evident *a* clear; obvious; visible.
evil *a* bad; depraved; ill-omened; *n* evil thing or act; *adv* **evilly.**
evince *v* show; demonstrate.
eviscerate *v* disembowel.
evoke *v* call forth; cause to appear; *n* **evocation;** *a* **evocative.**
evolve *v* develop, open out gradually, naturally; *n* **evolution** course of development of species; *a* **evolutionary.**
ewe *n* female sheep.
ewer *n* large water-jug; pitcher.
ex-, e-, ef- *prefix*: *forms compounds with meaning of* out from, from, out of. *Such words are not given, where the meaning may be deduced from the simple word.*
exacerbate *v* make worse; irritate; embitter; *n* **exacerbation.**
exact *a* absolutely correct, accurate; *v* demand; extort; insist on; *a* **exacting** severe; exhausting; *ns* **exactitude; exactness** accuracy.
exaggerate *v* over-emphasize; overstate; enlarge; *n* **exaggeration** overstatement.
exalt *v* raise to higher rank; extol; *n* **exaltation;** elevation; elation.
examine *v* scrutinize; investigate; question; test knowledge of; *ns* **examination; examiner.**
example *n* sample; precedent; warning instance; model.
exasperate *v* make angry; aggravate; provoke; *n* **exasperation;** *a* **exasperating** very annoying.
excavate *v* hollow out; dig out; unearth; *ns* **excavation; excavator.**
exceed *v* go beyond (limit etc.); surpass; *adv* **exceedingly** extremely.

excel *v* surpass, rise above; be very good at; *a* **excellent** very good; *ns* **excellence**; **excellency** title given to ambassadors etc.
except *v* exclude; object; *prep* omitting; *conj* unless; *n* **exception** thing excluded; objection; *prep* **excepting** excluding; *a* **exceptional** unusual; rare.
excerpt *n* selected passage, extract from book etc.
excess *n* amount, sum over normal, usual quantity etc.; over indulgence; *a* **excessive** extreme.
exchange *v* give (something), receive (another thing) in return; interchange; *n* act of exchanging; place where brokers, merchants transact business; district telephone office; *a* **exchangeable,** *n* **exchangeability.**
exchequer *n* treasury; State department dealing with finance, revenue.
excise *v* cut out, remove, cut away; *n* **excision.**
excise *n* duty on goods manufactured, consumed within a country; *n* **exciseman** collector of excise duties.
excite *v* rouse up; agitate; stimulate; *a* **excitable** easily excited; *n* **excitability**; *a* **exciting** thrilling; *n* **excitement.**
exclaim *v* cry out suddenly, loudly; *n* **exclamation** interjection (of surprise etc.); *a* **exclamatory.**
exclude *v* shut out; disallow; not include; *n* **exclusion**; *a* **exclusive** excluding; snobbish; unsociable.
excommunicate *v* expel from Church, & deprive of privileges; *n* **excommunication.**
excoriate *v* flay; graze, abrade skin; *n* **excoriation.**
excrement *n* waste matter from bowels; dung; *v* **excrete** discharge waste matter from body; *n* **excretion**; *n* & *a* **excretory,** (organ) serving to excrete.
excruciating *a* acutely painful, agonizing.
exculpate *v* vindicate; free from blame; *n* **exculpation.**
excursion *n* journey, *esp* pleasure trip; digression.
excuse *v* exonerate; overlook (fault etc.); apologize; release from obligation; *n* apology; pretext; *a* **excusable.**

exeat *n* leave of absence.
execrate *v* detest; loathe; curse; *n* **execration**; *a* **execrable** abominable.
execute *v* perform; carry out; kill; complete legal instrument; *ns* **execution**; **executioner** one who carries out capital punishment; *a* **executive** able to put into effect; *n* one charged with administrative, executive work; *n* **executor** (*fem* **executrix**) one appointed to carry out provisions of will.
exemplar *n* model, example; *a* **exemplary** worthy, commendable.
exemplify *v* serve as example; make official copy of.
exempt *v* from duty, obligation; *a* not liable to; *n* **exemption.**
exequies *n pl* funeral rites, ceremonies.
exercise *n* healthy physical activity; mental exertion; use of (rights etc.) (*mil*) manoeuvres; *v* take, give exercise to; use; train.
exert *v* make an effort; put into action; *n* **exertion** activity, mental or physical.
exhale *v* breathe out; evaporate; emit; *n* **exhalation.**
exhaust *v* drain off; use up; tire out; *n* waste gas, steam discharged from engine; *n* **exhaustion** intense fatigue; *a* **exhaustive** comprehensive.
exhibit *v* show in public; give evidence of; *n* thing exhibited, *esp* in museum, or as material evidence in court; *ns* **exhibition** display of works of art; etc.; grant to student; **exhibitor** one who exhibits *esp* in show.
exhilarate *v* enliven, cheer, raise spirits of; *n* **exhilaration.**
exhort *v* admonish; beg earnestly; *n* **exhortation.**
exhume *v* disinter; dig up *esp* corpse; *n* **exhumation.**
exigent *a* exacting; pressing, urgent; *n* **exigence, exigency** urgent need; *a* **exigible** capable of being exacted.
exiguous *a* too small; scanty.
exile *n* banishment; one banished; *v* banish; expel.
exist *v* live; be; occur; *n* **existence**; *a* **existent.**
exit *n* act of leaving, going out; way out; *v* leave stage; go out.

exodus *n* departure *esp* of many people; (*cap*) second book of Old Testament.
exonerate *v* free from blame; exculpate; acquit; *n* **exoneration.**
exorbitant *a* excessive; immoderate; *n* **exorbitance.**
exorcize *v* expel (evil spirit) by religious means; *n* **exorcism.**
exoteric *a* fit for, understandable by, general public.
exotic *a* foreign; rare, unusual; *n* **exoticism.**
expand *v* spread out; extend; dilate; develop; *ns* **expanse** wide, open tract of land; **expansion**; *a* **expansive** effusive.
expatiate *v* dilate, enlarge upon.
expatriate *v* banish; quit one's country; *a* **expatriated**; *n* expatriated person; *n* **expatriation.**
expect *v* await; anticipate; look for as due, right; *a* **expectant** awaiting; *ns* **expectancy** anxious, eager anticipation; **expectation** that which is expected; future prospects.
expectorate *v* spit; cough up (phlegm, etc.); *n* **expectoration.**
expedient *a* suitable; advantageous; convenient; *n* means to an end; device; *n* **expedience** fitness.
expedite *v* hasten, speed up (progress of); despatch; *n* **expedition** journey for set purpose *esp* military, exploratory; *as* **expeditionary**; **expeditious** rapid, prompt.
expel *v* drive out; dismiss; *n* **expulsion.**
expend *v* give out; spend; use up; *ns* **expenditure**; **expense** cost; disbursement; *a* **expensive** costly; **expendable** inessential, of little value.
experience *n* living through events, emotions etc.; knowledge, skill, gained by personal practice, observation etc.; event witnessed, lived through; *v* undergo, meet with; *a* **experienced** skilful, competent.
experiment *n* trial, undertaken to test theory, discover new facts; *v* make experiments; *a* **experimental.**
expert *a* skilled; dexterous; *n* one having special knowledge; *n* **expertise.**
expiate *v* atone for; make amends for; *n* **expiation.**

expire *v* exhale; die; come to an end; *ns* **expiration**; **expiry** conclusion.
explain *v* make intelligible; interpret; account for; *n* **explanation**; *as* **explanatory**; **explanative.**
expletive *a* superfluous; *n* exclamation, oath.
explicable *a* able to be explained.
explicit *a* clearly stated; unequivocal.
explode *v* burst violently, with loud report; cause to explode; *n* **explosion**; *a* & *n* **explosive.**
exploit *n* bold, adventurous deed; *v* make unfair use of; *esp* to one's own benefit; develop resources of; *ns* **exploitation**; **exploiter.**
explore *v* examine closely; travel in strange region and investigate it; probe; *ns* **exploration**; **explorer**; *a* **exploratory.**
export *v* send (goods) abroad for trade; *ns* **exportation**; **exporter.**
expose *v* lay bare; leave unprotected; display; reveal; *n* **exposure.**
expostulate *v* remonstrate; protest against; *n* **expostulation.**
expound *v* explain, set forth; *ns* **exponent**; **exposition** explanation; exhibition; *a* **expository**; *n* **expositor** interpreter.
express *v* make known by speech, visual image etc.; squeeze out; *a* explicit; of special kind; sent, travelling at fast speed; *n* fast postal, train service; *n* **expression** expressing; utterance; feeling; facial aspect; *a* **expressive.**
expropriate *v* deprive of possession of; *n* **expropriation.**
expunge *v* wipe out, erase; delete, *n* **expunction.**
expurgate *v* remove offensive material from text (of book etc.); *n* **expurgation.**
exquisite *a* select; extremely beautiful; tasteful; acutely sensitive.
extant *a* still surviving; still in existence.
extempore *a* & *adv* without preparation; *a* **extemporary**; *v* **extemporize** improvise; make up speech, song etc. on spur of moment.
extend *v* stretch out; expand; prolong; offer, bestow; last; reach; enlarge; *n* **extension** stretching out;

expansion; addition; *a* **extensive** widespread, comprehensive; *n* **extent** areas; scope; degree.

extenuate *v* lessen; minimize *esp* guilt, blame; *n* **extenuation**; *a* **extenuating**.

exterior *a* outside; external; *n* outward appearance.

exterminate *v* wipe out; extirpate; destroy; *ns* **extermination**; **exterminator**.

external *a* outward; visible, material.

extinct *a* having died out; no longer existing; inactive (of volcano); *n* **extinction**; *v* **extinguish** quench, stifle; *n* **extinguisher** device for putting out fire.

extirpate *v* root out, destroy; *n* **extirpation** total destruction.

extol *v* laud, praise highly.

extort *v* exact; obtain from by threats, force etc.; *ns* **extortion**; **extortioner**.

extra *a* additional; more than usual; *n* something extra.

extra- *prefix: forms compounds with meaning of* outside, beyond. *Where the meaning may be deduced from the simple word the compounds are not given here.*

extract *v* pull, draw out *esp* by force; excerpt; select; distil; *n* thing extracted; *ns* **extraction**; **extractor**.

extradition *n* surrender of an alleged criminal, by one State to another, under treaty; *v* **extradite** give, obtain such surrender.

extramural *a* outside walls of; associated with, not taking place in University.

extraneous *a* unrelated to; not essential; foreign.

extraordinary *a* unusual; exceptional; out of ordinary course.

extraterritorial *a* outside limits, jurisdiction of country.

extravagant *a* excessive; wasteful; flamboyant; *n* **extravagance**.

extreme *a* remotest; of highest degree; severe; last, final; beyond moderate; *ns* **extremist** one holding extreme views (in politics); **extremity** end; great distress, danger.

extricate *v* free from; disentangle; *n* **extrication**.

extrovert *n* one whose interests are directed outwards from self; vigorous personality.

extrude *v* thrust out; expel; *n* **extrusion.**
exuberant *a* full of vitality; overflowing; overabundant.
exude *v* ooze out; discharge through pores; *n* **exudation.**
exult *v* rejoice greatly; triumph; *n* **exultation**; *a* **exultant** jubilant.
eye *n* organ of sight; power of observation; anything resembling an eye; *v* look at; stare at; *ns* **eyebrow** ridge of hair above eye; **eyeglass** monocle; **eyelash** hair fringing eyelid; **eyesore** something offensive to eye: **eye-tooth** canine tooth; **eyelet** small hole in material.
eyot, ait *n* small island in river.

fable *n* short story with moral; myth; fiction; *as* **fabled** legendary; **fabulous** mythical; exaggerated; unbelievable.
fabric *n* structure, framework; woven cloth; *v* **fabricate** construct; concoct (lie); forge (document); *ns* **fabrication**; **fabricator.**
facade *n* front of building; outward appearance.
face *n* front of head *esp* human; right side of anything impudence; expression; *v* look, be turned towards; confront; cover surface of; *a* **facial** of face; *n* face massage; *n pl* **facings** trimming of different colour, material on garment.
facet *n* one small, cut surface of gem.
facetious *a* waggish; slyly humorous.
facia, fascia *n* flat strip of wood, metal on building; part of shop-front, showing name etc.; stripe.
facile *a* easily done; fluent; pliant; *v* **facilitate** make easier; *n* **facility** ease; dexterity; *pl* **facilities** helpful opportunities.
facsimile *n* exact copy.
fact *n* thing known to be true; actual experience; reality; *a* **factual.**
faction *n* discontented section *esp* in political party; dissension; *a* **factious** seditious.
factor *n* contributory force to a result; agent; *n* **factory** building in which goods are manufactured.

factotum *n* man of all work, handyman.
faculty *n* aptitude; inherent ability; natural or special function (of mind or body); division of University; collectively, members of such division.
fad *n* whim; passing craze; pet notion; *n* **faddiness**; *a* **faddy**.
fade *v* lose strength; wither; wane; become inaudible, faint; *a* **fadeless** unfading.
faeces *n* excrement; waste matter; *a* **faecal.**
fag *n* lower form boy who does jobs for senior; tiresome work; (*sl*) cigarette, *v* toil; weary; employ, act as fag.
faggot *n* bundle of sticks for firewood; bundle of steel rods; savoury chopped liver dish.
Fahrenheit *a* scale of temperature, having boiling point 212°, and freezing point 32°.
fail *v* be inadequate, insufficient; deteriorate; be defective; be unsuccessful; diminish; become weaker; *ns* **failing** fault, defect; **failure** that which fails; unsuccessful person; *prep* **failing** without.
faint *a* feeble; weak; vague; *v* swoon; *n* fainting fit.
fair *n* market for sale of goods, often with side-shows etc.; trade exhibition.
fair *a* lovely; clear; impartial; light-coloured; moderate; unblemished; *a* **fairish**; *ns* **fairness**; **fairway,** navigation channel; mown grass between tee & green (golf).
fairy *n* small supernatural being, in human form; *a* of, like fairy; magical, dainty; *ns* **fairyland**; **fairy-tale** story about fairies; white lie.
faith *n* trust; belief; sincerity; pledged word; *as* **faithful** reliable, true; accurate; **faithless.**
fake *v* make imitation of something rare, valuable; touch up; counterfeit; *n* sham; fabrication; forgery; *n* **faker.**
fakir *n* Hindu, Mohammedan ascetic beggar.
falcon *n* bird of prey, *esp* female trained in hawking; *ns* **falconer** one who keeps, hunts with, falcons; **falconry** hawking.
fall *v* drop; become lower; collapse; revert; be uttered; come to ground; succumb (to temptation); be captured; *pt* **fell**; *pp* **fallen**; *n* falling; drop; lowering in

value, degree etc.; autumn; stumble; *n* **fall-out** radio-active dust.

fallacy *n* misleading idea; illusion; *as* **fallacious** deceptive; **fallible** liable to error; *n* **fallibility**.

fallow *n* land ploughed up, left unsown; *a* uncultivated.

fallow *a* of brownish, reddish yellow (of deer).

false *a* wrong, mistaken; deceptive; disloyal; sham; artificial; *ns* **falsehood** lie; **falseness** disloyalty; **falsity** quality of being false; *v* **falsify** alter with intent to deceive; misrepresent; *n* **falsification**.

falter *v* stumble, be unsteady; stammer; hesitate; *a* **faltering**.

fame *n* renown, reputation; *as* **famed** well-known; **famous** celebrated.

familiar *a* intimate; well known; conversant with; vulgarly cordial; *n* **familiarity**; *v* **familiarize** accustom someone to something.

family *n* group of persons related by blood, marriage; all persons having a common ancestor; group of animals, plants descended from a common stock.

famine *n* acute shortage of food; starvation; *v* **famish** starve.

fan *n* device causing flow of air; ventilating machine; outspread tail feathers of bird; *v* direct currents of air on.

fan *n* (*sl*) enthusiastic supporter (of football team, actor etc.).

fanatic(al) *a* having violent, unreasoning belief in; *n* zealot; *n* **fanaticism**.

fancy *n* imagination; liking; desire for; whim; mental delusion; *a* imaginary; not plain; extravagant; (of animals) bred to special type; *v* imagine; feel inclined for; have liking for; *n* **fancier** one who has special knowledge (*esp* of animal breeding); *a* **fanciful** capricious; unreal.

fandango *n* lively Spanish dance.

fane *n* temple.

fanfare *n* flourish of trumpets.

fang *n* long, pointed tooth; poison tooth of snake.

fantasy *n* fancy; illusion; hallucination; *a* **fantastic** grotesque; fanciful; unbelievable.

far *adv* at, to, a distance; remote; considerably; *a* distant, not near; *comp a/adv* **farther** more distant; *sup a/adv* **farthest** most distant.
farad *n* unit of electrical capacity; *a* **faradic**.
farce *n* ludicrous, boisterous comedy; absurd, futile situation; *a* **farcical.**
fare *n* sum charged for conveyance of passenger; passenger; food; *v* travel; prosper; feed; get on.
farewell *n* leave-taking; *interj* good-bye.
farina *n* flour, meal, ground from corn, nuts etc.; *a* **farinaceous** mealy.
farm *n* land, buildings worked as unit for agricultural purposes; house in which farmer lives; *v* cultivate; rear cattle etc.; hire out; undertake care of (children) for payment; *ns* **farmer**; **farm-house.**
farrier *n* blacksmith who shoes horses.
farrow *n* litter of pigs; *v* give birth to pigs.
farthing *n* obsolete British copper coin.
farthingale *n* hooped petticoat.
fasces *n pl* bundle of rods, bound round an axe, symbol of ancient Roman authority.
fascia *n* stripe, band; name board over shopfront; dashboard of car.
Fascism *n* extreme right-wing dictatorial political system; *n* **Fascist.**
fascinate *v* enchant, bewitch; subdue by fixed stare; *n* **fascination**; *a* **fascinating.**
fashion *n* style; latest mode, vogue; method; *v* form, shape, make; *a* **fashionable** modish.
fast *a* firmly fixed; sure; rapid; (of clock) ahead of actual time; dissipated; *adv* fixedly; securely; rapidly; *v* **fasten** fix; secure; attach; seize (upon); *n* **fastness** secure place, stronghold.
fast *v* abstain from food or some kinds of food; *n* act of fasting.
fastidious *a* difficult to please; critical; discriminating; *n* **fastidiousness.**
fat *a* plump; obese; greasy; fertile; thick, stumpy; *n* oily, animal substance; best part; *v* **fatten** (*of cattle*) make fat for slaughter; *a* **fatted** fattened; *n* **fatness**; *a* **fatty**; *n* **fat-head** dull, stupid person.
fatal *a* ending in death; destructive; *ns* **fatality** calam-

ity; death by accident; **fatalism** doctrine that all events are preordained; **fatalist** believer in fatalism.

fate *n* supposed power controlling course of all events; destiny; one's lot, condition; evil fate, doom; *as* **fated** destined; **fateful** fraught with fate; decisive.

father *n* male parent; forefather; originator; title of respect *esp* of priest etc.; *v* beget; care for as father; be author of; *ns* **fatherhood**; **father-in-law** wife's, husband's father; **fatherland** native country; *as* **fatherly**; **fatherless**.

fathom *n* measure of depth, 6 ft.; *v* take soundings of; understand; *a* **fathomless** very deep.

fatigue *n* exhaustion; weariness, of body or mind; weakness in metal after repeated stresses; *v* weary; weaken.

fatuous *a* silly, stupid, futile; *n* **fatuity**.

faucet *a* tap for drawing liquid from cask, pipe etc.

fault *n* defect; error, culpability; fracture in earth's crust; offence; *as* **faulty**; **faultless**; *v* find fault with, blame.

faun *n* (*myth*) rural deity with horns & goat's feet.

fauna *n* all animal life of region or period.

favour *n* act of good will; partiality; rosette, badge; *v* approve; oblige; resemble; support; *a* **favourable** propitious; approving; *n* **favourite** favoured person or thing; *a* preferred, most liked; *n* **favouritism** undue partiality.

fawn *n* young deer; *a* pale, greyish brown.

fawn *v* (*of person*) cringe, act servilely towards; (*of dogs etc.*) show affection by grovelling.

fealty *n* fidelity of vassal to feudal lord.

fear *n* terror, dread; sinister anticipation; awe; *v* be afraid; feel dread; revere; *as* **fearful** apprehensive; awful; **fearsome** horrible; **fearless** courageous.

feasible *a* possible; practicable; *n* **feasibility**.

feast *n* religious day of rejoicing; lavish repast; village fete; *v* give, eat sumptuous banquet.

feat *n* exceptional deed, act of bravery, skill etc.

feather *n* one of quilled, soft appendages forming plumage of birds; *v* line, adorn with feathers; turn oar; *a* **feathery** soft light; *n* **feather-weight** very light person, or thing.

feature *n* part of face; noticeable or prominent part of anything; special article in newspaper etc.; *v* portray; give prominence to, present; *a* **featureless** without anything distinctive.

febrifuge *n* medicine reducing fever; *a* **febrile** feverish.

February *n* second month of year.

feckless *a* thoughtless, careless, irresponsible.

fecund *a* fruitful, fertile, prolific; *n* **fecundity**.

federal *a* relating to States which unite for external affairs, but remain internally independent; *v* **federate** unite to form federation; *n* **federation** federal union, society.

fee *n* charge for professional and other services; entrance money for examination, etc.

feeble *a* infirm, weak; ineffectual; frail; *adv* **feebly**.

feed *v* give food to; supply with fuel, material; eat; consume; *pt* & *pp* **fed**; *n* fodder; material supplied; *ns* **feeder** one who feeds; that which supplies; child's bib or bottle; **feed-pipe**; **feed-pump**; **feeding trough**; *a* **fed up** (*sl*) bored.

feel *v* experience sensation of; become aware of by touch; experience emotionally; be conscious of (cold, heat etc); *pt* & *pp* **felt**; *n* sense of touch; sensation; *ns* **feeler** tentative proposal; **feeling** physical, emotional sensation; *a* sensitive, sympathetic.

feign *v* pretend; assume; simulate.

feint *n* misleading action; pretence.

felicity *n* happiness, bliss; contentment; *a* **felicitous** happy; apt; *v* **felicitate** congratulate; *n* **felicitation**.

feline *a* of cats; catlike.

fell *n* rocky hill or mountainside.

fell *v* cut down (tree); knock down.

fellow *n* companion; associate; member (of society, governing body of college etc.).

felony *n* grave crime; more heinous than misdemeanour; *n* **felon** criminal guilty of felony; *a* **felonious**.

fel(d)spar *n* crystalline mineral.

felt *n* fabric made of compressed wool, mixed with size; *a* made of felt.

felucca *n* small Mediterranean sailing vessel.

female *a* of sex which bears offspring; of women; *n* one of this sex.
feminine *a* of women; having gender referring to females; *ns* **femininity**; **feminism** advocacy of complete equality between sexes; **feminist** supporter of feminism.
femur *n* thigh-bone; *a* **femoral**.
fen *n* low, flat, marshy land; *a* **fenny**.
fence *n* hedge, railing; swordsmanship; receiver of stolen goods; *v* enclose, protect with fence; fight with sword; avoid direct answer; *ns* **fencer**; swordsman; **fencing** protective fences; art of sword play.
fend *v* keep, ward off; provide (for oneself etc.); *n* **fender** wood, rope ball protecting ship from collision; surround to hearth.
fennel *n* fragrant herb used in cooking.
feral *a* fatal; gloomy; undomesticated; wild.
ferment *v* undergo chemical process involving effervescence; become excited; *n* substance causing fermentation, e.g. yeast; tumult, commotion; *n* **fermentation** act of fermenting.
fern *n* plant with fronds, feathery or plain; *a* **ferny** abounding in ferns.
ferocious *a* savage, fierce, cruel; *n* **ferocity**.
ferret *n* small, half-tamed animal of weasel family, used for driving rabbits out of holes; *v* hunt with ferret; (*fig*) search thoroughly.
ferric, ferreous, ferrous *a* of, containing iron; *a* **ferriferous** yielding iron; *n* **ferrite** type of iron ore; **ferro-** *prefix* denoting presence of iron.
ferrule *n* metal cap protecting end of stick, etc.
ferry *v* convey, cross, over river, channel etc., *n* boat, raft used for ferrying; place where ferry is.
fertile *a* fruitful; prolific; abundant; rich in ideas; *n* **fertility**; *v* **fertilize** make fertile; *ns* **fertilization**, **fertilizer**.
ferule *n* schoolmaster's rod.
fervent *a* burning, glowing; ardent, intense; *ns* **fervency**; **fervour**; *a* **fervid** hot, impassioned.
festal *a* of feast; festival; gay; joyous.
fester *v* suppurate; putrefy; rankle; *n* ulcer.
festival *n* joyful celebration; series of organized

musical, dramatic performances; *a* **festive,** joyous; convivial; *ns* **festivity** gaiety, joyousness; *pl* **festivities** joyful celebration.
festoon *n* chain or garland of flowers, ribbons etc. hung in loops; *v* decorate with festoons.
fetch *v* go and bring back; bring out; charm; be sold for; *a* **fetching** attractive.
fete *n* festival; fair, usually open-air; *v* honour with festivities.
fetid, foetid *a* stinking.
fetish *n* object worshipped by savages; object of exaggerated devotion; *n* **fetishism.**
fetlock *n* tufted pad at back of horse's leg, just above hoof.
fetter *n* shackle for feet; restraint (*pl*); *v* put in irons; impede; *a* **unfettered** unrestrained.
fettle *n* condition or state; *v* put in order; repair.
feu *n* (*Scot*) perpetual lease in return for fixed rent; *v* grant, let in feu.
feud *n* bitter, long-standing hostility between two persons, clans etc.
feud *n* land held in return for service to overlord.
feudal *a* pertaining to land held as feud; **f. system** medieval system of land tenure; *n* **feudalism.**
fever *n* disorder characterized by high temperature; extreme nervous excitement; *a* **feverish.**
few *a* & *n* not many; small number of.
fey *a* fated to die; full of whimsical beliefs, unnatural gaiety.
fez *n* red, brimless Moslem cap.
fiancé *n* betrothed man; (*fem* **fiancée**).
fiasco *n* total, utter failure.
fiat *n* decree; authorization.
fib *n* mild untruth; *v* tell fib; *n* **fibber.**
fibre *n* thread of animal, plant tissue; thread-like substance that can be spun; *a* **fibrous.**
fibula *n* outer bone of lower leg; *a* **fibular.**
fichu *n* small triangular lace shawl.
fickle *a* changeable; inconstant; *n* **fickleness.**
fiction *n* imaginary statement, account, story; novels collectively; *a* **fictitious** invented; false; assumed.
fiddle *n* violin; (*sl*) wangle; *v* play violin; fidget, move

restlessly; swindle, wangle; *ns* **fiddler; fiddlestick** violin bow.

fidelity *n* faithfulness; exactitude.

fidget *v* move restlessly; be uneasy; fuss; *n* one who fidgets; *pl* nervous restlessness; *a* **fidgety.**

fiduciary *a* of trustee; held in trust.

fief *n* land held by feudal tenure.

field *n* piece of enclosed land; tract of land yielding specified product (*e.g.* oil-field); area used for sport; game; scene of battle; scope of study, work etc.; all competitors but favourite; *v* (*cricket, etc.*) stop and return ball; *ns* **fielder; field-day** day of manoeuvres; gala occasion.

fieldfare *n* migratory bird, akin to thrush.

fiend *n* demon, devil; excessively evil person; *a* **fiendish,** crule, malevolent.

fierce *a* savage, wild, cruel; intense, strong; *n* **fierceness.**

fiery *a* of, resembling fire; flaming, glowing; choleric; spirited; *n* **fieriness**; *adv* **fierily.**

fife *n* shrill, flute-like instrument.

fifteen, fifth, fifty. *See* **five.**

fig *n* soft, sweet pear-shaped fruit, with many seeds, eaten fresh or dried; tree bearing figs.

fight *v* contend against violently; engage in single combat; manoeuvre troops, etc. in battle; oppose (by arguments etc.); *pt* & *pp* **fought**; *n* contest; struggle; *n* **fighter** one who fights; fast aircraft used for fighting.

figment *n* fantasy; something imagined.

figure *n* outer shape; bodily form (*esp* human); appearance; statue; ornament; diagram; numerical symbol; (*dancing, skating*) series of steps, movements; (*gram*) special use of words for effect; sum, amount; *v* imagine; depict; calculate; be conspicuous; *a* **figurative** metaphorical; symbolic; pictorial; *n* **figure-head** figure, bust, under bowsprit of ship; nominal leader.

filament *n* fine thread or fibre; fine conductor wire in electric light bulb, wireless valve.

filbert *n* cultivated hazel nut or tree.

filch *v* steal, pilfer.

file *n* hard steel tool with rough surface, for cutting or smoothing metal etc.; *v* use file on; *n* **filing** action of using file; *pl* particles of metal removed by filing.
file *n* stiff wire, box or folder for storing documents; collection of documents so kept for reference; *v* place in or on file; place on record.
file *n* line of persons, objects one behind another; *v* march, move in file.
filial *a* of, concerning son or daughter.
filibuster *n* irregular combatant; pirate; political obstructionist; *v*.
filigree *n* fine metal openwork; lace-like tracery of gold, silver wire.
fill *v* make full; occupy completely; cram, pack into; stop up; satisfy; imbue; appoint to post, office etc.; *n* full supply; *ns* **filling** tooth stopping; **filling-station** petrol station; *a* **filling** (*of food*) satisfying.
fillet *n* head-band; piece of boneless meat, fish; *v* slice and remove bones.
fillip *n* flip of finger against thumb; stimulus; *v* give fillip to, stimulate.
filly *n* female foal, young mare.
film *n* fine, thin skin or layer; thin flexible sensitized strip or roll used in photography, cinematography; motion picture; haze; *v* cover with film; make, direct, produce motion-picture; *a* **filmy** gauzy, delicate; *n* **filminess.**
filter *n* cloth, etc. used for straining liquids; device eliminating some light or electrical frequencies; traffic light allowing one lane to bypass the red light; *v* strain liquid; percolate; (*fig*) leak out; enter traffic lane gradually; move in direction shown by filter light; *n* **filtration.**
filth *n* nasty, revolting dirty; obscenity; *a* **filthy**; *n* **filthiness.**
fin *n* wing-like organ by which fish swim; projecting plane on aircraft etc.
final *a* at the end; decisive, *n* last examination, game or heat of series; *ns* **finalist** competitor in final of race, game etc.; **finality**; **finale** end; concluding movement, number of symphony, opera etc.

finance *n* management of (public) money; *pl* money resources of nation, company or individual; *v* supply money for; *a* **financial**; *n* **financier.**
finch *n* one of class of small seed-eating birds.
find *v* discover for first time; come upon (lost object, person); provide, equip with; return verdict; learn by experience; *pt* & *pp* **found**; *n* thing found; valuable or pleasing discovery; *ns* **finder**; **finding** verdict, result of enquiry.
fine *n* sum exacted as penalty; *v* punish by fine.
fine *a* thin, delicate; sharp; in minute particles; refined; not raining; showy; striking; excellent; finished; *v* refine, purify; make thinner; *ns* **fineness**; **finery** gay, elaborate dress; **finesse** subtlety; adroitness; (*cards*) attempt to take trick with low card, whilst holding higher one; *v*.
finger *n* one of five (or four, excluding thumb) members at end of hand; anything finger shaped; *v* touch with fingers, handle; *ns* **fingering** act of touching; fine knitting wool; (*music*) order of using specific fingers in playing; **fingerpost** signpost; **fingerprint** impression of whorls at tip of finger, used for identification.
finial *n* ornament at apex of pinnacle, gable etc.
finical, **finicking** *a* fussy, over-fastidious; *a* **finicky**.
finis *n* end, *esp* of book.
finish *v* bring to an end; complete; cease; put an end to, kill; make perfect; *n* end; final appearance; mode of finishing; *a* **finished** accomplished; perfect; *n* **finisher.**
finite *a* bounded, having limits.
fiord, fjord *n* narrow inlet of sea between cliffs, *esp* in Norway.
fir *n* coniferous, evergreen tree of pine family.
fire *n* state of burning; combustion; burning fuel; destructive burning; ardour, excitement, passion; discharge of firearms; *v* ignite; subject to heat; supply with fuel; animate, inflame; discharge gun; (*sl*) dismiss from work; *ns* **f.-alarm**; **f.-arm** weapon fired by explosion; **f.-brand** piece of burning wood; agitator; **f.-brigade** body of fire-fighters; **f.-damp** explosive gas found in coal mines **f.-dog** andiron;

f.-engine vehicle carrying pumps, ladders etc. to combat fires; **f.-escape**; **f.-fighter**; **f.-fly** insect emitting phosphorescent light; **fireman** a member of brigade; stoker; **fireplace** hearth; **f.-raiser** arsonist; **f.-water** strong liquor; **firework** container holding explosive material which gives off coloured lights, sparkles & loud bangs, when lit; **firing-party** soldiers detailed to shoot condemned man, or fire salute.

firkin *n* small cask; measure of capacity, 8-9 galls.

firm *a* solid; stable; resolute; steady; not fluctuating; *v* make firm; solidify; *n* partnership; business company.

firmament *n* whole expanse of sky.

first *a* earliest in order, time; highest in quality, rank, position; principal; *n* beginning; one who, that which, is first; highest prize; *n* **f.-aid** immediate aid given to injured; *as* **f.-hand** obtained directly; **f.-rate** of best quality.

firth *n* estuary; inlet of sea.

fiscal *a* concerned with public revenue; *n* high legal official.

fish *n* cold-blooded vertebrate, with fins, living in water; flesh of fish used as food; *v* catch, or try to catch, fish; try to get information; *ns* **fisher**; **fisherman** angler; man who catches fish for living; **fishery** fishing-ground; **fishmonger** one who sells fish; *a* **fishy** (*coll*) dubious; pertaining to fish.

fissure *n* cleft, chink, split; *a* **fissile** easily splitting; *n* **fission** splitting; reproduction by division; splitting of atomic nucleus.

fist *n* clenched fist; *v* strike with fist.

fistula *n* narrow, winding ulcer.

fit *n* sudden sharp attack of illness; seizure, spasm; passing whim; mood.

fit *a* suitable; competent; proper; strong; vigorous; *v* suit; be, adapted to, of correct size; supply, furnish; be properly adjusted to; *n* that which fits; adjustment; *ns* **fitness** suitability; good bodily health; **fitter** tailor who fits clothes; mechanic who adjusts machines; **fitment** built-in furniture; **fitting** action of fitting; *pl* furnishings and

equipment; *a* **fitting** suitable, proper, seemly.
five *a* & *n* cardinal number after four; *as* & *ns* **fifth** ordinal number; a fifth part; **fifteen** five pluś ten; **fifteenth**; **fifty** five tens; **fiftieth**; *n* **fives** ball-game played in walled court.
fix *v* make fast; stable; secure; arrange, appoint; determine; repair; gaze steadily at; (*sl*) get even with, bribe or trick; *ns* **fixation**; **fixative** fixing agent; **fixity**; immobility, **fixture** thing fixed in place; arranged match or game; (*leg pl*) furniture etc, attached to building and purchased with it.
fizz *v* hiss, splutter; effervesce; *n* (*sl*) champagne; noise of fizzing; *v* **fizzle** splutter weakly; come to end feebly.
flabbergast *v* dumbfound; astonish; disconcert.
flabby *a* hanging loosely; limp; flaccid; *n* **flabbiness.**
flaccid *a* limp; weak, without energy; *n* **flaccidity.**
flag *v* droop; become feeble.
flag *n* name of various kinds of iris.
flag *n* flat paving-stone; *n* **flagstone.**
flag *n* sheet of bunting, bearing emblem etc., attached to mast etc., used as standard or to signal; *v* signal by flag; *ns* **flag-officer** naval officer entitled to his own flag; **flagship** admiral's ship; **flagstaff** mast pole, for flag.
flagellate *v* scourge, whip; *n* **flagellation.**
flageolet *n* small flute-like instrument.
flagon *n* vessel for serving wine; large wine bottle.
flagrant *a* scandalous; blatantly evil; *ns* **flagrance, flagrancy.**
flail *n* implement for threshing grain by hand.
flair *n* natural aptitude; instinctive discernment.
flak *n* anti-aircraft fire.
flake *n* thin, light scale, layer; light, fleecy particle (of snow);; *v* peel come off in flakes; *a* **flaky.**
flamboyance *n* ostentation; showiness; exaggeration of speech, manner; *a* **flamboyant** showy; (*archi*) having wave-like tracery.
flame *n* burning gas or vapour; jet of fire; ardent passion, immagination; *v* emit flames; blaze; flare.
flamingo *n* scarlet:feathered aquatic bird, with long legs and neck.

flan *n* round, shallow, open pastry shell.
flange *n* projecting rim, edge, or rib.
flank *n* part of side of body between hip and ribs; side of hill, building, or body of troops; *v* guard, attack flank; be at side of.
flannel *n* soft woollen cloth; cloth for washing; *pl* trousers *esp* casual, sporting; *n* **flannelette** cotton imitation flannel.
flap *v* slap lightly; move (wings) up and down; sway; flutter; *n* act of flapping; flat piece of material partly attached and hanging; (*sl*) panic; *n* **flapper** flipper of seal etc.; (*sl*) young girl; **flapjack** powder case; pancake.
flare *n* bright, unsteady flame; vivid signal light; outburst of anger; outward spread, curve; *v* blaze up; spread outwards; *a* **flaring** gaudy.
flash *v* emit sudden bright light; gleam; pass rapidly by; signal by flashing; *n* sudden brief gleam of light; moment; cloth mark worn on uniform; *as* **flash, flashy** showy, tawdry; *n* **flashlight** small electric torch (USA); **flashpoint** temperature at which oil, spirit, vapour ignites.
flask *n* small, flattened pocket bottle for spirits etc.; wine-bottle; small narrow-necked bottle for scientific use.
flat *a* level; extended on ground; smooth; dull; listless; lower than true pitch; absolute; *n* what is flat; self-contained suite of rooms on one level; *n* **flatness**; *v* **flatten** make, become, flat, level,
flatter *v* praise insincerely; adulate; represent too favourably; congratulate oneself; *ns* **flatterer**; **flattery**.
flatulence, flatulency *n* wind, gas in stomach or intestines; *a* **flatulent** caused by, affected with flatulence; (*fig*) vapid.
flaunt *v* flourish, wave insolently; make display of.
flautist *n* flute player.
flavour *n* taste; distinctive quality; aroma; *v* give flavour to; season.
flaw *n* defect, blemish; crack; *v* crack, make flaw in; *a* **flawless** perfect; irreproachable.
flax *n* herb, whose fibres are spun into linen thread,

seeds produce linseed oil; *a* of, like flax; pale yellow.
flay *v* strip off skin; criticize savagely.
flea *n* small wingless, leaping, blood-sucking insect; *ns* **fleabane** plant supposed to keep away fleas; **flea-bite**, bite of flea; (*fig*) trifling thing.
fleck *n* spot; freckle; particle; *v* mark with flecks; dapple.
fledge *v* grow feathers on; provide feathers; *n* **fledg(e)ling** young bird; (*fig*) young inexperienced person.
flee *v* run away; avoid; shun; *pt* & *pp* **fled.**
fleece *n* sheep's wool; *v* swindle, plunder; *a* **fleecy** soft, woolly; resembling, covered with, fleece.
fleet *n* number of warships under one command; number of ships, aircraft, cars owned by one company or person; creek, inlet.
fleet *a* speedy, nimble, swift; *v* move swiftly, silently; *n* **fleetness**; *a* **fleeting** transient, transitory.
flesh *a* soft tissue of body, beneath skin, covering bones; edible animal tissue, meat; pulp of vegetable or fruit; animal nature of man, sensuality; *n* **flesher** butcher; *as* **fleshly** carnal; **fleshy** pulpy; plump.
fleur-de-lis *n* heraldic lily.
flex *v* bend, be bent; *n* flexible, insulated wire; *ns* **flexibility** ability to bend; **flexion** act of bending; inflexion; **flexor** muscle bending joint inwards; *a* **flexible** pliant; adaptable; versatile.
flibbertigibbet *n* flighty, unreliable person.
flick *v* tap, flip lightly and jerkily; *n* sharp light blow.
flicker *v* flutter waver; burn, shine unsteadily; *n* unsteady gleam; or movement.
flight *n* act of flying; distance flown; unit, formation of aircraft; volley (of arrows); series of stairs, steps; act of fleeing.
flighty *a* giddy, fickle, frivolous; *n* **flightiness**.
flimsy *a* thin, fragile; weak, paltry; *n* thin paper for carbon copy.
flinch *v* draw back in pain, fear; wince.
fling *v* throw, hurl; move with haste; lash out; flounce; *pt* & *pp* **flung**; *n* throw; vigorous dance; bout of dissipation.

flint *a* very hard dark grey quartz; anything hard, obdurate; piece of flint.
flip *v* flick, jerk; make smart light tap; *n* **flipper** limb or fin for swimming; *a* **flippant** lacking seriousness; frivolous; *n* **flippancy**; *a* & *adv* **flipping** nasty (*coll*), often used in place of stronger intensive.
flirt *v* jerk, flick quickly; move fitfully; play at courting; *n* coquette; sudden jerk, flick; *n* **flirtation**; philandering; *a* **flirtatious** fond of flirting.
flit *v* pass lightly, rapidly and quietly; (*sl*) move house secretly.
flitch *n* side of bacon.
float *v* rest, drift on surface of liquid; glide tnrough air; start, set going, launch (loan, company etc); *n* anything that floats, *esp* supporting something else on liquid; low-floored, shallow cart; cork on fishing net; *n* **flotation** act of floating, *esp* in commercial sense.
flock *n* lock, tuft of wool; wool, cotton fibres used as waste; *a* **flocculent** of, resembling wool or flock.
flock *n* number of animals (*esp* sheep) or birds, as unit; congregation; *v* assemble in large numbers; crowd together.
floe *n* sheet of ice floating on sea.
flog *v* beat hard; thrash with whip or stick; (*coll*) sell *esp* illicitly.
flong *n* paper matrices used for stereotyping.
flood *n* inundation; overflow of water in usually dry place; rising tide; (*coll*) floodlight; *v* inundate; overflow; overwhelm; *ns* **floodgate** sluice; **floodtide.**
floodlight *n* powerful artificial lighting; *v* illuminate by floodlights; *a* **floodlit.**
floor *n* lower surface of room etc.; storey; body of a hall etc., *v* furnish with floor; knock down; (*coll*) confound; *ns* **flooring** boards, blocks etc. forming floor; **floor-show** cabaret.
flop *v* move limply, heavily; fall clumsily, noisily; (*coll*) fail utterly; *adv* **floppily**; *n* act, noise of flopping; (*coll*) fiasco, failure; *a* **floppy** slack; loose, limp.
flora *n* flowers, plants, collectively, of particular area; classified list of species; *a* **floral** of flowers;

ns **florescence** season, state of flowering; **floret** small flower; **florist** grower of, dealer in flowers.
florid *a* flowery; over-elaborate; ruddy.
florin *n* obsolete British silver coin (equiv. to 10p).
floss *n* rough silk covering of cocoon; spun silk; *a* **flossy**.
flotilla *n* fleet of small ships or boats.
flotsam *n* floating wreckage or goods on the sea.
flounce *v* go, move jerkily, impatiently; *n* such movement.
flounce *n* ornamental strip, frill on garment.
flounder *n* kind of flatfish.
flounder *v* stagger, roll helplessly *esp* in water, mud; blunder, hesitate.
flour *n* finely ground meal *esp* of wheat; any very fine, soft powder; *v* cover with flour.
flourish *v* thrive; be florid in style, manner; brandish; sound fanfare; *n* act of brandishing anything; fanciful curved line; florid expression; fanfare.
flout *v* show scorn of; mock at; defy.
flow *v* (of water) glide along; gush; move along ceaselessly; (of blood) circulate; fall in loose folds, or masses; abound; *n* that which flows; rising tide; steady, copious supply.
flower *n* blossom, bloom; choicest, prime part; *v* produce blooms; reach highest state of development; *n* **floweret** small flower; *as* **flowery** abounding in flowers; florid; **flowered** decorated with floral pattern.
flu *n* influenza.
fluctuate *v* rise and fall; vary, be unstable; *a* **fluctuating**; *n* **fluctuation**.
flue *n* tube, pipe, shaft conveying air, smoke etc.; chimney.
fluent *a* flowing; able to, easily, rapidly; graceful; *n* **fluency**.
fluff *n* soft down, hair; light soft mass of wool, dust; *v* make into fluff; (*sl*) bungle; *a* **fluffy**.
fluid *n* liquid, gas, not solid; *a* flowing easily; *n* **fluidity**.
fluke *n* flat-fish; parasitic worm.
fluke *n* part of anchor; *pl* tail of whale.

fluke *n* lucky stroke, shot; happy chance; *v* make, gain by, fluke.
flume *n* artificial open water-channel.
flummox *v* bewilder; abash; disconcert.
flunkey *n* liveried man-servant, footman; toady.
fluor *n* mineral containing fluoride; *ns* **fluorine** non-metallic element; **fluoride** compound of fluorine; fluoridation.
fluorescence *n* property possessed by certain transparent bodies, of emitting light rays of different colour from those reflected; *a* **fluorescent.**
flurry *n* sudden gust; state of agitation of mind; death-throes of whale; *v* bewilder, fluster.
flush *v* fly, start up suddenly, as when startled; *n* flock of birds put up.
flush *v* flow suddenly, copiously; redden; cleanse by rush of water; elate, exhilarate; *n* rush of water; blush; sudden emotion; initial vigour; *a* full to brim; level with; (*sl*) having plenty (of money).
flush *n* hand of same suit (*cards*); run of same suit.
fluster *v* muddle, fuss, worry; be confused.
flute *n* wind-instrument, with side mouthpiece, and holes stopped by keys or fingers; narrow groove; *v* play flute; make grooves in; *a* **fluted** grooved, *ns* **fluting; flautist** player of flute.
flutter *v* move wings quickly, nervously; quiver; be excited; throb rapidly but feebly; move, wave (flag) quickly; *n* act of fluttering; nervousness; (*sl*) small bet.
fluvial *a* of rivers.
flux *n* flowing state, movement; morbid discharge of fluid (from body); substance added to help fusion; *v* fuse (metals) by melting.
fly *n* two-winged insect; imitation used as fish-bait; *a* **flyblown** tainted, maggoty; *n* **fly-catcher** small bird; **flyweight** boxer weighing 8st. or less.
fly *v* move on wings; control, travel in, aircraft; be propelled through air; flee from; flutter; spring, rush; *pt* **flew**; *pp* **flown**; *ns* **flying**; **flyover** long bridge over another road; **flying-boat** seaplane with floats; **flying-fish** tropical fish with wing-like fins; **flying-saucer** unidentified flying object;

flywheel heavy-rimmed wheel regulating speed of machine.
foal *n* young of horse, ass, etc.; *v* bear (foal).
foam *n* mass of small bubbles, froth, on surface of liquid; *v* form, emit foam; emit thick saliva, or sweat; *as* **foamy, foaming**.
fob *n* small pocket for watch, in waistband.
fob off *v* cheat, trick; delude into accepting (worthless article).
focus *n* point at which converging rays of light, heat, waves of sound, meet; centre of activity or intensity; *pl* **focuses, foci**; *v* adjust; cause to converge; concentrate; *a* **focal** pertaining to focus.
fodder *n* dried food for cattle, horses etc.
foe *n* enemy.
foetus, fetus *n* distinctly developed embryo in womb or egg; *a* **foetal**.
fog *n* thick mass of water vapour, smoke, dust etc. in lower atmosphere; thick mist; *v* cover in fog; confuse; *a* **foggy**; *ns* **fog-bank** belt of fog; **foghorn, fog-signal** audible warnings of fog.
fogey, fogy *n* fussy, slow old-fashioned person.
foible *n* weakness of character; idiosyncrasy.
foil *n* thin sheet of metal; quicksilver coating behind glass of mirror; person, thing enhancing another by contrast.
foil *n* light sword with button on end, used in fencing; *v* baulk, frustrate; repel (attack).
foist *v* palm off; impose fraudulently.
fold *v* bend over back on itself; double up; wrap round; clasp (in arms etc.) *n* crease made by folding; piece of folded material; hollow in hill; *n* **folder** folded printed circular, paper etc.; container for documents.
fold *n* enclosure, pen for sheep; *v* enclose in fold.
foliage *n* collectively, leaves of trees etc.; *a* **foliate** bearing leaves; leaf-like.
folio *n* sheet of paper folded once; large size paper; book made of such sheets; page number; *v* number pages of book.
folk *n* nation; people in general; *ns* **folk dance** traditional dance; **folklore** traditional beliefs etc.

follicle *n* small sac; seed-vessel; cocoon; *a* **follicular.**
follow *v* come, go after; go along, by; be later than; succeed in (office, position, etc.) grasp (meaning of); arise from (previous event etc.); obey; be disciple of; *ns* **follower** disciple; retainer; **following** body of followers; *a* **following** that is about to be mentioned.
folly *n* foolish act; rashness; useless, fantastic building.
foment *v* apply hot lotion, poultice to; stir up (trouble etc.); *n* **fomentation.**
fond *a* loving, affectionate; over-indulgent; *v* **be f. of,** have affection, liking for; *n* **fondness;** *v* **fondle** caress.
fondant *n* soft sweetmeat which melts easily.
font *n* bowl for baptismal holy water, in church.
food *n* matter which can be eaten, absorbed; solid nourishment; mental stimulus.
fool *v* stupid, silly person; dupe; clown; buffoon; *v* act with levity; dupe, hoax; mock; *a* **foolish** stupid; absurd; unwise; *n* **foolery** foolish behaviour; *as* **foolhardy** rash, foolishly daring; **foolproof** infallible; *ns* **foolhardiness; foolscap** dunce's cap; size of paper.
fool *n* dish of sieved fruit mixed with cream.
foot *n* lowest part of leg of man, animals, below ankles; part of sock, stocking covering foot; base; bottom; end of bed etc. where feet rest; infantry; lineal measure of 12 ins.; unit of scansion; *pl* **feet;** *v* walk, dance; put foot on stocking; **f. the bill** (*coll*) pay expenses; *ns* **football** inflated leather ball; game played with this; **footballer; footbrake; foot-fault** (tennis) service dissallowed, because server oversteps base line; **footing** secure standing; assured position; **footman** liveried servant; **foot-note** explanatory note at bottom of printed page; **footplate** driver's platform in locomotive; **footprint** impression of foot; *a* **footloose** free from ties.
footle *v* trifle; behave or talk in silly way; *n* nonsense, twaddle; *a* **footling** paltry.
fop *n* dandy; vain man; *a* **foppish.**
for *prep* suitable to; because of; toward; in favour of; instead of; during; at price of; in spite of; in search of; *conj* because.

for- *prefix: forms compounds (mostly verbs implying negative action) with meaning of* from, away, against, *e.g.* forget, forbid. *Also contraction of* **fore-** *(see later). Where the meaning may be deduced from the simple word, the compounds are not given here.*

forage *n* food for horses, cattle; *v* search for forage; rummage about; *ns* **forager; forage cap** military undress cap.

forasmuch as *conj* because, considering that.

foray *n* raid; plundering incursion; *v* raid, ravage.

forbear *v* refrain, abstain from; *pt* **forbore;** *pp* **forborne;** *n* **forbearance;** *a* **forbearing** patient, lenient

for(e)bear *n* ancestor.

forbid *v* prohibit; prevent; *pt* **forbade;** *pp* **forbidden** *a* **forbidding** threatening; sinister.

force *n* power; mental, moral strength; compulsion; body of troops, police etc.; violence; *v* compel; urge; break open; cause plants to flower, fruit before natural season; produce by effort; *as* **forced;** produced by special effort or necessity; strained; **forcible** done by force; convincing; **forceful** powerful; impressive.

forcemeat *n* seasoned minced meat and bread-crumbs for stuffing.

forceps *n* surgical pincers or tweezers.

ford *n* shallow place in river; *v* cross by means of ford.

fore *a* & *adv* before; in front (of); *comp* **former, further;** *sup* **foremost, first, furthest;** *n* front, forward part.

fore *interj* golfer's warning call.

fore- *prefix: forms compounds with meaning* earlier in time; in front; before (hand). *See* **for-.**

forearm *n* arm between elbow and wrist.

forebode *v* prophesy; portend; *n* **forboding,** presentiment.

forecast *v* estimate (result) beforehand; *n* prediction of future event.

forecastle *n* forward part of ship; crew's quarters.

foreclose *v* take away power of redeeming mortgage; debar, exclude; *n* **foreclosure.**

forefather *n* ancestor.
forego *v* precede, go without; *pp* **foregone**; *pr p* **foregoing**; *a* **foregone** preceding; already settled.
foreign *a* alien; pertaining to another nation; introduced from outside; *n* **foreigner**.
foremost *a* most distinguished; first in position, degree, dignity etc.
forensic *a* pertaining to law-courts; **f.medicine** medical jurisprudence.
forerunner *n* harbinger, precursor.
foreshadow *v* presage, indicate in advance.
foreshorten *v* represent according to viewing in perspective.
forest *n* large tract of land covered with trees; large unenclosed tract of waste land, heath etc.; *ns* **forestry** art of managing forests; **forester** one skilled in forestry; dweller in forest.
forestall *v* to get ahead of another by anticipation.
forethought *n* prudent thought for future.
forever *adv* always; *n* eternity.
foreword *n* preface.
forfeit *v* lose, as penalty; give up; *n* anything lost as penalty in law or game; *a* confiscated by law; *n* **forfeiture**.
for(e)gather *v* assemble, meet socially; associate.
forge *v* soften, shape (metal) by heating; imitate deceitfully, counterfeit; (*fig*) hammer out painstakingly; *n* smithy; workshop, plant for working red-hot metal; *ns* **forger** counterfeiter; **forgery** fraudulent making or alteration of signature, document etc.
forge *v* move forward slowly and steadily.
forget *v* cease to remember; accidentally omit; neglect; *pt* **forgot**; *pp* **forgot, forgotten**; *a* **forgetful** having bad memory; *n* **forget-me-not** marsh plant with small blue flower.
forgive *v* pardon; cancel, excuse; remit; *n* **forgiveness**.
fork *n* pronged tool, implement for digging, lifting; junction of two roads, rivers; meeting of bough and trunk of tree; *v* dig, lift, toss with fork; divide into branches; bifurcate.

forlorn *a* forsaken; desperate; neglected; **f.hope** very faint hope; *adv* **forlornly**; *n* **forlornness.**

form *n* shape, visible appearance; mode of expression; construction; type or kind: convention; model, pattern; printed formal document with blank spaces to be filled in with information; wooden bench; class in school; (also **forme**) type set and locked in chase; (also **forme**) hare's lair; *v* shape; create; act as; develop, educate; construct; assume shape; *a* **formal** according to rule; orderly; of outward form, lacking reality; stiff; *ns* **formality** propriety, conventionality; ceremony *esp* one without real meaning or use; **formation** forming; structure; *a* **formative** giving form; tending to shape, develop; *n* **format** shape and size of book etc.; *a* **formless** shapeless.

formaldehyde *n* colourless chemical compound; *n* **formalin** solution of formaldehyde used as antiseptic.

formic *a* pertaining to ants; **f.acid** irritant substance found in ants, stinging nettles etc., also produced artificially.

formidable *a* terrifying; overwhelming; presenting obstacles; huge.

formula *n* set form of words, prescribed for use on particular occasion; definition of dogma; recipe, prescription; method of solving problem; (*pl* **formulae, formulas**); *v* **formulate** express in formula; reduce to definite terms; *n* **formulation.**

fornication *n* sexual intercourse between unmarried persons; *v* **fornicate.**

forsake *v* abandon, desert; give up; *pt* **forsook**; *pp* **forsaken.**

forsooth *adv* in truth, certainly.

forswear *v* renounce on oath; perjure oneself; *pt* **forswore**; *pp* **forsworn.**

fort *n* fortress; fortified place, stronghold.

forte *n* special ability, strong point.

forte *adv* (*mus*) loudly; **fortissimo** very loudly.

forth *adv* forwards, onwards; *a* **forthcoming** about to appear; (*fig*) affable; communicative; *adv* **forthwith** at once, immediately.

forthright *a* outspoken, downright, candid.
fortify *v* strengthen; convert into fortress; *n* **fortification** act of strengthening; *pl* defensive works, walls etc.
fortitude *n* sustained courage, resoluteness in face of pain, danger etc.
fortnight *n* two weeks; *adv* **fortnightly.**
fortress *n* fortified place, stronghold.
fortuitous *a* due to chance, accidental; *n* **fortuity.**
fortune *n* chance, luck; lot in life; prosperity; wealth; *a* **fortunate** lucky; *ns* **fortune-hunter** unscrupulous person, trying to obtain wealth, *esp* by marriage; **fortune-teller** one who predicts one's future.
forty *a* & *n* four tens; **fortieth**
forum *n* public meeting place; tribunal, law court.
forward *a* in front of one; (*fig*) advanced; pert; early; precocious; *adv* towards front; at, in fore part (of ship etc.); onwards (in direction, time); *n* (*sport*) one of players in front line; *v* further; send, post on farther; dispatch; *n* **forwardness** pertness.
fosse *n* ditch, moat, trench; groove in bone.
fossil *n* petrified remains of prehistoric animal, vegetable organism found preserved in earth or rocks; (*fig*) antiquated person; *v* **fossilize** petrify; convert into fossil.
foster *v* rear another's child as one's own; encourage; cherish; *ns* **foster-child** one not related by blood to foster parents; **f.-mother**; **f.-father**; **f.-brother**.
foul *a* disgustingly filthy; clogged; (*of ropes etc.*) jammed, tangled; stormy (weather); vile; unfair; obscene; *n* (*sport*) unfair play; *v* become, make foul; jam; collide with.
foulard *n* thin silk or rayon material.
found *v* establish; institute; endow; base; *ns* **foundation** founding; substructure of building; basis; endowed institution; **foundation stone** one laid ceremonially at beginning of erection of building; **founder.**
found *v* melt (metal, minerals) and pour into mould; cast; *n* **foundry** place where founding, casting is carried out.

founder *v* (*of ship*) fill with water and sink: (*of horses*) fall, break down *esp* through lameness.
foundling *n* abandoned, deserted infant.
fount, font *n* set of printing type of one size & kind.
fount *n* fountain; (*fig*) source.
fountain *n* artificial, ornamental jet of water; jet of dtinking water; *ns* **f.head** source; origin; **f.pen** one with ink reservoir.
four *a* & *n* cardinal number next after three; *as* & *ns* **fourth** a fourth part; ordinal number; **fourteen** four plus ten; **fourteenth**; *ns* **four-in-hand** vehicle with four horses driven by one person; **four-poster** bed with four posts for curtains; **foursome** game, dance for four persons; *a* **foursquare** firm, steady; *n* **four-stroke** type of internal combustion engine.
fowl *n* bird, domestic cock or hen; flesh of birds (as food); *ns* **fowler** hunter of wild birds; **fowling-piece** light gun.
fox *n* reddish bush-tailed animal; crafty person; *v* act cunningly; mislead; *ns* **foxglove** plant with long spikes of tubular flowers; **foxhound** hound used for hunting fox; **fox-terrier** small terrier formerly used to drive fox from cover *a* **foxy** cunning
foyer *n* large hall, anteroom of theatre.
fracas *n* brawl, noisy quarrel.
fraction *n* numerical quantity less or more than integer; small piece; fragment; *a* **fractional** insignificant; **fractionary** fragmentary.
fractious *a* peevish, fretful, cross.
fracture *n* breaking, *esp* of bone; break, crack; *v* break.
fragile *a* easily broken; brittle; frail; *n* **fragility**.
fragment *n* piece broken off; unfinished part; *a* **fragmentary** incomplete; *n* **fragmentation** separation into fragments.
fragrant *a* sweet-scented; *n* **fragrance**.
frail *a* fragile; not robust (in health); morally weak; *n* **frailty**.
frail *n* rush basket for figs, raisins.
frame *v* construct; contrive; express in words; adapt;

cause to appear guilty; surround with, serve as, frame; *n* structure; border of wood etc. round picture setting; wood and glass structure protecting plants etc.; *ns* **framer**; **frame-up**, false evidence; **framework** substructure, skeleton.

franc *n* French, Belgian, Swiss etc. coin, monetary unit.

franchise *n* rights of citizenship; (*leg*) privilege, exemption.

Franciscan *n* & *a* (friar) of Order of St. Francis.

frangipane *n* rich almond pastry, perfume made from red jasmine.

frank *a* outspoken; sincere; candid; *n* signature, mark exempting letter from postal charges; *v* mark letter so; *adv* **frankly** openly; *n* **frankness** candour.

Frankenstein *n* monstrous creation beyond inventor's control.

frankfurter *n* German smoked sausage.

frankincense *n* sweet pungent gum resin used in incense.

frantic *a* violently excited *esp* with rage, grief, pain; frenzied; *adv* **frantically, franticly**.

fraternal *a* pertaining to brother; brotherly; *n* **fraternity** brotherhood; brotherliness; association of men with common interest; (U.S.) male student society; *v* **fraternize** be on friendly terms; *ns* **fraternization**; **fratricide** murder, murderer of brother or sister.

fraud *n* criminal deception, wilful dishonesty; impostor; *a* **fraudulent**; *n* **fraudulence**.

fraught *a* charged, teeming, full of.

fray *n* noisy fight, brawl; conflict.

fray *v* make, become ragged (as cloth) by rubbing, wear; ravel edges.

frazzle *v* fray; wear out; exhaust; *n* rags & tatters.

freak *n* abnormal form; monstrosity; whim; caprice; *a* **freakish**.

freckle *n* small brownish spot on skin, caused by sun; *v* mark or become marked with freckles; *a* **freckled**.

free *a* not enslaved; unconfined; unrestricted; frank, open; independent; exempt; unconditional; gratuitous; disengaged; unattached; (*chem.*) uncombined; spontaneous; *n* **freedom**; **freehold** land tenure without payment of rent or service; **freelance** independent journalist etc., not attached to any paper etc.; **freeman** one who enjoys freedom of a city; **Freemason** member of secret society for mutual benevolence; **Freemasonry** system, observances of Freemasons; (*fig*) instinctive understanding based on like experience.

freeze *v* become ice; feel very cold; congeal with cold; (*fig*) become rigid; horrify; refrigerate; chill; *pt* **froze**; *pp* **frozen**; *ns* **freezer** refrigerator; **freezing point** temperature at which liquids freeze; *a* **frozen** (*food*) preserved by freezing; (*assets etc.*) unrealizable.

freight *n* hire of ship for conveyance of goods; any load of goods for transport *esp* ship's cargo; *v* hire, load (vessel); *ns* **freighter** cargo vessel; **freightage** charge for transport of goods; **freightliner** fast goods train.

French *a* pertaining to France, its language and people; *ns* **French bean** haricot, kidney bean; **F.chalk** tailor's chalk; **F.horn** musical wind-instrument; **F.leave** absence without permission; **F.letter** condom; **F.window** glazed door to garden or balcony.

frenzy *n* violent excitement; paroxysm of rage, grief etc.; *a* **frenzied**

frequency *n* repeated occurrence; (*elect*) number of cycles per second of alternating current; **high f., medium f., low f.,** (*rad*) rate of vibration of sound waves.

frequent *a* happening often; numerous; common; *v* visit habitually.

fresco *n* method of water-colour painting on fresh plaster; mural so painted.

fresh *a* new; untainted; bracing; clean; inexperienced; (*sl*) impudent; (*of food*) not preserved or stale;)*of water*) not salt; (*of wind*) cool & brisk; *adv* **freshly** with freshness; anew; *n* **freshness**; *v* **freshen** make, become fresh; *ns* **freshet** freshwater stream flowing into sea; **freshman** undergraduate in first year.

fret *v* harass, vex, worry; *n* worry.

fret *n* complicated net-like carved work; bar on finger board of stringed instrument; *v* ornament with fret work; *ns* **fret-saw** fine-toothed narrow saw used for fret-work; **fret-work** ornamental lace-like carving on wood.
Freudian *a* pertaining to Sigmund Freud, psychologist, or his theories.
friable *a* easily crumbled; *n* **friability.**
friar *n* member of mendicant religious order; *n***friary** convent of friars.
fricasse *n* dish of meat, cut in pieces, cooked in rich white sauce; *v* cook thus.
friction *n* rubbing; resistance met when surface of body moves across another; (*fig*) antagonism; *a* **frictional.**
Friday *n* sixth day of week.
friend *n* person for whom one feels affection and respect; companion; helper; associate; member of Society of Friends (Quakers); *as* **friendless; friendly** kind, amiable; *ns* **friendship** amity; kindly feeling; **friendliness** kind attitude of mind.
frieze *n* kind of coarse woollen cloth; ornamental horizontal band in room or building.
frigate *n* light warship; sailing-warship.
fright *n* sudden alarm, fear, terror; grotesque ugly person; *v* **frighten** alarm, terrify; *a* **frightful** shocking, horrible; *n* **frightfulness.**
frigid *a* cold; distant, repellent; devoid of feeling; *n* **frigidity.**
frill *n* pleated, flounced ornamental trimming on edge of dress, curtains etc.; (*pl*) affected airs; *v* make into, adorn with frills; *a* **frilly.**
fringe *n* ornamental edging of threads, loops, tassels etc; border of hair cut & hanging over forehead; outer edge; border; limit; *v* adorn with, act as fringe.
frippery *n* finery.
frisk *v* gambol, frolic; *a* **frisky**; *n* **friskiness.**
fritter *n* slice of fruit etc., fried in batter.
fritter *v* waste, dissipate money, time etc.
frivolous *a* silly, futile; empty- headed; *n* **frivolity** levity.

frizz *v* hiss & splutter (as bacon being fried); curl, crisp (hair); *a* **frizzy** curly.
frizzle *v* fry, cook very crisply; (of hair) be tightly curled; crisp into small curls; fry thoroughly.
fro *adv* (*only in phrase* **to & fro**) back & forth; up and down.
frock *n* woman's dress; monk's robe; *v* invest as priest.
frog *n* tailless amphibian, developed from tadpole; horny pad in hoof of horse, etc.; attachment to belt supporting sword; ornamental loop and button on clothes; metal plate at junction of railway lines; *ns* **frogman** swimmer equipped and trained for underwater operations; **frog in the throat** hoarseness; *v* **frog-march** carry offender face downwards, four men holding limb each.
frolic *a* merry, jovial; *n* merry making; gaiety; *v* gambol, play pranks; *a* **frolicsome.**
from *prep* expressing source, distance, divergence, cause; unlike to; not near to.
frond *n* leaf-like organ, bearing spores, *esp* of ferns; anything resembling leaf.
front *n* forward part; battle area, forward line; promenade by sea-side; face of building; something, person acting as cover for illegal activities; forward part of weather change; *v* face; stand opposite to; *ns* **frontage**; extent of front; **frontier** boundary line between states etc; **frontispiece** illustration facing title page; *a* **frontal.**
frost *n* particles of frozen moisture on earth's or other surface; air temperature causing this; (*sl*) coolness of manner, fiasco; *v* affect with frost; make frosted (with sugar icing etc.); *a* **frosty** freezing; not genial; hoary; *n* **frost-bite** gangrenous injury to tissues, due to exposure to extreme cold; *a* **frost-bitten.**
froth *n* light mass of small bubbles; foam; (*fig*) futile talk; *v* cause to emit froth; *a* **frothy.**
froward *a* perverse, refractory.
frown *v* wrinkle forehead; seem gloomy, angry; *n* contraction of brows.
frowzy *a* stuffy, musty; dirty, unkempt.

fructify *v* render, become fruitful; yield results; *n* **fructification.**

frugal *a* sparing, thrifty; inexpensive; *n* **frugality.**

fruit *n* any vegetable product used by man; edible, pulpy seedcases; (*usu pl*) result; reward; offspring; *v* bear fruit; *ns* **fruiterer** dealer in fruit; **fruition** fulfilment, enjoyment; *as* **fruitful**; **fruitless**; **fruity.**

frump *n* plain, dowdy woman; *a* **frumpish.**

frustrate *v* baffle; circumvent; foil; *n* **frustration.**

fry *n* young fishes; **small f.**, young children; insignificant person.

fry *v* cook, be cooked in hot fat.

fuchsia *n* ornamental flowering shrub.

fuddle *v* make stupid by intoxication; tipple.

fudge *n* soft, sugary sweetmeat; nonsense.

fuel *n* any material used for burning; *v* provide with, take in fuel.

fug *n* fustiness; closeness of air; *a* **fuggy.**

fugitive *a* fleeing; transient; evanescent; *n* one fleeing from danger, captivity etc.

fugue *n* musical contrapuntal composition with recurring themes.

fulcrum *n* point on which lever moves.

fulfil *v* satisfy; comply with; carry out, perform; *n* **fulfilment.**

fulgent *a* shining, radiant, blazing; *n* **fulgency.**

full *a* filled to capacity; replete; abounding in; ample; crowded; (*of tones*) resonant; *adv* fully, completely; *n* **fulness, fullness**; *as* **fulsome** gushing, insincere; **fullblown** (*of flowers*) fully open; *n* **full-stop** punctuation mark (.) at end of sentence.

fuller *n* tradesman who shrinks, cleanses cloth; *v* **full** thicken, cleanse, dress, cloth; *n* **fuller's earth** clay used in fulling.

fulmar *n* sea-bird of petrel family.

fulminate *v* flash, explode; detonate; denounce violently; *n* highly explosive compound; *n* **fulmination.**

fumble *v* grope clumsily with hands, bungle; *n.*

fume *n* pungent smoke, vapour; (*fig*) anger; *v* emit fumes; (*fig*) fret, be angry; *v* **fumigate** disinfect by fumes; *ns* **fumigation, fumigator.**

fun *n* mirth, enjoyment, sport; joking; **make f. of** ridicule; **in f.**, as joke; *a* **funny** amusing; difficult to explain.

function *n* normal action, occupation or purpose; duty; official task, ceremony; large social gathering; (*math*) quantity whose value is linked to varying value of another; *v* work; act; *a* **functional** having special purpose; (*med*) affecting function; *n* **functionary** official.

fund *n* permanent stock; sum set apart for special purpose; (*pl*) money resources; *v* convert into, provide, invest in, permanent fund; *n* **funding** act, process of creating funded debt.

fundament *n* buttocks; *a* **fundamental** essential; basic; *n* basic rule; principle.

funeral *n* burial, interment of dead; *a* relating to funeral; *a* **funereal** mournful; dismal; black; **funerary** of, for funeral.

fungus *n* plant or allied growth reproducing by spores, *e.g.* mushroom, mildew; etc (*pl*) **fungi, funguses**; *a* **fungoid, fungous**; *n* **fungicide** substance which destroys fungi.

funicular *a* connected with, worked by rope.

funk *n* fear, terror; coward; *v* fear; try to avoid, through fear.

funnel *n* cone shaped tube for pouring liquids through to container; smoke stack of ship, locomotive; *v* pour off, as through funnel.

fur *n* short soft hair forming animal coat; dressed skin of animal; (*pl*) such skins collectively; coating. deposit (on tongue, in kettle etc.); *v* cover, become coated, with fur; *n* **furrier** dealer in furs; *a* **furry** of, like fur.

furbish *v* polish, clean up; burnish.

furcate *a* branched, forked.

furious *a* raging; violent; frenzied; savage, vehement; *ns* **fury, furiousness**.

furl *v* roll up and bind securely (sail, umbrella).

furlong *n* 1/8th. mile, 220 yards.

furlough *n* leave of absence *esp* to soldier, official.

furnace *n* enclosed chamber of brick, metal in which great heat can be generated.

furnish *v* provide; equip *esp* house, office etc with furniture; *ns* **furnisher** one who sells furniture; **furnishing** act of equipping house; (*pl*) furniture, fittings.
furniture *n* movable household equipment.
furore *n* widespread, enthusiastic admiration.
furrow *n* groove made in land by plough; deep wrinkle on face etc.; *v* make furrows.
further *v* forward, promote; *adv* besides; *a/adv* (*comp* of FAR) more distant; to greater degree, extent; *a/adv* **furthest** most distant; to greatest degree, extent; *n* **furtherance** promotion; *adv* **furthermore** besides; *a* **furthermost** most distant.
furtive *a* stealthy, secret, sly; *n* **furtiveness.**
fury *n* extreme anger; rage; avenging goddess; virago.
furze *n* thick growing, yellow flowered prickly shrub.
fuse *n* device to explode shells, mines etc.; soft wire with low melting point, used as safety device in electric circuits; *v* melt (metal) with heat; fit fuse to; *a* **fusible;** *n* **fusion** act of melting, blending; (*fig*) coalition.
fuselage *n* body of aircraft.
fusel-oil *n* mixture of crude alcohols.
fusil *n* light musket; *ns* **fusileer** soldier of regiment formerly armed with fusils; **fusillade** continuous fire from firearms.
fuss *n* nervous, anxious state of mind; needless bustle; *v* worry about; make nervous.
fustian *n* coarse twilled cloth, corduroy.
fustigate *v* cudgel, thrash with stick; *n* **fustigation.**
fusty *a* stale, stuffy; old-fashioned.
futile *a* vain, useless, ineffectual; *n* **futility.**
future *a* happening hereafter; of, connected with time to come; *n* time to come; fate; tense of verb indicating future; *ns* **futurity; futurism** non-representational art against tradition; *a* **futuristic.**
fuzz *n* stiff fluffy hair; (*sl*) police; *a* **fuzzy** fluffy; blurred.

gab *n* chatter; talkativeness; *v* **gabble** utter rapidly and indistinctly; *n* rapid, confused speech; jabbering.
gabardine, gaberdine *n* thin, ribbed woollen fabric;

rainproof coat of this; long, loose gown *esp* worn by Jews.

gable *n* triangular upper part of wall of building enclosed by roof ridges.

gaby *n* simpleton, ninny.

gad *v* wander about aimlessly or seeking pleasure; *n* **gadabout** pleasure-seeker.

gad-fly *n* horse-fly; infuriating person.

gadget *n* ingenious applicance, device, often useless.

Gaelic *n* Celtic speech *esp.* of Scotland; pertaining to Gaels; *n* **Gael** Scottish, Irish Celt.

gaff *n* iron hook for landing fish; light fishing-spear; spar extending top of fore-and-aft sail; *v* land (fish) with gaff.

gaffe *n* blunder, tactlessness.

gaffer *n* aged rustic; foreman.

gag *n* anything thrust into mouth to silence person; device for keeping mouth open during operation; unscripted remark; (*sl*) joke; *v* silence, by gag; put in jokes, remarks not in script; retch.

gage *n* pledge; symbol of challenge to fight; *v* pledge; stake.

gaggle *n* flock of geese; *v* cackle.

gain *n* obtain, secure; win; profit; improve; earn; *n* increase; improvement; *a* **gainful**, yielding gain.

gainsay *v* dispute, contradict, deny; *pt* & *pp* **gainsaid.**

gait *n* manner of walking, running.

gaiter *n* cloth, leather covering for lower leg.

gala *n* festivity; fete.

galantine *n* dish of spiced meat served in aspic.

galaxy *n* vast cluster of stars, as Milky Way; (*fig*) brilliant assembly.

gale *n* strong, violent wind.

galena *n* natural lead sulphide.

gall *n* bile, bitter secretion from liver; (*fig*) bitterness; effrontery; *ns* **g.-bladder** small bladder, containing bile; **g.-stone** calculus formed in gall-bladder.

gall *n* sore *esp.* on horse, caused by friction; growth on tree, *esp.* oak, produced by gall-fly; *v* make sore by rubbing; irritate.

gallant *a* brave, daring; chivalrous; attentive to women; *n* gay young man of fashion; lover; *n* **gallantry**.
galleon *n* old three- or four-decked sailing ship.
gallery *n* upper tier of seats in theatre, church etc; underground passage in mine; long narrow covered passage, open at one side; room, building for showing works of art.
galley *n* low, single decked ship with sails and oars; ship's cook-house; tray holding composed type; galley-proof; *ns* **g.-proof** proof before being made up into pages; **g.-slave** one condemned to row in galley; drudge.
Gallic *a* of, relating to Gaul; French; *n* **Gallicism** French word, idiom used in another language.
gallipot *n* jam-jar; small glazed earthenware pot.
gallium *n* rare silvery, metallic element with low melting point.
gallon *n* liquid or dry measure of capacity.
gallop *n* fastest pace of horse etc; quick ride; *v* move, ride at gallop; (*fig*) hurry.
gallows *n* structure from which criminals are hanged.
galop *n* lively dance; *v* dance galop.
galore *adv* plentifully; in great abundance.
galosh, golosh *n* protective overshoe worn in wet weather.
galvanism *n* electricity produced by chemical action; *a* **galvanic** (*fig*) spasmodic; *v* **galvanize** electrify by galvanism; coat with metal by galvanizing; *n* **galvanisation**.
gambit *n* (*chess*) opening move, when piece is intentionally sacrificed; initial move in action, conversation etc.
gamble *v* play games of chance for money stakes; place (money) at stake; (*fig*) take risk or chance; *n* act of gambling; risky chance; *n* **gambler**.
gamboge *n* yellow pigment.
gambol *v* skip about; frolic.
game *n* pastime; sporting contest; artful trick; jest; *v* gamble; *a* plucky; lame; *n* **gamester** gambler.
game *n* birds, animals hunted for food, sport;

game-keeper man employed to look after game.
gamete *n* reproductive cell which unites with another.
gamin *n* street urchin; neglected, impertinent child·
gamma *n* third letter of Greek alphabet; **g-rays** very short electro-magnetic waves.
gammon *n* lower end of flitch of bacon, including hind leg.
gammy *a* (*coll*) crippled, lame.
gamp *n* (*coll*) large, clumsy umbrella.
gamut *n* whole range, compass of voice, notes etc; (*fig*) whole extent, scope.
gander *n* male goose; (*sl*) look.
gang *n* group, squad; band of criminals; *n* **ganger** foreman.
ganglion *n* nerve-centre; hard globular swelling, usually on sinew.
gangrene *n* mortification of living tissue, necrosis; *a* **gangrenous**.
gangster *n* member of criminal gang; violent, armed criminal.
gangway *n* passage, road; movable bridge from ship to shore; way between rows of seats.
gannet *n* solan-goose; large fish-eating sea-bird.
gantry *n* bridge-like frame, carrying travelling crane, railway signals etc.
gaol *n* prison; *v* put in gaol; *ns* **gaoler** prison officer; **gaol-bird** convict.
gap *n* opening, cleft; space; interval; interruption.
gape *v* yawn; open mouth widely, in amazement; (*fig*) open.
garage *n* building for housing, repairing, refuelling, motor cars; *v* put (car) into garage.
garb *n* style of dress, costume etc; *v* dress, clothe.
garbage *n* refuse, rubbish.
garden *n* piece of cultivated land, for growing flowers,etc; *v* cultivate, work in garden; *ns* **gardener**; **garden-party** outdoor social gathering.
gardenia *n* tropical shrub with fragrant blossoms.
garfish *n* sea-fish, with long tapering jaws.
gargantuan *a* very large.
gargle *v* rinse mouth with liquid, kept agitated by breath; *n* liquid used for gargling.

gargoyle *n* ornamental rainwater spout from roof.
garish *a* gaudy, ostentatious.
garland *n* wreath of flowers, leaves, used as decoration, or sign of victory; *v* hang, adorn with garlands.
garlic *n* bulbous-rooted plant of onion family, used as flavouring.
garment *n* article of clothing.
garner *v* store up, accumulate.
garnet *n* red semi-precious stone.
garnish *v* decorate, improve appearance of (*esp* food); *n* material for this; *n* **garniture** ornamentation.
garret *n* room under roof of house, attic.
garrison *n* troops defending fortress, town etc; *v* furnish with, act as, garrison.
garrotte *v* execute by strangling; strangle; *n* instrument used for execution in Spain; cord so used; *n* **garrotter.**
garrulous *a* talkative, loquacious; *n* **garrulity.**
garter *n* band worn to keep stocking up; (*cap*) highest order of knighthood in G.B.
garth *n* enclosed space; court, yard, garden.
gas *n* one of various vapourous substances; air-like fluid; (*specif*) coal-gas used for heating, lighting, etc; poisonous vapour used in warfare; such vapour used as anaesthetic; *pl* **gases;** *v* use gas upon; (*sl*) talk nonsense at length; *a* **gaseous;** *n* **gasometer, gasholder;** *a* **gassy;** *n* **gas-mask** protective covering for face, worn with respirator.
gash *n* deep cut; slash; *v* cut deeply.
gasket *n* rope, cord for securing sail; tow, jointing, packing material; type of washer.
gasolene, gasoline *n* liquid distilled from petroleum; (U.S.) petrol.
gasp *v* catch breath suddenly, as in surprise or fear; *n* sudden catching of breath.
gast(e)ropod *n* one of class of molluscs, as snail, limpet, slug.
gastric *a* of, relating to stomach; *ns* **gastritis** inflammation of stomach; **gastronomy** art of good cooking & eating; *a* **gastronomic;** *n* **gastronome** epicure.
gate *n* hinged frame of wood or metal across opening,

path etc; sluice; way in or out of place; total number of spectators at sporting event; total amount paid by these for admission; *v* confine (undergraduate) to college; **gate-crasher** (*coll*) uninvited intruder at function, etc.

gateau *n* rich, fancy cake; *pl* **gateaux.**

gather *v* bring together; collect; acquire; infer; fester; pucker; *n* **gathering** assembly; purulent swelling; **gathers** small pleats in fabric.

gauche *a* clumsy, tactless, awkward; *n* **gaucherie.**

gaucho *n* S. American cowboy.

gaudy *a* showy; garish; vulgarly fine; *n* **gaudiness.**

ga(u)ge *n* standard of measure (diameter of wire, distance between rails, thickness of sheet metal, etc); instrument for measuring rainfall, force of wind, speed of current, etc; device for testing size of tools etc; *v* measure; (*fig*) estimate.

gaunt *a* lean, haggard; grim, forbidding.

gauntlet *a* glove with protective cuff; *v* throw down **g.**, issue challenge; run the **g.**, run (as punishment) between two rows of hostile men; (*fig*) be exposed to hostile attacks, criticism.

gauss *n* unit of intensity of magnetic field.

gauze *n* thin, transparent silk or other fabric; light haze; *a* **gauzy.**

gavel *n* chairman's, auctioneer's hammer.

gavotte *n* lively dance; music for this.

gawky *a* awkward, ungainly; *n* **gawk** such a person.

gay *a* lively, joyful, merry; bright-coloured; pleasure-loving; *n* **gaiety.**

gaze *v* look intently, fixedly.

gazebo *n* balcony, summer house, with wide view.

gazelle *n* small, delicately formed antelope.

gazette *n* official journal giving public notices, government & service appointments, bankruptcies etc; title of newspaper; *v* publish in gazette; *n* **gazetteer** geographical dictionary.

gear *n* apparatus, equipment, tackle, tools; harness; mechanism transmitting, regulating, or controlling movement; gear ratio; (*sl*) clothes; wheel, cog with teeth; *v* provide with, put in, gear; *ns* **gear-box, g.-case** case enclosing gear wheels etc; **gearing**

system of cog-wheels, forming gear; **out of g.** disengaged from gear; (*fig*) inharmonious.

gecko *n* house lizard.

Geiger counter *n* instrument that detects radio-activity.

geisha *n* Japanese singing and dancing girl.

gelatin(e) *n* glutinous substance, obtained by simmering animal tissue, bones etc; *a* **gelatinous** like gelatin, jelly.

geld *v* castrate; *n* **gelding** castrated horse.

gelid *a* ice-cold; frigid.

gelignite *n* highly explosive form of dynamite.

gem *n* precious stone, *esp* one cut and polished; *v* stud, set with gems.

geminate *v* double; *a* (*bot*) in pairs; *n* **gemination.**

gen *n* (*sl*) correct information.

gendarme *n* French soldier, employed as policeman; (*coll*) any policeman.

gender *n* classification of nouns, pronouns according to sex; sex.

gene *n* carrier of hereditary factor in chromosome.

genealogy *n* line of descent from ancestors; pedigree; study of this; *a* **genealogical**; *n* **genealogist.**

general *a* not specific; relating to whole class, group; usual; lacking details; miscellaneous; not specializing; *n* army rank above colonel; *ns* **generalissimo** supreme commander; **generality** undetailed statement; *v* **generalize** draw general conclusions; *ns* **generalization**; **generalship** skilful leadership.

generate *v* beget; produce; be cause of; *n* **generation** act of generating; all persons of approx. same age group; all persons in same degree of descent from common ancestor; period of approx. 30 years separating birth of parent and child; *a* **generative**; *n* **generator** apparatus for producing electricity.

generic *a* pertaining to genus or class.

generous *a* open-handed; magnanimous; abundant; (of wine) full bodied; *n* **generosity** quality of being generous; liberality.

genesis *n* origin; mode of production; *pl* **geneses**; *n* (*cap*) first book of Bible.

genetics *n* branch of biology, dealing with heredity; *a* **genetic.**
genial *a* kindly, amiable, cordial; (of climate) mild, warm; *n* **geniality.**
genie *n* Arabian demon or spirit; *pl* **genii.**
genital *a* relating to animal reproductive organs; *n pl* external organs of generation.
genetive *n* & *a* (*gram*) possessive case of nouns, pronouns.
genius *n* exceptional intellectual, artistic ability; person having such ability; natural aptitude; guardian spirit; *pl* **geniuses.**
genocide *n* deliberate murder of race.
genre *n* kind, style, species; painting of rustic life.
genteel *a* unnaturally polite, elegant or affected, (usually sarcastic).
gentian *n* herb usually having vivid blue flowers.
gentile *n* person who is not of Jewish race.
gentle *a* well-born; mild; serene; soft; moderate; docile; *ns* **gentility** gentle breeding; **gentleman** well-born man; honourable, courteous man; **gentleness** quality of being gentle; kindliness; **gentry** upper-class people, below nobility; **g's agreement** agreement binding by honour (not legally); *a* **gentlemanly.**
genuflect *v* bend knee in reverence etc; *n* **genuflexion** (also **genuflection**).
genuine *a* true, authentic, real; sincere.
genus *n* kind, sort, class, species; group of similar species; *pl* **genera.**
geo- *prefix* of the earth.
geocentric *a* having earth as centre; seen; measured from centre of earth.
geodesy *n* science of measuring earth & its surface.
geography *n* science describing earth's physical features, divisions, products, climate, plant and animal life, population etc; book on geography; *n* **geographer**; *a* **geographic(al).**
geology *n* science dealing with earth's crust, its history and structure; *n* **geologist**; *a* **geologic(al)**; *v* **geologize** study geology of.
geometry *n* mathematical science dealing with pro-

perties and relations of lines, surfaces etc; *n* **geometrician**; *a* **geometric(al)**.

geophysics *n* science dealing with earth's physics; *a* **geophysical**.

georgette *n* thin semi-transparent silk fabric.

Georgian *a* of period of George I, II, III, IV.

geranium *n* one of genus of flowering plants, as crane's bill; pelargonium (cultivated).

geriatrics *n* (*pl*) medical care and treatment of old people; *a* **geriatric** of old people.

germ *n* rudimentary form of organism from which new one can develop; microbe; (*fig*) elementary thing; *n* **germicide** substance capable of killing germs.

German *n* native, language of Germany; **g. measles** contagious disease.

germane *a* relevant, pertinent, appropriate.

germinate *v* begin, cause, to sprout or develop; *n* **germination**.

gerrymander *v* falsify facts; manipulate for personal political advantage.

gestation *n* carrying young in womb; pregnancy.

gesticulate *v* use motions of hands, arms, when speaking, for emphasis; *n* **gesticulation**.

gesture *n* movement of limbs, etc to convey meaning; something done for effect.

get *v* obtain; receive; earn; achieve; induce; (in *pt*) have to do; possess; reach; become; *pt* **got**; *pp* **got, gotten; get one's own back** obtain revenge; **get down** alight, descend.

gew-gaw *n* frivolous trifle; gaudy toy.

geyser *n* natural spout of hot water; device for heating domestic water.

ghastly *a* terrifying; horrible; shocking; pallid

gherkin *n* small cucumber used in pickles.

ghetto *n* Jewish quarter of city, town; any (*usu* poor) quarter inhabited by one racial group.

ghost *n* spirit, wraith, spectre; anything vague, shadowy; (*sl*) one who writes another's speeches, texts, etc for him; *v* write such work; *a* **ghostly**.

ghoul *n* evil spirit in East, supposed to feed on dead; human grave-robber; *a* **ghoulish** morbid, cruel.

ghyll, gill *n* ravine, gully, chasm.
giant *n* man, animal or plant of abnormally large size; mythical being of enormous size; *a* huge; *a* **gigantic** huge, immense.
gibber *v* talk, chatter incomprehensibly; *n* **gibberish** incoherent speech; meaningless words.
gibbet *n* gallows-post, used for execution by hanging.
gibbon *n* small, long armed ape.
gibbous *a* convex, bulging; humped; (of moon) between half and full.
gibe *v* deride; sneer; utter taunts.
giblets *n pl* edible inner parts of fowl.
giddy *a* dizzy; have feeling of, cause vertigo; flighty; *n* **giddiness.**
gift *n* something given; present; talent, aptitude; act, right of giving; *a* **gifted** talented.
gig *n* light, two wheeled carriage; racing-boat.
giggle *v* laugh in suppressed, nervous way, titter.
gigolo *n* professional male dancing-partner; young man kept by older woman.
gild *v* coat thinly, with gold; (*fig*) embellish; *pt* **gilded;** *pp* **gilded, gilt**; *a* **gilt** gilded; *n* **gilt** gold leaf or paint.
gill *n* liquid measure, ¼ pint.
gill *n* fish's breathing organ; flesh under chin and jaws of man.
gillie *n* (*Scot*) attendant on game fishermen & hunters.
gimbals *n pl* rings and pivot for keeping compass etc horizontal.
gimlet *n* small tool for boring holes.
gimmick *n* (*sl*) trick; gadget; device for attracting publicity.
gimp *n* plaited cord, braid used as trimming.
gin *n* alcoholic liquor distilled from grain, flavoured with juniper berries.
gin *n* snare, trap; kind of crane; machine separating seeds from cotton.
ginger *n* tropical spicy plant; (*sl*) energy, spirit; *a* sandy red colour; *v* **ginger up** (*sl*) stir up, stimulate; *ns* **g.-beer** drink of fermented sugar, ginger, yeast; **gingerbread** cake made with treacle,

ginger etc; *a* **gingery** of, like ginger; reddish; (*fig*) testy.

gingerly *a* cautious; *adv* carefully.

gingham *n* cotton cloth, often checked or striped.

gipsy, gypsy *n* member of wandering race of Indian origin; their language, Romany; roving, untrustworthy person.

giraffe *n* very tall African ruminant.

gird *v* encircle with belt, *esp* at waist; put on (belt etc); attach to (with belt); *pt* & *pp* **girded, girt**; *n* **girder** large metal or wooden beam.

gird *v* gibe, taunt (*obs*).

girdle *n* waist belt, band, cord; ring cut in bark round tree; light corset; *v* surround, encircle.

girl *n* female child; young unmarried woman; (*coll*) any young(ish) woman; *n* **girlhood**; *a* **girlish**.

girth *n* belly-band of saddle etc; circumference.

gist *n* essence, main points (of speech etc).

give *v* bestow; confer on; hand over; provide; inflict upon; impart; produce; devote; yield; transfer; *pt* **gave**; *pp* **given**; *pr p* **giving**; *n* elasticity, resilience.

gizzard *n* bird's second stomach.

glabrous *a* smooth, hairless.

glacé *a* glazed, shiny; coated with sugar.

glacier *n* slowly moving mass of ice, in mountain valleys; *a* **glacial** of ice, glaciers; very cold; (*fig*) frigid.

glad *a* happy, joyful; pleased; *v* **gladden** make glad; cheer; *n* **gladness**.

glade *n* opening, clearing in wood, forest.

gladiator *n* in ancient Rome, professional fighter with sword etc, in arena.

gladiolus *n* kind of iris, with sword-shaped leaves.

glamour *n* mysterious charm; magical illusion; fascination; *a* **glamorous**.

glance *v* strike obliquely; gleam; look rapidly; examine hastily; *n* brief look; flash; oblique blow.

gland *n* organ which secretes substance for use in body, and also transforms, excretes; *a* **glandular**; *n* **glanders** contagious disease of horses.

glare *v* emit dazzling light; stare angrily; *n* blinding brightness; *a* **glaring** dazzling; flagrant.

glass *n* hard, brittle substance, *usu* transparent, made by fusion of sand, soda, potash etc; drinking vessel of glass; its contents; mirror; barometer; telescope; optical lens; *pl* spectacles; *v* cover, protect with glass; *a* **glassy**; *n* **glass-house** greenhouse; (*sl*) military prison.
glaucoma *n* disease of the eye.
glaze *v* put glass into; coat with glassy substance; become glassy; *n* glass-like surface; vitreous coating for pottery; glossy coating; *n* **glazier** one who glazes windows.
gleam *v* emit beams of light; reflect light; *n* beam; transient flash of light.
glean *v* pick up stray ears of corn, scraps; (*fig*) gather (facts, etc) *n* **gleaner.**
glebe *n* land held by incumbent of benefice.
glee *n* light-hearted mirth; part-song; *a* **gleeful.**
glen *n* narrow valley (*usu* with woods & stream).
glengarry *n* (*Scot*) Highlander's woollen cap.
glib *a* fluent, plausible, smooth-spoken; *n* **glibness.**
glide *v* slide, move along smoothly, stealthily; fly (aircraft) without use of engine; fly in glider; *n* action, motion of gliding; musical slur; glancing stroke (cricket); *n* **glider** aircraft without engine.
glimmer *v* flicker, glow faintly; *n* **glimmering** fitful dream; (*fig*) faint idea.
glimpse *a* fleeting view; passing sight; *v* catch glimpse of.
glint *v* flash, reflect light faintly; glitter.
glissade *n* slide (*usu* on feet) down snow or ice slope; sideward glide in dancing.
glisten *v* glitter, shine, sparkle.
glitter *v* shine, sparkle intermittently; (*fig*) make brilliant show; *n*.
gloaming *n* (*Scot*) twilight.
gloat *v* dwell upon, exult in silently, with malicious joy.
globe *n* ball; sphere, *esp* the earth; model of earth or heavens; orb; *a* **global**; *ns* **globe-trotter** widely-travelled person; **globule** drop of liquid; **globulin** protein constituent of haemoglobin; *a* **globular** globe-shaped.

glomerate *v* collect into ball, cluster; *n* **glomeration.**
gloom *n* darkness; melancholy; *a* **gloomy** dismal, dark; pessimistic.
glory *n* splendour; earthly pomp; heavenly bliss; high degree of pride etc; *v* take delight in; boast; *v* **glorify** exalt; invest with glory; *n* **glorification**; *a* **glorious** sublime; famous; illustrious.
gloss *n* sheen; polished surface; *v* put gloss on; *a* **glossy.**
gloss *n* marginal note; explanation; *v* comment; explain away; *n* **glossary** explanatory list of words.
glottis *n* opening of larynx; *a* **glottal.**
glove *n* covering for hand and fingers; *v* provide with gloves; **hand in g.** very intimate; *n* **glover** one who sells, makes gloves.
glow *v* be incandescent; emit steady light without flame; be hot with emotion; be, look warm; *n* incandescence; sense of bodily warmth; ardour; *n* **g. worm** beetle; *a* **glowing.**
glower *v* scowl.
glucose *n* dextrose, grape-sugar.
glue *n* adhesive, *esp* one made from horns, hoofs, etc; *v* fasten with glue; (*pass*) be constantly with.
glum *a* morose, sullen, moody.
glut *v* surfeit, satiate; *n* superabundance.
gluten *n* protein found in wheat flour; *a* **glutenous.**
glutinous *a* of nature of glue; adhesive, sticky.
glutton *n* greedy feeder; insatiable enthusiast (for work, etc); wolverine; *a* **gluttonous** greedy; *n* **gluttony.**
glycerin(e) *n* sweet, colourless, viscous liquid extracted from fats and oils.
gnarled *a* knobby; rugged; weather-beaten.
gnash *v* grind teeth with rage.
gnat *n* small blood-sucking winged insect.
gnaw *v* chew, bite steadily at; wear away (by pain, worry etc).
gneiss *n* crystalline, banded granite-like rock.
gnome *n* dwarfish earth-goblin.
gnomon *n* rod, arm of sun-dial, casting shadow; indicator.

gnosis *n* special mystical knowledge; *a* **gnostic.**
gnu *n* South African antelope; wildebeest.
go *v* travel; move; leave; elapse; become; be, exist; work; result; *pt* **went**; *pp* **gone**; *n* **going** attempt; energy; *ns* **goer, going** pace of travelling etc, condition of ground for racing etc; **go-getter** (*sl*) thruster; *a* **go-ahead** enterprising.
goad *n* pointed stick for driving cattle; (*fig*) incentive; *v* urge on; (*fig*) provoke, incite.
goal *n* score posts in football etc; score so made; aim; purpose; destination.
goat *n* agile ruminant, often horned & bearded; *n* **goatee** small pointed beard.
gob *n* (*sl*) mouth; blob of spittle; *n* **gobbet** morsel of food; *v* **gobble** eat noisily, greedily; make throaty noise (as turkey); *n* **gobbler** turkey-cock.
goblet *n* drinking vessel without handles.
goblin *n* malicious ugly sprite.
god *n* supernatural being with divine powers; object of worship; idol; (*Cap*) the Supreme Creator and Ruler; *pl* (*coll*) gallery (theatre); (*fem*) **goddess;** *ns* **godfather, -mother** sponsor at baptism; **godchild** one who is sponsored at baptism; **godhead** godhood, divinity; **godliness** piety; *as* **godfearing, godly** pious; **godless** wicked; **godforsaken** desolate, depraved.
goffer *v* crimp, pleat with hot iron.
goggle *v* (of eyes) bulge; stare stupidly; *n* wide eyed stare; *n pl* protective spectacles; *a* **goggle-eyed** having bulging, staring eyes; *n* **goggle-box** (*sl*) T.V. set.
goitre *n* morbid enlargement of the thyroid gland.
gold *n* yellow, precious metal; gold objects *esp* coins; (*fig*) wealth; colour of gold; *a* of, like gold; *a* **golden;** *ns* **gold-digger** prospector for gold; (*sl*) woman who tries to get money etc from rich men; **goldfinch** British songbird; **goldfish** Chinese carp; **golden mean** middle course between two extremes; **golden wedding** 50th wedding anniversary; **goldsmith** a worker in gold & silver; **gold standard** monetary system in which unit of currency has precise value in gold.

golf *n* game in which small hard ball is struck by clubs into series of holes, on an open course; *v* play golf; *ns* **golfer, golf-course, -links** land laid out for golf.
golliwog *n* black-faced doll with fuzzy hair.
gonad *n* reproductive gland.
gondola *n* Venetian canal-boat; *n* **gondolier** rower of gondola.
gong *n* metal disc, giving resonant note when struck; anything used thus.
gonorrhoea *n* a venereal disease.
good *a* right; proper; meritorious; helpful; pious; efficient, valid; *n* integrity; benefit; *pl* wares; property; *ns* **goodness, goodwill** kindliness, value of business reputation; *a* **goodly** large; considerable.
good-bye *interj* & *n* farewell.
goof *n* (*sl*) stupid, awkward person; *a* **goofy** silly, stupid.
googly *n* off-break ball bowled with leg-break action (in cricket).
goon *n* (*sl*) foolish person.
goose *n* large web-footed bird; (*sl*) fool; tailor's iron; *pl* **geese**; *n* **gooseflesh** pimply bristling of skin due to cold, fear etc.
gooseberry *n* thorny shrub, with hairy, sweet edible berries; (*sl*) unwelcome chaperon or third party.
gopher *n* small American burrowing rodent.
gore *n* blood, shed and clotted; *a* **gory**.
gore *n* triangular gusset in garment.
gore *v* pierce with horn or tusk.
gorge *n* deep, narrow valley, ravine; throat; *v* eat greedily, in excess; *n* **gorget** throat-armour.
gorgeous *a* resplendent, dazzling, magnificent.
gorgon *n* mythical snake-haired woman; terrifying woman.
gorilla *n* largest anthropoid ape.
gormandize *v* eat like glutton.
gorse *n* spiny yellow-flowered shrub.
goshawk *n* large, fierce short-winged hawk.
gosling *n* young goose.

gospel *n* one of four books of New Testament; account of life and teaching of Christ; (*fig*) strongly held principle; (*coll*) absolute truth.

gossamer *n* filmy cobweb threads, floating in air, on bushes and grass; any thin filmy material.

gossip *n* idle talk, *esp* about others; ill-founded rumour; busy-body; *v* chat casually; spread rumours.

Gothic *a* of Goths; (*archi*) style of pointed arches, German black-letter type face.

gouache *n* opaque water-colour paint mixed with gum; picture painted in gouache.

gouge *n* concave chisel for making grooves; *v* cut with gouge.

goulash *n* rich stew of meat and vegetables, seasoned with paprika.

gourd *n* plant of melon, pumpkin class; fleshy fruit of plant; its dried rind used as vessel.

gourmand *n* greedy person, glutton.

gourmet *n* connoisseur of food and wine; epicure.

gout *n* painful, inflammatory disease of joints *esp* big toe; *a* **gouty**.

govern *v* direct, control, rule; determine, influence; restrain; (*gram*) decide (case etc); *a* **governable**; *ns* **governor** ruler; device regulating speed etc of machine; (*sl*) father; employer; **governess** private woman teacher; **government** ruling of state; ministry, persons responsible for this; political administrative system; *a* **governmental**.

gown *n* loose flowing garment; woman's dress; academic, official robe.

grab *v* snatch, grasp suddenly; take unjustly; *n* act of grabbing; device for picking up (soil etc).

grace *n* charm; elegance; virtue; kindness, mercy; prayer before, after meal; title of archbishop, duke; *as* **graceful** elegant, tactful; **graceless** depraved; clumsy; **gracious** charming, courteous, beneficent; *v* adorn; honour.

grade *n* step, degree; class, standard; slope; *v* classify; arrange in grades; *v* **gradate** (of colours) shade off; *ns* **gradation** arrangement in grades; gradual shading off in colour; **gradient** degree of slope; *a* **gradual** coming on by degrees; gentle.

graduate *v* take university degree; mark in degrees, grades; *n* holder of university degree; *n* **graduation.**
graft *n* bud, shoot inserted into another plant, to become scion; bribe; *v* insert (cutting etc) into stem of another plant; transplant living animal tissue; join inseparably; acquire (money) dishonestly; bribe; *n* **grafter** swindler.
grail *n* chalice; Holy Grail.
grain *n* small; hard, particle; hard seed *esp* of cereals; smallest unit of weight; texture, direction of fibres, (of wood etc); natural disposition; *v* give imitation wood graining to; *n* **graining**; *a* **granular** of, like grains.
gram, gramme *n* metric unit of weight.
grammar *n* science dealing with correct use of words, their classes, and structure; book on this; *n* **grammarian**; *a* **grammatic(al)** pertaining to, following rules of, grammar; *n* **grammar school** type of school.
gramophone *n* instrument for reproducing disc-recorded sounds.
grampus *n* killer- or spouting-whale; heavy breather.
granary *n* grain storehouse.
grand *a* splendid, imposing; chief, principal; noble; haughty; final; (*sl*) very good, enjoyable; *ns* **grandeur** magnificence; **grandfather, grandmother** parent's father, mother; **grandson, g.daughter** child of child; **grand piano** large harp-shaped piano; **g.stand** main section of raised seats for spectators; **grandiloquence** bombastic style of speech; *a* **grandiose** imposing; pretentious.
grange *n* country house, with farm buildings.
granite *n* very hard granular igneous rock.
grant *v* assent to; bestow; concede; *n* gift; money given to maintain student; scholarship allowance.
granule *n* small grain-like particle; *a* **granulous, granular**; *v* **granulate** reduce to particles; roughen surface; *n* **granulation** healing formation of grain-like bodies on wound.
grape *n* fruit of vine; *ns* **grape-fruit** large citrus fruit; **grape-sugar** glucose, dextrose.
graph *n* diagram showing relative positions, varia-

tions (of quantity, temperature etc); *a* **graphic** relating to writing, drawing, painting etc; vividly descriptive; *ns* **graphology** study of handwriting.

graphite *n* form of carbon, used in pencils, & as lubricant.

grapnel *n* hooked anchor for seizing, mooring ship.

grapple *n* grapnel; close hold, grip; *v* seize tightly; come to grips.

grasp *v* seize, hold firmly; clutch; understand; *n* firm hold, grip; comprehension; reach; *a* **grasping** eager for gain; rapacious.

grass *n* green herbage of fields, lawns etc; pasture-land; *v* sow with grass; put to grass; *ns* **grasshopper** small, leaping locust-like insect; **g.-roots** fundamentals; **g.-widow** woman whose husband is temporarily away.

grate *n* fire bars and framework of fireplace; *n* **grating** open framework of bars.

grate *v* rub, scrape with rough surface; grind into small pieces; make harsh noise, by rubbing; (*fig*) annoy, irritate; *n* **grater** kitchen utensil; *a* **grating** rasping; jarring.

grateful *a* thankful; feeling gratitude; *n* **gratefulness**.

gratify *v* please; satisfy; content; indulge; *ns* **gratification, gratitude** feeling of thankfulness, appreciation.

gratis *a* & *adv* free of charge.

gratuitous *a* freely given; unwarranted; *n* **gratuity** gift, *esp* money, for services rendered.

grave *n* hole dug in earth for burial; tomb; *n* **gravestone** tombstone.

grave *a* weighty, serious; solemn; low pitched; *n* **gravity**.

grave *v* incise, engrave, carve; scrape (ship's bottom); *n* **graving-dock** dry dock.

gravel *n* small pebbles, coarse sand; shingle; urinary crystals in bladder; *v* surface (path) with gravel; *a* **gravelly**.

gravid *a* pregnant.

gravitate *v* move by force of gravity; (*fig*) be attracted by; *n* **gravitation**.

gravity *n* force exerted by earth & other celestial bodies.

gravy *n* sauce made from juice of roasting meat.

grayling *n* freshwater fish; butterfly.

graze *v* feed in pastures; *n* **grazier** one who feeds and fattens cattle.

graze *v* touch by glancing blow, abrade; *n* slight abrasion caused by grazing.

grease *n* soft, melted animal fat; semi-solid oil as lubricant; *v* apply grease to; *a* **greasy**; *ns* **greasiness, grease-gun** lubricating appliance.

great *a* large, big; eminent; important; more remote by one generation; *n* **greatness, greatcoat** heavy overcoat; *n pl* **Greats** (at Oxford) final Honours School exam.

grebe *n* fresh water diving bird.

greedy *a* gluttonous; (*fig*) covetous; longing for; *ns* **greed** avarice; **greediness** gluttony.

Greek *n* native, language of Greece; *a* **Grecian** Greek.

green *a* of colour of mixed blue and yellow; grass coloured; unripe; immature; credulous; *n* green colour; grass plot, lawn; *pl* green vegetables; *ns* **greenery** vegetation; **greenfly** green aphis; **greengrocer** retailer of vegetables and fruit; **greenhorn** novice; **greenhouse** building with glass roof and sides, for rearing plants; **greenstick** partial fracture in bone; **greensward** turf.

greet *v* salute on meeting; welcome; meet; *n* **greeting**

gregarious *a* living in herds, flocks; sociable; *n* **gregariousness.**

gremlin *n* (*sl*) trouble-making imp, responsible for faults in (orig.) aircraft, now machinery generally.

grenade *a* small bomb thrown by hand; globular fire-extinguisher.

grenadine *n* thin silk fabric; pomegranate syrup; red dye.

grey, gray *a* of colour between black & white; pale, livid; clouded; grey haired; *a* **greyish**; *n* **greyhound** slender, tall, swift dog used for coursing and racing.

grid *n* grating; national network of electricity supply; luggage carrier on car; numbered network of squares on map, as reference.

griddle *n* metal plate for baking over fire.
gridiron *n* framework of metal bars for broiling over fire.
grief *n* sorrow, distress, woe; *v* **grieve** cause, feel grief; *n* **grievance** cause for complaint; *a* **grievous** distressing; painful.
griffin, griffon, gryphon *n* mythical animal, part eagle, part lion.
griffon *n* small coarse-haired terrier; vulture.
grig *n* small eel; grass-hopper.
grill *n* gridiron; food cooked on this; *v* cook, be cooked on grill; (*sl*) interrogate closely; *n* **grilling** severe cross examination; *a* very hot; *n* **grill, grill-room** room in restaurant etc where grilled food is served.
grille *n* open, metal framework over opening.
grilse *n* young salmon, on first return from sea.
grim *a* stern, forbidding; inflexible; cruel.
grimace *n* facial contortion, expressing ridicule, pain etc; *v* make grimaces.
grime *n* soot; ingrained dirt; squalor; *v* soil, begrime; *a* **grimy.**
grin *v* show teeth in smile, grimace etc; *n* broad smile; cruel smile.
grind *v* reduce to small pieces or powder by pressure; wear down; make smooth; sharpen; grate; *pt* & *pp* **ground**; *n* act of grinding; (*sl*) hard work; *ns* **grindstone** hard sandstone used for grinding; **grinder.**
grip *v* clutch, hold firmly; hold interest; *n* grasp; mastery; handle; suitcase; *a* **gripping** thrilling.
gripe *v* cause, feel spasms of pain of colic; (*sl*) complain; *n* spasm of pain in bowels.
grippe *n* influenza.
grisly *a* horrifying; gruesome, ghastly.
grist *n* corn for grinding; ground malt.
gristle *n* cartilage *esp* in cooked meat.
grit *n* small fragments of stone; coarse sand; (*fig*) courage; *pl* coarsely ground oats etc; *v* make grinding sound (with teeth); treat surface with grit; *a* **gritty**; *n* **grittiness.**
grizzly *a* greyish; *n* **g. bear** large N. American bear; *a* **grizzled** (of human hair) turning grey.

groan *v* utter deep sound of pain, grief etc; be overburdened; (of wood) creak; *n* sound made in groaning; moan.
groat *n* obsolete English silver coin.
groats *n pl* hulled grain; grits.
grocer *n* dealer in dry and canned goods, household requisites etc; *n* **grocery** grocer's trade; *pl* **groceries** goods sold by grocer.
grog *n* spirit (*usu* rum) with water; *a* **groggy** unsteady, shaky; weak.
groin *n* depression between thigh & abdomen; line made by intersection of two vaults; groyne; *v* form groin.
groom *n* servant in charge of horses; officer in royal household; bridegroom; *v* tend, care for (horse); keep one's clothes & person smart; *n* **groomsman** best man.
groove *n* narrow channel, furrow, *esp* cut by tool in wood, metal; fixed routine, rut; *v* cut groove in.
grope *v* feel round blindly, fumble; search cautiously.
gross *a* fat; coarse; obscene; flagrant; total, not net; *n* the whole; twelve dozen.
grotesque *a* fantastic; distorted; bizarre; (art) highly decorated with intertwined animal forms & foliage; *n*.
grotto *n* cave; artificial cavern; *pl* **grottoes**.
grouch *v* (*sl*) grumble persistently; *n*.
ground *n* soil, earth, land; sea-bottom; special area (for sport etc); reason, basis; background; *pl* estate around house; dregs; *v* place on ground; prevent (aircraft) from flying; run ashore; give basis to; *n* **grounding** basic instruction; *as* **grounded** (of aircraft) unable to fly; **groundless** unfounded; *ns* **groundnut** peanut; **groundwork** early preparation.
groundsel *n* common yellow-flowered weed.
group *n* collective unit of persons, things; class; number of persons sharing views, interests etc; (art) several figures forming one design; *v* place, form into group.
grouse *n* wild game-bird; its edible flesh.
grouse *v* (*sl*) grumble, complain; *n* **grouse**.
grout *n* liquid cement; *v* cover, fill, with grout.

grouts *n pl* dregs.
grove *n* small wood.
grovel *v* lie flat; (*fig*) humble oneself.
grow *v* develop; become larger; cultivate; flourish; *pt* **grew**; *pp* **grown**; *n* **growth** that which has grown, or is growing.
growl *v* utter deep rumbling sound of anger; grumble; grouse; *n* make growling sound.
groyne *n* breakwater on beach, to resist tidal erosion.
grub *v* dig, uproot; (*fig*) search arduously; *n* larva of insect; (*sl*) food; *a* **grubby** dirty.
grudge *v* envy; allow, give, unwillingly; *n* grievance, resentment.
gruel *n* thin watery oatmeal porridge; (*sl*) punishment; *a* & *n* **gruelling** exhausting; punishment.
gruesome *a* ghastly; macabre; horrible.
gruff *a* rough, surly; hoarse; *n* **gruffness.**
grumble *v* complain; murmur angrily; rumble; *n* complaint.
grumpy *a* surly, peevish, ill-tempered.
grunt *v* utter deep, rough, nasal sound; make this sound; *n* deep snort.
guano *n* droppings of sea-birds; fertilizer made from this.
guarantee *n* pledge, promise given that conditions of contract will be carried out; manufacturer's undertaking to make good defects in product; *v* undertake; give guarantee; *ns* **guaranty** surety; undertaking to be responsible for another's debts; **guarantor** one who gives guaranty.
guard *n* protector; sentry; state of wariness against danger; armed escort; railway official in charge of train; protective device or part; *v* protect; defend; restrain; *n* **guardian** protector; custodian; one who has custody of child.
guava *n* tropical tree, having egg-shaped fruit.
gudgeon *n* small fresh-water carp.
gudgeon *n* piston pin; socket, bearing.
guer(r)illa *n* irregular warfare; one engaged in it.
guernsey *n* thick knitted sweater; (*cap*) breed of dairy cows.

guess *v* conjecture; form opinion without material evidence; suppose.
guest *n* person enjoying another's hospitality; one staying in hotel etc.
guffaw *n* burst of loud, vulgar laughter.
guide *v* show way; direct; control; advise; *n* one who, that which, guides; guide-book; one who leads tourists, hunters etc; *ns* **guidance, Girl Guide** member of organization for girls based on lines of Boy Scouts.
guild *n* association of people with common trade, profession or aim; *n* **guildhall** meeting place of guild or corporation.
guile *n* deceit, wiliness; *as* **guileful, guileless.**
guillemot *n* web-footed sea-bird of auk family.
guillotine *n* machine for beheading; one for paper-cutting; *v* use guillotine.
guilt *n* condition, fact of having committed crime, or sin; culpability; *as* **guilty** having incurred guilt, **guiltless** innocent; *n* **guiltiness.**
guinea *n* obsolete English coin; *ns* **guinea-fowl** domesticated fowl, like pheasant; **guinea-pig** domesticated rodent.
guise *n* disguise; false appearance.
guitar *n* six-stringed musical instrument; *n* **guitarist**
gulch *n* deep ravine or torrent-bed.
gules *n* red (*her*).
gulf *n* large, deep, inlet of sea; chasm; (*fig*) impassable gap; *pl* **gulfs.**
gull *n* web-footed sea-bird; dupe, fool; *v* deceive, cheat *a* **gullible** credulous, easily duped; *n* **gullibility.**
gullet *n* passage from mouth to stomach.
gully, gulley *n* channel worn by water.
gulp *v* swallow noisily; choke back; *n* large mouthful.
gum *n* firm tissue around teeth; *n* **gumboil** abscess in gum.
gum *n* sticky viscid substance exuded by certain trees; liquid glue; chewing-gum; *v* stick with gum; *a* **gummy**; *npl* **gumboots** rubber boots.
gumption *n* shrewdness; common sense; intelligence.
gun *n* tubular weapon from which missiles are fired;

any fire-arm; *ns* **gunner, gunnery** art of artillery; **gunboat** small warship; **gun-cotton** high explosive; **gunman** armed gangster; **gunpowder** explosive used for fire-arms, blasting etc; **gunwale** upper edge of boat's side.

gunny *n* coarse, jute sacking.

gurgle *v* flow with, utter, bubbling sound; *n* **gurgling** sound.

guru *n* Hindu spiritual teacher.

gush *v* burst forth; flow out copiously; (*sl*) talk effusively; *n* violent flow; (*fig*) effusiveness; *n* **gusher** person who gushes; oil-well not needing pumps.

gusset *n* triangular section let into garment, to enlarge, or strengthen it.

gust *n* sudden, brief blast of wind, rain etc; (*fig*) brief, outburst of anger, passion etc; *a* **gusty.**

gusto *n* relish; zest, enjoyment.

gut *n sing* fine thread made from animal guts, used in surgery, violin-strings etc; narrow passage; *pl* bowels, intestines; *pl* (*sl*) courage, stamina; *v* remove guts of; destroy inner contents of (house etc *esp* by fire).

gutta-percha *n* elastic substance from dried sap of Malaysian tree.

gutter *n* narrow trough under eaves to carry rain water; open channel along road; (*fig*) lowest social class, slums; *v* form channels in; *n* **g.-urchin** street urchin.

guttural *a* pertaining to throat; (of voice) rasping, harsh.

guy *n* rope, wire, chain used to guide, steady or secure something; *v* steady with guy.

guy *n* grotesque effigy of Guy Fawkes burnt on Nov. 5th; scarecrow; badly dressed person; *v* mock; make fool of.

guzzle *v* drink, eat greedily and to excess.

gybe *v* (of boom or sail) swing from side to side; jib.

gymkhana *n* athletics display, *esp* equestrian events.

gymnasium *n* hall for physical training & gymnastics; *n pl* **gymnastics** physical exercises, with or without apparatus; *n* **gymnast** one skilled in gymnastics.

gynaecology *n* science dealing with functions and diseases of women; *a* **gynaecological**; *n* **gynaecologist.**
gypsum *n* sulphate of calcium, used for making plaster of Paris.
gypsy see entry for **gipsy.**
gyrate *v* revolve; whirl round; *n* **gyration**; *a* **gyratory** revolving, spinning.
gyro-compass *n* gyroscope with compass card attached.
gyroscope *n* fly-wheel capable of rotating about any axis, used to stabilize ships, aircraft etc; *a* **gyroscopic.**
gyve *n* shackle, fetter, handcuff (*usu* **gyves** *n pl*).

habeas corpus *n* writ issued requiring prisoner to be produced in court.
haberdasher *n* retailer of small articles of dress, sewing cotton, pins, etc; *n* **haberdashery.**
habit *n* usual behaviour; (*biol*) normal mode of growth; distinctive dress, (*esp* monk's, riding-habit); *a* **habitual** customary, usual; *v* **habituate** render familiar with; *ns* **habitat** natural home of animal; **habitude** usual custom; **habituè** regular visitor.
hachure *n* fine lines on map, showing slopes, coast.
hacienda *n* large plantation, ranch (Spain, S. America).
hack *v* cut roughly; chop; kick shins of; cough harshly; *n* act of hacking.
hack *n* hired horse, *esp* for riding; over-worked horse; (*fig*) badly-paid writer; *v* ride hack; ride at pace of hack; *n* **hack-work** literary drudgery.
hackle *n* long feathers on cock's neck; hair on neck and back of animal; artificial fly for fishing.
hackney *n* medium-sized ordinary riding horse.
haddock *n* edible sea-fish, akin to cod.
Hades *n* abode of dead, underworld.
haematin *n* pigment found in blood.
haemoglobin *n* protein substance of red blood corpuscles.

haemophilia *n* hereditary disease, in which blood fails to clot.
haemorrhage *n* bleeding; *v* to bleed (*med*).
haemorrhoids *n* piles (*med*).
haft *n* handle, hilt; *v* fit haft.
hag *n* ugly old woman, witch.
haggard *a* gaunt; having worn, wasted look.
haggis *n* Scottish culinary dish.
haggle *v* wrangle over price; dispute terms.
hagiology *n* study of saints or of their lives; *n* **hagiographer** writer of saint's life.
ha-ha *n* sunken fence, in wide ditch.
hail *n* small lumps of ice falling like rain; *v* shower down hail; *n* **hailstone.**
hail *interj* greeting; *v* greet; accost; **hail from** come from.
hair *n* fine threadlike growth from skin of animal; mass of such growth on human head; fur of animal; *a* **hairy**; *ns* **hairiness, hairdresser** one who cuts, sets, tints hair, *esp* women's hair; **hairspring** very fine spring in watch etc.
hake *n* coarse edible sea-fish, allied to cod.
halberd *n* long handled spiked battle-axe.
halcyon *n* kingfisher; *a* tranquil, peaceful; **h. days** period of calm weather, about winter solstice.
hale *a* healthy, robust, vigorous, *esp* of the elderly.
half *n* one of two precisely equal parts; (*pl* **halves**); *a* consisting of, equal to a half; partial; *ns* **half-breed, half-caste** person of mixed blood; *a* **half-hearted** not enthusiastic; **half-witted** imbecile.
halibut *n* large edible flat sea-fish.
halitosis *n* foul breath.
hall *n* large public room; passage, lobby at entrance to building; large private house; **hallmark** official mark on gold, silver plate, used by Goldsmith's Hall.
hallelujah *n* & *interj* praise the Lord!
hallo, hello *interj* cry of surprise; greeting.
halloo *n* call to hounds during chase; *v* shout loudly.
hallow *v* make holy; consecrate.
hallucination *n* fancied perception by senses of some non-existent thing; *v* **hallucinate** affect with hallucinations.

halo *n* ring of light round sun, moon etc; golden circle, disk around head of figure in picture, symbolizing holiness; (*pl* **haloes**).

halt *a* lame; *v* (*fig*) hesitate; *a* **halting** stumbling; hesitant.

halt *n* stoppage of movement; small railway station; *v* cause to stop; pause.

halter *n* rope, strap for leading, tying horses etc; rope with noose for hanging person.

halve *v* divide in halves; diminish by half; share.

halyard, halliard *n* rope used for raising sail, flags.

ham *n* back of thigh; thigh of hog, *esp* smoked and salted; amateur radio operator; *a* **ham-fisted, -handed** clumsy; *n* **hamstring** tendon at back of knee; tendon behind horse's hock; *v* lame by cutting hamstring.

hamburger *n* fried minced beef & onions in bread roll.

hamlet *n* small village.

hammer *n* long-handled tool with heavy head, for driving in nails, working metal, crushing etc; striking part of gun-lock; device for striking bell; auctioneer's mallet; *v* strike with, use hammer; knock loudly; **hammer out** solve problem by repeated discussion.

hammock *n* canvas or net bed, slung on cords.

hamper *n* large basket with lid.

hamper *v* hinder, impede, obstruct.

hamster *n* rodent with cheek pouches.

hand *n* extremity of arm, below wrist; style of writing; dexterity; direction, position; manual worker; cards dealt; one round in card game; aid; indicator on dial, clock; measure of 4 ins.; *v* pass, put into another's hands; give; *ns* **handbag** woman's light bag; **handbill** small printed notice; **handbook** guide book; **handcuff** one of pair of chained metal rings used as fetter; *v* put handcuffs on; **handful** (*fig*) small amount; **handiness** dexterity; nearness; **handkerchief** small square of fabric for wiping nose, eyes etc; **hand-out** something handed out, *esp* news, information etc for press; **handwriting**

manner, style of writing; *as* **handy** adroit; easily available; **handmade** not machine made.
handicap *n* disability (physical or mental); disadvantage in time, weight etc; race, contest where handicaps are imposed; *v* impose handicap.
handle *n* part of tool, utensile etc held in hand; *v* touch, feel with hands; control, manage; deal in.
handsome *a* good-looking; generous; having dignity.
hang *v* suspend; fix (wallpaper) to wall; attach (doors etc); be suspended; *pt* & *pp* **hung** execute by hanging by neck; *pt* & *pp* **hanged**; *a* **hangdog** looking guilty, sullen; *ns* **hanger-on** unwanted follower; **hangman** executioner; **hangover** unpleasant after effects of drinking bout; *v* **h. up** replace telephone receiver; **h. out** (*sl*) live.
hangar *n* covered shed, *esp* for aircraft.
hank *n* skein, coil, length, *esp* measure of yarn.
hanker *v* be eager for, crave.
hanky-panky *n* (*coll*) underhand dealing; trickery.
Hansard *n* official report of proceedings in Parliament.
hansom *n* light two-wheeled horse cab.
hap *n* chance; *a* **hapless** unlucky, wretched; **haphazard** random, accidental.
happen *v* take place; chance; *n* **happening** occurrence; (*sl*) fantastic, weird event.
happy *a* cheerful; content; fortunate; *adv* **happily**; *n* **happiness**; *a* **happy-go-lucky** carefree; easygoing.
hara-kiri, hari-kari *n* Japanese ritual suicide.
harangue *n* tirade; angry, ranting speech; *v*.
harass *v* worry, vex, annoy by repeated attack; *n* **harassment**.
harbinger *n* forerunner, precursor, herald.
harbour *n* haven, port; shelter; *v* shelter; conceal; lodge.
hard *a* firm; solid; difficult to do, understand; strenuous; cold; harsh; severe; merciless; (of water) not lathering well; (of lines, colours etc) too clear, too vivid; *v* **harden**; *adv* **hardly** harshly; scarcely, barely; *ns* **hardness, hardship** privation, suffering ill-luck; **hardware** ironmongery; *a* **hard-boiled**

(egg) boiled until solid; (*sl*) shrewd, callous; **hard of hearing** rather deaf; **hard up** short of money; **hardy** robust; bold; (*hort*) resisting frost and weather changes; *ns* **hardihood** boldness; **hardiness** audacity; robustness.

hare *n* swift rodent, resembling rabbit; *v* (*coll*) run wildly; run fast; *a* **hare-brained** rash, flighty; *n* **hare-lip** congenital fissure of human upper lip.

harebell *n* wild plant with blue bell-shaped flowers.

harem *n* women's quarters in Mohammedan house; seraglio.

haricot *n* french bean; stew of mutton, turnips & beans.

hark *v* listen to; **h. back** revert to a subject.

harlequin *n* comic character in pantomime; *a* multi-coloured; *n* **harlequinade** pantomime scene; buffoonery.

harlot *n* prostitute, whore.

harm *n* hurt, damage, physical or moral; *v* injure, hurt; *as* **harmful, harmless** without harm; innocent.

harmony *n* concord; agreement; melodious sound, chord; *a* **harmonic** of harmony; *n* one of components of complex musical tone; *n pl* **harmonics** science, art of musical harmony; *a* **harmonious** in harmony; melodious; *n* **harmonica** mouth-organ; *v* **harmonize** bring into harmony; reconcile; be in harmony; *n* **harmonization**; *n* **harmonium** small organ.

harness *n* straps, usually leather, and fastenings of horse; any gear resembling this; *v* put into harness; (*fig*) control, use.

harp *n* musical instrument, with strings plucked by hand; *v* play harp; refer to tediously; *ns* **harper, harpist**; **harpsichord** forerunner of piano.

harpoon *n* barbed spear with rope attached, for striking whales & large fish; *v* strike with h.; *ns* **harpooner, harpoon-gun** one used to fire harpoon.

harpy *n* mythical monster, half woman, half bird; cruel merciless person.

harridan *n* worn-out old woman; hag.

harrier *n* hound used in hunting hares; low-flying hawk.
harrow *n* spiked frame dragged over ground, to break it up; *v* use harrow; (*fig*) cause mental distress; *a* **harrowing** heart-rending.
harry *v* ravage; harass, annoy.
harsh *a* rough to touch; discordant; glaring; severe.
hart *n* adult male deer; *n* **hartshorn** salvolatile, formerly distilled from hart's antlers; *n* **hart's-tongue** fern with long narrow leaves.
harum-scarum *a* reckless; careless; irresponsible.
harvest *n* gathering in of crops; yield of the land or sea; season of gathering; *v* reap, gather in; *n* **harvester** reaping machine.
hash *n* dish of chopped cooked meat; (*coll*) mess, muddle; (*abb*) hashish; *v* chop up; mismanage.
hashish *n* dried Indian hemp, used as narcotic.
hasp *n* metal clasp, or hinged flap for fastening door etc.
hassock *n* tuft of coarse grass; kneeling cushion.
haste *n* speed, hurry, quickness; *v* **hasten** urge on; hurry, move with haste; *a* **hasty**; *adv* **hastily**.
hat *n* head-covering, usually with crown and brim; *n* **hatter** one who makes, sells hats.
hatch *n* trap door covering opening (in ship's deck; floor or roof); opening in wall between kitchen and dining room; *n* **hatchway** opening in ship's deck.
hatch *v* incubate; bring forth (young) from shell; emerge from egg.
hatch *v* shade in fine lines (for engraving).
hatchet *n* small axe; tomahawk.
hate *v* dislike intensely; detest; *n* loathing; *n* **hatred** profound ill-will; *a* **hateful**.
haughty *a* proud, disdainful; arrogant; *n* **haughtiness**.
haul *v* drag, pull with effort; transport; (*naut*) alter ship's course; *n* act of hauling; distance hauled; (*fig*) booty; *ns* **haulage** carting, conveying of goods; charge for this; **haulier** carter; man who hauls coal in mine.
haulm *n* dried stalks; stubble; straw.
haunch *n* hip, upper thigh & buttock; hind quarter.

haunt *v* visit habitually, frequent; (*fig*) fill mind of; *n* habitual resort of human or animal.
hautboy *n* oboe.
hauteur *n* haughty aloofness.
have *v* possess, own; be held, affected with; bear (offspring); obtain; be obliged to do; (as auxiliary, forms compound past tenses); *pt* & *pp* **had**; *pr p* **having**.
haven *n* harbour; (*fig*) refuge, shelter.
haversack *n* canvas bag for carrying rations, camping equipment etc.
havoc *n* devastation, destruction.
haw *n* red fruit of hawthorn; *ns* **hawthorn** thorny shrub with white, pink or red flowers.
haw *v* hesitate in speech; *n* inarticulate sound expressing doubt.
hawk *n* short-winged long-tailed falcon; *v* hunt with hawks.
hawk *v* sell from door to door; (*fig*) spread about; **hawker** *n* itinerant seller of wares.
hawk *v* clear throat noisily; spit phlegm.
hawse *n* part of ship's bows where anchor cables pass through holes.
hawser *n* large rope or small cable.
hay *n* grass mown and dried for fodder; *ns* **haycock** heap of hay; **hayseed** grass seed; **haystack** rick of hay; **hay-fever** allergic catarrh of nose and throat.
hazard *n* game of chance, played with dice; chance, risk, danger; *v* expose to risk; *a* **hazardous** risky.
haze *n* mist, vapour; *a* **hazy** misty, obscured; vague, confused (mental state).
hazel *n* tree with edible nuts; light brown colour; *a*.
he *masc nom pron* (*3rd pers sing*) male person etc just referred to; as *prefix* **he-** denotes male animal; *n* **he-man** (*coll*) virile man.
head *n* top or foremost part of body consisting of bony cavity containing brain, sense organs, face, jaws, ears etc, top upper part of anything; leader; (*fig*) intelligence; promontory; side of coin with ruler's head on it; froth on beer etc; crisis; source of river; (*sl*) headache; *v* lead; divert course of; be at top; hit (ball) with head; make for; *a* chief, senior;

ns **headache** pain in head; worrying problem; **header** plunge head first; **heading** title over chapter, at top of page; **headland** steep cliff jutting into sea; **headline** large type summary in newspaper; **headquarters** (*pl*) centre of operations of any organization; **headway** progress; *as* **headlong** head fore-most; (*fig*) hurried, rash; **headstrong** self-willed; **heady** rash; intoxicating.

heal *v* make, become sound or healthy; cure; *n* **health** state of well-being; bodily condition; toast drunk wishing one health & prosperity; *as* **healthful** promoting good health; **healthy** in good health; vigorous; *n* **healthiness.**

heap *n* piled-up mass of things; large number or quantity; *v* amass; form into heap.

hear *v* perceive by ear; listen to; (*leg*) try as judge; learn; *pt* & *pp* **heard**; *ns* **hearer, hearing** sense by which sound is perceived; formal, official listening; **hearsay** rumour.

hearken *v* listen attentively.

hearse *n* funeral carriage for coffin.

heart *n* muscular organ which pumps blood round the body; (*fig*) seat of human emotions, affection, courage etc; core, central part; *v* **hearten** cheer up, encourage; *as* **heartfelt** sincere; **heartfree** not being in love; **heartless** unfeeling, cruel; **heart-rending** deeply moving; **hearty** vigorous; cordial; jovial; *n* **heartsease** wild pansy.

hearth *n* place where domestic fire is made; (*fig*) home.

heat *n* hotness; sensation of warmth; (*fig*) strong emotion; period of sexual desire in female mammals; eliminating round or course in race or contest; *v* make, become hot; *a* **heated** excited, vehement.

heath *n* open, shrubby ground; heather, ling.

heathen *n* one who does not believe in God; barbarous, irreligious person; *a* unenlightened; savage; *a* **heathenish** (*fig*) barbarous; pagan.

heather *n* plant of heath family, growing on heaths and mountains.

heave *v* lift up; drag along; throw (something heavy); utter (sigh); (of waves) rise up, swell; retch; *n.*

heaven *n* abode of God; sky; (*fig*) state of extreme felicity; *a* **heavenly** of, from heaven; (*sl*) delightful, beautiful.

heavy *a* weighty; difficult to lift; serious; dull; overcast; severe; clumsy, indigestible; sad, gloomy; *ns* **heaviness, h. water** water in which hydrogen has been replaced by deuterium; deuterium oxide.

hebdomadal *a* weekly.

hebetude *n* dullness, stupidity.

hecatomb *n* sacrifice of 100 oxen; (*fig*) massacre.

heckle *v* interrupt public speaker with questions; *n* **heckler.**

hect-, hecto *prefix* hundred.

hectic *a* consumptive; flushed; (*sl*) exciting, rushed, busy.

hector *v* bully, browbeat, bluster at.

hedge *n* shrubs planted closely as fence or boundary; *v* enclose with, plant, hedge; (*fig*) place secondary bet as protection against loss; (*coll*) refuse to commit oneself; *ns* **hedgehog** small wild spiny mammal; **hedger** man who makes, repairs hedges; **hedgerow** wild hedge; **hedge sparrow.**

hedonism *n* theory that pleasure is the chief good; *n* **hedonist.**

heed *v* take notice; regard carefully; *a* **heedless** careless; reckless.

heel *n* hind part of foot; part of shoe, boot supporting this; last part; *v* supply with heel; pass (ball) out of scrum with heel.

heel *v* tilt to one side, *esp* of ship; cause to do this; *n* list.

hefty *a* weighty; muscular; big and strong.

hegemony *n* leadership; political control.

heifer *n* young cow that has not yet calved.

height *n* vertical dimension; loftiness; culmination; hill; *v* **heighten** make, become higher; augment.

heinous *a* hateful; atrocious; odious.

heir *n* one who succeeds to another's rank, property, on the death of the latter; (*fem*) **heiress;** *n* **heirloom** object inherited from ancestors; chattel that goes with real estate.

helical *a* spiral.

helicopter *n* aircraft deriving lift from horizontally rotating rotors.
heliograph *n* signalling device using reflected rays of sun.
heliotrope *n* plant of borage family, with fragrant purple flowers; *a* colour of flowers; *a* **heliotropic** turning towards sun.
helium *n* light non-inflammable gaseous element.
hell *n* abode of damned souls; place, state of intense suffering, misery, cruelty; (*fig*) gambling den; *a* **hellish** (*coll*) very unpleasant.
hellebore *n* Christmas rose.
Hellenic *a* Greek.
helm *n* steering wheel of ship, tiller; (*fig*) place of control; *n* **helmsman** steersman.
helmet *n* protective covering for head.
help *v* aid, assist; serve, supply; alleviate; be able, unable to avert (something); *n* **helper**; *as* **helpful, helpless** powerless; useless; *n* **helpmate, helpmeet** comrade, partner, husband or wife.
helter-skelter *adv* in disorderly haste.
hem *n* edge of cloth turned up and stitched; *v* sew thus; confine; *n* **hemstitch** decorative stitch.
hemisphere *n* half a sphere; half of earth's surface; *a* **hemispherical**.
hemlock *n* plant producing powerful sedative; poison extracted from it.
hemp *n* plant, fibre of which is used for rope; narcotic drug made from it; *a* **hempen**.
hen *n* female domestic fowl, or any bird; *a* **hen-pecked** nagged by wife.
hence *adv* from this; therefore; *adv* **henceforth, henceforward** from now onwards.
henchman *n* trusty attendant; staunch supporter.
henna *n* Asiatic shrub; red dye for hair made from it.
henry *n* international unit of inductance.
hepatic *n* pertaining to liver.
hepta- *prefix* seven; *n* **heptagon** plane figure with seven sides; **heptateuch** first seven books of Bible.
her *a obj* & *poss* case of SHE; *pron* **hers** of her; *pron* **herself**.
herald *n* official who makes public announcements

or arranges ceremonies; one charged with care of armorial bearings etc; forerunner, harbinger; *v* announce; usher in; *a* **heraldic**; *n* **heraldry** study of use of armorial bearings.

herb *n* plant whose stem dies down annually; one used in medicine, or flavouring; *as* **herbaceous** dying down in winter; perennial flowering; **herbal** of herbs; *ns* **herbage** grass, pasture; **herbalist** dealer in medicinal herbs; **herbarium** collection of preserved plants.

herd *n* group, flock of animals, usually of same species, living, feeding together; (*fig*) rabble, mob; *v* tend (herd); huddle together; *n* **herdsman.**

here *adv* in, towards this place; at this point; *adv* **hereafter** in future; *n* life after death; *adv* **herewith.**

heredity *n* passing of bodily, mental characteristics from parent to child; *a* **hereditary** passing by inheritance or heredity; *n* **hereditament** thing that can be inherited.

heresy *n* erroneous religious belief; opinion contrary to orthodox one; *n* **heretic** one guilty of religious heresy; *a* **heretical.**

heritage *n* inheritance; characteristic derived from ancestors; *a* **heritable.**

hermaphrodite *n* human being, animal, plant with both male and female characteristics.

hermetic *a* air-tight; *adv* **hermetically** so as to be perfectly closed.

hermit *n* one living in solitude, for prayer, meditation; (*fig*) recluse; *n* **hermitage** cell of hermit.

hernia *n* rupture *esp* abdominal.

hero *n* one noted for valour, noble qualities; chief male character in play, book etc; demigod; (*pl*) **heroes**; (*fem*) **heroine**; *a* **heroic** courageous; larger than life; (*n pl*) **heroics** bombastic talk, behaviour; *ns* **heroism** courage; **hero worship** excessive admiration of someone.

heroin *n* narcotic, habit-forming drug, derived from morphine.

heron *n* long-necked, long-legged wading bird.

herpes *n* skin disease; shingles.

herring *n* edible sea-fish; *n* **herring-bone** pattern of criss-cross lines.
hesitate *v* pause in doubt; falter; be reluctant; *a* **hesitant** undecided; *ns* **hesitancy, hesitation** indecision; speech impediment.
heterodox *a* unorthodox.
heterogenous *a* composed of unrelated kinds.
heterosexual *a* of different sex; normally sexual.
hew *v* chop, hack; fell with axe; *pt* **hewed**; *pp* **hewed, hewn**; *n* **hewer**.
hexagon *n* plane figure with six sides; *a* **hexagonal** six-sided.
hexameter *n* verse of six feet.
hey-day *n* peak, acme, prime.
hiatus *n* gap; break in continuity; slight pause between two vowels.
hibernate *v* pass winter in torpid state; *ns* **hibernation, hibernator**.
Hibernian *n* & *a* (native) of Ireland.
hibiscus *n* rose-mallow; showy flowering plant.
hiccup, hiccough *n* spasm of diaphragm, with closure of glottis; sound made by this; *v* utter this sound.
hickory *n* N. American hardwood tree bearing nuts.
hide *n* raw or dressed animal skin; *n* (*sl*) **hiding** thrashing; *a* **hidebound** (*fig*) narrow-minded.
hide *v* conceal; cover up; keep secret; *pt* **hid**; *pp* **hidden**; *pr p* **hiding**.
hideous *a* repulsive, horrible.
hie *v* hasten.
hierarchy *n* rank, order, class of sacred persons; any graded system of officials.
hieroglyph *n* symbol used in ancient Egyptian picture writing; (*fig*) secret writing; *a* **hieroglyphic**.
higgledy-piggledy *a* & *adv* completely disordered; jumbled up.
high *a* tall, lofty; exalted in rank, office; main; intense, very great; (of sound) shrill, acute; (of meat) tainted; *adv* to, at high level, degree; at high pitch; *n* **highbrow** intellectual; **Highlands** mountainous country, *esp* of Scotland; **highlight** best, most conspicuous part; *v* emphasize; *n* **high-**

way public road; **highwayman** robber, *esp* mounted, of travellers by road; **highflown** bombastic; **high-handed** domineering; **high-strung** excitable; *n* **highness** quality of being high; title given to Royal princes.

hijack *v* (*coll*) steal by force; steal (goods) from smuggler.

hike *v* tramp; walk through country; *n* walking excursion; *n* **hiker.**

hilarity *n* cheerfulness, mirth, jollity; *a* **hilarious.**

hill *n* small elevation of earth's surface; small artificial mound; *n* **hillock** little hill; *a* **hilly.**

hilt *n* handle of sword, dagger.

him *pron* objective case of HE; *pron* **himself** emphatic form.

hind *n* female of red deer.

hind, hinder *a* at back, posterior.

hinder *v* impede, obstruct; prevent; *n* **hindrance.**

Hindu *n* Aryan non-Moslem of N. India; *n* **Hindi** language of N. India.

hinge *n* joint on which door, lid etc hangs and turns; *v* provide hinge; (*fig*) depend on.

hint *n* indirect suggestion; brief advice; *v* give hint of; make hint.

hinterland *n* district behind coast, or that served by port.

hip *n* projecting part of upper thigh; fruit of briar or rose.

hippodrome *n* arena for chariot-racing, horse-shows etc.

hippopotamus *n* large ungainly amphibious African mammal.

hircine *a* goat-like.

hire *n* payment for services of person, or use of thing; *v* engage for wages; pay for temporary use; *ns* **hireling** mercenary person; **hire purchase** payment by instalments, with right of use after first payment.

hirsute *a* hairy.

his *pron* & *a* belonging to him.

hiss *v* make noise like sound of prolonged S; express disapproval, scorn by this sound; *n* **hissing.**

hist *interj* hush! be silent!
histology *n* study of structure of organic tissues; *n* **histologist**.
history *n* systematic record of past events in existence of nation, individual, etc; study of such events; methodical account of evolution of language, art etc; *n* **historian** writer of history; *as* **historic** famous; epoch-making; **historical** based on, recorded in history; *n* **natural h.** zoology; botany.
histrionic *a* pertaining to actors, acting; dramatic *n pl* acting for effect.
hit *v* strike, knock with blow, missile; injure; find by design or luck; reach target; *pt* & *pp* **hit**; *n* blow, stroke; (*coll*) popular success; *adv* **h. or miss** casual; *v* **h. it off** get on well with.
hitch *v* raise with jerk; fasten by hook; become entangled; *n* jerk; knot; slight hindrance; *v* **hitch-hike** travel by getting free lifts in cars, lorries etc; *a* **hitched** (*sl*) married.
hither *adv* to, towards this place; *a* nearer, on this side; *adv* **hitherto** until now, up to this time.
hive *n* box for honey bees to live in; (*fig*) busy place; *v* gather, place in hive.
hives *n pl* skin eruption; croup.
hoard *n* secret store; hidden treasure; *v* amass, gather and keep hidden.
hoarding *n* temporary wooden fence, *esp* one used for posters.
hoarfrost *n* frozen dew; *a* **hoar** covered with hoar frost.
hoarse *a* husky, rough, harsh; *n* **hoarseness**.
hoary *a* grey with age; (*fig*) ancient; greyish-white.
hoax *n* practical joke; mischievous trick; *v* play practical joke upon; *n* **hoaxer**.
hob *n* ledge beside grate for keeping things hot; peg used as mark in quoits etc.
hobble *v* limp, walk clumsily; tie two legs (of horse etc) together to prevent straying; *n* straps, rope used to hobble animal.
hobbledehoy *n* awkward, bad mannered youth.
hobby *n* favourite leisure occupation; *n* **h.-horse** rocking-horse; (*fig*) hobby.

hobby *n* small European species of falcon.
hobgoblin *n* mischievous imp; *n* **hob** rustic elf.
hobnail *n* large headed nail for studding boots.
hobnob *v* be on familiar terms with.
hobo *n* tramp; migratory worker.
hock *n* joint in middle of hind leg of horse, ox etc; *v* hamstring.
hock *n* Rhenish white wine.
hockey *n* game played with ball and curved sticks, in field or on ice.
hocus-pocus *n* trickery; conjuror's jargon; nonsense; *v* **hocus** dupe; swindle; stupefy with drugs.
hod *n* small trough on handle for carrying bricks, mortar etc.
hoe *n* tool for breaking soil, weeding etc; *v* use hoe.
hog *n* adult male pig, *esp* castrated one; (*fig*) greedy, filthy person; *n* **hogshead** large cask; liquid measure, 52½ imp. gallons.
Hogmanay *n* (*Scot*) New Year's Eve.
hoiden, hoyden *n* ungainly, rough girl; tomboy.
hoi-polloi *n* common people; the masses.
hoist *v* raise with tackle; heave, lift up; *n*.
hold *v* grasp, keep in hand; keep in position; occupy; maintain (opinion); remain fixed; enclose; retain (in mind); restrain; be valid; detain; celebrate; occur; *pt* & *pp* **held**; *n* grip; control; fortress; *ns* **holdall** roomy portable bag; **hold-up** armed robbery; traffic delay.
hold *n* space below deck, for cargo, in ship.
hole *n* cavity; opening; tear, rent; outlet; den, burrow; *v* make, go into hole.
holiday *n* day, time of rest from work; time of recreation; religious festival; *a* festive.
hollo, holloa *interj* loud call for attention; *v* shout.
holland *n* coarse unbleached linen fabric.
hollow *n* cavity; depression; hole; small valley; *a* not solid; sunken; echoing; (*fig*) insincere; *v* make hollow; scoop out.
holly *n* evergreen shrub with glossy, prickly leaves and red berries.
hollyhock *n* tall, spiked, flowering garden plant.
holm *n* islet, *esp* in river; rich land near river.

holmoak, holm *n* evergreen oak, ilex.
holocaust *n* complete destruction by fire.
holograph *n* document hand-written by signatory.
holster *n* leather case for pistol, hung from belt etc.
holt *n* copse; wooded hill.
holy *a* pertaining to God; sacred, deeply pious; *n* **holiness** sanctity; title of Pope; *n* **Holy Week** one before Easter Sunday.
homage *n* declaration of allegiance; (*fig*) honour, respect, devotion.
home *n* family dwelling-place; family, native place; place of rest, asylum; *a* pertaining to home or country; native; *adv* to, at home; *as* **homeless, homely** simple; plain; **homesick** pining for home; *n* **homespun** home-made cloth; **homestead** farm; *adv* **homeward, -s** towards home; *v* **h. on to** be automatically guided to (target).
homicide *n* killer, killing of human being; *a* **homicidal.**
homily *n* sermon; (*fig*) tedious lecture.
homo-, homoeo- *prefix: forms compounds with meaning* same, same kind. *Where the meaning may be deduced from the simple word, the compounds are not given here.*
homoeopathy *n* treatment of disease, by minute doses of drug, which in normal person produces symptoms like those of disease itself.
homogeneous *a* belonging to same category; uniform.
homonym *n* word differing in meaning, but sounded alike.
homosexual *a* morbidly attracted to one's own sex; *n* **homosexuality.**
hone *n* whetstone; *v* sharpen.
honest *a* straightforward, not criminal, sincere; open frank; *n* **honesty** integrity; trustworthiness; garden herb, with transparent seed pods.
honey *n* sweet sticky fluid made from nectar by bees; *n* **honeycomb** mass of hexagonal wax cells, made by bees, to store honey or larvae; *v* pierce with many holes; riddle; *ns* **honeydew** sweet deposit on plants; **honeysuckle** climbing plant

with fragrant flowers; **honeymoon** holiday spent alone by newly-married couple.

honk *n* cry of wild goose; similar sound *esp* of motor horn; *v* to make this sound.

honour *n* respect, esteem; good reputation; moral dignity, high rank; mark of esteem; *pl* distinction in University exam; court cards; *v* esteem highly; confer honour on; pay (bill, draft etc) when due; *as* **honourable, honorary** given, done as honour; giving services without pay; **honorific** conferring, expressing honour; *n* **honorarium** voluntary payment for services.

hood *n* soft covering for head and neck; cowl; folding roof of car etc; chimney-cowl; *v* cover with hood; *v* **hoodwink** deceive.

hoodoo *n* bad luck; curse.

hoof *n* horny sheath protecting animal's foot; (*pl*) **hoofs** or **hooves.**

hook *n* curved piece of metal, wood, plastic or other substance, for holding, hanging, catching or pulling something; curved cutting implement; blow with bent arm in boxing; *v* grasp, seize, hold, fasten with hook; hit ball to striker's left; *n* **hook-worm** parasitic worm.

hookah *n* Oriental pipe, in which smoke passes through tube and water-bottle.

hooligan *n* noisy, destructive (*usu* young) ruffian.

hoop *n* circular band of wood, metal *esp* to bind cask; large ring of wood, bowled along, as toy; *v* bind with hoop.

hoopoe *n* bird with handsome crest and plumage.

hoot *n* cry of owl; sound of motor-horn etc; cry of derision; *v* utter hoots; cause to hoot.

hop *n* plant whose flowers are used in making beer; (*pl*) dried flower cones; *v* gather, produce hops; *ns* **hopping** gathering hops; **hop-garden.**

hop *v* jump on one leg; advance so; *n* leap; informal dance; (*coll*) short aircraft flight.

hope *n* confident expectation of something desired; likelihood that something desired will happen; thing, person, action which inspires hope; *v* entertain hope; desire and expect; *a* **hopeful**; *n* **young h.** promising boy or girl; *a* **hopeless.**

hopper *n* funnel-like device for feeding grain to mill, coal to machine etc; self-discharging dredging barge, or rail truck; that which hops; hop picker.

horal, horary *a* pertaining to an hour; hourly; lasting an hour.

horde *n* band of warlike nomads; destructive gang, rabble.

horizon *n* circle bounding visible part of earth's surface; line where earth and sky seem to meet; (*fig*) limits of interest, mental outlook; *a* **horizontal** parallel with horizon; level.

hormone *n* internal secretion by glands, which stimulates functional activity of organs of body.

horn *n* one of hard bony pointed growths on head of cow etc; substance of horns; various things made of, or like it; wind-instrument; warning device on car, lighthouse etc; *as* **horned** having horns; **horny**; *n* **hornpipe** old wind-instrument; sailors' dance.

hornbeam *n* deciduous tree, resembling beech.

hornblende *n* mineral found in granite & other igneous rocks.

hornet *n* large species of wasp.

horology *n* art of clock-making, or measuring time; *n* **horologer** clock- or watch-maker.

horoscope *n* calculation of positions of heavenly bodies at particular moment, *esp* of person's birth, to predict fortune, character etc.

horror *n* terror; disgust; repulsion; its cause; *as* **horrible** causing horror; shocking; terrifying; **horrid** frightful, disgusting; *v* **horrify** excite horror in; *a* **horrific** horrifying.

hors d'oeuvre *n* light savoury dish served before meal as appetizer.

horse *n* large four-footed domesticated mammal, used for riding on, or draught; stallion; cavalry; frame with legs, for support; vaulting-block; *ns* **horse-chestnut** tree bearing glossy brown nuts; **horse-power** unit of power, force required to raise 550 lb. one ft. per sec.; **horseshoe** strip of

metal nailed to rim of horse's hoof, to protect it; **horseman, horsewoman** rider on horse; *a* **horsy** fond of, having to do with horses, horse-racing.
hortative, hortatory *a* exhorting; admonitory.
hosanna *interj* Hebrew exclamation of praise.
hose *n* flexible tube for carrying water or other liquids; (*pl*) **hose** socks, stockings; *ns* **hosiery** men's underwear, socks, collars etc; shop dealing in this; stockings; **hosier.**
hospice *n* house of rest for travellers, *esp* one kept by monks; home for sick or poor.
hospital *n* place where sick and injured are cared for; *v* **hospitalize** send, admit to hospital; *n* **hospitalization.**
hospitality *n* cheerful, friendly entertainment, feeding and lodging of guests; *a* **hospitable** inviting, generous, friendly.
host *n* one who entertains a guest; hotelkeeper; (*fem*) **hostess.**
host *n* army; great number.
hostage *n* one given or taken as pledge that promises will be kept.
hostel *n* lodging-house for students, workers, young people etc.
hostile *a* unfriendly; warlike; *n* **hostility** enmity; (*pl*) **hostilities** acts of war.
hot *a* of high temperature; feeling, giving heat; pungent; (*fig*) violent; lustful; (*coll*, of news) exciting & fresh; (*sl*, of stolen goods) sought by police; angry; *n* **hotness, hotbed** bed of fermenting manure; (*fig*) place conducive to rapid growth (*usu* of vice etc); *a* **hot-headed** rash, impetuous; *ns* **hothouse** forcing house for plants; **hot water** (*coll*) trouble.
hotchpotch *n* thick stew with many ingredients; medley.
hotel *n* large, superior inn; *n* **hotelier.**
hound *n* dog, hunting by scent; *v* pursue, persecute.
hour *n* sixty minutes; 1/24th part of day; fixed point of time; (*pl*) regular time of work; *adv* **hourly** every hour; *n* **hour-glass** sand-glass which runs out in 1 hour.

houri *n* nymph in Mohammedan paradise; seductive woman.
house *n* dwelling designed for human habitation; hotel, inn etc; business firm; legislative assembly or building used for such; family, lineage; *v* provide house for; harbour; *ns* **housebreaker** burglar; demolisher of houses; **household** persons living together in house; **householder** head of household; **housekeeper** woman employed to run house; **housemaid** maidservant; **house-warming** party to celebrate entry into new home; **housewife** mistress of household; **housey-housey** game of chance, bingo; **housing** providing with house; protective covering.
hovel *n* mean dwelling.
hover *v* (of birds) float motionless in air; (*fig*) linger, hesitate; *n* **hovercraft** craft moving along, on cushion of air, over land or water.
how *adv* in what way; by what means; to what degree; *adv* **however** nevertheless; all the same.
howdah *n* covered seat on elephant's back.
howitzer *n* gun with high-angle firing, at low velocity.
howl *v* utter loud dismal cry; *n* such cry; *n* **howler** person, animal or thing that howls; (*sl*) stupid mistake.
hub *n* central part of wheel; (*fig*) centre of activity or importance.
hubbub *n* uproar; riot.
huckaback *n* strong, rough, linen towelling.
huckleberry *n* N. American shrub; its fruit.
huckster *n* hawker; pedlar; *v* haggle; carry on petty trade.
huddle *v* heap, gather into confused mass; crowd together; *n* such a crowd.
hue *n* colour, tint; complexion.
hue and cry *n* loud outcry; angry pursuit.
huff *v* bully, hector; take offence; (draughts) remove opponents piece as forfeit; *n* sulkiness; *a* **huffy**; *adv* **huffily**.
hug *v* embrace warmly; clasp tightly in arms; (*fig*) keep close to; *n* act of hugging.

huge *a* very great, enormous.
hula *n* Hawaiian woman's dance.
hulk *n* derelect, dismantled ship; (*fig*) clumsy, unwieldy person; *a* **hulking** big and clumsy.
hull *n* body of ship; pod, shell of pea; *v* pierce hull of ship; remove hull from pea.
hullabaloo *n* uproar, din, clamour.
hum *v* produce low buzzing, droning sound, as bee; utter musical sound with closed lips; *n* continuous low drone; *n* **humming-bird** small tropical bird making humming noise with wings.
human *a* pertaining to mankind; associated with man; *adv* **humanly** in human manner; *a* **humane** kind; merciful; *ns* **humanism** system of thought dealing with human interests; **humanist** classical scholar; **humanity** human race as whole; kindness of heart (*pl*) **Humanities** classical literary studies; **humanitarian** philanthropist; *v* **humanize** make, become human, humane.
humble *a* lowly, meek, modest; not exalted in rank, position; *v* abase; put to shame; *adv* **humbly**.
humble-bee *n* large wild stingless bee.
humbug *n* hoax; nonsense; empty, boastful person; peppermint sweetmeat; *v* deceive, dupe.
humdrum *a* commonplace, dull.
humerus *n* bone of upper arm in man; *a* **humeral** of shoulder.
humid *a* moist, damp; *n* **humidity**; *v* **humidify**.
humiliate *v* put to shame; lower pride of; abase; *n* **humiliation**.
humility *n* quality of being humble; meekness.
hummock *n* knoll, hillock; ridge of ice.
humour *n* mood, state of mind; fun; jocular action, saying; whim, fancy; *v* indulge moods; act tactfully; *n* **humourist, humorist** one who makes jokes; comic writer, artist or actor; *a* **humorous** laughable, funny; amusing.
hump *n* rounded lump, bulge or mound; (*sl*) mental depression; *v* carry on back; **humpback** person with spinal deformity; *a* **humpbacked** having hump.
humus *n* decayed plant and animal tissue in soil.

hunch *n* hump, hunk; (*sl*) premonition; *v* stoop, draw shoulders up; *n* **hunchback** humpback.

hundred *n* cardinal number, ten times ten; subdivision of county; *a* **hundredth** ordinal number; *a* & *adv* **hundredfold**; *n* **hundredweight** measure of weight = 112 lbs. or 1/20th ton.

hunger *n* desire for food; exhaustion, emaciation due to lack of food; (*fig*) craving; *v* **h. strike** refusal of all food, as protest; *a* **hungry** feeling hunger; starving; *adv* **hungrily**.

hunk *n* thick piece.

hunt *v* pursue (animals), often with hounds in order to kill, or catch; pursue (person); search for, track down; *n* search; local association of persons with their horses, hounds engaged in hunting; *ns* **huntsman** man in charge of hounds; **hunter**; (*fem*) **huntress**.

hurdle *n* light wooden framework, as temporary fence or to jump over; *n* **hurdler** one who runs in hurdle races; **hurdle-race** race in which series of fences or hurdles are leapt.

hurl *v* throw violently; hurtle; *ns* **hurling** Irish or Cornish ball-game; **hurler**.

hurrah *interj* shout of joy, applause.

hurricane *n* violent wind-storm, of 75 m.p.h. or more; tropical cyclone; *n* **hurricane-lamp** lamp with well-shielded flame.

hurry *v* move, do quickly; hasten; urge to haste; *v* & *n* **hurry-scurry** rush.

hurt *v* cause pain to; injure, distress; damage; *pt* & *pp* **hurt**; *n* harm; wound; pain; *a* showing, feeling pain, offence; *a* **hurtful**.

hurtle *v* move violently; dash against; whirl.

husband *n* married man; *v* manage thriftily; *n* **ship's h.**, agent managing ship's business for owners.

hush *v* make, become silent, quiet; *n* silence, stillness.

husk *n* dry covering of certain seeds; *v* strip husk from; *a* **husky** dry as husk; hoarse; harsh, rasping.

husky *n* Eskimo sledge dog.

hussar *n* light cavalryman.

hussy *n* pert, ill-mannered girl.

hustings *n pl* Guildhall Court; electioneering platform; election proceedings.
hustle *v* hurry; jostle; urge along roughly; *n* bustle, hurry; *n* **hustler** one who gets things done.
hut *n* shed, small wooden building; hovel; *n* **hutment** encampment of huts.
hutch *n* box, bin, chest; box-like coop for rabbits etc.
hyacinth *n* bulbous plant of lily family, with spikes of bell-like flowers.
hyaena *n* carnivorous dog-like animal.
hyaline *a* crystalline, transparent.
hybrid *n* animal or plant produced by parents of different species; (*fig*) anything derived from mixed origins; *a* cross-bred; *v* **hybridize** cross-fertilize; interbreed.
hydra *n* (*myth*) many-headed serpent; freshwater polyp.
hydrant *n* pipe from water-main, with attachment for hose.
hydraulic *a* conveying water; water-powered; *n pl* science dealing with flow of liquids.
hydr-, hydro- *prefix: forms compounds with meaning of* water, e.g. **hydroplane** *n* seaplane. *Where the meaning may be deduced from the simple word, such compounds are not given here.*
hydrodynamics *n pl* mathematical study of liquids in motion.
hydroelectric *a* pertaining to electricity generated by water power.
hydropathy *n* water-cure.
hydrogen *n* colourless gas combining with oxygen to form water; **h. bomb** highly destructive atom bomb.
hygiene *n* science and principles of maintaining health; cleanliness; *a* **hygienic.**
hygrometer *n* instrument for measuring humidity of atmosphere.
hymeneal *a* of marriage.
hymn *n* song of praise *esp* to God; *a* **hymnal** of hymns.
hyoscine *n* poisonous alkaloid, used as nerve sedative.

hyper- *prefix: forms compounds with meaning of* excessive, above; *e.g.* **hypercritical** *a* too critical. *Where the meaning may be deduced from the simple word, such compounds are not given here.*
hyperbola *n* curve formed by section of cone when cutting plane makes larger angle with base than side makes.
hyperbole *n* rhetorical exaggeration.
hyperborean *a* & *n* (inhabitant) of extreme North.
hyphen *n* mark (-) indicating that two words or syllables are connected; *a* **hyphenated.**
hypnosis *n* induction of sleep; artificially induced state resembling deep sleep; *a* **hypnotic** inducing sleep; *v* **hypnotize** affect with hypnosis; *ns* **hypnotist, hypnotism.**
hypo-, hyph-, hyp- *prefix: forms compounds with meaning of* below, less, under. *Such compounds are not given where the meaning may be deduced from the simple word.*
hypo *n* solution of hyposulphite used in developing film negatives.
hypochondria *n* morbid obsession with one's health; *n* **hypochondriac;** *a* **hypochondriacal.**
hypocrisy *n* pretending to be better morally than one is; *n* **hypocrite, hypocritical.**
hypodermic *a* under the skin; *n* **h. syringe** one used for giving such injection.
hypotenuse *n* side of right-angled triangle opposite the right angle.
hypothermia *n* very low body temperature, *esp* in old people.
hypothesis *n* supposition; unproved theory; *pl* **-eses;** *a* **hypothetical.**
hyrax *n* small African & Asian mammal; rock-rabbit.
hyssop *n* kind of aromatic, pungent mint.
hysterectomy *n* surgical removal of uterus; *n* **hysterotomy** incision of uterus.
hysteria *n* extreme emotional excitability, and loss of will-power; *a* **hysteric(al);** *n pl* **hysterics** fit of hysteria.

I *pron* (1st per sing nom) myself; (*pl* **we**).
iambus *n* metrical foot of short & long syllable.
ibex *n* large-horned wild goat.
ibis *n* wading bird with long curved bill.
ice *n* frozen water; ice-cream; *v* chill, cover with ice; cover with sugar; *ns* **iceberg** large mass of floating ice; **ice-cream** frozen cream, etc, sweetened & flavoured; **ice-floe** sheet of floating ice; **icicle** hanging spike of ice formed by freezing, trickling water; *a* **icy** ice-like; very cold; (*fig*) frigid; *adv* **icily**.
ichneumon *n* small Eastern animal, like weasel; *n* **ichneumon fly** parasitic insect.
ichor *n* thin fluid discharge from wounds or sores.
ichthyology *n* branch of zoology, dealing with fish; *n* **ichthyosaurus** extinct marine reptile.
icon *n* image; sacred portrait; *n* **iconoclast** (*fig*) one who attacks established customs and beliefs.
id *n* (*psych*) instinctive impulses of the individual.
idea *n* notion; opinion; scheme, plan; thought; imagination; *a* **ideal** visionary; of highest standard; *n* supreme perfection; standard of excellence to be copied; *ns* **idealism** practice of seeking perfection in all things; unrealistic attitude to life; **idealist** one who believes in idealism; impractical person; *v* **idealize** to make ideal; exaggerate good qualities of; *n* **idealization**; idealized view.
identity *n* individuality; absolute sameness; *a* **identical** the very same; *v* **identify** prove identity of; associate closely with; *n* **identification**.
ideograph *n* symbolic representation of an object, without naming it; *n* **ideography** shorthand writing; symbolic writing.
ideology *n* science of ideas; visionary theorizing; ideas forming basis of social, political, etc. system.
Ides *n pl* (Roman Calendar) 15th. March, May, July, October, 13th. of other months.
idiom *n* mode of expression; one peculiar to a language; dialect; *a* **idiomatic** characters of language; fluent & colloquial.
idiosyncrasy *n* individual peculiarity of manner, thought, way of speaking etc.
idiot *n* imbecile; person of defective intellect;

n **idiocy**; *a* **idiotic** utterly foolish, senseless; *adv* **idiotically.**

idle *a* inactive; lazy; futile; empty, trivial; *v* do nothing; (of engine) tick over; *ns* **idleness**; **idler**; time-waster; *adv* **idly.**

idol *n* image representing deity; false god; person, object of extreme devotion; *ns* **idolater** worshipper of false gods (*fem* **idolatress**); **idolatry**; *a* **idolatrous**; *v* **idolize** make an idol of; love, admire excessively.

idyll *n* short, simple poem on homely, pastoral subjects; romantic incident, usually rural; *a* **idyllic.**

if *conj* supposing that; even though; whenever; whether.

igloo *n* Eskimo hut of frozen snow blocks.

igneous *a* fiery; produced by volcanic action.

ignite *v* set on fire; be kindled; *n* **ignition** setting on fire; means of firing of explosive gaseous mixture by electric spark.

ignoble *a* base, degraded; humiliating, shameful; *adv* **ignobly.**

ignominy *n* dishonour, degradation; public disgrace; *a* **ignominious** shameful; humiliating.

ignorance *n* lack of education; inexperience; *a* **ignorant** uninformed; unaware; *n* **ignoramus** ignorant person.

ignore *v* disregard; refuse to consider.

iguana *n* large, crested S. American tree lizard.

iguanodon *n* huge, extinct herbivorous lizard.

ileum *n* lower part of small intestine.

ilex *n* holm-oak; evergreen oak.

ilk *a* (*Scots*) same; **of that ilk** of same name etc.; (*coll*) of that kind.

ill *a* sick, unwell; bad; unfavourable; sullen; imperfect; *n* harm; evil; misfortune; *n* **illness**; *as* **ill-advised** unwise; **ill-fated** unfortunate; **ill-favoured** ugly; **ill-natured** surly; **ill-omened** unlucky; *v* **ill-treat** treat unkindly; *n* **ill-will** malice.

illegal *a* unlawful; *n* **illegality.**

illegible *a* difficult to read; *n* **illegibility.**

illegitimate *a* unlawful; not born in wedlock; *n* **illegitimacy.**

illicit *a* prohibited; forbidden.
illimitable *a* boundless; vast, unlimited.
illiterate *a* unable to read or write; *n* **illiteracy.**
illogical *a* irrational; unsound.
illuminate *v* make light; adorn with lights; decorate (manuscript) with gold and colours; *n* **illumination**; *v* **illumine** enlighten.
illusion *v* deceptive appearance; delusion; *n* **illusionist** conjuror.
illustrate *v* make clear, explain; furnish (book etc.) with pictures; *ns* **illustration**; illustrator.
illustrious *a* famous, distinguished, glorious.
image *n* statue; simile; counterpart; idea; reflection (in mirror); *n* **imagery** images; mental pictures.
imagine *v* form image, idea in mind; suppose; *as* **imaginable**; **imaginary** not real; *n* **imagination** power of calling up mental images; fancy; *a* **imaginative.**
imago *n* final state of insect, *esp* of winged one.
imbecile *a* mentally deficient; *n* such a person; *n* **imbecility.**
imbibe *v* drink in; absorb; drink.
imbricated *a* overlapping; *v* imbricate.
imbroglio *n* complicated, confused situation.
imbue *v* saturate; dye; (*fig*) fill mind with.
imitate *v* copy closely; mimic; *n* **imitation** act of imitating; copy; counterfeit; *a* **imitative**; *n* **imitator.**
immaculate *a* pure; unsoiled; innocent.
immaterial *a* not consisting of matter; spiritual; unimportant.
immature *a* not adult; unripe; *n* **immaturity.**
immediate *a* next to; at once; contiguous.
immemorial *a* beyond living memory; very ancient.
immense *a* very great, vast; (*sl*) very good; *n* **-sity.**
immerse *v* dip, plunge into liquid; (*fig*) engross; *n* **immersion**; **i.heater** electric water heater.
immigrate *v* come to foreign country to live; *ns* **immigration**; **immigrant** (also *a*) person settling in foreign country.
imminent *a* impending; threatening; about to happen; *n* **imminence.**

immobile *a* not moving; fixed; *n* **immobility**; *v* **immobilize** render immobile.
immoderate *a* excessive; unrestrained.
immolate *v* kill; (*fig*) sacrifice; *n* **immolation**.
immortal *a* never dying; everlasting; *n* **immortality**.
immune *a* free from; exempt from; resistant to (disease); *v* **immunize**; *ns* **immunization** act of making immune; **immunity** state of being immune.
immure *v* shut up; enclose; imprison.
imp *n* little devil; mischievous child.
impact *n* collision; (*fig*) strong impression; *v* press strongly together.
impair *v* weaken; injure; *n* **impairment**.
impale *v* transfix *esp* on pointed stake; *n* **impalement**.
impart *v* transmit; make known; bestow.
impartial *a* unprejudiced; just; fair; *n* **impartiality**.
impassable *a* not capable of being crossed over.
impasse *n* deadlock; blind alley.
impassioned *a* ardent; passionate.
impassive *a* without emotion; calm; *n* **impassivity**.
impatient *a* intolerant of restraint; irritable, restless; *n* **impatience**.
impeach *v* indict, charge with crime *esp* high treason; *n* **impeachment**.
impeccable *a* faultless; incapable of sin; *n* **impeccability**.
impecunious *a* poor, hard up; *n* **impecuniosity**.
impede *v* obstruct; delay; *n* **impediment**.
impel *v* drive forward; urge on; force.
impend *v* overhang; be about to happen; threaten.
imperative *a* peremptory; urgent; necessary; *n* imperative mood.
imperfect *a* faulty; *n* **imperfection** blemish.
imperial *a* of empire or emperor; *n* type of beard; paper size; *ns* **imperialism** belief in colonial empire; **imperialist**.
imperil *v* endanger.
imperious *a* dominating; dictatorial; haughty.
impersonal *a* not distinctive; automatic; without feelings; (of verb) without personal subject.

impersonate *v* pretend to be another; act part of; *ns* **impersonation**; **impersonator**.
impertinent *a* irrelevant; impudent, insolent; *n* **impertinence**.
imperturbable *a* calm; not liable to be ruffled.
impervious *a* not allowing entry; (*fig*) insensible to.
impetigo *n* pustular skin disease.
impetuous *a* violent; rash, hasty; impulsive; *n* **impetuosity**.
impetus *n* momentum; driving force; (*fig*) stimulus.
impinge *v* fall on, against; infringe.
impious *a* without piety; ungodly.
implacable *a* inexorable; relentless; *n* **implacability**
implant *v* insert; (*fig*) instil (into mind).
implement *n* tool, utensil, instrument; *v* carry into effect; complete.
implicate *v* entangle; involve; include; *n* **implication**; *a* **implicit**; hinted at; unquestioning; *v* **imply** mean; hint, insinuate.
implore *v* ask for earnestly; entreat.
import *v* bring in (*esp* goods from abroad); signify, imply; *n* thing imported; consequence; *ns* **importation**; **importer**; *a* **important** distinguished; of consequence; essential; pompous; *n* **importance**.
importune *v* pester with troublesome demands; *a* **importunate**; *n* **importunity**.
impose *v* exact (tax etc.); palm off, foist upon; deceive; *ns* **imposition** act of imposing; tax; deception; task given as school punishment; **imposter** deceiver; charlatan; fraudulent person; **imposture**; **impost** tax, duty; weight carried by race-horse; *a* **imposing** impressive.
impossible *a* not feasible; (*coll*) insufferable; *n* **impossibility**.
impotent *a* powerless; feeble; lacking sexual capacity (*esp* of males); *n* **impotence**.
impound *v* confiscate; confine; enclose in pound.
impoverish *v* make poor; weaken; *n* **impoverishment**.
imprecation *n* curse.
impregnable *a* unassailable; invincible.

impregnate *v* make pregnant; fertilize; saturate; *n* **impregnation.**
impressario *n* theatrical, operatic manager.
impress *v* stamp; (*fig*) affect deeply; fix mark on; *n* **impression** number of copies of book etc. printed at one time; effect produced *esp* on mind; belief; *a* **impressionable** easily influenced; *ns* **impressionism** style of painting giving general effect without detail; **impressionist**; *a* **impressive** making great effect.
impress *v* compel to serve in army, navy.
imprest *n* loan made to individual by the State.
imprint *v* stamp; fix in mind; *n* mark, stamp made by pressure; publisher's, printer's name etc. in book.
imprison *v* put in prison; confine; *n* **imprisonment.**
impromptu *adv* & *a* without preparation; unrehearsed.
improve *v* make, become better; make good use of; *n* **improvement.**
improvident *a* imprudent; wanting foresight; *n* **improvidence.**
improvise *v* compose, do on spur of moment, *esp* with makeshift materials; *n* **improvisation.**
impudent *a* insolent, bold, saucy; *n* **impudence.**
impugn *v* criticize; challenge.
impulse *n* push; sudden inclination to act; stimulus; *n* **impulsion** impetus; *a* **impulsive** rash, acting without thought.
impunity *n* freedom, safety from penalty.
impure *a* dirty; adulterated; unchaste; *n* **impurity.**
impute *v* ascribe to; credit with; *n* **imputation** reproach; accusation.
in *prep* contained by; during; into; at end of (time); *adv* in, into some state, place etc.
in- *prefix*: *with forms* **il-, im-, ir-** *gives negative sense to simple words such as* **incapable, irreligious, illegal, immodest**; *also forms compounds with meaning of* in, upon, *eg* **ingress, irradiate**; *Such compounds are not given here, where the meaning may be deduced from the simple word.*
inadvertent *a* careless; unintentional; accidental.
inane *a* senseless; frivolous; *n* **inanity** silly remark.

inasmuch *adv* only **inasmuch as** seeing that, since.
inaugurate *v* install in office with ceremony; begin, open *esp* formally; *a* **inaugural**; *n* **inauguration.**
inauspicious *a* ill-omened; unlucky; unfavourable.
inboard *a* within, near centre on, ship.
inborn, inbred *a* inherent; natural; *n* **inbreeding** breeding from closely related stocks.
incalculable *a* beyond calculation; unpredictable; uncertain.
incandescent *a* luminous with heat; brilliant; *n* **incandescence**; *v* **incandesce.**
incantation *n* magic spell; charm.
incapacitate *v* render unfit; disable; disqualify; *n* **incapacity.**
incarcerate *v* imprison, confine; *n* **incarceration.**
incarnate *a* embodied in human form; personified; *v* give bodily form to; *n* **incarnation.**
incendiary *n* & *a* (one) who maliciously sets property on fire; inflammatory; *n* **incendiarism** arson.
incense *n* fragrant smoke from burning spices etc.
incense *v* anger, enrage.
incentive *n* stimulus; motive; *a* rousing, inciting.
inception *n* beginning, commencement.
incessant *a* constant, unceasing.
incest *n* sexual intercourse between close blood relations; *a* **incestuous.**
inch *n* 1/12th. linear foot; *v* mark in inches; advance by small degrees.
inchoate *a* undeveloped; rudimentary.
incident *n* happening, event; *a* associated with; *n* **incidence** fact of affecting; scope of occurrence; *a* **incidental** casual, accidental.
incinerate *v* consume by fire; *ns* **incineration**; **incinerator.**
incipient *a* beginning, in early stages.
incise *v* cut into; carve; *n* **incision**; **incisor** cutting tooth; *a* **incisive** sharp; (*fig*) pointed; vigorously clear.
incite *v* inflame; urge, rouse; *n* **incitement.**
inclement *a* (of weather) cold, severe, rough.
incline *v* slope, lean; bend; tend, be disposed; *n* slope,

slant; *n* **inclination** slope; bow; tendency, liking.
include *v* contain; regard as part of whole; *n* **inclusion**; *a* **inclusive**.
incognito *a* passing under assumed name; *n* such a name; person adopting it.
incoherent *a* rambling, disconnected, lacking cohesion; *n* **incoherence**.
income *n* money received (*esp* annually) from investments, salary etc.
incommode *v* disturb; trouble; *a* **incommodious** inconvenient.
incongruous *a* inconsistent; unsuitable; *n* **incongruity**.
inconsequent *a* irrelevant; disconnected.
incorporate *v* include; blend; form legal corporation; *n* **incorporation**.
increase *v* grow, become larger; enlarge; multiply; *n* enlargement, growth.
incredible *a* unbelievable; (*coll*) remarkable.
incredulous *a* unbelieving; sceptical; *n* **incredulity**.
increment *n* addition; increase.
incriminate *v* accuse; render liable to accusation.
incubate *v* hatch, sit on eggs; *ns* **incubation** (*med*) period between infection and appearance of symptoms; **incubator** apparatus for artifically hatching eggs, or rearing premature babies.
inculcate *v* implant, impress on mind; *n* **inculcation**.
incumbent *a* lying, resting on; morally binding; *n* holder of church benefice; *n* **incumbency**.
incur *v* run into, become liable to (debt etc.); *n* **incursion** attack, invasion, inroad.
incurable *a* that cannot be cured; inveterate.
indebted *a* owing; under obligation; *n* **indebtedness**.
indeed *adv* truly, in fact; certainly.
indefatigable *a* untiring, unremitting.
indefeasible *a* not to be made void, forfeited.
indefensible *a* untenable; inexcusable.
indefinite *a* vague; not precise; *a* **indefinable** vague.
indelible *a* not capable of being erased or effaced; *n* **indelibility**.
indemnity *n* security from loss, injury etc.; compensation for loss etc.; *v* **indemnify** compensate.

indent *v* notch; carve out; make official order for; *n* notch; marginal cut; requisition; *ns* **indentation** dent; **indenture** deed, contract drawn up in duplicate, *esp* one binding apprentice to employer.

independent *a* not subordinate; free; financially self-supporting; *n* one not attached to any political party; *ns* **independence, independency** self-reliance; independent state.

indescribable *a* indefinable; vague.

index *n* pointer; indicator; forefinger; alphabetical list of words, subjects in book; (*math*) exponent *pl* **indexes** or (*math*) **indices**; *v* provide with index; enter in index.

india-rubber *n* pencil eraser.

Indian *a* of India or American Indians; *ns* **Indian corn** maize; **Indian summer** warm spell in autumn.

indicate *v* point out; reveal; imply; *ns* **indication** sign; suggestion; **indicator** one who, that which indicates.

indict *v* accuse formally; *n* **indictment**; *a* **indictable**

indifferent *a* uninterested; callous; mediocre; impartial; *n* **indifference**.

indigenous *a* native, not foreign; natural to a country.

indigent *a* very poor; *n* **indigence**.

indigestion *n* dyspepsia; inability to digest food.

indignant *a* feeling, expressing righteous anger; *ns* **indignation**; **indignity** insult; humiliating treatment.

indigo *n* blue dye got from indigo plant; *a* deep blue.

indisposition *n* slight illness; reluctance; *a* **indisposed** unwell; averse.

individual *n* one particular person, animal or thing; single person; *a* distinct; characteristic of single person, thing; *n* **individuality** personality; individual character.

indoctrinate *v* teach; imbue with particular doctrine.

indolent *a* lazy, inactive; *n* **indolence**.

indomitable *a* unyielding.

indoor *a* pertaining to inside of house, etc.; domestic; *adv* **indoors**.

indubitable *a* beyond doubt.
induce *v* persuade; bring about; *n* **inducement** incentive, motive.
induct *v* install formally; *n* **induction** installation; transference of electric force without physical contact; *a* **inductive**; *n* **inductor**.
indulge *v* gratify; give way to; pamper; *n* **indulgence** favour; gratification of one's desires; (R.C.) remission of punishment for sins; *a* **indulgent**.
industry *n* diligence; manufacture, trade; particular branch of manufacture, trade; *as* **industrious** hard-working; **industrial** of industry.
inebriate *v* intoxicate; *n* **inebriation** drunkenness.
inedible *a* not suitable to be eaten.
ineffable *a* unutterable; inexpressibly great.
inefficient *a* unable to work properly; *n* **inefficiency**.
ineligible *a* unqualified, unsuitable; *n* **ineligibility**.
inept *a* fatuous; absurd, senseless, *n* **ineptitude**.
inert *a* without power of action; slow, inactive; *ns* **inertia**; **inertness** tendency to remain inactive; sluggishness.
inestimable *a* not to be estimated; invaluable.
inevitable *a* unavoidable; certain to happen; *n* **inevitability**.
inexorable *a* relentless.
infallible *a* never mistaken; certain; unerring; *n* **infallibility**.
infamous *a* disgraceful; notorious; shameful; *n* **infamy**.
infant *n* very young child; legal minor; *ns* **infancy**; **infanticide** murder of child; *esp* new-born; *a* **infantile**.
infantry *n* foot soldiers.
infatuate *v* make foolish; inspire with extreme passion; *a* **infatuated** besotted; *n* **infatuation**.
infect *v* pass disease to; pollute; affect by example; *n* **infection**; *a* **infectious** catching, spreading.
infer *v* draw conclusions; deduce; *n* **inference**.
inferior *a* lower; of less value, quality; *n* one lower in rank etc.; *n* **inferiority**; **inferiority complex** (*psych*) lack of self-confidence.
infernal *a* devilish, fiendish; (*sl*) confounded.

infest *v* swarm in; overrun; *n* **infestation.**
infidel *n* unbeliever; pagan; *n* **infidelity** disbelief in religion; unfaithfulness; disloyalty.
infiltrate *v* filter through; permeate; penetrate by stealth; *n* **infiltration.**
infinite *a* boundless; *a* **infinitesimal** minute; *n* **infinity** unlimited time, quality, space etc.; *n* (*gram*) **infinitive** mood expressing action only, not person, number etc.
infirm *a* feeble, physically weak; *ns* **infirmity; infirmary** hospital; sick-quarters.
inflame *v* set on fire; (*med*) make, become red, hot, swollen; (*fig*) rouse passion in; *a* **inflammable** easily set on fire; excitable; *ns* **inflammability; inflammation** morbid condition of redness, swelling, pain; *a* **inflammatory.**
inflate *v* swell, distend with air, gas; increase (currency) in circulation; raise (prices) artificially; *n* **inflation.**
inflect *v* bend, curve inwards; modify forms of words; *n* **inflection; inflection** intonation; variation of words; *a* **inflexible** unbending; *n* **inflexibility.**
inflict *v* cause to undergo; impose; *n* **infliction** punishment; suffering.
inflorescence *n* arrangement of flowers on stem; flowering.
influence *v* affect; sway; persuade; *n* effect produced; moral power (over); power of influencing important persons; *a* **influential.**
influenza *n* infectious virus disease.
influx *n* flowing in, inflow.
inform *v* tell; instruct; bring charge against; *ns* **informant** giver of information; **information** knowledge; accusation made to magistrate; **informer**; one who informs *esp* against criminal; *a* **informative.**
infra *adv* below; further down, on; **i.dig** (*coll*) beneath one's dignity; **i. red rays** invisible heat radiation.
infrequent *a* rare, unusual; *ns* **infrequence, -quency**
infringe *v* transgress, disobey; break; *ns* **infringement, infraction** violation, transgression.
infuriate *v* enrage, drive to frenzy.

infuse *v* steep, soak in liquid; (*fig*) permeate; *n* **infusion** liquid extract so obtained.
ingenious *a* clever at inventing; cleverly made; *n* **ingenuity**.
ingenue *n* artless, inexperienced girl; actress playing such a girl.
ingenuous *a* frank, candid; guileless.
ingestion *n* taking (of food) into stomach.
ingle *n* fire on hearth; *n* **ingle-nook** chimney corner.
ingot *n* block of cast metal.
ingratiate *v* obtain another's good will.
ingredient *n* component, one part of mixture.
ingress *n* entry; power, right of entry.
inhabit *v* dwell in; occupy; *ns* **inhabitant**; **inhabitation**.
inhale *v* breathe in; *n* **inhalation**.
inherent *a* innate; naturally associated with.
inherit *v* derive from parents, ancestors; succeed as heir; *ns* **inheritance**; **inheritor** heir, one who inherits.
inhibit *v* restrain; hinder, obstruct; *n* **inhibition** (*psych*) unconscious restraint, or suppression of natural urge; *a* **inhibitory**.
inimical *a* hostile, unfriendly; antagonistic.
inimitable *a* incapable of being imitated; unrivalled.
iniquity *n* injustice; wickedness, sin; *a* **iniquitous** unfair, wicked.
initial *a* occurring at beginning; *n* initial letter; *v* write, mark with, one's initials; *v* **initiate** originate; admit (to society etc.); *n* initiated person; *ns* **initiation**; **initiative** first move; enterprise.
inject *v* introduce, drive in (fluid) by force; fill by this means; *ns* **injection**; **injector**.
injunction *n* writ issued to restrain; order, command.
injury *n* harm, hurt; wound; moral hurt, insult etc.; *v* **injure** do harm, hurt to; *a* **injurious**.
injustice *n* wrong; injury; unjust act.
ink *n* coloured fluid used for printing and writing; *v* mark with ink; *a* **inky**.
inkling *n* hint, vague idea; suspicion.

inland *n* interior of country; *a* away from sea; *adv* in, towards inland.
inlay *v* decorate by embedding pieces of substance, in contrasting colour, in groundwork; *n* inlaid material.
inlet *n* creek; entrance.
inmate *n* inhabitant, lodger.
inmost *a* deepest; most intimate; *sup* of **in.**
inn *n* public house providing lodging etc. for travellers; *n* **innkeeper**; *n* **Inns of Court** four legal societies admitting to English Bar.
innate *a* native, instinctive, inborn, inherent.
inner *a* inside; interior; *comp* of **in**; *n* ring next to bull on target.
innings *n pl* (cricket) period of batting; (*fig*) period of active life.
innocent *a* blameless; guileless; not guilty; simple; *n* guileless child or person; *n* **innocence.**
innocuous *a* harmless, inoffensive.
innovate *v* introduce new methods, changes; *n* **innovation.**
innuendo *n* hint, insinuation; (*pl* **-does**).
innumerable *a* countless; too many to be counted.
inoculate *v* introduce (disease etc.) into system, as protection; render immune by infecting with specific germ; *n* **inoculation.**
inoffensive *a* harmless; giving, causing no offence.
inoperable *a* not suitable for treatment by surgical operation.
inopportune *a* ill-timed, unseasonable.
inordinate *a* excessive, extravagant.
inorganic *a* not result of natural growth; of substances without carbon.
input *n* electric current, data, material fed into machine (*esp* computer) or factory; tax paid on goods received.
inquest *n* legal, judicial inquiry.
inquire, enquire *v* seek information; find out; *ns* **inquirer, enquirer**; **inquiry, enquiry** investigation.
inquisition *n* searching examination; ecclesiastical court for suppression of heresy; *n* **inquisitor**; *as* **inquisitorial**; **inquisitive** curious, prying.

inroad *n* invasion, incursion.
insane *a* mad; crazy, senseless; *n* **insanity** lunacy, madness.
inscribe *v* write, engrave on, in; dedicate, draw geometric figure within another; *n* **inscription**.
inscrutable *a* enigmatic; impenetrable, mysterious; *n* **inscrutability**.
insect *n* invertebrate aninal having six legs and segmented body, usually two or four wings; *n* **insecticide** substance for killing insects; *a* **insectivorous** insect-eating.
inseminate *v* implant, impregnate.
insensate *a* unreasoning; inanimate; foolish.
insensible *a* not feeling; unconscious; unaware.
insert *v* set in; introduce; *ns* **insertion**; **inset** something added, inserted.
inshore *adv* & *a* near shore.
inside *a* within; *adv* on the inner side; *n* inner side.
insidious *a* cunning; treacherous, sly.
insight *n* discernment; knowledge.
insignia *n* (*pl*) badges of office; distinguishing marks (of honour etc).
insinuating *a* ingratiating; *v* **insinuate** hint at; gradually penetrate; *n* **insinuation**.
insipid *a* lacking flavour; dull; *n* **insipidity**.
insist *v* emphasize; assert; demand urgently; *a* **insistent**; *n* **insistence**.
insolent *a* insulting; rude; haughty; *n* **insolence**.
insomnia *a* inability to sleep; sleeplessness.
insouciant *a* indifferent, unconcerned; *n* **insouciance**.
inspect *v* examine closely, thoroughly; *ns* **inspection**; **inspector**.
inspire *v* inhale; influence, arouse; stimulate thoughts, action; *n* **inspiration**.
install *v* place in office, formally; establish; put in position for use etc.; *n* **installation**.
instalment *n* one part-payment of debt; one part of thing appearing, supplied at intervals.
instance *n* example; request; *v* cite, refer to; *a* **instant** urgent, immediate; of current month; *n* precise moment; *a* **instantaneous** occurring in an instant; *adv* **instanter** instantly, immediately.

instead *adv* in place of; as alternative to.
instep *n* upper surface of foot in front of ankle.
instigate *v* incite, urge; stir up; *ns* **instigation**; **instigator**.
instil *v* implant; infuse; *n* **instillation**.
instinct *n* natural aptitude; impulse; intuition; *a* **instinctive**.
institute *v* set up, found; begin, set going; *n* scientific, social, etc. society; building occupied by such society; *n* **institution** established custom, system, law etc.; institute; *a* **institutional**.
instruct *v* teach, give orders to; *n* **instruction**; *a* **instructive** informative; *n* **instructor**.
instrument *n* tool, implement; device for producing musical sounds; legal document; *a* **instrumental** acting as means, or instrument; produced by musical instruments; *ns* **instrumentality** means **instrumentation** arrangement of music for particular instruments.
insubordinate *a* rebellious; disobedient; unruly; *n* **insubordination**.
insufficiency *n* inadequacy; lack; *a* **insufficient**.
insular *a* of, like an island; (*fig*) narrow-minded; *n* **insularity**.
insulate *v* isolate; prevent passage of electricity by use of non-conducting material; *ns* **insulation**; **insulator**.
insulin *n* extract from animal pancreas, used in treating diabetes, etc.
insult *v* abuse, treat with contempt; *n* affront; insolence; *a* **insulting**.
insuperable *a* not to be overcome or surmounted.
insure *v* enter into contract to secure payment in event of loss of (life, health etc.); make safe; make sure; *ns* **insurance**; **insurer**; **insurance-policy** written contract of insurance; *a* **insurable**.
insurgent *a* rebellious; *n* **insurrection** rebellion.
insusceptible *a* not capable of being moved by feeling; unimpressed.
intact *a* untouched; entire; uninjured.
intaglio *n* design carved, engraved on hard surface; jewel carved so (a cameo).

intake *n* what is taken in; air-shaft in mine; (in car) air passage to carburettor.
intangible *a* insubstantial; impalpable; vague.
integer *n* anything complete, entire; whole number; *a* **integral** essential; whole, complete; *v* **integrate** abolish segregation; form into whole; *ns* **integration**; **integrity** original completeness; honesty, probity; **integral calculus** branch of mathematics.
integument *n* outer covering, skin; rind, shell.
intellect *n* faculty of knowing, reasoning; *a* **intellectual** of, exercising intellect; inclined to mental activity *n* intellectual person; *n* **intellectuality**.
intelligence *n* intellect; mental ability; quickness in learning; news, information *esp* military etc.; **i.quotient** number indicating level of intelligence; **intelligent** clever; well-informed; *n* **intelligencer** informant, secret agent; *a* **intelligible** clear in meaning; *n* **intelligentsia** cultured, intellectual classes.
intemperate *a* unrestrained; given to excess.
intend *v* design, destine; mean, contemplate.
intense *a* excessive, extreme, violent; ardent, eager; *v* **intensify** increase; deepen; make stronger; *ns* **intensification**; **intensity** strength, depth; *a* **intensive** thorough; concentrated on.
intent *a* concentrating; earnest; *n* purpose, motive; *n* **intention** aim, meaning **intentness**; *a* **intentional**.
inter *v* bury *n* **interment**.
inter- *prefix* among, between, mutual; *forms compounds, eg* **interaction** acting on each other; **interrelation** relation between things, persons. *Such words are not given here where the meaning may be deduced from the simple word.*
intercede *v* plead for, mediate; *n* **intercession**.
intercept *v* hinder, prevent passage of; *ns* **interception**; **interceptor**; *a* **interceptive**.
interchange *v* exchange; alternate with; *a* **interchangeable**.
intercommunicate *v* communicate with; (of rooms) open one into another; *n* **intercom** internal telephone system.
intercourse *n* mutual dealings, relations; coition.

interdict *n* prohibition; exclusion from sacraments & religious rites; *v* prohibit; restrain; *n* **interdiction.**
interest *n* concern; benefit; influence; payment made for use of money; advantage; intellectual curiosity; *v* rouse, hold attention; concern; *a* **interesting.**
interfere *v* meddle; hinder; mediate; *n* **interference** hindrance; interruption of radio reception.
interim *a* temporary, meantime.
interior *a* inner, internal; inland; *n* inside; inland.
interject *v* interrupt by, break in with (word etc.); *n* **interjection** exclamation.
interlace *v* twist together.
interleave *v* insert blank pages among others in book.
interlocutor *n* person taking part in dialogue; *n* **interlocution.**
interloper *n* intruder; meddler in another's affairs.
interlude *n* interval between two acts of play; short entertainment during such interval.
intermediate *a* in the middle; *ns* **intermediary; intermediator** mediator.
interminable *a* endless; unduly prolonged.
intermission *n* interval; respite; *a* **intermittent** ceasing at intervals.
intern *v* confine to specified area; *n* **internment.**
internal *a* inner; interior; *n* **i. combustion engine** one driven by explosion of air and fuel in cylinder.
international *a* pertaining to relations between nations; *n* game, match between different countries; player taking part in such contest.
internecine *a* mutually destructive.
interplay *n* reciprocal action; interaction.
interpolate *v* insert (spurious matter) in book etc.; *n* **interpolation** words etc. added by another author
interpose *v* insert, interrupt; intervene; obstruct.
interpret *v* explain; construe; translate; *ns* **interpreter; interpretation.**
interregnum *n* interval between reigns.
interrogate *v* ask searching questions of; *ns* **interrogation; interrogator**; *as* **interrogative** questioning; **interrogatory.**
interrupt *v* break in on; obstruct; cut off continuity of; *n* **interruption.**

intersect *v* cut through; cross each other; *n* **intersection.**
intersperse *v* scatter among; diversify.
interstice *n* chink; small opening.
interval *n* intervening space or time; pause, break; difference of pitch.
intervene *v* come between; interfere; take part in; *n* **intervention.**
interview *n* formal meeting and conversation; one arranged to test suitability of applicant for position, or to obtain views, opinions of a personality; *v* have interview with; *n* **interviewer.**
intestate *a* not having made a will; *n* **intestacy.**
intestine *n* lower part of alimentary canal, bowel; *a* (*fig*) internal; domestic.
intimate *a* inward; closely linked; familiar; having sexual relationship; *n* **intimacy.**
intimate *v* make known; hint; *n* **intimation** notice.
intimidate *v* frighten, terrorize; restrain by threats; *n* **intimidation.**
into *prep* from outside to inside; to place of, condition of, form of.
intone *v* chant; recite in monotone; *n* **intonation** modulation of voice; sounding of musical notes.
intoxicate *v* make drunk; (*fig*) excite greatly; *ns* **intoxicant** intoxicating liquor; **intoxication.**
intransigent *a* obstinately hostile; uncompromising.
intrepid *a* brave, fearless; *n* **intrepidity.**
intricate *a* involved; entangled; puzzling; *n* **intricacy.**
intrigue *n* secret plot; illicit love affair; *v* carry on intrigue; interest; *n* **intriguer.**
intrinsic *a* inherent, real, genuine.
intro- *prefix* within, into; forms compounds as **intrude**; **intravenous**; *etc.*
introduce *v* bring into use, notice etc.; make known formally; insert; *n* **introduction,** *a* **introductory** preliminary.
introit *n* hymn, etc. sung as priest approaches altar.
introspection *n* self-analysis; *a* **introspective** dwelling on one's own thoughts.
introvert *n* self-centred, introspective person;

v direct, cause to turn inwards; *n* **introversion**;
intrude *v* thrust in; force in uninvited; *ns* **intruder**. **intrusion**; *a* **intrusive.**
intuition *n* immediate instinctive knowledge, without reasoning; instinct; *a* **intuitive.**
inundate *v* flood, swamp; (*fig*) overwhelm; *n* **inundation.**
inure *v* accustom; harden.
invade *v* enter with hostile intent; (*fig*) assail; encroach on; *ns* **invader; invasion.**
invalid *a* not valid; *n* **invalidity**; *v* **invalidate.**
invalid *n* & *a* (person) suffering from ill-health, weakness; *v* render infirm; remove from active service.
invaluable *a* priceless; very valuable.
invariable *a* constant; unchanging.
invective *n* abuse; vituperation.
inveigh *v* attack violently with words.
inveigle *v* delude, lure, entice; *n* **inveiglement.**
invent *v* originate; contrive for first time; make up; *n* **invention** something that is invented; fabrication; ability to invent; *a* **inventive** originative; resourceful; *n* **inventor.**
inventory *n* detailed list of stock etc; catalogue.
invert *v* turn upside down; reverse order, position of; *a* **inverse** opposed; contrary; *n* **inversion.**
invertebrate *n* animal without backbone; *a* spineless; (*fig*) irresolute.
invest *v* clothe, array; endue; besiege, put money into (business etc.) for profit; *ns* **investiture** formal ceremony of presenting with office, insignia, order etc.; **investment** (*usu*) money invested, stocks and shares bought; **investor.**
investigate *v* enquire into; examine carefully; *ns* **investigation; investigator.**
inveterate *a* persistent; long-established; obstinate; confirmed.
invidious *a* giving offence by injustice; likely to arouse ill-will.
invigorate *v* strengthen; refresh, animate.
invincible *a* unconquerable; *n* **invincibility.**
inviolable *a* unprofaned; not to be dishonoured or

violated; *a* **inviolate** strictly preserved; kept sacred; uninjured.
invisible *a* not capable of being seen; *n* **invisibility.**
invite *v* ask person to come to social gathering etc.; request; attract; provoke; *n* **invitation.**
invoice *n* list of goods sent, with prices; *v* make out invoice.
invoke *v* appeal to; implore; call on; *n* **invocation.**
involuntary *a* unintentional; automatic, instinctive.
involve *v* entangle; complicate; implicate; entail; imply; *a* **involute** intricate; spirally curved; *n* **involution.**
inward, inwards *adv* towards interior; into the mind; *a* **inward** internal; spiritual, mental; *n* (*pl*) entrails; *adv* **inwardly** privately.
iodine *n* non-metallic element used in medicine.
iodize *v* treat with iodine.
ion *n* electrically charged atom; *v* **ionize** charge ions with electricity; *n* **ionization.**
iota *n* Greek letter *i*; very small part, jot.
I.O.U. *n* signed acknowledgement of debt.
ipecacuanha *n* root of S Amer. plant, used as emetic.
ire *n* wrath, anger; *as* **irate** enraged; irascible irritable; *n* **irascibility.**
iridescent *a* changing in colour, like rainbow; *n* **iridescence.**
iridium *n* hard silvery metallic element.
iris *n* coloured part of eye, around pupil; tuberous-rooted plant.
irk *v* weary, worry; *a* **irksome** tiresome.
iron *n* very hard metallic element; most common metal used for tools, weapons etc. and the raw material of steel; appliance for smoothing, pressing cloth etc; metal-headed golf-club; *n* (*pl*), fetters; *a* of iron; (*fig*) very strong; unyielding; hard; *v* smooth, cover, fetter with iron; *ns* **Iron Age** era of use of iron tools etc.; **Iron Curtain** frontier, and ideological barrier between Communist and non-Communist states; **iron lung,** apparatus for giving artificial respiration; **ironmonger** dealer in hardware; **ironmould** spot made by rust or ink.
irony *n* way of speaking, in which the meaning is the

opposite of apparent meaning; sarcasm; *a* **ironic** of irony.

irradiate *v* shine on, illumine; diffuse; *n* **irradiation** exposure to therapeutic rays.

irrefutable *a* indisputable.

irrespective *a* without regard, reference to; not taking into account.

irrigate *v* water by artificial channels; *n* **irrigation.**

irritate *v* annoy, exasperate; provoke; inflame, make sore; *n* **irritation**; *as* **irritant** causing irritation; **irritable** irascible; easily angered; (of wounds etc.) inflamed, sore.

irruption *n* invasion; sudden violent incursion.

isinglass *n* kind of gelatin obtained from fish.

Islam *n* Mohammedan religion or world; *a* **Islamic.**

island *n* piece of land surrounded by water; detached isolated patch, mound; *n* **islander** one who lives on island.

isle *n* island; *n* **islet** small island.

isobar *n* line on map joining places with equal mean atmospheric pressure.

isolate *v* set apart; keep (infected person) away from others; *ns* **isolation**; **isolationism** policy of avoiding involvement in world politics; **isolationist.**

isosceles *a* of triangle, having two equal sides.

isotherm *n* line on map joining places of same mean temperature.

isotope *n* atom of element having different atomic weight from other atoms in same element; *a* **isotopic.**

issue *n* flowing, coming out; publication; outlet; offspring; result; problem; *v* go out; emit; publish; be derived from; distribute.

isthmus *n* narrow strip of land between two seas, connecting two land areas.

it *pron* 3rd pers. neuter; *a* **its** belonging to it; *pron* **itself** emphatic form; *n* **it** (*sl*) sex-appeal.

italic *a* of type, with letters sloping up to right; *n pl* this type, used for emphasis; *v* **italicize** print in italics.

itch *n* irritating sensation of skin; *v* feel itch; have restless desire; *a* **itchy.**

item *n* single detail in list; piece of news; subsection of agenda etc.; *adv* likewise; *v* **itemize.**
iterate *v* repeat; *n* **iteration.**
itinerant *a* travelling from place to place; wandering; (of judges, preachers etc.) on circuit; *n* **itinerary** route; record of travel; guide book.
ivory *n* hard white substance from tusks of elephants etc.; **i. black** black pigment made from burnt ivory.
ivy *n* climbing evergreen plant.

jab *v* poke suddenly, with force; thrust roughly.
jabber *v* speak rapidly, gabble; chatter.
jabot *n* frill, ruffle on bodice, shirt-front.
jacaranda *n* tropical American hard-wood tree.
jacinth *n* reddish-orange variety of zircon.
jack *n* device for raising load from below; (in cards) knave; (bowls) ball used as mark; ship's flag; *prefix* male; large; *v* **j. up** raise by jack.
jackal *n* wild scavenging animal, allied to dog.
jackanapes *n* pert child.
jackass *n* male ass; *n* **laughing jackass,** large Australian kingfisher.
jackboot *n* large boot reaching above knee.
jackdaw *n* small kind of crow.
jacket *n* short coat; outer casing, covering.
jack-knife *n* large pocket knife.
jackpot *n* pool in poker-game; money prize increasing in value until won.
Jacobean *n* of reign of James I; *n* **Jacobite** adherent of Stuarts after abdication of James II.
jade *n* hard green or white gem stone; colour green.
jade *n* worn-out horse; *a* **jaded** tired, wearied.
jag *n* sharp, pointed projection; ragged tear in cloth; *a* **jagged.**
jaguar *n* large carnivorous S. Amer. mammal.
jam *n* fruit preserve; crush; traffic hold-up; *v* block, fill up; cease to work.
jamb *n* side post of door; window-frame.
jamboree *n* spree; social gathering; Boy Scout rally.
jangle *v* make harsh, clanging sound; *n* such sound.
janitor *n* doorkeeper; caretaker.

January *n* first month of year.
japan *n* hard black lacquer; *v* cover with this.
jape *n* joke.
jar *n* round glass, earthenware vessel.
jar *v* be, sound discordant; grate upon; cause to shake, vibrate; *n* harsh sound, shock.
jargon *n* gibberish; excessively technical language.
jasmin(e), jessamin(e) *n* fragrant flowering shrub.
jasper *n* opaque reddish, yellow or brown quartz.
jaundice *n* morbid state, characterized by yellow tint of eyes & skin; *a* **jaundiced** (*fig*) jealous, biassed.
jaunt *n* short pleasure trip; *v* go on jaunt, *n* **jaunting-car** Irish two-wheeled cart.
jaunty *a* care-free; sprightly; swaggering.
javelin *n* light throwing spear, or shaft.
jaw *n* two bones, in which teeth are set, and their muscles; *pl* mouth; gripping device (*fig*) opening, entrance; *v* (*sl*) talk at length; lecture.
jay *n* noisy, brightly-coloured bird of crow family; *n* **jay-walker** careless pedestrian.
jazz *n* syncopated rhythmical music of Negro origin; *v* play, dance to, jazz; *a* **jazzy** bizarrely patterned.
jealous *a* envious; grudging; suspicious; distrustful; *n* **jealousy**.
jean *n* twilled cotton fabric; (*pl*) trousers, overalls of this cloth.
jeep *n* light, open truck, with four-wheel drive.
jeer *v* mock, scoff at; *n* taunt, gibe.
jejune *a* poor, barren; void of interest.
jelly *n* semi-solid, transparent food made with gelatine, any substance of similar consistency; *v* **jell** turn to jelly, set, (*sl*) take definite form; *n* **jelly-fish** free floating sea-creature; medusa.
jemmy *n* burglar's crow-bar.
jenny *n* spinning machine; female ass.
jeopardy *n* hazard, peril, danger; *v* **jeopardize** imperil.
jerboa *n* small African burrowing rodent; desert rat.
jeremiad *n* lamentation.
jerk *n* quick pull, twitch; sudden, sharp movement; *v* move with jerk; *a* **jerky**; *adv* **jerkily**; *n* **jerkiness**.
jerk *v* cure (meat) by slicing and drying in sun.

jerkin *n* close-fitting leather jacket.
jerry-built *a* hastily, flimsily constructed.
jersey *n* close-fitting knitted jumper; breed of cow.
jest *n* joke; *v* make jokes; *n* **jester** joker.
Jesuit *n* member of R.C. religious order.
jet *n* hard black mineral, used for ornaments etc.
jet *n* stream, spurt of liquid, gas, forced from small opening; nozzle; aircraft propelled by jet engine; *v* gush, give out in jet; *n* **j.-propulsion** in which ejected stream of gas provides the thrust; **j.-engine** one propelled by jets.
jetsam *n* things thrown overboard to lighten vessel, and washed ashore; *v* **jettison** throw overboard; (*fig*) get rid of; abandon.
jetty *n* pier, mole, quay.
Jew *n* member of Hebrew race; (*sl*) misér; (fem) **Jewess**; *n* **Jewry** collectively Jews; *n* **jew's harp** small nusical instrument held in mouth.
jewel *n* precious stone, gem; ornament set with one; precious object; *ns* **jeweller** dealer in jewels; **jewellery**.
jib *n* ship's triangular foremost stay-sail; projecting arm of crane etc.; *v* pull over (sail) to other side; (of horse) balk; (*fig*) refuse to proceed.
jig *n* lively dance; template guiding cutting tool; *v* move jerkily up and down; dance jig.
jigsaw *n* machine fretsaw for cutting curved, irregular patterns; *n* **j.puzzle** picture mounted on wood, etc. and cut in irregular pieces, to be re-assembled.
jilt *v* reject (lover) after encouraging him.
jingle *n* light, ringing, tinkling sound, as of small bells; verses with simple, catchy words; *v* make, cause to make this sound.
jingo *n* warmonger; *n* **jingoism** aggressive patriotism.
jinx *n* hoodoo, bringer of bad luck.
jitters *n pl* (*sl*) extreme nervousness; panic; *a* **jittery** nervy, jumpy; *n* **jitterbug** one who dances convulsively; one who panics easily.
jive *n* very emotional swing, or jazz music; form of dance; *v* dance to this style.

job *n* piece of work; task, employment, matter, affair; *v* work at piece-rate; hire out; act as broker; *ns* **jobber** odd jobman; dealer in Stock Exchange securities; **jobbery** corrupt practice in public position.

jockey *n* professional rider in horse-racing; *v* cheat, trick; manoeuvre.

ocose *a* facetious; playful, jesting *n* **jocosity**; *a* **jocular** joking; *n* **jocularity**.

jocund *a* merry, gay, cheerful; *n* **jocundity**.

jodhpurs *n pl* riding-breeches.

jog *v* push, nudge, keep moving steadily; (*fig*) stimulate memory; *n* **jog-trot** slow steady trot.

joggle *v* move jerkily; shake slightly.

join *v* connect; unite; become member of; fasten; **j. up** enlist; *n* place of joining; *ns* **joiner** craftsman in wood; **joinery**.

oint *n* point where two things join; articulation of two bones in body; piece of meat cut ready for cooking; (*sl*) low club or resort; *a* shared by two or more; *v* fasten, fit together by joints; divide at joints; *n* **joint-stock** share capital.

jointure *n* estate settled on woman at her marriage.

joist *n* one of parallel beams, supporting floor or ceiling.

joke *n* jest; something not meant to be serious; *v* make jokes; talk jestingly; *n* **joker** one who jokes; odd card in pack.

jolly *a* jovial, merry, hearty; pleasant; *v* cajole; persuade by flattery; *ns* **jollity**; **jollification** merrymaking.

jolly-boat *n* ship's boat.

jolt *v* shake with sudden jerk; jog; *n* sudden jerk or bump.

jonquil *n* type of scented narcissus.

joss *n* Chinese idol; *ns* **joss-house** Chinese temple; **joss-stick** incense.

jostle *v* knock or bump against.

jot *n* trifle, small amount; *v* make brief written note; *n* **jotter** notebook.

joule *n* unit of electrical energy.

journal *n* daily record; diary; periodical; daily

newspaper; part of axle resting on bearings; *ns* **journalism** profession of producing, editing, writing in newspapers etc.; **journalist**; *a* **journalistic.**

journey *n* act of travelling; distance travelled; *v* travel.

journeyman *n* qualified artisan, craftsman.

joust *n* encounter between two armed, mounted knights; *v* take part in tournament; tilt.

jovial *a* convivial; cheery, hearty; festive; *n* **joviality.**

jowl *n* lower part of face, jaw; dewlap of cattle.

joy *n* great pleasure, gladness; happiness; cause of this; *as* **joyless**; **joyful.**

joystick *n* control column of aircraft.

jubilation *n* rejoicing; *a* **jubilant** exultant, elated.

jubilee *n* fiftieth anniversary; festive celebration.

Judaism *n* Jewish religion, custom.

judge *n* official appointment to preside over court of justice; one who decides a dispute; umpire; arbiter; *v* try (case) in law court; form opinion, decide on; estimate worth; *n* **judgement** sentence of court; opinion; divine retribution; faculty of judging.

judicature *n* administration of justice; body of judges; judicial system; *as* **judicial** of, befitting court of law, judge; impartial; **judicious** wise, prudent; *n* **judiciary** body of judges.

judo *n* Japanese system of unarmed combat.

jug *n* vessel with handle and lip or spout, for holding liquids; its contents; (*sl*) prison; *v* stew in jug (*esp* hare).

Juggernaut *n* idol of Hindu god Krishna; (*fig*) relentless, destructive force.

juggle *v* perform conjuring tricks; (*fig*) deceive; *ns* **jugglery**; **juggler.**

jugular *a* of, relating to neck, throat.

juice *n* liquid part of animal or vegetable tissue; (*sl*) petrol; *a* **juicy** succulent; (*sl*) spicy, suggestive.

ju-jitsu, ju-jutsu *n* judo.

ju-ju *n* W. African fetish; charm, taboo.

jujube *n* lozenze made of sugar, gelatine etc.

juke-box *n* automatic coin-operated record player.

julep *n* sweet, soothing, medicated drink; iced mint-flavoured alcoholic drink.

Julian *a* of Julius Caesar, *esp* of calendar introduced by him.
July *n* seventh month.
jumble *v* mix up, confuse together; *n* disorded heap; **j. sale** charitable sale of second-hand goods.
jump *v* spring, leap, bound; start, jerk; omit, ignore; **j. at** accept eagerly; **j. claim** steal another's land etc.; **j. the gun** act prematurely; *n* leap, jerk etc.; *n* **jumper** one who jumps; woman's loose pullover; sailor's blouse; *a* **jumpy** nervous.
junction *n* joining; place, point of union; station where branches of railway meet.
juncture *n* position of affairs; critical point.
June *n* sixth month.
jungle *n* wild, uncultivated land, with thick undergrowth; (*fig*) confused, tangled mass.
junior *a* younger; of lower status; *n* subordinate; one who is younger.
juniper *n* evergreen tree.
junk *n* old rope; (*sl*) useless articles; rubbish; salt meat.
junk *n* large flat-bottomed Chinese sailing vessel.
junket *n* milk curdled with rennet.
junta *n* Spanish or Italian council of state; political faction.
Jupiter *n* supreme Roman god; the largest planet.
Jurassic *a* pertaining to fourth geological period.
jurisdiction *n* authority to administer law; area covered by authority; *a* **juridical** legal; *n* **jurisprudence** science, knowledge of law; *a* **jural** of law *n* **jurist** law graduate; writer on law.
jury *n* body of persons sworn to return verdict in court of law; *ns* **juror, juryman** member of jury; **jury-box** enclosed place, in court, for jury to occupy.
jury-mast *n* temporary mast erected in place of broken one.
just *a* fair, upright; well-grounded; well-deserved; *adv* barely, scarcely; exactly; *n* **justice** fairness; administration of law; punishment for crime; judge, magistrate; *v* **justify** prove to be right; vindicate; exonerate; *a* **justifiable**; *n* **justification.**

jut *v* project, stick out.
jute *n* fibre of Indian plant, used for rope, canvas etc.
juvenile *a* young; suited to, characteristic of youth; *n* young person; youth; *n* **juvenility.**
juxtapose *v* put side by side; *n* **juxtaposition.**

Kaffir, Kafir *n* negro of S. African Bantu race; (*pl*) S.A. gold mining shares.
kale, kail *n* cabbage with curly leaves, cole.
kaleidoscope *n* tube containing pieces of coloured glass and reflectors, showing varying patterns, when tube is moved; *a* **kaleidoscopic** ever-changing.
kangaroo *n* Australian marsupial with powerful hindlegs; *n* **k. court** (*sl*) irregular, illegal court.
kaolin *n* china clay, used medicinally and for manufacture of porcelain.
kapok *n* soft fibre from silk-cotton tree seeds, used to fill cushions etc.
kaput *a* (*sl*) broken; dead.
karma *n* fate, destiny; ethical causation.
katabolism *n* destructive metabolism.
kayak *n* Eskimo canoe made of stretched sealskin.
kedge *n* small anchor for mooring etc.; *v* move (ship) by hauling on kedge.
keel *n* ship's lowest longitudinal timbers or plates, on which hull is built; *v* **k. over** capsize; *v* **keelhaul** (*fig*) rebuke severely.
keen *a* sharp; acute; eager; shrewd.
keen *n* Irish funeral lament; *v* wail over, lament.
keep *v* observe; retain possession of; maintain; preserve; detain; remain (sound); defend; *pt* & *pp* **kept**; *n* sustenance; cost of naintaining; stronghold; *ns* **keeper**; **keeping** custody; suitability; **keepsake** gift kept in memory of giver.
keg *n* small cask.
kelp *n* large brown seaweed, source of iodine.
kelpie *n* (*Scots myth*) malevolent water sprite.
ken *v* (*Scots*) know; *n* range of knowledge.
kennel *n* hut, shelter for dog; (*fig*) hovel; (*pl*) boarding, training establishment for dogs; *v* keep, put in kennel.

kennel *n* gutter.
kepi *n* French flat-topped military cap, with peak.
kerb *n* stone edging of pavement.
kerchief *n* head-covering, scarf.
kernel *n* inner, germinating part of nut, or fruit-stone; (*fig*) essential, vital part.
kerosene *n* paraffin oil distilled from petroleum.
kersey *n* coarse, ribbed woollen cloth.
kestrel *n* small migratory falcon or hawk.
ketch *n* small two-masted fishing vessel.
ketchup *n* spicy sauce made from tomatoes, etc.
kettle *n* metal vessel with spout and handle, used for boiling water.
kettledrum *n* cauldron-shaped brass or copper drum, having variable musical pitch.
key *n* metal instrument to fasten or unfasten lock; (*fig*) tone; explanation; clue; set of related musical notes; dominating position; lever, button on typewriter, piano etc. *v* secure with wedge; (*music*) adjust pitch, tune up; *ns* **keyboard** set of keys on piano, typewriter etc.; **keynote** lowest note of musical key; dominant idea; **keystone** central wedge-shaped stone of arch.
key *n* reef,, small island.
khaki *a* dull brownish-fawn, earth coloured; *n* military uniform.
kibbutz *n* Israeli collective farm settlement.
kibosh *n* (*sl*) rubbish, nonsense; *v* **put the k. on** put an end to.
kick *v* strike out with foot; recoil; resist; *n* blow by foot; recoil (of gun); (*sl*) thrill; stimulant.
kid *n* young goat; leather made of its skin; (*coll*) child; *v* (*sl*) tease, hoax.
kidnap *n* steal (child); abduct, *esp* for ransom etc.; *n* **kidnapper.**
kidney *n* one of a pair of glandular organs, secreting urine; (*fig*) kind, class.
kill *v* cause to die; destroy; neutralize; pass (time); *n* act of killing; that which is killed.
kiln *n* furnace, oven.
kilo- *prefix* thousand, as in **kilometre** 1000 metres; **kilowatt** 1000 watts.

kilt *n* short pleated skirt, usually tartan; *v* tuck up (skirt) in pleats; *a* **kilted.**

kimono *n* loose wide-sleeved Japanese robe, with sash; dressing-gown in this style.

kin *n* relatives; *a* related by blood; *n* **kindred** blood-relationship; *a* (*fig*) similar, congenial; *ns* **kinship**; **kinsman**; **kinswoman.**

kind *n* sort, variety, class; *a* good, considerate, affectionate; *n* **kindliness**; *a* **kindly.**

kindergarten *n* infant school.

kindle *v* set light to; (*fig*) excite, stir up; *n* **kindling** small sticks to start fire.

kinematics *n* science of pure motion; *a* **kinematic.**

kinetics *n* science of motion in relation to force; *a* **kinetic.**

king *n* male ruler of nation; monarch; card with picture of king; piece in game of chess; *a* **kingly** noble, royal; *n* **kingdom** state ruled by king; monarchy; domain, sphere *esp* of nature.

king-cup *n* marsh marigold.

kingfisher *n* small brilliantly coloured fish-eating bird.

king-pin *n* swivel-pin; (*fig*) chief person.

kink *n* twist, bend in rope, hair etc.; (*fig*) eccentricity; *v* make, put kink in; *a* **kinky** eccentric; perverted.

kiosk *n* open pavilion; refreshment, newspaper stall; telephone booth.

kip *n* (*sl*) bed; sleep; *v* (*sl*) go to bed.

kipper *n* smoked, salted herring; salmon at spawning time; *v* cure fish by smoking, salting.

kirk *n* (*Scots* & N) church.

kismet *n* destiny, fate.

kiss *v* caress with lips; (of billiards) touch lightly; *n* act of kissing.

kit *n* small wooden tub; equipment; outfit; *v* provide with kit; *n* **kit-bag** bag for holding soldier's or traveller's belongings.

kitchen *n* place where food is cooked; *n* **kitchen-garden** vegetable garden.

kite *n* bird of prey; light framework covered with paper, flown in wind; *n* **kite balloon** captive observation balloon.

kith and kin *n* family and relations.
kitsch *n* trash; inferior, pretentious art.
kitten *n* young cat; *a* **kittenish** like kitten; playful.
kittiwake *n* kind of seagull.
kitty *n* pool of money in some gambling games; jointly held fund; (*bowls*) the jack.
kiwi *n* flightless N. Zealand bird; (*sl*) N. Zealander.
kleptomania *n* morbid impulse to steal; *n* **kleptomaniac.**
knack *n* aptitude, talent; habit; trick.
knacker *n* dealer in worn-out horses for slaughter.
knapsack *n* bag carried on back, small rucksack.
knave *n* rogue; jack, lowest court card; *n* **knavery** villainy; *a* **knavish.**
knead *v* squeeze and press with hands *esp* to work bread dough; massage.
knee *n* joint between upper and lower leg; *n* **knee-cap** patella.
kneel *v* rest on knees; *pt* & *pp* **knelt**; *n* **kneeler** hassock.
knell *n* sound of tolling bell; omen of doom.
knickerbockers *n pl* loose, baggy breeches; *n pl* **knickers** woman's undergarment.
knick-knack *n* trifle, trinket.
knife *n* cutting implement with blade set in handle; *v* cut, stab with knife.
knight *n* one who receives non-hereditary honour, carrying title (*Sir*); *n* **knighthood**; *v* create (man) knight; *a* **knightly.**
knit *v* make fabric by fastening loops of wool, etc. together with needles (*pt* & *pp* **knitted**); draw close together, make compact (*pt* & *pp* **knit**); *ns* **knitter**; **knitting** knitted work.
knob *n* rounded protuberance; door-handle.
knock *v* strike, rap; collide; *n* blow, rap; tapping noise in car engine due to over-compression; *as* **knock-kneed** having incurved legs; **knocked-up** tired, exhausted.
knoll *n* small rounded hill, mound.
knot *n* tightly tied loop of string, rope etc.; (*fig*) difficulty; hard lump where branches join trunk; unit of ship's speed; one nautical mile an hour;

v tie into, make knot; become entangled; *a* **knotty** full of knots; (*fig*) complicated.

know *v* be aware of, acquainted with; understand; be informed of; *pt* **knew**; *pp* **known**; *a* **knowing** shrewd; *n* **knowledge** that which is known; understanding; information; *a* **knowledgeable** clever; well informed.

knuckle *n* bone at finger-joint; knee-joint of veal, pork etc.; *v* clench hand, showing knuckles; **knuckle under** submit, yield; *n* **knuckle-duster** metal guard worn on knuckles to add force to blow.

knurl *n* ridge, knob; *a* **knurled.**

koala *n* small Australian marsupial, living in trees.

kohl *n* powdered antimony, used as eye-shadow.

kola *n* bitter, stimulating extract from kola nut.

Koran *n* sacred book of Mohammedans.

kosher *a* ceremonially fit, pure, clean, as laid down by Jewish law.

kotow, kowtow *n* in China, humble salutation; *v* bow to; (*fig*) be servile to.

kraal *n* S. African fenced village.

krait *n* venomous Indian snake.

krypton *n* rare gaseous element.

kudos *n* (*sl*) fame; credit.

kukri *n* short, curved Gurkha knife.

kummel *n* liqueur flavoured with caraway.

kursaal *n* assembly room for visitors to spa.

laager *n* (S. Africa) temporary camp.

label *n* slip of paper etc. attached to object giving information on it; *v* fix label to.

labial *a* of lips; sound made by lips.

laboratory *n* scientific establishment for research and experiment.

labour *n* hard work; task; pains of childbirth; body of workers; *v* toil, work hard; (of ship) toss in heavy seas; be in child-birth; (*fig*) stress to excess; *n* **labourer**, one who labours *esp* manual worker; *a* **laborious**, industrious; wearisome.

laburnum *n* tree with pendulous yellow flowers.

labyrinth *n* maze; network of winding paths.

lace *n* patterned net-like fabric; string, cord used as fastening; *esp* for shoes; *v* fasten with laces; add spirits to (coffee etc.).

lacerate *v* tear, mangle; (*fig*) distress; *n* **laceration**.

lachrymal *a* of tears; *as* **lachrymatory**, causing flow of tears; **lachrymose**, tearful.

lack *n* deficiency; absence, need; *v* be short of, want.

lackadaisical *a* dreamy; affectedly languid.

lackey *n* manservant in livery; (*fig*) servile person.

laconic *a* brief; using few words; terse.

lacquer *n* hard glossy varnish; *v* paint with this.

lacrosse *n* ball-game played with long-handled racquet, or crosse.

lactic, lacteal *a* of milk; *n* **lactation**, secreting of milk; period of suckling.

lacuna *n* gap, hiatus; empty space *esp* in book; cavity (in bone or tissue).

lad *n* boy, young man.

ladder *n* climbing device of two poles joined by rungs; vertical flaw in stocking; *v* (of stockings etc.) cause, develop vertical flaw.

lade *v* load, put cargo into; (*fig*) burden.

ladle *n* long-handled, deep-bowled spoon; *v* serve with ladle.

lady *n* gentlewoman; (*coll*) any woman; (*cap*) title of wives of knights, baronets and peers below rank of duke; title of daughters of peers above rank of viscount; *prefix* feminine, female; *a* **ladylike** refined, elegant; *ns* **Ladyship** form of address; **Our L.** the Virgin Mary; **L. Day** the Annunciation; quarter day; **ladybird** small red black-spotted beetle; **lady-killer** man very attractive to women.

lag *v* loiter; walk, move slowly; *n* **laggard** loiterer.

lag *v* wrap boiler, pipes etc. to conserve heat; *n* **lagging**.

lag *n* (*sl*) convict *esp* recidivist.

lager *n* light German beer.

lagoon *n* shallow salt water channel, enclosed by reef, sandbank or atoll.

lair *n* den, resting-place *esp* of wild animals.

laird *n* Scottish landowner.

laissez-faire *n* policy of non-interference by

government, allowing things to take natural course.
laity *n* persons not in Holy Orders, laymen.
lake *n* large sheet of water enclosed by land.
lake *n* reddish pigment.
lam *v* (*sl*) beat, flog, thrash; *n* **lamming.**
lama *n* Buddhist priest in Tibet; *n* **lamasery** monastery of lamas.
lamb *n* young sheep; its meat; (*fig*) gentle, innocent child, person; *v* give birth to lamb; *a* **lamblike** gentle; *n* **lambkin** very young lamb; term of affection.
lambent *a* twinkling; softly shining; (*fig*) light & witty.
lame *a* disabled, *esp* feet and legs; (*fig*) unconvincing; *v* cripple; *n* **lameness.**
lamé *n* fabric interwoven with metallic threads.
lamella *n* thin plate, scale; layer; (*pl*) – **ae.**
lament *v* bewail, mourn; feel, express deep grief; *n* expression of deep grief; dirge; **lamentation**; *a* **lamentable** deplorable.
laminate *v* roll, beat into thin plates; cover with thin sheets (of metal, plastic etc.); split into layers; *n* thin plate, layer.
Lammas *n* 1st August.
lamp *n* any of various devices for giving light or therapeutic rays; *ns* **lamp-black** pigment made from soot; **lamplighter** lighter of street lamps.
lampoon *n* venomous, abusive personal satire; *v* satirize in lampoon.
lamprey *n* eel-like fish, with sucker lips.
lance *n* long, ceremonial cavalry spear; fish-spear; *v* pierce, cut with lance or lancet; *ns* **l.-corporal** N.C.O. in army; **lancet** double-edged pointed surgical instrument; **lancer** mounted soldier armed with lance; (*pl*) kind of quadrille; *a* **lanceolate** lance-shaped.
land *n* dry solid surface of earth; country, nation; ground, area, estate; *v* put on shore; disembark; set (aircraft) down; *ns* **landfall** first sighting of land, after voyage; **landing** act of landing; platform where one lands, or at top of stairs; **landing-stage**

pier, jetty; **landlord, landlady** man or woman who lets property; innkeeper; **land-lubber** one unused to sea, ships; **land-mark** something serving as guide for direction etc.; (*fig*) outstanding event; **landrail** corncrake; **landscape** rural scenery, or painting etc. of this; **landslide** fall of earth; (*fig*) overwhelming political victory; *as* **landward** facing land; **landed** possessing lands.

landau *n* four-wheeled carriage with folding top.

lane *n* narrow road, street; regular route for shipping, aircraft.

language *n* speech; particular form of speech of nation, race, profession etc.; any symbols, gestures expressing meaning.

languish *v* become languid; pine; droop from misery etc.; *a* **languid** weak, spiritless; *n* **languor** want of interest; lassitude; *a* **languorous.**

lank *a* limp; long and thin; lean; *a* **lanky.**

lanolin *n* refined wool-grease.

lantern *n* transparent case for lamp etc.; lamp-room of lighthouse; structure on dome to admit light.

lanyard *n* short cord (for securing whistle or knife); short nautical rope.

lap *n* part between knees and waist of seated person; circuit of race-track; *v* enfold; surround; complete, or have lead of, one circuit of race-track; *n* **lap-dog** small pet dog.

lap *v* drink by scooping up movement of tongue, as animal; splash softly; (*fig*) listen eagerly to.

lapel *n* front part of coat folded back to shoulders.

lapidary *a* of stones; *n* cutter, engraver of stones.

lapiz lazuli *n* semi-precious bright blue stone.

lapse *n* fall; error; passing (of time etc.); *v* fall away; cease to exist.

lapwing *n* crested plover, or peewit.

larboard *n* port side of ship.

larceny *n* stealing, theft.

larch *n* coniferous tree.

lard *n* refined, rendered pig fat; *v* insert strips of fat in meat; enrich (style of speech) with; *a* **lardy.**

larder *n* storeroom for food.

large *a* great in size, number; roomy; copious;

liberal; *n* **largesse** liberality; gift; *a* **large-hearted** generous; tolerant.
largo *adv* (*mus*) slowly and nobly; *n* such music.
lariat *n* lasso; long rope with noose.
lark *n* singing wild bird, sky-lark.
lark *n* jest, sport; piece of fun; *v* play about, jest.
larva *n* caterpillar, worm-like stage of butterfly, fly etc.; (*pl*) – **ae**; *as* **larval, larviform.**
larynx *n* back of throat, containing vocal chords.
Lascar *n* East Indian sailor.
lascivious *a* lustful, wanton.
lash *v* strike with whip; (*fig*) strike violently; (*fig*) scold fiercely; fasten, bind tightly; *n* whip; eyelash.
lashings *n* (*sl pl*) plenty, large quantity.
lass *n* young girl.
lassitude *n* weariness, weakness.
lasso *n* rope with noose; *v* catch with lasso.
last *n* shoemaker's model of foot.
last *a* & *adv* after all others; latest; *n* last person, thing; that which is most recent; *adv* **lastly** finally.
last *v* continue, endure; suffice; be durable.
latch *n* fastening for doors and windows; spring lock; *v* fasten with latch.
late *a* behindhand; towards end; earlier than present; no longer living; (*comp*) **later**; (*sup*) **last, latest**; *adv* (also **lately**) recently.
lateen *a* of triangular sail.
latent *a* hidden; dormant.
lateral *a* at, from side.
latex *n* white, milky juice, secreted by plants, *esp* rubber tree; *a* (*bot*) **lactiferous** bearing latex.
lath *n* thin strip of wood, or other material.
lathe *n* machine used in turning wood, metal.
lather *n* froth of soap and water; (of horse) foamy sweat; *v* form lather; (*sl*) beat.
Latin *a* of ancient Rome; of languages and races descended from this; *n* member of Latin race.
latitude *n* (*geog*) distance N & S from equator; freedom from restriction; scope; (*pl*) regions; *a* **latitudinal.**
latrine *n* privy, *esp* in camp, barracks.
latter *a* later; second of two; *adv* **latterly.**

lattice *n* structure of criss-cross laths, or metal strips; window with glass crossed by lead strips; *a* **latticed.**

laud *v* praise, extol; *a* **laudable** praiseworthy.

laudanum *n* tincture of opium.

laugh *v* utter sounds expressing amusement, joy, scorn; *n* such sound; *a* **laughable** funny; *ns* **laughter, laughing-stock** object of general ridicule; **laughing-gas** nitrous oxide, mild anaesthetic.

launch *v* hurl, fling; initiate; set afloat; (*fig*) embark on; *n* act of launching.

launch *n* largest boat carried by warship; large power-driven pleasure boat.

launder *v* wash and iron linen etc.; *ns* **laundress** washerwoman; **laundry** place where linen etc is laundered; clothes sent to laundry; **launderette** place where washing machines can be used on payment of fee.

laureate *a* crowned with laurels; *n* **Poet L.** poet appointed to Royal Household.

laurel *n* evergreen, glossy-leaved shrub; (*pl*) its leaves; symbol of victory, fame.

lava *n* molten rock thrown out by volcano.

lavatory *n* room with wash-basin & water-closet.

lavender *n* shrub with fragrant pale mauve flowers.

lavish *a* profuse; extravagant; abundant; *v* bestow, spend recklessly.

law *n* rule imposed by authority; jurisprudence; sequence of natural processes in nature; sequence of causes and effects; *as* **law-abiding** well behaved; **lawful** legitimate; **lawless** regardless of laws; *ns* **lawgiver** legislator; **lawyer** member of legal profession; **lawsuit** action at law.

lawn *n* fine linen.

lawn *n* stretch of close-mown grass; *ns* **l.-mower, l.-tennis** ball game played on grass or hard court.

lax *a* loose, slack; careless; (of bowels) relaxed; *a* **laxative** having loosening effect on bowels; *ns* **laxity, laxness** slackness; lack of moral principles.

lay *v* deposit; cause to lie; produce egg; *pt* & *pp* **laid;** *pr p* **laying;** *vs* **l. off** dismiss (workers); **l. on** apply;

supply; **l. it on** (*sl*) flatter; **l. waste** devastate; *n* **lay-by** roadside stopping place for traffic; *n* **layer** stratum; shoot of plant pegged in earth to make roots; *v* propagate by layers.

lay *a* not clerical or professional; *n* ballad; *n* **lay-figure** jointed figure used by artists; (*fig*) nonentity; **layman** one who is not expert.

layette *n* outfit of clothes etc. for new born child.

laze *v* be idle; rest oneself; *a* **lazy** indolent; *n* **laziness.**

lea *n* meadow, open grassland.

lead *n* heavy bluish white metal element; piece of this used for sounding depth of water; graphite; metal strip separating lines of type; *v* cover, space with lead; *pt* & *pp* **leaded**; *a* **leaden** of, like lead; (*fig*) heavy; inert.

lead *v* conduct, guide; act as chief; govern; be ahead; excel; produce; *pt* & *pp* **led**; *ns* **leader** one who leads; editoral article in newspaper; **leadership, leading question** question which suggests required answer.

leaf *n* one of lateral growths from plant stem; flat expanded green organ of photo-synthesis; thin sheet; two pages of book etc.; movable flap of table etc.; (*pl*) **leaves**; *v* **l. through** glance briefly at book etc.; *n* **leaflet** small leaf; single printed sheet for distribution, pamphlet; *as* **leafy, leafless.**

league *n* compact, alliance for mutual protection etc.; association, group of persons, clubs etc. with common interest; *v* form alliance, league.

leak *n* crack, hole through which liquid or gas passes; amount of liquid, gas that leaks; *v* allow liquid, gas etc. to pass slowly through crack; prematurely disclose (news etc.); *n* **leakage** leaking; gradual escape or loss; *a* **leaky.**

lean *a* thin; containing no fat; (*fig*) unproductive.

lean *v* bend, incline, slope; rely on; prop against; *pt* & *pp* **leant** or **leaned**; *n* **leaning** inclination; tendency.

leap *v* spring, jump; **l. at** (*fig*) accept eagerly; *pt* & *pp* **leapt** or **leaped**; *n* jump; *ns* **leapfrog** game of vaulting over another player's bent back; **leap year** every fourth year in which February has 29 days.

learn *v* acquire knowledge, skill; commit to memory; be taught; find out; *pt* & *pp* **learnt** or **learned**; *a* **learned** well-informed, erudite; *ns* **learner, learning** knowledge acquired by study.
lease *n* contract whereby land, property is rented for stated time by owner to tenant; *v* let, rent by lease; *a* **leasehold** held on lease.
leash *n* chain or strap holding dog; set of three dogs so held; thong holding hawk; *v* hold by leash.
least *a/adv* (*sup* of LITTLE) smallest; to the smallest degree.
leather *n* skin of animal prepared by tanning; *as* **leathern** of, like leather; **leathery** tough; *n* **leather-jacket** larva of crane-fly.
leave *v* allow, cause to remain; go away; deposit; forsake; bequeath; *pt* & *pp* **left**; *pr p* **leaving.**
leave *n* permission; permission to be away from duty etc.; time spent away from work etc., holiday.
leaven *n* yeast; (*fig*) stimulating, spiritual influence; *v* raise with yeast; influence.
lecher *n* lustful, sensual person; *n* **lechery** inordinate sexual indulgence; *a* **lecherous.**
lectern *n* reading-desk in church.
lecture *n* instructive discourse; admonishment; *v* deliver lecture; reprove; *n* **lecturer.**
ledge *n* narrow shelf projecting from wall, cliff-face etc.
ledger *n* principal account book of business, etc.; flat stone; *n* **ledger-line** fishing line; (*mus*) additional line above or below stave.
lee *n* side protected from wind; *a* **leeward** on lee side; *n* **leeway** leeward drift of ship; (*fig*) loss of progress.
leech *n* blood-sucking worm; (*fig*) usurer.
leek *n* vegetable like onion.
leer *v* glance lustfully, slyly; *n* such a look.
lees *n pl* sediment of wine; dregs.
left *a* denotes side opposite to right; *n* left hand side, part; (*pol*) radical, socialist, party; *a* **left-wing** tending to more radical views.
leg *n* one of limbs on which animal, person stands, walks etc.; anything which supports, as leg of chair

etc.; part of garment covering leg; area of cricket field to left of r. handed batsman (& v.v.); **legging(s)** outer covering of leather etc. for leg; *a* **leggy, long-legged.**

legacy *n* gift, bequest by will; (*fig*) something handed down; *n* **legatee.**

legal *a* pertaining to law; lawful; *n* **legality**; *v* **legalize** make legal; *n* **legalization.**

legation *n* diplomatic body; chief of such body and his staff; his official residence.

legato *adv* (*mus*) smoothly, without breaks.

legend *n* traditional story, myth; inscription, on map or medal; *a* **legendary** fabulous, mythical.

legerdemain *n* conjuring trick; sleight of hand.

leghorn *n* plaited straw; breed of domestic fowl.

legible *a* easily read; *n* **legibility.**

legion *n* unit of ancient Roman infantry; body of troops; multitude; large organized group; *a* & *n* **legionary.**

legislator *n* maker of laws; *v* **legislate** make laws; *a* **legislative**; *n* **legislature** legislative body.

legitimate *a* lawful; justifiable; born in wedlock; *v* make lawful; *n* **legitimacy** state of being legitimate; *vs* **legitimatatize, legitimise** to legitimate.

leguminous *a* pod-bearing (pea, bean etc.).

leisure *n* freedom from work; free, unoccupied time; *as* **leisurely** unhurried, deliberate; **leisured** having much leisure.

leitmotif *n* (*mus*) recurring theme; (*fig*) recurrent association of ideas.

lemming *n* small arctic rat-like animal.

lemon *n* very acid pale yellow fruit; its colour; *ns* **lemonade** drink flavoured with lemon; **lemon sole** flat fish, type of plaice.

lemur *n* nocturnal animal resembling monkey.

lend *v* grant temporary use of; let out for hire, or interest; impart; consent to do; *pt* & *pp* **lent**; *n* **lender.**

length *n* quality of being long; total duration or extent; *v* **lengthen** make, become longer; *a* & *adv* **lengthwise**; *a* **lengthy** long; **at length** at last; in detail.

lenient *a* merciful, tolerant; not severe; *ns* **lenience, leniency.**
lens *n* piece of glass with curved surfaces, used in cameras, telescopes, spectacles etc.; (*pl*) **lenses.**
Lent *n* period of penance and fasting from Ash Wednesday to Easter; *a* **Lenten.**
lentil *n* dried seed of leguminous food plant.
lento *adv* (*mus*) slowly.
leonine *a* like a lion.
leopard *n* large, spotted carnivore of cat tribe.
leper *n* sufferer from leprosy; *n* **leprosy** infectious chronic skin disease, also affecting tissues and nerves; *a* **leprous.**
lepidoptera *n pl* insects with four scaly wings, including moths and butterflies.
leprechaun *n* Irish sprite.
lesbian *n* female homosexual; *n* **lesbianism** homosexuality between women.
lèse-majesté *n* treason.
lesion *n* injury; morbid change affecting body functions.
less *a/adv* (*comp* of LITTLE) not so much; to a lesser degree, amount; *n* smaller amount, quantity; *prep* with deduction of; *v* **lessen** reduce, diminish.
lessee *n* one to whom lease is granted.
lesson *n* anything learnt or taught; warning example portion of Scripture read in Church.
lessor *n* one who grants a lease.
lest *conj* for fear that.
let *v* allow, cause; grant use of for rent; be leased; *pt* & *pp* **let**; *pr p* **letting**; *1st* & *3rd pers imp* expressing wish, command.
let *n* hindrance, stoppage; accidental obstruction of tennis ball in serving, not counted as fault.
lethal *a* fatal, deadly.
lethargy *a* abnormal drowsiness; indifference, apathy; *a* **lethargic.**
letter *n* written symbol expressing a sound of speech; written message; (*pl*) literary culture, literature; *v* mark with letters; *a* **lettered** having education; marked with letters; *ns* **letterpress**

printing from type; **letters patent** legal document granting certain rights, or privileges.
lettuce *n* plant used for salads.
leucocyte *n* white blood corpuscle.
levee *n* reception held by sovereign, for men only.
levee *n* natural or artificial river embankment, to prevent inundation.
level *a* horizontal; even; of same height; equable; *n* plane surface; usual height; moral, intellectual, social standard; horizontal passage in mine; instrument for testing horizontal plane; *v* make flat; bring to same level; aim (gun); *a* **level-headed** calm, sensible.
lever *n* rigid bar (usually supported at fixed point) which lifts or moves weight at one end when power is brought to bear on the other; *n* **leverage** action, power of lever; *v* use lever.
leveret *n* young hare.
leviathan *n* sea-monster; (*fig*) something of huge size, *esp* ship.
levitation *n* power of raising solid body into air by non-physical means; *v* **levitate** cause to do this.
levity *n* frivolity; facetiousness; lightness.
levy *n* collection of tax; sum thus collected; forced military enlistment; *v* impose tax etc.; conscript (troops).
lewd *a* indecent; obscene; *n* **lewdness.**
lexicon *n* dictionary; *ns* **lexicography** art, process of making dictionaries; **lexicographer.**
liable *a* likely to have or suffer; answerable to; apt, inclined to; *n* **liability** obligation.
liaison *n* connection; co-operation; illicit sexual relationship; *v* (*coll*) **liaise** act as means of co-ordination with; *n* **liaison officer** officer who acts as link between units, etc.
liana *n* tropical climbing plant.
libation *n* drink-offering to gods.
libel *n* written, printed statement likely to damage person's reputation; *v* publish libel; defame character *a* **libellous** defamatory.
liberal *a* generous; tolerant; belonging to political

party favouring reforms; *n* member of this party; *n* **liberality** generosity; *v* **liberalize.**

liberate *v* set free; *ns* **liberation, liberator.**

libertarian *n* advocate of liberty, freedom of will.

libertine *n* debauched, dissolute man; *a* dissolute.

liberty *n* freedom; offensive act or remark; (*pl*) privileges, rights, conferred by grant.

libido *n* life-force; sexual desire; *a* **libidinous.**

library *n* collection of books; place where books are kept, or may be borrowed; *n* **librarian.**

libretto *n* words of an opera or musical play.

licence *n* permission granted by authority; document granting it; excessive freedom; dissoluteness; **poetic l.** deviation from rules of his art by writer or artist; *v* **license** grant licence to; *ns* **licensee** holder of licence; **licentiate** one authorized to practice profession or art.

licentious *a* dissolute, immoral.

lichen *n* flowerless, moss-like plant growing on trees, rocks etc.; *a* **lichened.**

lichgate, lychgate *n* roofed gateway into churchyard.

lick *v* pass tongue over; flicker round; (*sl*) beat, defeat; *a* act of licking; *n* **licking** (*sl*) beating, thrashing.

lid *n* movable cover; eyelid.

lido *n* open air swimming-pool.

lie *v* recline, be in resting position; be situated, placed; *pt* **lay**; *pp* **lain**; *pr p* **lying**; *n* direction.

lie *v* make false statement; *pt* & *pp* **lied**; *pr p* **lying**; *n* deliberate untruth; *ns* **white lie** justifiable falsehood; **liar** one who tells lies.

lief *adv* (*ar*) willingly, gladly.

liege *a* bound to render feudal service; *n* lord, sovereign; *n* **liegeman** vassal, subject.

lien *n* (*leg*) right to hold property of another until debt is paid.

lieu *n* place; **in lieu** instead of.

lieutenant *n* deputy; rank below naval lieut.-commander or army captain.

life *n* animate existence; duration of existence; living beings in general; biography; period of usefulness;

way of living; vitality; (*pl*) **lives**; *as* **lifeless** dead; dull; **lifelong** lasting for lifetime; *n* **lifetime** duration of life.

lift *v* raise to higher position; take up; (of fog) disperse; *n* that which lifts; elevator.

ligament *n* band of fibrous tissue connecting bones; connecting band; *n* **ligature** anything which binds; thread for tying severed artery.

light *a* not heavy; loose, friable; mild; trivial; *adv* in light manner; *v* **lighten** make less heavy; make, become less gloomy; *n* **lightness**; *v* **l. on** discover by chance; *as* **l.-headed** delirious; **l.-hearted** gay, cheerful.

light *n* form of energy, acting on optic nerve; making vision possible; brightness; source of this; knowledge; aspect; *a* bright; pale in colour; *v* set fire to; illuminate; *pt* & *pp* **lighted** or **lit**; *v* **lighten**, give light to; become brighter; *ns* **lighter** instrument for lighting; boat for unloading goods into; **lightning** visible discharge of electricity from atmosphere; **lighthouse, – ship** tower on coast or anchored ship with powerful light to guide others; **l. year** distance light travels in year, approx. 6,000,000 miles.

ligneous *a* like, made of wood; *n* **lignite,** soft woody brown coal.

like *a* similar; *adv* in same way; *prep* in manner of; *a* **likely** probable; *n* **likelihood**; *v* **liken** compare, *n* **likeness** resemblance; portrait; *adv* **likewise** also, moreover.

like *v* be fond of; be attached to; *a* **likeable** agreeable, attractive.

lilac *n* flowering shrub; pale mauve colour.

Lilliputian *a* diminutive.

lilt *v* sing sweetly with spirit; *n* well-marked beat or rhythm in music; swing.

lily *n* bulbous flowering plant.

limb *n* leg, arm, wing; bough of tree.

limber *n* detachable part of gun-carriage.

limber *a* pliable, supple; *v* **limber up** make supple by exercise.

limbo *n* (*theo*) condition, or region allotted to souls of unbaptised children; (*fig*) place for neglected and forgotten things; W. Indian dance.

lime *n* calcium oxide obtained by burning limestone; sticky substance for catching birds, birdlime; *v* dress, mix, treat with lime; *ns* **limelight** bright white light; (*fig*) glare of publicity; **limestone** kind of rock, calcium carbonate.

lime *n* kind of tree; its round acid fruit; *ns* **lime-juice** sweetened juice of lime used as cordial; **limey** (*U.S.* & *Aust. sl*) Briton.

lime *n* linden tree.

limerick *n* nonsense verse of five lines.

limit *n* boundary; (*fig*) intolerable person or thing; *v* restrict; curb; *n* **limitation**; *as* **limitable, limited.**

limn *v* paint, depict.

limousine *n* large, closed type of motor car.

limp *a* flaccid; not firm; *n* **limpness.**

limp *v* walk lamely; *n* lameness.

limpet *n* rock-clinging marine shell-fish.

limpid *a* clear, transparent; *n* **limpidity.**

linch-pin *n* metal pin holding wheel on to axle.

linden *n* lime-tree.

line *n* string, cord; very thin threadlike mark, made by pen etc.; wrinkle; row; mode of action; organized system of transport by road, sea, air etc.; occupation; hobby; lineage; that which has length but no breadth; *v* mark with lines; insert lining; bring into line; *ns* **lineage** descent; pedigree; **lineament** feature; **liner** large passenger-carrying ship or aircraft; **lining** material used to cover inner surface; *a* **linear** of, in lines.

linen *n* cloth made of flax; underclothes, bed-linen, tablecloths etc.; *a* made of linen.

ling *n* kind of heather.

ling *n* species of coarse sea-fish, allied to cod.

linger *v* delay, loiter; be slow to disappear.

lingerie *n* women's underwear.

lingo *n* outlandish jargon, *esp* foreign.

lingual *a* of, formed by tongue; *n* lingual sound; *n* **linguist** one skilled in foreign languages; *a* **linguistic** of languages.

liniment *n* embrocation.

link *n* loop, ring of chain; unit of measurement (7.92″); connection; *v* join together, as with link; connect; *n* **linkage**.
links *n* golf course.
linnet *n* song-bird of finch family.
linoleum *n* type of floor-covering; *n* **linocut** relief engraving on linoleum; print made from this.
linotype *n* type-setting machine which casts whole line in one piece.
linseed *n* flax seed.
lint *n* soft material for dressing wounds.
lintel *n* horizontal stone or timber bar over doorway or window.
lion *n* large powerful carnivore of cat tribe; (*fig*) celebrity; (*fem*) **lioness**; *v* **lionize** treat as celebrity.
lip *n* one of fleshy flaps of tissue round mouth; edge, rim; (*sl*) impertinence; *n* **lipstick** cosmetic for colouring lips.
liqueur *n* strong, sweetened alcoholic liquor.
liquid *n* substance between solid and gas, fluid; *a* (of sounds) harmonious; flowing smoothly; fluid; *v* **liquefy** become, make liquid; melt; *ns* **liquefaction, liquidity**; *a* **liquescent**.
liquidate *v* pay (debt); wind up financial affairs and dissolve company; (*coll*) kill; *ns* **liquidation, liquidator** official appointed to liquidate business.
liquor *n* liquid substance, *esp* alcoholic one.
liquorice *n* black, very sweet substance extracted from root of plant of same name, used in medicine, and as sweetmeat.
lisle *n* fine cotton thread or fabric.
lisp *v* speak with imperfect pronunciation of sibilants; *n*.
lissom *a* lithe, supple.
list *n* roll, catalogue of names, words etc.; inventory; *v* make, write list.
list *n* inclination, leaning (of ship etc.) towards one side; *v* slope, lean.
listless *a* languid, apathetic.
listen *v* attend closely so as to hear; *n* **listener**.
litany *n* prayer with responses from congregation.
literal *a* of letters; based on exact words of original;

accurate; word for word; *adv* **literally** (*coll*) absolutely.
literate *a* educated, able to read & write; *n* educated person; *n* **literacy** ability to read & write.
literature *n* writings of country or period; written works on any subject; (*coll*) any book or printed matter; *a* **literary** of, learned in literature.
lithe *a* supple, flexible; pliant; *n* **litheness.**
lithography *n* art of printing copies from designs on prepared stone or metal plates; *ns* **lithograph** print so made; **lithographer**; *a* **lithographic.**
litigate *v* contest at law; make subject of lawsuit; *ns* **litigant, litigation.**
litmus *n* vegetable substance turned red by acids and blue by alkalis; *n* **litmus-paper.**
litre *n* metric unit of capacity (about 1$\frac{3}{4}$ pints).
litter *n* scattered oddments of rubbish; portable couch, stretcher; all young born at one time; straw etc. as bedding for animals; *v* make untidy with litter; give birth to.
little *a* small; brief; *n* small amount; *adv* slightly.
littoral *a* pertaining to seashore; *n* coastal region.
liturgy *n* prescribed public worship.
live *v* exist; dwell; subsist; pass one's life; *n* **living** way of life; livelihood, maintenance; church benefice.
live *a* having life; vital; flaming, glowing; *ns* **l. broadcast** one not pre-recorded; **l. wire** electrified wire; (*fig*) lively person; *a* **lively** brisk, vivid; merry; *ns* **liveliness, livelihood** subsistence, support.
livelong *a* lasting throughout the day.
liver *n* organ secreting bile; *a* **liverish** of liver; irritable, touchy.
livery *n* distinctive uniform of City Company, or servants of one employer; food-allowance for horses; *n* **l. company** City of London Company; **liveryman** member of City Company; **l. stable** one where horses are boarded, or hired out.
livid *a* of bluish pale colour, as by bruising; (*sl*) very angry.
lizard *n* four-footed reptile.
llama *n* woolly S. American ruminant.
load *n* that which is carried; burden; (*elect*) amount

of energy drawn from source; *v* place burden on, in; charge (gun); *n* **loadline** Plimsoll mark.

loadstone, lodestone *n* magnet, magnetic iron oxide.

loaf *n* mass of bread of definite size, weight; small cone of sugar; (*pl*) **loaves.**

loaf *v* loiter, work lazily; *n* **loafer.**

loam *n* rich vegetable soil.

loan *n* something lent; act of lending; money lent; *v* lend.

loath, loth *a* unwilling; *v* **loathe** detest; abhor; *n* **loathing** great disgust, repulsion; *a* **loathsome** disgusting, revolting.

lob *n* high-pitched underhand ball in cricket; high ball in tennis; *v* bowl, hit shot thus.

lobby *n* hall, anteroom; room in House of Commons where M.P.s and public meet; corridor where M.P.s vote; *v* try to influence M.P.s (to favour particular group, interests etc.); *n* **lobbying** frequent lobby for such purpose.

lobe *n* soft pendulous lower part of ear; rounded projecting part of liver, etc.; *a* **lobed**

lobelia *n* genus of herbaceous plants.

lobster *n* large edible marine crustacean.

lobworm *n* large worm used as fish bait.

local *a* of, in, confined to particular place, region, part of body; *n* person belonging to district; (*sl*) public house; *ns* **locale** scene of event; **locality** position, district; *v* **localize** restrict to particular area; give local character to.

locate *v* discover, set in, particular place or position; *n* **location** position; outdoor set where scenes for film are shot.

loch *n* Scottish lake or arm of sea.

lock *n* tress of hair; tuft of wool.

lock *n* device for closing door, safe etc., operated by key, combination; mechanism for firing gun; blockage; enclosure on river, canal in which boats can be moved from one level to another; *v* fasten with lock; become rigidly fixed; block; *ns* **locker** box, small cupboard with lock; **lockjaw** tetanus; **lockout** refusal by employer to allow work to continue;

locksmith maker, repairer of locks; **lock-up** prison; private garage.
locket *n* small metal case for photograph etc., worn as ornament.
locomotive *a* having power of moving from place to place; *n* steam, diesel, electric engine moving by its own power; *n* **locomotion** action, power of moving.
locum tenens *n* one acting temporarily as deputy, *esp* of doctor.
locus *n* exact place; (*math*) line tracing path of point through space.
locust *n* destructive winged insect; *n* **l. tree** carob tree; **l. bean** its fruit.
locution *n* mode, style of speech; phrase.
lode *n* vein of metal ore; **lodestone** see **loadstone**.
lodge *n* gate-keeper's house; local branch, meeting place of Freemasons; *v* house; deposit; be embedded; lay accusation, charge against; occupy lodgings; *ns* **lodging(s)** room(s) let to lodger; **lodger** one who pays rent for part of another's house; **lodg(e)ment** lodging place; (*mil*) stable position gained by effort.
loft *n* attic; room over stable; gallery in church; *v* hit golf ball high; *a* **lofty** of great height; (*fig*) noble, sublime; haughty; *adv* **loftily**.
log *n* unhewn piece of timber; apparatus for measuring ship's speed; daily record of ship's voyage, aircraft flight etc.; (*abbrev*) logarithm; *v* cut into logs; enter in log-book; *ns* **logging** felling, sawing, transporting logs to river; **logger; log-book** daily record of journey.
loganberry *n* hybrid fruit, cross between blackberry and raspberry.
logarithm *n* exponent of power to which invariable number must be raised to produce given number, tabulated for use in calculation.
loggerhead *n* blockhead; **at loggerheads** quarrelsome.
loggia *n* roofed, open extension to house.
logic *n* art of reasoning; *a* **logical** of logic; consistent; rational *n* **logician**.
logistics *n pl* science of moving & supplying troops.
loin *n* part of body between ribs and hip.

loiter *v* linger; loaf; delay; *n* **loiterer.**
loll *v* sit, lie lazily; hang out tongue.
lollipop *n* sweetmeat.
lone *a* solitary; isolated; *a* **lonely** feel conscious of solitude; unfrequented; *n* **loneliness**; *a* **lonesome.**
long *a* having length; protracted; (of series, list etc.) having many items; *adv* for long time; *a* **long-winded** tiresomely long.
long *v* desire earnestly; yearn, crave for; *n* **longing** yearning, desire.
longeron *n* longitudinal member of body of aircraft.
longevity *n* prolonged duration of life.
longitude *n* distance in degrees, E or W from given meridian; *a* **longitudinal** of longitude; lengthwise.
longshoreman *n* man employed on wharves; or doing odd jobs on shore; in-shore fisherman.
loofah *n* fibrous part of tropical gourd, used as sponge.
look *v* use eyes; seem to be; gaze, stare; (*fig*) consider; *n* looking; expression; appearance; *ns* **looking-glass** mirror; **look-out** one who keeps watch; *v* **l. after** tend; **l. down on** despise.
loom *n* weaving machine.
loom *v* emerge indistinctly; (*fig*) appear important and menacing.
loon *n* lout, fool; guillemot.
loop *n* bend in cord, string etc., made by crossing ends; noose; railway line branching from main line and rejoining it farther on; *v* form loop; **l. the l.** aerial manoeuvre in which aircraft describes complete vertical circle.
loophole *n* vertical slit in castle wall; (*fig*) means of evasion, or escape.
loose *a* free; not tight; lax, dissolute; not firmly fixed, fastened; vague; *v* unfasten; free; shoot (arrow), fire (gun); *v* **loosen** make loose; *ns* **looseness, loose-box** stable or van where horse is free to move about.
loot *n* & *v* plunder.
lop *v* trim, shorten by chopping (branches etc.).
lop *v* hang limply; *n* **lop-ear** drooping ear; rabbit with such ears; *a* **lop-sided** unevenly balanced.

lope *v* run with long, easy, bounding pace.
loquacious *a* talkative; *n* **loquacity.**
lord *n* ruler, governor, master; owner; any peer of realm; God; *v* dominate; *a* **lordly** magnificent; haughty; *ns* **lordliness, lordship** power of lord; domain; title of peers.
lore *n* knowledge of special kind, often derived from tradition.
lorgnette *n* eyeglasses on handle, opera-glass.
lorikeet *n* small green and blue parrot.
lorry *n* large, heavy, open wagon or truck used for road transport.
lory *n* kind of parrot.
lose *v* suffer loss; get rid of; fail to retain, find; be bereaved of; be defeated; *pt* & *pp* **lost**; *pr p* **losing**; *n* **loss** act, result of losing; bereavement.
lot *n* one's fate, fortune; item at auction; large quantity; **cast (draw) lots** decide fate or fortune by chance fall of die or similar marked object.
lotion *n* medicinal or cosmetic liquid for external use.
lottery *n* gamble; competition in which prizes are allotted by chance drawing of tickets.
lotto *n* game of chance, played as bingo.
lotus *n* Egyptian water-lily; (*myth*) plant whose fruit caused forgetfulness and bliss.
loud *a* producing much sound; noisy; (*fig*) boisterous, vulgar; *n* **loud-speaker** amplifier which radiates sound waves.
lough *n* Irish loch.
lounge *v* recline lazily; be idle; *n* comfortably furnished room; sofa; *n* **lounger** idler, loafer.
lour, lower *v* scowl; glare sullenly; (*fig*) grow dark (sky, clouds etc.).
louse *n* parasitic insect; (*pl*) **lice**; *a* **lousy** having lice; (*sl*) unpleasant; bad; **lousy with** full of; having plenty of.
lout *n* clumsy, mannerless fellow; *a* **loutish.**
louver, louvre *n* window frame with inclined boards or slats for admitting air, without rain; ventilating structure resembling this.
love *n* affection; charity; devotion; sexual passion; sweetheart; (tennis) no score; *v* be fond of; desire

passionately; delight in; feel love for; *ns* **lover** one who loves *esp* sexually outside marriage; **love-bird** small green parrot; **loveliness, loving-cup** large cup passed among several persons, each drinking from it; *as* **lovely** beautiful, delicious; **loving** affectionate.

low *a* not high, tall; not intense; humble; vulgar; not loud; melancholy; inferior in order of merit; *v* **lower** cause to descend; decrease, diminish; degrade; *ns* **low-brow** not an intellectual; **lowliness** humility; **low frequency** (*elect*) one having less than 1000 periods per second; **low-down** (*sl*) inside information.

low *n* cry of a cow; *v* utter this sound.

loyal *a* faithful to Crown, cause, person etc.; upright, honourable; *ns* **loyalty, loyalist.**

lozenge *n* diamond-shaped figure, rhombus; small flat medicinal tablet.

lubber *n* clumsy, stupid person; untrained seaman.

lubricate *n* make slippery, smooth with oil, grease; *ns* **lubrication, lubricant** substance used to reduce friction; (*sl*) bribe; **lubricator, lubricity** smoothness; (*fig*) lewdness.

lucent *a* shining, bright; clear.

lucerne *n* clover-like plant, used as fodder.

lucid *a* clear; easy to understand; clear-headed; *ns* **lucidity, lucidness.**

luck *n* fate, chance; good fortune; *as* **lucky** fortunate; **luckless**; *adv* **luckily** fortunately.

lucre *n* material profit, gain; **filthy l.** (*sl*) money, wealth; *a* **lucrative** profitable.

lucubrate *v* work hard, study *esp* at night; *n* **lucubration** learned writing.

ludicrous *a* absurd, ridiculous, comical.

ludo *n* simple game played with counters and dice.

luff *n* sail ship close to the wind; *n* part of fore-and-aft sail nearer wind.

lug *n* ear-like projection used as handle; *v* pull, drag with effort.

lug *n* common worm used as fish bait.

luggage *n* baggage, trunks, suitcases etc.

lugsail *n* oblong sail on oblique yard; *n* **lugger** small vessel with lugsails.

lugubrious *a* mournful, woe-begone; funereal.
lukewarm *a* tepid; (*fig*) lacking enthusiasm.
lull *v* soothe, make quiet; subside; *n* temporary pause; *n* **lullaby** cradle-song; soothing sound.
lumbar *a* of, near loins; *n* **lumbago** rheumatic pain in loins, or lower part of spine.
lumber *v* move clumsily, heavily; encumber, obstruct; *n* useless odds and ends; sawn timber; *n* **lumberjack** man who fells and prepares timber for sawmill.
luminary *n* light-giving body, *esp* heavenly; (*fig*) distinguished, learned person; *a* **luminous** bright, glowing; (*fig*) clear; *n* **luminosity**.
lump *n* shapeless mass; swelling, bump; *v* throw together in one mass; *as* **lumpish** clumsy; shapeless; **lumpy** uneven; *v* **lump it** (*sl*) put up with, endure.
lunar *a* of, relating to moon.
lunatic *a* insane; *n* insane person; *n* **lunacy**.
lunch, luncheon *n* light mid-day meal.
lung *n* respiratory organ in vertebrates.
lunge *n* sudden thrust, blow made with weapon; sudden movement of body; plunge; *v* make lunge.
lupin *n* garden plant with long spikes of flowers.
lupine *a* like a wolf.
lupus *n* tuberculous skin disease.
lurch *v* pitch, roll to one side; *n* sudden stagger; **leave in the lurch** leave in difficulties.
lurcher *n* dog, cross between collie and greyhound.
lure *n* bait used to recall hawk; decoy; (*fig*) anything which entices; *v* recall (hawk); attract.
lurid *a* ghastly; sensational; crude, garish; glaring.
lurk *v* remain hidden; lie in wait.
luscious *a* delicious; excessively sweet.
lush *a* (of grass etc) juicy, luxuriant.
lust *n* sexual appetite; (*fig*) excessive desire; *as* **lustful, lusty** vigorous, powerful.
lustration *n* purificatory, expiatory ceremony.
lustre *n* gloss, sheen; (*fig*) renown, glory; *a* **lustrous** shining, luminous.
lute *n* stringed musical instrument; *n* **lutanist**.
lute, luting *n* cement for making joints air-tight.

luxury *n* state, mode of life of great ease and comfort; expensive but unnecessary thing; great comfort or enjoyment; *a* **luxurious** extravagant; sumptuous; *v* **luxuriate** indulge in luxury; revel in; grow profusely; *a* **luxuriant** abundant; exuberant; *n* **luxuriance** excessive abundance.
lyceum *n* building with lecture-halls, library etc.
lyddite *n* powerful explosive.
lye *n* alkaline solution of wood-ash in water.
lymph *n* colourless fluid found in lymphatic vessels; fluid exuding from inflamed tissues; *n pl* vessels in body conveying lymph; *a* **lymphatic** of lymph; (*fig*) sluggish.
lynch *v* put to death, by mob violence, without trial; *n* **lynch law** rapid, summary justice.
lynx *n* fierce wildcat with short tail and tufted ears; *a* **lynx-eyed** keen sighted.
lyre *n* old form of harp.
lyric *n* words for song; short emotional poem; *a* **lyric(al)** of poems expressing emotion.

macabre *a* gruesome; terrible.
macadam *n* broken stone for road surfacing; *v* pave road with this.
macaroni *n* tubular form of Italian wheat paste.
macaroon *n* small sweet cake or biscuit made of ground almonds.
macaw *n* kind of parrot.
mace *n* staff of office, *esp* of mayors etc.
mace *n* spice made of dried outer layer of nutmeg.
macerate *v* soften by soaking; become thin through fasting.
Mach *n* ratio of speed of aircraft etc. to speed of sound.
machete *n* large, heavy chopping knife.
machination *n* intrigue, subtle contrivance; *v* **machinate** plot; contrive, conspire.
machine *n* apparatus, contrivance that applies power to perform work, or direct movement; organized system to carry out specific functions; *v* print, sew with machine; *ns* **machinery** machines; parts of

machine; **machinist** one who makes, invents, operates machines; **machine gun** *n* quick-firing mechanically operated gun.
mackerel *n* type of edible sea-fish.
mackintosh *n* rubber-coated cloth; waterproof coat made of this.
macrocosm *n* the great world, the universe.
mad *a* insane; irrational; angry; wildly gay; (of dog) suffering from rabies; *ns* **madman, madness** insanity; excitement; **madcap** rash person; *v* **madden** drive mad; infuriate.
madam *n* formal mode of addressing women.
madder *n* climbing plant; red dye from its root.
Madonna *n* Virgin Mary; picture, statue of her; **M. lily** large-flowered white lily.
madrigal *n* type of part song for three or more voices.
maelstrom *n* whirlpool; (*fig*) turmoil.
maenad *n* Bacchante; nymph attendant.
maestro *n* eminent composer, musician or conductor.
Mafia *n* Sicilian secret criminal organization.
magazine *n* store-house for ammunition, weapons etc.; periodical containing articles, stories etc. by different authors; cartridge chamber of repeating rifle.
magenta *n* purplish-red aniline dye; *a* of this colour.
maggot *n* grub, larva *esp* of blow-fly; *a* **maggoty.**
magic *n* feigned superhuman control over natural forces and objects; sorcery; unexplained mysterious influence; conjuring; *a* **magical;** *n* **magician** one skilled in magic; wizard; conjurer.
magistrate *n* civil official administering law; *a* **magisterial** of, pertaining to magistrates.
magnanimous *a* of generous, noble character; incapable of pettiness, resentment; *n* **magnanimity.**
magnate *n* prominent, influential man, *esp* in finance, industry.
magnesium *n* metallic element; *n* **magnesia** alkaline compound of this used in medicine.
magnet *n* piece of iron or steel etc. having property of attracting or repelling other pieces of metal; loadstone; (*fig*) anything that attracts; *a* **magnetic;**

n **magnetism** magnetic phenonema; science of this; (*fig*) power of attracting, influencing others; *v* **magnetize** turn into magnet; attract, fascinate (someone); *n* **magneto** small dynamo with magnet, *esp* one producing ignition spark in internal combustion engine.

magnificent *a* splendid; of surpassing beauty, quality, generosity; *n* **magnificence.**

magnify *v* cause to appear larger, as with lens; exaggerate; *n* **magnification.**

magniloquent *a* speaking pompously; grandiose; *n* **magniloquence.**

magnitude *n* size, greatness; extent.

magnolia *n* genus of flowering trees.

magnum *n* two-quart bottle.

magpie *n* black and white bird of crow family.

Magyar *n* dominant race in Hungary; their language.

maharajah *n* title of some Indian princes; *ns* **maharanee** maharaja's wife.

mahatma *n* Indian spiritual adept; one endowed with wisdom & power.

mah-jong *n* Chinese game played with 144 'tiles'.

mahogany *n* reddish-brown, fine-grained, hard wood.

mahout *n* Indian elephant keeper and driver.

maiden *n* young unmarried woman, *a* virginal; unused; done or experienced for first time; *ns* **maid** young girl; woman servant; **maidenhead** virginity; **maidenhood**; *a* **maidenly** modest.

mail *n* armour of interlaced metal rings or plates; *a* **mailed** wearing such armour.

mail *n* postal system; letters conveyed at one time; *v* send by post; **mail order** order for goods sent by post.

maim *v* cripple; mutilate.

main *a* chief, most important, leading; *n* principal pipe or cable iu water, sewage, electricity, or gas system; *ns* **mainland** main part of country; **mainspring** chief spring of watch or clock; **mainstay** rope from mainmast; (*fig*) chief support.

maintain *v* keep up; carry on; support; preserve; assert; *a* **maintainable**; *n* **maintenance** act of preserving; livelihood; upkeep.

maisonette *n* small house; part of house used as flat.
maize *n* Indian corn.
majesty *n* sovereignty; dignity; title of sovereign; *a* **majestic** stately, dignified.
major *a* greater; more important; elder; *n* person of full age; army rank above captain; *ns* **majority** greater number; number of votes by which one party leads in election; full age; **major-domo** chief steward of household.
make *v* construct; prepare for use; create; earn; produce; compel; promote; reach; appoint; *pt* & *pp* **made**; *pr p* **making**; *n* style, shape, mode of structure; *ns* **makeshift** temporary inferior substitute; **make-believe** pretence; **make-up** arrangement of type etc. into page form; cosmetics; **making** forming; (*pl*) potential qualities.
mal-, male- *prefix* bad, ill, wrong. *Forms compounds e.g.*: *as* **maladroit** clumsy; **malicious** spiteful; *ns* **malcontent** discontented person; **malediction** curse; **malefactor** evil-doer; **malevolence** ill-will; **malformation** deformity; **malice** ill-will, spite; **malpractice** wrong-doing.
malacca *n* kind of bamboo cane.
malachite *n* green mineral.
malady *n* sickness, disease, ailment.
malaise *n* slight physical discomfort.
malapropism *n* ridiculous misuse of word.
malaria *n* fever transmitted by mosquito-bite.
male *a* belonging to sex which begets offspring; *n* male person or animal.
malign *v* defame; speak evil of; *a* **malignant** filled with ill-will; (of disease) likely to prove fatal; *ns* **malignancy, malignity** spite, malice.
malinger *v* feign illness to escape duty, work etc.; *n* **malingerer**.
mall *n* level shaded walk *esp* public avenue.
mallard *n* common wild duck.
malleable *a* capable of being hammered, pressed into shape; amenable; *n* **malleability**.
mallet *n* wooden-headed hammer; polo-stick; croquet-mallet.
mallow *n* common wild flower.

malmsey *n* sweet white wine.
malt *n* dried fermented barley or other grain used in brewing; *n* **maltster** maker of malt.
mamba *n* deadly African tree-snake.
mammal *n* animal which suckles its young; *a* **mammary** pertaining to breast; **mammary gland** milk gland.
mammon *n* personified wealth, as object of pursuit.
mammoth *n* extinct type of elephant; *a* colossal.
man *n* human being; adult male person; human race; piece used in chess, draughts etc.; man-servant; (*pl*) **men**; *v* supply with men for defence, work etc.; fortify; *v* **man-handle** move without mechanical aid; treat roughly; *ns* **manhole** hole giving access to drains, pipes etc; **mannikin** dwarf; lay figure; **manliness; manslaughter** unlawful, unpremeditated homocide; *as* **manful** bold, resolute; **manlike, manly** virile; bold; **mannish** (woman) like man.
manacle *n* & *v* handcuff.
manage *v* conduct, handle; succeed in doing; see to; influence; *a* **manageable** docile; *ns* **management** process of managing; administration; body of persons managing business; **manager** one who manages; one in charge of business etc.; (*fem*) **manageress**; *as* **managerial, managing**.
mandarin *n* former Chinese high official; small sweet type of orange.
mandate *n* command, commission to follow specified policy, *esp* given by electors to their representative; placing of small, backward country's affairs in care of major power; *n* **mandatary** holder of mandate; *a* **mandatory, mandated** entrusted to a mandate.
mandible *n* jaw-bone; either part of bird's beak.
mandolin(e) *n* musical stringed instrument.
mandrake, mandragora *n* narcotic plant.
mandrel *n* rod or bar on which articles are fixed while being turned.
mandrill *n* large baboon with blue face & red rump.
mane *n* long hair on neck of horse, lion etc.
manganese *n* metallic element.
mange *n* skin disease of dogs etc.; *a* **mangy**.
mangel-wurzel *n* large kind of beet.

manger *n* feeding-trough in stable etc.
mangle *n* machine with rollers for pressing linen etc.; *v* press in mangle.
mangle *v* mutilate, spoil, hack.
mango *n* tropical fruit; tree bearing it.
mangrove *n* tropical tree, growing in swamps.
mania *n* violent madness; (*fig*) obsession, craze; *a* **maniacal**; *n* **maniac** mad person.
manicure *v* treat and care for hands and nails; *n*; *n* **manicurist.**
manifest *a* obvious; undoubtedly; *v* make manifest; *n* list of cargo for Customs; *ns* **manifestation, manifesto** public declaration of policy.
manifold *a* numerous; varied; *n* pipe with several outlets.
manila, manilla *n* fibrous hemp.
manipulate *v* handle; manage skilfully; alter fraudulently; *ns* **manipulation, manipulator**; *a* **manipulative.**
manna *n* miraculous food of Israelites in wilderness; (*fig*) spiritual food; gum of Arabian tamarisk.
mannequin *n* live model employed to display clothes.
manner *n* way thing happens or is done; custom, style; (*pl*) social behaviour; *n* **mannerism** peculiarity of style; *a* **mannerly** polite.
manoeuvre *n* strategic movement of troops; clever move; (*pl*) mock warfare; *v* manage with skilfulness; perform manoeuvres.
manor *n* feudal unit of land; estate, owner or lord of which retains ancient rights over land; *n* **manor-house** house of lord of manor; *a* **manorial.**
mansard *n* roof with two angles of slope.
manse *n* minister's house *esp* in Scotland.
mansion *n* large house.
mantel *n* structure round fireplace; *n* **mantelshelf, mantelpiece** shelf at top of mantel.
mantilla *n* ornamental Spanish shawl.
mantis *n* genus of insects.
mantle *n* loose cloak; incandescent mesh covering gas flame; *v* cover; flush, blush.
manual *a* of, done with hands; *n* handbook; organ keyboard.

manufacture *n* process of making articles, goods etc.; *v* produce goods *esp* in large quantities; (*fig*) fabricate, concoct (story etc.) *n* **manufacturer** owner of factory; person, company making goods.
manure *n* dung, compost used to fertilize land; *v* apply manure to (land).
manuscript *a* written by hand; *n* hand-written document; draft of book etc. for printing.
Manx *a* of Isle of Man; **M. cat** tailless breed of cat.
many *a* numerous; *n* large number.
Maori *n* New Zealand aboriginal; their language.
map *n* plane representation of earth's surface or part of this; chart of heavens; *v* make map.
maple *n* tree of sycamore family; its wood.
maquis *n* dense scrubby undergrowth in Corsica; French resistance movement in World War II.
mar *v* spoil; ruin.
maraschino *n* liqueur made from cherries.
marathon *n* long-distance race; (*fig*) endurance competition.
marauder *n* roving thief; raider; *v* **maraud.**
marble *n* hard kind of limestone, capable of being highly polished; small ball used in game; (*pl*) child's game; *v* stain with streaks of colour.
March *n* third month of year.
march *n* boundary; frontier; *v* border.
march *v* walk, proceed in steady rhythmic step, *esp* in military formation; *n* act of marching; distance covered; music to accompany march.
marchioness *n* wife or widow of marquis.
mare *n* female horse; **mare's tails** wispy cirrus clouds.
margarine *n* manufactured butter substitute.
margin *n* edge, limit; extra amount beyond what is necessary; space round printed page; *a* **marginal.**
marguerite *n* ox-eye daisy.
marigold *n* plant with yellowy-orange flowers.
marijuana, marihuana *n* addictive narcotic prepared from hemp.
marine *a* of, connected with sea or shipping; *n* soldier serving on warship; *n* **mariner** seaman, sailor.
marionette *n* puppet moved on strings.

marital *a* of, pertaining to husband, marriage.
maritime *a* connected with, situated near sea; having a navy, sea-coast or sea-trade.
marjoram *n* aromatic herb.
mark *n* visible sign, symbol; target; spot, scar; *v* make mark; assign marks to (examination paper etc.); observe; *ns* **marksman** sharpshooter; **marker** person or thing that marks; one who, that which marks scores; *a* **marked** prominent; noticeable.
mark *n* unit of German currency.
market *n* public assembly, place for buying and selling; demand for goods; *v* buy, sell in, take to market; *a* **marketable.**
marl *n* limy clay soil used as fertilizer.
marline *n* two-ply cord; **m. spike** pointed hook for separating strands of rope to be spliced.
marmalade *n* jam usually made of oranges etc.
marmoreal *a* of, like marble.
marmoset *n* small, bushy-tailed monkey.
marmot *n* hibernating rodent of squirrel family.
maroon *a* brownish-crimson; *n* loudly detonating firework; *v* abandon on desert island etc.; (*fig*) desert; *n* descendant of escaped Negro slaves.
marquee *n* large tent *esp* one used at fêtes etc.
marquetry *n* inlaid wood-work.
marquis, marquess *n* title of nobleman between duke and earl.
marrow *n* soft fatty substance inside bones; edible gourd; **marrowfat** large green pea.
marry *v* take as husband or wife; join in marriage; *n* **marriage** state of being married; (*fig*) close union; *a* **marriageable.**
Mars *n* Roman god of war; planet of solar system.
Marseillaise *n* French national anthem.
marsh *n* low-lying water-logged land; *a* **marshy**; *n* **marsh-mallow** marsh plant; sweetmeat formerly made from its root.
marshal *n* official of royal household etc. who directs ceremonies etc.; *v* arrange in position; lead with ceremony.
marsupial *n* animal which carries young in pouch, as kangaroo etc.; *a* pertaining to pouch.

mart *n* trading-centre; auction room.
marten *n* weasel-like animal, valued for its fur.
martial *a* suitable for, pertaining to war; warlike.
martin *n* species of swallow; **martlet** martin; (*her*) bird without feet.
martinet *n* strict, pedantic disciplinarian.
martingale *n* strap to prevent horse from tossing head up, or rearing.
martyr *n* one who dies rather than give up faith; (*fig*) sufferer (from pain etc.); *n* **martyrdom** suffering or death of martyr.
marvel *n* something wonderful, amazing; *v* wonder; be surprised; *a* **marvellous** wonderful.
marzipan *n* paste made of ground almonds, sugar etc.
mascara *n* cosmetic for darkening eyelashes and eyebrows.
mascot *n* supposed bringer of good luck; talisman.
masculine *a* relating to males; strong; vigorous; of gender denoting males; *n* **masculinity**.
maser *n* amplifier of radar & radio astronomy signals.
mash *n* soft pulpy mass, warm food given to animals; *v* beat, crush into soft pulp.
mashie *n* golf-club for lofting, no. 5 iron.
mask *n* covering for face; *v* cover with mask; (*fig*) conceal, dissemble.
masochism *n* sexual perversion, in suffering physical pain and humiliation; *n* **masochist**.
mason *n* stone worker; Freemason; *a* **masonic** of Freemasonry; *n* **masonry** trade of mason; stonework; Freemasonry.
masque *n* theatrical tableaux; *n* **masquerade** masked ball; *v* be disguised; (*fig*) assume character of.
Mass *n* celebration of Eucharist *esp* in R.C. church.
mass *n* quantity of matter in one body, lump; large amount, number; (*pl*) **the masses** proletariat; *v* put, come together in mass; *a* **massive** large, heavy; *n* **mass meeting** large public meeting; *v* **mass produce** manufacture large quantities of standardized articles.

massacre *v* slaughter indiscriminately; *n* killing of helpless persons.
massage *n* remedial treatment consisting of rubbing and kneading affected part; *v* treat with massage; *n* **masseur** one who practices massage; (*fem*) **masseuse.**
massif *n* group of mountains forming unit.
mast *n* pole to support ship's rigging etc.; flagpole.
mast *n* fruit of beech, oak, chestnut etc.
master *n* person having authority; head of household; owner; employer; captain of merchantman; teacher; expert; *v* overcome; acquire knowledge of, skill in; *as* **masterful** imperious; **masterly** showing great talent, skill; *n* **mastery** authority; supremacy.
mastic *n* kind of resin.
masticate *v* chew with teeth; *n* **mastication.**
mastiff *n* large, thickset kind of dog.
mastoid *a* nipple-shaped; of process of bone behind ear; *n* **m. process.**
masturbate *v* artificially stimulate one's own genital organs; *n* **masturbation** sexual self-abuse.
mat *n* piece of plaited straw or coconut fibre etc. for wiping feet on, or covering part of floor; small rug; tangled hair; *v* become tangled; (*sl*) **on the mat** reprimanded.
mat, matt *a* having dull surface; lustreless.
matador *n* man who kills bull in bull-fight.
match *n* thing exactly like another; person equal to another in quality, power etc.; contest of skill, strength etc.; marriage; eligible person; *v* be equal to in contest; pit against in fight etc.; marry; correspond; *a* **matchless** peerless, unequalled; *n* **matchmaker** one who schemes to bring about marriages.
match *n* small strip of wood, tipped with combustible material; fuse for firing gun; *ns* **matchwood** small splinters; **matchbox.**
mate *n* & *v* checkmate (in chess).
mate *n* comrade; husband, wife; (of animals etc.) one of pair; officer in merchant ship; *v* marry; pair *esp* animals; *a* **matey** (*sl*) friendly.
material *n* stuff of which thing is made; fabric,

cloth; *a* of matter or body; essential, important; *ns* **materialism** theory that matter is the only reality; **materialist** one engrossed in material interests; *a* **materialistic**; *v* **materialize** make material; (of spirits etc.) assume bodily form; *adv* **materially** in relevant way; essentially.

maternity *n* motherhood; *a* **maternal** related through mother; motherly.

mathematics *n pl* abstract science concerned with properties of and relations between quantities; *a* **mathematical**; *n* **mathematician.**

matinee *n* afternoon theatrical or musical performance; *n pl* **matins** morning service of C. of E.

matriarch *n* mother as head of family or household; *n* **matriarchy** social system where descent is traced through female line.

matricide *n* act of killing one's own mother.

matriculate *v* register as student in university or college; pass necessary examination; *n* **matriculation** act of matriculating.

matrimony *n* marriage; *a* **matrimonial.**

matrix *n* mould in which type is cast; rock etc. in which gems, stones etc. are embedded; (*pl*) **matrices**

matron *n* married woman; woman in charge of nursing and domestic staff of hospital; house-keeper, domestic superintendent in institution or boarding-school; *a* **matronly** dignified; plump.

matter *n* substance of which physical object is made; subject of book, discussion etc.; affair, reason; pus; cause of complaint, trouble; *v* signify; discharge pus.

mattock *n* grubbing axe for loosening soil.

mattress *n* large cushion placed on bed, above springs & below bedclothes; similar padding with extra wires built into it.

mature *a* ripe; fully developed; prudent, wise; *v* ripen; complete; (of insurance policy, etc.) become due for payment; *n* **maturity**.

matutinal *a* pertaining to early morning.

maudlin *a* tearfully sentimental; self-pitying.

maul *v* beat, bruise; lacerate; handle roughly.

maulstick, mahl- *n* stick used to steady painter's hand.

maundy *n* ceremonial foot-washing and distribution of alms to poor people; royal alms given on Maundy Thursday, before Easter.
mausoleum *n* large stately tomb.
mauve *n* pale lilac, violet colour; *a* of this colour.
maw *n* stomach; open jaws; crop of birds.
mawkish *a* sickly; feebly emotional.
maxim *n* rule of conduct; proverb.
maximum *n* greatest size, number, degree; *a* greatest.
May *n* fifth month; hawthorn blossom; *n* **mayfly** ephemeral fly; imitation used in fishing.
may *v aux* expresses permission, possibility, hope; *pt* **might** (no *pp*); *advs* **maybe** possibly; **mayhap** perhaps.
mayhem *n* loss of, injury to limb, part of body as basis for action for damages.
mayonnaise *n* sauce of egg yolk, olive oil & vinegar.
mayor *n* chief officer of city or borough; *a* **mayoral**; *ns* **mayorality** office, period of office of mayor; **mayoress** mayor's wife.
maze *n* labyrinth; network of paths, hedges or lines; *v* bewilder.
mazurka *n* lively Polish dance; music for this.
me *pron* accusative and dative case of I.
mead *n* alcoholic drink made of fermented honey.
meadow *n* grassy field; hay-field; *n* **meadow-sweet** fragrant white-flowered plant.
meagre *a* thin, lean; scanty, inadequate; limited.
meal *n* coarsely ground grain; *as* **mealy, mealy-mouthed** apt to mince words.
meal *n* taking of food; repast.
mean *n* average; midway between two extremes; *pl* mode, way, agent, cause; money, resources; *ns* **meantime, meanwhile** intervening time.
mean *a* inferior, mediocre; shabby; parsimonious; *n* **meanness.**
mean *v* have in mind; signify; intend; have meaning; *pt* & *pp* **meant**; *n* **meaning** sense, significance; *a* expressive.
meander *v* flow windingly; (*fig*) ramble.
measles *n* infectious disease, characterized by red

rash and fever; *a* **measly** (*sl*) miserable; meagre.

measure *n* size, quantity etc. as units; standard; system, device for measuring; metre; limit; statute, law; plan of action; *v* ascertain size, proportion etc.; be of (specified size, quantity etc.); deal out (specified amount etc.); *a* **measured** of certain measure; steady; careful; *n* **measurement** act of measuring; (*pl*) dimensions.

meat *n* flesh of animals used as food; *a* **meaty** (*fig*) substantial.

mechanic *a* of machine; *n* skilled, trained workman, *esp* one working with machinery; (*pl*) science of motion and force; *a* **mechanical** concerned with; produced by, machines; (*fig*) acting without thinking.

mechanism *n* machinery; *n* **mechanization** making; mechanical *esp* change from manpower to machines; *v* **mechanize**; *a* **mechanized.**

medal *a* small metal disc *usu* with inscription used to mark achievement etc.; *ns* **medallion** large medal; round panel, ornament; **medallist** one who gains medals.

meddle *v* interfere; tamper with; *a* **meddlesome.**

mediaeval, medieval *a* of, belonging to Middle Ages; *n* **medievalism** cult, spirit of Middle Ages.

median *n* & *a* middle; average; **medial** in middle.

mediate *v* intervene as peace-maker; *a* through intermediary, not direct; *ns* **mediation** reconcilement; **mediator**.

medicine *n* science of preventing, treating and curing disease; substance taken internally to cure disease; *a* **medical** of medicine; *n* **medicament** remedy, drug; *v* **medicate** treat, impregnate with medicinal substance; *n* **medication**; *a* **medicinal** curative.

mediocre *a* ordinary, average, of medium quality; second rate.

meditate *v* contemplate; ponder; *n* **meditation** concentrated thought, solemn contemplation; *a* **meditative** contemplative.

medium *n* that which is between extremes; agency, channel; environment; intermediate substance conveying force; one who receives messages from

spirit world; (*pl*) **mediums, media**; *a* between two extremes.
medlar *n* small stone fruit eaten when rotten; tree bearing this fruit.
medley *n* confused, miscellaneous assortment.
meek *a* submissive, mild; humble; *n* **meekness.**
meet *a* fitting, suitable.
meet *v* encounter, come face to face; assemble; confront; converge at given point; *pt* & *pp* **met**; *n* hunt meeting; *n* **meeting** encounter; assembly.
megalith *n* huge prehistoric stone, menhir.
megalomania *n* (*psyc*) abnormal, excessive belief in one's own importance; *n* **megalomaniac.**
megaphone *n* funnel-shaped device used to increase volume of sound, and carry it farther.
megrim *n* migraine; (*pl*) depression.
melancholy *n* gloom, sadness, dejection; *n* **melancholia** emotional insanity accompanied by extreme depression; *a* **melancholic.**
melee *n* confused fight, skirmish.
meliorate *v* improve; *n* **melioration** amendment.
mellifluous *a* sweet-sounding, dulcet; *n* **mellifluence.**
mellow *a* ripe; well-matured; grown gentle through age, experience; (*sl*) merrily drunk; *v* make, become mellow.
melodrama *n* sensational, high-flown, sentimental play; *a* **melodramatic.**
melody *n* air, tune in music; sweet agreeable sounds; *as* **melodious** tuneful, musical; **melodic** of melody.
melon *n* edible gourd with sweet juicy flesh.
melt *v* become liquid by heat; dissolve; blend; (*fig*) soften, make tender; *as* **melting** sweet, soft; languishing; **molten** of, like melted metal.
member *n* part, limb of human or animal body; single part of complex whole; person belonging to group, society etc.; *n* **membership** status as member; total number of members of club, society etc.
membrane *n* thin, supple tissue covering or lining part of organ or body.
memento *n* souvenir, keepsake; reminder.

memoir *n* biography; (*pl*) personal experiences and observations of writer.
memory *n* ability to remember; recollection of past events etc.; period of such recollection; *n* **memorial** thing commemorating person, event etc.; *a* bringing to mind; *v* **memorize** commit to memory; *a* **memorable** noteworthy; remarkable; *n* **memorandum** note made to aid memory; summary of terms of contract etc.
menace *n* threat, impending danger; *v* threaten.
menagerie *n* collection of wild animals, *esp* travelling exhibition.
mend *v* repair; correct; improve (in health); rectify; *n* repaired hole, patch, darn.
mendacious *a* lying, untruthful; *n* **mendacity**.
mendicant *n* beggar; *a* begging; *ns* **mendicancy, mendicity**.
menhir *n* prehistoric monolith.
menial *a* of household servants; servile, mean; *n* domestic servant.
meningitis *n* inflammation of membranes of brain.
menopause *n* time in life when menstruation ceases.
menstruation *n* monthly discharge from womb; *v* **menstruate**; *a* **menstrual**.
mensurable *a* capable of being measured; *n* **mensuration**.
mental *a* of, relating to mind; (*sl*) crazy, mad; *n* **mentality** mental quality, attitude.
menthol *n* substance obtained from oil of peppermint.
mention *v* speak of, refer to; *n* brief reference.
mentor *n* counsellor; wise, prudent adviser.
menu *n* list of dishes available, or to be served.
mercantile *a* connected with trade, commercial.
mercenary *a* working only for payment; eager for gain; *n* soldier hired by foreign country.
mercer *n* dealer in fabrics, cloth; *n* **mercery** his trade, goods; *v* **mercerize** give appearance of silk to cotton fabric, by treating with chemicals.
merchant *n* wholesale trader *esp* with foreign countries; *ns* **merchandise** his wares; **merchantman** trading ship.
mercury *n* silvery fluid metallic element, quicksilver;

(*cap*) Roman god of oratory; planet nearest sun; *a* **mercurial** lively; erratic.
mercy *n* compassion; clemency; leniency shown to offender; *as* **merciful, merciless.**
mere *n* lake.
mere *a* only; simple; nothing but.
meretricious *a* specious; tawdry, flashy.
merge *v* lose identity; absorb; fade gradually into; *n* **merger** absorption of smaller thing by greater; combine (*esp* of commercial interests).
meridian *a* relating to noon; *n* noon; line of longitude passing through poles and cutting equator at right angles; zenith.
meringue *n* cake of stiffly beaten egg whites mixed with sugar and baked in cool oven.
merino *n* breed of sheep; soft woollen yarn or fabric.
merit *n* worth, excellence; quality deserving punishment or reward; (*pl*) intrinsic rightness or wrongness; *v* deserve; *a* **meritorious** praiseworthy.
merlin *n* small, strong falcon.
mermaid *n* fabulous creature (half woman, half fish).
merry *a* gay, joyous, lively; *ns* **merriment, merry-go-round** roundabout with hobby horses.
mesh *n* one of open spaces in net; (*pl*) **meshes** network; (*fig*) snares, toils; *v* catch in meshes; (of gear wheels) be engaged; **in mesh** in gear.
mesmerism *n* hypnotism; method of artificially inducing sleep and other conditions; *a* **mesmeric**; *v* **mesmerize** hypnotize; *n* **mesmerist** hypnotist.
meson *n* type of elementary particle with mass between electron and proton.
mess *n* muddle, disorder; difficult position; group of persons habitually eating together, *esp* in armed forces; mess-room; *v* eat thus; make muddle of; potter about; *n* **mess-room.**
message *n* oral or written communication; *n* **messenger** carrier of message.
Messiah *n* Christ; promised deliverer of the Jews.
messuage *n* (*leg*) dwelling-house with attached land & outbuildings.
metabolism *n* process of chemical changes in living organism; *a* **metabolic**; *v* **metabolize.**

metal *n* mineral substance that is opaque, ductile, malleable & capable of conducting heat or electricity; broken stone for road-surfacing; *a* **metallic**; *ns* **metallurgy** science and technology of metals; **metallurgist**.

metamorphosis *n* transformation; remarkable change; (*pl*) **metamorphoses**.

metaphor *n* figure of speech in which word is used to denote something different from its usual meaning; *a* **metaphorical** figurative.

metaphysics *n* branch of abstruse study concerned with nature and causes of being and knowledge; *a* **metaphysical**.

mete *v* (*usu* **mete out**) allot, distribute.

meteor *n* shooting star; (*fig*) any bright but transient object; *a* **meteoric** like meteor; dazzling but brief; *ns* **meteorite** stony or metallic mass fallen from outer space; **meteorology** science of weather; **meteorologist**; *a* **meteorological**.

meter *n* mechanical device for measuring quantity, volume etc.

methane *n* inflammable hydrocarbon gas, marsh gas, fire-damp.

method *n* mode, manner of procedure; systematic, orderly arrangement; *a* **methodical** orderly.

meths *n* methylated spirit (*abbrev*).

methyl *n* chemical basis of wood spirit.

meticulous *a* over-careful about details; punctilious.

metier *n* profession, occupation; one's line.

metre *n* poetical rhythm; group of metrical feet; unit of length in metric system; *as* **metrical** of measurement of poetic metre; **metric** measuring by metres.

metronome *n* (*mus*) mechanical device for beating time.

metropolis *n* capital, chief city of country.

metropolitan *a* of metropolis; *n* bishop having authority over other bishops of province.

mettle *n* spirit, courage; ardour; **on one's m.** eager to do one's best; *a* **mettlesome** high-spirited.

mew *n* cry of cat, gull; *v* utter this cry.

mew *v* (of hawk) moult; *v* put (hawk) into cage; (*fig*) confine, as in cage; *n pl* **mews** stables, originally place where falcons were kept.

mezzanine *n* low storey between two higher ones.

mezzo-soprano *n* voice between contralto & soprano.

miasma *n* unwholesome vapour, damp mist.

mica *n* mineral silicate, found in glittering scales.

micro- *prefix* very small; a millionth part.

microbe *n* microscopic organism, bacterium, *esp* as cause of disease.

microcosm *n* man as epitome of universe; representation in miniature.

microfilm *n* film reducing book etc. to minute scale.

micrometer *n* instrument for making minute, exact measurements.

microphone *n* instrument used to intensify sounds.

microscope *n* optical instrument that magnifies minute objects; *a* **microscopic** very small.

micturition *n* morbid desire to urinate.

mid *a* denoting middle part or position; *ns* **midday**, noon; (*pl*) **Midlands** central England; **midnight** 12 o'clock at night; *a* & *adv* **midway** half way.

midden *n* dung-hill; pile of refuse.

middle *a* equidistant from extremes; halfway; *n* middle part or point; *n* **m. class** section of society neither working-class nor aristocratic; **middleman** trader, agent between producer and consumer; *a* **middling** moderate; fairly well; *n pl* **middlings** second-rate, coarse flour.

midge *n* tiny flying, biting insect; *n* **midget** dwarf.

midriff *n* diaphragm.

midst *prep* in middle of; *n* central part.

midwife *n* woman who assists women in childbirth; *n* **midwifery** science, skill of midwife; obstetrics.

mien *n* manner, demeanour; appearance.

might *n* power, strength, force; *pt* of MAY; *a* **mighty** powerful, strong; *adv* (*coll*) very.

mignonette *n* sweet-scented garden plant.

migraine *n* nervous headache, often on one side only.

migrate *v* move from one region to another, *esp* as certain birds etc.; *a* & *n* **migrant**; *n* **migration** act of migrating; periodical movement of birds, fishes etc.; body of individuals migrating; *a* **migratory** having habit of migration; wandering.

milch *a* (*of cow*) yielding or kept for milk.

mild *a* gentle, kind; placid; temperate; not strong in flavour; *n* **mildness.**

mildew *n* parasitic fungus growing on plants; mould growing on damp food, paper etc.; *v* affect, be affected by mildew.

mile *n* measure of linear distance, 1760 yards; *ns* **mileage** miles travelled in certain time; miles travelled per gallon of petrol; **mileometer** instrument in motor-car for recording miles travelled; **milestone** stone indicating distance in miles from place.

military *a* of, suitable to or performed by soldiers, or army; *n* army; *a* **militant** warlike, combative; *ns* **militancy**; **militarism** reliance on, enthusiasm for armed strength; **militia** auxiliary infantry force, called out in emergency.

milk *n* white fluid secreted by female mammals, as food for young; *v* draw milk from; (*coll*) extract all possible profit from; *ns* **milksop** feeble effeminate man; **milk tooth** one of first set of temporary teeth; *a* **milky** like milk; white, opaque; *n* **Milky Way** luminous belt of stars and nebulae.

mill *n* machine for grinding grain; building containing this; small machine for grinding pepper, coffee etc.; works, factory for processing cotton, paper etc.; *v* treat in mill; serrate rim (of coin etc.); (*sl*) pummel; (of cattle etc.) move in circles; *ns* **miller** one who owns, works, flour mill; **millrace** current of water driving mill-wheel; **millstone** stone used for grinding corn etc.

millenium *n* period of thousand years, *specif.* that of Christ's second Advent; *a* **millenial.**

millet *n* small-seeded cereal grass, used as food.

milli- *prefix.* one thousandth (part of weight, measure in metric system), as **milligram** thousandth part of gram; **millimetre** etc.

milliard *n* 1000 millions.

milliner *n* maker, seller of women's hats, ribbons,

trimmings etc.; *n* **millinery** milliner's business, or articles sold by milliner.
million *n* 1000 thousands; *n* **millionaire** man possessing a million pounds, dollars etc.; very rich man; (*fem*) **millionairess**; *a* **millionth.**
milt *n* roe of male fish.
mime *n* art of communication by use of gestures and facial expression; *v* imitate; act in mime.
mimeograph *n* apparatus for making stencil copy of typewritten matter.
mimic *v* copy, resemble closely; ridicule by imitating speech, action; *n* one who mimics; *n* **mimicry.**
mimosa *n* genus of plants with small, fluffy yellow flowers, and sensitive leaves.
minaret *n* tall slender turret on a mosque.
minatory *a* menacing, threatening.
mince *v* cut, chop in small pieces; speak, behave affectedly; *n* finely chopped meat; *n* **mincemeat,** mixture of raisins, candied peel, suet, brandy etc. **mince-pie** small covered pie containing mincemeat.
mind *n* intellectual faculties; memory; opinion, thought; intention; *v* pay attention to; look after; object (to); intend; *a* **mindful** bearing in mind; careful.
mine *poss pron* belonging to ME.
mine *n* deep excavation from which coal, minerals (except stone) are dug; buildings, machinery connected with this; (*fig*) rich source of supply; tunnel under enemy position; *v* sink mine; extract from mine; undermine; *n* **miner.**
mine *n* charge of explosives detonated in container; *v* lay mines in sea, on land; *ns* **minefield** area where mines have been laid; **minelayer**; ship laying mines; **minesweeper** ship for clearing minefield.
mineral *n* natural, inorganic substance found in earth; anything not animal, vegetable; anything dug up by mining; *a* inorganic; *ns* **mineralogy** science of minerals; **mineralogist**; **mineral water** water naturally containing mineral salts, *esp* medicinal ones; (*coll*) aerated drink.
mingle *v* mix, blend; join, combine.

miniature *n* small painting, *esp* on ivory; very small copy or model; *a* minute, very small.
minim *n* (*mus*) note equal to two crotchets; 1/60th of fluid drachm; *v* **minimize** reduce to smallest possible amount; underestimate, understate; *n* **minimum** smallest, least amount, point possible; *pl* **minima,-mums**; *a* least possible.
minion *n* favourite; toady, hireling.
minister *n* clergyman; person in charge of state department; diplomatic agent or representative below ambassador; *v* supply; help; serve; *a* **ministerial**; *n* **ministry** office, function of minister; act of ministering; *a* **ministrant** acting as minister; *n* helper; *n* **ministration** service, help.
miniver *n* white fur; ermine.
mink *n* animal of weasel family; its valuable fur.
minnow *n* small freshwater fish; stickleback.
minor *a* less; inferior; unimportant; *n* person not legally of age; *n* **minority** state of being a minor; smaller number.
Minotaur *n* fabled monster (half man, half bull).
minster *n* abbey church; cathedral.
minstrel *n* medieval singer; itinerant singer, musician; *pl* performers of negro songs.
mint *n* place where money is legally coined; *v* coin money; (*fig*) invent word etc. **m. condition** (of stamps, coin etc.) unused.
mint *n* aromatic herb, used for flavouring.
minuet *n* slow, stately dance; music for this.
minus *prep* & *a* less, deducted, subtracted; lacking; *n* minus sign (−).
minute *a* very small; insignificant; precise; *n* **minutiae** small details.
minute *n* 1/60th. of hour or degree; moment; memorandum; (*pl*) summary of proceedings at meeting; *v* record in form of minutes.
minx *n* impudent, saucy girl; hussy.
miocene *a* of less recent geologic time.
miracle *n* marvel; abnormal event that cannot be explained; *a* **miraculous**.
mirage *n* optical illusion; (*fig*) misleading delusion.
mire *n* mud; swampy ground; *v* dirty with mud.

mirror *n* polished surface which reflects image; (*fig*) pattern model; *v* reflect.
mirth *n* merriment, gladness; hilarity; *a* **mirthful**.
mis- *prefix meaning* unfavourable, amiss, bad, wrong. *Forms compounds as* **misadventure** ill-luck; **miscalculate** calculate wrongly. *Such compounds are not given where the meaning may be deduced from the simple word.*
misanthrope *n* one who distrusts or hates mankind; *a* **misanthropic**; *n* **misanthropy**.
miscarry *v* go awry, astray; give birth prematurely; *n* **miscarriage**.
miscegenation *n* interbreeding of races, *esp* between black and white.
miscellaneous *a* mixed; consisting of various kinds; *n* **miscellany** medley of various kinds.
mischief *n* harm, injury; immoral influence; troublesome conduct; *a* **mischievous** injurious, causing needless, thoughtless, minor damage.
miscreant *n* scoundrel, villian, ruffian.
misdemeanour *n* misdeed; minor indictable offence.
miser *n* one who hoards money and lives wretchedly; *a* **miserly** avaricious; *n* **miserliness**.
miserable *a* unhappy; squalid, wretched; scanty; pitiable; *n* **misery** unhappiness; discomfort; squalor.
misgiving *n* doubt, mistrust; fear.
mishap *n* accident, bad luck.
mislay *v* lose temporarily.
mislead *v* deceive; lead astray; *pt* & *pp* **misled**; *a* **misleading** deceptive.
misnomer *n* wrong name; incorrect description.
misogamy *n* hatred of marriage; *n* **misogamist**.
misogyny *n* hatred of women; *n* **misogynist**.
misprision *n* (*law*) misdemeanour; concealment of another's crime.
Miss *n* title of unmarried woman, girl.
miss *v* fail to hit, secure, meet, catch, notice; omit; feel want of; *n* failure to hit, secure etc.; *a* **missing** absent; lost.
missal *n* mass book.
missel-thrush *n* large species of thrush.

missile *n* object thrown or shot (*usu* as weapon).
mission *n* act of sending or being sent as representative; delegation; vocation; centre for missionary or social work; *n* **missionary** one sent on religious mission; *a* of religious missionary.
missive *n* letter.
mist *n* visible watery vapour; *a* **misty** covered by mist; dim, obscure.
mistake *v* make error in understanding; identify wrongly; be in error; *pt* **mistook**; *pp* **mistaken**; *n* error; fault.
Mister *n* title of address to man, written **Mr.**
mistletoe *n* evergreen parasitic plant.
mistral *n* cold dry N.W. wind of S. France.
mistress *n* female holding authority; female teacher; kept woman; (*cap*) courtesy title given to married women, written **Mrs.**
mite *n* very small insect; enything very small; very small child.
mitigate *v* make less severe; alleviate; *n* **mitigation.**
mitre *n* headdress worn by Pope, bishops etc.; angled joint between two pieces of wood; *v* join with mitre.
mitten *n* glove with finger & thumb ends open;
mix *v* put together; mingle; blend; associate; *n* **mixer** one who, that which, mixes; **good mixer** one who has social tact; *n* **mixture.**
mi(z)zen *n* fore-and-aft sail set on mizzen-mast, or aftermost mast.
mnemonic *n* (phrase, rhyme etc.) helping memory.
moan *n* low, mournful sound expressing pain, groan; *v* utter moan.
moat *n* defensive trench (*usu* filled with water) round castle, etc.
mob *n* lawless, rough crowd; rabble; excited mass of people; *v* jostle, attack in mob; crowd round.
mob-cap *n* woman's frilled cap.
mobile *a* movable; moving, changing easily; *n* **mobility**; *v* **mobilize** call up (armed forces) for service; gather resources, forces; *n* **mobilization.**
moccasin *n* soft shoe (*usu* deerskin) of N. Amer. Indian.

mock *v* ridicule; deride; mimic; (*fig*) delude; *a* sham, imitation; *ns* **mocker**; **mockery** ridicule; travesty.
mode *n* method; style; fashion; *a* **modish** fashionable.
model *n* pattern; small-scale reproduction; mannequin; one who poses for artist etc; *v* work into shape; act as model, pose.
moderate *a* not going to extremes; restrained, medium; *v* make, become less extreme or violent; *n* one holding moderate views; *ns* **moderation**; **moderator** arbitrator; president of Presbyterian assembly.
modern *a* of present or recent times; up-to-date; *n* **modernism** movement expressing present day views, methods etc.; *v* **modernize** make modern; adapt to present day usage; *n* **modernization**.
modest *a* moderate; diffident; humble; chaste; *n* **modesty**.
modicum *n* small amount or quantity.
modify *v* qualify; alter slightly; *n* **modification**.
modulate *v* regulate, adapt; vary, inflect (voice etc.); (*mus*) change key; *ns* **modulation**; **modulator**.
modus *n* method; style.
mohair *n* fine cloth of Angora goat's hair.
Mohammedan *n* & *a* (follower) of Mohammed; Moslem.
moiety *n* half-share; part.
moiré *n* watered silk or other fabric.
moist *a* damp, humid; *v* **moisten**; *n* **moisture** dampness; condensed watery vapour.
moke *n* (*sl*) donkey.
molar *n* double grinding tooth; *a*.
molasses *n* thick dark syrup drained from raw sugar.
mole *n* dark-coloured spot on skin; small burrowing animal; breakwater, jetty.
molecule *n* smallest particle of element or compound that can exist without chemical change; *a* **molecular**.
molest *v* trouble, pester; accost illegally.
mollify *v* pacify, appease; soften; *n* **mollification**.
mollusc *n* soft-bodied animal usually having hard shell (e.g. snail, oyster).

moment *n* brief period of time; importance; *a* **momentary** brief, quick; **momentous** of great importance; *n* **momentum** impetus, increasing force.
monarch *n* sovereign; supreme ruler; *ns* **monarchy** state ruled by monarch; **-ist** supporter of monarchy.
monastery *n* house lived in by religious community; *a* **monastic** of monastery; of monks, nuns; *n* **monas ticism** monastic life and system.
Monday *n* second day of week.
money *n* coins, banknotes in general; wealth; **make m.** grow rich; **money's worth** full value; *a* **monetary** relating to coinage or currency.
mongoose *n* small Indian animal that kills snakes; (*pl*) **-gooses.**
mongrel *n* animal (*esp* dog) of mixed breed; hybrid; *a* of mixed breeding or origin.
monitor *n* one who warns, advises; school prefect; large lizard; heavy gun-boat; master screen in TV studio; *v* listen to foreign broadcasts; *a* **monitory.**
monk *n* member of religious order, living under vows of poverty, chastity etc.
monk's hood *n* aconite.
monkey *n* any of primates, other than man or lemurs, *esp* long-tailed; mischievous child; (*pl*) **-keys**; *v* play tricks; meddle with; *ns* **monkey-nut** ground-nut, peanut; **monkey-puzzle** tree with broad prickly spines, Chile pine.
mono- *prefix* single, alone.
monochromatic *a* of one colour.
monocle *n* single eye-glass.
monogamy *n* practice of marrying only one partner at a time.
monogram *n* single figure made of two or more interwoven initials.
monolith *n* single block of stone as monument.
monologue *n* speech by single actor.
monomania *n* obsession of mind by single idea.
monopoly *n* exclusive right of trading in specified commodity; *v* **monopolize** engross, enjoy to exclusion of others.
monosyllable word of one syllable.

monotone *n* single, unvaried tone; *a* **monotonous** lacking in variety; dully repetitive.
monotype *n* machine casting type in single letters.
monsoon *n* seasonal wind of Indian Ocean; rainy season in India.
monster *n* person, animal, thing of abnormal shape or huge size; abnormally wicked, cruel person; *a* monstrous, like monster; shocking; hideous; *n* **monstrosity** freak; badly made, hideous object.
montage *n* final selection and arrangement of shots to form cinema film; two or more pictures imposed on single background.
month *n* one of twelve parts into which year is divided; period of moon's revolution; *a* **monthly** occurring once a month; *n* magazine published monthly.
monument *n* tombstone, building, statue etc. erected as memorial; *a* **monumental** of, serving as monument; massive, enormous.
moo *n* cry of cow; *v* utter moo, low.
mooch *v* (*sl*) loiter, slouch, slink about.
mood *n* temporary state of mind, feelings; *a* **moody** varying in mood: sulky; gloomy.
mood *n* (*gram*) form of verb indicating its function.
moon *n* earth's satellite; satellite of another planet; *v* wander about dreamily, aimlessly; *ns* **moonlight**; **moonshine** nonsense; (*sl*) illicitly distilled whisky; **moonstone** translucent semi-precious stone.
moor *n* tract of open country, usually hilly and heather-clad; *n* **moor-hen** water hen.
moor *v* fasten, secure (ship) by cables, chains etc.; *n pl* **moorings** place where vessel is moored; cables, buoys etc. by which it is secured.
Moor *n* member of mixed Berber & Arab race.
moose *n* N. American elk.
moot *v* raise in debate; *a* arguable, debatable.
mop *n* bundle of yarn on long handle; *v* clean, wipe with mop; **mop up** (*fig*) round up, defeat.
mope *v* be low-spirited, depressed.
moraine *n* debris of earth, stones etc. deposited by glacier.
moral *a* relating to generally accepted ideas of right

and wrong; virtuous; of right conduct; *n* lesson taught by experience, fable; (*pl*) principles of right and wrong conduct; *n* **morality** good moral conduct; virtue; *v* **moralize** draw moral lesson from, think on moral aspect; *n* **moralist** teacher of, writer on, morals.

morale *n* mental state, *esp* regarding courage etc.

morass *n* swamp, marsh.

moratorium *n* legal authorization to delay or defer payment of debt etc.

morbid *a* abnormal; pathological; unwholesome.

mordant *a* sarcastic; corrosive; (of dyeing) serving to fix colours.

more *a* greater in quantity, extent etc.; *comp* of MANY, MUCH; *adv* in addition, to greater degree; *adv* **moreover** besides.

morello *n* dark red, bitter cherry.

morganatic *a* **m. marriage** marriage of man of royal rank with woman of inferior status, children of which have not the right of succession.

morgue *n* place where corpses await identification.

moribund *a* dying; decaying.

Mormon *n* member of religious sect.

morning *a* first part of day, from dawn until noon; *n* **morn** morning.

morocco *n* fine, flexible leather.

moron *n* mentally deficient person; (*sl*) fool.

morose *a* surly, sullen, gloomy.

morphia, morphine *n* narcotic alkaloid of opium, used to relieve pain.

Morris *n* old form of dance, in fancy costume.

morrow *n* next following day; tomorrow.

morse *n* system of telegraphic signalling, built up of dots, dashes.

morsel *n* small piece, fragment.

mortal *a* liable to die; causing death; implacable; *n* human being; *n* **mortality** condition of being subject to death; death-rate.

mortar *n* vessel in which substances are pounded; short-barrelled cannon; cement of lime, sand, water for holding bricks etc. together; *n* **mortar-board** square flat college cap.

mortgage *n* conveyance of property as security for debt; *v* convey on mortgage; (*fig*) pledge; *ns* **mortgagee; mortgagor.**
mortify *v* discipline by self-denial; humiliate; become gangrenous; *n* **mortification**
mortise, mortice *n* hole cut in piece of wood etc. to receive tenon; *v* join by, make mortise in; *n* **mortise lock** one embedded in door.
mortuary *a* of, pertaining to death and burial; *n* building where corpses are kept before burial.
mosaic *n* pattern made by fitting together small pieces of coloured marble, stone etc.
Moslem, Muslim *n* Mohammedan; *a* of, belonging to Mohammedans.
mosque *n* Mohammedan temple.
mosquito *n* one of various kinds of biting gnat.
moss *n* low growing tufted plant found on moist surfaces; lichen; *a* **mossy** covered with moss.
most *a* greatest in number, quantity, degree; *sup* of MANY, MUCH; *adv* to greatest degree; *adv* **mostly** generally.
mot *n* witty saying or remark.
mote *n* speck of dust.
motel *n* hotel specially designed for motorists.
motet *n* sacred vocal composition.
moth *n* night-flying insect, related to butterfly; **clothes m.,** whose larvae feed on woollen fabrics, furs etc.; *a* **moth-eaten** damaged by clothes-moth; (*fig*) shabby.
mother *n* female parent; head of convent, nunnery; (*fig*) source; *v* look after, tend, as mother; *n* **motherhood**; *a* **motherly**; *n* **m.-in-law** wife's, husband's mother; **m.-of-pearl** iridescent lining of some shells
motif *n* recurrent theme *esp* in music; ornamental needlework partern.
motion *n* movement; proposal put to meeting; gesture; evacuation of bowels; (*leg*) application for ruling; *v* indicate, make gesture towards; *a* **motionless** at rest; still.
motive *n* cause; incentive; that which influences behaviour or action; *v* **motivate** impel, induce; *n* **motivation.**

motley *a* of various colours; of mixed ingredients; *n* parti-coloured garment *esp* jester's.
motor *n* that which imparts movement; machine supplying motive power; engine; *v* travel in motor-car; *ns* **motoring**; **motorist**.
mottle *v* mark with blotches of different colours; *n* blotch; pattern of blotches.
motto *n* short phrase expressing maxim, rule of conduct, *esp* on coat-of-arms.
mould *n* loose crumbling earth; soil generally.
mould *n* furry, fungoid growth caused by dampness; *a* **mouldy** musty, decaying; *v* **moulder** crumble, decay.
mould *n* pattern, hollow shape, matrix for shaping or casting soft materials; (*fig*) character; *n* **moulding** modelling; ornamental strip of wood.
moult *v* shed feathers, fur etc. periodically; act or time of moulting; *n* **moulting**.
mound *n* raised heap of earth, stones etc.; hillock.
mount *v* climb, ascend; get on horseback; rise, increase; provide frame, setting for (picture etc) *n* that on which thing is mounted; gun-carriage.
mountain *n* large, lofty hill; *n* **mountaineer** dweller in, expert climber of, mountains; *a* **mountainous** very high; enormous; *n* **mount** high hill.
mountebank *n* charlatan, quack.
mourn *v* lament; grieve for; show sorrow; *n* **mourner** *a* **mournful**; *n* **mourning** grief *esp* for death; clothes worn as sign of such grief; time these are worn.
mouse *n* small rodent; (*fig*) shy person; (*pl*) **mice**; *v* catch, hunt mice; *n* **mouser** cat good at catching mice.
mousse *n* dessert of flavoured whipped eggs & cream.
moustache *n* hair on upper lip.
mouth *n* opening in animal's head by which it eats and utters sounds; opening, outlet, aperture; *v* speak with exaggerated lip and jaw movement; *n* **mouthpiece** part of pipe, tube etc. placed between lips; spokesman.
move *c* change position of; set in motion; affect

feelings; make formal motion (in court of law etc.); *n* movement; (*fig*) device; step; *a* **movable**; *n* **movement** act, fact, process of moving; moving part of mechanism, *esp* of watch; division of musical composition.

movies *n* (*sl*) cinema; cinema film.

mow *v* cut down (grass etc.); (*fig*) **m. down** kill indiscriminately; *pt* **mowed**; *pp* **mowed, mown**; *n* **mower** mowing machine, one who mows.

much *a* great in quantity; *n* great deal; *adv* greatly; nearly.

mucilage *n* gummy substance obtained from plants.

muck *n* filth, dirt, manure; refuse; *a* **mucky** dirty; distasteful.

mucus *n* slimy, viscous secretion of mucous membrane; *a* **mucous** secreting mucus; slimy.

mud *n* very wet, moist earth; *a* **muddy**.

muddle *v* bewilder, confuse; bungle; *n* disorder; mess, confusion.

muff *n* covering, for keeping hands warm.

muff *v* (*sport*) miss, bungle; *n* fool; blunderer.

muffin *n* round cake of yeast dough eaten hot with butter.

muffle *v* wrap with covering, for warmth, or to deaden sound; *n* **muffler** thick, warm scarf.

mufti *n* expounder of Muslim law; civilian clothes.

mug *n* drinking cup; (*sl*) face; simpleton; *v* (*sl*) rob with violence, in open air; (*coll*) swot.

muggy *a* damp, close, oppressive.

mulatto *n* child of negro and white parents.

mulberry *n* tree with reddish purple edible berries.

mulch *n* straw etc. spread round roots of plants etc.; *v* protect (plants) with mulch.

mule *n* hybrid between horse and ass; stubborn person; spinning machine; heelless slipper; *n* **muleteer** mule driver; *a* **mulish** obstinate.

mull *v* heat (wine etc.) with spices.

mullein *n* wild herbaceous plant with woolly leaves.

mullet *n* edible sea-fish.

mulligatawny *n* soup made with curry powder.

mullion *n* upright shaft, *usu* of stone, between window panes.

multi-, mult- *prefix: forms compounds meaning* many. *Where the meaning may be deduced from the simple word, the compounds are not given here.*
multifarious *a* of many kinds.
multiple *a* having many parts; *n* number which contains another number an exact number of times; *n* **multiplicity** great number; *v* **multiply** increase in number.
multitude *n* great number; crowd of people; *a* **multitudinous** very numerous.
mum *a* silent; *v* mime; *n* **mummer** actor in dumb-show; *n* **mummery** miming.
mumble *v* speak indistinctly, mutter.
mummy *n* childish term for mother (*abbrev* **mum**).
mummy *n* embalmed body, esp of ancient Egyptian; *v* **mummify**; *a* **mummified.**
mumps *n pl* contagious disease, inflammation of parotid and salivary glands.
munch *v* crunch, chew noisily and vigorously.
mundane *a* earthly, worldly.
municipal *a* belonging to affairs of borough, city, town; *n* **municipality** town, borough etc. enjoying local government; local authority.
munificent *a* lavishly generous; *n* **munificence.**
munitions *n pl* military stores.
mural *a* of, on wall; *n* wall-painting.
murder *n* unlawful, intentional homicide; *v* kill thus; *n* **murderer**; (*fem*) **murderess**; *a* **murderous** intending to murder; deadly.
murk *n* thick darkness; *a* **murky** dark, cloudy.
murmur *v* make low, continuous sound; speak in low voice; grumble; *n* act, sound of murmuring.
muscat *n* raisin; musky grape; *n* **muscatel** muscat; sweet wine made from it.
muscle *n* animal elastic fibrous tissue, highly contractile, by which movement is effected; (*fig*) bodily force, strength; *a* **muscular** having, strong, well-developed muscles; of muscle; *a* **muscle-bound** with muscles strained and inelastic through over-exercise.
Muse *n* one of nine goddesses associated with the

arts, sciences and literature; *n* (*fig*) **muse** poetic inspiration; *v* ponder, meditate.

museum *n* collection of natural, scientific, historical or artistic objects; building housing such collection.

mush *n* soft, pulpy mass; *a* **mushy** soft, pulpy.

mushroom *n* quick-growing edible fungus; *v* (*fig*) grow, expand rapidly; gather mushrooms; *a* of, like mushroom.

music *n* art of producing rhythmical, melodious, sounds; written or printed score of musical composition; (fig) pleasing sound; *a* **musical** of, like music; melodious; skilled in, fond of music; *n* play with songs etc.; *ns* **musician**; **music-hall** variety theatre.

musk *n* strong scent obtained from male musk-deer; plant with similar scent; *a* **musky**; *ns* **musk-deer** small hornless deer; **musk-ox** Arctic ox; **musk-rat** N. American water rat.

musket *n* early form of hand-firearm; *ns* **musketeer**; **musketry** skill in use of firearms.

muslin *n* fine cotton fabric.

musquash *n* fur of musk-rat.

mussel *n* edible bivalve mollusc.

must *n* new unfermented wine.

must *v aux* expressing compulsion, obligation, certainty; *pt* **had to**; no *pp*; *n* (*coll*) an essential.

mustang *n* American wild or semi-wild prairie horse.

mustard *n* hot, pungent powder made from pounded seeds of mustard plant, used as condiment; *n* **m. gas** poisonous irritant gas.

muster *v* assemble; summon; *n* assembly of troops etc. for inspection etc.;

musty *a* mouldy, stale; *n* **mustiness.**

mutable *a* liable to change; *n* **mutation** change; sudden genetic change.

mute *a* dumb; silent; *n* dumb person; professional mourner; device used to soften tone or reduce sound of musical instrument; *a* **muted** muffled (sound).

mutilate *v* maim; cut off; render imperfect; *n* **mutilation.**

mutiny *n* revolt against authority *esp* in armed forces; *v* revolt; *a* **mutinous**; *n* **mutineer.**

mutter *v* speak indistinctly in low voice; grumble.
mutton *n* flesh of sheep used as food.
mutual *a* performed by joint action; reciprocal, common to both.
muzzle *n* mouth and nose of animal; cover for these to prevent biting; mouth of gun; *v* put muzzle on; impose silence on.
muzzy *a* dazed; vague; fuddled; *n* **muzziness.**
my *a* belonging to ME; *reflex pron* **myself** I, me.
mycology *a* science of fungi.
myopia *n* short-sightedness; *a* **myopic.**
myriad *n* ten thousand; endless number; *a* countless.
myrrh *n* aromatic gum.
myrtle *n* evergreen, flowering shrub.
mystery *n* strange, secret, obscure fact or thing; religious rite; biblical play; *a* **mysterious.**
mystic *a* havine inner, secret meaning; esoteric; *n* one who believes in attainment, through contemplation, of inaccessible truths; *a* **mystical;** *n* **mysticism.**
mystify *n* puzzle, bewilder; *n* **mystification.**
myth *n* fictitious story or legend; imaginary person or thing; *a* **mythical;** *n* **mythology** collection, body of myths concerning ancient religious belief; *a* **mythological.**
myxomatosis *n* highly fatal disease of rabbits.

nab *v* (*sl*) catch suddenly; arrest.
nabob *n* very wealthy man.
nacelle *n* framework containing engine of aircraft.
nadir *n* point opposite zenith; lowest point.
naevus *n* birth-mark, mole; (*pl*) **naevi.**
nag *n* small riding pony; horse.
nag *v* find fault persistently; scold; (*fig*) give constant pain.
naiad *n* water-nymph.
nail *v* horny plate at end of fingers and toes; talon; metal spike for fixing things together; *v* fix, fasten to, with nail.
naïve *a* natural, ingenuous; foolishly simple; *n* **naïveté, naïvety.**

naked *a* unclothed; nude; exposed; bare; without normal covering; *n* **nakedness.**

name *n* word by which person, thing, idea is known or called; fame; lineage, family; reputation; *v* call by, give name to; appoint; identify by name; *a* **nameless** anonymous; unknown; *adv* **namely**; that is to say; *n* **namesake** one having same name as another.

nanny *n* child's nurse; **n. goat** female goat.

nap *n* downy surface of cloth; *v* put, raise nap on.

nap *n* short sleep; *v* doze; **be caught napping** be caught unawares.

napalm *n* jellified petrol, used in flame-throwers etc.

nape *n* back of the neck.

naphtha *n* inflammable oil distilled from crude petroleum, etc.

napkin *n* small cloth used at meals to protect clothes and wipe fingers, lips; baby's nappy.

nappy *n* (*coll*) baby's diaper; small cloth used for nursery purposes.

narcissus *n* genus of bulbous plants; (*pl*) **narcissi**; *n* **narcissism** morbid self-admiration.

narcosis *n* unconsciousness induced by drugs; *n* **narcotic** drug causing sleep, insensibility *a* inducing sleep etc.

nark *n* (*sl*) spy, police informer.

narrate *v* relate, tell story of; *ns* **narration, narrative** story, account; *a* **narrating**; *n* **narrator.**

narrow *a* of small breadth in proportion to length; *v* become, cause to become narrow; *adv* **narrowly** closely; only just; *a* **narrow-minded** prejudiced, bigoted.

narwhal *n* kind of Arctic whale.

nasal *a* of or in nose; *n* nasal sound (phonetics).

nascent *a* just appearing; about to be born.

nasturtium *n* climbing garden plant.

nasty *a* offensive to taste or smell; disgusting; disagreeable; *n* **nastiness.**

natal *a* of, at, belonging to birth.

natation *n* act of swimming, floating; *as* **natant** floating, as of plants; **natatory** pertaining to swimming.

nation *n* large group of people having common language, culture etc., and living in one area under one government; *a* **national** of, common to a nation; *n* citizen of a state; *n* **nationality** status of belonging to a particular nation; *n* **nationalist** one devoted to his national interests; *v* **nationalize** transfer (land, railways etc.) from private to state ownership; *n* **nationalization** act of nationalizing.

native *a* belonging to by birth; inborn; innate; indigenous; *n* one born in particular place; member of primitive race, usually coloured.

nativity *n* birth *esp* of Christ.

natterjack *n* yellow striped toad.

natty *a* neat, trim, dapper; skilful.

natural *a* of, arising from external physical world; not artificially prepared; uncultivated, wild; normal; innate; born out of wedlock; *n* simpleton; (*mus*) sign to show note is neither flat nor sharp; (*coll*) one to whom skills come easily. *adv* **naturally** innately; without artificial aid; of course; *n* **naturalist** student of natural history; *v* **naturalize** confer rights of citizenship on; (of plants, animals) acclimatize; *n* **naturalization**; **natural history** study of botany, zoology; **naturism** nature-worship.

nature *n* sum of forces, processes and phenomena underlying the physical, external world; essential, innate qualities of person or thing; instinctive behaviour; physical, material world as whole.

naught *n* nothing; arithmetical symbol nought (0).

naughty *a* mischievous, disobedient, badly behaved; immoral; *n* **naughtiness**.

nausea *n* sickness; disgust; *v* **nauseate** sicken; disgust; *a* **nauseous** causing nausea; loathsome.

nautical *a* pertaining to ships, sailors, etc.

nautilus *n* one of group of molluscs.

nave *n* central part of church, west of chancel.

navel *n* rounded depression in abdomen, umbelicus.

navigate *v* cause to sail or travel on set course; direct ship or aircraft; *ns* **navigation** act, science of navigating; **navigator** one skilled in science of navigation; *a* **navigable**.

navvy *n* labourer engaged in heavy manual work.

navy *n* all warships of state; fleet; naval personnel; *a* **naval** pertaining to navy.
Nazi *n* member of Hitler's National-Socialist party.
neap *a* (of tide) very low.
near *adv* close to; not far from; *a* close in relationship, degree; about to come, happen; niggardly; (of horse, car etc.) left side; *v* approach; *a* **nearby** close at hand, adjacent; *adv* **nearly** almost; closely.
neat *a* trim, well-kept; skilful; (of utterances) apt; (of alcoholic liquor) pure, undiluted; *n* **neatness**.
nebula *n* luminous cloud-like patch in sky; cluster of stars; *a* **nebulous** cloudy, misty; (*fig*) vague, indefinite.
necessary *a* inevitable; indispensable, requisite; obligatory; *n* that which is essential or indispensable; *n* **necessity** compulsion; anything inevitable because of natural law; poverty, want; *v* **necessitate** render necessary, compel; *a* **necessitous** poor; destitute.
neck *n* part of body joining head to trunk; narrow connecting part; isthmus; *v* (*sl*) kiss and cuddle; *ns* **neckcloth** cravat; **necklace** string of jewels, gold chain etc. worn round neck.
necromancy *n* sorcery; black magic; communication with the dead; *n* **necromancer** wizard.
necropolis *n* large cemetery.
nectar *n* (*myth*) drink of the gods; sugary liquid produced by flowers; *ns* **nectary** honey-gland of flower; **nectarine** variety of peach with smooth skin.
need *n* that which is required; necessity; poverty, want; *as* **needful** necessary; **needless** unnecessary; **needy** poor, in want.
needle *n* small sharp instrument with eye to take thread, for sewing; pointed end of hypodermic syringe; thin rod of metal, plastic etc. used in knitting; magnetized bar of compass; leaf of pine or fir; *v* (*coll*) annoy, goad; *n* **needlewoman** skilful woman sewer; sempstress; **needlework** sewing, embroidery.
ne'er-do-well *n* improvident good-for-nothing.
nefarious *a* unlawful; wicked.
negate *v* deny; nullify; *n* **negation** contradiction;

denial; *a* **negative** expressing denial; lacking in positive qualities; (*photo*) reversing lights and shades; (*elect*) cathode; *n* word, statement which denies, refuses, forbids; *v* veto; disprove.

neglect *v* pay no heed to; disregard; omit, fail to do; *n* fact of neglecting or being neglected; *a* **neglectful.**

negligée *n* loose robe, as dressing gown; informal state of dress.

negligence *n* heedlessness; lack of care, attention; *as* **negligent**; **negligible** not worth considering.

negotiate *v* arrange, settle business matter, by discussion; get cash for a security; discuss terms of peace with; surmount (obstacle); *a* **negotiable**; *ns* **negotiation**; **negotiator.**

negro *n* member of black-skinned race of Africa or of African origin; (*fem*) negress; *a* **negroid** of appearance of negro.

neigh *v* utter cry of horse; *n* this cry.

neighbour *n* one who lives next door, or nearly so; *a* **neighbouring** adjacent; placed near together; *n* **neighbourhood** proximity; district surrounding one's house; *a* **neighbourly** kindly, friendly.

neither *a* & *pron* not either; also *adv* & *conj*.

Nemesis *n* goddess of vengeance; retributive justice.

neolithic *a* of later Stone Age.

neon *n* one of inert gases occurring in atmosphere; **neon light** glowing light obtained by ionizing gas in tube or bulb.

neophyte *n* new convert; novice, beginner.

nephew *n* brother's, sister's son.

nephritis *n* inflammation of kidneys.

nepotism *n* favouritism towards one's relatives.

Neptune *n* god of the sea; third largest planet.

nerve *n* cord-like fibre, bundle of fibres, transmitting sensory and motor impulses from brain to parts of body; (*fig*) courage; (*coll*) audacity; (*pl*) irritability; apprehension; *v* give courage, strength to; *as* **nerveless** weak, numb; without vigour; **nervous** of nerves; timid; excitable; *n* **nervousness** apprehension; *a* **nervy** easily excited, jumpy.

nescient *a* not knowing, ignorant; *n* **nescience** agnosticism.

ness *n* headland, promontory.
nest *n* structure built by bird in which it lays eggs and rears young; snug shelter; *v* build, occupy nest; *n* **nest-egg** real or dummy egg left in hen's nest to stimulate laying; money saved up.
nestle *v* settle cosily; lie, press closely against.
nestling *n* young bird before it leaves nest.
net *n* meshwork of knotted, woven cord, thread etc.; length of this used to catch anything, or for protection; *v* catch in, cover with net; *ns* **netting** string, wire network; **net-ball** team game in which ball is thrown through circular net.
net, nett *a* free of all deductions; remaining after all necessary expenses; *v* yield as clear profit.
nether *a* lower, below.
nettle *n* plant with stinging hairs on leaves and stalks; *v* irritate, vex.
network *n* meshed structure of wire, cords etc.; system of interlocked streets etc.; chain of radio, T.V. transmitting stations.
neural *a* of nerves, *ns* **neuralgia** acute pain, *us* along nerve; **neuritis** inflammation of nerve; **neurosis,** functional disorder of nervous system; *a* **neurotic** (*coll*) abnormally sensitive; morbidly emotional.
neuter *a* neither masculine nor feminine; *n* noun, pronoun of neuter gender; animal deprived of sexual organs.
neutral *a* impartial; not taking either side in dispute, *esp* war; disengaged (of gears); *n* state or subject of state taking neither side in conflict; *n* **neutrality** non-participation *esp* in war; *v* **neutralize** make, treat as neutral; counteract, make in effectual.
neutron *n* electrically uncharged atomic particle.
never *adv* not ever; emphatic negative; *adv* **nevertheless** notwithstanding.
new *a* not previously existing; recently discovered; fresh, newly grown, produced; untried, novel; *ns* **newness**; **newcomer** person just arrived; *a* **newfangled** of modern fashion, design (as opposed to old style).
newel *n* core of spiral staircase; post of stair-rail.

news *n* information, reports of recent events; tidings; *ns* **newsagent** one who sells papers, periodicals etc.; **newspaper** daily or weekly publication containing news of day; **newsprint** paper on which newspapers are printed; **newsreel** film showing recent events.
newt *n* small lizard-like amphibian.
next *a* & *adv* nearest in order, rank time etc.; *n* **next-of-kin** nearest blood relative.
nib *n* split pen-point; *pl* crushed cocoa beans.
nibble *v* bite gently, with small bites; (*fig*) show signs of being attracted by (offer etc.); tentative bite.
niblick *n* golf club with well-lofted, heavy head.
nice *a* fastidious; punctilious; pleasing; delicate; agreeable; *n* **nicety** accuracy; (*pl*) subtle details.
niche *n* small recess in wall; (*fig*) place, scope suitable for person's work, condition etc.
nick *n* notch, slit; (*sl*) police-station; exact point of time; *v* cut notch in; (*sl*) steal; arrest.
nickel *n* hard, silvery-white metallic element.
nickname *n* extra name given in affection or derision.
nicotine *n* oily, poisonous alkaloid in tobacco.
niece *n* brother's or sister's daughter.
niggard *n* covetous, miserly person; *a* **niggardly.**
nigger *n* (in contempt) Negro, coloured person.
niggle *v* fret, be fussy over petty details; *a* **niggling** too fussy; small but persistent.
nigh *a adv* & *prep* near.
night *n* period between sunset and sunrise; darkness; *ns* **nightcap** cap worn in bed; drink taken before going to bed; **nightingale** small migratory bird which sings at night; **nightmare** bad, frightening dream; horrible experience; **nightshade** name of various poisonous plants; *a* & *adv* **nightly** (happening) every night.
nihilism *n* systematic rejection of all religious beliefs and moral principles; violent revolutionary beliefs, doctrines etc.; anarchism; *n* **nihilist.**
nil *n* nothing.
nimble *a* quick, agile; alert, clever.
nimbus *n* halo; rain-cloud.
nincompoop *n* simpleton; brainless person.

nine *a* & *n* cardinal number next above eight; *as* & *ns* **ninth** ordinal number; a ninth part; **nineteen** nine plus ten; **nineteenth**; **ninety** nine tens; **ninetieth** *n* **ninepins** skittles.

ninny *n* fool, simpleton.

nip *v* pinch sharply with fingers, claws; pinch off (buds, leaves etc.); (of wind) cut off, blight; *n* pinch; sharp, keen bite of wind, or frost; small drink; *n* **nipper** (*sl*) small boy; (*pl*) pincers; *a* **nippy** quick, active; frosty, cold.

nipple *n* teat of woman's breast; artificial teat of feeding bottle; any similar projection.

nirvana *n* (Buddhism) state of complete blessedness when individual is absorbed into divine infinity.

nisi *conj* (*leg*) becoming valid after certain interval unless cause is shown for rescinding it.

nit *n* egg of louse or other parasitic insect.

nitwit *n* fool, idiot.

nitre *n* potassium nitrate; saltpetre; *ns* **nitrate** compound of nitric acid and alkali; **nitrogen** colourless gaseous element, forming 78% of the air; *a* **nitric**; *n* **nitroglycerine** explosive liquid.

nix *n* (*sl*) nothing; water-sprite.

no *n* refusal; negative word, vote; (*pl*) **noes**; *a* not any; *adv* in no respect; none.

nobble *v* (*sl*) interfere with horse before race (by drugging or injury); obtain money etc by dishonest means.

noble *a* famous; having high ideals; admirable; of high rank; *n* person of noble birth; *ns* **nobility** quality of being noble; body of those with hereditary titles; **nobleman** member of nobility, a peer.

nobody *n* no person; person of no account.

nocturnal *n* of, in, by night; active at night.

nocturne *n* (*mus*) pensive, short composition (*usu* for piano; night-scene.

nod *v* bow head slightly, sharply in assent, greeting etc.; droop head when drowsy; *n* act of nodding.

node *n* knot, joint on stem of plant; hard swelling on muscle; point of intersection; *n* **nodule** small rounded lump; *a* **nodular** of nodes; having nodules.

noggin *n* small mug; liquid measure, 1 gill.

noise *n* clamour; loud sound; din; *as* **noiseless**; **noisy** making much noise; *n* **big noise** (*sl*) important person.
noisome *a* unhealthy; harmful; disgusting.
nomad *n* member of wandering, pastoral tribe; wanderer; *a* **nomadic**.
nom-de-plume *n* writer's assumed name, pen-name.
nomenclature *n* system of names or naming used in classifying; terminology.
nominal *a* pertaining to name; existing in name only; inconsiderable.
nominate *v* name, propose person for post, office; *ns* **nominator**; **nomination**; **nominee** person nominated.
non- *prefix* not, contrary of. *Such negative compounds are not given here, where the meaning may be deduced from the simple word.*
nonage *a* under age; *n* immaturity.
nonagenerian *n* person aged between 90 and 100.
nonce *n* **for the n.,** for the present; once only.
nonchalant *a* indifferent; *n* **nonchalance**.
noncommital *a* refusing to take sides, neutral.
nonconformist *n* dissenter *esp* from C. of E.
nondescript *a* not easily classified; vague, indefinite.
none *pron* no one; *adv* in no way.
nonentity *n* unimportant person; non-existent thing.
nonpareil *a* unequalled; matchless, unique.
nonplussed *a* in state of perplexity, bewilderment; being taken aback.
nonsense *n* lack of sense; meaningless words, statement; absurdity; *a* **nonsensical** absurd, ridiculous.
noodle *n* simpleton.
noodle *n* thin flat strip of macaroni paste.
nook *n* corner; retreat, hiding-place.
noon *n* midday, twelve o'clock.
noose *n* running knot, slip-knot, as in lasso.
nor *conj* and not.
Nordic *a* pertaining to Germanic races of Europe, *esp* Scandinavian.
norm *n* recognized standard; pattern, type; *a* **normal** average, ordinary; conforming to accepted standard, type; *n* **normality**.

north *n* cardinal compass point opposite midday sun; northern parts of earth or country generally; *a* to, from, in north; *as* **northern** pertaining to north; **northerly** from, to direction of north; *n* **northerner** inhabitant of northern region of country.
nose *n* external organ of smell, used in breathing; any projection like a nose; *v* nuzzle, sniff at; move cautiously; (*fig*) discover; *ns* **nose-dive** vertical descent of aircraft; **nosegay** bunch of sweet smelling flowers; *a* **nosy, nosey** (*sl*) inquisitive.
nosh *n* (*sl*) food, *v* (*sl*) to eat.
nostalgia *n* home-sickness; longing for what is past.
nostril *n* one of two external orifices of nose.
nostrum *n* quack medicine; favourite remedy.
not *adv* expressing denial, negation, refusal.
notable *a* remarkable; conspicuous; *n* notable person; *n* **notability** person of distinction.
notary *n* public official legally entitled to attest, certify deeds, contracts etc.
notation *n* system of symbols for representing numbers, musical notes etc.
notch *n* V-shaped cut, nick; *v* make notches in.
note *n* symbol for musical sound; brief informal letter; memorandum; written, printed promise of payment; brief comment; fame; *v* observe; record in writing; *as* **noted** well-known; **-worthy** remarkable.
nothing *n* not anything; zero; *adv* not at all.
notice *n* announcement; attention; dismissal (of servant); written warning; review (of play, book etc.); *v* observe; refer to; heed; *a* **noticeable** striking, easily seen; appreciable.
notify *v* report; make known; tell officially; *a* **notifiable**; *n* **notification**.
notion *n* idea, conception; inclination, fancy; belief.
notoriety *n* quality of being well-known in bad sense; *a* **notorious** commonly known in unfavourable sense.
notwithstanding *prep* in spite of; *adv* & *conj* although.
nougat *n* sweetmeat of sugar paste and nuts, fruit etc.

nought *n* nothing; symbol 0.
noun *n* word used as name of person, thing, action quality; substantive.
nourish *v* feed, sustain with food; (*fig*) foster, encourage; *n* **nourishment.**
nous *n* intelligence; common-sense.
nova *n* star whose brilliance flares briefly.
novel *a* new, strange; unfamiliar; *n* **novelty** newness; newly-marketed knick-knack.
novel *n* fictional prose story in book form; *ns* **novelist** author of novels; **novelette** short novel or story.
November *n* the eleventh month.
novice *n* inexperienced beginner; monk, nun who has not taken monastic vows; *n* **novitiate, noviciate** period of being a novice; apprenticeship.
now *adv* at present time; *adv* **nowadays** in these days.
nowhere *adv* in no place; not anywhere.
nowise *adv* in no way, by no means.
noxious *a* harmful, corrupting, offensive.
nozzle *n* projecting spout or vent.
nuance *n* delicate distinction in colour, meaning, feeling, tone of voice etc.
nubile *a* marriagable (of a girl).
nuclear *a* of, pertaining to nucleus; *n* **nuclear energy** energy released by nuclear fission; **n. fission** breaking of heavy atom into two or more atoms; **n. reactor** structure in which nuclear energy can be released under control.
nucleus *n* central core or kernel; (*fig*) startingpoint; core of atom; (*pl*) **nuclei.**
nude *a* naked, bare; *ns* **nudity**; **nudism** practice of going naked for health or religious reasons; **nudist.**
nudge *v* push slightly with elbow; *n* such touch.
nugget *n* lump of metal *esp* of native gold.
nuisance *n* something harmful, offensive, annoying.
null *a* of no effect, void; *n* **nullity**; *v* **nullify** make useless; cancel.
numb *a* deprived of feeling *esp* through cold; *v make* numb, deaden.
number *n* sum, amount; abstract mathematical

unit; numerical symbol; single issue of periodical etc; song, single item in variety show; collection of persons or units; *v* give number to; *a* **numberless** countless.

numeral *a* of, expressing number; graphic symbol of number; *v* **numerate** count; *n* **numeration** in fractions, figure denoting number of fractional units; *as* **numerical** of numbers; **numerous** many.

numismatics *n pl* study of coins and medals; *a* **numismatic**; *n* **numismatist**.

numskull *n* dolt, dunce.

nun *n* member of woman's religious order, living in convent; *n* **nunnery** community of nuns, convent.

nuncio *n* Papal ambassador.

nuptial *a* of, relating to marriage; *n pl* wedding ceremony.

nurse *n* person trained to care for sick or injured; woman employed to look after children; *v* suckle (an infant); act as nurse to; *ns* **nursery** room set apart for children's use; place for rearing young plants; **nurseryman** man who grows plants for sale.

nurture *n* nourishment; fostering care; training; *v* rear; educate.

nut *n* hard-shelled fruit of certain plants, containing edible kernel; hollow metal collar threaded to fit screw or bolt; (*sl*) head; *a* **nutty** of, like nut; (*sl*) crazy, mad; *n* **nutmeg** pungent spice.

nutria *n* fur of coypu.

nutrient *a* nourishing; *ns* **nutriment** nourishing food; **nutrition** process of receiving nourishment; *as* **nutritious, nutritive** nourishing; maintaining growth.

nuzzle *v* press nose against, or in.

nylghau *n* large Indian antelope.

nylon *n* synthetic plastics material having properties similar to those of silk.

nymph *n* legendary maiden deity, spirit of woods, hills, rivers etc.; insect pupa, chrysalis.

nymphomania *n* morbid sexual desire in women; *n* **nymphomaniac**.

nystagmus *n* involuntary twitching of eyelid.

oaf *n* clumsy, awkward fellow, lout.
oak *n* type of common tree; oak timber; *a* of oak; *n* **oak-apple** fleshy excrescence on oak caused by gall-flies.
oar *n* long pole with flattened blade, used to propel boat; *v* row; impel by rowing; *n* **oarsman.**
oasis *n* fertile place in desert; (*pl*) **oases.**
oast *n* kiln for drying hops; *n* **oast-house** building containing oast.
oat *n pl* (*usu*) cereal plant; its seeds; *n* **oatmeal.**
oath *n* solemn appeal to God or some sacred thing, as witness to truth of statement; curse, profanity.
obduracy *n* stubbornness; impenitence.
obdurate *a* stubborn, unyielding; hard-hearted.
obedience *n* submission to authority; act of obeying.
obedient *a* submissive, willing to obey.
obeisance *n* bow, formal gesture of respect etc.
obelisk *n* upright, four-sided, tapering stone pillar.
obese *a* extremely fat, corpulent; *n* **obesity.**
obey *v* carry out commands of; submit; follow rules of.
obfuscate *v* obscure, bewilder, confuse.
obituary *n* notice of death of person, often with short biography.
object *n* material thing; aim, purpose; noun, clause governed by verb or preposition; *a* **objective** relating to objects; existing outside the mind; *n* object, purpose aimed at.
object *v* be opposed to; feel dislike to; protest against; *n* **objection;** *a* **objectionable** liable to objection; offensive, unpleasant; *n* **objector.**
oblation *n* solemn, religious offering; *n* **oblate** one dedicated to monastic life.
obligato, obbligato *n* instrumental accompaniment to voice & another instrument, essential to effect.
oblige *v* compel by legal, moral force; do favour to; *n* **obligation** binding promise, contract etc.; duty; indebtedness for kindness, favour etc.; *a* **obligatory** compulsory; necessary to be done; *v* **obligate** bind legally, morally; *a* **obliging** helpful, courteous.
oblique *a* slanting; (*fig*) not straightforward; *n* **obliquity** deviation from straight line.

obliterate *v* blot out, erase; efface, wipe out; *n* **obliteration.**
oblivion *n* forgetfulness; being forgotten: *a* **oblivious** unaware; not realizing.
oblong *n* & *a* (rectangle) longer than broad.
obloquy *n* reproach; calumny; disgrace.
obnoxious *a* disagreeable; offensive; odious.
oboe *n* woodwind musical instrument.
obscene *a* indecent; lewd; disgusting; *n* **obscenity.**
obscure *a* dim, indistinct; not clear in meaning; unimportant; *n* **obscurity** darkness; ambiguity; state of being unknown.
obsequies *n pl* funeral rites, ceremonies.
obsequious *a* cringing, servile; excessively humble.
observe *v* pay attention to; watch; consider carefully; comment, remark; take notice ; *a* **observant** attentive; alert, vigilant; *ns* **observance** act of observing (laws etc.); commemoration; **observation** act of noticing; surveillance; (*pl*) record, remarks; critical comment on action or event etc.; **observatory** building with instruments for watching stars etc.; **observer** one who observes.
obsess *v* haunt, occupy mind; *n* **obsession** fixed idea, exclusive preoccupation of mind.
obsidian *n* glassy, very hard volcanic rock.
obsolescence *n* state of becoming obsolete or slowly disappearing through disuse; *a* **obsolescent.**
obsolete *a* disused; out-of-date.
obstacle *n* hindrance; obstruction, impediment.
obstetrics *n pl* science of midwifery; *a* **obstetric** of child-birth; *n* **obstetrician** specialist in midwifery.
obstinacy *n* stubborness; persistence.
obstinate *a* stubborn; persistent; intractable.
obstreperous *a* noisy; unruly, turbulent.
obstruct *v* block; hinder; impede; *ns* **obstruction**; **obstructionism** system of impeding Parliamentary or other business; **obstructionist**; *a* **obstructive** causing obstruction.
obtain *v* gain; acquire; be valid; *a* **obtainable** procurable.
obtrude *v* force upon; intrude; *n* **obtrusion**; *a* **obtrusive** thrusting; intrusive.

obtuse *a* blunt; (of persons) dull, dense; (of angle) greater than right angle.
obverse *a* facing an observer; *n* side of coin with head of sovereign etc; complement.
obviate *v* get rid of; make unnecessary.
obvious *a* easily seen; clear; lacking subtlety.
ocarina *n* small musical wind-instrument.
occasion *n* point of time when some event takes place; cause, reason; special event; *v* give rise to; cause; *a* **occasional** not continuous; composed for special purpose; rare.
Occident *n* the west; Western hemisphere; *a* **occidental.**
occlude *v* close, shut in or out; *n* **occlusion**; *a* **occlusive.**
occult *a* hidden, esoteric; supernatural; *ns* **occultation** eclipse; **occultism** study of supernatural.
occupancy *n* act of taking possession and residing in house etc; term of such occupation; *ns* **occupant**; **occupation** possession; employment; *a* **occupational**; of one's trade or habitual employment; *n* **occupier** tenant.
occupy *v* take & keep possession of (country etc); reside in (house); busy oneself with; fill (space).
occur *v* happen, take place; be found to exist; suggest itself; *n* **occurrence** incident; happening.
ocean *n* one of great expanses of salt water; *pl* (*coll*) plenty, vast amount; *a* **oceanic**; *ns* **oceanology, oceanography** branch of science concerned with oceans.
ocelot *n* large S. American wild cat.
ochre *n* earthy metallic oxide of iron, used for making yellow-brown pigments.
oct-, octa-, octo- *prefix* eight.
octagon *n* plane figure with eight sides.
octane *n* liquid ingredient of petroleum.
octave *n* eighth note above, below any note.
octavo *n* size of book or page made up of sheets folded into eight.
octennial *a* lasting, coming every eight years.
octet, octette *n* group of eight.

October *n* tenth month (eighth in old Roman calendar).
octogenarian *n* person aged between 80 and 90.
octopus *n* mollusc with eight arms bearing suckers.
octoroon *n* offspring of quadroon & white person, having 1/8th negro blood.
ocular *a* of eye or sight; *n* **oculist** specialist in diseases of eye.
odalisque *n* female slave or concubine in harem.
odd *a* not even; not divisible by two; not part of a set; not ordinary, casual; *n* **oddity** strangeness; odd person, thing; *n pl* **oddments** trifles; remnants; *n pl* **odds** difference in favour of one person, thing over another; ratio between stake and amount payable if bet is won; **odds and ends** bits and pieces.
ode *n* poem in complicated lyrical form.
odium *n* hatred; blame; *a* **odious** hateful, detestable.
odontology *n* study of teeth and their diseases.
odour *n* smell, scent; (*fig*) reputation; *v* **odorize** perfume; *as* **odorous** fragrant; (*coll*) bad smelling; **odoriferous** fragrant.
oedema *n* swelling of tissue caused by increased fluid content; local dropsy.
oesophagus *n* part of alimentary canal leading from mouth to stomach.
of *prep* belonging to; coming from; deprivation; due to; containing; distant from; made by.
off *adv* away; *prep* away from; *a* distant; not on; not working; (of horses, cars etc.) right; (cricket) to right of r.handed batsman.
offal *n* edible internal organs of animals; garbage; waste matter.
offend *v* annoy; do wrong; *ns* **offence** wrong-doing; affront; **offender; offensive** position of attack, aggression; *a* causing annoyance.
offer *v* proffer for acceptance or refusal; give as sacrifice or sign of worship; present for sale at price; bid as price for; show signs of; *n* bid; expression of willingness to do something *esp* to help; *ns* **offering** something offered *esp* sacrifice to God; money

donated; **offertory** collection taken in church service.

office *n* duty; function; position of trust, authority; public, state department; building, room where administrative, clerical work is done; form of worship; (*pl*) kitchen etc. and lavatories; *ns* **officer** one in command in armed forces; one who holds position of trust, authority.

official *n* one holding office *esp* in public organization; *a* having authority; **officialdom** body of public or state officials; bureaucratic outlook; red tape.

officiate *v* perform duty of; preside (at); conduct Divine service.

officinal *a* (of drugs etc.) of recognized medical value; stocked by chemists.

officious *a* meddling; offering uninvited advice; overbearing.

offing *n* the sea as far as can be seen from land; (*fig*) **in the offing** likely to appear, happen.

offset *n* beginning; side-shoot; method of printing from rubber roller; *v* compensate for.

offspring *n* child or children; (*fig*) result.

oft, often *adv* many times, frequently.

ogee *n* (*archi*) S-shaped moulding.

ogle *v* make eyes at; look at amorously.

ogre *n* evil man-eating giant; (*fig*) coarse, cruel man. (*fem*) **ogress.**

ohm *n* unit of electrical resistance.

oil *n* viscous organic or mineral substance, insoluble in water, and inflammable; *v* lubricate with oil; take oil in as fuel; *ns* **oilcake** cattle food from crushed oil-containing seeds; **oil-colour** pigment blended with oil; **oilskin** cloth treated with oil and used for waterproof clothing; *a* **oily** like oil; (*fig*) unctuous.

ointment *n* oily substance for healing wounds, or softening skin.

okapi *n* African ruminant, allied to giraffe.

okay, O.K. *adv* & *a* (*coll*) all right; approved; *v* (*coll*) sanction; *n* (*coll*) agreement; sanction.

old *a* aged; not young; having lived long; belonging to past; worn out; (*comp*) **older, elder**; (*sup*) **oldest,**

eldest; *n* old people, things; *as* **olden** old; **old-fashioned** out-of-date; antiquated; *n* **old maid** middle-aged spinster; *a* **old-time** of, like past times; *n* **Old World** Europe, Asia, Africa.
oleaginous *a* oily, greasy.
oleander *n* evergreen Mediterranean shrub.
olfactory *a* pertaining to sense of smell.
oligarchy *n* government by few persons; state so governed.
olive *n* evergreen tree; oil-yielding fruit; *a* yellowish green; *n* **olive branch** symbol of peace.
Olympiad *n* period of four years between Olympic Games; *as* **Olympian** god-like; **Olympic, O.Games** modern revival of ancient Grecian athletic meeting.
omega *n* last letter of Greek alphabet.
omelet, omelette *n* beaten eggs, seasoned and fried.
omen *n* sign, portent of things to come.
ominous *a* threatening evil.
omission *n* something left out, not done.
omit *v* leave out; fail to do or include.
omni- *prefix* all.
omnibus *n* large passenger-carrying road vehicle, on fixed route; *a* having many uses.
omnipotent *a* all-powerful, almighty; *n* **omnipotence.**
omniscient *a* infinitely wise; *n* **omniscience.**
omniverous *a* eating all kinds of food; (*fig*) assimilating everything.
on *prep* resting upon, covering; near, close to; at date of; concerning; *adv* forward; continuously; functioning; *a* **onward** forward.
once *adv* on single occasion; formerly; *n* **once-over** (*sl*) brief, preliminary survey.
oncoming *a* approaching.
one *n* lowest cardinal number; particular single person or thing; unity; *a* of number less than two; forming single whole; certain; *prons* somebody; anybody; **oneself** *reflx* & emphatic form of 'one'; *as* **one-sided** lop sided; (*fig*) biassed; **one-way** street where traffic is allowed in one direction only.
onerous *a* burdensome, weighty; *n* **onerousness.**
onion *n* strong-smelling edible bulbous plant.

onlooker *n* spectator.
only *a* single, sole; *adv* solely; exclusively; *conj* except (that).
onomatopoeia *n* formation of words by imitation of sounds associated with object named e.g. cuckoo.
onset *n* beginning; attack.
onslaught *n* violent attack.
onto *prep* to and upon.
onus *n* burden; responsibility.
onyx *n* variety of agate.
oodles *n pl* (*sl*) abundance.
oology *n* study of birds' eggs; *n* **oologist**.
ooze *n* liquid mud, slime *esp* on sea-, river-bed; slow trickle; *v* exude (liquid); flow slowly out.
opacity *n* state of being opaque.
opal *n* white iridescent gem-stone; *a* **opalescent**.
opaque *a* not allowing light through; dark, obscure.
open *a* not shut or closed; accessible; free to be used, shared, entered by all; not secret; frank, sincere; not decided, settled; *v* unfasten; uncover; lay bare; begin; make accessible; *n* open space: outdoors; unprotected position; *n* **opening** hole; beginning; *a* first; *as* **opencast** mining of surface area only; **open-handed** generous; **open-minded** unprejudiced.
opera *n* drama set to music, sung to orchestral accompaniment; *a* **operatic**; *n* **operetta** short, light opera.
operation *n* action; plan, project; undertaking; act of surgery; *v* **operate** work; cause to function; perform act of surgery; *a* **operative** working; valid; *n* worker; artisan; *n* **operator** one who works machine.
ophthalmia *n* inflammation of eye; *a* **ophthalmic** pertaining to eye.
opinion *n* considered belief, judgement; point of view; *v* **opine** utter opinion; *a* **opinionated** obstinate in beliefs etc.; dogmatic.
opium *n* narcotic, intoxicant and sedative drug obtained from white poppy; *v* **opiate** mix with opium; *n* drug containing opiate; (*fig*) anything that soothes or calms; *a* inducing sleep.

opossum *n* small nocturnal marsupial of America.
opponent *n* antagonist; rival.
opportune *a* seasonable, suitable, well-timed; *n* **opportunity** lucky chance, favourable occasion or time; *n* **opportunism** policy of taking advantage of circumstances; **opportunist**.
oppose *v* place against; withstand, contend against; *n* **opposer**; *a* **opposite** situated facing; entirely different, in position, in nature, in direction; *n* the contrary; *n* **opposition** resistance; political party opposing that in power.
oppress *v* crush, treat unjustly, cruelly; weigh heavily on, depress; *a* **oppressive** tyrannical; hard to bear; (of weather) heavy, tiring; *ns* **oppression** harshness; tyranny; **oppressor**.
opprobium *n* reproach; infamy, disgrace; *a* **opprobrious** shameful, infamous.
opt *v* choose; **opt out** choose to take no part in; *a* **optative** expressing wish, desire.
optic *a* pertaining to eyes or sight; *pl* science of vision *esp* in relation to light; *a* **optical**; *n* **optician** one who makes and sells optical instruments and spectacles.
optimism *n* habit of looking at brighter side of things; doctrine that good ultimately prevails over evil; *a* **optimistic**; *n* **optimist**.
optimum *n* best, most favourable state, condition.
option *n* choice; privilege of buying or selling at certain price within specified time; *a* **optional** not obligatory; voluntary.
opulent *a* wealthy, abundant; luxuriant; *n* **opulence**.
opus *n* work or composition *esp* in music.
or *conj* introduces alternative; offering choice.
oracle *n* prophecy or answer, divinely inspired, given by ancient Greek, Roman priest; place, shrine where answer, often ambiguous, was given; the inspired priest; *a* **oracular** of oracle; ambiguous.
oral *a* by mouth; spoken.
orange *n* large red-gold citrus fruit; tree bearing this; colour of fruit.
orang-outang, orang-utan *n* large anthropoid ape of Borneo.

orator *n* eloquent, public speaker; *n* **oration** set, formal speech; *a* **oratorical** ; *n* **oratory** eloquence, rhetoric; small private chapel.
oratorio *n* musical composition *usu* of sacred nature for solo voices, chorus and orchestra.
orb *n* sphere, globe; *a* **orbicular**; *n* **orbit** eye-socket; path of heavenly body or artificial satellite.
orchard *n* plantation of fruit trees.
orchestra *n* band of musicians playing instrumental music; front part of theatre where such band plays; *a* **orchestral**; *v* **orchestrate** compose, arrange music for orchestra; *n* **orchestration.**
orchid, orchis *n* kind of plant with exotic flowers.
ordain *v* admit to holy orders; decree, enact, appoint; *n* **ordination.**
ordeal *n* severe, searching experience; test of courage, endurance.
order *n* relative position in series; sequence; tidiness; classification; command; group of monks etc.; instruction; *v* arrange; command; direct (goods) to be supplied; *a* **orderly** tidy; law-abiding; *n* soldier in attendance on officer; hospital attendant; *n* **orderliness**; *a* **ordinal** indicating position in series; *n* ordinal number.
ordinance *n* decree, regulation; religious ceremony.
ordinary *a* normal, usual; average; commonplace; *n* cleric having authority in his own right; fixed-price meal; inn serving this.
ordnance *n* artillery; military stores, equipment, material; **o. survey** official geographical survey of Britain.
ordure *n* dung, filth.
ore *n* metal-yielding mineral.
organ *n* part of animal or plant performing particular function; keyboard wind-instrument; means of action; agency for information etc. *i.e.* newspaper; *a* **organic** pertaining to, affecting bodily and vital organs; systematic; *ns* **organism** individual capable of reproduction and growth; **organist** one who plays organ.
organize *v* arrange, group separate parts into systematic whole; make efficient; unite into society

etc.; *ns* **organization** act of organizing; body of persons having common purpose; **organizer.**
orgasm *n* violent excitement, paroxysm, *esp* in sexual act.
orgy *n* drunken revelry; continuous round of pleasure.
oriel *n* projecting bay or recessed window.
Orient *n* the East; lustre of finest pearl; *v* **orientate** face, be pointed to East; (*fig*) take mental attitude towards; take bearings; *a* & *n* **oriental;** *ns* **orientation** adjustment in relative position; **orientalist** expert in Eastern customs and languages.
orifice *n* mouth, outer opening of tube, pipe etc.
origin *n* source, beginning; initial cause; ancestry.
original *a* earliest; new creative, inventive; made, done for first time; *n* that from which copies are made; first pattern, model; eccentric person; *n* **originality** creative faculty; novelty; *v* **originate** bring about; have origin in.
oriole *n* yellow and black bird of crow family.
orison *n* prayer.
ormolu *n* gilded bronze; gold coloured alloy of copper, zinc and tin; furniture etc. decorated with this.
ornament *n* decoration; adornment; trinket; *v* decorate, embellish; *a* **ornamental;** *n* **ornamentation.**
ornate *a* excessively adorned.
ornithology *n* scientific study of birds; *a* **ornithological;** *n* **ornithologist.**
orphan *n* child who has lost one or both parents; *n* **orphanage** institution for care of orphans.
orrery *n* mechanism showing movement in solar system.
orris *n* gold or silver lace or braid.
orris root *n n* fragrant root of kind of iris.
ortho- *prefix* right, correct.
orthodox *n* holding conventional views.
orthopaedics *n pl* branch of surgery dealing with bone deformities; *a* **orthopaedic** pertaining to orthopaedics.
oscillate *v* swing to and fro; (*fig*) waver; *ns* **oscilla-**

tion; oscillator apparatus generating electromagnetic waves.
osculate *v* kiss; *n* **osculation**; *a* **osculatory.**
osier *n* species of willow, used in basket-making.
osmosis *n* passage of liquid through permeable membrane.
osprey *n* sea-eagle.
osseous *a* bony; of, like bone; *v* **ossify** change into bone; (*fig*) harden; *n* **ossification.**
ostensible *a* apparent; pretended.
ostentation *n* pretentious show of wealth etc.; *a* **ostentatious** given to showing off; pretentious.
osteopathy *n* treatment of disease by manipulation of bones; *n* **osteopath** one who practises osteopathy.
ostler *n* groom, stableman at an inn.
ostracise *v* refuse to associate with; banish; *n* **ostracism** exclusion from social group etc.
ostrich *n* large, flightless, African bird.
other *a* different; additional; not the same; *pron* other person or thing; *adv* **otherwise** differently; *conj* if not.
otiose *a* superfluous; futile.
otter *n* web-footed aquatic mammal.
Ottoman *a* Turkish; *n* low, padded seat without back.
ought *v aux* expressing obligation, desirability, probability.
ouija *n* lettered & numbered board used in seances etc.
ounce *n* unit of weight, sixteenth of pound avoirdupois; (*fig*) small amount.
ounce *n* snow-leopard; lynx.
our *a* belonging to us; *pron* **ours**; *pron* **ourselves** emphatic form of WE.
ousel, ouzel *n* one of various kinds of thrush.
oust *v* turn out, expel; eject.
out *adv* away from inside; expressing exclusion, termination, insuffiency; deviation; no longer confined; *a* **outer** external; *n* **outing** pleasure trip; *a* & *adv* **outward(s).**
out- *prefix*: *forms compounds with meaning* outside, remote, excess, *eg* **outfit** equipment, kit. *Such com-*

pounds are not given here, when the meaning may be deduced from the simple word.

outback *n* (*Aust*) uncultivated remote inland area.

outclass *v* surpass; excel.

outcrop *n* part of rock stratum coming to surface; *v.*

outflank *v* get the better of.

outlandish *a* foreign-looking; uncouth.

outline *n* lines defining edge of visible figure; (*fig*) general scheme, plan, *v* draw outline; summarize.

output *n* product of physical or mental effort; rate of production; computer-processed data; telecommunications signal; tax charged on goods sent out.

outrage *n* violation, rape; violent transgression of law; *v* violate; offend against.

outré *a* exaggerated; in bad taste.

outrigger *n* mast with tackle for hoisting; metal stay with rowlock; boat with one.

outright *adv* openly; *a* direct, positive.

outside *n* external part, surface; extreme limit; *a* external; unconnected; unlikely; *adv* out of doors; *prep* on outer side of; apart from.

outskirts *n pl* outer areas (of city, subject etc).

outwork *n* detached fort or defensive work; work done away from factory.

oval *a* egg-shaped, elliptical; *n* figure of this shape.

ovary *n* female organ of reproduction; *a* **ovarian.**

ovation *n* enthusiastic welcome or applause.

oven *n* heated metal or brick receptacle, in which food is baked; small kiln, or furnace.

over *adv* above; away; past; excessively; *prep* above; crossing, spanning; more than; *n* in cricket, six balls bowled in succession from one end.

over- *prefix forms compounds with meaning* too, in excess, above, *eg* **overall** protective outer garment. *Such compounds are not given here, when the meaning may be deduced from the simple word.*

overbearing *a* dictatorial, domineering.

overhaul *v* examine closely for faults, or needed repairs; overtake.

overhead *a* above one's head; *adv* above; *n pl* **overheads** general expenses of a business.

overland *adv* by land, rather than water.

overmuch *n* superfluity; *a* & *adv* excessive(ly).
overpass *n* bridge crossing motorway.
overpower *v* get better of, conquer.
override *v* disregard, nullify.
oversea(s) *a* & *adv* over, across sea; abroad; foreign.
overseer *n* foreman, supervisor; *v* **oversee** supervise.
oversight *n* mistake; accidental omission to do something.
overt *a* openly done; apparent.
overtake *v* catch up and pass; overhaul.
overthrow *v* upset; defeat, *pt* **overthrew**; *pp* **overthrown**; *n* ruin; defeat.
overtime *n* time worked after normal hours; wages for this.
overture *n* musical composition played at beginning of opera etc; *usu pl* friendly or formal approach.
overwhelm *v* flow, cover over; overpower; engulf; *a* **overwhelming** irresistible.
overwrought *a* too excited; exhausted by emotion.
oviform *a* egg-shaped; *n* **ovoid** egg-shaped figure; *a* **oviparous** egg-laying.
ovine *a* of, like sheep.
ovum *n* female egg-cell; *n* **ovule** unfertilized seed.
owe *v* be indebted to; have to repay; *a* **owing** unpaid; due; **owing to** as result of; caused by.
owl *n* night bird of prey; *n* **owlish** stupidly solemn; *n* **owlet** young owl.
own *v* possess; admit, confess; acknowledge; *a* emphasises possession; *ns* **owner** one who possesses; **ownership** possession.
ox *n* castrated adult male of domestic cattle; (*pl*) **oxen**; *ns* **oxbow** horseshoe bend in river; **oxeye, oxslip** types of flowering plants.
oxalis *n* plant, wood-sorrel; *a* **oxalic**; **o. acid** organic poisonous acid, originally obtained from oxalis.
oxide *n* compound of oxygen and another element; *v* **oxidize** unite with oxygen, make, become rusty, or dull; *n* **oxidation**.
oxygen *n* colourless, odourless gas in the atmosphere, essential to life; *prefix* **oxy** of oxygen; of an oxide; *v* **oxygenate** combine, treat with oxygen; *a* **oxy-**

acetylene of, consisting of, mixture of oxygen and acetylene; cutting, burning with flame of such gas.
oyez *n* call by court-usher, or town crier, to demand attention, or silence.
oyster *n* edible marine bivalve mollusc.
ozone *n* concentrated form of oxygen, with pungent smell; (*pop*) bracing sea-side air.

pace *n* one step in walking; rate, speed of moving; gait; *v* walk slowly with measured tread; set speed for (runner etc.); *n* **pacemaker** one who sets rate of speed for runner, cyclist etc.
pachyderm *n* thick-skinned animal, as elephant.
pacify *v* make peaceful; appease; *a* **pacific** peaceable; *ns* **pacification**; **pacifism** systematic opposition to war, or violence; **pacifist** believer in pacifism.
pack *n* bundle; number of animals hunting together; set of hounds; forwards of Rugby team; set of playing cards; *v* put closely together (in case, box); fill with things; *ns* **package** parcel; **p.deal** one in which bad factors must be accepted with the good; **packet** small parcel; (*sl*) large sum of money; (*sl*) trouble; **packet-boat** mail-boat; **pack-horse** horse used for carrying loads; **pack-ice** floating mass of broken ice.
pact *n* agreement, compact, covenant.
pad *v* go on foot softly; trudge along.
pad *n* anything composed of or stuffed with soft material, used as protection or to prevent friction; under-part of paw; block of sheets of paper; *v* make soft, protect with pad etc.; *n* **padding** soft material used for stuffing; space-, time-filling material used in speech, novel etc.
paddle *n* short, broad oar without rowlock; *v* propel by paddle; walk barefoot in shallow water.
paddock *n* small grass field, or enclosure.
paddy *n* growing rice; *n* **paddyfield** rice-field.
padlock *n* detachable lock with hinged loop to be hooked through staple etc.; *v* fasten thus.
padre *n* chaplain in armed forces.
paean *n* song of praise, triumph, thanksgiving.

paediatrics *n pl* branch of medicine dealing with children's diseases; *n* **paediatrician.**
pagan *n* & *a* heathen; barbarian; *n* **paganism.**
page *n* boy attendant or servant; *v* call name of person (in hotel, club etc).
page *n* one side of leaf of book; *v* mark page numbers.
pageant *n* splendid, imposing display in costume; series of richly costumed, historical tableaux or scenes; *n* **pageantry** gorgeous display.
paginate *v* number book pages.
pagoda *n* Oriental temple, tapering pinnacled tower with several storeys.
pail *n* bucket; *n* **pailful.**
pain *n* bodily, mental suffering, anguish; penalty; (*pl*) effort, trouble; *v* inflict pain on; be source of pain; *as* **painful**; **painless**; **painstaking**; careful, industrious.
paint *n* colouring matter used to give colour to surface; pigment; *v* colour, coat, portray with paint; (*fig*) describe vividly; *ns* **painter**; **painting** act of colouring with paint; painted picture, *esp* hand-painted.
painter *n* rope fastening bow of boat to mooring.
pair *n* set of two similar things normally used together; mated couple of animals; *v* arrange in twos; mate; match.
pal *n* (*sl*) mate, close friend.
palace *n* residence of sovereign or bishop; large public hall; *a* **palatial** splendid, sumptuous, spacious; **palatine** with royal privileges.
paladin *n* chivalrous person, knight-errant.
palaeolithic *a* belonging to earlier Stone Age.
palaeontology *n* study of fossils & extinct forms of life.
palanquin *n* light covered litter, used in Orient.
palate *n* roof of mouth; sense of taste.
palaver conference; idle talk.
pale *a* whitish, wan; faint, dimly coloured; not bright.
pale *n* wooden stake; *n* **paling** fencing.
palette *n* small board on which colours are mixed; range of colours.

palfrey *n* saddle-horse.
palindrome *n* word, line etc., reading same backwards and forwards.
palisade *n* fence of pointed stakes.
pall *n* cloth spread over coffin.
pall *v* satiate; weary, become tedious to.
pallet *n* small, hard straw mattress.
palliasse *n* straw mattress.
palliate *v* mitigate; relieve without curing; excuse; *a* & *n* **palliative** (giving) temporary relief.
pallid *a* excessively pale; *n* **pallor**.
pall-mall *n* old game, resembling croquet.
palm *n* inner surface of hand; tropical tree; leaf of this tree as symbol of victory; *v* conceal in palm; transfer by sleight of hand; *ns* **palmistry** fortune-telling from lines on palm of hand; **palmist**; **palmer** pilgrim; **palm-oil** oil from palm tree; (*fig*) bribe; **Palm Sunday** Sunday before Easter.
palpable *a* capable of being felt, touched; obvious.
palpate *v* (*med*) examine by touch.
palpitate *v* beat irregularly; flutter; throb; *n* **palpitation** throbbing; irregular, quickened action of heart.
palsy *n* paralysis, *esp* with trembling of limbs.
paltry *a* trifling, petty; insignificant.
pampas *n* grassy plains of S. America.
pamper *v* over-indulge; cosset, coddle.
pamphlet *n* short unbound treatise, *usu* on some current topic.
pan *n* broad, shallow vessel *usu* for cooking; *v* wash (gravel etc) to extract gold; (*fig*) **pan out** result, turn out.
pan-, panto- *prefix* all.
panacea *n* remedy for all ills.
panache *n* ostentation, swagger.
panama *n* hat made from strawlike material.
pancake *n* thin flat cake of fried batter; *v* (of aircraft) land flatly and abruptly.
panchromatic *a* (of photographic film) sensitive to light of all colours.
pancreas *n* gland secreting digestive juices & insulin.

panda *n* large black and white Himalayan bear; small bear-cat.
pandemonium *n* complete confusion; wild disorder, uproar.
pander *n* procurer, pimp; *v* act as pander; *v* **p. to** gratify, encourage (unworthy desires, etc.).
pane *n* single sheet of glass in window.
panegyric *n* extravagant speech of praise.
panel *n* rectangular piece of material set into surface (of door, dress etc.) list of persons called for jury service; group of persons taking part in quiz, or game before audience; *v* fit, ornament with panels; *n* **panelling** series of panels.
pang *n* sudden sharp pain.
panic *n* sudden, excessive, infectious terror, alarm; *a* (*sl*) **panicky** very nervous; *a* **panic-stricken** terrified.
pannier *n* basket carried on back (of mule etc.)
pannikin *n* small metal cup.
panoply *n* complete equipment of armour.
panorama *n* wide, unbroken view; series of scenes, pictures showing historical or other views; *a* **panoramic.**
pansy *n* wild or garden plant of violet family; (*sl*) effeminate youth; male homosexual.
pant *v* gasp for breath; (*fig*) long intensely; *n* short, laboured breath.
pantaloon *n* foolish old man in pantomime; long tight trousers (*ar*).
pantechnicon *n* furniture removal-van or store.
pantheism *n* belief that universe is God; *n* **pantheist**; *n* **pantheon** temple for worship of all gods.
panther *n* spotted carnivore of cat tribe.
pantile *n* roofing-tile.
pantograph *n* instrument for reproducing drawing, plan etc. on larger or smaller scale.
pantomime *n* theatrical performance, based on legend or fairy tale, *usu* given at Christmas; dumb-show.
pantry *n* room where food, plates etc. are kept.
pants *n pl* knickers, drawers; trousers.
pap *n* soft, sloppy food; mash; nipple of breast.

Papacy *n* office of Pope; papal system; *a* **papal** pertaining to Pope, or Papacy; *a* & *n* **papist** (adherent) of Papacy; Roman Catholic.
pa(w)paw *n* tropical tree or its edible fruit.
paper *n* substance made of pulped rags or vegetable fibre, formed into thin sheets, used for writing, drawing etc.; newspaper; article, essay; set of questions for examination; (*pl*) documents etc., credentials; *v* cover, decorate (walls etc.) with paper.
papier-mâché *n* paper pulp mixed with glue, moulded while soft, and dried.
papoose *n* N. American Indian infant.
paprika *n* red, capsicum pepper.
papyrus *n* sedge-like plant; writing material of this; (*pl*) **papyri** manuscript written on this.
par *n* equality of value; nominal value (esp. of stocks, shares); (*fig*) normal state of health etc.; (*golf*) number of strokes reckoned as perfect score for hole, course; *a* **parity** equality; analogy.
para- (**par-** before vowel or h mute) *prefix* beside, beyond; contrary, wrong; ancillary to; defence against (*e.g.* **parachute** *abbrev* **para** itself used as prefix—**paratroop, parafoil** etc).
parable *n* brief story with moral lesson.
parabola *n* plane curve formed by intersection of cone by plane parallel to cone's side.
parachute *n* umbrella-like apparatus used to retard descent of falling body; *v* leap, fall to earth using parachute; *n* **parachutist**.
parade *n* proud display; military review; ground where this takes place; promenade; *v* muster; march solemnly past; display.
paradise *n* Garden of Eden; heaven; place of perfect happiness.
paradox *n* statement apparently absurd or self-contradictory yet really true; *a* **paradoxical.**
paraffin *n* inflammable hydrocarbon obtained from wood, petroleum, shale etc.
paragon *n* model of excellence or perfection.
paragraph *n* section in prose writing; short, separate news item.
parakeet, paroquet *n* small, long-tailed parrot.

paraldehyde *n* narcotic drug.
parallax *n* apparent displacement of object caused by actual displacement of observer.
parallel *a* (of lines etc.) equidistant in all parts; markedly similar; *n* line equidistant from another; line of latitude; comparison; *v* compare; *n* **parallelogram** four-sided plane figure with parallel opposite sides.
paralysis *n* loss of sensation and motive power in any part of body; (*pl*) **-yses**; *v* **paralyse** affect with paralysis; (*fig*) check, render inoperative; *n* & *adj* **paralytic** (person) suffering from paralysis.
paramount *a* having supreme authority; pre-eminent, chief.
paramour *n* illicit lover.
parang *n* heavy Malayan straight-edged knife.
paranoia *n* mental disorder, accompanied by delusions of grandeur or power.
parapet *n* low wall; (*mil*) rampart in front of troops.
paraphernalia *n pl* miscellaneous belongings, accessories, equipment.
paraphrase *n* free rendering of any passage; free translation; *v* express in other words.
parasite *n* useless hanger on; (*biol*) organism which lives on or within another organism; *a* **parasitic** of, caused by, parasite.
parasol *n* sunshade.
paratroops *n pl* airborne troops landed by parachute *n* **paratrooper**.
paratyphoid *n* infectious disease resembling typhoid, but caused by different bacilli.
paravane *n* contrivance for cutting moorings of submerged mines.
parboil *v* boil partially.
parbuckle *n* rope for raising cask etc.
parcel *n* object, objects wrapped, *esp* in paper, to form single package; piece of land; *v* divide into parts; wrap up.
parch *v* make, cause to become excessively dry; scorch.
parchment *n* animal skin dressed and prepared for writing on; manuscript, etc. written on parchment.

pardon *n* forgiveness; excuse; remission of punishment; *v* forgive; grant pardon to; *a* **pardonable.**
pare *v* trim; cut away edge or surface; gradually reduce; *n* **paring** thin slice pared off.
paregoric *n* tincture of opium, that soothes pain.
parent *n* father or mother; *a* **parental**; *n* **parentage** ancestry, origin.
parenthesis *n* word, clause etc. inserted into sentence which is grammatically correct without it; *n pl* **parentheses** brackets ( ) enclosing parenthesis.
pariah *n* very low caste Hindu; (*fig*) social outcast; **p. dog** vagabond mongrel dog in India.
pari-mutuel *n* French form of totalisator.
parish *n* smallest local unit in civil or ecclesiastical administration; *n* **parishioner** inhabitant of parish.
park *n* public garden in town; area of grass & trees surrounding mansion; country area set aside as nature reserve etc.; place where cars etc. may park; *v* put car etc. in car park or leave elsewhere; (*coll*) leave object in one place, *usu* temporarily.
parky *a* (*sl*) sharply cold.
parlance *n* manner of speaking; words, idiom.
parley *n* conference *esp* between opponents, on peace terms; *v* discuss terms.
parliament *n* supreme legislative body of U.K.; representative law-making body; *a* **parliamentary**; *n* **parliamentarian** one experienced in parliamentary procedure; (*hist*) Roundhead.
parlour *n* sitting-room; room for receiving guests.
parlous *a* dangerous; critical.
parochial *a* pertaining to parish; (*fig*) narrow-minded.
parody *n* mocking imitation of author's style or work; bad imitation, travesty; *v* make fun of by imitating.
parole *n* word of honour, solemn pledge *esp* one given by prisoner, not to escape.
parotid *a* near the ear; *n* parotid or salivary gland.
paroxysm *n* sudden spasm, fit of emotion, pain etc.
parquet *n* flooring made of inlaid wooden blocks.
parr *n* young salmon.
parricide *n* murder murderer of parent.

parrot *n* tropical bird with hooked beak, and faculty of imitating human speech; (*fig*) imitator.
parry *v* ward off, avert; evade; *n*.
parse *v* describe (word), analyse (sentence), grammatically.
parsimony *n* undue economy; stinginess; *a* **parsimonious.**
parsley *n* culinary herb.
parsnip *n* plant with edible, cream-coloured root.
parson *n* rector, vicar; clergyman; *n* **parsonage** house of parson.
part *n* portion; section; component; share; actor's role; member of living organism; *v* separate; sunder; go in different ways; **part with** give up, dispense with; *adv* **partly** in part.
partaker *n* participant; one who takes part in, of; *v* **partake** take share in; *pt* **partook**; *pp* **partaken.**
parterre *n* level space with flower-beds.
partial *a* forming part of whole; biased; fond of; *n* **partiality** bias in favour; fondness.
participate *v* have share in; partake; *ns* **participant, participation.**
participle *n* verbal adjective, having some functions of verb.
particle *n* very small amount, part; minor, indeclinable part of speech.
particular *a* distinct, separate; peculiar, not general; *n pl* detailed account, specification; *n* **particularity.**
partisan *n* adherent of party, cause etc.; guerilla fighter *esp* in resistance movement; *a* showing blind devotions.
partition *n* division; minor dividing wall in house; *v* divide into parts, sections.
partner *n* member of commercial partnership: (golf, tennis etc.) one who plays with another, against opponents; one who dances with another; husband or wife; *n* **-ship** state of being partner; association of two or more persons in business, etc.
partridge *n* game bird related to grouse.
parturition *n* act of giving birth.
party *n* group of persons holding same opinions *esp* in politics; social gathering; squad of soldiers etc.;

(*coll*) person; *ns* **p. line** policy laid down by political party; shared telephone line; **p.-wall** common wall separating two properties.
parvenue *n* upstart.
Paschal *a* of Passover or Easter.
pasha *n* title of high-ranking Turkish, Egyptian officials.
pass *v* move forward; go beyond; hand to; transfer; sanction; be accepted by; take examination successfully; pronounce (judgement); elapse; *n* narrow way, channel; permit to go into, through; free ticket; satisfactory standard in exam.; *a* **passable** capable of being passed; fairly good, tolerable.
passage *n* voyage, crossing; accommodation on ship; part of book etc. referred to separately; means of access; *v* (of horse) move, cause to move sideways.
passenger *n* one who travels in ship, car, train etc.
passerine *a* of order of perching birds.
passion *n* strong feeling, enthusiasm; sexual desire; wrath; (*cap*) sufferings and death of Christ; *a* **passionate** violent, quick-tempered, intense, ardent; *n* **passion flower** large-flowered climbing plant.
passive *a* inactive; offering no active resistance; grammatical form of verb that shows subject as acted upon.
Passover *n* annual Jewish feast.
passport *n* official document granted to enable holder to travel abroad etc.
password *n* secret word, phrase identifying person as entitled to enter (camp, society etc); countersign.
past *a* gone by, ended; taking place in past; *n* time gone by; earlier life; *prep* beyond, after.
paste *n* soft, slightly moist compound; adhesive compound; vitreous compound used for artificial gems; *v* fasten, affix with paste.
pastel *n* crayon made of powdered pigment mixed with gum, or oil; drawing in pastel; *a* delicately coloured.
pasteurization *n* sterilization (of milk etc.) by heating; *v* **pasteurize.**
pastil(le) *n* aromatic paste burnt as fumigator; small lozenge, often medicated.

pastime *n* recreation, amusement.
pastor *n* priest, minister; *a* **pastoral** of office of pastor; connected with shepherds; (of land) used for pasture.
pastry *n* baked paste of flour and fat; pie, tart etc. made of this; small rich cream-filled cake.
pasture *n* grass for food of cattle; land on which cattle are grazed; *v* graze; *n* **pasturage** cattle-grazing; pasture.
pasty *n* small pie of meat and potatoes, baked without dish; *a* pale, unhealthy-looking.
pat *n* quick light touch; small shaped lump of butter; *v* tap (dog, horse etc.) lightly with hand.
patch *n* piece of material used to cover, repair hole in garment etc.; black spot worn as facial ornament; small plot of land; *v* mend by means of patch; *a* **patchy** not consistent in quality etc.; *n* **patchwork** needlework of patches of different colours; (*fig*) medley, jumble.
pate *n* head.
patella *n* knee-cap.
paten *n* plate, *usu* gold or silver, for holding bread at the Eucharist.
patent *a* obvious; protected by patent; *n* licence granting sole right to make and sell invention; **letters patent** open letter issued by sovereign granting privilege etc.; *v* secure patent.
paternal *a* of father, fatherly; *n* **paternity** fatherhood.
paternoster *n* The Lord's Prayer; eleventh bead of rosary.
path *n* way, track, footpath; (*fig*) line of conduct; *n* **pathway** track for pedestrians.
pathology *n* science of diseases; *a* **pathological** caused by, of nature of disease; morbid; *n* **pathologist**.
pathos *n* that which evokes sympathy, sorrow or pity; *a* **pathetic** affecting emotions; pitiable.
patient *a* enduring provocation or pain; persistent in; *n* person under medical treatment; *n* **patience** forbearance; endurance without complaint; card-game.

patina *n* greenish film on old copper, bronze; fine gloss on old woodwork.
patois *n* local, provincial form of speech.
patriarch *n* father, head of family, clan etc.; *a* **patriarchal** venerable.
patrician *n* member of ancient Roman nobility; one of noble birth; *a* of noble birth.
patricide *n* murder of one's own father.
patrimony *n* property inherited from one's father or ancestors.
patriot *n* one who is devoted to and loyally supports his country; *n* **patriotic** inspired by patriotism; *n* **patriotism** love of one's country.
patrol *v* walk regularly up and down (in); go the rounds; be on guard duty; *n* small body of troops, police etc. patrolling; unit of six Boy Scouts.
patron *n* one who encourages and supports social or charitable undertaking; regular customer; guardian saint; *n* **patronages** pecial support; right of presentation to church benefice; *v* **patronize** encourage; support by being customer; treat condescendingly.
patronym *n* name derived from father, surname.
patten *n* clog, raised wooden shoe.
patter *v* run with quick, light steps; utter, speak hurriedly; *n* succession of light taps; speech, jargon (of thieves, conjurers, comedians etc.)
pattern *n* model, shape as guide in constructing anything; sample; design.
paucity *n* scarcity; smallness of number or amount.
paunch *n* belly; *v* remove entrails (of rabbit etc.).
pauper *n* destitute person supported by charity or at public expense.
pause *n* brief stop or rest; *v* stop for a while; hesitate,
pave *v* cover surface with flat stones etc.; *n* **pavement** paved walk for pedestrians.
pavilion *n* large tent; building attached to games-, sports-field; summer-house.
paw *n* foot of quadruped with claws; *v* scrape with forefoot; handle roughly and unnecessarily.
pawn *v* deposit article with (pawnbroker); *n* loan thus raised; chess piece; *n* **pawnbroker** one who lends money at interest on articles pledged.

pax *interj* (*sl*) truce, peace.
pay *v* give, hand over money etc. for goods or services; produce profit for; discharge (debt); let out (rope) *pt* & *pp* **paid**; *n* salary, wages; *a* **payable** due; *ns* **payee** one to whom payment is made; **payer**; **payment** amount paid.
pea leguminous climbing plant, with edible seeds enclosed in pod; *n* **peanut** ground-nut.
peace *n* calm; freedom from strife, war; tranquility; *as* **peaceable** at peace, not quarrelsome; **peaceful** free from war; calm, tranquil.
peach *n* stone-fruit with pink velvety skin; tree bearing this; (*sl*) pretty girl; anything very pleasant.
peach *v* (*sl*) inform against.
peacock *n* bird with brilliantly coloured fan-shaped tail; (*fem*) **peahen.**
peak *n* pointed top or end; highest point, degree, volume; *a* **peaked** having peak; **peaky** having drawn, emaciated look.
peal *n* loud ringing of bells; set of bells tuned to each other; loud, reverberant sound; *v* ring loudly.
pear *n* sweet juicy oval fruit; tree bearing this; **prickly pear** type of cactus; its edible fruit.
pearl *n* lustrous concretion found in some molluscs, *esp* pearl-oyster, and used as jewel; imitation pearl; mother-of-pearl; (*fig*) outstandingly fine person or thing; *n* **p.-barley** barley with outer skin rubbed off; **pearlie** costermonger wearing pearly buttons.
peasant *n* countryman, rustic; *n* **peasantry** peasants collectively.
pease *n* peas; **pease-pudding** porridge of split peas.
peat *n* fibrous, partly decomposed vegetable matter found in bogs; this used for fuel.
pebble *n* small rounded stone; **pebble-dash** small pebbles sprayed on outside walls of house; *a* **pebbly.**
pecan *n* N. American nut, allied to walnut.
peccadillo *n* slight offence; petty crime.
peccary *n*. N. American gregarious, pig-like quadruped.
peck *n* $\frac{1}{4}$ bushel; (*fig*) large amount.
peck *v* strike with beak; nibble half heartedly; (*coll*) nag; (*coll*) kiss hurriedly; *n* blow of beak; *n* **pecker-**

pointed instrument; (*coll*) nose, courage; **peckish** *a* (*coll*) hungry.

pectin *n* gelatinous substance found in some fruits.

pectoral *a* of, in connection with breast.

peculation *n* embezzlement; *v* **peculate** embezzle.

peculiar *a* one's own; individual; unusual; *n* **peculiarity** distinguishing characteristic; eccentricity; oddity; *adv* **peculiarly** strangely, specially.

pecuniary *a* relating to, connected with money.

pedagogue *n* schoolmaster; narrow-minded teacher.

pedal *n* lever, operated by foot, for transmitting power or movement; foot-lever to modify tone of piano, organ etc.; *v* use pedals of organ etc.; work, drive by pedals.

pedant *n* one who attaches exaggerated importance to minor details; one who makes tiresome display of learning; *a* **pedantic**; *n* **pedantry** tiresome display of learning.

peddle *v* retail goods from house to house; *n* **pedlar** licensed itinerant vendor of small wares.

pedestal *n* base of large column or statue.

pedestrian *a* going on foot; (*fig*) prosaic, uninspiring; *n* person on foot; walker.

pedicure *n* chiropody, care and treatment of feet.

pedigree *n* genealogy, ancestry; *a* of animals bred from known stock.

pediment *n* triangular structure forming gable-end.

pedometer *n* instrument recording distance walked.

peek *n* glance with half-closed eyes.

peel *n* skin of fruit or vegetable; *v* strip off, remove any form of covering.

peep *v* look hastily, furtively; *n* such a look.

peer *v* look closely, gaze fixedly at.

peer *n* person or thing of equal merit, quality etc.; nobleman; *a* **peerless** unrivalled, without equal; *ns* **peerage** rank of peer; body of peers; (*fem*) **peeress.**

peevish *a* fretful, irritable; *a* **peeved** (*coll*) annoyed; *n* **peevishness.**

peewit *n* bird of plover family, lapwing.

peg *n* wooden or metal pin, bolt; *v* fasten with pegs; fix price etc. by regulations; *a* **off the peg** ready made (clothes).

pejorative *a* disparaging, depreciatory.
pekinese *n* small Chinese dog, allied to pug.
pekoe *n* choice kind of black tea.
pelagic, pelagian *a* of, in, deep sea.
pelf *n* (*sl*) money, material wealth.
pelican *n* large, fish-eating water bird, with food-storing pouch beneath its beak.
pelisse *n* long cloak, *esp* fur-lined.
pellagra *n* chronic eruptive nutritional disease.
pellet *n* small ball; small shot; pill.
pellicle *n* thin skin, membrane; *a* **pellicular.**
pell-mell *adv* headlong, confusedly; *n* disordered haste.
pellucid *a* translucent, transparent; (*fig*) clear, lucid.
pelmet *n* strip of board or cloth concealing curtain rail etc.
pelt *v* throw things at; (of rain etc.) beat down heavily; run quickly.
pelt *n* raw animal skin with fur or wool.
pelvis *n* bony girdle formed by hip-bones and sacrum; *a* **pelvic.**
pemmican *n* cake of pounded meat, dried and smoked.
pen *n* small enclosure for domestic animals, fowl etc; *v* put in pen; imprison; *a* **pent** confined; repressed.
pen *n* instrument for writing; *v* write, put on paper.
penal *a* connected with punishment, *esp* legal; *n* **p. servitude** imprisonment with hard labour; *n* **penalty** legal punishment; loss, suffering as result of folly etc.; (sport) disadvantage imposed for breaking rule; *v* **penalize** punish; handicap.
penance *n* act performed as proof of repentance.
penchant *n* inclination, partiality, liking.
pencil *n* instrument for writing etc., consisting of graphite or crayon enclosed in wood; small brush used by painters; *v* draw, write with pencil.
pendant, pendent *n* hanging ornament; locket; *a* hanging, suspended.
pending *a* not decided, unfinished; *prep* during; awaiting.
pendulous *a* hanging freely; swinging to and fro.

pendulum *n* swinging weight, *esp* one regulating clock mechanism.
penetrate *v* pierce; enter; permeate; (*fig*) see through; reach mind of; *a* **penetrable; penetrating** piercing; shrill; discerning; *n* **penetration** acute, subtlety of mind.
penguin *n* flightless Antarctic sea-bird.
penicillin *n* one of anti-infective class of antibiotics, obtained from mould.
peninsula *n* piece of land nearly surrounded by water; *a* **peninsular.**
penis *n* male organ of copulation.
penitence *n* sorrow for sin; *a* **penitent** having sense of sin; repentant; *n* one who repents of sin; *n* **penitentiary** reformatory; prison.
pennant *n* long narrow flag; pennon.
pennon *n* small swallow-tailed or pointed flag.
penny *n* bronze coin; 100th part of £1; (*pl*) **pennies. pence**; *a* **penniless** poor, destitute.
pennyroyal *n* aromatic herb of mint family.
penology *n* study of methods of punishment and prevention of crime.
pensile *a* hanging down, suspended.
pension *n* periodic payment made to retired public servants, old people etc.; *n* **pensioner.**
pensive *a* immersed in sad thoughts; wistful.
penta- *prefix* five.
pentagon *n* plane figure with five sides; (*cap*) U.S. Department of Defence building.
pentateuch *n* first five books of Old Testament.
Pentecost *n* Whitsunday; Jewish harvest festival.
penthouse *n* small house or apartment on flat roof of building.
pentstemon *n* hardy herbaceous plant.
penultimate *a* last but one.
penumbra *n* partially shaded region round complete shadow *esp* in eclipse; *a* **penumbral.**
penury *n* want, destitution; *a* **penurious** poor; mean.
peony *n* shrub with large red, pink or white flowers.
people *n* race, nation, human beings in general; relatives, family; lower classes; followers, servants; *v* populate.

pep *n* (*coll*) vigour; *v* (*coll*) **pep up** stimulate.
pepper *n* pungent aromatic condiment, made from dried berries of pepper plant; *v* sprinkle with pepper; pelt with missiles; *a* **peppery** tasting of pepper; (*fig*) irritable.
peppercorn *n* dried berry of pepper plant; **p. rent** nominal rent for leasehold premises.
peppermint *n* pungent aromatic herb of mint family.
pepsin *n* digestive ferment in gastric juice; *a* **peptic** pertaining to digestion.
per *prep* by means of; for each.
per- *prefix* through; completely.
peradventure *adv* perhaps.
perambulate *n* walk up and down; walk about.
perambulator *n* light carriage for child, (*coll*) **pram.**
perceive *v* become aware of through senses; apprehend; *a* **perceptible** that can be perceived; *n* **perception** faculty of perceiving; immediate awareness; *a* **perceptive** quick to notice; aware.
percentage *n* rate, allowance, proportion per hundred.
perch *n* edible freshwater fish.
perch *n* rod, branch for birds to roost on; measure of length, 5½ yds.; *v* (of birds) alight, come to rest; sit, balance on high position.
perchance *adv* perhaps, possibly.
percolate *v* filter, ooze, drip slowly (through); *ns* **percolation; percolator** coffee-pot with filter.
percussion *n* impact; violent collision; musical instruments played by being struck.
perdition *n* damnation; ruin.
peregrinate *v* travel, roam about; *n* **peregrination.**
peremptory *a* imperious, dictatorial; precluding opposition, appeal etc.
perennial *a* lasting year after year; never failing; *n* plant lasting more than two years.
perfect *a* faultless; complete; of highest state of excellence; *n* verbal tense expressing complete action; *v* improve; make highly competent; *n* **perfection** state of being perfect.
perfidy *n* treachery, faithlessness; *a* **perfidious.**

perforate *v* pierce, penetrate, make hole(s) in; *n* **perforation** act, result, of perforating; holes made in paper to make tearing easy.
perforce *adv* by necessity.
perform *v* accomplish, carry out; enact (play) in public; play on musical instrument; *ns* **performance; performer** one who performs.
perfume *n* pleasant small; scented liquid applied to body or clothing; *v* impart fragrance to; *ns* **perfumery** place where perfumes are made or sold; **perfumer.**
perfunctory *a* superficial; hasty; indifferent.
pergola *n* stone or wooden arched structure on which plants climb, bordering a path.
perhaps *adv* possibly.
peri- *prefix* round.
peril *n* danger, hazard; *a* **perilous** dangerous, risky.
perimeter *n* distance all round plane figure; outer edge, boundary.
period *n* interval of time; era, epoch; phase of menstrual cycle; full stop (.); *a* characteristic of certain period of time (of furniture, dress etc.); *a* **periodic** recurring at regular intervals; *a* **periodical** periodic; *n* magazine published at regular intervals, i.e. weekly etc.
peripatetic *a* walking about; itinerant.
periphery *n* circumference; outside, outer surface.
periscope *n* apparatus for seeing objects above eye-level, where direct view is obstructed.
perish *v* die; decay; *a* **perishable** liable to speedy decay; *n pl* goods specially liable to decay; *a* (*coll*) **perished** exhausted by cold or hunger.
peritoneum *n* membrane lining inner surface of abdomen; *n* **peritonitis** inflammation of peritoneum.
periwig *n* wig.
periwinkle *n* trailing plant; small edible mollusc.
perjure *v* bear false witness; forswear oneself; *n* **perjury** deliberately false testimony under oath; crime of making false statement under oath.
perk up *v* regain one's health, spirits; *ns* **perkiness** jauntiness; **perk** perquisite; *a* **perky** cheeky, gay.

perm *n* (*coll*) permutation in football pools; (*coll*) permanent wave (hairstyling).
permanent *a* continuing without change, lasting; *ns* **permanence** state of being permanent; **permanency** something that is permanent.
permeate *v* pass through, saturate; *a* **permeable** allowing free passage of liquids.
permit *v* allow; give permission to; tolerate; *n* warrant, licence; document giving formal permission; *n* **permission** leave, consent, sanction; *a* **permissible** allowable; **permissive** allowing.
permute *v* put in different order; interchange; *n* **permutation.**
pernicious *a* highly injurious; deadly; fatal.
peroration *n* concluding part of a speech.
peroxide *n* oxide with larger proportion of oxygen than normal oxide, *specif* **peroxide of hydrogen** used as bleach and antiseptic.
perpendicular *a* exactly upright, vertical; *n* line at right angles to another line or surface.
perpetrate *v* commit, be guilty of; *ns* **perpetration**; **perpetrator.**
perpetual *a* everlasting; unceasing, constantly repeated; *n* **perpetuity** indefinite period.
perpetuate *v* cause to last indefinitely; preserve from oblivion; *n* **perpetuation.**
perplex *v* puzzle; make confused; *n* **perplexity** bewilderment, confusion.
perquisite *n* profit, monetary or in kind, in addition to regular wages or salary.
perry *n* drink of fermented pear-juice.
persecute *v* harass; oppress; treat cruelly, *esp* on account of religious or political reasons; *ns* **persecution**, persecutor.
persevere *v* persist, doggedly, patiently in attaining purpose; *n* **perseverance** prolonged, steadfast effort.
persiflage *n* light flippant banter; frivolous, airy talk.
persimmon *n* Amer. hardwood tree; its fruit, date-plum.
persist *v* continue in spite of opposition; remain;

endure; *a* **persistent** obstinate; tending to recur; *n* **persistence** tenacity of purpose; **persistency** obstinacy.

person *n* human being; individual; (*gram*) one of three changes in pronoun or verb showing person speaking; *a* **personable** good-looking; *n* **personage** person of importance; *a* **personal** individual; private; of bodily state, appearance; of grammatical change; *ns* **personality** distinctive character; **personalty** (*leg*) property excluding land; *v* **personate** assume identity; pretend to be; *n* **personation.**

personify *v* represent as person; typify, embody; *n* **personification.**

personnel *n* all members of staff; man-power.

perspective *n* art of depicting three-dimensional objects on plane surface; **in p.** (*fig*) relative importance.

perspicacious *a* having keen mental judgement or understanding.

perspicuous *a* clearly expressed; lucid.

perspire *v* sweat; exude moisture through pores; *n* **perspiration.**

persuade *v* induce to think, believe; *n* **persuasion** creed; way of thinking; *a* **persuasive.**

pert *a* impudent, saucy.

pertain *v* belong to; have reference to; concern.

pertinacious *a* obstinate, tenacious; *n* **pertinacity** persistance.

pertinent *a* relevant, to the point.

perturb *v* disturb; throw into disorder, confusion; *n* **perturbation** agitation of mind; disorder; deviation of planet from true orbit.

peruse *v* read through, look over; *n* **perusal.**

pervade *v* penetrate thoroughly; *a* **pervasive**; *ns* **pervasiveness, pervasion.**

pervert *v* turn, divert from proper use; *n* apostate; one with abnormal sexual habits; *n* **perversion**; *a* **perverse** intractable; self-willed; *n* **perversity.**

pervious *a* permeable; penetrable.

peseta *n* Spanish coin.

pessary *n* contraceptive device; vaginal suppository.

pessimism *n* tendency to look on dark side of things; doctrine that world is essentially evil; *n* **pessimist**; *a* **pessimistic.**
pest *n* troublesome, vexatious or harmful person, animal or thing; garden parasite, blight; mildew etc.
pester *v* worry, plague *esp* with trivialities.
pestilence *n* fatal infectious, contagious disease; *esp* bubonic plague; *as* **pestilential, pestilent.**
pestle *n* instrument for pounding substances in mortar.
pet *n* tame animal kept as object of affection; favourite, cherished child; *v* treat as pet; fondle.
pet *n* ill-humour; peevishness; *a* **pettish** sulky, fretful.
petal *n* one section of corolla of flowers; *a* **petal(l)ed** having petals.
petard *n* (*obs*) small bomb; **hoist with his own petard** (*fig*) person caught in his own trap.
peter out *v* (*coll*) gradually diminish.
petite *a* (of woman) of small, dainty build.
petition *n* entreaty; urgent request; formal application *esp* one to sovereign, or courtof law; *v* address petition to; *n* **petitioner.**
petrel *n* small black and grey sea-bird.
petrify *v* turn into stone; (*fig*) paralyse with fear etc.
petroleum *n* inflammable mineral oil; *n* **petrol** spirit made from refined petroleum, used as fuel.
petrology *n* study of origin and structure of rocks; *a* **petrous** of, like stone.
petticoat *n* women's underskirt.
pettifogging *a* given to petty, mean tricks, quibbles; *n* **pettifogger** one who uses dishonest tricks in law.
petty *a* trivial; of small worth, scale; *ns* **p. cash** money for small payments; **p. officer** naval N.C.O.
petulance *n* peevishness, irritability; *a* **petulant.**
petunia *n* genus of herbs with funnel-shaped purple, cerise, white, etc. flowers.
pew *n* fixed bench, used as seat in church; (*coll*) seat, chair.
pewter *n* alloy of tin and lead; vessel, plate etc. made of this.
phaeton *n* light open carriage.
phagocyte *n* white blood-corpuscle; leucocyte.

phalanx *n* body of closely-massed soldiers; (*fig*) resolute group of persons.
phalarope *n* small wading-bird of snipe family.
phallus *n* penis; image of it used in some primitive forms of religion; *a* **phallic.**
phantasm *n* illusion; apparition; *n* **phantasmagoria** series of optical illusions; *a* **phantasmagoric.**
phantom *n* spectre; supernatural or imaginary figure; delusion.
Pharaoh *n* title of kings of ancient Egypt.
pharisee *n* self-righteous person; hypocrite.
pharmacy *n* preparation and dispensing of drugs; chemist's shop; *n* **pharmacist** one skilled in preparation of drugs; *a* **pharmaceutic** of pharmacy; *n pl* science of pharmacy; *n* **pharmacopoeia** authoritative list of drugs and directions for their use and preparation.
pharos *n* lighthouse; beacon.
pharynx *n* cavity at back of nose and mouth opening into larynx.
phase *n* stage in development; aspect of planet.
pheasant *n* game-bird with brilliant colouring.
phenobarbitone *n* sedative and soporific drug.
phenol *n* carbolic acid.
phenomenon *n* anything perceived by senses; uncommon, remarkable event; (*pl*) **phenomena**; *a* **phenomenal** relating to phenomena; extraordinary.
phial *n* small glass bottle.
phil- *prefix* loving; studying.
philander *v* make love insincerely; *n* **philanderer.**
philanthropy *n* love of mankind; benevolence; *n* **philanthropist.**
philately *n* stamp-collecting; *n* **philatelist.**
philharmonic *a* devoted to music (chiefly of societies).
philology *n* study of linguistics.
philosophy *n* theory of knowledge; mental balance, calmness in dealing with events, circumstances; *n* **philosopher**; *a* **philosophic(al)**; *v* **philosophize** indulge in philosophical theories; moralize.
philtre *n* love-potion.

phlebitis *n* inflammation of lining of veins.
phlegm *n* viscid substance secreted by mucous membranes, *esp* in nose and throat; apathy, indifference; calmness; *a* **phlegmatic** not easily excited; sluggish.
phlox *n* garden plant with clusters of pink, mauve, red, or white flowers.
phobia *n* morbid, irrational fear.
phoenix *n* fabulous bird; unique thing.
phone *n*, *v* & *a* (*coll*) telephone.
phonetic *a* of, relating to vocal sounds; *n pl* science of vocal sounds.
phoney *a* (*sl*) sham; insincere; bogus; *n* (*sl*) insincere person.
phono- *prefix* of sounds (*esp* vocal).
phonograph *n* obsolete instrument for recording and reproducing sounds; (*USA*) gramophone.
phonology *n* study of sound changes in a language.
phosgene *n* colourless poison gas.
phosphorus *n* non-metallic element emitting glow in the dark; *ns* **phosphate** salt of phosphoric acid **phosphide**; compound of phosphorus; **phosphorescence** property of emitting slight glow in dark, without heat.
photo- *prefix* of light; of photography.
photo *n* & *v abbrev* photograph.
photoelectric *a* pertaining to effect of light on electrons; *n* **p. cell** device that detects, measures light.
photo-finish *n* photo taken to decide winner of race.
photogenic *a* having qualities that make attractive photograph.
photograph *n* picture produced by action of light on sensitized film; *v* take photograph of; *n* **photographer**; *a* **photographic** *n* **photography.**
photogravure *n* process of reproducing, by photography, an engraving.
photometer *n* instrument for measuring intensity of light.
photostat *n* apparatus which makes direct photographic copies of drawings, documents etc.; facsimile so produced; *v* take photostat of.

photo-synthesis *n* process by which plant-cells make carbohydrates from carbon dioxide and water.
phrase *n* group of words forming part of sentence; striking remark; idiomatic expression; *v* express in words; *n* **phraseology** selection of words used.
phrenology *n* theory that one's character, intelligence etc. can be deduced from shape of skull; study of shape of skull; *n* **phrenologist.**
phthisis *n* tuberculosis of the lungs.
phylloxera *n* vine-killing genus of aphides.
physic *n* medicine; *v* give physic to; *n* **physician** one trained in medical profession, who diagnoses and treats disease, but does not operate.
physical *a* pertaining to matter; pertaining to nature and natural features of universe; connected with human or animal body.
physics *n* study of properties of matter and energy; *n* **physicist** one skilled in, or student of physics.
physiognomy *n* art of judging character from face; general appearance and expression of face; (*sl*) face.
physiology *n* study of functions and vital processes of living beings; *n* **physiologist.**
physiotherapy *n* remedial treatment by massage, heat, exercise etc; *n* **physiotherapist.**
physique *n* physical form, structure; constitution.
piano *adv* (*mus*) softly; *a* & *n* soft (passage); *n* pianoforte; *n* **pianist** one who plays the piano; *n* **pianoforte** keyboard musical instrument with strings struck by hammers.
piazza *n* public square *esp* in Italy.
pibroch *n* form of Scottish bagpipe music.
pica *n* largest size of type used in books, six lines to the inch; 12 pt. size type.
picador *n* mounted bullfighter, armed with lance.
picaroon *n* rogue; pirate ship.
piccolo *n* small shrill flute.
pick *n* tool with wooden shaft, long curved head pointed at one end and chisel-edge at other; *n* **pickaxe** tool for breaking ground.
pick *v* break up, pierce with pick; probe; gather, pluck; choose; nibble; open (lock) without key; *n* best part of; choice; *v* **p. holes in** find fault; *v* **p. up**

acquire; take in (passengers); call for (someone); improve; *n* act of picking up; sound-converting device in gramophone; car with rear portion made like truck; *ns* **pickings** trifles left over; dishonest profits.

pickaback *adv* on back of another person.

pickaninny, piccaninny *n* small Negro child.

picket *n* pointed stake; striker posted outside place of employment to dissuade others from working; (*mil*) patrol on special duty; *v* fence with pickets; act as picket in strike.

pickle *n* brine, vinegar etc. used to preserve food; food so preserved; (*coll*) trouble; mischievous child; *v* preserve in pickle; *a* (*sl*) **pickled** drunk.

picnic *n* casual meal eaten out-of-doors; (*coll*) thing easily done; *v* go on, take, picnic.

Pict *n* member of race formerly inhabiting Scotland.

picture *n* painting, drawing, photograph; mental image; vivid verbal description; (*pl*) cinema; *v* make picture of; imagine; describe; *a* **pictorial** expressed in pictures; *n* journal, mainly consisting of pictures; *a* **picturesque** like, forming striking picture; vivid, graphic; *n* **p. gallery** room, building where paintings etc. are exhibited.

pidgin *n* mixture of English & native tongues to be heard in some Oriental & African countries.

pie *n* magpie; kind of woodpecker; *a* **piebald** irregularly marked in black and white blotches.

pie *n* dish of meat, fruit etc., covered with pastry and baked.

piece *n* bit, part; item; literary, artistic or musical composition; (*sl*) girl; *v* put together; join; *a* **piecemeal** piece by piece.

pier *n* column, mass of stone, supporting arch etc.; projecting wharf, or landing-place; jetty.

pierce *v* make hole in; penetrate; stab; *a* **piercing** keen, sharp, penetrating.

pierrot *n* pantomime character; one of troupe of seaside entertainers.

piety *n* devotion to God; dutiful, loyal feelings.

piffle *n* (*sl*) rubbish, nonsense.

pig *n* swine, hog; (*coll*) greedy, selfish person; oblong

casting of metal; *v* (*sl*) **pig it** live in dirty, untidy way; *as* **piggish** greedy, stubborn; **pigheaded** stupidly obstinate; *n* **pigsty** pen for pigs; very dirty room or house.
pigeon *n* wild or domesticated bird of dove species; (*sl*) dupe; *n* **pigeon-hole** small compartment in desk for storing papers etc.
pigment *n* substance for colouring, paint, dye; natural colour in living tissue.
pike *n* large freshwater fish; short spear; *n* **pikestaff** shaft of pike.
pikelet *n* small round kind of tea-cake.
pilaster *n* rectangular column, *usu* projecting from wall.
pilau, pilaff *n* dish of meat, rice and spices.
pilchard *n* large-scaled fish of herring family.
pile *n* pointed beam driven into ground, bed of river etc.; *n* **pile-driver** machine for driving in piles.
pile *n* heap or mass; large building; **atomic p.** nuclear reactor; *v* heap up; make into pile; stack.
pile *n* nap *esp* of velvet; high standing fibres of cloth.
piles *n pl* haemorrhoids in veins of lower rectum.
pilfer *v* steal small quantity; *n* **pilferer.**
pilgrim *n* one who visits sacred place, shrine for religious reasons; *n* **pilgrimage.**
pill *n* small ball of medicinal drugs, swallowed whole; (*sl*) ball *esp* billiard ball; *n* **pill-box** small box for pills; small round concrete fort.
pillage *v* plunder, rob openly, loot; *n.*
pillar *n* slender supporting column; (*fig*) outstanding supporter (of society etc.); *n* **pillar-box** low, hollow pillar for posting letters in.
pillion *n* seat, cushion for another person placed behind rider (of horse, motor-cycle).
pillory *n* framework with holes for neck and wrists, where offenders were secured and exposed to public ridicule; *v* punish by putting in pillory; (*fig*) expose to public disgrace, scorn etc.
pillow *n* cushion for head, *esp* in bed; *v* rest on, as on pillow.
pilot *n* one who directs course of vessels *esp* one licensed to navigate into or out of port; one quali-

fied to fly aircraft; (*fig*) guide, leader; *v* act as pilot; *a* experimental; preliminary; *n* **pilotage** fee paid for pilot's service.

pimento *n* allspice, Jamaica pepper.

pimp *n* & *v* pander.

pimpernel *n* small annual plant with scarlet flowers, closing in dull weather.

pimple *n* small pustule on skin; *a* **pimply**.

pin *n* short, stiff, pointed wire with head, used for fastening; wooden, metal peg or rivet; cask holding 4½ galls; *pl* (*coll*) legs; *v* fasten, attach with pin; hold firmly *esp* under weight; **p. down** (*fig*) bind (person) to; *n* **p.- money** allowance, pocket money; *v* **pin-point** mark precisely.

pinafore *n* loose sleeveless garment.

pince-nez *n* armless eye-glasses kept on nose by spring-clip.

pincers *n pl* gripping tool.

pinch *v* nip, squeeze; (*fig*) cause to become thin etc.; (*sl*) steal; arrest; *n* painful squeeze, *esp* of skin, with finger and thumb; as much as can be taken up between finger and thumb; emergency.

pinchbeck *n* zinc and copper alloy; jewellery of this; *a* sham, not genuine.

pine *n* evergreen coniferous tree; pineapple.

pine *v* languish; waste away through sorrow etc.; long intensely (for).

pineapple *n* large, cone-shaped edible fruit; plant with spiny leaves bearing this fruit.

ping-pong *n* (*coll*) table-tennis.

pinion *n* wing feather of bird; smaller of two geared wheels; *v* cut one pinion of bird to prevent it from flying; confine by binding arms.

pink *n* garden plant allied to carnation; acme, perfection; fox-hunter's red coat; *a* of pale, delicate reddish colour; *v* decorate (edge) with zig-zags; *n* **pinking shears** scissors cutting with zig-zag line.

pink *v* (of motor engine) knock run unevenly; *n* **pinking**.

pinnace *n* warship's boat; small boat used as tender.

pinnacle *n* ornamental tapering turret; slender mountain peak; (*fig*) culminating point.

pint *n* liquid measure; half a quart; 1/8th. gallon.
pioneer *n* one who is first in experiments or exploration; early settler in new country; one of party of troops preceeding army on march and preparing roads etc.; *v* take lead in; be first to introduce.
pious *a* devout; faithful in religious duties.
pip *n* spot on playing card; (*coll*) rank-denoting star on officer's shoulder; *n* seed in fruit.
pipe *n* long tube conveying water, gas etc.; tube with small bowl at end for smoking tobacco; tube-shaped musical wind instruments; measure of wine; shrill voice, or bird call; *v* play on pipe; convey by pipe; ornament (cake or garment) with piping; *ns* **pipe-clay** fine white clay; **piper** player on bagpipes; **piping** act of playing on pipes; series, system of pipes for water etc.; trimming on garments; decoration of icing on cake.
pipette *n* small graduated tube used in chemistry.
pipit *n* small bird akin to wagtail.
pipkin *n* small earthenware pot.
pippin *n* name for several varieties of apples.
piquant *a* stimulating, lively; pleasantly sharp to taste; *n* **piquancy.**
pique *n* resentment; sense of being slighted; *v* wound pride of.
piqué *n* heavy, corded cotton fabric.
piquet *n* card game for two players.
pirate *n* person illegally plundering vessels on high seas; privately-owned radio transmitter operating without licence; one who infringes another's copyright etc.; *n* **piracy**; *a* **piratical.**
pirouette *n* & *v* rapid spin round on toe in dancing.
piscatory *a* of fishing, or fishes.
pistachio *n* edible green nut.
pistil *n* seed-bearing organ of flower.
pistol *n* small fire-arm held in one hand when fired; *v* shoot with pistol.
piston *n* short cylinder within cylindrical vessel, working up and down, used to generate and apply pressure; sliding valve in musical instrument; *n* **p. rod** rod which connects piston to crankshaft.
pit *n* deep hole in ground *esp* one dug to excavate

coal, gravel etc.; hollow depression; indentation on skin; part of theatre behind stalls; *v* enclosure where animals were kept or set to fight; *v* mark with small hollows; **p. against** match in rivalry; set to fight; *n* **pitfall** concealed pit as trap for animals or man; (*fig*) hidden snare, unexpected obstacle.

pit-a-pat *adv* & *n* (sounding like) succession of light taps, beats.

pitch *n* thick, dark, resinous substance obtained from coal-tar, turpentine etc.; *v* coat with this; *a* **pitch-black, pitch-dark** very dark.

pitch *v* set up erect; hurl, cast; (music) set key; (of ship) plunge lengthwise; fall headlong; *n* customary position; act of throwing; (cricket) area between wickets; (football, hockey etc) marked area of play; *n* **pitchfork** fork for lifting hay etc.

pitchblende *n* mineral ore, mainly uranium oxide, chief source of radium.

pitcher *n* large jug, usually earthenware.

pith *n* soft cellular tissue in plant stems and branches; (*fig*) essential part; *a* **pithy** of, full of, pith; (*fig*) terse, forceful.

pittance *n* meagre, inadequate allowance of money.

pituitary *a* secreting mucus; **p. gland** ductless gland at base of brain.

pity *n* grief, sympathy for suffering of another; source of disappointment, regret etc.; *v* feel pity for; *as* **piteous** exciting pity; **pitiable** compassionate; contemptible; **pitiless** ruthless, hard.

pivot *n* shaft, fixed point on which something turns; *v* (*lit* & *fig*) turn on, as on pivot; depend.

pixie, pixy *n* elf or fairy.

placard *n* public notice or advertisement, *esp* one displayed on hoarding; poster; *v* fix poster to.

placate *v* appease, pacify; conciliate; *a* **placatory**.

place *n* specific building, position, condition; station in life; duty, business; space or seat; town, village etc.; *v* put in any situation; identify; arrange.

placenta *n* mass of tissue in womb connecting foetus with mother; after-birth.

placid *a* calm, serene, unruffled; *n* **placidity**.

plagiarize *v* adopt, reproduce as one's own, the work

of another; *ns* **plagiarism** act of copying without permission; **plagiarist.**

plague *n* pestilence, serious epidemic; (*sl*) annoying person or thing; *v* vex, harass, annoy.

plaice *n* edible flat-fish.

plaid *n* cloth with tartan pattern, worn as cloak by Scottish Highlanders.

plain *a* clear, obvious; easily understood; without decoration; simple; not beautiful; *n* tract of flat land; *n* **plain-clothes** civilian, not official or uniform dress; *a* **plain-spoken** frank, candid.

plaint *n* statement of complaint in law court; lament; *n* **plaintiff** one who brings action in court of law; *a* **plaintive** mournful; complaining.

plait *n* flattened fold, pleat; braid of three or more strands (of hair etc.) *v* weave into plait.

plan *n* drawing, diagram of structure projected on flat surface; map of district etc.; mode of action; scheme; *v* make, draw up plan for; think out beforehand.

planchette *n* small heart-shaped board on castors, used in psychical experiments.

plane *n* wide-spreading tree with broad leaves.

plane *n* flat surface; carpenter's tool for smoothing wood; *v* use plane; *a* completely flat, level.

plane *n* (*abbrev*) aeroplane; wing of aircraft; *v* glide in aircraft, without use of engine.

planet *n* large solid body orbiting sun or other star; *a* **planetary**; *n* **planetarium** model of solar system; building containing such model.

plank *n* long, flat, broad piece of sawn timber

plankton *n* microscopic plant and animal organisms drifting in seas, lakes etc.

plant *n* vegetable organism; complete mechanical equipment *esp* for factory; (*sl*) hoax, swindle; *v* put plant, seed etc. into soil that it may grow; fix firmly in position; colonize; (*sl*) conceal (plunder) in another's possession.

plantain *n* low-growing perennial herb; species of banana.

plantation *n* collection of growing trees; large estate producing cotton, tobacco, sugar etc.

plaque *n* memorial plate or wall-tablet.
plash *n* gentle, splashing sound; *v* dabble in water.
plasma *n* colourless liquid forming part of blood; protoplasm.
plaster *n* medical dressing applied to wound etc.; mixture of lime, sand and water for coating walls etc.; immobilizing cast (for broken limb etc.) **p. of Paris** finely ground gypsum which sets hard when mixed with water; *v* apply plaster to; apply lavishly; *n* **plasterer**; *a* **plastered** (*sl*) drunk.
plastic *a* that can be moulded, or shaped; made of synthetic plastic; *n pl* **plastics** man-made substances which be moulded or pressed, and are extremely durable; **p. surgery** restoration of damaged tissue, or alteration of appearance, by transferring skin or bone.
plastron *n* guard to protect breast in fencing.
plate *n* thin sheet of metal or other material; various articles of silver, electro-plate etc. used at table; shallow flat dish for food; contents of such dish; *v* cover with thin coating of gold, silver etc.; *ns* **p. glass** large thick sheets of glass, used for shop windows etc; **plater; plate-mark** hall-mark on gold or silver; mark on engraving left by pressure of plate.
plateau *n* elevated flat stretch of land.
platen *n* plate which presses paper against inked type; typewriter roller.
platform *n* raised floor or stage; part of railway station where passengers enter and leave trains; declared political programme, policy.
platinum *n* heavy, malleable, silvery-white metal element.
platitude *n* commonplace remark; triteness, dullness.
platonic *a* of, derived from Plato; **P. love** love without sex, between man and woman.
platoon *n* military unit.
platter *n* large flat dish or plate.
platypus *n* duck-billed, egg-laying mammal.
plaudit *n* act of applauding *esp* by clapping; (*fig*) praise.
plausible *a* seeming fair or reasonable; specious; *n* **plausibility**.

play *v* (of wind, light etc) move capriciously; flicker, flutter; gamble; amuse oneself; take part in (game, sport etc.); perform on musical instrument; act part of; toy with; *n* stage performance; sport, frolic; freedom of movement; gambling; *n* **player**; *a* **playful** gay, skittish; *ns* **playhouse** theatre; **plaything** toy; **playwright** dramatist; **playing card** one of set used in card games.

plea *n* urgent demand; excuse; statement made by litigant, or answer by defendant; *v* **plead** argue before court of law; put forward as excuse; entreat.

pleach *v* (of tree branches) interlace, intertwine.

pleasant *a* agreeable, affable; pleasing; *ns* **pleasantness**; **pleasantry** jocular remark, jest.

please *v* be agreeable to; delight, gratify; impress favourably; *n* **pleasure** enjoyment; satisfaction; desire, will; *a* **pleasurable** giving pleasure.

pleat *n* variant of PLAIT; three-fold crease in cloth; *v* form into pleats.

plebeian *a* of common people; low born; *n* proletarian.

plebiscite *n* expression of public opinion by direct ballot of electorate.

plectrum *n* small thin piece of metal, horn etc. used for plucking strings of guitar, zither etc.

pledge *n* object given as security for repayment of loan etc.; solemn undertaking; token; toast; *v* give as security; promise; drink toast.

pleistocene *n* denoting Ice Age; *n* geological formation containing greatest number of fossils.

plenary *a* full, absolute, unlimited; representing all sections.

plenipotentiary *a* & *n* (ambassador, envoy) having full powers.

plenitude *n* fullness, completeness.

plenty *n* prosperity; ample supply, abundance; *as* **plenteous** plentiful, abundant; **plentiful** ample; present in large quantities.

plesiosaurus *n* extinct lizard-like marine reptile.

plethora *n* superabundance; pathological condition due to excess of red blood corpuscles; *a* **plethoric**.

pleurisy *n* inflammation of pleura, membraneous covering of lungs.

plexus *n* intricate network of nerves, bloodvessels etc.
pliable *a* easily bent; (*fig*) flexible, yielding; *a* **pliant** flexible; *n* **pliancy.**
pliers *n pl* pincers, able also to cut wire etc.
plight *v* engage, betroth.
plight *n* distressing condition; awkward predicament.
Plimsoll-mark,-line mark on ships showing maximum draught allowed when loaded.
plimsolls *n pl* rubber soled canvas shoes.
plinth *n* square base to column or pedestal.
pliocene *n* & *a* (geological formation) of the Upper Tertiary period.
plod *v* walk laboriously; (*fig*) work conscientously.
plot *n* small piece of land; conspiracy; series of events etc. forming story of play, novel etc.; *v* conspire; divide into plots of land; make chart, map of; *n* **plotter** conspirator; one who plots course etc.
plough *n* implement for turning up soil; *v* furrow; (*fig*) make track through; (*sl*) fail in exam; *ns* **ploughman; ploughshare** blade of plough.
plover *n* wading bird allied to lapwing.
ploy *n* prank; plan.
pluck *v* pull, pick off; strip feathers from; *n* courage; *a* **plucky** brave, courageous.
plug *n* piece of wood, metal etc., used to fill hole; wedge, bung, stopper; electrical connection; flushing mechanism in water-closet; sparking plug; *v* close with plug; (*coll*) work hard at, plod.
plum *n* tree bearing stone fruit with sweet juicy flesh; this fruit; (*fig*) best of its kind; (*coll*) easy, well paid job.
plumage *n* feathers of a bird; *n* **plume** a feather; tuft; *v* dress, preen feathers.
plumb *n* weight, lump of lead on line used to test perpendicular; *a* vertical; (*fig*) absolute; *v* test, sound with plumb-line; (*fig*) see to bottom of, understand fully; *n* **p.-line** one used to test perpendicular.
plumbago *n* graphite, black-lead; genus of herbs.
plummet *n* sounding-weight; plumb-line; *v* plunge headlong.
plump *a* of rounded form, chubby; *n* **plumpness.**

plump *v* fall heavily; (*fig*) **p. for** show strong preference for.
plunder *v* seize by force; loot, despoil; *n* booty, loot.
plunge *v* dive, thrust suddenly into liquid; enter with violence; *n* dive; **take the p.** (*coll*) embark on new, doubtful course of action.
pluperfect *n* & *a* (*gram*) tense expressing action already completed before past point of time.
plural *n* & *a* (form) denoting more than one; *n* **pluralism** holding more than one office at a time.
plus *prep* with addition of; *n* symbol (+) denoting addition, positive electric charge.
plush *n* velvet-like fabric with deeper pile.
plutocracy *n* government by wealth, or wealthy; state ruled thus; *n* **plutocrat** one whose wealth makes him influential.
plutonium *n* artificially produced radioactive element.
pluvial *a* rainy; caused by rain.
ply *n* fold, layer of cloth, wood etc.; strand of wool etc.; *n* **plywood** thin, cross-laminated sheets of wood.
ply *v* wield; work at; supply excessively, in pressing manner; **p. for hire** (of taxi etc.) travel to and fro; run regularly.
pneumatic *a* of air, gases; containing or inflated by air; operated by air pressure.
pneumonia *n* inflammation of lungs.
poach *v* cook eggs, without shell, in boiling water.
poach *v* take game or fish illegally; encroach on another's sphere of action; *n* **poacher** one who trespasses to take game etc.
pock *n* pustule on skin; pit, scar left by this.
pocket *n* small bag or pouch in garment for carrying money etc.; small cavity containing mineral ore; space where density of air causes aircraft to drop suddenly; small hollow; *v* put into one's pocket; take as profit; accept meekly; *a* meant for putting in pocket; miniature; *n* **p.-money** allowance for small expenses.
pod *n* long, narrow seed-vessel of peas, beans etc.; group of whales; *v* form seed-pods; shell (peas etc.).

podgy *a* fat, thick, stumpy, short.
poem *n* literary composition in metrical form, rhymed or unrhymed; *ns* **poet** writer of poems; (*fem*) **poetess**; **poetry** work, art of poet; *a* **poetic**; *n* **poetaster** inferior poet, scribbler of verse.
po-faced *a* looking stupidly solemn.
pogrom *n* organized massacre *esp* of Jews in Russia.
poignant *a* affecting with feeling of unhappiness; highly pathetic.
poilu *n* French private soldier.
point *n* dot; full stop; item; mark indicating position in space or time; essential part of argument; sharp end; (*fig*) that which is pointed, as remark, joke etc.; *v* sharpen; aim; show direction etc. by extending finger; *a* **pointed** tapering; (*fig*) satiric, critical; *n* **pointer** one who, that which points, as hand of clock etc.; indicator; dog trained to point muzzle towards bird, game etc.; *as* **pointless** blunt; purposeless; **point-blank** (of gun) fixed directly at mark; *ns* **point-duty** duty of policeman at fixed point to direct traffic etc.; **point-to-point** steeplechase.
poise *n* self-possession; calmness; equilibrium, balance; *v* put in position; keep in balance; hover.
poison *n* any substance which when absorbed by living organism will kill or seriously harm it; *v* administer poison to; kill by poison; (*fig*) corrupt, pervert; *a* **poisonous**; *n* **poisoner**.
poke *v* push; thrust into; jab, nudge; *n* act of poking; jab; *v* **p. about** (*coll*) investigate; *n* **poker** rod for poking fire; card game; *a* **poky** cramped.
polar at, near, pertaining to North, South or magnetic poles; having positive & negative electricity; *n* **polarity**; *v* **polarize** give polarity to; limit vibrations of light to single plane; (*fig*) give unity of direction to; *ns* **polarization**; **polar bear** large white Arctic bear.
pole *n* either ends of earth's axis; either terminals of electric battery; (*fig*) opposite extreme.
pole *n* long rounded piece of wood; measure ($5\frac{1}{2}$ yds, $30\frac{1}{4}$ sq. yds); *v* propel boat by means of pole.

pole-axe *n* butcher's slaughtering axe.
pole-cat *n* small carnivore related to weasel.
polemic *a* controversial; *n* dispute, discussion.
police *n* civil administration for maintaining public order; force of men, women so organised; *v* (*fig*) control; *n* **p. constable** lowest-ranking police officer.
policy *n* course of action, *esp* of government; political ideals of party; contract of insurance.
poliomyelitis *n* abbrev. **polio**; inflammation of spinal cord; infantile paralysis.
polish *v* make smooth and glossy, *esp* by rubbing; (*fig*) make elegant, refine; *n* smoothness, glossiness; substance used for polishing; (*fig*) refinement.
polite *a* well-bred, courteous; refined; *n* **politeness.**
politic *a* prudent, wise; cunning; opportune; *n pl* art of government; political affairs, principles, aims etc. *a* **political** of government or administration of state; *n* **p. economy** science concerned with production, distribution of wealth; *ns* **politician** one engaged in party politics; **polity** organized system of state government.
polka *n* lively, gay dance; music for this.
poll *n* register of electors; act of voting at election; number of electors voting; *v* vote; receive (certain number of votes).
poll *v* remove top; remove horns of (cattle, etc.) lop off (branches), pollard.
pollard *v* lop top branches of tree, to make thick, bushy new head; *n* tree so cut back or polled.
pollen *n* fertilising powder on flower anther.
pollination *n* fertilization of flower by pollen.
pollute *v* make foul; defile; contaminate; *n* **pollution.**
polo *n* ball game resembling hockey played by two teams of four players on horseback.
polonaise *n* slow Polish dance; music for this.
polony *n* kind of sausage.
poltergeist *n* noisy hobgoblin or ghost.
poltroon *n* coward, mean-spirited person.
poly- *prefix* many; several.
polyandry *n* custom of having two or more husbands at same time.

polyanthus *n* cultivated form of primula.
polychromatic *a* many-coloured.
polygamy *n* custom of having two or more wives at same time.
polyglot *a* written in, speaking, made of up, several languages.
polygon *n* multi-sided plane figure.
polyhedron *n* multi-faceted solid figure.
polymer *n* complex molecule made up of several similar ones; *v* **polymerise**; *n* **polymerisation.**
polyp *n* sea-anenome or similar creature.
polysyllabic *a* having many syllables.
polystyrene *n* thermoplastic material.
polytechnic *a* pertaining to many arts, crafts and technical sciences; *n* polytechnic school or institution
polythene *n* tough, flexible plastic material.
polyurethane *n* & *a* resinous plastic polymer.
pomade *n* scented ointment for hair.
pomegranate *n* reddish, many-seeded fruit of African, Asiatic tree.
pommel, pummel *n* knob of sword-hilt; rounded high front part of saddle; *v* strike repeatedly; pound with fists.
pommy *a* & *n* (*Aust. sl*) English (man).
pomp *n* splendid display, parade; pageantry; *a* **pompous** self important; (of speech) florid, bombastic; *n* **pomposity.**
pompadour *n* style of dressing hair swept back from forehead.
pom-pom *n* automatic, quick-firing gun.
pom-pom *n* small, rounded ornamental tuft of ribbon etc.
poncho *n* rectangular cloak with hole for head.
pond *n* small lake or pool of still water.
ponder *v* consider, think over; muse, cogitate.
ponderous *a* heavy, unwieldy; massive; dull.
poniard *n* dagger.
pontiff *n* high priest; bishop; Pope; *n* **pontificate**; dignity or office of bishop; *v* act as bishop; (*fig*) speak pompously; *a* **pontifical.**
pontoon *n* flat-bottomed boat or metal drum supporting temporary bridge; card game.

pony *n* small horse; (*sl*) £25; small glass.
poodle *n* breed of curly haired dog.
pool *n* small body of still water; deep place in river where water is slow-flowing.
pool *n* stakes played for in various games; form of billiards; common fund; combination for gambling, as on football results etc.; commercial combination; *v* put into common fund; amalgamate.
poop *n* raised deck at stern of ship.
poor *a* having little money; unfortunate; scanty; unproductive; of low quality; *a* **poorly** not in good health.
pop *n* short, explosive sound; (*coll*) fizzy drink; *v* make such sound; put on, into with sudden light movement; *vs* **p. in** visit unexpectedly; **p. off** go away, suddenly; (*coll*) die.
pop *a* (*coll abbrev*) popular; of or producing light dance music, jazz etc.; *n* (*coll*) very popular song, tune etc.; **p. art** art style inspired by & copying contemporary advertisements, posters etc.
Pope *n* head of Roman Catholic church and bishop of Rome; *a* **popish** (derogatory) R.C.
popinjay *n* parrot; dandy, fop.
poplar *n* straight, slender, tall tree.
poplin *n* ribbed fabric of silk or cotton & wool.
poppet *n* pretty child; term of endearment.
poppy *n* any plant of genus *Papaver*.
populace *n* common people, the masses.
popular *a* of, pertaining to populace liked by, suited to the average person; *n* **popularity** quality of being popular or being generally liked; *v* **popularize** make popular; make familiar to average person.
populate *v* furnish with inhabitants; *n* **population** total number of inhabitants of country, town etc.; *a* **populous** thickly inhabited.
porbeagle *n* kind of shark.
porcelain *n* fine, translucent white earthenware; china-ware.
porch *n* projecting, covered entrance to doorway.
porcine *a* of, like pigs.
porcupine *n* rodent covered with sharp quills.
pore *n* minute opening *esp* in skin; small interstice

between particles of any body; *a* **porous** full of pores; permeable by liquids; *n* **porosity**.

pore *v* fix eyes on; become absorbed in.

pork *n* pig's flesh as food; *n* **porker** pig raised for food; *a* **porky** fleshy, fat.

pornography *n* indecent, obscene writing; obscenity generally; *a* **pornographic**.

porpoise *n* blunt-nosed marine mammal, like dolphin.

porridge *n* oatmeal boiled in water or milk; *n* **porringer** small bowl.

port *n* harbour; town having harbour; (*fig*) refuge; left side of ship; gateway; opening in side of ship; *v* turn helm of ship to left or port side. *ns* **porthole** round window in side of ship; **portal** large gateway.

port *n* strong, sweet, red wine of Portugal.

portable *a* capable of being carried, moved; not fixed; *ns* **portability**; **portage** carriage; transport; also cost of this.

portcullis *n* heavy grating in castle gateway.

portend *v* foretell, presage; *n* **portent** omen *esp* of evil; marvel; *a* **portentous** ominous, marvellous; pompous.

porter *n* door-keeper; one employed to carry burden, load; kind of dark-brown bitter beer.

portfolio *n* flat case for carrying papers etc.; State ministerial office; list of securities owned.

portico *n* covered colonnade or walk.

portion *n* part; share; one's fate, destiny; *v* divide into shares.

portly *a* corpulent, stout.

portmanteau *n* large suitcase.

portray *v* depict. describe vividly in words; represent on stage; *ns* **portrait** picture of person; **portraiture** art of portraying; **portrayal** act of portraying.

pose *v* lay down; place in, assume attitude; pretend to be; *n* attitude; assumed attitude of mind; pretence; *n* **poseur** one who assumes affected attitudes.

poser *n* puzzling, baffling question.

position *n* place; posture; condition; situation, employment; *v* place in position; localize.

positive *a* definite; convinced; absolute; real; not negative; *n* positive degree; photographic print in which light and shade is not reversed; (*elect*) positive pole, anode.
positron *n* positive electron.
posse *n* force of men a sheriff can call out to aid him; body of armed men.
possess *v* own; dominate; control; *a* **possessed** controlled by evil spirit; *n* **possession** act of possessing; ownership; thing owned; *n* **possessor**; *a* **possessive** selfishly domineering; indicating possession; *n* possessive case or pronoun.
posset *n* hot milk with ale, wine, spices etc.
possible *a* capable of existing; feasible; that may or may not happen; (*coll*) tolerable; acceptable; *n* **possibility**.
post *n* upright stake or pole supporting structure; *v* fix (notice) on post or notice-board; *n* **poster** large advertising notice in public place.
post *n* official collection, transport and delivery of letters etc.; act, time of delivering or collecting letters; letters etc. sent or to be delivered; station, place of duty; fort; office, situation; *v* place in official box for carriage by post; keep (person) informed; bring (ledger) up to date; station or appoint (person) to specific place or duty; *ns* **postage** charge for carrying letters etc.; **postmaster**, **postmistress** official in charge of post-office; **postman** man who delivers and collects mail; **postmark** mark cancelling stamp on letters, etc. *as* **postfree** prepaid; **postal** of post office.
post- *prefix* after, behind, later. *Where the meaning may be deduced from the simple word, such compounds are not given here.*
post-date *v* assign, affix later date than actual one.
posterior *a* situated behind; *n* buttocks; rear part.
posterity *n* descendants; future generations.
postern *n* back door or gate.
postgraduate *a* of studies carried on after graduation.
posthumous *a* after death.
postmeridian *a* after midday; of or in afternoon.

postmortem *n* autopsy.
postpone *v* defer, delay.
post-prandial *a* after dinner or lunch.
postscript *n* addition to letter, written after and below signature.
postulate *v* stipulate; take for granted.
posture *n* attitude; position, carriage of body; *v* assume affected attitude.
posy *n* flower, nosegay; motto inscribed in ring.
pot *n* rounded vessel of any material, for holding liquids etc.; flower-pot; cooking vessel; tea-pot; (*sl*) marijuana; *v* put into pot; preserve in sealed pot; *ns* **pot-boiler** artistic or other work done simply to earn money; **pothole** deep hole in river bed or rock; hole in road surface; *a* **pot-luck** whatever maybe available as food.
potable *n* drinkable; *n* **potation.**
potash *n* crude potassium carbonate; alkali used in soap and fertilizers; *n* **potassium** malleable metallic alkaline element.
potato *n* cultivated plant with edible tuber.
poteen, potheen *n* illicitly distilled Irish whisky.
potent *a* powerful; convincing; (of men) sexually vigorous; *ns* **potency** power; efficiency; **potential** that which has latent power; possibility; *a* latent, possible; *n* **potentate** king, ruler.
potion *n* draught, dose of medicine or poison.
pot-pourri *n* mixture of dried flower petals, spices etc.; literary, musical medley.
pottery *n* earthenware; art of making it; place where it is made; *n* **potter** one who makes pottery.
potter *v* dawdle; be busy in desultory manner.
potty *a* (*sl*) slightly mad; trivial.
pouch *n* small bag, sack; bag in which marsupials carry young; *a* **pouched** in form of, provided with pouch.
poult *n* young chicken, turkey, pheasant; *ns* **poulterer** dealer in poultry; **poultry** domestic fowls.
poultice *n* soft mass of hot meal, mustard etc., applied to inflamed part of body; *v* apply poultice.
pounce *v* swoop down suddenly; leap on; *n* sudden swoop, movement to take something.

pound *n* measure of weight (16oz. avoirdupois, 12 oz. troy); British monetary unit (100p); *n* **poundage** percentage charged as commission on monetary transaction; charge of so much per pound (weight).
pound *n* enclosure for straying cattle, or dogs.
pound *v* reduce to pieces, powder; beat, thump; run, walk with heavy steps.
pour *v* flow or cause to flow freely; rain heavily; move in continuous stream; (*fig*) emit copiously (words, ideas etc).
pout *v* thrust out lips; look sulky, displeased; *n* act of pouting; *n* **pouter** breed of fancy pigeon.
poverty *n* state of being poor; unproductiveness; *a* **poverty-stricken** very poor.
powder *n* solid reduced to fine, dry particles by grinding; drug in this form; gunpowder; cosmetic powder; *v* sprinkle with powder; reduce to powder; *a* **powdery**.
power *n* capacity, ability to do or act; strength; energy; authority; (*math*) product of number multiplied by itself; (*optics*) magnifying capacity; *as* **powerful, powerless**; *n* **power-house, -station** building in which electric power is generated.
pox *n* name for various eruptive diseases, causing pustules on skin, *esp* syphilis.
practical *a* of, concerning action; efficient; not theoretic; virtual; *a* **practicable** able to be done; capable of being used; *n* **practicability**.
practice *n* habitual action; exercise of profession; clients, patients collectively; rules of procedure in court of law; *v* **practise** do habitually; train, exercise in skill, action etc.; pursue profession; *n* **practitioner** one who carries on profession *esp* medicine.
pragmatic *a* relating to affairs of state; officious; dogmatic; *n* **pragmatism**.
prairie *n* wide, flat, treeless grassland; *ns* **prairie dog** squirrel-like rodent; **prairie-wolf** coyote.
praise *n* commend highly; express approval of, glorify (God); *n* expression of approval; *a* **praise-worthy** commendable, laudable.
praline *n* sweetmeat of cooked nuts and sugar.
pram *n* *abbrev* perambulator.

prance *v* move with bounds; swagger; (of horse) spring from hind legs.
prank *n* mischievous trick, practical joke.
prate *v* chatter; prattle; talk idly.
prattle *v* babble; talk like child; *n* childish talk; *n* **prattler.**
prawn *n* edible, marine crustacean.
pray *v* beg for, ask earnestly; offer prayers *esp* to God; *n* **prayer** act of praying to God; prescribed form of words used; formal petition, request.
pre- *prefix* prior to, in front; before. *Such compounds are not given here where the meaning may be deduced from the simple word.*
preach *v* deliver sermon; advocate strongly; exhort morally; *n* **preacher.**
preamble *n* preface; opening part of speech etc.
prebend *n* stipend of member of chapter of cathedral; benefice or living in gift of chapter; *n* **prebendary** holder of prebend; honorary canon.
precarious *a* uncertain, insecure; risky, dangerous.
precaution *n* careful foresight; measure taken beforehand to guard against danger; *a* **-ary.**
precede come, be before in time, order, rank etc.; *n* **precedence**; priority derived from birth, official status etc.; *n* **precedent** something that has happened before, serving as model for future conduct etc; (*leg*) previous judicial decision, *esp* as guide for present parallel case.
precentor *n* director of singing in cathedral.
precept *n* rule of action or conduct; maxim; *n* **preceptor** teacher.
precinct *n* enclosure within outer walls of building *esp* of cathedral etc.; *pl* environs, neighbourhood.
precious *a* of great value; beloved; affected, over-refined.
precipice *n* sheer, perpendicular cliff-face; (*fig*) crisis; *a* **precipitous** sheer, steep.
precipitate *v* throw, hurl down; cause (vapour) to fall as rain, snow etc.; cause to be deposited as solid substance, from solution; *a* rash, impetuous; *n* **precipitation** undue haste; that which is precipitated; act, process of precipitating.

précis *n* short summary of document; abstract.
precise *a* exactly defined; punctilious; definite; formal, *ns* **precisian** formalist; pedant; **precision** accuracy, exactness.
preclude *v* exclude, prevent, make impracticable.
precocious *a* prematurely developed; *ns* **precocity precociousness.**
precursor *n* forerunner, harbinger.
predatory *a* living by plunder, robbery; (of animals) living by preying on others; *n* **predator.**
predecessor *n* one who precedes another in office, rank etc.; ancestor.
predestine *v* settle beforehand; foreordain.
predicament *n* unfortunate or puzzling situation.
predicate *v* declare; affirm, assert; *n* that which is affirmed, denied of something; (*gram*) that which is stated about subject of sentence; *a* **predicative.**
predict *v* foretell, prophesy; *n* **prediction.**
predilection *n* preference; preconceived liking.
predominate *v* be in majority; be chief element or factor in; *n* **predominance.**
pre-eminent *a* superior to, excelling all others; *n* **pre-eminence.**
pre-empt *v* acquire, appropriate by anticipation; *n* **pre-emption;** *a* **pre-emptive.**
preen *v* (of bird) dress feathers with beak; (*fig*) show self-complacency.
prefabricate *v* construct sections (of houses etc.) for quick assembly; *n* **prefab** (*coll*) house so made.
preface *n* initial, introductory part of book, speech etc.; *v* begin, introduce.
prefect *n* ancient Roman official; senior boy in school, with authority over others.
prefer *v* like better; promote; *a* **preferable** more to be desired; *n* **preference** favour; prior claim; *a* **preferential** giving, receiving preference; *n* **preferment** advancement, promotion.
prefix *n* word placed before another; (*gram*) particle forming first part of compound word; *v* put as introduction.
pregnant *a* with child, with young; (*fig*) full of meaning, ideas; *n* **pregnancy.**

prehensile *a* (of animals) capable of grasping and holding; *n* **prehensility.**
prehistoric *a* pertaining to periods before recorded history; *n* **prehistory** prehistoric archaeology.
prejudge *v* judge or decide upon before hearing or enquiry.
prejudice *n* preconceived unreasonable opinion, bias; (*leg*) injury, damage, loss; **without p.** without detraction from any claims or rights; *v* bias, influence person; *a* **prejudicial** detrimental, causing harm, injury.
prelate *n* church dignitary; *esp* archbishop, bishop.
preliminary *a* introductory, preceding; *n pl* **prelims** (*print*) pages preceding actual text.
prelude *n* introductory act, performance, event; *v* serve, act as prelude to; usher in.
premature *a* happening before normal time; earlier than expected.
premier *a* first in rank, degree etc.; principal; *n* Prime Minister; *n* **premiership.**
premise *n* assumption, proposition on which inference is based; (*leg*) introductory part of document, *esp* lease; (*pl*) building; house etc. with grounds *v* **premise** assume.
premium *n* reward, bonus; fee paid by pupil for admission to profession; sum paid for insurance; excess of market price over par; **at a p.** (*fig*) highly valued; difficult to buy.
premonition *n* presentiment, foreboding.
preoccupy *v* occupy and engross thoughts to exclusion of other things; *n* **preoccupation** absent-mindedness.
prepare *v* make ready for use; construct; teach, train; accustom; lead up to; *n* **preparation** act of preparing; school work, homework done before lesson; period when this is done; *abbrev* **prep**; *a* **preparatory** serving to prepare; **p. school** school where boys, girls are prepared for public or higher school.
prepay *v* pay in advance; *pt* & *pp* **prepaid.**
preponderate *v* exceed in number, importance; *n* **preponderance.**

preposition *n* part of speech, word placed before noun or pronoun, indicating its relation to another word in sentence; *a* **prepositional.**
prepossess *v* influence *esp* favourably; *a* **prepossessing** attractive; *n* **prepossession.**
preposterous *a* unreasonable absurd.
prerogative *n* exclusive, peculiar right or privilege.
presage *n* omen. portent; *v* foretell, give warning of.
presbyter *n* P. church elder, minister; *n* **presbytery** P. church court; R.C. priest's house; E. end of chancel; *a* & *n* **Presbyterian** (members) of Church governed by one order of ministers, called presbyters
prescience *n* foresight, foreknowledge; *a* **prescient.**
prescribe *v* ordain, dictate; (*med*) advise treatment, or use of medicine; *n* **prescription** prescribing; written directions given by physician; medicine prescribed; (*leg*) uninterrupted possession over long period.
preselector *n* mechanism enabling gear position to be selected before changing into it.
present *a* existing now, not absent; *n* present time, tense; *adv* **presently** soon; *n* **presence** being present; mien; nearness, (of danger etc.).
present *v* introduce (person) formally; show; give, bestow; *n* gift; *a* **presentable** suitable for presentation; well-bred; *n* **presentation** bestowal; formal gift; introduction *esp* at court.
presentiment *n* apprehension, foreboding.
preserve *v* protect, save from injury, harm etc.; prevent (food) from decaying; *n* that which is preserved, as jam, bottled fruit etc., game coverts preserved for shooting; river etc. preserved for fishing; *n* **preservation**; *n* & *a* **preservative** (substance) which keeps (food etc.) from going bad.
preside *v* take control at formal meeting; superintend; *ns* **president,** head of republic, society, college, public corporation etc.; **presidency** office, tenure of, president; *a* **presidential.**
press *v* apply weight, force on, squeeze; exert pressure; urge strongly; push against; *n* throng, crowd; machine for pressing *esp* printing machine;

newspapers etc. collectively; *a* **pressing** urgent; *n* **press-agent** one who manages publicity etc. for another.

pressure *n* act of pressing; (*fig*) compulsion, constraint; force exerted on suroundings by solid, liquid, gas; thrust of one body against another; *n* **pressure-cooker** saucepan in which food is cooked by steam pressure.

pressurize *v* maintain normal atmospheric pressure at high altitudes (in aircraft); force to do something; *n* **pressurization.**

prestidigitator *n* conjurer, juggler.

prestige *n* good repute; power to influence; *a* designed to impress; *a* **prestigious** highly honoured.

presto *adv* (*mus*) very rapidly.

presume *v* take for granted, believe as probable; take liberties; *a* **presumable**; probable; *n* **presumption** act of presuming; probability; effrontery; *a* **presumptive** giving reasonable grounds for belief; **heir p.** one who is heir at present; *a* **presumptuous** over-confident; arrogant.

pretend *v* lay false claim to; feign; imagine oneself as; *ns* **pretender** claimant to throne; **pretence** pretext, fraud; *a* **pretentious** assuming great merit or importance; conceited; snobbish.

preter- *prefix* beyond, more than.

preterite *n* & *a* (tense) expressing past action.

preternatural *a* beyond what is natural; supernatural.

pretext *n* reason, motive put forward to conceal real one; excuse.

pretty *a* superficially attractive, pleasing, charming; considerable, large; **p. penny** (*coll*) large sum of money; *adv* moderately; considerably; *n* **prettiness** charming, trivial personal beauty.

prevail *v* triumph; be prevalent; be in use; **p. on** persuade; *n* **prevalence** common occurrence; frequency; *a* **prevalent** widely practised; rife.

prevaricate *v* make evasive answer; quibble; *ns* **prevarication, prevaricator.**

prevent *v* guard against; hinder, thwart; stop; *n* **prevention**; *n* & *a* **preventative**; *a* **preventable.**

preview *n* advance, private showing of pictures. film etc.
previous *a* prior, preceding; (*coll*) too hasty; *adv* **previously** before.
prey *n* animal hunted by another, as food; victim; *v* **p. on, upon** kill and eat; oppress; plunder; *n* **bird of p.** one that kills and eats other birds or animals.
priapism *n* lewdness, lustfulness.
price *n* that which is paid or asked for anything; cost; value; betting odds; *v* fix price; value; *a* **priceless** invaluable.
prick *n* sharp point; small wound or puncture made by prick; slight sharp pain; goad; spur; *v* pierce slightly with sharp point; (*fig*) cause mental pain; (of animals) raise ears alertly; **p. out** transplant seedlings; *n* **prickle** small thorn; *v* tingle as if pricked; *a* **prickly; p. heat** inflammation of sweat glands causing irritation; **p. pear** edible fruit of cactus.
pride *n* excessive opinion of one's merits etc.; justifiable self-respect; satisfaction at achievement; anything causing this; group of lions; *v reflex* be proud of; take credit for.
priest *n* official minister of religion; clergyman; (*fem*) **-ess**; *n* **priesthood**; *a* **priestly**.
prig *n* conceited, self-satisfied person; *a* **priggish**.
prim *a* neat, precise; stiffly formal; easily shocked.
primacy *n* position of being first; pre-eminence; *a* **primal** first, original; *a* **prima** first; **p. donna** leading female operatic singer.
primate *n* archbishop; highest order of mammals, including man, monkeys etc.
prime *a* first in time, rank, quality; initial; principal; *n* first, best period; **P. Minister** chief minister of Government; *v* **prime** put explosive charge into; fill up (with food, drink, information); lay on preparatory coat of paint; *a* **primary** earliest; chief original; elementary; *adv* **primarily** originally; firstly; *n* **priming** first coat of paint etc; explosive charge.
prim(a)eval *a* of first ages of world; prehistoric.

primitive *a* not elaborate; underdeveloped; old-fashioned; simple.
primogeniture *n* (*leg*) system by which title & real estate pass to eldest son on death of father.
primordial *a* of earliest origin; primeval.
primrose *n* wild plant with pale yellow flowers.
primula *n* genus of plants including primrose and polyanthus.
prince *n* ruler; son of king or queen; (*fem*) **princess**; *a* **princely** magnificent, lavish; *n* **princeling** petty ruler.
principal *a* most important; *n* head of college, or school; capital on which interest is paid; one who employs another to act for him; *n* **principality** territory ruled by prince.
principle *n* basic moral truth or conviction; fundamental belief; constituent; uprightness.
print *n* stamp, impression; printed lettering; photographic positive; printed fabric; *v* impress; reproduce words or pictures on paper etc. from inked type, blocks, plates; obtain positive photograph from; stamp with coloured design; *ns* **printer** one engaged in printing; **printing** process, art, style of printing.
prior *a* earlier; *n* head of religious order or house; (*fem*) **-ess**; *n* **priory** monastery, nunnery.
priority *n* superiority, precedence.
prise, prize *v* raise, as by means of lever.
prism *n* solid figure whose bases are equal, parallel planes and whose sides are parallelograms; transparent triangular prism for refracting light; *a* **prismatic** of, like prism.
prison *n* place of captivity, gaol; *n* **prisoner** captive; person under arrest and in custody.
pristine *a* original, primitive; unspoiled.
private *a* not public; secret, confidental, unofficial, secluded; not holding any rank; *n* **privacy** seclusion; freedom from observation, interruption.
privateer *n* privately-owned, armed vessel, having government authorization to attack enemy shipping.
privation *n* want of necessities and comforts of life; hardship.

privet *n* evergreen shrub, used for garden hedges.
privilege *n* individual right, advantage; immunity, exemption enjoyed by some; prerogative; *v* grant privilege to; *a* **privileged** enjoying privilege; completely confidential.
privy *a* private; secretly knowing; *n* water-closet; **p. council** body of advisers appointed by sovereign; **p. purse** allowance for sovereign's personal use.
prize *n* reward given for merit, success in competition; thing won in lottery, contest etc.; that which is captured in war, *esp* vessel; *v* value, esteem highly; *ns* **p. fight** boxing match for money prize; **p. money** share of proceeds of sale of war prizes; money given as prize in competition etc.
pro- *prefix* before, in front of; instead of; for.
proa *n* Malayan sailing canoe.
probable *n* likely to happen, to be true; *n* **probability** likelihood; likely event.
probate *n* proving of will; certified approved copy of will.
probation *n* trial, test of person to prove suitability for duty, position etc.; (*leg*) system of releasing young offenders, under supervision; *n* **probationer** one serving on probation *esp* nurse during first part of training.
probe *n* (*med*) instrument for esploring wound etc.; (*coll*) investigation; exploratory spacecraft; *v* examine thoroughly.
probity *n* honesty, integrity.
problem *n* question set for discussion, or solution; difficult situation; *a* **problematic(al)** doubtful questionable.
proboscis *n* elongated flexible snout; elephant's trunk; elongated mouth-parts of some insects.
proceed *v* advance; go on; make progress; come forth, arise from; take legal action; *n pl* product, realized profit; *ns* **procedure** mode of action; manner of conducting business, *esp* parliamentary; technique; **proceeding** action; (*pl*) record of transactions of society etc.
process *n* series of continuous actions and changes; method of operation; system of manufacture; whole

course of legal proceedings; *n* **procession** body of persons marching, riding in formal order; act of marching forward; progress; *a* **processional.**

proclaim *v* announce, declare officially; make known publicly; *n* **proclamation.**

proclivity *n* inclination; tendency, propensity.

procrastinate *v* delay, defer, postpone; *ns* **procrastination**; **procastinator.**

procreate *v* beget, generate; *n* **procreation.**

proctor *n* university official with disciplinary powers.

procure *v* gain, obtain; act as pimp, pander; *a* **procurable** obtainable; *ns* **procurator** one who manages affairs for another; **procuration**; **procurement** act of procuring; **procurer** pander, pimp.

prod *n* goad; poke, thrust; *v* poke with pointed instrument; (*fig*) stir up, incite.

prodigal *a* lavish, open-handed; wasteful, improvident; *n* **prodigality** profusion; extravagance.

prodigy *n* extraordinarily gifted person; wonder, marvel; monstrosity; *a* **prodigious** huge, vast; amazing.

produce *v* bring forward; bring forth; give rise to; make; continue; yield; *ns* **produce** that which is yielded or made, **producer**; **product** result of natural growth; anything manufactured; **production** act of producing, manufacturing; that which is produced; *a* **productive** creative; fertile; efficient; *n* **productivity** rate at which something is produced *esp* in industry.

profane *a* not sacred, irreverent; pagan; *v* desecrate; *n* **profanity** blasphemous language or behaviour.

profess *v* affirm; make public declaration of; practise, have as one's business; teach as professor; *n* **profession** confession (of faith); occupation requiring training and intellectual ability; body of persons following such occupation; *a* **professional** practising specified profession; engaged in sport or game for money; *n* paid player; *ns* **professionalism** position (*esp* in sport) of professional as distinguished from amateur; **professor** university teacher of highest rank.

proffer *v* offer.

proficient *a* skilled, expert; *n* **proficiency.**
profile *n* outline of side view of object, *esp* of face; short biographical sketch.
profit *n* benefit; financial gain; *v* benefit; *a* **profitable** advantageous; lucrative; *n* **profiteer** one who makes exorbitant profits at expense of consumer.
profligate *a* dissolute, depraved; recklessly extravagant; *n* **profligacy.**
profound *a* deep; very learned; *n* **profundity.**
profuse *a* abundant; prodigal. *n* **profusion.**
progeny *n* children, descendants; *n* **progenitor.**
prognathous *a* having projecting jaws.
prognosis *n* act of prognosticating; (*med*) opinion formed as to probable future course and outcome of disease; *a* **prognostic**; *v* **prognosticate** foretell; predict, warn; *n* **prognostication.**
programme *n* printed details of performers, items etc. in play, concert, broadcast etc.; summary of things to be done; data for computer; *v* prepare programme of work for.
progress *n* advance; forward, onward movement; improvement; *v* go forward; develop favourably; *n* **progression** act of moving forward; (*math*) series of numbers each of which increase, decrease by regular law; (*mus*) succession of notes, chords; *a* **progressive** progressing; advocating reform.
prohibit *v* forbid; prevent; *n* **prohibition** act of forbidding; forbidding by law of supplying and consuming alcoholic drinks; *a* **prohibitive** tending to check, forbid, or exclude.
project *n* plan, scheme; *v* throw, propel; scheme, plan; jut out; cast (photographic image etc.) on screen; *n* **projectile** heavy missile, shell, bullet; *ns* **projection**; **projector** one who plans projects; apparatus to project picture on screen.
prolapse *n* falling down or out of place.
proletariate *n* lowest class of society; working class, *esp* manual workers; *a* **-arian.**
proliferate *v* reproduce by budding, or rapid cell-division; *n* **proliferation.**
prolific *a* productive; fertile, fruitful.
prolix *a* lengthy, tedious, verbose; *n* **prolixity.**

prologue *n* preface to poem, play etc.; introductory act or event.
prolong *v* extend, lengthen in space or time; *n* **prolongation.**
promenade *v* stroll about for pleasure, exercise; *n* such a walk; seaside esplanade (*coll abbrev* **prom**); **prom. concert** concert where some of audience (**promenaders**) walk about.
promenader one who attends p. concert.
prominent *a* standing, jutting out, conspicuous; well-known; *n* **prominence.**
promiscuous *a* indiscriminate *esp* in sexual intercourse; *n* **promiscuity.**
promise *n* undertaking, assurance to do or not to do something; likelihood of success; *v* make promise; give cause for hope; *as* **promising** likely to develop well or achieve success etc; **promissory** containing promise.
promontory *n* headland jutting out into sea.
promote *v* raise, move to higher rank; assist in formation of (company, scheme etc.); publicize; *n* **promotion; promoter.**
prompt *a* done quickly; at right time, not late; immediate; *v* help (actor etc.) by suggesting forgotten word; *ns* **prompter; promptitude.**
promulgate *v* proclaim; put into effect; announce publicly; *n* **promulgation.**
prone *a* lying with face downwards; inclined (to); liable; *n* **proneness** inclination, tendency.
prong *n* sharp pointed piece of metal; tine of fork; point of stag's antler.
pronoun *n* word used in place of noun; *a* **pronominal** of, like pronoun.
pronounce *v* declare, utter solemnly and publicly; articulate, utter word, sound; give as expert opinion; *a* **pronounced** emphasized; strongly marked; *n* **pronouncement** formal declaration; **pronunciation** way in which word, syllable etc. is pronounced; articulation.
proof *n* act of proving truth of fact etc.; demonstration; test, trial of quality, truth etc.; standard of alcoholic strength; trial impression from type,

plates etc.; *a* having standard quality of strength, hardness; **p. against** strong enough to be impenetrable, unmoved by; *v* make proof against.

prop *n* support, stay, strut; *v* act as prop; furnish with support.

propaganda *n* act, method of spreading opinions, beliefs to promote a cause; views, doctrines thus spread; *n* **propagandist** zealous supporter of cause, etc.

propagate *v* reproduce, have offspring; disseminate; cause to multiply by reproduction; *ns* **propagation** act, process of propagating; **propagator** one who propagates; garden frame used for propagating plants.

propel *v* drive forward; impel; *ns* **propeller** (*abbrev* **prop**) screw of ship or aircraft; **propulsion**; act of driving forward; *a* **propulsive** having power of propelling; *a* & *n* **propellent** propelling (agent).

propensity *n* inclination, addiction, tendency.

proper *a* suitable; peculiar; particular; respectable; prim; one's own; **p. noun** one denoting particular person or place.

property *n* characteristic, inherent quality, power etc.; that which is owned; possessions etc., estate, land, goods, money; object, costume used in play etc. (*usu pl abbrev* **props**).

prophet *n* interpreter, teacher of Divine Will; religious leader, teacher; one who foretells the future; *n* **prophecy** prediction, foretelling of future; *v* **prophesy** make predictions; foretell; *a* **prophetic**.

prophylactic *a* serving to prevent, preserve from disease; *n* **prophylaxis**.

propinquity *n* nearness, proximity in time, space, relationship.

propitiate *v* appease, conciliate; *n* **propitiation**; *a* **propitious** favourable; fortunate.

proportion *n* part or share; comparative relation in size, number, amount, degree; harmonious relation of parts in whole; symmetry; (*pl*) dimensions; **out of p.** (*fig*) exaggerated; *as* **proportional** being in proportion; corresponding in size, number etc.; **proportionate** in due proportion.

propose *v* bring forward, submit for consideration; offer marriage; intend; *ns* **proposal** plan; offer *esp* of marriage; **proposer**; **proposition** proposal; (math) theorem, problem; project.

propound *v* put forward, offer for consideration.

proprietor *n* owner; (*fem*) **proprietress**; **proprietary** belonging to owner; made, patented, sold under exclusive ownership.

propriety *n* correct behaviour; appropriateness; decency.

prorogue *v* terminate (session of Parliament) without dissolution.

prosaic *a* matter-of-fact; unromantic; dull.

proscenium *n* part of stage between curtain and orchestra.

proscribe *v* outlaw; denounce and forbid; *n* **proscription.**

prose *n* language, spoken or written without rhyme or metre; *a* **prosy** dull, uninspired; *n* **prosiness.**

prosecute *v* follow, pursue further; start legal proceedings against; *ns* **prosecution**; **prosecutor** one who prosecutes, *esp* in criminal court.

proselyte *n* convert; *v* **proselytize.**

prosody *n* art of versification; *n* **prosodist.**

prospect *n* wide outlook; something expected or thought likely; possible customer etc.; *pl* future expectations *esp* financial; *v* inspect, search for, *esp* for gold etc.; *a* **prospective** anticipated; future; *ns* **prospector** one who explores for minerals etc.; **prospectus** descriptive pamphlet issued by company, school etc.

prosper *v* excel, succeed, flourish; be fortunate; *n* **prosperity** success; good fortune; *a* **prosperous** doing well, rich; thriving.

prostate *n* gland accessory to male generative organs

prostitute *n* woman who sells her body for sexual intercourse; *v* (*fig*) put to base, dishonourable use; *n* **prostitution.**

prostrate *a* lying flat, prone; (*fig*) crushed, spent, utterly dejected; *v* cast to ground; (*fig*) abase oneself, cringe; *n* **prostration** extreme bodily exhaustion; extreme depression and distress.

protagonist *n* principal character in play etc.; lead.
protect *v* keep safe; guard; *n* **protection** act of protecting; safeguard; *a* **protective**; serving to protect; *ns* **protector** one who protects; one appointed as regent; **protectorate** rule by protector; State so ruled.
protégé *n* person under patronage of another.
protein *n* complex organic compound of numerous amino-acids.
protest *v* affirm; raise objection; *n* declaration of objection, disapproval; *n* **protestation** solemn affirmation.
Protestant *a* belonging to any Christian Church outside the Roman Catholic communion; *n* member of such church; *n* **Protestantism.**
proto-, prot- *prefix* first.
protocol *n* diplomatic etiquette; first draft agreement for treaty.
proton *n* positively charged particle in nucleus of atom.
protoplasm *n* basic material of which cells are composed.
prototype *n* original, model, pattern.
protract *v* lengthen; prolong; draw to scale; *a* **protracted** long drawn out; tedious; *ns* **protraction**; **protractor** instrument for measuring angles.
protrude *v* project, stick out; *n* **protrusion**: *a* **protrusive** thrusting forward.
protuberant *a* bulging out; *n* **protuberance** projection, swelling
proud *a* feeling or displaying pride; arrogant; splendid; gratified.
prove *v* establish truth of; turn out to be; test quality, accuracy; *a* **proven** proved.
provenance *n* place of origin, source.
provender *n* fodder for cattle; (*coll*) food.
proverb *n* short, pithy, traditional saying; maxim; *a* **proverbial** generally known.
provide *v* procure and supply; equip; furnish with means of support.
providence *n* fate; benevolent provision of God; foresight; thrift.

provident *a* looking ahead; far-seeing; thrifty; *a* **providential** lucky, merciful, beneficial.
province *a* division of country; region; sphere of knowledge, thought, action etc.; *pl* any part of country outside capital; *a* **provincial** countrified; local, limited; *n* inhabitant of provinces; countryman.
provision *n* act of providing, supplying; something provided, *esp* (*pl*) food; (*leg*) stipulation, condition; *v* supply with food; *a* **provisional** temporary, conditional.
proviso *n* condition.
provoke *v* give rise to; stir up; make angry; incite; *n* **provocation**; *a* **provocative.**
provost *n* head of certain colleges: (*Scot*) chief magistrate of burgh, corresponding to mayor; *n* **p.-marshal** head of military police.
prow *n* forepart of ship, bow.
prowess *n* bravery, valour; skill, success.
prowl *v* go about stealthily, furtively, *esp* in search of prey, plunder; *n* **prowler.**
proxy *n* authority given to person to act as agent; person acting as agent or substitute.
prude *n* woman of affected modesty and propriety in dress, speech etc.; *a* **prudish.**
prudence *n* careful behaviour; sagacity.
prudent *a* careful; discreet; circumspect; provident; *a* **prudential** showing prudence.
prune *n* dried plum.
prune *v* cut out, shorten unwanted branches (of trees, shrubs etc.)(*fig*) shorten by omission.
prurient *a* having morbidly indecent, obscene ideas etc.; *n* **prurience.**
prussic acid *n* solution of hydrocyanic acid.
pry *v* search into; peer, spy, *esp* with unnecessary curiosity; break open, as with lever.
psalm *n* sacred song or hymn; *ns* **psalmist** composer of psalms; **psalmody** art of singing sacred songs; **psalter** Book of Psalms, arranged for use in Prayer Book.
pseudo- *prefix* false, pretended, seeming. *Such compounds are not given where the meaning may be deduced from the simple word.*

pseudonym *n* fictitious name; nom-de-plume.
psittacine *a* pertaining to parrot tribe; *n* **psittacosis** contagious influenza of parrots.
psyche *n* human soul or spirit; mentality; mind; *a* **psychedelic** relating to a relaxed, ultra-perceptive mental state, or to drugs causing this; *ns* **psychiatry** treatment, cure of mental illness; **psychiatrist** one who practises this; *as* **psychic, -al** of soul or mind *esp* in reference to spiritualistic phenomena.
psycho- *prefix* mental; *ns* **p.-analysis** method of treating certain mental disorders; investigation of subconscious mind; **psycho-analyst.**
psychology *n* branch of science studying mental processes & motives; *a* **psychological;** *n* **psychologist** one who studies, practises psychology.
psychopathic *a* suffering from mental disorder.
psychosis *n* form of insanity due to grave mental disorder.
psychosomatic *a* caused by mental disorder.
psychotherapy *n* treatment of disease by mental influence.
ptarmigan *n* bird of grouse family.
pterodactyl *n* extinct flying reptile.
ptomaine *n* poisonous alkaloid substance formed by putrefaction of animal or vegetable matter.
puberty *n* state of sexual maturity.
public *a* pertaining to people as community; not concealed, or secret; *n* general body of people; community as whole; *ns* **public-house** (*abbrev* **pub**) inn, tavern licensed for sale of alcoholic liquor; **publican** innkeeper; **public school** school under public management; (in U.K.) fee-paying boarding school; **p. relations** relationship between organisation & its customers, etc.; maintenance of (good) p.r.; **p. spirit** interest in welfare of community.
publicity *n* state of being generally known; advertisement; notoriety; *v* **publicize** make known to public, *esp* by adertisement.
publish *v* make generally known; prepare and issue for sale (books, journals etc.); *ns* **publisher; publication.**
puce *n* & *a* brownish purple colour.

puck *n* rubber disc used as ice-hockey ball.
puck *n* mischievous sprite or goblin.
pucker *v* wrinkle; fall into creases; *n* crease, fold.
pudding *n* soft, cooked mixture of flour, milk, eggs etc.; any solid sweet dish.
puddle *n* shallow muddy pool; rough cement lining for ponds etc.; *v* apply watertight mixture to pond; stir molten cast iron to make it wrought iron.
pudency *n* modesty, bashfulness.
puerile *a* childish; foolish, silly, weak.
puerperal *a* pertaining to child-birth.
puff *n* short blast of wind, breath etc.; laudatory notice; kind of pastry; *v* blow out, send out in puff; swell with air; smoke; *a* **puffy** swollen; *n* **puff-ball** type of fungus.
puffin *n* sea-bird with large parrot-shaped beak.
pug *n* breed of dog, resembling small bull-dog; foot-print of wild beast; *a* **pug-nosed** snub-nosed.
pugilist *n* boxer; *n* **pugilism**; *a* **pugilistic.**
pugnacious *a* fond of fighting; *n* **pugnacity.**
puisne *a* (*leg*) junior, of lower rank.
puissant *a* powerful, mighty, strong; *n* **puissance.**
puke *v* vomit.
pulchritude *n* beauty.
pull *v* draw, tug; remove by pulling; pluck; propel (by rowing); *n* act of pulling; force exerted by it; quantity (of beer etc.) drawn at one time; (*coll*) influence, advantage; **pull off** (*sl*) bring off successfully; **pull in, out** (of train) arrive, depart; **pull through** recover (from illness, difficulty etc.); *n* **pull-in** roadside cafe.
pullet *n* young hen.
pulley *n* small grooved wheel, carrying cord, used to change direction of power.
pullover *n* knitted jersey without fastening.
pulmonary *a* of lungs.
pulp *n* soft, moist vegetable or animal substance; flesh of fruit or vegetable; *v* reduce to pulp.
pulpit *n* raised enclosed structure from which preacher delivers sermon.
pulse *n* throb of blood in arteries etc.; any regular vibration or beat; *v* **pulsate** throb, vibrate; (*fig*)

throb with excitement, emotion etc.; *n* **pulsation.**
pulse *n* edible seeds of leguminous plants.
pulverize *v* reduce to fine powder, dust or spray; (*fig*) destroy utterly; *n* **pulverization.**
puma *n* large, carnivorous feline mammal, cougar.
pumice *n* light, porous volcanic stone.
pummel see POMMEL
pump *n* device for raising water etc. by suction; or for taking out, and putting in air etc. by piston and handle; *v* raise, compress; take out, put in (air, liquids etc.); (*fig*) extract information from.
pump *n* light patent-leather shoe.
pumpkin *n* edible fruit, resembling vegetable marrow.
pun *n* play upon words; *v* make pun.
punch *n* tool for stamping, perforating; blow with fist; *v* strike with fist; perforate, make holes in.
punch *n* drink of spiced spirits or wine (*usu* hot).
punctilious *a* very exact, particular.
punctual *a* in good time; prompt; *n* **punctuality.**
punctuate *v* divide up written or printed words by stops, commas etc.; *n* **punctuation** commas, semicolons etc. put in writing to help make sense clear.
puncture *v* make hole in; prick; *n* small hole made by sharp point.
pundit *n* learned Brahmin; very learned man.
pungent *a* sharp, piercing; highly-seasoned; (of mode of expression) piquant, pointed.
punish *v* inflict retribution on; handle roughly; *a* **punishable**; *n* **punishment**; *a* **punitive**; inflicting or designed to inflict punishment.
punnet *n* small, flat, chip basket for fruit.
punt *n* flat-bottomed boat with square ends, propelled by long pole thrust against river-bed; *v* convey, travel in punt.
punt *n* kick given to football dropped from hands, before it touches ground; *v* kick thus.
punt *v* (cards) lay stake against bank; bet, *esp* on horse; *n* **punter** one who bets, gambles.
puny *a* weak, feeble, undersized.
pupa *n* stage between larva and imago; chrysalis of insect; *v* **pupate** become pupa.
pupil *n* person being taught; opening of iris in eye.

puppet *n* small jointed figure, moved by strings, wire; (*fig*) person who is unable to act on his own; *ns* **puppet-show**; **puppetry** art of manipulating puppets.
puppy, pup *n* young dog; conceited, impudent young man.
purblind *a* short-sighted.
purchase *v* buy; (*fig*) obtain by effort etc.; move by leverage; *n* that which is bought; lever, pulley etc.; *n* **purchaser.**
purdah *n* curtain or screen shutting off Indian women's quarters.
pure *a* clean; unmixed; not tainted; chaste; simple; *v* **purify** make pure; *ns* **purification** cleansing, purifying; **purism** strict adherence to correct usage etc. in language; **purist**; **purity** state of being pure.
purée *n* soft food passed through sieve.
purge *v* cleanse, purify; (*leg*) clear oneself of accusation; cause evacuation of bowels; expel unwanted members from political party, armed forces etc.; *n* that which cleanses; *n* & *a* **purgative** (medicine) causing evacuation of bowels; *n* **purgatory** (*eccles*) state or place of torment etc. where souls of dead are purified; (*fig*) any such state or place.
Puritan *n* member of extreme Protestant party in 16th. and 17th. centuries; one holding very strict religious and moral views; *a* **puritanical.**
purl *n* knitting stitch producing ridge; ornamental looped edging to lace etc.; *v* knit purl stitch.
purl *v* flow with gentle murmur; babble.
purlieu *n* (*usu pl*) outskirts of any place; slums.
purloin *v* steal; pilfer.
purple *n* red-blue colour; *a* of this colour.
purport *v* mean to be; seem to signify; *n* significance; bearing.
purpose *n* intention; aim, design, object; *v* intend.
purr *v* (of cats etc.) express pleasure by making low vibrating noise; *n* this sound.
purse *n* small bag, pouch for money; funds; sum of money offered as prize etc.; *v* pucker, wrinkle up (lips); *n* **purser** ship's officer in charge of accounts and passenger's requirements.

pursue *v* follow closely; chase; follow to desired end; continue (speaking); *n* **pursuance** performance; *a* **pursuant** according; confirming; *ns* **pursuer**; **pursuit** chasing after; quest; employment, occupation.
pursy *a* stout and short-winded; puckered.
purvey *v* provide, supply *esp* provisions; *n* **purveyor**.
pus *n* yellowish matter produced by suppuration; *a* **purulent** full of, discharging pus; septic; *n* **purulence.**
push *v* cause to move by pressure; propel forward; *n* thrust; self-assertive energy; *n* **pusher** one who pushes; (*sl*) dope-pedlar; *a* **pushful, pushing** self-assertive; too ambitious.
pusillanimous *a* cowardly; *n* **pusillanimity.**
puss, pussy *n* (*coll*) cat; mischievous girl.
pussyfoot *v* (*sl*) walk softly; conceal one's plans; *n* (*sl*) advocate of prohibition.
pustule *n* pimple containing pus; *a* **pustular.**
put *v* place; lay; set; express; throw; arrange; *pt* & *pp* **put.**
putative *a* reputed, supposed; presumed.
putrid *a* decomposed; decayed, rotten; (*sl*) very unpleasant; *v* **putrefy** make, become putrid; *ns* **putrefaction**; process of putrefying; rotten, foul-smelling substance; **putrescence**; *a* **putrescent**, rotting; stinking.
putt *v* strike golf ball gently across green; (athletics) throw weight (shot) from shoulder; *n* distance that ball, weight is putted; *n* **putter** golf-club used for putting.
puttee *n* strip of cloth wound round leg.
putty *n* soft cement made of linseed oil & clay; gem- polishing powder made of tin & lead.
puzzle *v* perplex; baffle; try to solve; *n* difficult problem; verbal mechanical contrivance to test ingenuity.
pygmy, pigmy *n* dwarf; *a* very small, dwarfish.
pyjamas *n pl* sleeping suit of jacket and trousers.
pylon *n* tall structure *usu* of steel girders, carrying electric cables etc.
pyorrhoea *n* disease of gums; discharge of pus.

pyramid *n* figure with square base and four triangular sides sloping to apex; Egyptian tomb of this shape; *a* **pyramidal.**
pyre *n* pile of wood for burning corpse.
pyrethrum *n* genus of composite plants.
pyrogenic, pyrogenetic *a* productive of heat or fever.
pyrometer *n* instrument for measuring high temperatures.
pyrotechnics *n pl* display of fireworks; (*fig*) display of brilliant, ironical oratory.
Pyrrhic *a* **P. victory** one won at enormous and ruinous cost.
python *n* large non-venomous snake that crushes its prey.
pyx *n* vessel in which Host is kept in churches; box at Royal Mint for, holding specimen coins.

quack *n* cry of duck; *v* utter such sound.
quack *n* one who pretends to have skill, knowledge *esp* in medicine; charlatan.
quadrangle *n* four-angled plane figure; square or rectangular court with buildings round it; *n* **quadrant** quarter of circle; instrument for measuring angles; *n* & *a* **quadrate** square; *a* **quadratic** (of equation) involving square of unknown quantity.
quadrilateral *n* & *a* (figure) having four sides and four angles.
quadrille *n* dance for four persons; music for this.
quadroon *n* offspring of white person and mulatto; quarter-blooded person.
quadruped *n* four-footed animal.
quadruple *a* fourfold; *v* multiply by four.
quaff *v* drink deeply, eagerly; drain.
quag, quagmire *n* soft, marshy, quaking ground.
quagga *n* S. African animal related to zebra.
quail *n* small game-bird related to partridge.
quail *v* cower, flinch; lose heart.
quaint *a* attractively strange; odd, eccentric.
quake *v* shake, tremble, rock from side to side; *n* tremor; (*coll*) earthquake.

Quaker *n* member of religious body (Society of Friends).
qualify *v* give quality to; describe; obtain official qualification by study etc.; limit; become competent; *n* **qualification** restriction, modification; act of becoming fit, suitable for; attribution of quality.
quality *n* essential nature or characteristic; degree of value; high social rank; *a* **qualitative** having to do with quality.
qualm *n* feeling of nausea; misgiving, scruple.
quandary *n* difficult perplexing situation; dilemma.
quantity *n* number, amount, extent; specified amount; *a* **quantitative**; *n* **quantum** amount; sufficiency.
quarantine *n* isolation to prevent spreading of infection; *v* put, keep in quarantine.
quarrel *n* angry dispute; squabble; *v* disagree; dispute; become estranged; *a* **quarrelsome.**
quarry *n* one who that which, is hunted or pursued.
quarry *n* open pit from where stone, sand, etc. is excavated; *v* dig, excavate from quarry.
quart *n* quarter of gallon, two pints.
quarter *n* fourth part; part, region, area; clemency; (*pl*) lodgings; *v* divide into quarters; lodge; *ns* **quarterdeck** area of upper deck restricted to officers; **quartermaster** military, naval rank; *a* **quarterly** occurring, due each quarter of year; *n* periodical published quarterly; *ns* **quartet(te)** group of four musicians; musical composition for four performers; **quarto** size of paper or book.
quartz *n* form of crystalline silica.
quash *v* annul, make void; suppress.
quasar *n* extra-galactic source of radiation.
quasi *a*, *adv* & *prefix* as if; in certain sense; almost.
quatrain *n* four-line stanza rhymed a b a b.
quaver *v* tremble, shake, vibrate; speak tremulously; *n* (music) note, time value of half crotchet; *n* **quavering** tremulous sound, *esp* made by voice.
quay *n* pier, jetty, wharf; landing-place.
queasy *a* causing, feeling nausea; easily shocked; *n* **queasiness.**
queen *n* wife of king; female sovereign; court card;

piece in chess; fertile female bee, wasp etc.; female cat; (*sl*) homosexual man; *a* **queenly.**

queer *a* odd, strange; suspicious, doubtful; slightly mad; unwell; (*sl*) spoil; *a* & *n* (*sl*) homosexual; **q. the pitch** spoil chances of success.

quell *v* suppress; stifle; allay, pacify.

quench *v* extinguish, put out; allay, slake (thirst).

quern *n* hand-mill for grinding corn, pepper etc.

querulous *a* complaining; whining.

query *n* question; interrogation mark (?); *v* question; express doubt about.

quest *n* search; *v* search for.

question *n* act of asking; sentence requiring reply; interrogation; point of discussion; *v* ask question of; dispute; *a* **questionable** dubious; dishonest; *n* **questionnaire** list of formal questions, devised to obtain information etc.

queue *n* line of waiting people or vehicles; man's pigtail; *v* line up, wait in queue.

quibble *n* play on words; *v* evade point; make puns.

quick *a* rapid, keen, brisk; hasty; living; *n* sensitive flesh below finger- or toe-nail; *v* **quicken** cause to be quick; give life to; become living; become faster; *ns* **quicklime** unslaked lime; **quicksand** very loose, wet, soft sand; **quicksilver** mercury; *a* **quick-witted** reacting quickly.

quid *n* (*sl*) £1-00 sterling; chew of tobacco.

quiescent *a* still; calm; inactive; passive; *n* **quiescence** inactivity.

quiet *a* peaceful; motionless; serene; monotonous; *v* **quiet, quieten** make, become quiet; *ns* **quietness, quietude.**

quietus *n* riddance, final discharge from; death.

quiff *n* tuft or curl of hair over forehead.

quill *n* hollow stem of bird's feather; long wing feather; spine of porcupine.

quilt *n* padded bed-cover; *v* stitch two pieces of cloth together with padding in between; *n* **quilting.**

quince *n* pear-shaped fruit with sharp flavour.

quinine *n* bitter-tasting drug.

Quinquagesima *n* Sunday before Lent.

quinquennial *a* occurring once in or lasting five years.

quinsy *n* suppurative tonsilitis.
quintessence *n* purest form of some quality.
quintet(te) *n* (*mus*) composition for five instruments or voices; group of five performers.
quintuplets *npl* (*abbrev* **quins**) five children born at one time.
quip *n* witty remark; jest, clever repartee.
quire *n* twentieth part of ream of paper.
quirk *n* quick twist or turn; quip; individual trait.
quirt *n* riding-whip.
quisling *n* traitor.
quit *a* free, clear, rid of; *v* leave, abandon; cease from; give up, retire from; *n* & *a* **quits** (state of) being on equal terms; *ns* **quittance** receipt, discharge; **quitter** one who abandons task in face of difficulty etc.
quitch *n* coarse, creeping grass; couch-grass.
quite *adv* wholly, completely; entirely; *interj.* exactly, certainly.
quiver *n* case for holding arrows.
quiver *v* tremble, shake; *n* **quivering**.
quixotic *a* extravagantly generous & chivalrous.
quiz *v* question closely; stare at inquisitively; *n* game of answering questions, or solving problems, *esp* as public entertainment.
quod *n* (*sl*) prison.
quoin *n* salient angle of building; corner-stone; wedge used for locking type in forme.
quoit *n* ring for throwing at, or over, peg; (*pl*) game using this.
quorum *n* minimum number of members that must be present before meeting may proceed.
quota *n* proportional share; allocation; allowance; amount of goods allowed to be imported during certain period.
quote *v* repeat or cite something said, written by another; name price, give estimate; *n* **quotation**.
quoth *v* (*ar poet*) said, spoke.
quotidian *a* daily.
quotient *n* number resulting from division of one number by another.

rabbet *n* groove in woodwork; *v* join by rabbet.
rabbi *n* Jewish teacher of law, or minister of religion; *a* **rabbinical.**
rabbit *n* burrowing rodent akin to hare; (*sl*) unskilful player of game, beginner; *v* hunt rabbits.
rabble *n* disorderly, riotous crowd or mob.
Rabelaisian *a* outspokenly broad and coarsely humorous.
rabid *a* affected with rabies; furious; violently fanatical; *n* **rabies** infectious disease of dogs etc; canine madness.
race *n* contest of speed in running, riding, sailing etc; strong current of water *esp* leading to water-mill; (*pl*) horse-races; *v* run, cause to run swiftly; compete in speed (against); *n* **racer.**
race *n* group of persons descended from same original stock; distinct variety; lineage; breed; *a* **racial;** *ns* **racialism** belief that one race of people is superior to another; **racist** adherent of such belief.
raceme *n* flower cluster in which simple flowers grow on stems along main stem; *a* **racemose.**
rack *n* framework to hold things (hats, baggage, letters etc.); medieval instrument of torture; in mechanics, straight bar with teeth on its edge to work with pinion; *v* cause great pain or distress to; **r. one's brains,** make painful effort to think.
racket, racquet *n* bat used in tennis; (*pl*) game akin to tennis played in paved, walled court.
racket *n* loud noise, din; illegal business or way of making money; *n* **racketeer** one who operates illegal business.
rac(c)oon *n* small, carnivorous nocturnal mammal.
racy *a* spirited, piquant, spicy; *n* **raciness.**
radar *n* electronic system for direction finding, and observation of distant objects, by reflection of radio waves.
radiate *v* emit rays of light, heat etc; spread from centre; *a* **radial** of rays; *ns* **radiation** emission of rays (of heat, light etc;) **radiance** brightness; brilliance; *a* **radiant** shining; displaying delight; *n* (*geom*) straight line assumed to rotate round fixed point; *n* **radiator** that which radiates; device for

cooling car engine; apparatus for heating rooms etc.

radical *a* of root or origin; (politics) advanced, progressive; complete; *n* number expressed as root of another; politician of advanced liberal views.

radicle *n* minute root of plant.

radio- *prefix* of rays, of radium, of radiation.

radio *n* transmission of sounds by electromagnetic waves, without wires; *v* broadcast; send message by wireless telegraphy; *ns* **radiogram** combined wireless set and gramophone; **radiophone** wireless telephone.

radioactivity *n* spontaneous disintegration & emission of gamma rays etc; *a* **radioactive.**

radiology *n* science of X-radiation & radioactivity.

radiologist *n* specialist in use of rays in medicine.

radiotherapy *n* treatment of disease by X-rays.

radish *n* plant with edible, pungent root.

radium *n* rare, radioactive, metallic element.

radius *n* straight line from centre to circumference of circle; shorter bone of forearm; (*pl*) **radii, radiuses.**

radix *n* number or quantity taken as basis for calculations.

raffia *n* fibre from leaves of Madagascar palm, used for tying up plants etc.

raffish *a* rakish, disreputable.

raffle *n* sale of article by means of lottery; *v* dispose of by raffle.

raft *n* flat, buoyant structure of logs, planks etc.

rafter *n* one of pieces of timber supporting roof.

rag *n* shred, tatter of cloth; (*pl*) old clothes; *a* **ragged** jagged, uneven; clothed in torn clothes; rough; *ns* **rag trade** (*sl*) manufacture of clothes and fabrics etc; **ragamuffin** ragged, dirty person or child; **ragstone** rough blueish limestone; **ragtime** strongly syncopated music.

rag *v* tease good-naturedly; play practical jokes on; be noisy, riotous; *n* good-natured mischievous prank, *esp* by students.

rage *n* violent anger; frenzy; fury; (*coll*) person, thing temporarily widely admired etc; *v* speak, act with violent anger; (of storm etc.) be extremely violent, rough; **all the rage** very popular.

raglan *a* of sleeves not set into armhole.
ragoût *n* highly seasoned stew of meat and vegetables.
raid *n* attack, invasion; police search on suspect premises, as low night-club etc; *v* make raid on, into; attack.
rail *n* horizontal wooden or metal bar; (*pl*) system of railway lines; *v* send by rail; *ns* **railway** permanent track on which trains run; **railroad** railway; *v* (*sl*) force through despite opposition; **off the rails** (*sl*) (*fig*) mistaken; eccentric.
rail *v* utter complaints against; reproach bitterly; *n* **raillery** good-humoured banter.
rail *n* kind of bird, corncrake etc.
raiment *n* dress, garments, clothing.
rain *n* condensed moisture of atmosphere falling in drops; *v* fall as rain; (*fig*) arrive in large numbers, in continuous succession; *a* **rainy**; *ns* **rainbow** arc showing colours of spectrum, formed by refraction of sunlight in water-drops; **rainfall** total amount of rain falling on given area of given time.
raise *v* cause to rise; erect; increase amount or value of; evoke; breed, rear; increase in intensity; **raise Cain** (*sl*) cause trouble; **raise land** (*naut*) come within sight of land.
raisin *n* dried grape.
rajah *n* Indian or Malayan prince or ruler; *n* **raj** rule, *esp* British sovereignty in India.
rake *n* long handled tool with cross bar set with teeth for gathering hay, leaves etc, or for breaking, scraping ground; *v* use rake; sweep target with fire lengthways; (*fig*) ferret about, search; *n* **rake-off** (*sl*) share of profits *usu* on illegal deal.
rake *n* dissolute or immoral man; *a* **rakish** dashing, showy.
rake *v* incline backwards from perpendicular; *n* (of ship's mast, stage) slope.
rally *v* gather together again; re-form after repulse etc; recover health, strength etc; revive; *n* act of rallying; mass-meeting; gathering of car-drivers etc. for long competitive drive; in tennis, exchange of strokes.

ram *n* adult male sheep; device for bettering or piercing; hydraulic machine; *v* collide forcibly with; crush by repeated blows; crush, cram; (*fig*) instil (ideas etc.) by persistent effort.
Ramadan *n* great feast, lasting throughout 9th. month of Moslem year.
ramble *v* wander, walk about idly; stroll for pleasure; chatter, speak incoherently; (of plants) grow in long shoots; *n* casual walk; *n* **rambler** one who rambles; climbing, trailing plant, *esp* rose.
ramify *v* spread, branch out; subdivide; *n* **ramification** branching, subdivision in complex system.
ramjet *n* type of jet aero-engine.
ramp *n* inclined plane joining two level surfaces; (*sl*) swindle; (*coll*) storm of anger, rampage.
rampage *v* rage, behave turbulently; *n* wild behaviour; *as* **rampageous** violent, uncontrolled; **rampant** violent; wide-spread; (*her*) standing on hind legs.
rampart *n* defensive mound with parapet; (*fig*) defence.
ramshackle *a* rickety; tumbledown; worn-out.
ranch *n* large American cattle farm; *n* **rancher.**
rancid *a* having offensive smell and taste *esp* of stale fat or oil.
rancour *n* deep-rooted hatred, ill-will; malice, spite; *a* **rancorous.**
random *a* haphazard; made, done by chance; heedless.
randy *a* (*coll*) lustful.
ranee, rani *n* Hindu queen or ruler; wife of rajah.
range *n* line, row; extent, area, scope, sphere; distance that can be reached by weapon, vehicle etc; shooting area; cooking stove; *v* place; set in rows; (of animals, plants etc.) frequent, be found in; wander; vary within limits; *ns* **range-finder** instrument for measuring distance away of target etc; **ranger** forest, or park official; rover.
rank *n* line, row, series; (*pl*) body of soldiers; social class, order; grade, class; *v* take rank; classify; *n* **ranker** soldier in ranks; officer promoted from ranks.
rank *a* overgrown, coarse; rancid; flagrant.

rankle *v* fester; (*fig*) be remembered with bitterness, resentment; cause anger.
ransack *v* hunt for something; plunder, pillage.
ransom *n* money, price paid for release of prisoner, or captured goods etc; *v* pay ransom for.
rant *v* speak wildly, extravagantly; use violent language; *n* **ranter.**
ranunculus *n* one of genus of plants, including buttercup.
rap *n* light, smart blow; *v* tap, strike with quick blow.
rap *n* something worthless, of trifling value.
rapacious *a* greedy, hungry; grasping, avaricious; *n* **rapacity.**
rape *n* plant grown as fodder for sheep; seed of this used as food for birds, and producing oil.
rape *v* violate; ravish; assault sexually; *n* act of raping; *n* **rapist.**
rapid *a* swift, fast-moving; done quickly; *n* (*usu pl*) swift current in river owing to sudden fall in bed; *n* **rapidity** speed, velocity.
rapier *n* light, thrusting duelling sword.
rapine *n* plunder, violent robbery.
rapport *n* harmony; sympathetic relationship.
rapprochement *n* renewal of cordial relations; reconciliation.
rapscallion *n* rascal, ne'er-do-well, scamp.
rapt *a* carried away in body or mind; completely absorbed; intent; *a* **raptorial** predatory; of order of birds of prey; *n* **rapture** ecstasy; great delight; *a* **rapturous.**
rare *a* uncommon; infrequent; exceptional, not dense; *adv* **rarely** seldom; *n* **rarity** state of being rare; rare object or quality.
rare *a* (of meat) underdone.
rarebit *n* **Welsh r.** toasted cheese.
rarefy *v* make rare or thin; reduce density of; (*fig*) refine.
rascal *n* rogue, scamp; mischievous child (term of affection); *a* **rascally.**
rash *n* skin eruption.
rash *a* impetuous; spoken, done without caution or thought; *n* **rashness.**

rasher *n* thin slice of bacon or ham.
rasp *n* coarse file; grating sound; *v* file, scrape with rasp; grate upon (ear), irritate.
raspberry *n* juicy, bright-red fruit growing on canes; the plant.
rat *n* small, long-tailed rodent, allied to mouse; (*fig*) cowardly traitor; *v* hunt rats; desert a cause etc *a* **ratty** (*sl*) angry, ill tempered.
ratafia *n* liqueur distilled from almonds, crushed fruit kernels; small macaroon biscuit.
ratchet *n* set of teeth on bar or wheel, allowing motion in one direction only.
rate *n* amount, degree measured in relation to something else; charge; tax levied by local authorities; *v* estimate value of; assess for local taxation; *a* **rateable** that may be valued; liable to taxation; *n* **ratepayer** one who pays local rates.
rate *v* scold, take to task.
rather *adv* sooner; more; slightly; preferably.
ratify *v* confirm, make valid; *n* **ratification**.
rating *n* act of assessing; classification; sailor who is not commissioned; scolding, rebuke.
ratio *n* proportion; fixed numerical relations.
ration *n* fixed amount or allowance of food, goods; *v* supply with, limit to certain amount.
rational *a* reasonable, sensible; *ns* **rationalism** doctrine that reason is only source of knowledge; **rationalist**; *v* **rationalize** give rational explanation of; *ns* **rationalization** reorganization of an industry or related group; **rationality** reasonableness.
ratlines *n pl* ropes fastened across shrouds of ship, forming a rope ladder.
rattan *n* species of climbing palm; cane of this.
rattle *v* give out succession of short, sharp sounds; move with clatter; talk rapidly, briskly; (*coll*) disconcert, confuse; *n* this sound; device or child's toy, making this sound; horny rings on rattlesnake's tail; *n* **rattlesnake** venomous American snake, which can rattle its tail.
raucous *a* hoarse, harsh-sounding.
ravage *v* devastate by violence; plunder; *n* ruin waste.

rave *v* speak wildly in delirium; talk enthusiastically about; *n* (*coll*) praise; (*sl*) party, dance.
ravel *v* entangle, confuse; fray; **r. out** disentangle.
raven *n* large black bird related to crow; *a* jet-black.
ravenous *a* voracious, famished with hunger.
ravine *n* deep narrow valley or gorge.
ravioli *n pl* Italian dish of small squares of pasta holding seasoned, chopped meat etc.
ravish *v* fill with rapture; violate, commit rape upon; *n* **ravishing** delightful, entrancing.
raw *a* uncooked; in natural state; crude; sore; cold, damp; untrained; *n* **rawhide** untanned hide; *a* **raw-bone** thin, gaunt; **in the raw** unprocessed; crude; (*sl*) naked.
ray *n* single beam, shaft of light, heat etc; any one of group of radiating lines; *v* radiate.
ray *n* flat-fish, skate.
rayon *n* artificial silk made from cellulose.
raze *v* obliterate; lay level with ground; destroy.
razor *n* cutting instrument for shaving.
re, in re *prep* in the matter of; concerning.
re- *prefix* repetition, again; back. *Forms compounds, these are not given where the meaning may be deduced from the simple word.*
reach *v* extend; touch, take with outstretched hand; achieve; *n* act, power of touching; range; stretch of water, *esp* on river.
react *v* act in response to stimulus; *ns* **reaction** response to stimulus; reciprocal action; contrary action; depression following over-excitement; **reactionary** one who opposes progress and reform; *a* inclined to such action, retrograde.
reactor *n* (*phys*) apparatus for generating heat by nuclear fission; atomic pile.
read *v* see and understand printed, written words, symbols etc; read and utter; learn by reading; (of thermometer etc.) indicate, register; *pt* & *pp* **read**; *a* **readable** that can be read; interesting, not tedious; *ns* **readability**; **reader** student, lover of books; one who reads MSS submitted to publishers: one who reads and corrects proofs for press; official university lecturer; reading-book.

ready *a* prepared for use; immediately available; prompt; *n* **readiness**; *adv* **readily** easily; willingly; promptly.
reagent *n* substance used to produce chemical change or reaction.
real *a* existing in fact; genuine; actual; *n* **r. estate** landed property; *ns* **realism** practical outlook; ability to see things as they are; attempt to depict life etc. as it actually exists; **realist** adherent of realism; one who claims to have no illusions; *a* **realistic**; *n* **reality** state of being real; *v* **realize** become aware of; convert into, sell for money; *ns* **realization** act of realizing; **realty** (*leg*) real estate, property.
realm *n* kingdom; (*fig*) sphere, region.
ream *n* 20 quires of paper, 480 or 500 sheets.
ream *v* bevel out, countersink; (*naut*) open for caulking; *n* **reamer** tool for this.
reap *v* cut and gather (corn etc.); (*fig*) obtain as reward, result of action, conduct; *n* **reaper.**
rear *n* raise, lift up; bring up, educate; (of horse etc.) stand on hind legs.
rear *n* hind part; part of army behind front line; position of being at back; *ns* **rear-admiral** lowest flag rank in Royal Navy; **rearguard** body of troops protecting rear of army on march.
reason *n* faculty of thinking logically; cause, motive; sanity; common sense; *v* persuade by logical argument; *a* **reasonable** rational; fair, just; not extravagant.
rebate *n* deduction; discount; rabbet; *v* cut rebate or rabbet in.
rebel *v* revolt; resent control, constraint; take up arms against; *n* one who rebels; *n* **rebellion** organized, open resistance to authority etc; *a* **rebellious** taking part in rebellion; revolting against control or authority.
rebore *v* bore through (cylinder) again to regain true shape; *n* act, process of reboring or being rebored.
rebound *v* bound, spring back; recoil on; *n* act of rebounding; **on the r.** (*fig*) reacting against disappointment (in love etc.).

rebuff *n* repulse; snub; check; *v* check; snub; defeat.
rebuke *v* reprove, reprimand; censure for fault; *n* reproof.
rebus *n* riddle in which names, syllables etc. are represented by pictures and letters.
rebut *v* repel, check *esp* accusations etc; refute; *n* **rebuttal.**
recalcitrant *a* refractory; obstinately disobedient; *n* **recalcitrance.**
recall *v* summon, order back; remember; restore; revoke; *n* summons to return.
recant *v* take back; disavow opinions, beliefs etc; repudiate publicly; *n* **recantation.**
recapitulate (*coll abbrev* **recap**) *v* summarize; restate briefly; *n* **recapitulation.**
recede *v* move back; slope backwards; retreat.
receipt *n* written acknowledgement of money, goods received; act of receiving or getting; recipe.
receive *v* take, obtain (something given, sent, offered etc.); undergo; greet, welcome; allow into one's presence; *n* **receiver** official appointed to collect money or administer property under litigation; ear-piece of telephone; wireless receiving set; one who receives stolen goods.
recent *a* new, fresh; modern.
receptacle *n* vessel, container; that which receives or contains.
reception *n* act of receiving; formal act of receiving guests, clients, hotel visitors etc; quality of broadcasting signals received; *n* **receptionist** person employed to receive hotel guests, patients etc; and arrange accommodation, appointments etc.
receptive *a* able, quick to receive, *esp* new ideas etc.
recess *n* cessation, suspension of business; alcove; secret place.
recession *n* act of receding; period of reduction, slackening in industry and trade.
recessional *n* hymn sung as clergy leave chancel.
recherché *a* choice, select; of refined, rare quality.
recidivist *n* one who relapses into crime.
recipe *n* formula, directions for making, cooking something; prescription.

recipient *n* & *a* (person, thing) that receives.

reciprocal *a* felt, done in return; mutual; alternating; *v* **reciprocate** exchange mutually; alternate; move backwards and forwards; *ns* **reciprocation**; **reciprocity**.

recite *v* repeat aloud from memory *esp* to audience; *ns* **recital** act of reciting; (*mus*) performance by soloist or small group, or of works of one composer; **recitation** recital of poetry or prose *usu* from memory.

reckless *a* heedless, careless; rash, incautious.

reckon *v* count; include; consider; cast accounts; *ns* **reckoner** one who reckons; book of tables as aid to calculations etc; **reckoning** calculation; account.

reclaim *v* bring back; demand return of; reform from vice etc; recover (land) from sea or waste state; *n* **reclaimable**; *n* **reclamation**.

recline *v* sit, lean backwards; rest, repose.

recluse *n* hermit; one who chooses to live alone in retirement; *n* **reclusion**.

recognize *v* know again; acknowledge; admit to be true, valid; *ns* **recognition**; **recognizance** obligation to fulfil some condition, undertaken before court; sum forfeited if party fails to meet this obligation.

recoil *v* draw back; retreat; rebound; (*fig*) feel disgust, horror; *n* rebound *esp* of gun; backward motion.

recollect *v* recall to mind; remember; *n* **recollection**.

recommend *v* represent as being suitable; advise; entrust to care of; *n* **recommendation**.

recompense *v* make equal return for; reward; compensate; *n* that which is given as reward, compensation etc.

reconcile *v* settle (dispute, quarrel etc); bring into logical agreement; be resigned to; *ns* **reconciliation** restoration of friendship; act, state of being reconciled; **reconcilement**; *a* **reconciliatory**.

recondite *a* obscure; concerned with abstruse subjects.

reconnoitre *v* make preliminary survey (of enemy's position etc.); explore, examine beforehand; *n* **reconnaissance** act of reconnoitring.

record *v* write down for future information; store

sound) on gramophone disc or magnetic tape for (subsequent reproduction; *n* written account, document; sound recording on gramophone disc; best, finest achievement *esp* in sport; **off the r.** (*coll*) confidential; *ns* **recorder** one who, that which records; judge who presides over Quarter Sessions of city or borough; musical instrument like flute; **recording** record of sounds made on disc or tape.

recount *v* narrate, relate; count again.

recoup *v* compensate; make good (financial losses).

recourse *n* act of seeking help; application for help.

recover *v* get, win back what has been lost; *n* **recovery**.

recreant *a* false to one's principles etc; cowardly; *n* apostate.

recreate *v* create, form anew; restore, revive; *n* **recreation** relaxation; amusement, game, sport; pastime.

recriminate *v* express mutual reproach; make counter-charges; *n* **recrimination** mutual abuse and reproach.

recrudesce *v* break out afresh; *n* **recrudescence**; *a* **recrudescent**.

recruit *n* newly enlisted member of armed forces; newly enrolled member of society etc; *v* enlist, seek to enlist (new soldiers etc, members); recover health; *n* **recruitment**.

rectangle *n* right-angled parallelogram; *a* **rectangular**.

rectify *v* put right; purify; adjust; refine by distillation; *n* **rectification** act of rectifying; refining; conversion of alternating current into direct current; *n* **rectifier**.

rectilineal, rectilinear *a* consisting of, in, straight lines.

rectitude *n* moral uprightness; integrity; honesty of purpose.

rector *n* C. of E. parish priest entitled to tithes; head of certain religious and educational institutions; *n* **rectory** rector's house.

rectum *n* lowest, terminal part of large intestine; *a* **rectal**.

recumbent *a* lying down, reclining; *n* **recumbence.**
recuperate *v* recover, regain health etc; recover from financial losses; *n* **recuperation.**
recur *v* happen again; return to one's mind; (*math*) be repeated indefinitely; *n* **recurrence;** *a* **recurrent.**
recusant *n* & *a* (one) refusing to obey, conform to laws etc, *esp* religious matters.
red *a* of colour like blood, crimson, scarlet etc; *n* this colour; (*fig*) Communist; *ns* **R. Admiral** red and black butterfly; **redbreast** robin; **R. Cross** international society helping victims of war or disaster; **r. deer** largest British wild deer. **R. Ensign** flag of British merchant navy; **r. flag** symbol of Communism; Communist song; danger signal; **r. herring** misleading fact or clue; **r. tape** (*fig*) excessive attention to official rules and formalities; *v* **redden** make, become red; blush.
redeem *v* buy back; fulfil; make amends for; ransom; (of God, Christ) save from damnation; *ns* **redeemer** one who redeems, *specif* **the R.** Jesus Christ; **redemption;** *a* **redeemable.**
redolent *a* fragrant; giving out sweet scent; **r. of** (*fig*) steeped in; reminiscent of; *n* **redolence.**
redouble *v* double again; increase; refold.
redoubt *n* small independent outwork in chain of defences.
redoubtable *a* formidable; valiant.
redound *v* contribute, lead to.
redress *v* male good, set right; make amends for; *n* reparation, compensation.
reduce *v* lessen, decrease; break down to simpler form; (*med*) replace dislocated joint; cause to grow, try to become, slim; bring by force or necessity to some inferior position, state etc; *n* **reduction;** *a* **reducing.**
redundant *a* superfluous, unnecessary; *n* **redundancy.**
reed *n* various aquatic or marsh grasses; stem of these; vibrating cane or metal strip of some musical instruments; *a* **reedy** full of reeds; harsh, piping, shrill.
reef *n* part of sail which can be folded up to shorten

sail; ridge of rock just below surface of water; lode of auriferous quartz; *v* reduce area (of sail) by taking in reef; *n* **reefer** sailor's short double-breasted jacket; (*sl*) marijuana cigarette.

reek *n* fumes, stench; *v* emit smoke, fumes; smell, stink.

reel *n* small spool or bobbin round which thread is wound; lively Scottish dance; music for it; unit of length of cinema film (approx. 1000 ft); act of staggering; *v* wind on reel; stagger, sway.

reeve *n* steward, bailiff; female ruff.

refectory *n* room for meals, *esp* in monastery, school etc.

refer *v* assign to, identify with; send to for information; allude; submit for decision; *ns* **reference** act of referring; testimonial; relation, respect; **referendum** submitting of question to electorate.

referee *n* one to whom a thing is referred; umpire *esp* in football (*coll abbrev* **ref**); *v* act as umpire.

refine *v* purify, clarify; make, become more elegant; *ns* **refinement** act of refining; culture; fineness of feeling, taste etc.; **refinery** place where materials are refined or purified.

reflect *v* throw back, give out (light, heat etc.); reproduce visual image; think deeply; cast doubt on; *n* **reflection, reflexion** act of reflecting; that which is reflected (rays of light, heat etc.); reflected visual image (by mirror etc.); meditation; *a* **reflective**; *n* **reflector** polished surface which reflects (rays of light etc.).

reflex *a* directed backwards; **r. action** involuntary muscular, nervous reaction to stimulus; **r. angle** angle greater than 180° and less than 360°; *a* **reflexive** (*gram*) denoting action coming back on agent; **r. pronoun** one referring to subject of sentence.

reform *v* change for better; improve condition, by removal of abuses etc; *n* improvement.

reformation *n* amendment; **the R.** 16th century religious revolt.

reformatory *n* corrective institution for young offenders; *a* producing reform.

refract *v* deflect rays or waves from direct course; *n* **refraction**; *a* **refractive.**
refractory *a* unmanageable, stubborn; (*med*) resistant to treatment, hard to cure.
refrain *n* recurring lines, words at end of song, etc.
refrain *v* abstain, forbear; keep oneself from.
refresh *v* revive, invigorate; renew; provide with fresh supply; *n* **refresher** that which refreshes; additional fee paid to counsel; **r. course** course of instruction given to persons already qualified etc; to bring knowledge up to date; *n* **refreshment** that which refreshes *esp* food or drink.
refrigerate *v* freeze; keep at very low temperature; *ns* **refrigeration; refrigerator** machine for cooling, freezing (food etc.); ice-box.
refuge *n* shelter, protection; sanctuary, hiding place; *n* **refugee** one who seeks refuge, *esp* in another country.
refulgent *a* shining; radiant; *n* **refulgence** brightness; splendour.
refund *v* repay; restore.
refurbish *v* renovate.
refuse *v* decline; reject; (of horse) be unwilling to jump; *n* rubbish, discarded matter; *n* **refusal** act of refusing; option.
refute *v* reject; disprove; *a* **refutable**; *n* **refutation.**
regal *a* of, like king; *n pl* **regalia** insignia of royalty; insignia, clothes etc. of a society; *n* **regality.**
regale *v* feast; give great delight to.
regard *v* gaze at intently; consider; esteem, value; *n* look; esteem; care, attention; *pl* expression of goodwill; **with r. to** concerning; *a* **regardless** heedless; negligent.
regatta *n* race-meeting for boats or yachts.
regenerate *v* bring new life to; reorganize after decay; recreate; be reformed morally; *a* **regenerative**; *n* **regeneration; regenerator** device in furnace for saving fuel by heating incoming air.
regent *n* one who rules during absence, minority or illness of sovereign; *n* **regency** office or position of regent; *a* of, in style prevailing during regency (*esp* 1810-20 in England & 1715-23 in France).

regicide *n* killer, killing of king or sovereign.
régime *n* system, method of government, administration.
regimen *n* course of treatment *esp* in matters of diet, exercise etc.
regiment *n* military unit; (*fig*) large quantity; *a* **regimental** of regiment; *n pl* uniform of particular regiment.
region *n* area, district, tract of country; area of body; sphere, realm; *a* **regional**.
register *n* record of names, events etc. *esp* official one kept for reference; range, compass of voice, instrument; mechanical device for regulating draught in stove etc; *v* set down in writing; indicate automatically; (*print* & *photo*) adjust exactly.
registrar *n* one who keeps public records (births, deaths etc); **registration** act of registering.
registry *n* place, office where register is kept; **r. office** local registry for births, marriages and deaths.
regius *a* appointed, founded by crown.
regnant *a* reigning.
regorge *v* vomit; swallow again.
regress *n* return, going back; relapse; *a* **regressive** falling back; *n* **regression** backward movement.
regret *v* be sorry for; remember with grief, sorrow; repent of; *n* grief; repentance; sorrow; *as* **regretful**; **regrettable** to be regretted.
regular *a* orderly; according to rule, law, type; normal; habitual; symmetrical; of professional soldier; *n* **regularity**.
regulate *v* put in order; control by law; make clock etc. work correctly; *ns* **regulation** act of regulating; rule, order; **regulator** lever of watch etc.
regurgitate *v* flow, gush back; bring up again (swallowed food etc); *n* **regurgitation**.
rehabilitate *v* restore normal capacity; reinstate; *n* **rehabilitation**.
rehash *v* rearrange old literary material, and produce under new title.
rehearse *v* perform, practise (play, piece of music etc.) in private, before publish performance; *n* **rehearsal**.

reign *n* rule, supreme power of sovereign; period of ruler's reign; *v* rule as monarch; be supreme; predominate.
reimburse *v* refund; compensate by payment; *n* **reimbursement.**
rein *n* leather strap fastened to bit for leading, holding horse; (*fig*) that which restrains; *v* hold in, control with reins; **give r. to** allow full play to; **tight r.** severe restraint.
reincarnation *n* return of soul to earth, after death, in fresh form; *v* **reincarnate** cause to be reborn in other form.
reindeer *n* large, domesticated deer of northern regions; **r. moss** grey arctic lichen.
reinforce *v* (*mil*) strengthen with additional troops, supplies etc; strengthen (fabric etc.) by increasing thickness etc; *ns* **reinforcement; reinforced concrete** concrete strengthened by steel bars embedded in it.
reinstate *v* restore to former state, position; *n* **reinstatement.**
reiterate *v* repeat many times; *n* **reiteration** repetition.
reject *v* discard as imperfect, valueless, useless; refuse to accept; disallow; *n* that which is rejected; *n* **rejection** refusal.
rejoice *v* make, be glad; feel, express joy; delight; *n pl* **rejoicings** outward expression of joy, festivities.
rejoin *v* join again; make answer; *n* **rejoinder** retort; answer to a reply.
rejuvenate *v* renew youth of; become young again; *n* **rejuvenation.**
relapse *v* fall back into former bad state; become ill again; backslide; *n.*
relate *v* narrate; have connection with; refer (to) belong to same family as; *n* **relative** that which is relative; one belonging to same family; *a* having relation; not absolute; *n* **relativity** fact or state of being relative; Einstein's theory based on principle that space & time are inseparable; *ns* **relation** narrative; connection between things; connection by blood or marriage; **relationship.**

relax *v* loosen; slacken; make,become less rigid, tense; unbend, become less severe; *n* **relaxation** act of relaxing; slackening of strain, tension etc; recreation.
relay *n* team of men, horses or dogs etc. replacing tired ones; broadcast sent from one station to another; *v* pass on (information); transmit from relay station; to lay again; **r. race** race between teams, each member running part of distance and handing baton to next runner.
release *v* give up; set free; discharge; *n* liberation; formal discharge; catch releasing mechanism.
relegate *v* send, dismiss to inferior position; transfer; *n* **relegation.**
relent *v* become less hard, severe, stern or obstinate; *a* **relentless** pitiless; inexorable.
relevant *a* bearing on point at issue; pertinent, applicable; *n* **relevance.**
relic *n* object surviving from past, *esp* one associated with saint; memento.
relict *n* (*ar*) widow; *a* left behind; surviving.
relief *n* alleviation of pain, distress, anxiety etc; assistance given to those in need; release from duty; that which breaks monotony; projection of carved design from surface; representation of elevations of land surface by hachures, shading etc, as on **relief map**; *v* **relieve** bring relief to; lessen; provide contrast to.
religion *n* belief in and worship of God or gods; *a* **religious** pertaining to religion; devout, pious; (*fig*) conscientious.
relinquish *v* abandon, surrender; let go.
reliquary *n* casket, box for keeping relics.
relish *n* flavour, aroma; (*fig*) any stimulating quality; (*fig*) zest, gusto; *v* enjoy; (*fig*) smack of.
reluctant *a* unwilling, disinclined; difficult to treat; *n* **reluctance.**
rely *v* trust, depend on; *a* **reliable** dependable; trustworthy; *ns* **reliability; reliance** ground of trust or confidence; *a* **reliant** confident; trusting.
remain *v* stay, be left behind; endure, persist; stay, continue in same place; *n pl* what is left or survives; relics; dead body; *n* **remainder** remaining persons

or things; quantity left after subtraction; copies of books etc. unsold in publisher's stock; *v* offer unsold books etc. at reduced prices.

remand *v* send back *esp* into custody; *n* **r. home** institution for young delinquents.

remark *v* take notice of; observe; utter comment; *n* observation, comment; *a* **remarkable** noticeable; unusual.

remedy *n* substance, treatment which cures disease etc; action or method tending to mitigate an evil or wrong; *v* put right; *a* **remedial**.

remember *v* call to mind; retain in memory; have in mind; *n* **remembrance** memory; keepsake, souvenir; (*pl*) greeting.

remind *v* put in mind of, cause to remember; *n* **reminder** that which reminds.

reminiscence *n* memory, recollection; (*pl*) memoirs; *a* **reminiscent** serving to remind; tending to recall past.

remiss *a* negligent; careless.

remit *v* forgo, give up in whole or part; send back; transmit; *a* **remissible**; *ns* **remission** abatement; pardon; **remittance** sending of money; sum of money sent as payment or allowance.

remnant *n* remaining fragment; short length of fabric, oddment.

remonstrate *v* protest; expostulate, plead, with; *n* **remonstrance**.

remorse *n* repentance, regret, *as* **remorseful**; **remorseless** ruthless, pitiless; relentless.

remote *a* far away; aloof, distant; *n* **r. control** device for controlling machine, weapon etc. from distance by radio waves.

remove *v* take, carry (thing) away, off; withdraw; erase; relieve of office, rank etc; move from one place to another *esp* residence; *n* **removal** act of removing *specif* of furniture from house.

remunerate *v* pay, compensate; *n* **remuneration**; *a* **remunerative** profitable.

renaissance *n* rebirth, revival; *specif* **the R.** revival of art and learning in 15th. and 16th. centuries (also **Renascence**).

renal *a* of the kidneys.
renascent *a* reviving, springing into fresh life.
rend *v* tear apart; split; (*fig*) cause anguish to; *pt* & *pp* **rent.**
render *v* give in return; tender; depict by art; interpret; melt and clarify (fat); put on first coat of plaster etc; *n* **rendering** version, interpretation; **rendition** interpretation, performance.
rendezvous *n* meeting-place fixed beforehand; popular, general resort.
renegade *n* apostate; deserter, turncoat.
renew *v* restore to original condition or state of freshness; begin again; prolong, extend existence or validity of; grow again; *n* **renewal** revival, restoration; *as* **renewable; renewing** regenerating, quickening.
rennet *n* preparation (*usu* from membrane of calf's stomach) used to curdle milk, and in cheese-making.
renounce *v* formally give up, disclaim; repudiate; not to follow suit at cards; *n* **renunciation.**
renovate *v* restore to good condition; renew; repair; *ns* **renovation; renovator** one who renovates.
renown *n* fame, celebrity; *a* **renowned** famous.
rent *n* payment made for use of house, land etc; *v* occupy (house etc.) for payment; hire out; let; *n* **rental** amount payable as rent.
rep, repp *n* thick corded, ribbed material.
rep *n* (*coll abbrev*) representative; *n* & *a* (*coll abbrev*) repertory theatre.
repair *v* mend; set right, compensate for; *n*; *as* **reparable, repairable;** *n* **reparation** redress, amends.
repair *v* have recourse to; frequent.
repartee *n* readiness in making witty reply or retort.
repast *n* meal, feast.
repatriate *v* send back, return to native country; *n* **repatriation.**
repay *v* pay back, refund (money); make return for, reward; *pt* & *pp* **repaid;** *n* **repayment.**
repeal *v* revoke, abrogate; annul (law etc); *n* revocation.
repeat *v* say again, reiterate; recite; do again; repro-

duce; recur; *n* repetition; thing repeated *esp* programme or order for goods; *adv* **repeatedly** over and over again; *n* **repeater** one who, that which repeats; watch that strikes hours; repeating fire-arms; *n* **repetition** act of repeating; recital, recitation; *a* **repetitive** tending to repeat.

repel *v* drive back; spurn; rouse dislike, disgust in; *n* **repellence**; *a* **repellent** disgusting, revolting; *n* that which repels (insects etc.).

repent *v* feel penitence, regret for deed or omission; *a* **repentant**; *n* **repentance**.

repercussion *n* rebound, recoil; (*fig*) indirect effect, consequence *usu pl*.

repertory *n* store; stock; *n* **repertoire** stock of songs, plays that person or company can perform; **repertory theatre** theatre with permanent company, depending on constant change of plays.

repine *v* fret, complain; be discontented.

replace *v* put back; supersede; substitute for; *n* **replacement**.

replenish *v* fill up again; restock; *n* **replenishment**.

replete *a* well-filled; sated, gorged; *n* **repletion** surfeit.

replica *n* duplicate, copy of anything; *esp* of work of art, done by the artist himself.

reply *v* & *n* answer in speech or writing.

report *v* relate, state; take down verbatim; present oneself for service, duty etc; lodge complaint officially; *n* account; written statement *esp* by schoolmaster; rumour; loud noise; *n* **reporter** one who reports, *esp* for newspaper.

repose *v* place; rest; rely on; lean on; be supported by; *n* act of reposing; *n* **repository** place where things may be deposited, stored; warehouse.

repoussé *a* embossed by hammering on reverse.

reprehend *v* rebuke; censure, blame; *a* **reprehensible** not good; deserving reproof.

represent *v* depict by painting, etc; describe; mean, signify; symbolize; take place of; act on behalf of; *n* **representative** one who acts as agent, delegate; *a* typical.

repress *v* suppress, put down; curb, check, overcome;

n **repression** suppression, restraint; (*psyc*) result of mental conflict.

reprieve *v* cancel or defer punishment *esp* death sentence; give respite (to); *n* cancellation or suspension of criminal sentence; respite.

reprimand *n* rebuke, censure severely; *n* severe reproof.

reprisal *n* retaliation.

reproach *v* scold, upbraid, charge with some fault; *n* rebuke; thing bringing disgrace etc; *a* **reproachful.**

reprobate *a* & *n* depraved (person); (one) without honour or principles.

reproduce *v* become parent of; produce afresh; repeat; present again; *n* **reproduction** process of reproducing; copy, facsimile; *a* **reproductive** pertaining to, used in, reproduction; fertile.

reprove *v* chide, rebuke; *n* **reproof.**

reptile *n* cold-blooded, air-breathing vertebrate, which crawls, as snake, lizard etc; (*fig*) sly person; *a* **reptilian.**

republic *n* State having no monarch & governed by representatives elected by people; *a* & *n* **republican.**

repudiate *v* reject; disown, disclaim; *n* **repudiation.**

repugnant *a* distasteful, offensive; inconsistent; *n* **repugnance** dislike, aversion; contradiction.

repulse *v* drive, beat back; (*fig*) snub, rebuff; *n* **repulsion** aversion; dislike, disgust; *a* **repulsive** loathsome; repellent.

repute *v* be generally thought or spoken of; *n* **esteem** good, bad name; *a* **reputable** of good repute; held in esteem; *n* **reputation** opinion commonly held of person or thing.

request *n* act of asking for something; petition; *v* ask for; demand politely.

requiem *n* dirge; R.C. mass for the dead.

require *v* ask, claim as right; command; need, want; *n* **requirement** need; condition, provision.

requisite *n* & *a* (something) needed, essential.

requisition *n* formal demand or request; *v* demand supply of.

reredos *n* ornamental screen at back of altar.

rescind *v* cancel; make void; *n* **rescission** act of rescinding.
rescue *v* save from danger, injury etc; *n* **rescuer.**
research *n* diligent search and investigation *esp* with view to gaining new knowledge etc; *n* **researcher.**
resemble *v* be like; have qualities, features in common with; *n* **resemblance.**
resent *v* feel and show displeasure, irritation at; regard as offensive; *n* **resentment**; *a* **resentful.**
reserve *v* keep, hold back; keep for specific person or use; order in advance; *n* that which is reserved; (*fig*) aloofness, self-restraint; part of army only called up in emergency; *n* **reservation** act of reserving; unexpressed doubt; tract of land reserved for use of natives, or for preservation of animals; *a* **reserved** not showing feelings.
reservoir *n* large storage tank or artificial lake for water supply of town etc; any receptacle holding liquids; (*fig*) reserve supply.
reside *v* dwell in permanently or for long time; *ns* **residence** abode, habitual dwelling; **residency** official residence of British Government agent in semi-dependent State; *a* & *n* **resident** (one) dwelling permanently in given place; *a* **residential** of part of town etc. mainly of residences.
residue *v* remainder, what is left; *as* **residual residuary.**
resign *v* give up or back; retire from office etc; abandon; (*reflex*) accept calmly; *n* **resignation** act of resigning office etc; submission to will of God; *a* **resigned** content to endure; uncomplaining.
resilient *a* capable of returning to original shape, state; *n* **resilience** elasticity; recuperative power.
resin *n* sticky substance secreted by most plants *esp* pines, firs.
resist *v* withstand; oppose; *n* **resistance** act of resistance; organized armed opposition by civilians in occupied country; (*elect*) opposition of conductor to flow of electricity; **passive r.** non-violent act done as protest against abuse etc; *as* **resistant**; **resistless** inevitable.
resolute *a* firm; steadfast; determined; *n* **resolution**

firm intention; vote or decision of public assembly or legislative body; analysis.

resolve *v* separate component parts of; make clear; decide, firmly intend; form by vote or resolution; *n* determination; firmness of purpose; *as* **resolvable** capable of being resolved; *n* & *a* **resolvent** (substance) that can disperse, dissolve.

resort *v* have recourse to; frequent; use as means; *n* frequently-visited place, *esp* for holidays etc; recourse.

resound *v* echo, ring with prolonged sound; (*fig*) (of deed, fame etc.) be widely known; *a* **resonant** echoing; sonorous; *n* **resonance**.

resource *n* inventiveness, skill in adapting things to one's purpose; (*pl*) means of support; stock that can be drawn on; *a* **resourceful**.

respect *v* pay heed to; hold in esteem; treat as binding; *n* attention; esteem; special aspect, point; reference; *a* **respectable** estimable; decent; moderate, passable; *n* **respectability**; *as* **respectful** deferential; **respective** of each in relation to each.

respire *v* breathe; *ns* **respiration**; **respirator** apparatus worn over mouth and nose to protect lungs from fumes, gas etc; *a* **respiratory** pertaining to breathing.

respite *n* temporary rest from work, effort, duty, pain etc; pause; reprieve.

resplendent *a* gorgeously bright, brilliant; magnificent, splendid; *n* **resplendence**.

respond *v* reply, make answer; act as result of another's action; react *usu* in good sense; *ns* **respondent** one who answers *esp* to lawsuit for divorce; **response** answer; reaction to stimulus; *a* **responsive** sympathetic: readily reacting to stimulus; *n* **responsiveness**.

responsible *a* legally, morally answerable for actions etc; capable of assuming responsibility; of good credit, repute etc; *n* **responsibility** moral obligation, liability; duty, charge; state of being answerable.

rest *n* cessation of activity or movement; repose; place of rest; support, prop; pause; take, give rest to; be supported; *as* **restful**; **restless**.*v*

rest *n* what is left; residue; others; *v* remain in (specified state or condition).
restaurant *n* place where meals can be bought and eaten; *n* **restaurateur** restaurant-keeper.
restitution *n* reparation; act of giving back something that has been taken or lost; *v* **restitute.**
restive *a* restless, fidgety; stubborn; impatient of control; *n* **restiveness.**
restore *v* bring back to former place, state etc; reinstate; renovate, repair; give back; *n* **restoration** act of restoring, *specif* **R.** of Charles II to his kingdom; *n* & *a* **restorative** (medicine, treatment) restoring health etc.
restrain *v* check, control; confine legally; *n* **restraint** control of emotions; limitation; confinement.
restrict *v* impose limits on; limit by law; *n* **restriction** limitation; law, regulation that restricts; *a* **restrictive** limiting.
result *v* happen, follow as consequence; have as natural effect; end (in); *n* consequence; outcome; (in games) final score; *a* **resultant** arising as result.
resume *v* assume, occupy again; begin again; summarize; *n* **resumé** summary; *n* **resumption** starting again; resuming.
resurge *v* rise again; *n* **resurgence;** *a* **resurgent.**
resurrection *n* rising again, *specif* **the R.** rising of Christ from the grave; *v* **resurrect** restore to life; resuscitate; use once more.
resuscitate *v* restore to life, consciousness, activity; *n* **resuscitation.**
retail *n* sale in small quantities to consumer; *a* concerned with such sale; *adv* by retail; *v* sell by retail; repeat (gossip, news etc); *n* **retailer.**
retain *v* hold; keep control of; engage services of; remember; *n* **retainer** fee to retain services of barrister; dependant, follower; *n* **retention;** *a* **retentive** able to, capable of retaining.
retaliate *v* pay back in kind; take vengeance; *n* **retaliation** return of like for like; reprisals; *a* **retaliatory.**
retard *v* delay, make slow or late; reduce speed or rate; *n* **retardation.**

retch *v* try to vomit, strain as in vomiting.
reticent *a* reserved in speech; uncommunicative; secretive; *n* **reticence.**
reticulate, reticulated *a* of, like network; *v* **reticulate** make, be like network; *n* **reticulation.**
retina *n* sensitive layer of nerve fibres at back of eye.
retinue *n* suite, train of retainers, attendants.
retire *v* withdraw; give up profession, occupation etc; go to bed; *a* **retired** private, secluded; having withdrawn from active life, business etc; *n* **retirement**; *a* **retiring** shy, unobtrusive.
retort *v* answer sharply; repay in kind; reply with counter-charge; *n* sharp, witty reply; glass vessel with long, bent neck used in chemistry, distilling etc.
retouch *v* touch up; add finishing touches to (photograph etc.).
retract *v* draw back; disavow, recant; *a* **retractable**; *ns* **retraction** recantation; **rectractor** muscle which draws back; surgical instrument.
retread *v* walk over or along again; put new tread on (tyre); *n* used tyre given new tread.
retreat *v* retire; move, cause to move backwards; *n* act of retreating; military signal to retire; secluded, quiet, private place.
retrench *v* cut down *specif* expenditure; curtail, lessen; *n* **retrenchment.**
retribution *n* punishment for evil deeds; fitting recompense.
retrieve *v* search for & fetch; regain; make good; atone; *ns* **retrieval; retriever** kind of dog trained to retrieve shot game; *a* **retrievable.**
retro- *prefix* backwards in place, time etc.
retrocession *n* act of yielding, granting back; movement backwards; *v* **retrocede** more backwards; retire; *a* **retrocessive.**
retrograde *a* moving, going backwards; deteriorating; *n* **retrogression.**
retrospect *n* mental review of past; *a* **retrospective** referring to past; *n* **retrospection.**
retroussé *a* (of nose) turned up at end.
return *v* give, come, send back; report officially; elect (M.P.); *n* act of returning; profit; renewal.

rev *n* (*coll abbrev*) revolution (of engine); *v* **r. up** speed up, increase revolutions per minute.
reveal *v* make known or visible; divulge; *n* **revelation**.
reveillé *n* signal sounded by bugle at sunrise.
revel *v* feast, carouse; enjoy thoroughly; *n pl* rejoicing, merrymaking; *ns* **reveller**; **revelry** unrestrained merrymaking.
revenant *n* ghost, apparition.
revenge *v* avenge; make retaliation for; *n* vindictiveness; vengeance; (sport, cards etc.) return game; *a* **revengeful**.
revenue *n* total income, *esp* of State; **Inland R.** government department dealing with collection of national revenue.
reverberate *v* echo, resound; throw back, reflect (sound etc); *n* **reverberation**
revere *v* venerate; regard with great or religious respect; *n* **reverence** feeling of awe and admiration; deference; *a* **reverend** worthy to be revered; *esp* as mode of address to clergyman; *a* **reverential** caused, marked by reverence.
reverie *n* day-dream, dreamy contemplation; musical composition reflecting this state of mind.
revers *n* lapel; part of garment turned back.
reverse *v* turn upside down; cause to go backwards; cancel, annul; *n* what is contrary, opposite; less important side; set-back; defeat; financial loss; *a* contrary, opposite; *ns* **reversal** act of reversing; state of being reversed; **reversion** (*leg*) return of estate to grantor or his heirs at expiry of grant; (*biol*) return to ancestral type; *a* **reversionary** (*leg*) of, pertaining to reversion; *n* **reverse gear** mechanism causing backward motion.
revert *v* pass back legally to grantor; refer to again; return to former state; go back to more primitive or ancestral, type.
revet *v* cover, face (surface) with stone etc. to strengthen; *n* **revetment** protective covering.
review *v* recall to mind in detail; inspect formally, officially; write critical notice of book etc; *n* revision; formal inspection *esp* of armed forces; written

criticism of book etc; periodical with critical articles and discussion of current events; *n* **reviewer**.

revile *v* abuse; bitterly reproach; *n* **reviler**.

revise *v* look over and amend; *n* **revision** act of revising; something that has been revised.

revive *v* come, bring back to life, consciousness, health etc; *ns* **revival**; rebirth, *esp* of religious fervour; **revivalist** organizer of or preacher at revival meeting.

revoke *v* annul; (of cards) fail to follow suit, although possible to do so; *a* **revocable**; *n* **revocation** act of revoking *esp* (law) repeal, annulment.

revolt *v* rebel; feel nauseated by; disgust; *n* rebellion; *a* **revolting** repulsive, disgusting; *n* **revulsion** marked repugnance.

revolve *v* go round, rotate; move, occur, in cycles; *n* **revolution** complete rotation or turning round; complete overthrow of political system; *a* **revolutionary** of, causing, radical change of outlook, methods etc; *n* person taking part in revolution; *v* **revolutionize** make fundamental changes in.

revolver *n* pistol with revolving magazine; that which revolves.

revue *n* theatrical entertainment, with songs, sketches, dancing etc.

reward *v* repay, recompense for service, conduct etc; *n* that which is given in return for goods received, or for return of lost articles etc.

rhapsody *n* highly emotional, enthusiastic utterance; emotional musical composition; *v* **r. over** express enthusiastic delight in.

rheostat *n* instrument for regulating value or resistance in electrical circuit.

rhesus *n* small long-tailed money; **R. factor** substance found in blood of many human-beings.

rhetoric *n* art of oratory; flowery, high-sounding language; *a* **rhetorical**.

rheum *n* discharge from mucous membrane of mouth, nose etc; nasal catarrh; *a* **rheumy**.

rheumatism *n* name of various diseases attended with painful inflammation of joints and muscles; *as* **rheumatic; rheumatoid** of, like rheumatism.

rhinoceros *n* large, thick-skinned, tropical quadruped, with one or two horns on nose.
rhodium *n* hard, greyish-white metal resembling platinum.
rhododendron *n* evergreen, flowering shrub.
rhombus *n* equilateral parallelogram with two acute and two obtuse angles; *a* **rhomboid.**
rhubarb *n* perennial garden herb, with thick pink stalks which are cooked and eaten as fruit; (*sl*) nonsense; squabble.
rhyme, rime *n* close similarity of sound in words or final syllables, *esp* at ends of lines of verse; *v* make rhymes.
rhythm *n* regular increase and decrease of sounds, movements; pleasant rise and fall *esp* of words, musical sounds; *a* **rhythmic(al).**
rib *n* one of bones curving forward from spine, and enclosing thorax, curved timber or framework of boat; *v* furnish with ribs; (*sl*) tease.
ribald *a* coarse, irreverent; scurrilous; *n* **ribaldry** coarse, indecent joking.
ribbon, riband *n* narrow woven strip of silk, satin etc; (*fig*) long, narrow strip; *n* **r. development** act of building single row of houses, factories etc. along each side of main road.
rice *n* cereal plant grown on marshy or flooded ground in tropical climates; seeds of this plant used as food; *n* **rice-paper** edible paper used for packing sweets etc.
rich *a* wealthy; abundant; costly; (of food) very fatty, sweet or highly seasoned; (of colours, sound) full, deep intense; *n* (*collect*) wealthy people; *n pl* **riches** wealth; abundance.
rick *n* stack of corn, hay, thatched for storing in open.
rickets *n* deficiency disease of children, marked by deformation of bones; *a* **rickety** suffering from rickets; shaky, tottering.
rickshaw *n* light, two-wheeled, Oriental carriage drawn by man.
ricochet *n* rebounding of projectile or other object from flat surface; *v* rebound; cause to glance off surface.

rid *v* free, deliver from; clear away; *pt* & *pp* **rid**; *n* **riddance** act of getting rid; **good r.** welcome relief from unwelcome, unwanted person or thing.

riddle *n* enigma; puzzling question *esp* with pun; puzzling thing or person.

riddle *n* large meshed sieve; *v* sift by means of riddle; make many holes in; **riddled with** seriously damaged by.

ride *v* go on horseback; travel in, be carried by any vehicle; (of ship) float, lie at anchor; (*coll*) exasperate by continual criticism; *pt* **rode**; *pp* **ridden**; *n* journey on horseback, or in any vehicle; track for horse-riding; *n* **rider** one who rides; supplementary clause to document or verdict; *as* **riderless**; **riding** used for riding.

ridge *n* long raised strip; elongated summit of mountain, etc; line where two slopes of roof meet; elevated part between furrows; *v* form ridges.

ridiculous *a* absurd; preposterous, foolish; *v* **ridicule** make fun of; deride; *n* mockery, derision.

Riding *n* one of three administrative divisions of Yorkshire.

rife *a* prevalent; frequent, common.

riffraff *n* rabble; worthless people.

rifle *v* search and rob; furnish gun barrel with spiral grooves; *n* type of firearm; *n* **rifling** spiral grooves in gun barrel; plundering.

rift *n* opening, cleft, rent, split.

rig *v* (of ship) fit out with spars, ropes etc; **r. out** equip with clothes; **r. up** arrange hastily, *esp* in makeshift way; *n* way ship's masts and sails are arranged; style of dress; *n* **rigging** complete system of ship's ropes, sails, spars etc.

rig *v* manipulate dishonestly; arrange by underhand means; *n* dishonest dealing (also **rigging**).

right *a* straight, direct; proper, correct; towards east when thing, person faces north; opposite of left; morally good, desirable; in politics, Conservative; true; *v* put right; win justice for; put in correct position; *n* opposite side from left; outer, more finished side of fabric; *n* **r. angle** angle of 90°; *a* **rightful** based on justice; having just claim; *n* **right-of-way**

public right of free passage over roads, fields etc; *a* **righteous** upright, virtuous; *n* **righteousness.**

rigid *a* stiff, inflexible; stern, severe; *n* **rigidity.**

rigmarole *n* long, rambling, incoherent string of words.

rigor *n* shivering, with sense of chill; **r. mortis** stiffening of body after death.

rigour *n* severity; inflexibility; austerity; harshness; *a* **rigorous.**

rile *v* make angry; annoy, irritate.

rill *n* small stream.

rim *n* edge, margin, brim; outer part of wheel.

rime *n* hoar-frost; *a* **rimy.**

rind *n* peel, bark, crust; tough outer layer of bacon, cheese.

ring *n* line enclosing round space; flat circular object with large hole in middle; hoop of gold, silver etc. for finger; area within roped square for boxing etc; coil; *v* put ring around; put identifying ring or tag on (bird's leg etc); *ns* **ringlet** curl of hair; **ringleader** leader, organizer of riot etc; **ringworm** skin disease with circular eruptions, usually on scalp.

ring *v* give our loud, clear, resonant sound, as bell; cause (bell) to sound; *pt* **rang**; *pp* **rung**; *n* sound of ringing; telephone call; *vs* **ring up** telephone to; raise curtain in theatre; **r. off** end telephone call.

rink *n* sheet of ice for skating or curling; floor for roller skating; one of divisions of bowling green.

rinse *v* wash in clean water; *n* act of rinsing; hair-dye.

riot *n* disturbance of public peace; tumult; (*fig*) unrestrained profusion; noisy behaviour; *v* take part in riot; revel in; *a* **riotous** unrestrained; turbulent; dissipated; luxuriant.

rip *v* cut, slit; slash, tear with violence; *n* rent, tear; *ns* **rip-cord** cord to open parachute; **rip-tide** tide causing violent currents.

rip *n* worn-out, useless horse; reprobate.

riparian *a* of, pertaining to river bank.

ripe *a* ready to harvest as food etc; fully matured, developed; ready for specific use; *v* **ripen** grow, become ripe; mature.

riposte *n* quick return lunge or thrust in fencing; (*fig*) quick retort.
ripple *v* flow in, form, small slight waves; *n* slight wave; light, soft sound; ruffling of surface.
ripsaw *n* hand-saw with coarse, narrow-set teeth.
rise *v* ascend; stand up; get up; increase in value, price; appear above horizon (of sun, moon etc); *pt* **rose**; *pp* **risen**; *n* increase in amount, volume, intensity etc; upward slope; *n* **riser** upright face of step, between two treads; person or thing that rises.
risible *a* capable of laughing; tending to laugh; *n* **risibility**.
risk *n* possibility, likelihood of danger; amount covered by insurance; *v* expose to danger; venture, hazard; face result of; *a* **risky** dangerous, hazardous.
risqué *a* verging on, tending towards impropriety.
rissole *n* ball, cake of minced meat, fish etc. fried in egg and breadcrumbs.
rite *n* solemn act *usu* religious ceremony; *a* **ritual** of rites; *n* system of religious or magical ceremonies; book of prescribed ceremonies; *n* **ritualism** practice of, and insistence on, ritual.
rival *n* one who competes against another for success, favour etc; *v* vie with, equal, be comparable to; *n* **rivalry** close approach to equality in merit etc; keen competition.
rive *v* split, tear apart; *pt* **rived**; *pp* **riven**.
river *n* large body of water flowing in natural channel to sea; plentiful flow.
rivet *n* bolt or pin for fastening metal plates; *v* fasten with rivets; (*fig*) hold attention of; *n* **riveter**.
rivulet *n* small stream, brook.
roach *n* freshwater fish.
road *n* track with surface prepared for use by vehicles, *esp* as means of communication between places; highway; direction, route; (*fig*) mode, line of action by which aim is attained; *ns* **r.-hog** selfish reckless motorist; **r.-house** country inn or restaurant on main road; **r. sense** ability to use road carefully and safely; **roadstead, roads** piece of water near shore where ships may ride in safety; **roadster** horse or bicycle suited for road; touring car.

roam *v* wander; ramble aimlessly.
roan *n* & *a* (horse, dog) of bay, sorrel, chestnut mingled with white, grey; of mixed reddish colour.
roar *n* loud, deep, resonant sound; bellow; burst of laughter; *v* make such sound.
roast *v* cook in hot oven, bake; make, be very hot; *n* roasted joint of meat etc; *n* **roaster** animal, bird suitable for roasting.
rob *v* steal; plunder; deprive of unlawfully; *ns* **robber; robbery.**
robe *n* long, loose outer garment; (*esp* in *pl*) official, ceremonial dress; *v* dress; put on robe.
robin *n* small, brown, singing bird with red breast.
robot *n* mechanical man; (*fig*) one who works mechanically, with unthinking efficiency.
robust *a* strong, sound, healthy, vigorous; *n* **robustness.**
roc *n* large, fabulous Arabian bird.
rock *n* mass of hard mineral matter; crag, boulder; hard sweetmeat; *n* **rockery** mound of earth and rocks, where alpine plants are grown; *a* **rocky** full of, made of, rocks; (*fig*) firm, rugged.
rock *v* sway, move from side to side; shake violently; *n* **rocker** curved support of cradle, rocking-chair; (*sl*) tough, rowdy youth; *n* **rock (-n'-roll)** form of jazz; dance in this rhythm.
rocket *n* projectile driven through space by explosion produced in it; large jet-powered missile; explosive firework, used for signalling, display or carrying life-line; *v* rise straight upwards; (*fig*) increase sharply (in price etc.).
rococo *a* (of furniture, architecture) florid; flamboyantly ornamented in style of 17th. & 18th. century; *n* this style.
rod *n* slender piece of wood; long, light, pole of metal; wood etc; wand; cane; (*fig*) corporal punishment, measure of length, 5½ yds.
rodent *a* gnawing; *n* gnawing animal, as rat.
rodeo *n* rounding-up of cattle on ranch; display of skill in rounding up cattle.
roe *n* small species of deer.
roe *n* mass of fish eggs.

Rogation days *n* three days preceding Ascension Day.
rogue *n* scoundrel, rascal; criminal, dishonest person; mischievous child or person; savage, wild beast, living apart from herd; *a* **roguish** arch; mischievous; *n* **roguery**.
roister *v* swagger; behave boisterously.
role *n* part played by actor; specific function or action.
roll *v* move round & round; turn like wheel; (of ship) wallow; form into ball or cylinder; pass roller over something to flatten it; wrap round on itself; *n* packet, bundle formed by folding into cylindrical shape; small rounded loaf, bun, rissole; cylindrical mass; list of names; swaying motion; *ns* **roll-call** act of calling over list of names; **roller** cylinder of wood, metal etc. revolving on axis, used for crushing, smoothing, pressing etc; long swelling wave; **roller-skate** skate with wheels; **rolling-pin** roller for pastry etc; **rolling-stock** locomotives, carriages etc collectively.
rollicking *a* boisterously jovial.
Roman *a* of Rome, or Church of Rome; *n* **Roman Catholic** member of Christian Church of which Pope is head; *n* **Roman type** ordinary style used in printing.
romance *n* sentimental, adventurous novel; happy love-affair; medieval tale of chivalry; glamorous charm, atmosphere; *v* invent fanciful stories, exaggerate.
romantic *a* connected with romance; (of literature etc) seeking to rouse personal feelings, expressing sentiment and imaginative episodes etc; glamorous; emotional; *v* **romanticise** make seem romantic; have romantic ideas.
romany *n* gipsy; gipsy language.
romp *v* play noisily; **romp home** (*coll*) win race easily; *n* wild, noisy game.
rondo *n* musical composition with principal theme repeated after each subordinate one.
röntgen rays *n pl* X-rays.
rood *n* crucifix *esp* one over junction of nave and

choir; **r. screen** one separating nave from chancel.
rood *n* measure of land, ¼ acre.
roof *n* outer covering over top of building; **roof of mouth** palate; *v* put roof on.
rook *n* bird of crow family; *v* cheat, swindle; *n* **rookery** colony of rooks; (*fig*) crowded tenement building.
rook *n* piece at chess, castle.
room *n* space; separate apartment in a building; scope, opportunity; *pl* lodgings; *a* **roomy** large, spacious.
roost *n* perch for birds at night; *v* sleep on perch; *n* **rooster** domestic cock.
root *n* source, origin; downward-growing part of plant; essential element; basic element of word; factor of quantity which gives that quantity when multiplied by itself; *v* implant roots firmly; be firmly established, *esp* by development of roots; **r. out** uproot; (*fig*) eradicate; have basis in.
rope *n* thick cord; *v* secure, tie up, with rope; *a* **ropy** (of liquid) sticky, forming glutinous threads; *n* **ropiness.**
Roquefort *n* French cheese of goats' and ewes' milk.
rose *n* any of genus Rosa; flower of this; perforated nozzle; pinkish colour; method of cutting gems; *n* **rosary** rose-garden; string of beads used by R.C.s to count prayers; *a* **roseate** rose-coloured; *n* **rosette** rose-shaped bunch of ribbon etc; **-wood** dark-coloured fragrant wood used in cabinetmaking; *a* **rosy** flushed; optimistic; favourable.
rosemary *n* evergreen fragrant flowering bush.
rosin *n* resin.
roster *n* list showing rotation of duty etc; list of names.
rostrum *n* platform, pulpit.
rot *v* decompose naturally; *n* decay; fungus disease of timber, plants, etc; (*coll*) nonsense; *a* **rotten** decomposed; (*coll*) deplorably bad; unwell.
rota *n* roster; round of duties; tribunal in R.C. Church.
rotary *a* turning like wheel; *v* **rotate** revolve round axis; follow regular succession; *n* **rotation** act of

rotating; recurrence; *a* **rotatory;** *ns* **Rotary Club** one of international association of business men's clubs; **Rotarian** member of such; **rotary engine** one turning like wheel.

rote *n* **by rote** by heart, from memory.

rotor *n* revolving part of dynamo, etc.

rotund *a* round, plump; *n* **rotundity.**

rouble *n* Russian coin.

roué *n* dissolute person; rake.

rouge *n* red cosmetic used to colour cheeks and lips; silver polish; *v* colour with rouge.

rough *a* shaggy, rugged; not smooth, even or glossy; stormy, boisterous; rude, lacking refinement; not precise, approximately; *v* make rough; draft in outline; *n* rough part of anything; incomplete state; hooligan; *v* **roughen** make, become rough; *ns* **rough-house** (*sl*) boisterous fight; **roughage** coarse, bulky food that promotes proper bowel action.

roulette *n* game of chance, played with revolving wheel and ball.

round *a* spherical, circular, curved; approximate; plump; blunt, outspoken; *n* circle, ring; thing round in shape; fixed circuit; type of song; complete slice of bread as in sandwich; single shot from rifle; series of actions, duties etc; game (of golf); single bout (in boxing etc); *prep* about, on all sides of; *a* **roundabout** indirect; *n* merry-go-round; circular obstacle at cross-roads, causing one-way traffic flow; **Roundhead** supporter of Parliament in Civil War; *adv* **roundly** bluntly; vigorously; *n pl* **rounders** ball-game; *v* **round up** collect forcibly; gather cattle for branding.

rouse *v* wake up; cause to rise; stimulate; excite to action.

rout *n* rabble, mob; overwhelming defeat; *v* defeat, put to flight; drag out by force.

route *n* road, way; (*mil*) order to march; plan way for.

routine *n* customary actions; regular procedure; boringly automatic procedure.

rove *v* wander at random; *n* **rover** one who wanders.

row *n* number of things or persons in straight line.

row *v* propel (boat) by oars; transport by rowing; *n* act of rowing; trip in rowing boat.
row *n* disturbance; dispute, quarrel; *v* quarrel, brawl.
rowan *n* mountain ash (tree).
rowdy *a* disorderly, noisy rough; *n* hooligan.
rowel *n* small spiked wheel on spur.
rowlock *n* forked support in boat serving as leverage for oar.
royal *a* of, pertaining to, patronized by, king or queen; majestic; *ns* **royalist** supporter of monarchy; **royalty** state of being royal; royal persons collectively; percentage paid to author by publisher; payment to owner of land for right to exploit it; or to inventor for use of his invention.
rub *v* apply friction to; abrade, make sore; become frayed, worn by friction; *n* **rubber** one who rubs; india-rubber; eraser; thing for rubbing.
rubber *n* series of odd number of games; two out of three games won.
rubbish *n* refuse, waste material; nonsense; *a* **rubbishy** valueless.
rubble *n* broken, crushed pieces of stone; builders' rubbish.
rubicund *a* reddish, ruddy.
rubric *n* instruction, chapter-heading printed, written distinctively *esp* in red; liturgical direction.
ruby *n* deep red, transparent, precious stone; its colour; *a* of this colour.
ruche *n* pleated trimming for dress etc.
ruck *n* irregular fold, crease; *v* crease, wrinkle.
rucksack *n* bag, knapsack strapped on back.
rudd *n* fresh water fish, red eye.
rudder *n* steering device at stern of boat, or tail of aircraft.
ruddy *a* of fresh, red colour; rosy.
rude *a* primitive; rough, crude; uncivil; insulting.
rudiment *n* beginning; first principle; slight trace, vestige; *a* **rudimentary** in undeveloped, unformed state; vestigial.
rue *n* small, perennial herb with bitter leaves.
rue *v* grieve for, regret; repent of; *a* **rueful** sorry; dejected.

ruff *n* starched frilled collar; bird allied to sandpiper, *fem* **reeve**; *n* **ruffle** gathered or pleated frill; *v* wrinkle; (*fig*) upset temper of.
ruff *v* to trump at cards; *n* act of trumping.
ruffian *n* rough, violent, lawless person; bully.
rug *n* thick, woollen wrap; coverlet; floor-mat *esp* with long pile.
rugby *n* form of football, played with oval ball which may be carried in hands; (*coll*) **rugger.**
rugged *a* rough; harsh; ill-finished.
ruin *n* state of decay, collapse; destruction; cause of ruin; (*pl*) remains of buildings etc; *v* reduce to ruins; spoil; impoverish; *n* **ruination**; *a* **ruinous** tending to cause financial ruin; wasteful; likely to cause destruction.
rule *n* principle, line of conduct; government; regulations of society, game etc; custom; graduated metal or wooden bar for measuring; *v* govern; give judicial decision; draw straight lines; *n* **ruler** governor, sovereign; instrument of wood etc. for measuring, or drawing straight lines.
rum *a* (*sl*) odd, peculiar, queer.
rum *n* alcoholic spirit distilled from sugar-cane.
rumba, rhumba *n* dance of Cuban origin.
rumble *v* make low, continuous, rolling noise, as of thunder, or heavy cart etc; *n* such noise.
ruminate *v* chew cud; (*fig*) meditate, think deeply over; *ns* **rumination** act of chewing cud; (*fig*) deep thought; **ruminant** animal which chews cud; *a* thoughtful.
rummage *v* grope about, turn over roughly; search thoroughly; *n* ransacking; jumble.
rummy *n* card-game.
rumour *n* gossip, hearsay; story, statement without basis.
rump *n* buttocks; (*fig*) last, inferior part.
rumple *v* crease, wrinkle; crush.
rumpus *n* noisy disturbance, confusion.
run *v* move along on foot, more swiftly than walking; flee; compete in race; flow; melt; cross by running; manage; *pt* **ran**; *pp* **run**; *n* act of running; rush; course, tendency; motor-car, bicycle trip; *v* **r. down**

disparage; stop working; *ns* **runway** prepared track for aircraft landing and taking off; **runner** one who runs; slender stem of plant, which puts out roots; blade of skate or sledge; *a* **running** flowing; entered for race; continuous; **in the r.** having chance of success.

rune *n* angular character of Teutonic alphabet; magic sign.

rung *n* cross-bar of ladder, or chair.

runnel *n* gutter; small rivulet.

runt *n* stunted animal; undersized person.

rupee *n* Indian coin.

rupture *n* breaking; split; hernia; *v* burst, break; produce hernia.

rural *a* of country; rustic.

ruse *n* stratagem, trick.

rush *n* aquatic herb, stems of which are used for basket-making etc.

rush *v* move with violent rapidity; take by storm; enter hastily; *n* impetuous forward movement; sudden increase; eagerness to obtain.

rusk *n* piece of crisp baked bread or biscuit.

russet *a* of reddish-brown; *n* this colour; homespun fabric; kind of apple.

rust *n* reddish-brown coating produced on iron etc. by oxidation; disease of plants, caused by fungus.

rustic *a* of country life or people; rural; unsophisticated; *n* **rusticity**; *v* **rusticate** send down temporarily from University; live country life; *n* **rustication.**

rustle *v* emit soft, crisp, whispering sound, as of dry leaves etc; *n* this sound.

rut *n* sexual excitement *esp* of deer; *v* be affected with rut.

rut *n* groove, wheel-track; (*fig*) settled habit.

ruthless *a* pitiless, merciless, cruel.

rye *n* cereal plant, grain used for fodder, and bread; **rye whisky** distilled from rye grains; *n* **rye-grass** grass grown for fodder.

Sabbath *n* day of rest and worship, observed by Jews on Saturday and Christians on Sunday; *ns* **Sabba-**

tarian strict observer of Sunday; **sabbatical year** one allowed to some university teachers, as working holiday; *a* **sabbatical** of or like Sabbath.
sable *n* small Arctic carnivore, having valuable dark brown fur; *a* black.
sabot *n* wooden shoe.
sabotage *n* deliberate damage to industrial plant, materials etc by strikers or spies; *n* **saboteur.**
sabre *n* curved cavalry sword.
sac *n* membraneous bog or pouch in animal or vegetable body.
saccharin(e) *n* very sweet white substance from coal-tar; (*fig*) *a* too sweet, sentimental.
sacerdotal *a* priestly.
sachet *n* small soft bag for holding handkerchiefs or scented powder etc.
sack *n* large, narrow bag of coarse fabric; (*coll*) dismissal; loose waistless dress; *v* loot; pillage (captured town); (*coll*) dismiss; *ns* **sackcloth, sacking** coarse textile fabric used for sacks.
sack *n* dry, white wine.
sackbut *n* old musical instrument.
sacrament *n* one of solemn religious ceremonies of Christian Church *esp* Eucharist; any sacred, solemn obligation; *a* **sacramental.**
sacred *a* holy, dedicated to God, a god; set apart; inviolable.
sacrifice *n* making offering to God or deity; thing offered; giving up (something valued) for sake of someone else; *v* offer as sacrifice; give up (something valued); *a* **sacrificial.**
sacrilege *n* violation of something sacred; *a* **sacrilegious** profane.
sacristan *n* official in charge of sacred vessels and vestments; sexton.
sacrum *n* bone at lower end of spine, formed by five fused vertebrae.
sad *a* sorrowful; mournful; lamentable; *v* **sadden** make sad; *n* **sadness.**
saddle *n* rider's seat on horse, bicycle etc; part of animal's back; mountain ridge; joint of mutton or venison; *v* put saddle on; (*coll*) place burden on; *ns*

saddler maker of saddles; **saddlery** trade, shop of goods sold by saddler.
sadism *n* sexual perversion marked by cruelty; love of inflicting pain; *n* **sadist**; *a* **sadistic.**
safari *n* hunting or shooting expedition.
safe *a* free from danger; uninjured; involving no risk; not reckless; trustworthy; likely, certain to occur; *n* strong box; cool store-cupboard; *ns* **safety** quality, state of being safe; **safe-conduct** document, etc, ensuring safe passage through hostile territory; **safeguard** defence; proviso; **safety-valve** automatic valve to prevent explosion; (*fig*) any outlet as relief for emotion etc.
saffron *n* variety of orange-yellow crocus; dye and flavouring substance from this; *a* of this colour.
sag *v* sink, droop downwards in middle; buckle; (*fig*) become low-spirited; (*fig*) (of prices) drop in value.
saga *n* ancient Norse prose epic; long novel or series about family or group; romantic tale of adventure and heroism.
sagacious *a* shrewd, keenly intelligent; *n* **sagacity** sound judgement; quality resembling reason in lower animals.
sage *a* wise; serious, characterized by sagacity; *n* person of great wisdom.
sage *n* shrubby aromatic herb, used in cooking.
sago *n* edible starchy pith of certain Malayan palms.
sahib *n* title of respect in India; member of former British ruling class in India.
sail *n* piece of canvas etc arranged to catch wind, to drive ship; *esp* sailing vessel; voyage on ship; various sail-like objects (*eg* revolving part of windmill etc); *v* travel across water; start sea trip; navigate; *n* **sailor** mariner; seaman below rank of petty officer; **bad (good) s.** person (not) liable to be seasick.
saint *n* one recognised and venerated as holy etc by Christian Church; title of canonized person; *a* **sainted** venerated, regarded as saint; *n* **saintliness** piety, holiness of life.
sake *n* cause, behalf; aim, purpose; in order to secure; **for the s. of** in order to please, benefit, obtain.
saké *n* Japanese drink made from fermented rice.

salaam *n* ceremonial bow; Eastern mode of greeting; *v* make salaam.
salacious *a* lewd, lecherous; *n* **salacity.**
salad *n* dish of raw, or cold cooked vegetables or fruit; lettuce; **s. days** age of youth and immaturity.
salamander *n* lizard-like amphibian, supposed to be able to live in fire.
salame *n* highly seasoned Italian sausage.
salary *n* fixed payment for work (*usu* non-manual) made at regular intervals of month or more; *a* **salaried.**
sale *n* act of selling; auction; offering of goods for sale *esp* at reduced prices; *ns* **salesman** one engaged in selling; **salesmanship** business skill of salesman.
Salic law *n* law forbidding succession of women to crown.
salient *a* projecting; prominent, *n* body of troops projecting from main line.
saline *n* metallic, alkaline salt; *n* **salinity** saltness.
saliva *n* fluid secreted in mouth to aid digestion; *a* **salivary.**
sallow *n* species of willow.
sallow *a* having sickly, yellow colour.
sally *n* sudden rush out, *esp* from fortress etc; (*fig*) witty remark; *v* rush out; go out of doors.
salmon *n* large edible silvery fish, with pink flesh; *n* **salmon-trout** sea-trout.
salon *n* reception room; private reception of people notable in the arts; annual exhibition of pictures.
saloon *n* large reception room; main cabin in passenger ship; more expensive bar in public house; public room for specific use (*eg* hairdressing, billiards etc); closed car without partition between driver and passengers.
salt *n* chemical substance (sodium chloride) used to season and preserve food; any of compounds formed by replacing hydrogen of acid, by metal; wit, pungency; *n* **old s.** sailor; *a* preserved with, tasting of, salt; **with a pinch of s.** with reserve or disbelief; *a* **salty** salt-tasting; *ns* **salt-cellar** small receptacle for salt at table; **saltpetre** potassium nitrate.
saltire, saltier *n* (*her*) diagonal cross.

salubrious *a* healthy, beneficial; promoting health.
saluki *n* gazelle hound.
salutary *a* wholesome; having good effect.
salute *v* greet, acknowledge by words or customary gesture; perform military salute; *n* greeting; (*mil*) formal gesture made by hand to superior; *n* **salutation** act of saluting, usually by spoken or written words.
salvage *n* saving, rescue of ship, cargo etc from shipwreck, fire etc; reward for this act; ship, cargo etc, so saved; saving goods from fire etc; property so rescued; saving and utilization of waste material; *v* save from shipwreck, fire, destruction.
salvation *n* fact or state of being saved.
salve *n* healing, soothing ointment.
salver *n* flat tray for presenting letters, visiting cards etc.
salvo *n* discharge of artillery etc.
sal-volatile *n* alcoholic aromatic preparation of ammonia.
Samaritan *n* inhabitant of Samaria; helpful, charitable person.
samba *n* dance of Brazilian origin.
sambo *n* child of negro and mulatto; (*coll*) Negro.
same *a* identical; unchanged; aforesaid; monotonous; **all the same** after all, nevertheless; *n* **sameness.**
samite *n* (*ar*) fine, thick, silk material.
samovar *n* Russian tea-urn.
sampan *n* light, flat-bottomed Chinese river boat.
sample *n* specimen, example; *v* test quality of, take, sample; *n* **sampler** piece of embroidery, needlework.
samurai *n* member of extinct class of Japanese warriors.
sanatorium *n* hospital, *esp* one for treatment of tuberculosis; *pl* **sanatoria.**
sanctify *v* purify from sin; regard as holy; *ns* **sanctity** saintliness; inviolability.
sanctimonious *a* making outward show of piety; *n* **sanctimoniousness** hypocritical piety.
sanction *n* authorization, consent; measure taken to compel nation to obey international law; justification; *v* permit, allow, approve.

sanctuary *n* holy place; place of refuge for fugitives from justice; *n* **sanctum** any private or inviolate retreat.

sand *n* fine, dry, gritty substance; mass of this found on seashore and in deserts etc; *pl* stretches of sand; *v* cover with sand; *a* **sandy** containing, covered with, sand; *ns* **sandstone** porous rock of compacted sand; **sandbag** sack filled with sand; **sandman** imaginary being who makes children sleepy; **sand-martin** small swallow which nests in sandy cliffs etc; **sandpaper** paper encrusted with sand and used to smooth wood etc.

sandal *n* open shoe consisting of sole secured by straps.

sandalwood *n* hard, yellowish sweet-scented wood of E. Indian tree.

sandwich *n* two slices of bread with meat, cheese or other filling between them; *v* insert between two other things; squeeze in; **s. boards** advertising boards hung on **s. man** who carries them about the street etc.

sane *a* sound in mind, mentally normal; sensible, rational; *n* **sanity**.

sang-froid *n* coolness, presence of mind; composure.

sanguine *a* ruddy, florid; hopeful, optimistic; *a* **sanguinary** accompanied by bloodshed; bloody; bloodthirsty; *adv* **sanguinely** hopefully, confidently.

sanitary *a* hygienic; having to do with health and cleanliness; *n* **sanitation** public hygiene; system of drainage, disposal of sewage, ventilation and pure water supply.

Sanskrit, Sanscrit *n* ancient language of Hindus.

sap *n* juice, fluid circulating in plant tissue; (*fig*) vigour, vitality; *v* (*fig*) weaken, drain-away strength of.

sap *n* (*mil*) covered trench; *v* (*mil*) construct these; undermine; *n* **sapper** (*specif*) member of Royal Engineers.

sapient *a* wise; shrewd; knowing; *n* **sapience**.

saponaceous *a* containing soap, soapy; (*fig*) unctuous.

Sapphic *a* of Sappho, Greek poetess; kind of verse.
sapphire *n* deep blue translucent precious stone.
sarcasm *n* bitter, ironic remark; sneer; mocking taunt, intended to wound; *a* **sarcastic.**
sarcophagus *n* large coffin, usually of stone, used in ancient Egypt.
sard *n* semi-precious stone, variety of chalcedony.
sardine *n* small fish of herring family, usually preserved in oil; **packed like s.** packed close together.
sardonic *a* bitter, sneering; insincere.
sardonyx *n* semi-precious stone of layers of red sard and white chalcedony.
sargasso *n* species of sea-weed, found floating in Sargasso Sea.
sari, saree *n* robe worn by Hindu women.
sarong *n* principal garment of Malay men and women.
sarsaparilla *n* species of smilax; its dried root used medicinally.
sarsen *n* large block of hard sandstone, as used in Stonehenge.
sartorial *a* pertaining to trade and work of tailor.
sash *n* ornamental scarf worn over shoulder, or round waist.
sash *n* one of two sliding frames holding glass of window.
Satan *n* the Devil; *a* **satanic(al)** fiendish, malignant, wicked.
sate *v* satisfy; gratify to the full; glut surfeit.
sateen *n* glossy, imitation satin, cotton fabric.
satellite *n* hanger-on; planet revolving round another; projectile in orbit round the earth.
satiate *v* satisfy; dull; cloy by over-indulgence; *ns* **satiety** feeling of having had too much; **satiation.**
satin *n* soft silk fabric with glossy surface; *n* **satinwood** fine, hard yellowish wood used in cabinet-making.
satire *n* holding up of human follies, vices to ridicule; literary work of this nature; bitter contempt, sarcasm directed against faults, hypocrisies of society in general; *a* **satiric(al)**; *n* **satirist** writer of satires; *v* **satirize** make object of satire.

satisfy *v* gratify; suffice for; comply with discharge (debt); set doubts at rest; *n* **satisfaction**; *a* **satisfactory.**
saturate *v* soak thoroughly; (*chem*) cause substance to combine completely; (*fig*) be steeped in, affected by; *n* **saturation** act, result of saturating; **s. point** stage at which greatest possible amount of something has been absorbed.
Saturday *n* seventh day of week.
Saturn *n* Roman god; large planet surrounded by rings; *a* **saturnine** gloomy, glowering, morose; *n* **saturnalia** revelry; orgy.
satyr *n* woodland deity (half beast, half man); lecherous man.
sauce *n* spiced or flavoured liquid used to add to taste of food; gravy; (*coll*) impudence; *ns* **saucepan** cooking pot; **sauce-boat** small vessel for serving sauce at table; *a* **saucy** impudent.
sauerkraut *n* chopped raw cabbage fermented in brine.
saunter *v* walk slowly, stroll; *n* leisurely walk.
saurian *n* member of group of extinct reptiles.
sausage *n* minced, seasoned meat packed into skin or thin membrane.
sauté *a* lightly, quickly fried.
Sauterne *n* light, sweet white French wine.
savage *a* wild, uncivilized; fierce, cruel, brutal; *v* bite and worry ferociously; *n* **savagery.**
savanna *n* prairie; extensive grassy treeless plain.
savant *n* man of learning, scholar.
save *v* rescue; preserve untouched for future use; guard against; prevent need of; put by (money); *prep, conj* or *adv* except; *n* **saving** act of economizing; (*pl*) money put by.
saveloy *n* highly seasoned, dried sausage.
saviour *n* one who redeems; (*cap*) Jesus Christ.
savory *n* aromatic culinary herb.
savour *n* taste, flavour; (*fig*) slight trace; *v* have particular flavour; enjoy taste of; (*fig*) **s. of** suggest presence of; *a* **savoury** taste, appetizing; *n* light tasty dish, flavoured with salt, cheese etc.
savoy *n* kind of cabbage with curled leaves.

savvy *v* (*sl*) understand; *n* common sense.
saw *n* maxim, traditional saying.
saw *n* tool with toothed edge, for cutting wood etc; *v* cut with saw; (*fig*) make to and fro movement, as of sawing; *pt* **sawed**; *pp* **sawn**; *n* **sawdust** fine particles of wood made in sawing.
saxifrage *n* Alpine rock plant.
saxophone, saxhorn *n* reeded brass wind instrument with many keys or valves.
say *v* utter, express in words; state, report; be of opinion; *pt* & *pp* **said**; *n* expressed opinion; opportunity of stating it; *n* **saying** proverb, adage, maxim.
scab *n* dry crust which forms over wound in healing; skin disease; plant disease; (*coll*) blackleg.
scabbard *n* sheath for sword or dagger.
scabies *n* contagious itching skin disease.
scabious *n* herbaceous plant having round cushion-like mauve flowers.
scabrous *a* having rough surface; scurfy; controversial; indecent.
scaffold *n* temporary structure of poles and planks to support workmen; gallows; *n* **scaffolding** collective term for planks and poles used as scaffold, *esp* by builders.
scald *v* injure tissues of body with hot liquid, steam; heat almost to boiling point; *n* burn caused by hot liquid, steam etc.
scale *n* one of hard, thin flakes covering fish and reptiles; any flaky deposit in boilers, kettles etc; *v* clear scales from; flake off.
scale *n* one of two pans of balance; *pl* weighing-machine; *v* be weighed.
scale *n* (*mus*) series of graduated notes, *esp* in octave; system of grading by size, rank, amount, degree etc; ratio of size; *v* climb up, clamber up; increase, reduce according to fixed ratio.
scalene *a* (of triangle) having unequal sides.
scallop *n* edible bivalve mollusc; (*pl*) series of curves, like edge of scallop shell, used as ornamental edging; *v* ornament (dress) with scallops.
scallywag *n* rogue, scamp.

scalp *n* skin and hair on top of head; *v* strip, cut scalp off.
scalpel *n* small, slender, surgical knife.
scamp *n* rogue, rascal.
scamper *v* run about gaily, caper; run off hastily.
scan *v* look closely at; analyse (verse) into metrical elements; *n* **scansion.**
scandal *n* damaging, malicious or idle talk, act or thing that brings disgrace on reputation; *v* **scandalize** arouse indignation in; shock feelings of; *a* **scandalous**; *n* **scandalmonger** one who spreads scandal.
scant *a* small; inadequate in amount; *a* **scanty** insufficient, meagre.
scapegoat *n* one who takes blame, or is punished, for faults of others.
scapula *n* shoulder-blade; *pl* **-lae, -las**; *a* **scapular** of scapula; *n* short cloak worn by monks of certain religious orders.
scar *n* mark left by wound, burn or sore, after healing; *v* mark, heal with scar; *a* **scarred.**
scar, scaur *n* craggy & precipitous part of mountainside.
scarab *n* sacred beetle of ancient Egyptians; seal or gem shaped like beetle.
scaramouch *n* stock buffoon character in old Italian farce; boastful rogue.
scarce *a* not plentiful, rare, infrequent, uncommon; *adv* **scarcely** not quite, only just; *n* **scarcity** deficiency of supply; rarity.
scare *v* startle, frighten; *n* ill-founded alarm; widespread fear; *n* **scarecrow** dummy figure used to scare birds from crops; badly dressed person; guy.
scarf *n* long piece of material worn round neck; loose neckerchief; *pl* **scarves** or **scarfs.**
scarify *v* scratch, cut (skin); break, loosen surface (of soil); (*fig*) lacerate feelings of; *ns* **scarification**; **scarifier** agricultural implement.
scarlatina *n* scarlet fever.
scarlet *n* brilliant, vivid red; cloth, clothing of this colour *esp* robes of High Court Judges etc; *a* of this

colour; *ns* **scarlet fever** infectious disease, accompanied by high temperature and scarlet rash.

scarp *n* steep slope or face below rampart or hill; escarpment.

scatheless *a* unharmed, uninjured; *a* **scathing** damaging; (of remarks, comments etc) cutting, bitter

scatter *v* sprinkle; spread over; be dispersed; drive off in disorder; *n* **scatterbrain** flighty, thoughtless person.

scavenger *n* one employed to clean streets, remove house refuse etc; animal which feeds on carrion.

scene *n* place of action; background for fictional events, as in play etc; (*coll*) outburst of anger etc; view; sub-division of play within an act; *n* **scenery** painted scenes in theatre; landscape; woods, hills etc collectively as view; *a* **scenic** theatrical; picturesque, pertaining to natural scenery; *n* **scenario** complete outline of play, film etc, with stage-directions, situations etc.

scent *v* smell; track by smell; make fragrant; *n* odour; pleasant smell; liquid perfume.

sceptic *n* one who refuses to accept statement without positive proof; agnostic; *a* **sceptical**; *n* **scepticism.**

sceptre *n* ornamental rod carried as symbol of sovereignty; *a* **sceptred** wielding royal power.

schedule *n* written or printed list; tabulated statement; time-table; *v* set out, put into, form of schedule; **on s.** on time.

scheme *n* plan, design; project, enterprise; outline, synopsis; *v* plan as scheme; plot dishonestly, intrigue; *n* **schemer** one who schemes, *esp* in bad sense.

scherzo *n* (*mus*) lively, playful movement or passage.

schism *n* division in organized body or society *esp* in Church.

schist *n* type of crystalline rock.

schizophrenia *n* psychosis or mental disorder marked by split personality etc; *as* **schizophrenic**; **schizoid** tending towards schizophrenia.

schnapps *n* kind of Hollands gin.

schnorkel *n* tube for supplying submarine or underwater swimmer with air. Also **snorkel.**

school *n* establishment for education & instruction, *esp* of children; buildings of such institution; group of writers, artists etc. of similar principles, opinions; (*pl*) Oxford examinations for degree; *v* train, educate; discipline, bring under control; *n* **scholar** one taught in school; learned person; member of school or college entitled to sum of money annually; *a* **scholarly** learned; *n* **scholarship** learning; yearly grant of money for tuition fees etc; *a* **scholastic** of schools or scholars; academic, pedantic.

school *n* large shoal of fish; shoal of whales or porpoises.

schooner *n* fore-and-aft rigged vessel with two or more masts; large glass (for beer, sherry etc).

schottische *n* lively round dance; music for this.

sciatica *n* neuralgia of sciatic nerve, causing acute pain in back of thigh; *a* **sciatic** of, pertaining to hip.

science *n* systematized knowledge of natural or physical phenomena; investigation of this; knowledge or skill based on study, experience and practice; *a* **scientific** based on principles and methods of science; systematic; objective; *n* **scientist** one learned, trained in natural science.

scimitar *n* short oriental curved sabre.

scintillate *v* sparkle, twinkle; (*fig*) be witty and brilliant in conversation; *ns* **scintilla** spark; (*fig*) particle, atom; **scintillation** act of sparkling.

scion *n* slip for grafting; young member of family, descendant.

scission *n* act of cutting; split, division; *a* **scissile.**

scissors *n pl* cutting instrument of two blades pivoted together; style of high jumping; wrestling hold; movement in Rugby football.

scoff *n* taunt; expression of contempt, derision; *v* jeer at, mock.

scold *v* reprove angrily, noisily; find fault with; *n* nagging woman.

sconce *n* metal bracket candlestick on wall; socket of candlestick; earthwork; *v* entrench.

scone *n* thin flat cake baked on griddle or in oven.

scoop *n* article for ladling, dipping, or shovelling; tool for hollowing out; (*sl*) unexpected and profitable piece of luck; in journalism, exclusive news item; *v* ladle, shovel out; hollow out; (*sl*) obtain as profit, before others.

scoot *v* (*coll*) run quickly; run away; *n* **scooter** low-powered motor-cycle with small wheels; child's toy.

scope *n* range of activity; extent of view; area; outlet.

scorbutic *a* affected with, of scurvy.

scorch *v* burn superficially (of plants etc), dry up, wither.

score *n* notch, mark drawn or scratched; reckoning; number of points made in game; set of 20 persons, or objects; (*pl*) indefinite, large number; printed, written copy of orchestral music; *v* notch; cross out; record, make points in game; (*fig*) gain advantage; *n* **scorer** one who keeps or makes score in game.

scorn *n* contempt; disdainful state of mind; *v* feel, show contempt of; treat with derision; *a* **scornful** full of contempt.

scorpion *n* small arachnid insect with sting in tail and lobster-like claws.

scot *n* tax, rate; *a* **scot-free** free from payment; unpunished; unhurt.

Scot *n* native of Scotland; *a* **Scottish** (contracted to **Scotch**), **Scots** of Scotland; *ns* **Scotch** whisky from Scotland; **Scotsman** native of Scotland.

scotch *v* crush, render harmless; thwart; hinder; *n* wedge to prevent wheel etc from slipping.

scoundrel *n* blackguard, rogue; *a* **scoundrelly**.

scour *v* clean and polish by friction; search thoroughly; wash away by rapid flow of water; get rid of, free from.

scourge *n* whip, lash; affliction; pest; *v* flog, chastise; oppress.

scout *n* person sent out to reconnoitre; Boy Scout; college servant at Oxford; *v* go out, act as scout; reconnoitre.

scowl *v* frown; look sullen, angry; *n* sullen, angry frown.

scrabble *v* scratch; scramble about; *n* scrawl.

scrag *n* bony end of neck of mutton; *a* **scraggy** skinny, thin , lean; *v* wring or tackle neck.

scramble *v* clamber, climb using arms and legs; struggle roughly with; cook eggs beaten with butter, until partly solid; *n* act of scrambling; rough hill climb in motor-cycle racing; disorderly proceeding.

scrap *n* small detached piece; waste material; (*pl*) odds and ends of waste food; (*sl*) fight; very small piece of anything; *v* break up; dispose of as useless; (*sl*) fight; *ns* **scrap book** book with blank sheets for pasting in press-cuttings etc; **scrap heap** dust heap; (*fig*) limbo of forgotten things.

scrape *v* gaze, abrade surface with sharp edge; clean thus; scratch; *n* act, sound of scraping, (*coll*) awkward predicament; *n* **scraper** instrument for scraping.

scratch *v* leave slight mark on skin or surface with claws, or anything pointed; (*fig*) withdraw from game, competition etc; *n* wound or mark made by scratching; zero, par, in games scored by numerical points; *a* arranged at short notice, impromptu.

scrawl *v* write, draw hastily; scribble; *n* shapeless, untidy handwriting etc.

scream *v* utter shrill, piercing cry; laugh wildly and shrilly; *n* shriek, shrill cry.

scree *n* loose shifting broken particles of stones on steep hill etc.

screech *v* utter shrill harsh cry; *n* scream.

screed *n* long tedious speech or letter.

screen *n* structure giving shelter from heat, cold, wind, or concealing something; large white surface on which cinema films, photographic slides are projected; coarse sieve; *v* shelter, protect with screen; conceal; project (film etc); examine (person) for political motives; riddle, sift (*esp* coal).

screw *n* cylindrical piece of metal with spiral groove running round it and used as fastening; ship's propeller; action of twisting, turning; (*sl*) wages etc; *v* fasten with screw; turn, twist; distort; (*fig*) extort; *n* **screw-driver** chisel-shaped tool for turning screws.

scribble *v* write carelessly, illegibly; make meaningless marks with pencil etc; *n* something scribbled.

scribe *n* writer, author; *n* **scriber** tool for marking lines on stone etc; *v* **scribe** mark with scriber.

scrimmage *n* scuffle, confused struggle.
scrimp *v* make small; be niggardly; *a* **scrimpy** scanty.
scrip *n* small wallet or satchel.
scrip *n* share-, or stock-certificate.
script *n* handwriting; text of play, film etc.
scripture *n* sacred writings; the Bible.
scrofula *n* tuberculosis of lymphatic glands; *a* **scrofulous.**
scroll *n* roll of parchment or paper; ornamental spiral or curved design.
scrotum *n* pouch of skin containing testicles.
scrounge *v* (*sl*) cadge, pilfer; *n* **scrounger** cadger.
scrub *n* brushwood; land covered with such; *a* **scrubby** insignificant; undersized; inferior *esp* of sports team.
scrub *v* clean by hard rubbing *esp* with brush and water; (*sl*) cancel; *n* act of scrubbing; *ns* **scrubbing-brush** hard stiff brush; **scrubber** one who scrubs; (*sl*) unattractive woman.
scruff *n* nape of neck.
scrummage *n* scrimmage; *abbrev* **scrum** struggle between opposing forwards in Rugby football, with ball on ground between them; *n* **scrum-half** player who puts ball into scrum, etc.
scruple *n* small weight, 20 grains; doubt, hesitation about proposed action; conscientious objection; *a* **scrupulous** punctilious; conscientious; meticulous; *n* **scrupulousness.**
scrutiny *n* searching look; careful, official examination (of voting papers etc); *n* **scrutineer** examiner *esp* of ballot papers; *v* **scrutinize** examine carefully, look into closely.
scud *v* move quickly, *esp* of wind-driven clouds.
scuff *v* scratch (shoes) by dragging feet; *a* **scuffed** (of shoes) roughened or grazed.
scuffle *v* struggle, push roughly; *n* confused struggle.
scull *n* light, one-handed oar; *v* propel, move (boat) by means of scull(s).
scullery *n* room off kitchen, where rough work and cleaning of pots etc is done; *ns* **scullery-maid**; **scullion** (*ar*) boy who cleans dishes etc.

sculpture *n* art of carving or chiselling stone, wood etc to form figures in relief or solid; example of this art; *v* represent by sculpture; *n* **sculptor** artist who models in clay, carves wood or stone figures; (*fem*) **sculptress.**

scum *n* froth or other floating matter on liquid; waste part of anything; (*fig*) lowest, most degraded people; *a* **scummy.**

scumble *v* soften outline of painting with wash of opaque colour.

scupper *n* hole in ship's side to carry off water from deck; *v* (*sl*) disable (ship); ruin.

scurf *n* thin flakes of dried skin on scalp; dandruff; *a* **scurfy.**

scurrilous *a* coarsely abusive; *n* **scurrility.**

scurry *v* run, hurry, scuttle.

scurvy *n* disease of malnutrition, due to lack of fresh vegetable food; *a* mean, low, contemptible; scurfy.

scut *n* short stumpy tail *esp* of rabbit, hare.

scuttle *n* receptacle for holding coal, in a room.

scuttle *v* run away hurriedly; bolt.

scuttle *n* covered hole in deck of ship, or in wall, roof etc; *v* make holes in ship, to sink it.

scythe *n* tool for mowing, with long curved blade set at right angles to handle; *v* cut with scythe; mow.

sea *n* mass of salt water covering larger part of earth; tract of this; (also **seas**) state, condition of sea in relation to weather; large expanse of anything; *ns* **seaboard** sea-coast; **seafarer** traveller by sea; mariner; **sea-lion** species of large seal; **sea-urchin** marine animal with brittle, spiny shell; **seaweed** plant growing in sea; *a* **seaworthy** (of ships) fit to go to sea.

seal *n* marine, amphibious fish-eating mammal with flippers; *v* hunt seals; *ns* **sealer** ship or man hunting seals; **sealskin** fur of seals.

seal *n* piece of metal etc or die engraved with device for impression on wax; piece of wax thus impressed (on documents etc); *v* affix seal to; ratify; close, shut closely; confirm; decide finally; *n* **sealing wax** hard-setting wax for sealing.

seam *n* join between two edges (of cloth, or planks);

thin layer, vein, stratum; *v* join by sewing together; mark with furrows, wrinkles; *a* **seamless**; *n* **seamstress, sempstress** needlewoman; *a* **seamy** showing rough side; **s. side** least pleasant aspect of life etc.

séance *n* meeting of spiritualists.

sear *v* dry up; scorch, burn surface of; brand.

search *v* go through and examine closely; scan, reconnoitre; seek, try to find; *n* act of searching; *n* **searcher**; *a* **searching** penetrating; piercing; rigorous; *n* **searchlight** powerful beam of light.

season *n* one of four divisions of year; period during which certain natural processes occur; time of year devoted to particular sports and amusements; *v* bring into fit condition for use; flavour (food); *n* (*coll*) **season (-ticket)** one issued at reduced rate for specified period; *as* **seasonable** usual, suitable for particular season of year; **seasonal** varying with seasons; *n* **seasoning** spice, flavouring.

seat *n* anything made to sit on; right to sit (as in Parliament, theatre etc); way of sitting *esp* when horse-riding; buttocks; locality of trouble, disease etc; large house *esp* in country; *v* sit down; provide with seating accommodation.

sebaceous *a* fatty, **s. glands** sweat-glands, or glands of hair follicles.

secant *n* reciprocal of cosine of angle.

secateurs *n pl* pruning shears.

secede *v* withdraw voluntarily from federation etc; *n* **secession** act of seceding.

seclude *v* shut up, keep apart from others; *a* **secluded** remote, withdrawn *esp* of place; *n* **seclusion**.

second *a* ordinal number of two; nest after first; inferior; *n* one who that which comes second; one who assists and helps another, *esp* boxer, duellist; one sixtieth of minute; instant; (*pl*) inferior goods; *v* support; (*mil*) detach officer for temporary special duty; *n* **seconder** one who supports motion; *a* **secondhand** bought or for sale, after use by previous owner; unoriginal.

secondary *a* subsidiary; between primary and university stage of education; minor; inferior.

secret *a* hidden, meant to be kept from common

knowledge; mysterious; clandestine; remote, secluded; *n* thing kept secret; *n* **secrecy** ability, fidelity, in keeping secret; *a* **secretive** unduly reticent; furtive; *n* **secretiveness.**

secretary *n* one employed to deal with correspondence, keep records, and generally act in confidential manner; head of state department; *a* **secretarial**; *n* **secretariat** body of secretaries; building occupied by secretarial staff; *n* **secretary-bird** long-legged S. African bird, resembling heron.

secrete *v* hide, conceal; (of gland etc) collect and distribute material from blood as secretion; *n* **secretion** process of collecting substances from blood for use of body or expulsion as excreta; *a* **secretory** secreting.

sect *n* group holding minority views in religion; religious denomination; *a* **sectarian** characteristic of sect; *n* **sectary** member of sect.

section *n* act of cutting; severed part; any separate, distinct part of anything; smallest military unit; drawing of an object cut vertically; *a* **sectional.**

sector *n* portion of circle enclosed by two radii and arc which they cut off; (*mil*) part of fortified front or position.

secular *a* worldly; not ecclesiastical; age-long, persistent; *v* **secularize** transfer from ecclesiastical to civil ownership or use etc; make secular.

secure *a* free from care; made safe; firm, stable; certain; *v* make safe; insure, make certain; fasten, firmly; get hold of; *n* **security** safety; protection; safeguard; guarantee; (*pl*) bonds, title-deeds, share certificates etc; *a* surety.

sedan *n* covered chair carried on two poles; large closed motor-car.

sedate *a* calm; staid, decorous; *n* **sedateness.**

sedative *a* allaying anxiety; soothing; *n* sedative drug; *n* **sedation** act of administering sedative drug.

sedentary *a* sitting; requiring little bodily exertion.

sedge *n* coarse, perennial, grass-like plants, growing in marshy ground; *n* **sedge-warbler** summer migrant bird.

sediment *n* matter which settles at bottom of liquid; dregs.

sedition *n* offence against State authority, not amounting to treason; public commotion, riot; *a* **seditious.**

seduce *v* corrupt, lead astray; induce (someone) to surrender chastity; charm, entice; *n* **seduction**; *a* **seductive** alluring; attractive; persuasive.

sedulous *a* diligent; assiduous; careful, painstaking; *n* **sedulity.**

see *v* perceive with eyes; grasp mentally; come upon; make sure that; consider; interview; inspect; *pt* **saw**; *pp* **seen**; *conj* **seeing** since; in view of.

see *n* diocese, office, jurisdiction of bishop.

seed *n* fertilized reproductive germs of flowering plants; one grain of this; sperm, milt etc; (*fig*) offspring; seeded player; *v* form seed; remove seed; arrange draw for lawn-tennis or other tournament so that best players, or those of same nationality do not meet in early rounds; *n* **seedling** young plant raised from seed; *a* **seedy** run to seed; (*coll*) shabby; (*coll*) out of sorts.

seek *v* look out for; investigate; make search; *pt* & *pp* **sought.**

seem *v* look like; give one impression; appear to be *as* **seeming** ostensible; apparent; **seemly** decent; proper; appropriate.

seep *v* trickle through slowly; percolate; leak.

seer *n* prophet.

seersucker *n* lightweight, puckered, cotton fabric.

see-saw *n* children's play apparatus, plank resting on central support, child sitting on each end, moving up and down alternately; any motion as this; *v* move up and down.

seethe *v* boil, bubble up; (*fig*) be violently agitated by.

segment *n* section, portion cut or marked off; *v* divide into parts.

segregate *v* separate from main body; isolate; *n* **segregation.**

seine *n* large vertical fishing net with floats and sinkers; *v* catch fish with seine.

seismic *a* pertaining to earthquakes; *ns* **seismograph** instrument for recording earth tremors; **seismology** science of earthquakes.

seize *v* grasp, take by force; grasp rapidly with mind; (of machinery etc) stick, bind, *esp* from overheating or undue friction; *n* **seizure** forcible taking; sudden attack of illness *esp* stroke or fit.

seldom *adv* rarely, not often.

select *v* pick out, choose; *a* chosen; exclusive, fastidious; *a* **selective** having power of selection, able to discriminate; *ns* **selection** act of selecting; collection of samples; **selector**; **selectivity** ability to discriminate.

self *n* person's own identity, and individual character; personality; ego; essential quality, inmost nature of anything; (*pl*) **selves**.

self- *prefix* expressing reflexive action to, by, for oneself; automatic; acting upon agent. *Such compounds are not given here where the meaning may be deduced from the simple word.*

self-centred *a* preoccupied with one's own affairs or personality.

self-confidence *n* confidence in one's own ability etc.

self-conscious *a* easily embarrassed, shy.

self-contained *a* compact or complete within itself; of reserved personality.

self-denial *n* voluntary abstention from pleasures.

self-determination *n* right, power of race, nation to decide on its own form of government.

self-devotion *n* giving up of one's time to cause etc.

self-importance *n* conceited, pompous manner; exaggerated idea of own importance.

self-possessed *a* composed; having presence of mind.

self-respect *n* proper regard for one's own character etc.

self-satisfied *a* conceited.

self-service *a* (of stores etc) where customers serve themselves.

self-will *n* obstinacy; being headstrong.

-self suffix forming reflexive or emphatic persona pronouns (**oneself; myself** etc).

sell *v* dispose of by sale; deal in (something); betray, cheat; find buyers for; *pt* & *pp* **sold**; *n* **seller.**

selvedge, selvage *n* edge of cloth woven to prevent ravelling.
semantics *n pl* branch of linguistic study dealing with development of meaning of words.
semaphore *n* post with two movable arms worked by levers, for signalling; signalling by use of person's arms & flags; code used for such signals; *v* signal thus.
semblance *n* appearance; similitude; outward show.
semen *n* spermatic fluid of male animal.
semester *n* university term of six months.
semi- *prefix* partly, half.
semibreve *n* musical note equal to two minims or four crotchets.
semicircle *n* half-circle; *a* **semicircular.**
semicolon *n* punctuation mark (;).
semi-detached *a* (of house) having another joined to it on one side.
semi-final *n* round before the final.
seminary *n* school, place of education.
semiquaver *n* musical note half length of quaver.
Semite *n* member of racial group including Jews, Arabs; Jew; *a* **Semitic** pertaining to Semites and their languages.
semitone *n* musical half-tone.
semolina *n* hard, coarsely ground grains of wheat, used in making macaroni.
senate *n* ancient Roman legislative assembly; upper legislative council of State (as of U.S.A.); academic governing body of university; *n* **senator;** *a* **senatorial**; *n* **senate house** building where senate meets.
send *v* cause to go, be conveyed; dispatch; compel; (of natural processes) emit; (*sl*) rouse to ecstasy; *pt* & *pp* **sent; s. down** expel from University.
seneschal *n* steward, bailiff of medieval palace etc.
senile *a* showing weakness and decay of mental faculties, due to old age.
senior *a* older, of higher degree, rank, position; *n* older person; superior; *n* **seniority.**
sensation *n* effect felt by senses; state of excitement; event, person etc causing such state of mind; *a* **sen-**

sational arousing, tending to arouse, great interest, curiosity etc; *n* **sensationalism** crude, melodramatic presentation of news items *esp* sex & violence.

sense *n* faculty of bodily perception of feeling; one of five bodily faculties, sight, hearing, smell taste, touch; consciousness; meaning, sound judgement; (*pl*) sanity; *as* **senseless** insensible; foolish; **sensible** conscious; shrewd; aware; *n* **sensibility.**

sensitive *a* feeling acutely; keenly perceptive; easily distressed; reacting quickly to slight changes; *n* **sensitiveness** state of being sensitive; **sensitivity** degree of sensitiveness; *v* **sensitize** (*photo*) make sensitive to light.

sensual *a* pertaining to body senses; lustful, voluptuous; *ns* **sensuality** proneness to sexual indulgence; **sensualism** sexual indulgence; *a* **sensuous** pertaining to, based on bodily senses.

sentence *n* judgement, decision of court, declaring punishment to be inflicted on criminal; combination of words which convey complete meaning; *v* condemn.

sententious *a* full of maxims; uttering trite, pompous expressions.

sentient *a* having sense or feeling.

sentiment *n* tender emotion; tendency to be influenced more by emotion than reason; verbal expression of feeling; *a* **sentimental** arising from sentiment, rather than logical motives; foolishly emotional; *ns* **sentimentalist** one affected by or working up sentiment; **sentimentality** tendency to be sentimental; sloppy.

sentinel *n* one who keeps watch; sentry.

sentry *n* armed military guard.

sepal *n* one of leaves forming calyx of flower.

separate *v* divide; cut up, off; come, go apart; part; *a* divided; distinct physically; isolated; kept apart; *a* **separable**; *ns* **separation** act, process of separating; in law, formal arrangement when married couple live apart, without divorce; **separator** that which separates; device for separating cream from milk.

sepia *n* dark brown pigment, made from ink of cuttle fish; *a* of this colour.
sepoy *n* native soldier in Indian army.
September *n* 9th month (7th in old Roman calendar).
septennial *a* lasting, occurring every seven years.
septet(te) *n* music for, group of, seven instruments or voices.
septic *a* of, caused by blood-poisoning or putrefaction; *ns* **sepsis** infection of blood by micro-organisms; **septicaemia** blood-poisoning.
septuagenarian *a* aged between 70 and 80; *n* person so aged.
Septuagesima *n* third Sunday before Lent.
sepulchre *n* tomb; burial vault; *a* **sepulchral** of pertaining to grave, burial or dead; funereal; (of voice etc) deep, hollow; *n* **sepulture** burial.
sequel *n* consequence; result, effect.
sequent *a* following; *n* **sequence** order in which events, object follow; series; succession.
sequester *v* set apart, isolate; *v* **sequestrate** confiscate; (*law*) take (property) by process of law and divert income to meet claims against owner; *n* **sequestration.**
sequin *n* ornamental disc or spangle; old Venetian gold coin.
sequoia *n* one of species of giant Californian conifers.
seraglio *n* Turkish sultan's palace; harem.
seraph *n* one of highest orders of angels; *pl* **seraphim**; *a* **seraphic** angelic.
sere *a* withered, dry.
serenade *n* music sung or played at night (*esp* by lover) beneath lady's window); nocturne; *v* sing serenade to.
serendipity *n* faculty of finding valuable or interesting things by chance.
serene *a* calm, placid; unclouded; tranquil; *n* **serenity.**
serf *n* feudal labourer; slave; *n* **serfdom.**
serge *n* hard-wearing, twilled woollen cloth.
sergeant, serjeant *n* N.C.O. in army; police officer;

s.-at-arms ceremonial official of Parliament; **sergeant-major** senior N.C.O. of regiment etc.
serial *a* of, forming series; *n* story, novel etc published in successive instalments; *v* **serialize** arrange in series; publish, produce as serial.
series *n* sequence; set, succession; linear, end-to-end arrangement.
serif *n* (*print*) short thin line at top or bottom of letters.
serious *a* solemn; meant in earnest, genuine; grave; critical.
sermon *n* discourse on moral and religious subjects forming part of church service; *v* **sermonize** preach *esp* tediously.
serpent *n* snake; malevolent person; obsolete wind instrument.
serrated *a* having notches like teeth of saw; *n* **serration.**
serried *a* in compact order; closely packed.
serum *n* watery fluid remaining after coagulation of blood; such fluid prepared by culture for use in inoculation.
servant *n* one employed by another; one who follows; adheres to, another.
serve *v* work for; perform duty for; wait upon (with food); satisfy; undergo (prison sentence); deliver (writ); (tennis etc) deliver ball to opponent, by striking it; be useful for.
service *n* occupation of servant; official duty, as in Civil, Consular Service; serving of meal, set of dishes, cutlery etc; **active s.** service in armed forces involving fighting; *v* overhaul; *a* **serviceable** useful; lasting; profitable.
serviette *n* table-napkin.
servile *a* pertaining to slaves, slavery; cringing, obsequious; *n* **servility.**
servitude *n* slavery, bondage.
sesame *n* annual E. Indian herb, with seeds yielding oil.
session *n* formal assembly or meeting; period during which legislative body sits *esp* Parliament; continuous series of such meetings.

set *v* put, lay in specified place etc; put; fix in right position; (of hair) arrange and dry in waves etc; (of sun) sink below horizon; become firm, solid; *pt* & *pp* **set** *a* deliberate; formal; unvarying; *n* (radio) apparatus for reception or transmission; number of things, persons, considered as whole; *v* **s. up** establish; *n* **setting** act, process of setting; background; that in which gems are set.

sett *n* badger's burrow.

settee *n* sofa, couch.

setter *n* breed of dog trained to point at game.

settle *n* wooden bench with high back and arms; *v* arrange; establish, make firm, or quiet; decide on; endow legally; end dispute; subside; pay; become clear; take up abode; *n* **settlement** act of settling; property conveyed to some person; colony or other place occupied by settlers; *n* **settler** colonist.

seven *n* & *a* cardinal number next above six; *ns* & *as* **seventh** ordinal number; seventh part; **seventeen** seven plus ten; **seventeenth**; **seventy** seven tens; **seventieth.**

sever *v* separate, cut off; divide; *n* **severance.**

several *a* separate, distinct; more than two, not many; *adv* **severally** apart from others.

severe *a* harsh, strict; rigorous; intense; austere; violent; *n* **severity.**

sew *v* fasten, work with needle and thread; *pt* **sewed**; *pp* **sewed, sewn**; *n* **sewing** needlework.

sewage *n* waste matter, excreta etc carried away in sewers; *ns* **sewer** underground conduit or drain for carrying off sewage; **sewerage** public drainage.

sex *n* fact or quality of being male or female; physiological difference between male and female; *as* **sexual** pertaining to sex; **sexy** having great sexual attractiveness; *n* **sexuality** sexual desire; **sex-appeal** strong sexual attractiveness.

Sexagesima *n* second Sunday before Lent.

sexennial *a* lasting, happening once in, six years.

sextant *n* navigator's instrument for determining latitude and longitude.

sextet(te) *n* group of six instruments or players; music for this group.

sexton *n* man employed by church as caretaker, gravedigger etc.
shabby *a* wearing old, worn out clothes; well worn; mean, squalid; shameful; *n* **shabbiness.**
shack *n* hut, shanty.
shackle *n* (*pl*) fetters, chains; link, staple; *v* fasten with shackles; (*fig*) hamper.
shad *n* edible marine fish of herring family.
shaddock *n* tropical fruit of orange family; grapefruit.
shade *n* partial darkness; shadow; depth of colour; something which gives shelter, protection from light; spirit, ghost; slight amount, degree; *v* darken; screen from light; represent light and shade in drawing; *a* **shady** affording, standing in, shade; (*coll*) disreputable.
shadow *n* patch of shade; person who follows closely; phantom; indistinct, imperfect image; very slight amount or degree; *v* cast shadow over; follow closely, *esp* as detective or bodyguard; *a* **shadowy** unsubstantial; dim.
shaft *n* handle, stem; arrow; beam of light; vertical opening to mine etc; ventilating channel; *pl* poles between which horse is harnessed; revolving rod transmitting power.
shag *n* long-napped cloth; fine-cut tobacco; *a* **shaggy** rough, unkempt.
shag *n* small crested cormorant.
shagreen *n* kind of untanned leather; sharkskin.
Shah *n* king of Persia.
shake *v* tremble; totter; vibrate; rock to and fro; agitate (contents of bottle etc); *pt* **shook**; *pp* **shaken** *n* act of shaking; jolt; *a* **shaky** insecure, unsteady; (*fig*) unreliable; *n* **shakedown** makeshift bed.
shako *n* peaked military cap with plume.
shale *n* clay rock formation, which flakes easily.
shall *v aux* used to denote promise, obligation, intention, command, futurity; *pt* **should**; no *pp*.
shallot *n* kind of onion.
shallow *a* not deep; (of thought, feeling etc) superficial, trivial; *n* shallow place in body of water.

sham *n* imposture; counterfeit, faked article; imitation; *v* pretend, imitate.
shamble *v* walk with stumbling, shuffling gait.
shambles *n pl* slaughter-house; butcher's stall; (*fig*) place of bloodshed, carnage; (*sl*) muddle.
shame *n* emotion of regret and contrition, caused by consciousness of guilt, dishonour etc; disgrace; (*coll*) unfair happening, hard luck; *v* make ashamed; bring shame, disgrace on; *as* **shamefaced** ashamed of oneself; **shameful** outrageous; disgraceful; **shameless** impudent, brazen; immodest.
shampoo *v* wash (hair) with shampoo; wash carpet, car etc. with special preparations; *n* special preparation for washing hair, carpet, etc.
shamrock *n* trefoil plant, probably wood-sorrel, taken as national emblem of Ireland.
shank *n* lower leg; shin; handle, shaft, stem.
shantung *n* tussore silk; natural Chinese silk.
shanty *n* small hut; temporary wooden building.
shanty, chanty *n* sailor's song.
shape *n* external form or appearance; pattern, mould; *v* form, fashion; assume shape; *as* **shapely** well proportioned; **shapeless.**
shard *n* broken fragment of pottery.
share *n* portion; part played in action; one of equal portions into which capital of joint-stock company is divided; *v* give, allot, take a share; *n* **shareholder.**
share *n* blade of plough.
shark *n* one of large group of voracious sea-fishes; (*fig*) rapacious, grasping swindler.
sharkskin *n* shagreen; stiff, heavy rayon fabric.
sharp *a* having keen edge, piercing point; clearly seen; intense; shrill; alert; brisk; dishonest; *n* (music) note raised semitone in pitch; (*sl*) swindler, cheat; *v* **sharpen** whet edge or point; (*fig*) make keen; *ns* **sharper** one who cheats *esp* at cards; **sharpness**; *as* **sharp-set** hungry; **sharp-witted** very quick and intelligent; *n* **sharpshooter** skilled marksman.
shatter *v* break in fragments, smash; (*fig*) cause to crumble.
shave *v* cut off (hair) with razor; pare; graze; *pt* **shaved**; *pp* **shaved, shaven**; *n* act of shaving; (*fig*)

narrow escape; *ns* **shaver** one who, that which shaves; (*coll*) lad; **shaving** thin slice, *esp* of wood.

Shavian *a* after, in manner of George Bernard Shaw.

shawl *n* large square of fabric worn round shoulders, or for wrapping babies in.

she *fem nom pron* (*3rd pers sing*) female person etc just referred to; *a* female.

sheaf *n* bundle of things tied together—*esp* cut corn stalks; *pl* **sheaves.**

shear *v* clip, remove (fleece) from; cut off by one stroke; *pt* **sheared, shore;** *pp* **shorn, sheared;** *n pl* **shears** large cutting implement with blades like scissors; *n* **shearer** one who shears *esp* sheep.

sheath *n* case, covering *esp* for knife etc; *v* **sheathe** put into sheath; cover with protective casing or sheath.

shed *n* wooden hut; outhouse; shelter for cattle, tools etc.

shed *v* cast off; emit; moult; cause to flow; *pt* & *pp* **shed.**

sheen *n* gloss, lustre; *a* **sheeny.**

sheeny *n* (*sl*) Jew.

sheep *n* ruminant mammal with woolly coat and edible flesh; *a* **sheepish** bashful; *ns* **sheepcote** shelter for sheep; **sheep-dip** liquid insecticide used to preserve wool and kill vermin.

sheer *a* clear; unmixed; perpendicular; (of fabric) transparent.

sheet *n* large piece of fabric used to cover bed; broad, piece of any thing material; thin flat piece of metal; rope fastened to sail; *n* **sheet-anchor** large emergency anchor; (*fig*) person, thing which can be relied on.

sheikh *n* Arab chieftain; Muslim title of respect.

shekel *n* old Jewish weight; (*sl*) money, cash.

shelf *n* horizontal projecting board on wall etc; horizontal ledge of rock etc; reef; *pl* **shelves;** *v* **shelve** place on, fit with shelves; (*fig*) put aside, postpone indefinitely; defer.

shell *n* hard outer covering of animal or vegetable object; explosive projectile; framework; ruined building with only walls standing; *v* remove shell from (nut etc); fire at (with shells); *n* **shellfish** edible marine mollusc or crustacean; *n* **shell-shock** functional nervous disorder, caused by experience of bursting shells etc.

shellac *n* coloured resin used in varnishes, sealing wax etc; *v* coat with shellac.

shelter *n* protection, cover, screen; place of refuge; *v* give, afford cover to; protect; seek safety; screen.

shepherd *n* one who tends sheep; (*fig*) minister of religion; **the Good S.** Christ; *fem* **shepherdess.**

sherbet *n* Eastern drink of fruit juice etc; effervescent drink; powder for making this.

sheriff *n* county official (formerly representing Crown); chief judge of Scottish county; (in U.S.A.) chief officer enforcing law, order in county.

sherry *n* type of Spanish, fortified, brown wine.

shield *n* piece of protective armour carried on arm; that which serves as protection or defence; *v* protect, guard, screen.

shift *v* remove, get rid of; change position; veer; (*coll*) go fast; *n* contrivance, dodge; set of workmen; time worked by these; change in position; *as* **shiftless** feckless, inefficient; **shifty** evasive, dishonest; furtive.

shillelagh *n* stout cudgel *esp* of oak, blackthorn.

shilling *n* former British silver coin worth 12 old pence or 5 new (decimal) pence.

shilly-shally *n* indecision, needless delay; *v* hesitate, waver.

shimmer *v* shine with faint light; *n* faint, tremulous light; glimmer.

shin *n* front of lower leg; *v* climb, swarm up by using legs and arms.

shindy, shindig *n* (*coll*) noisy party; disturbance.

shine *v* emit, reflect light; sparkle; excel in; show great intelligence; *pt* & *pp* **shone**; *n* polish; brilliance; *a* **shiny.**

shingle *n* wooden tile for roofing, outside walls etc; woman's short hair-style; *v* cover with shingles; cut hair in shingle.

shingle *n* coarse rounded stones, pebbles found on seashore.

shingles *n* acute inflammatory disease of nerve endings.
Shinto *n* national religion of Japan.
shinty *n* game like hockey.
ship *n* large sea-going vessel; *v* send (goods etc) by ship; embark, serve in ship; *n* **shipment** act of shipping; consignment; **ship-chandler** supplier of ship's stores and fittings; **ship-broker** one who secures cargoes for, or charters ships; *a* **shipshape** trim, tidy, orderly.
shire *n* county.
shirk *v* evade, refuse to face (danger, duty etc); *n* **shirker.**
shirt *n* sleeved garment, worn under jacket.
shiver *v* splinter, break in pieces.
shiver *v* tremble, shake with cold or fear; *n* shudder, quivering movement; *a* **shivery** inclined to shiver.
shoal *n* large mass of fish swimming together; submerged sandbank; *v* form shoal; become shallow.
shock *n* violent jolt, collision; feeling of horror, surprise, disgust etc; that which causes such feeling; discharge of electric current through body; upset of nervous system and vital functions of body following accident, operation etc; *v* cause, produce shock; *n* (*sl*) **shocker** sensational novel.
shock *n* group, pile of sheaves of corn.
shoddy *n* cheap material made of waste or old woollen cloth; anything made of cheap inferior material; *a* cheap and nasty.
shoe *n* covering for foot; metal rim, or plate, nailed to hoof of horse; part of brake which presses on rim of wheel; *v* protect, furnish with shoes; *pt* & *pp* **shod** (*ar* **shoed**).
shoot *v* dart; move swiftly, suddenly; discharge weapon; kill or injure with gun shot; be carried rapidly over; (football, hockey etc) aim ball directly at goal; grow rapidly; produce bud; *pt* & *pp* **shot**; *n* act of shooting; sprout; shooting-party, ground over which shooting takes place; **shooting star** meteorite.
shop *n* place where goods are retailed; workshop; (*fig*) one's business etc; *v* visit shops to buy goods;

(*sl*) betray to police; *ns* **shop assistant** one who serves in shop; **shop-lifter** one who steals from shop; **shop-steward** trade union official in factory, works etc; *v* **talk shop** talk about one's business, etc, or special interest.

shore *n* land at edge of sea or lake.

shore *n* thick beam used as prop; *v* prop, support.

short *a* brief, not tall; scanty; concise; abrupt; deficient; reduced; friable; *adv* suddenly; without reaching end; (*pl*) short trousers; *n* **shortage** deficiency; *v* **shorten** make short; make crumbly, as pastry; **shorthanded** understaffed; *adv* **shortly** briefly, abruptly; soon; *a* **short-winded** easily out of breath.

shortbread, shortcake *n* easily crumbled cake made with much butter and sugar etc.

short-circuit *n* shortening of electric circuit by accidental contact; *v* develop short-circuit; (*fig*) by-pass, take shorter path to objective.

short-coming *n* failing.

shorthand system of rapid writing using symbols and contractions.

shot *a* woven so as to change colour, according to angle of light.

shot *n* small lead pellet in cartridge; act of firing; noise of this; attempt, try; (*sl*) injection, injected dose *esp* of drug; **big s.** important person; **s. in the dark** random guess.

shoulder *n* part of body to which arm or foreleg is attached; strip of land bordering road; *v* put on one's shoulder; (*fig*) undertake responsibility for; *n* **shoulder-blade** shoulder bone.

shout *n* loud outcry; *v* utter with loud voice.

shove *v* & *n* push.

shovel *n* broad spade, used for lifting earth etc; *v* lift, move with shovel.

show *v* expose to view; demonstrate; guide; exhibit; appear; *pt* **showed**; *pp* **shown, showed, shewn** *n* display; ostentation; appearance; indication; *a* **showy** gaudy, ostentatious; *n* **showman** owner, producer of travelling show etc; **show-down** unmasking, final revelation of plans etc; *v* (*coll*) **s. off**

make display of one's attainments, abilities etc; **s. up** expose, reveal bad side of.

shower *n* short fall of rain; copious discharge (of missiles); shower-bath; *v* fall as shower; give out abundantly; take shower; *n* **shower-bath** ablutionary device where water falls in shower from overhead; *a* **showery** with frequent rain-showers.

shrapnel *n* shell filled with bullets or pieces of metal which scatter on bursting; piece of such metal.

shred *n* tattered fragment; strip; *v* pare, tear into shreds.

shrew *n* virago; mouselike carnivorous mammal; *a* **shrewish** nagging.

shrewd *a* astute, sharp-witted; piercing; *n* **shrewdness.**

shriek *v* & *n* screech; scream.

shrievalty *n* office or rank of sheriff.

shrike *n* butcher-bird, bird of prey.

shrill *a* piercing, high-pitched in tone.

shrimp *n* small edible, long-tailed crustacean; (*fig*) small person; *v* fish for, catch shrimps.

shrine *n* sacred place, chapel etc, associated with saint; casket containing holy relics; (*fig*) something held sacred in memory; *v* **enshrine.**

shrink *v* contract, diminish; recoil, retreat, flinch; *pt* **shrank**; *pp* **shrunk** (*occ* **shrunken**); *n* **shrinkage.**

shrive *v* give absolution to; *pt* **shrove**; *pp* **shriven**; *n* **shrift** absolution and confession; (*fig*) **short s.** summary treatment.

shrivel *v* curl, roll up; wither.

shroud *n* cloth wound round corpse; (*fig*) covering; *pl* ropes from masthead; *v* wrap in shroud; hide, cover, veil.

Shrovetide *n* three days before Lent; **Shrove Tuesday** day before Ash Wednesday.

shrub *n* low-growing bushy, woody plant; *n* **shrubbery** plantation of shrubs.

shrub *n* drink of sweetened fruit-juice with rum.

shrug *v* lift and draw up shoulders slightly, as sign of doubt etc; **s. off** make light of; *n* shrugging.

shrunk(en) *a* contracted, shrivelled, reduced.

shuck *n* husk, pod of peas, etc; *v* remove pods etc.
shudder *v* quake, tremble violently; feel aversion, be disgusted at; *n* shuddering.
shuffle *v* move feet without lifting them; speak, act evasively; mix cards up; *n* shuffling; *n* **shuffler**.
shun *v* avoid; keep clear of.
shunt *v* turn, switch (train) to side line; (*fig*) push to one side.
shut *v* close; lock up; imprison; exclude; *pt* & *pp* **shut**; *n* **shutter** hinged window screen; device in camera for screening lens.
shuttle *n* weaver's instrument for carrying weft; sliding thread holder in sewing machine; *v* move regularly back and forwards between two places.
shuttle-cock *n* feathered & weighted cork, used in badminton or battledore.
shy *a* timid; bashful; reluctant; (*sl*) short of; *v* (of horse) start and swerve nervously; **s. at** be unwilling to face or do; *pt* & *pp* **shied**.
shy *v* (*coll*) fling, throw; *n* act of throwing; (*pl*) **shies**.
Siamese *a* of Siam; *n* native, language of Siam; blue eyed, creamy-brown coloured domestic cat; **S. twins** human twins linked at birth by fleshy ligature.
sibilant *n* & *a* (consonant) uttered with hissing sound.
sibyl *n* wise woman, soothsayer; witch; *a* **sibylline** oracular.
siccative *n* & *a* (substance) causing drying.
sick *a* ill; vomiting, suffering from nausea; (*coll*) furious, annoyed, disgusted; (of joke etc.) macabre; *v* **sicken** make, become sick; disgust; weary; *a* **sickly** weakly; ailing; nauseating; *n* collectively sick people; **sickness, sickliness**.
sickle *n* reaping hook.
side *n* external or internal surface; area; space that is to right or left; edge, margin; team, group; area between ribs and hip in human body; line of descent through one parent; (*sl*) arrogance, conceit; *v* support (person, party etc); *ns* **sideboard** piece of dining-room furniture holding cutlery, dishes, etc; **sidecar** small carriage for one, attached to side of motor-bicycle; *a* **sidelong** to one side, oblique; *adv* **side-**

ways obliquely; edgewise; *ns* **siding** short line of rails beside main line, used for shunting; **side effect** unintended effect (*usu* unpleasant) accompanying intended effect; **side issue** one subordinate to main issue; **sideslip** skid; *v* **side-track** divert (person) from his purpose; shelve.

sidereal *a* relating to, measured by apparent motion of stars.

sidle *v* move, walk sideways in cringing, fawning manner.

siege *n* besieging of fort or town.

sienna *n* brownish-yellow earthy pigment.

sierra *n* mountain chain with jagged ridges.

siesta *n* short rest, sleep in early afternoon.

sieve *n* framework of mesh or net for sifting; *v* pass through sieve, sift.

sift *v* pass through sieve or riddle; separate coarse from fine particles; examine carefully; sprinkle; *n* **sifter**.

sigh *v* utter long audible breath; express grief, fatigue etc. by this act; **s. for** long for; lament; *n* act, sound of, sighing.

sight *n* faculty of seeing, vision; that which is seen; device (on gun etc.) for helping vision; view; spectacle; *v* get, come in, sight of; adjust sights of (rifle etc.); *a* **sightless**; *ns* **sight-seer** visitor to places of notable interest; **sightseeing**.

sign *n* indication, token, symbol which conveys meaning; visible mark; agreed word, gesture expressing meaning; omen; *v* write one's name on; ratify; indicate by word or gesture.

signal *n* message conveyed to distance; indication, warning of something else; apparatus whereby message is conveyed; *v* make signal to; send, notify by signals; *a* remarkable; conspicuous.

signatory *n* representative of party or state who signs document, treaty etc.

signature *n* person's name written by himself; **s. tune** one associated with programme or performer on radio etc.

signet *n* small seal.

significant *a* meaningful; noteworthy; suggesting

covert meaning; *ns* **significance** import, meaning; **signification** exact meaning or implication.
signify *v* mean; imply; matter; be of importance.
signor *n* Italian form of address to man.
Sikh *n* member of military sect in Punjab.
silence *n* absence of noise or sound; refraining from speech; *v* cause to be silent; (*fig*) put to shame; *a* **silent**; *n* **silencer** device for reducing, muffling noise of machinery or firearms.
silhouette *n* portrait in outline or profile, cut from black paper, or done in solid black, against white background; outline, profile, of object seen as dark against light background; *v* show up in outline.
silica *n* hard, white mineral; *n* **silicate** salt of silicic acid; *as* **silicic** pertaining to silica; **siliceous** flinty; *n* **silicon** non-metallic element, one of principal constituents of earth's surface.
silicone *n* one of various compounds of silicon and hydrocarbon, used in lubricants, polishes etc.
silicosis *n* lung disease, caused by inhaling coal dust or other gritty dust.
silk *n* fine filament produced by pupae of certain moths; thread, fabric made from this; *as* **silken** made of, like silk; **silky** glossy, fine, soft to touch; *ns* **silkiness**; **silkworm** silk-producing caterpillar.
sill *n* horizontal block or slab at base of window or door; slab of igneous rock between sedimentary layers.
silly *a* foolish; trivial; weak-minded; *n* **silliness**.
silo *n* pit, tower for fodder or grain; *n* **silage** cattle fodder partly fermented and stored.
silt *n* mud etc. deposited by water; *v* **silt up** become choked, blocked with silt.
silvan, sylvan *a* of woods, forests; rural.
silver *n* white precious metal element; objects made of, plated with silver; silver coins; *a* made of, resembling silver; (*fig*) shining, lustrous; (of sound) ringing, clear, soft; *v* coat with silver; *a* **silvery**; *ns* **silverside** top side of round of beef, *usu* salted; **silverfish** small, flattish wingless insect found in houses *esp* in dark, damp places.
simian *a* of, like apes.

similar *a* like, resembling; *n* **similarity** likeness, resemblance.
simile *n* figure of speech in which one thing is directly compared to another.
similitude *n* comparison; likeness; similarity.
simmer *v* boil gently; be just below boiling point; (*coll*) be in condition of suppressed rage or excitement; *n* state of simmering.
simony *n* crime of buying or selling church preferment.
simoom *n* hot, suffocating wind of Arabian desert.
simper *v* smile affectedly; smirk; *n*.
simple *a* clear, intelligible; easy; austere; ingenuous; credulous; foolish; not complex or compound; *n* herbal medicine; *ns* **simpleton** foolish, weak-minded person; **simplicity** quality state of being; simple; *v* **simplify** make less complicated or easier *n* **simplification**.
simulate *v* imitate; pretend to be, have or feel; *n* **simulation** act of simulating; **simulacrum** deceptive shadowy likeness; sham.
simultaneous *a* occurring at same time; *n* **simultaneousness**.
sin *n* transgression of divine law, moral code; any offence in general; vice; iniquity; *v* be sinful; commit sin; *a* **sinful** guilt of, of nature of, sin; *n* **sinner**.
since *adv* from then until now; ago; *prep* after, succeeding; *conj* because; seeing that.
sincere *a* genuine; honest, true; free from deceit or pretence; *n* **sincerity**.
sine *n* perpendicular drawn from one extremity of arc to diameter drawn through other extremity; ratio of this perpendicular to radius of circle.
sinecure *n* paid office or work with few or no duties.
sinew *n* tendon; (*pl*) muscles; (*fig*) (of war) money and material resources; *a* **sinewy** muscular.
sing *v* utter musical notes; (of birds) utter natural cries; (*fig*) rejoice; *pt* **sang**; *pp* **sung**; *ns* **singer**; **singing**.
singe *v* burn superficially; scorch; *n* slight burn.
single *a* one only; not double; alone, unmarried; sincere; (of ticket) valid for one journey; *v* select, pick

out; *a* **single-handed** unaided; *n* **singleton** single card of suit in hand; *adv* **singly** one by one; alone.

singlet *n* undervest.

singular *a* of, relating to one person or thing; remarkable, unusual, eminent; *adv* **singularly** oddly; outstandingly; *n* **singularity**.

sinister *a* evil; ominous; malevolent; (*her*) on left hand side.

sink *v* be, become, submerged in liquid; subside; become lower (in value, degree, health etc); penetrate deeply; excavate; *pt* **sank**; *pp* **sunk** (*occ* **sunken**); *n* kitchen trough or basin, with outlet for waste water; (*fig*) sordid place where corruption exists; *ns* **sinker** weight for fishing net or line; **sinking fund** one formed by setting apart yearly sums of money to pay off liability; *as* **sunk** (*coll*) ruined, doomed, lost; **sunken** submerged; below ground or water level.

sinuous *a* curving, bending; snaky, undulating; *n* **sinuousity**.

sinus *n* cavity in tissue or bone *esp* in facial bone; *n* **sinusitis** inflammation of nasal sinus.

sip *v* drink in very small quantities; *n* very small mouthful of liquid.

siphon *n* bent tube used for transferring liquid from one level to lower one; bottle with tap at top, through which aerated water is forced by gas pressure; *v* draw off by siphon. Occasionally **syphon**.

sir *n* term of respect for man; title of knight or baronet.

sire *n* form of address to monarch; male parent, *esp* of horse, dog; *v* beget, be sire of.

siren *n* mythological sea-nymph; (*fig*) alluring woman; loud warning hooter or signal.

sirloin *n* upper part of loin of beef.

sirocco *n* hot Mediterranean wind, blowing from Libyan desert.

sisal *n* fibre of American agave, used for rope-making.

siskin *n* olive green bird of finch family.

sister *n* daughter, woman, born of same parents; nun; nurse in charge of ward; *a* closely related, of same type; *n* **sisterhood** community of nuns etc; **sister-in-law** sister of husband of wife; wife of brother.

sit *v* rest on buttocks or haunches; take one's place in assembly; pose for portrait; fit, hang well; (of birds) remain on eggs; sit upon (horse); undergo examination; *pt* & *pp* **sat**; *ns* **sitter** one who sits; **baby s.** one who looks after children in absence of parents; **sitting-room** living-room; space sufficient, reserved for sitting in.

site *n* ground, situation; local position.

situate(d) *a* placed, having particular site; *n* **situation** place; employment; state of affairs.

six *n* cardinal number one above five; *a* & *n* **sixth** ordinal number; a sixth part; *n* **sixpence** silver coin worth six old pennies, two and half decimal pence; *ns* & *as* **sixteen** six and ten; **sixteenth**; **sixty** six times ten; **sixtieth**.

size *n* standard measure of length, weight, quantity; magnitude; fixed dimension; *v* arrange according to size.

size *n* thin glue used to glaze and stiffen paper, etc; *v* apply size to.

sizzle *v* make hissing noise; *n* hissing, spluttering sound *esp* in frying.

skate *n* edible flat fish of ray family.

skate *n* one of pair of steel blades, attached to boot, for gliding over ice; roller-skate; *v* move on skates.

skedaddle *v* (*sl*) run away, clear out; *n* hasty flight.

skein *n* quantity of coiled and knotted yarn (of cotton, silk etc); flock of wild geese in flight.

skeleton *n* bony framework of human or animal body; such bones preserved in their natural position; (*coll*) very thin person; outline, draft; framework; *a* **skeletal** pertaining to, attached to skeleton; *n* **skeleton key** key used for picking locks.

sketch *n* rough drawing serving as study for finished picture; rough draft; short play; *v* make sketch of; *a* **sketchy** depicted in outline; unfinished, inadequate.

skew *a* oblique; crooked; sloping; *a* **skewbald** (of horse) irregularly marked white and another colour (not black).

skewer *n* thin pointed pin of wood or metal for keeping piece of meat in shape; *v* pierce or fasten with skewer.

ski *n* long wooden runner, fastened to foot, for moving over snow; *v* use skis for travelling over snow; *n* **skier** one who skis.

skid *n* drag fixed to wheel, to reduce speed; *v* (of vehicle) slip sideways out of control; (*fig*) slip & fall; *ns* **skid-lid** (*coll*) crash-helmet; **skid-pan** slippery area where motorists may practise skid-control.

skiff *n* small rowing, sculling boat.

skiffle *n* jazz folk-music; *n* **s. group** musical group using guitar and improvised percussion instruments.

skill *n* deftness, manual dexterity; cleverness, ingenuity; *as* **skilled** skilful, expert; trained in some specific trade etc; **skilful** clever, dextrous.

skim *v* remove scum, fat or other substance from surface of liquid; pass lightly over; (*fig*) read through (book) rapidly and perfunctorily.

skimp *v* stint; supply in too small an amount; do carelessly; *a* **skimpy** meagre; fitting too tightly.

skin *n* outer covering of anything, as of human or animal body, fruit etc; *v* remove skin of; *n* **skinner** dealer in pelts and hides; *as* **skin-deep** superficial; **skinny** thin; **skin-tight** very close fitting; *ns* **skin-flint** miser; **skin-diving** under-water swimming with oxygen cylinders but no diving suit.

skip *v* leap lightly; gambol; jump on spot, while rope passes underneath one; (*coll*) decamp, bolt; omit, pass rapidly over in reading.

skipper *n* captain of ship; (*coll*) captain of team; *v* act as skipper.

skirl *n* shrill, piercing sound of bagpipes.

skirmish *n* fight between small groups of soldiers etc; (*fig*) brief, slight contest or argument; *v* engage in skirmish.

skirt *n* woman's garment hanging below waist; flank of beef; (*sl*) woman; outlying part; *v* border, go round; *n* **skirting** board running round bottom of walls of room.

skit *n* light, satirical, humorous sketch or burlesque; *a* **skittish** playful, lively; frolicsome.

skittles *npl* game of ninepins.
skua *n* large dark-brown gull.
skulk *v* lurk in concealment; sneak away; *n* **skulker.**
skull *n* bony case containing brain of animals; *n* **skull-cap** close-fitting cap.
skunk *n* small, carnivorous N. American mammal emitting offensive odour when attacked; (*coll*) contemptible person.
sky *n* upper part of earth's atmosphere; (*fig*) heaven *pl* **skies**; *v* throw, hit (ball) high up; hang (picture) high up; *a* of colour of blue, cloudless sky; *ns* **skylight** window in roof or ceiling; **skyscraper** very high building.
skylark *n* common bird, noted for its song and soaring flight.
slab *n* thick, squarish piece.
slack *a* sluggish; loose, relaxed; lazy; not busy; *n* anything left slack or loose; (*pl*) loose sports trousers; *v* loosen; sag; be idle, lazy; *v* **slacken** abate, diminish; reduce (speed).
slack, slag *n* dross or refuse of coal or smelted metal.
slake *v* quench, allay; mix (lime) with water.
slam *v* shut, close with bang; put down noisily; *n* loud bang or noise; **grand s.** (cards) taking of all tricks in one deal.
slander *n* (law) malicious, false spoken statement; *v* utter such statement; *a* **-ous**; *n* **slanderer.**
slang *n* colloquial word, phrase not recognized as suitable for serious usage; *v* scold, abuse violently.
slant *v* slope; incline from perpendicular; *n* slope; (*coll*) point of view; *adv* **slantwise** obliquely.
slap *v* smack, strike smartly with open hand; *n* such blow; *a* **slapdash** head-long, happy-go-lucky; *n* **slapstick** rough knockabout farce or comedy; *a* **slap-up** (*coll*) lavish.
slash *v* gash; make cuts or slits in; lash violently at; reduce (prices) abruptly; *n* long cut; slit; act of slashing.
slat *n* thin narrow strip of wood or metal.
slate *n* hard, grey, shaly rock which splits easily into thin layers; piece of this used for roofing, or writing upon; *v* cover with slates; (*coll*) abuse, find fault

with; *ns* **slating** rebuke, severe criticism; **slate-club** club whose members pay weekly subscriptions, which are repaid at specified time.

slattern *n* slut; *a* **slatternly** untidy, dirty, sluttish.

slaughter *n* butchering of animals for food; needless killing (of humans, animals) in large numbers; *v* kill animals for meat; kill needlessly, massacre; *n* **slaughter-house** abattoir; place where cattle are butchered for market.

slave *n* one held in bondage to another; drudge; one dominated by desire, passion or devoted to cause, principle; *v* work like slave; *n* **slavery** bondage; serfdom; drudgery; *a* **slavish** servile; *n* **slaver** person, ship engaged in slave trade.

slaver *v* let saliva run from mouth; (*fig*) flatter.

slay *v* kill; *pt* **slew**; *pp* **slain**; *n* **slayer** killer.

sleazy *a* flimsy; (*coll*) sordid.

sledge, sled *n* vehicle on runners, for sliding on snow; toboggan; *v* travel, convey by sledge.

sledge-hammer *n* heavy hammer with long handle.

sleek *a* glossy, smooth, oily.

sleep *n* natural unconscious state recurring regularly in man and animals; period during which one sleeps; (*fig*) lethargy; death; *v* slumber; take rest by sleeping; (*coll*) provide beds for; *pt* & *pp* **slept**; *ns* **sleeper** one who sleeps; wooden support for railway lines; sleeping-car; **sleepiness**; **sleeping partner** one with financial interest in, but not taking active part in business; **sleeping sickness** tropical disease caused by tsetse fly; *as* **sleepless**; **sleepy.**

sleet *n* mixture of rain & snow falling together; *v* fall as sleet.

sleeve *n* part of garment which covers arm; tubular case or cover enclosing smaller tube or rod; decorative outer cover of gramophone record; *v* furnish with sleeves; *ns* **sleeve-link**, cuff-link; **sleeve valve** sliding valve; *as* **sleeved; sleeveless.**

sleigh *n* sledge.

sleight *n* dexterity, cunning; **s. of hand** conjuring trick *esp* by substitution.

slender *a* thin; slight; scanty.

sleuth *n* detective; (*ar*) trail, scent left by animal or

man; *v* track by scent; *n* **sleuth hound** bloodhound.
slew *v* swing round.
slice *n* flat, thin piece; cross-section; broad serving implement; slicing stroke, *esp* in ball games; *v* cut in slices; hit ball so that it turns to right.
slick *a* smooth, sleek; (*coll*) glib; *v* make smooth, glossy.
slide *v* slip, glide easily, down or off; (*fig*) pass over lightly; propel, push, thrust along slowly; *pt* & *pp* **slid**; *n* act of sliding; strip of smooth ice; shoot; slip of glass holding picture for projection, or object to be examined under microscope; *n* **slide-rule** mathematical instrument for rapid calculations; **sliding-scale** schedule for raising, lowering taxes, wages etc. in agreement with fluctuations in cost of living etc.
slight *a* slim, slender; mild; trivial; *v* neglect, disregard; *n* act, utterance of disrespect; humiliation.
slim *a* slender, slight, reverse of stout, thick; *v* make thin; reduce weight by diet etc; *ns* **slimness**; **slimming.**
slime *n* soft wet dirt; liquid mud; moisture secreted by snails etc; *a* **slimy** like smeared with, slime; (*fig*) fawning, servile.
sling *n* loop of leather etc. for hurling stones or other missiles; strip of cloth supporting injured limb; rope, band etc. for hoisting weights; *v* throw, suspend by sling; *pt* & *pp* **slung**; **s. out** throw out forcibly.
slink *v* move furtively, secretively; *pt* & *pp* **slunk.**
slip *v* slide; miss one's footing; go, steal away; pass rapidly; release (dog); escape from; give birth to prematurely; *n* act of slipping; error in judgement; moral lapse; loose cover for pillow; cutting for grafting; thin narrow strip; petticoat; young sole or plaice; *pl* **slips** fielding position in cricket.
slip-knot *n* knot that slides along string; one untied by pulling on it.
slip-on *n* garment easily put on.
slip-over *n* light, sleeveless jersey.
slipper *n* light, soft indoor shoe; *a* **slippered.**
slippery *a* difficult to hold; too greasy etc. for safety; (*fig*) artful, unreliable; *n* **slipperiness.**
slippy *a* (*coll*) fast, quick; slippery.

slip-road *n* minor local bypass road.
slipshod *a* slovenly; careless in working.
slipstream *n* current of air driven backwards by propeller or jets of aircraft.
slip-up *n* (*coll*) mistake.
slipway *n* slope on which ships are launched or laid up for repair.
slit *v* cut open, make incision in; *pt* & *pp* **slit** or **slitted**; *n* narrow opening, incision.
slither *v* slip and slide slowly along or down.
sliver *n* small, narrow piece, cut, torn off anything; splinter.
slob *n* (*sl*) fool, lout.
slobber *v* allow saliva to run out of mouth; dribble; (*fig*) show sentimental affection for; *n* dribbling saliva; (*fig*) sentimentality.
sloe *n* bluish-black fruit of blackthorn; **sloe gin** liqueur of sloes steeped in gin.
slog *v* work hard and persistently; hit hard (*esp* at cricket).
slogan *n* catchword or phrase used in advertising etc; Highland war-cry.
sloop *n* single-masted sailing vessel; small warship.
slop *v* spill, be spilt; overflow; *n* (*pl*) dirty water, liquid waste; soft food for invalids; *a* **sloppy** wet; (*fig*) maudlin; slipshod.
slope *n* inclined direction or surface; steepness; *v* be, have inclined (in) surface; (*sl*) run away.
slot *n* narrow slit; aperture, *esp* for insertion of coins; *n* **slot-machine** automatic machine, worked by insertion of coins.
slot *n* track of animal.
sloth *n* indolence, laziness; sluggish S. American mammal; *a* **slothful** lazy, inactive.
slouch *n* careless, clumsy, slovenly gait; *v* walk thus; *n* **slouch hat** soft hat with turned down brim.
slough *n* swamp, bog.
slough *n* cast-off skin of snake; *v* shed skin; come off, discard.
sloven *n* lazy, dirty & untidy person; **slovenly** *a* untidy in appearance; careless, slipshod; *n* **slovenliness.**

slow *a* moving at low rate of speed; taking longer than usual; behind correct time; not alert, stupid; inactive; *v* reduce speed; *ns* **slowness; slowcoach** person slow in acting, thinking etc; *adv* **slowly.**

slow-worm *n* blind-worm, limbless lizard.

sludge *n* thick, greasy mud; slush; any slimy deposit.

slug *n* land snail with no shell; small bullet for air-gun etc; (*print*) line of type-metal used for spacing; *v* hit hard, slog; *a* **sluggish** slow; inactive; lazy; *n* **sluggishness.**

sluice *n* flood-gate; (*coll*) brisk wash with water; *v* provide with sluices; (*coll*) wash down with, splash water over.

slum *n* dilapidated, squalid street or area, *usu* over-crowded; *v* go visiting slums.

slumber *v* sleep; (*fig*) lie dormant; *n* sleep.

slump *n* sudden fall in prices, value etc; *v* fall in price, demand; financial depression; (*fig*) decline in esteem.

slur *v* pass lightly over; pronounce indistinctly; (*mus*) sing, play legato; *n* act of slurring; stain, stigma.

slush *n* liquid, soft mud; melting snow; (*coll*) sickly sentiment; drivel; *a* **slushy.**

slut *n* dirty, untidy woman; slattern; *a* **sluttish.**

sly *a* cunning, underhand; not frank; artful; *n* **slyness.**

smack *n* taste, trace of; suggestion of; *v* have flavour of; be suggestive of.

smack *n* smart explosive sound (of lips); crack of whip; slap; *v* make such sound.

smack *n* small fishing-vessel.

small *a* little, very young; trivial, unimportant; petty, paltry; *ns* **smallness; small-arms** revolvers and rifles; **small fry** young fish; (*fig*) children; **small-holding** small plot of agricultural land let out; very small farm; **smallpox** acute infectious and contagious disease; **small-talk** trivial conversation; *a* **small-minded** narrow-minded, petty.

smarmy *a* (*coll*) ingratiatingly polite, flattering.

smart *a* sharp, forcible; brisk; alert, clever; well-dressed, fashionable; *v* feel sore and painful; feel hurt, resentful; *n* sharp pain.

smarten *v* make, give spruce appearance to; *a* **smartly** fashionably; quickly; *n* **smartness.**
smash *v* break to pieces, shatter; hit violently; defeat utterly; ruin *esp* financially; collide with; *n* violent shattering; bankruptcy, ruin; violent collision of vehicles; *n* **smash-hit** (*coll*) highly popular song, film etc; *a* **smashing** devastating; (*coll*) outstanding, delightful.
smattering *n* slight, superficial knowledge of subject.
smear *n* stain, mark made by contact with oily, greasy substance; (*coll*) malicious rumour; *v* mark with smear; damage by rumour.
smell *v* perceive, inhale, emit, odour; stink; (*fig*) track, discover; suspect; *n* odour, scent; act of smelling; *pt* & *pp* **smelt, smelled.**
smelt *n* small edible silvery fish.
smelt *v* extract metal from ore, by heat.
smile *v* curve, part lips in expression of pleasure, amusement; (*fig*) be favourable to; *n* act of smiling; facial expression showing happiness, affection, amusement.
smirch *v* dirty; stain; disgrace.
smirk *v* simper in self-satisfied manner; *n* conceited; knowing smile.
smite *v* wound; afflict; affect strongly *esp* with love, fear; *pt* **smote**; *pp* **smitten.**
smith *n* worker in metal; *n* **smithy** smith's workshop; forge.
smock *n* loose outer protective garment, formerly worn by shepherds; *v* adorn with honeycomb needlework; *n* **smocking.**
smog *n* dense mixture of smoke and fog.
smoke *n* fine particles, emitted by burning matter suspended in vapour; act of smoking tobacco; *v* emit smoke; inhale and expel smoke of burning tobacco; cure (fish etc.) by exposing to wood smoke; *n* **smoker**; *a* **smoky.**
smooth *a* polished; even; level; calm; soothing; unruffled; *v* make smooth.
smoulder *v* burn slowly without flame.
smudge *n* smear, blur, blot; *v* make smudge.
smug *a* complacent; prudish, prim; *n* **smugness.**

smuggle *v* import or export (goods) without payment of customs duties; convey secretly; *n* **smuggler**
smut *n* particle of soot, dirt, etc; parasitic fungus; obscene talk, writing etc; *a* **smutty**.
snack *n* hasty, light meal; *n* **snack-bar** bar in restaurant where snacks are served; café.
snaffle *n* light bit for horse; *v* (*sl*) steal, pinch.
snag *n* tree-stump *esp* in river bed; (*fig*) unexpected obstacle; run or catch in stocking.
snail *n* shell-bearing, slow-moving mollusc, leaving slimy trail; (*fig*) slow-moving person.
snake *n* scaly limbless reptile, serpent; *a* **snaky** of, like snakes; winding; *v* move like snake; twist, wind.
snap *n* make quick bite or snatch; break sharply, abruptly; *n* quick sharp sound; *a* **snappy** irritable; quick, lively; (*coll*) smart; *ns* **snap-dragon** antirrhinum; **snapshot** quickly-taken photograph.
snare *n* device for catching birds, animals etc; *v* catch in snare.
snarl *v* growl threateningly; entangle; *n* facial expression, sound made in snarling; traffic jam.
snatch *v* seize, make quick grab at; *n* act of snatching; disconnected fragment, portion.
sneak *v* move, creep furtively; (*sl*) inform against; *n* mean, furtive person; tell-tale.
sneer *v* smile, speak scornfully; *n* act of sneering.
sneeze *v* eject air through nostrils with sudden involuntary noise and spasm; *n* sneezing.
snick *n* small cut, notch; *v* cut thus.
snicker *v* laugh furtively, slyly; neigh; *n* such sound.
sniff *v* inhale audibly through nose; **sniff at** express scorn etc. by sniffing; *n* act of sniffing.
snip *v* cut, clip with scissors, shears; *n* short, quick cut; (*sl*) profitable bargain; *n* **snippet** small piece.
snipe *n* bird of plover family; *v* shoot at enemy from cover; *n* **sniper**.
snivel *v* whine, whimper peevishly; sniff repeatedly; *n* **snivel**.
snob *n* one who pretends to be better than he is; one who puts exaggerated importance on rank, wealth etc; *n* **snobbery**; *a* **snobbish**.
snood *n* ornamental hair net.

snooker *n* game combining pool and pyramids played on billiard table.
snoop *v* (*sl*) pry; peer into.
snooze *v* take short, light nap; doze; *n*.
snore *v* breathe heavily, noisily when asleep; *n* act, sound of snoring.
snort *v* make loud noise by drawing air through nostrils; *n*.
snot *n* (*sl*) mucus from nose.
snout *n* projecting nose of animal.
snow *n* frozen vapour falling as flakes from sky; (*sl*) powdered cocaine; *v* fall as snow; **snowed under** (*fig*) overwhelmed; *a* **snowy** covered with snow; inclined to snow; *n* **snowball** snow pressed into hard ball; something growing bigger; *v* play with snowballs; increase in size rapidly; *ns* **snowdrop** early spring flower; **snowshoe** racquet-shaped framework attached to foot for travelling on snow.
snub *v* rebuff by sneering remark; slight, insult; *n* snubbing; *n* **snub nose** one turned up at end.
snuff *n* powdered tobacco for sniffing up nose; *v* put out (candle).
snug *a* warm, cosy; trim; *n* **snuggle** nestle, lie close to; cuddle.
so *adv* & *conj* in such manner; in order that; to such extent; *a* **so-called** called thus, but not entitled to name.
soak *v* steep, drench; wet thoroughly; *n* soaking.
soap *n* compound of fatty acid and base which cleans and washes; *a* **soapy** pert. to soap; obsequious.
soar *v* fly high; (*fig*) rise to heights of imagination etc; *n* **soaring**.
sob *v* weep noisily; catch breath in weeping; *n* sobbing; *n* (*sl*) **sob stuff** exaggerated pathos or sentimentality.
sober *a* temperate, moderate; quiet in colour; not drunk; *v* make, become sober; *n* **sobriety** state of being sober.
sobriquet, soubriquet *n* nick-name; assumed name.
soccer *n* (*coll*) *abbrev.* Association football.
sociable *a* companionable; affable; *n* **sociability**.

social *a* relating to society; gregarious; sociable; *n* **socialite** member of high society.
socialism *n* political movement advocating public ownership of means of production, distribution and exchange; *n* **-ist** member of socialist party.
society *n* organized community of mutually dependent individuals; companionship; association, club, group; fashionable people collectively.
sociology *n* social science.
sock *n* short stocking; inner sole of shoe.
sock *v* (*sl*) hit, thrash.
socket *n* hollow, recess into which something fits.
sod *n* flat piece of turf.
soda *n* any of various sodium compounds; (*coll*) soda-water; *n* **soda-water** aerated water.
sodden *a* soaked, saturated; (*fig*) heavy, stupid.
sodium *n* metallic alkaline element.
sodomy *n* unnatural sexual intercourse; (*coll*) *abbrev* **sod**, *n* **sodomite** one practising this.
sofa *n* long padded couch with back and arms.
soft *a* not hard; smooth; flabby; gentle; not loud; feeble-minded; *v* **soften** make, become soft; *n* **soft drink** non-alcoholic drink; **soft soap** (*fig*) flattery; *a* **soft-hearted** merciful.
soggy *a* soaked with water, sodden.
soil *n* surface earth; land, country.
soil *v* make, become dirty; tarnish, sully.
sojourn *v* stay for a time; *n* short visit; *n* **sojourner**.
solace *n* consolation; *v* comfort in distress.
solar *a* pertaining to sun; *v* **solarize** expose to action of sun; **solar plexus** network of nerves in pit of stomach; **solar system** system of planets. comets, asteroids etc. which revolve round the sun.
solder *n* fusible metal alloy used for joining metal; *v* join with this; *n* **soldering-iron**.
soldier *n* one enlisted in army; *v* serve as soldier; *n* **soldiery** soldiers collectively.
sole *n* under surface of foot; under part of shoe etc; edible marine flat-fish; (of shoes etc) fit with (new) sole.
sole *a* one and only; single.
solecism *n* grammatical error; social mistake.
solemn *a* serious, formal; grave, deliberate; *n* **solem-**

nity; *v* **solemnize** perform with legal formalities; make solemn; *n* **solemnization.**

solicit *v* request earnestly; accost (person) for immoral purpose; *ns* **solicitation**; *n* **solicitor** lawyer; *a* **solicitous** eager; anxious; *n* **solicitude** anxiety, concern.

solid *a* not liquid or gaseous; compact; not hollow; financially sound; unanimous; *n* solid body of three dimensions; *n* **solidity**; *v* **solidify** make, become solid; *ns* **solidification**; **solidarity** unanimity.

soliloquy *n* talking to oneself; monologue not addressed to anyone; *v* **soliloquize.**

solitary *a* alone, single; lonely; *n* **solitude** state of being alone; loneliness; *n* **solitaire** single gem set on its own; card game for one.

solo *n* (*music*) composition for single instrument or voice; (*fig*) display, performance by one person; card-game like whist; *n* **soloist**; *a* **solo** alone; unaccompanied.

solstice *n* time of year when sun reaches point furthest N or S of equator.

solve *v* work out; find answer to; *as* **soluble** capable of being dissolved in liquid; **solvable** able to be solved; *ns* **solubility**; **solution** answer to problem; liquid containing dissolved solid; *a* **solvent** able to pay all debts; *n* substance that can dissolve something; *n* **solvency** ability to pay debts.

sombre *a* dark, gloomy.

sombrero *n* wide-brimmed hat.

some *pron* certain number, not specified; *a* unspecified person, thing, number or account; (*sl*) remarkable, great; *n* **somebody**; *adv* **somehow** by means still unknown; *n* **something** thing not clearly defined; *a* **sometime** formerly; *advs* **sometimes** now and then; occasionally; **somewhat** rather; **somewhere** in unspecified place.

somersault *v* turn, fall head over heels; *n.*

somnambulist *n* sleep-walker; *n* **somnambulism.**

somnolent *a* sleepy, drowsy; *n* **somnolence.**

son *n* male child; *n* **son-in-law** daughter's husband.

sonar *n* apparatus used in locating underwater objects.

sonata *n* musical composition in several movements; *n* **sonatina** short sonata.
song *n* musical utterance by human voice, or by birds; *n* **songster** singer; *esp* singing-bird.
sonic *a* of sound; *n* **s. bang, s. boom** sound of shock waves set up by aircraft flying through sound barrier.
sonnet *n* short poem of fourteen lines.
sonorous *a* deep, resonant.
soon *adv* in short time; early; readily; immediately.
soot *n* black flaky substance produced by burning matter; *a* **sooty**; *v* cover with soot.
soothe *v* appease; make calm; allay pains etc.
soothsayer *n* prophet; diviner.
sop *n* bread dipped in liquid; (*fig*) concession, bribe; *a* **soppy** (*sl*) soft, sloppy; (*coll*) weakly sentimental; *v* **sop up** absorb (liquid).
sophist *n* plausible reasoner, quibbler; *n* **sophism** fallacious argument; *v* **sophisticate** deprive of naturalness; corrupt; *a* **sophisticated** worldly-wise; artificial; (engine etc) having latest refinements; *n* **sophistication.**
sophomore *n* second-year student at American university.
soporific *n* & *a* (drug) causing sleep.
soprano *n* highest voice in women and boys; singer with this voice; musical part for this.
sorcerer *n* wizard, magician; *n* **sorcery** witchcraft; enchantment.
sordid *a* mean; ignoble; squalid; obscene; *n* **sordidness.**
sore *a* painful; affronted; grieved; *n* boil, ulcer, (*fig*) painful memory; *n* **soreness.**
Soroptimist *n* member of women's Rotary Club.
sorrel *n* herb with reddish-brown acrid-tasting leaves; *a* of this colour.
sorrow *n* grief; mental pain; regret; *v* grieve, mourn; *a* **sorrowful.**
sorry *a* regretful; gloomy, mean; poor.
sort *n* class; kind; (*print*) letters of particular fount of type; *v* arrange, select in groups; *n* **sorter.**
sortie *n* sudden attack by besieged troops.

S.O.S. *n* international signal of distress.
so-so *a* (*coll*) neither good nor bad; mediocre.
sot *n* habitual, persistent drunkard; *a* **sottish.**
sotto voce *adv* in an undertone.
soufflé *n* light dish made with beaten whites of egg.
soul *n* spiritual, non-material part in man; immortal part, separated from body; human being; *as* **soulful** emotional; sentimental; **soulless** without emotion; cruel; impersonal.
sound *n* what is heard; noise; *v* emit, cause to emit noise; seem; *n* **sound-barrier** moment when aircraft's speed equals that of sound-waves.
sound *a* healthy, in good condition; logical; reliable; strong; *adv* **soundly** thoroughly.
sound *v* measure depth of (water); plunge to bottom; (*fig*) ascertain views of; test with stethoscope; *n* strait, channel; *n pl* **soundings** depth of water taken with lead.
soup *n* thick or clear liquid food made from meat or vegetables; (*sl*) **in the s.** in trouble.
sour *a* acid; rancid; fermented; (of soil) poor, damp; morose; *v* make, become sour; *n* **sourness.**
source *n* spring; starting-point; origin.
souse *v* pickle; soak with water; *a* **soused** pickled; (*sl*) very drunk.
soutane *n* cassock.
south *n* cardinal point opposite N; region in this direction; *a* & *adv* towards south; *as* **southerly** towards, coming from south; **southern** pertaining to south; *ns* **sou'wester** waterproof hat; **Southdown** breed of sheep.
souvenir *n* keepsake; memento.
sovereign *n* monarch, supreme ruler; British gold coin worth £1; *a* supreme; efficacious, effectual; *n* **sovereignty** supreme power or rule.
soviet *n* political unit of U.S.S.R.; council of workers, soldiers etc; **S. Union** modern name of Russia.
sow *n* fully grown female pig.
sow *v* scatter, cast seed on ground; *pt* **sowed;** *pp* **sown** or **sowed;** *n* **sower.**
soya *n* species of oil-yielding bean; **s. flour** flour made from ground soya beans.

sozzled *a* (*sl*) drunk.
spa *n* mineral spring; health resort having mineral spring.
space *n* area, distance; period of time; region beyond earth's atmosphere; room; empty place; *a* **spacious** extensive, roomy; *n* **spaceship** vehicle capable of passing beyond earth's atmosphere.
spade *n* digging tool with flat blade; card of suit of spades; **spade work** preliminary work.
spaghetti *n* thin macaroni.
span *n* distance between tip of thumb and little finger, when fully extended; approx. 9″; full extent; space between supports of bridge; extreme breadth *esp* of birds or aircraft across wings; team of oxen; *v* measure with hand; stretch across, over.
spangle *n* small disc of brilliant metal, used as ornament.
spaniel *n* breed of sporting dog with long drooping ears and silky hair.
spank *v* slap with open hand; move briskly; *n* **spanking** series of slaps, as punishment; *a* brisk, rapid; *n* **spanker** fast horse; fore-and-aft sail on mizzen mast.
spanner *n* tool for tightening or loosening nuts and bolts.
spar *n* pole used as mast.
spar *n* kind of crystalline mineral.
spar *v* practise boxing blows; contest in friendly manner; *n* **sparring partner** one against whom boxer practises.
spare *a* meagre; lean, thin; additional, extra; in reserve; *n* spare part for machine *esp* motor-car; *v* refrain from killing etc; do without; show mercy; give away.
spark *n* glowing particle thrown off by burning substance; brief flash of light accompanying electric discharge; (*fig*) vitality, life; *v* emit sparks; **sparking plug** device for securing electric ignition in internal combustion engine.
sparkle *v* glitter; effervescence; *n* brilliance; gaiety, wit; *a* **sparkling** scintillating; intellectually brilliant (of wine) effervescent.

sparrow *n* small common brown birds; **s.-hawk** small hawk.
sparse *a* thinly scattered; scanty.
spartan *a* austere, hardy; unflinching.
spasm *n* sudden violent, involuntary muscular contraction; *a* **spasmodic** jerky; intermittent.
spastic *a* suffering from lack of muscular control, due to congenital brain damage; *n* person suffering from such damage.
spat *n* short gaiter.
spatchcock *n* quickly cooked fowl.
spate *n* sudden flood of river after rain; *fig* excessive amount.
spatial *a* pertaining to space.
spatter *v* splash drops on; *n* shower, sprinkling.
spatula *n* blunt, broad-bladed knife used for mixing paint, and in cooking.
spavin *n* disease of hock-joint of horse; *a* **spavined.**
spawn *n* eggs of fish, frogs etc; offspring; *v* (of fish etc) lay eggs; (*fig*) generate in mass.
speak *v* utter words; convey meaning; give speech, lecture etc; converse; *pt* **spoke**; *pp* **spoken**; *n* **speaker** one who delivers, speech, lecture etc; (*cap*) presiding officer in House of Commons.
spear *n* long-shafted weapon with pointed head; *v* pierce, catch with spear.
spearmint *n* common garden mint.
special *a* particular, exceptional; not for public, general use; for specific purpose; distinctive; *n* **specialist** one who devotes himself to a particular branch of science, art or profession; *v* **specialize** make special; limit; particularize; *n* **specialty, speciality** special product, distinctive feature etc.
specie *n* coined money.
species *n* class; group; sort, kind.
specific *a* characteristic of species; definite; (*med*) of, for a particular disease; *n* remedy for particular disease; **s. gravity** ratio of density of substance to that of water; *v* **specify** state definitely, precisely; *n* **specification** detailed description or statement.
specimen *n* representative example or sample; (*coll*) odd person.

specious *a* plausible.
speck *n* small spot, mark; *v* **speckle** mark, be marked with small spots; *a* **speckless** spotless.
spectacle *n* show, display; *pl* pair of optical lenses in frame; *a* **spectacular** impressive, remarkable; *n* **spectator** onlooker.
spectre *n* ghost, apparition; *a* **spectral.**
spectrum *n* series of bands of coloured light formed when beam has passed through prism; *pl* **spectra**; *n* **spectroscope** instrument for analysing spectra.
speculate *v* form theory about; invest in uncertain security; *n* **speculator**; *a* **speculative** given to guessing; risky; *n* **speculation.**
speculum *n* reflector; mirror of telescope.
speech *n* act, faculty of speaking; language; formal public discourse; *v* **speechify** make long, tedious speeches; *a* **speechless** dumb; at loss for words.
speed *n* swiftness; velocity; *v* move quickly; drive (vehicle) at high speed; *pt* & *pp* **sped** or **speeded**; *n* **speeding** exceeding speed limit; **speedometer** instrument to show speed of vehicle; *a* **speedy** rapid; prompt; *n* **speed limit** legal limit of speed of vehicle; *n* **speedway** motor-cycle racing track.
speedwell *n* flowering herb.
spell *n* magical formula, charm; fascination; *a* **spell-bound** bewitched, entranced.
spell *n* bout, short period of activity.
spell *v* say or write letter by letter; *pt* & *pp* **spelled** or **spelt**; *n* **spelling** way in which word is spelt.
spelter *n* zinc.
spend *v* pay out; expend; wear out, exhaust; *pt* & *pp* **spent**; *n* **spend-thrift** one who squanders; wasteful person.
sperm *n* male generative substance.
spermaceti *n* white, waxy substance obtained from head of sperm-whale; *n* **sperm-whale** large whale.
spew *v* vomit.
sphagnum *n* peat-moss.
sphere *n* ball, globe; scope, range; status; *ns* **spherical**; *n* **spheroid** nearly spherical body.
Sphinx *n* fabulous human-headed lion; Egyptian statue of this; (*fig*) inscrutable person.

spice *n* aromatic pungent vegetable seasoning; (*fig*) that which adds interest or excitement; *a* **spicy**.
spick and span *a* bright, fresh, tidy.
spider *n* small eight-legged animal, which spins web to catch prey; *a* **spidery**.
spigot *n* plug for stopping air hole in cask.
spike *n* sharp pointed rod, nail etc; ear of corn; *v* drive spike into; furnish, set with spikes; impale.
spill *n* splinter, strip of paper, or wood used as taper.
spill *v* (of liquid) flow, be upset, out of vessel; (of persons) fall from vehicle etc; *pt* & *pp* **spilt** or **spilled**; *n* fall.
spillikins *n* game played with set of small rods or pegs.
spin *v* twist (wool etc. into thread); whirl; (of spiders etc) exude filament for web; *pt* **spun** (*ar* **span**); *pp* **spun**; *n* act of spinning; twist, whirl; *ns* **spinning** act of making web; process of forming thread; **spinneret** silk-spinning organ of silkworm, spider etc.
spinach *n* garden vegetable with edible leaves.
spindle *n* rod, axis on which anything rotates; *a* **spindly** long and slender.
spindrift *n* spray blown over water.
spine *n* backbone; thin, sharp thorn, or growth on animal; back of book; *a* **spinal**.
spinet *n* keyboard instrument.
spinnaker *n* large, triangular sail on yacht.
spinney *n* small wood.
spinster *n* unmarried woman.
spiraea *n* kind of plant allied to meadowsweet.
spire *n* pointed part of steeple.
spiral *a* winding constantly about centre, like thread of screw; *n* spiral curve.
spirit *n* life essence; soul, ghost; immaterial part of man; courage, liveliness; *pl* powerful alcoholic drink; liquid got by distillation; *v* remove secretly; *as* **spiritual** pertaining to soul or spirit, not material; **spiritless** listless, apathetic; *ns* **spiritualism** belief that spirits of dead can communicate with living; **spiritualist** believer in spiritualism; *a* **spirituous** alcoholic.
spit *n* sharp rod for roasting meat on; sandy point projecting into sea; *v* thrust through.

spit *v* eject saliva; *pt* & *pp* **spat**; *n* saliva; *ns* **spittle** saliva; **spittoon** vessel to spit into.
spite *n* malice; *v* act maliciously towards; **in spite of** notwithstanding; *a* **spiteful.**
spiv *n* one who makes living by dishonest, but not criminal means.
splash *v* fall in drops on; scatter (liquid) on; *n* result, sound, of splashing.
splay *v* slant; dislocate (joint); *n* slanting edge; *a* **splay-footed** having flat, turned-out feet.
spleen *n* ductless gland in abdomen; ill-humour; *a* **splenetic.**
splendid *a* magnificent; illustrious; (*coll*) excellent; *n* **splendour** brilliance; magnificence.
splice *v* join by interweaving strands; join (wood) by overlapping; (*coll*) marry.
splint *n* rigid piece of wood etc. *esp* when keeping fractured bone in place; *v* support with splint; *n* **splinter** small, sharp broken off piece of wood, glass etc; *v* break into fragments.
split *v* divide; tear apart; gape open suddenly; *pt* & *pp* **split**; *n* cleft, tear (in fabric).
splotch *n* splash; irregular stain, daub of colour.
splurge *n* ostentation; *v* make vulgar display.
splutter *v* split slightly while speaking; utter indistinctly.
spoil *v* injure; damage; deteriorate; cause to become badly-behaved, selfish etc; by over-indulgence; *pt* & *pp* **spoiled** or **spoilt**; *n pl* booty; *n* **spoil-sport** one who prevents others from enjoying themselves.
spoke *n* radial bar of wheel; *n* **spokeshave** kind of plane.
spokesman *n* one deputed to speak for others; representative.
spolation *n* robbery with violence; act of spoiling.
sponge *n* marine animal whose fibrous skeleton is used to absorb liquids, or for cleaning; light cake; *v* wipe with sponge; *v* (*sl*) **s. on** cadge from; *n* (*sl*) **sponger** cadger; *a* **spongy** elastic, soft, absorbent.
sponsor *n* guarantor; patron; godparent.
spontaneous *a* (of persons) voluntary; self-acting, or self-originated; *n* **spontaneity.**

spoof *n* & *v* hoax.
spook *n* ghost, wraith.
spool *n* reel, bobbin.
spoon *n* implement consisting of shallow bowl on handle, used in cooking and conveying food to mouth etc; *v* use, lift with, spoon; (*sl*) make love.
spoor *n* track of wild animal.
sporadic *a* scattered; occurring in single cases.
spore *n* minute reproductive organism, of flowerless plant, or as in bacteria.
sporran *n* leather pouch worn in front of kilt.
sport *n* outdoor pleasurable activity; outdoor games; fun; freak; *pl* athletic meeting; *v* joke; amuse oneself; wear conspicuously; *a* **sportive** playful; *n* **sportsman** one engaging in sport; good loser.
spot *n* small mark *esp* if round; pimple; small place; (*fig*) moral blemish; *v* mark with spot; (*coll*) see, catch sight of; *a* **spotless** without blemish; perfectly clean; *n* **spotlight** strong beam of light able to be focussed on one spot; *v* illuminate with spotlight; (*coll*) draw attention to.
spouse *n* husband or wife.
spout *v* gush, pour out; *n* projecting lip or tube for pouring liquid; gushing jet of liquid, water.
sprain *v* & *n* twist or wrench (of muscles, tendons etc).
sprat *n* small edible fish of herring family.
sprawl *v* lie, be stretched out awkwardly; straggle.
spray *n* sprig, twig with smaller branches or flowers.
spray *n* fine droplets of liquid; wind-blown particles of sea-water; atomizer; device for spraying; *v* squirt, treat, with spray; become spray; *n* **sprayer** device for spraying.
spread *v* cover (surface) with; stretch out, extend in all directions; become widely diffused, circulated; *pt* & *pp* **spread**; *n* extent; increase; feast.
spree *n* frolic; drinking bout.
sprig *n* small twig; small nail; scion; *a* **sprigged** ornamented with spray-like design.
sprightly *a* lively, brisk; *n* **sprightliness.**
spring *v* leap; discharge; pounce; bubble, gush forth; sprout up; *pt* **sprang**; *pp* **sprung**; *n* source, well;

first season of year; recoil; piece of coiled resilient metal etc; leap; *a* **springy** elastic; *n* **springer** variety of spaniel.

sprinkle *v* scatter in small drops; strew; *ns* **sprinkler; sprinkling** small quantity of drops, particles; few, scattered, people or objects.

sprint *v* run at full speed for short distance; *n* such run; *n* **sprinter.**

sprit *n* spar extending diagonally upwards from mast.

sprite *n* fairy, elf.

sprocket *n* projecting tooth on wheel for engaging chain.

sprout *v* put forth shoots, begin to grow; *n* young shoot; *n pl* **Brussels sprouts** vegetable like miniature cabbage.

spruce *n* type of coniferous tree; *a* smart and neat in dress.

spry *a* nimble, agile; alert.

spud *n* small spade for digging up weeds etc; (*sl*) potato.

spume *n* & *v* foam, froth.

spunk *n* tinder; courage, pluck.

spur *n* pricking wheel fixed on horseman's heel, for urging on horse; pointed projection on cock's leg; projecting ridge or part of mountain range; stimulus; *v* prick with spurs; urge; ride hard.

spurious *a* not genuine; false; sham.

spurn *v* reject scornfully; repel.

spurt, spirt *n* jet; short vigorous effort, *esp* in race; *v* gush out suddenly; make sudden brief effort (to increase speed etc).

sputum *n* saliva, spittle.

spy *n* agent employed to obtain secret information; *v* act as spy; catch sight of; *n* **spy-glass** small hand telescope.

squab *n* young, fat, unfledged pigeon or rook.

squabble *n* petty quarrel; *v* quarrel, bicker.

squad *n* (*mil*) small number of men; small group of persons; *n* **squadron** body of cavalry; group of aircraft or warships.

squalid *a* foul, dingy; sordid, mean; *n* **squalor.**

squall *n* harsh, shrill shriek; brief, violent storm; *v* scream; *a* **squally** gusty.
squander *v* spend, use, wastefully.
square *n* equilateral rectangle; open space of this shape in town etc; product of number multiplied by itself; *a* square in form; genuine; *v* make square; bribe; pay; make even; multiply number by itself.
squash *v* crush, press; flat; (*coll*) snub; *n* drink of crushed fruit; pulpy mass; game for two, played with rackets and soft ball in walled court; packed crowd.
squat *v* sit on heels; *a* short and thick; *n* **squatter** illegal settler in unoccupied house or land.
squaw *n* N. American Indian married woman.
squawk *n* loud, harsh cry; *v* utter such cry.
squeak *v* utter weak, thin cry of fright etc; make high, grating noise, as of unoiled hinge; *n* such noise.
squeal *v* utter shrill prolonged cry; (*sl*) betray secrets; *n* long shrill cry.
squeamish *a* easily nauseated; over sensitive.
squeegee *n* rubber broom for cleaning wet floors.
squeeze *v* press; wring; extort; extract; *n* act of squeezing.
squelch *v* produce sucking, gurgling sound; *n* such sound.
squib *n* small hissing firework.
squid *n* cuttle-fish.
squiggle *v* wriggle, squirm; *n* twisty illegible writing.
squint *v* look in different directions with each eye; *n* this eye affection, strabismus; (*coll*) glance.
squire *n* county landowner; formerly, attendant on knight; man escorting woman; *v* escort woman.
squirm *v* & *n* wriggle, writhe.
squirrel *n* small bushy-tailed rodent.
squirt *v* eject, be forced out, in jet; *n* jet (of liquid); syringe.
stab *v* pierce with pointed weapon; *n* wound so inflicted.
stabilize *v* make stable; restore to equilibrium; *ns* **stabilization**, **stabilizer** device for keeping ship, aircraft etc. in equilibrium.
stable *a* firmly fixed; not easily upset; resolute; *n* **stability** steadiness, firmness.

stable *n* building where horses are kept; *v* put in stable.
staccato *a* (*mus*) with each note played in sharply detached manner.
stack *n* heap, pile *esp* of hay, straw etc; tall chimney; (*coll*) large amount; *v* pile in stack.
stadium *n* open-air arena for athletics etc.
staff *n* tall pole; organized body of workers; servants of one employer; (*mus*) five lines on which notes are written; *pl* **staffs, staves.**
stag *n* male deer; *a* (*sl*) for men only, as **s. party.**
stage *n* raised floor or platform in theatre; scene of action; fixed stopping place (of bus etc); point of development; *v* put (play) on stage; do for effect; *a* **stagy** theatrical.
stagger *v* walk, move unsteadily; reel; shock; prevent from coinciding; *n* unsteady gait; *n pl* disease of horses and cattle.
stagnate *v* remain stationary; cease to flow; (*fig*) become sluggish; *n* **stagnation.**
staid *a* sedate, sober, steady; *n* **staidness.**
stain *v* discolour; impart colour deliberately; soil, blemish; *n* spot, blemish; *a* **stainless** of rustless steel alloy.
stairs *n pl* series of steps *usu* in building; *ns* **staircase, stairway** structure enclosing stairs; flight of stairs.
stake *n* pointed stick or post; prize; money wagered; *v* wager, risk; mark with posts etc.
stalactite *n* tapering lime formation hanging from roof of cave etc; *n* **stalagmite** similar formation rising from floor.
stale *a* not fresh; (*fig*) out of practice; tired by too much work.
stalemate *n* chess position when King cannot move without being in check; (*fig*) deadlock.
stalk *n* stem of plant.
stalk *v* walk in stiff, dignified way; pursue (prey, game etc) stealthily; *ns* **stalker; stalking-horse** horse used as cover by hunter; (*fig*) pretext.
stall *n* division in stable etc; booth in market for sale of goods; front seat in theatre etc; seat in chancel; *v*

unintentionally stop (engine); (of aircraft) lose flying speed.

stallion *n* uncastrated male horse.

stalwart *a* strong; brave, unflinching; *n* stalwart person.

stamen *n* pollen-bearing male organ of flower.

stamina *n* power of endurance; vigour, vitality.

stammer *v* speak hesitantly, with repetition of speech sounds; stutter; *n* this speech defect; *n* **stammerer.**

stamp *v* put foot down heavily; affix postage stamp; impress mark on; **s. out** (*fig*) destroy utterly; *n* act of stamping; imprinted mark, or instrument making it; gummed label printed with device as evidence of postage paid; class, character.

stampede *n* sudden frightened rush, *esp* of cattle; crowd etc; *v* flee in panic; cause to stampede.

stance *n* attitude in standing, *esp* when about to strike ball in golf etc.

stanchion *n* upright bar; prop, support.

stand *v* assume upright position; be situated; endure; remain valid; be candidate for; *pt* & *pp* **stood;** *n* stoppage; resolute resistance; structure on which something is placed, displayed; raised platform on which persons may sit or stand; *v* **stand by** support; be ready to help; **s. out** be conspicuous; **s. up for** defend; **s. in** deputize; *n* **standing** *a* erect; lasting; *ns* **standpoint** position, repute; point of view; **standstill** complete cessation of progress etc.

standard *n* flag; fixed rule; quality; approved model; *v* **standardize** regulate.

stannary *n* tin-mine; *a* of, pertaining to tin-mines.

stanza *n* group of verse-lines.

staple *n* U-shaped piece of metal with pointed ends, for fastening; paper-fastener; principal commodity; chief raw material; thread, fibre of wool, cotton; *a* leading, principal; *v* fasten with staple; grade (wool etc); *n* **stapler** grader of wool etc; machine for wire-stitching paper etc.

star *n* luminous heavenly body; figure, device resembling apparent shape of star; popular actor etc;

leading player; asterisk (*); *v* mark with asterisk; appear, present as, leading actor; *a* **starry** covered with, shining like, stars.

starboard *n* right-hand side of ship, looking forward; *a* of, on this side.

starch *n* carbohydrates, main food element in vegetables; white soluble powder mixed with water for stiffening linen etc; *v* make stiff thus; *a* **starchy** containing starch; stiff, formal.

stare *v* look, gaze at intently, fixedly; *n* prolonged intent look.

stark *a* stiff, rigid; absolute, utter.

starling *n* glossy black gregarious bird.

start *v* begin; set going; move with jerk; *n* sudden jerk; beginning; advantage in contest; *n* **starter** signaller for race to start.

startle *v* alarm; shock, surprise.

starve *v* die, suffer, from lack of food; suffer from cold; *ns* **starveling** thin, underfed person or thing; **starvation.**

state *n* condition; rank, position; nation and its government; self-governing division of country; pomp; *v* **state** express in words; *as* **stated** definitely fixed, settled; **stately** grand, impressive; imposing; *ns* **statement** assertion; utterance; official report of financial position of firm; **statesman** person taking part in state government; **statesmanship** statecraft; **state room** ceremonial reception room; private cabin on ship.

static *a* stationary; **s. electricity** electricity at rest; **statics** radio atmospherics.

station *n* place, position where thing stops or is placed; walk in life; employment, occupation; *v* place in specific spot; *a* **stationary** at rest; not moving; not changing.

stationery *n* writing materials, pens, paper, ink etc; *n* **stationer** dealer in writing materials.

statistics *n pl* systematic collection and arrangement of numerical facts; study of these; *n* **statistician** one skilled in dealing with statistics; *a* **statistic(al).**

statue *n* carved or moulded figure of human or animal etc; *n* **statuary** statues collectively; *a*

statuesque having dignity or serenity of statue; *n* **-uette** small statue.
stature *n* bodily, height, size.
status *n* rank, social position; legal position.
statute *n* law made by Parliament; *a* **statutory** depending on, enacted by statute.
staunch, **stanch** *v* stop flow (of blood); *a* trustworthy, loyal.
stave *n* curved wooden strip forming part of cask; stanza; (music) staff; *v* break hole in; keep off; *pt* & *pp* **stove** or **staved.**
stay *v* check; remain in place as visitor etc; last out; pause; *n* rest, visit; (*leg*) suspension of proceedings, restraint.
stay *n* prop, strut; rope supporting mast etc; *pl* corsets; *v* support, sustain.
stead *n* place; service; **in (one's) stead** in place of; **in good stead** be of good service; *n* **steading** farmstead.
steady *a* firm; regular; sober; reliable; *v* make, become steady; *a* **steadfast** unwavering; resolute; *n* **steadiness.**
steak *n* thick slice of meat *esp* beef, or fish.
steal *v* rob, thieve; move furtively, silently; *pt* **stole**; *pp* **stolen**; *n* **stealth** secret, furtive action; *a* **stealthy.**
steam *n* water-vapour; *v* cook, treat with steam; give off steam; move by steam power; *ns* **steam-engine** one worked or propelled by steam; **steamer** utensil for cooking with steam; steamship; **steam-roller** heavy roller for levelling roads; (*fig*) massive force; *a* **steamy** covered with steam; misty.
steed *n* (*poet*) horse.
steel *n* iron containing carbon; tool, weapon of steel; (*fig*) harden; *a* **steely.**
steelyard *n* weighing-machine.
steep *a* sharply inclined; (*coll*) exorbitant; incredible.
steep *v* soak, saturate; (*fig*) imbue.
steeple *n* tall tapering structure on church; *ns* **steeplechase** cross-country horse race; **steeplejack** man employed to repair, clean steeples, tall chimneys etc.

steer *v* guide, direct course of (car, ship, etc); aim one's course; *n* **steerage** act, method of steering; stern; cheapest accommodation on ship.
steer *n* young ox, bullock.
stellar *a* of stars.
stem *n* stalk, trunk; part of word to which inflexional endings are added.
stem *v* check flow of; resist.
sten gun *n* type of machine gun.
stench *n* offensive smell.
stencil *n* thin plate of metal etc. perforated with design, or letters; pattern, design produced by applying colouring matter through holes of stencil plate; *v* decorate, make copy of, by using stencil.
stenography *n* shorthand writing; *n* **stenographer.**
stentorian *a* very loud.
step *v* lift and set down foot; walk; *n* act of stepping; sound, mark made by foot; gait; pace; procedure; stair; (*fig*) degree, stage; *pl* portable ladder with hinged prop.
stepchild *n* child of husband or wife by previous marriage; *ns* **stepfather; stepmother.**
steppe *n* broad, open, treeless plain in Russia.
stereophonic *a* (of sound) giving effect of coming from many directions.
stereoscope *n* optical instrument producing illusion of relief and distance by presenting two different images of same subject, one to each eye.
stereotype *n* metal plate cast from mould of set-up type; *a* **stereotyped** repeated without variations; printed from stereotype.
sterile *a* barren; unproductive; *n* **sterility**; *v* **sterilize** make incapable of reproduction; destroy bacteria; *ns* **sterilization** act, process of sterilizing; **sterilizer.**
sterling *a* in British money; genuine, pure; (*fig*) dependable.
stern *a* severe, strict; *n* **sternness.**
stern *n* after part of ship; rump of animal.
sternum *n* breast-bone.
stertorous *a* breathing loudly, as with sound of snoring.

stet *n* direction to printer, on proof, to cancel correction made.
stethoscope *n* instrument for listening to action of heart or lungs.
stevedore *n* one who stows and unloads cargoes at docks.
stew *v* cook slowly in closed vessel; *n* food so cooked; (*sl*) agitated condition.
steward *n* salaried manager of large household or estate; catering manager of club etc; waiter, attendant on ship's, aircraft's passengers; official helping to organize race-meeting, etc; (*fem*) **stewardess.**
stick *v* thrust into, stab; attach; adhere; (*coll*) bear bravely; come to a stop; *pt* & *pp* **stuck**; (*sl*) **stick up** threaten, rob at gun point (*n* also); **s. out** protrude; be obvious; **s. with** remain loyal to; *as* **sticky** adhesive; (*coll*) awkward; (*sl*) difficult, unpleasant; **stuck-up** (*coll*) conceited.
stick *n* slender rod of wood or other substance.
stickleback small fish with spiny dorsal fin.
stickler *n* one who insists on trivial points of procedure.
stiff *a* rigid; not easily moving; thick, formal; difficult; *v* **stiffen** make, become, stiff; *n* **stiffness**; *a* **stiff-necked** obstinate.
stifle *v* smother.
stigma *n* moral reproach; (*bot*) part of pistil receiving pollen; *v* **stigmatize** mark out (something discreditable); *n* **stigmatism.**
stile *n* steps, rail for climbing hedge or fence.
stiletto *n* small dagger; small pointed boring instrument.
still *a* motionless; silent; (of wine) not sparkling; *v* calm; quieten; *n* **stillness**; *as* **stilly** quiet; **stillborn** born dead; *n* **still life** picture of inanimate objects.
still *n* apparatus for distilling; *n* **still-room** store room for liquors, preserves etc.
stilt *n* (*usu pl*) pole with foot rests, for raising walker above ground; wading bird; *a* **stilted** stiff in manner.
stimulus *n* anything which excites action; incentive; *pl* **stimuli**; *v* **stimulate** rouse up; urge, incite; *n* & *a*

stimulant (drink, drug etc.) producing temporary increase of energy; *n* **stimulation.**

sting *n* sharp, pointed defensive, offensive organ of insect, reptile etc; sharp pain caused by sting; *v* thrust sting into; cause, feel sharp pain; *pt* & *pp* **stung.**

stingy *a* mean; niggardly; *n* **stinginess.**

stink *v* give out bad smell; *pt* **stank** or **stunk**; *pp* **stunk**; *n* stench; offensive smell.

stint *v* grudge; be niggardly with; *n* limitation.

stipend *n* salary, *esp* of clergyman; *a* **stipendiary** salaried; *n* **s. magistrate** one appointed by State.

stipple *v* paint, engrave in dots; *n* this method.

stipulate *v* make conditions in bargain; insist on; *n* **stipulation** proviso.

stir *v* set in motion; mix round and round with spoon etc; rouse, excite; *n* mental excitement *esp* public.

stirrup *v* metal hoop hung by strap from saddle for supporting foot of rider.

stitch *n* movement of needle in sewing; result of such movement; sharp pain in side; *v* sew.

stoat *n* animal of weasel family.

stock *n* bole, stem of tree, plant; handle; trader's supply of material for sale; lineage; capital of corporation or company; scented garden plant; *pl* timber framework supporting ship when building; *pl* frame with holes for head, hands and feet, for punishing offenders; *v* supply with, keep in stock; *ns* **Stock Exchange** place where stocks and shares are bought and sold; **stockbroker** member of Stock Exchange who buys stock etc. for clients; **stockjobber** member of Stock Exchange who deals in stocks etc. with broker; *as* **stock** constantly kept in stock; habitually produced; commonplace; **stocky** thickset, sturdy.

stockade *n* barrier, wooden fence for defence.

stocking *n* close-fitting covering for leg and foot.

stodgy *a* heavy, indigestible; dull.

stoic *n* person of rigid calm, fortitude; *a* **stoic(al)**, impassive; *n* **stoicism.**

stoker *n* one who tends furnace; fireman.

stole *n* long, narrow wrap of fur etc. worn about

shoulders; narrow strip of cloth or silk worn by priests.
stolid *a* impassive; lacking animation or action.
stomach *n* sac in abdomen in which food is digested; abdomen; (*fig*) liking; wish; *a* **stomachic** pertaining to stomach; *n* digestive medicine.
stone *n* fairly small piece of rock; gem; hard seed-case in certain fruits; hard deposits formed in kidneys, bladder etc; measure of weight, 14 lbs; *v* throw stones at; remove stone from fruit; *as* **stone-blind** quite blind; **stone deaf**; *n* **stone ware** coarse pottery; *a* **stony** full of stones; (*fig*) hard, cruel; (*sl*) penniless.
stonewalling *n* (cricket) batting with little effort to make runs; (*fig*) obstruction of business.
stooge *n* one who is butt of comedian's jokes; (*coll*) dupe, butt; *v* **s. around** wander about purposelessly, idly.
stool *n* backless seat; footstool; matter evacuated from bowels.
stoop *v* bend forwards or down; be round-shouldered, condescend; (of hawk) swoop; *n* position of stooping.
stop *v* cease, cause to cease motion; prevent; close opening; discontinue; stay, remain; *n* act of stopping; any device for altering pitch of note; peg, block; punctuation mark; *ns* **s.-gap** temporary substitute; **s.-press** late news; **s.-watch** watch with hand which can be stopped instantly, used for timing race etc; **stoppage** cessation of action, flow, etc; **stopper** plug, *esp* for bottle.
store *n* reserve supply, stock; warehouse; large general shop; *v* accumulate and keep supplies etc; hold storage room for; *ns* **storage** act of storing, being stored; **storage battery** accumulator; **s. heater** one using stored electrical heat.
storey *n* horizontal division, floor of building.
stork *n* large wading bird.
storm *n* violent atmospheric disturbance; tempest; (*mil*) violent assault; *v* assault; (*fig*) express rage, scold; *a* **stormy** tempestuous; passionate.
story *n* spoken or written narrative; tale; account; (*coll*) untruth; *n* **storyteller** reciter, writer of stories; (*coll*) liar.

stout *a* durable; resolute; fat; *n* strong dark beer; *n* **stoutness.**
stove *n* cooker; apparatus for heating.
stow *v* pack away; fill (hold) with goods; *ns* **stowage** space for stowing; **stowaway** one who hides in ship, aircraft, to get free passage.
straddle *v* spread legs wide; bestride.
strafe *v* shell, bomb heavily; (*coll*) damage; scold severely.
straggle *v* loiter, be apart from main group; *n* **straggler.**
straight *a* not bent or crooked; (*lit* & *fig*) upright; in order; (of spirits) neat; *n* straight stretch of road, river etc; (cards) sequence; *v* **straighten** make, put, become straight; *a* **straightforward** open, frank; *advs* **straight** direct; **straightaway** at once.
strain *v* make taut; over-exert, over-tax; wrench by too sudden effort; *n* tautness; severe bodily, mental effort; sprain; (*fig*) tone, manner etc; *a* **strained** showing nervous fatigue, forced.
strain *n* breed, stock, ancestry.
strainer *n* sieve, colander; *v* filter.
strait *a* (*ar*) narrow, strict; *n* narrow channel of water between two seas; (often *pl*) difficult position; *as* **straitened** impoverished, in financial difficulty; **straitlaced** austere, strict; *n* **strait-jacket** coat to confine arms of violent lunatics etc.
strand *n* shore; *v* run aground; leave, be left helpless, destitute.
strand *n* single thread of wool, fibre, rope etc; lock of hair.
strange *a* unfamiliar; unusual; foreign; singular; *ns* **strangeness; stranger** unknown person; foreigner.
strangle *v* kill by compressing windpipe, throttle; *n* **strangulation.**
strap *n* strip of leather or metal for fastening; *v* fasten with strap; beat with strap; *a* **strapping** tall, well-made; *n* **strap-hanger** standing passenger in train etc. who holds on to strap to steady himself.
stratagem *n* trick, plan for deceiving enemy; *ns* **strategy** art of military manoeuvring; (*fig*) battle of wits; **strategist;** *a* **strategic(al).**

stratosphere *n* upper atmospheric layer beginning approx. 6 miles above earth's surface.
stratum *n* (*geol*) layer; (*fig*) social division, class; *pl* **strata.**
straw *n* dry cut stalks of corn; *ns* **strawberry** plant bearing red sweet juicy fruit; **strawboard** cardboard made from straw.
stray *v* wander, lose one's way; *a* strayed; occasional; *n* lost animal or child.
streak *n* long line, stripe; (of lightning) flash; *v* mark with streaks; (*coll*) rush quickly past; *a* **-y.**
stream *n* body of flowing water or other liquid, rivulet, brook; *v* flow, run with liquid; fly out, float on air; *n* **streamer** ribbon, flag to fly in air.
streamlined *a* of curved shape, offering minimum resistance to water or air.
street *n* road in town or village with buildings on both sides; *n* **street-walker** prostitute.
strength *n* power; intensity; quality of being strong; force; *v* **strengthen** make stronger.
strenuous *a* energetic; unremitting.
streptococcus *n* bacterium in chain formation; *pl* **streptococci.**
streptomycin *b* antibiotic substance.
stress *n* strain; emphasis; intense pressure; (*mech*) force exerted on solid body; *v* emphasize; accent; subject to mechanical stress.
stretch *v* extend; be elastic; reach out; exert to utmost; *n* stretching; expanse; period of time; *n* **stretcher** one who, that which stretches; light framework for carrying disabled person.
strew *v* scatter, spread on surface; *pt* **strewed**; *pp* **strewn** or **strewed.**
stricken *a* affected by grief, illness, terror etc.
strict *a* exact; inflexible; stern, rigorous; *ns* **strictness**; **stricture** (*med*) contraction of duct or vessel; (*fig*) severe criticism.
stride *v* walk with long steps; crossover with one long step; *pt* **strode**; *pp* **stridden**; *n* single step or its length.
strident *a* harsh, shrill, grating.
strife *n* conflict, discord.

strike *v* hit; collide; aim, deliver blow; (of clock) sound time; affect; ignite; take down (tent, flag etc); make (coin, medal); stop work to enforce demand; *pt* **struck**; *pp* **struck, stricken**; *n* stoppage of work; *n* **striker** one who, that which, strikes; *a* **striking** noteworthy.
string *n* cord, twine; series of objects, chain; (of musical instrument) cord of catgut, wire; *pt* & *pp* **strung**; *as* **stringed**; furnished with strings; **stringy** fibrous.
stringent *a* strict, rigid, binding; *n* **stringency** severity.
strip *v* tear off, deprive of (covering etc); undress; *n* long, narrow piece; *n* **strip-tease** female entertainer who undresses in public.
stripe *n* narrow mark, band; chevron worn as symbol of military rank.
stripling *n* youth, lad.
strive *v* try earnestly; fight, contend; *pt* **strove**; *pp* **striven.**
stroke *n* blow; line made by single movement of pen, brush etc; single movement of hands or hand-operated instrument (as in swimming, cricket etc); rower in stern setting rate; a sudden attack of illness; *v* pass hand lightly over, caress; row stroke in boat.
stroll *v* take short leisurely walk, saunter; *n*.
strong *a* powerful; tough; healthy; affecting senses acutely; *n* **stronghold** fortess.
strop *n* leather strap for putting edge on razor; *v* apply strop to razor.
structure *n* formation, construction; that which is made up of many parts; building; *a* **structural.**
struggle *v* fight; grapple with; make strenuous effort; move convulsively; *n* contest; violent tussle.
strum *v* play noisily, idly or badly on stringed instrument.
strumpet *n* prostitute.
strut *n* prop, stay; affected, pompous gait; *v* support with struts; swagger.
strychnine *n* white poisonous alkaloid, used medicinally.
stub *n* tree-stump; end part, remnant (of cigarette,

pencil etc.); *v* hit one's toe accidentally on something; **stub out** extinguish (cigarette etc.).

stubble *n* short stalks of corn etc. left in ground after reaping; short growth of hair.

stubborn *a* resolute, unyielding; obstinate, pigheaded; *n* **stubbornness.**

stucco *n* fine plaster for coating walls.

stud *n* large headed projecting nail or peg; double headed button for cuff or collar of shirt; *v* set, decorate with studs.

stud *n* number of horses kept for breeding, hunting etc; *n* **stud-book** register of pedigree of thoroughbred horses etc.

studio *n* work-room of artist, photographer etc; room or premises where films are made or radio broadcasts are transmitted.

study *v* learn systematically; analyse; show concern for; *n* subject studied; experimental painting, sketch; room in which to study; *n* **student** person engaged in study, not yet graduate; one who studies; *as* **studied** premeditated; **studious** eager; careful; devoted to learning.

stuff *n* substance, material; textile fabric; (*fig*) nonsense; *v* fill, cram tightly with stuffing; (*coll*) overeat; *n* **stuffing** that which is used for filling; savoury seasoning used inside bird, meat; *a* **stuffy** close, lacking fresh air.

stultify *v* make a fool of; make ineffectual; *n* **stultification.**

stumble *v* trip up; falter; **s. across, on,** come upon by chance; *n* **stumbling-block** impediment, obstacle.

stump *n* stub, remainder, remnant; (cricket) sticks of wicket; *v* walk noisily; (cricket) put batsman out by striking bails off wicket; (*coll*) **s. up** pay out; *a* **stumpy** short, thickset.

stun *v* knock senseless; shock, amaze; *a* **stunning,** causing loss of senses; (*coll*) excellent; very beautiful.

stunt *v* (*coll*) spectacular feat or display, *esp* involving danger; sensational newspaper article etc.

stunt *v* check growth of; *a* **stunted** undersized; retarded.

stupefy *v* make stupid, dull; amaze; *n* **stupefaction.**
stupendous *a* astonishing; extraordinary.
stupid *a* slow-witted, dull; lacking intelligence; *n* **-ity.**
stupor *n* dazed condition; torpor; mental dullness.
sturdy *a* robust; vigorous; well-developed; *n* **sturdiness.**
sturgeon *n* large fish from which caviare and isinglass are obtained.
stutter *v* speak with hesitation and repetitions; stammer; *n* speech-defect.
sty *n* pen for pigs; (*fig*) filthy place.
sty, stye *n* inflamed swelling on eyelid.
style *n* manner of doing, expressing; deportment; sort, variety; correct mode of address; manner; *v* designate; *a* **stylish** smart, fashionable.
stymie *n* position on golfing green when opponent's ball blocked line to hole; *v* (*fig*) hinder, check.
styptic *n* & *a* (preparation) which stops bleeding.
suave *a* bland, urbane, affable; *n* **suavity.**
sub- *prefix*: *forms compounds with meaning* under almost, about, inferior, smaller. *Such compounds are not given here, when the meaning may be deduced from the simple word.*
subaltern *n* commissioned officer in army below rank of captain.
subconscious *n* not fully realized by mind; *n* (psycho-analysis) part of mind outside personal awareness of individual.
subcutaneous *a* under the skin.
subdue *v* overcome.
subject *a* under authority; exposed, liable to; *n* person owing, giving allegiance; one who, that which, is dealt with in specific way; that about which something is predicated; one under power of another; *v* conquer; make liable, cause to undergo; *n* **subjection** act of bringing, or state of being, under control; *a* **subjective** existing in mind; nominative; *n* **subjectivity.**
subjugate *v* conquer; force under control; *n* **subjugation.**
subjunctive *n* (*gram*) mood of verb expressing wish, possibility; *a* of, in that mood.

sublet *v* let to another, property of which one is tenant.
sublimate *v* refine; purify by heating from solid to vapour and restoring solidity; *n* sublimated substance; *n* **sublimation** act of sublimation; (*psych*) expression of undesirable impulses in desirable form.
sublime *a* majestic, exalted; awe-inspiring; *ns* **sublimity; sublimeness.**
submarine *a* below surface of sea; *n* ship designed to remain, travel, under water for long period; *n* **submariner** seaman serving in submarine.
submerge *v* plunge, cause to go, beneath surface of water; *n* **submersion.**
submit *v* surrender; suggest, put forward for consideration etc; *n* **submission**; *a* **submissive** resigned, docile.
subordinate *a* inferior in rank or importance; dependent upon; *n* **subordination.**
suborn *v* bribe, induce to commit crime; *n* **suborner.**
subpoena *n* writ summoning person to attend court; *v* serve with such writ.
subscribe *v* write one's name at end of document; agree, approve; pay (contribution, instalment) regularly; *ns* **subscriber; subscription** fee, sum subscribed.
subsequent *a* later; following as result; *n* **subsequence.**
subservient *a* submissive, servile; *n* **subservience; -viency.**
subside *v* settle, sink down; diminish, abate; *n* **subsidence.**
subsidy *n* grant of money by State; *v* **subsidize** give; support by, subsidy; *a* **subsidiary** additional, auxiliary; secondary.
subsist *v* sustain life; continue in being; *n* **subsistence** means of supporting life.
subsonic *a* of less than speed of sound.
substance *n* matter, material; essential, most important elements or parts; portion of solid matter; means, wealth; *a* **substantial** solid; considerable; wealthy; *n* **substantiality**; *v* **substantiate** give reality to; prove, establish truth; *n* **substantiation**;

a **substantive** having real existence; (*gram*) **ex**pressing existence; *n* noun.
substitute *n* person, thing taking place of another; deputy; *v* put, use in place of another; deputy; *v* put, use in place of another; *n* **substitution.**
substratum *n* underlying layer; basis; *pl* **-ta, -tums.**
subterfuge *n* equivocation; means of evasion.
subterranean, -eous *a* situated, existing underground.
subtle *a* elusive; keen, discriminating; ingenious; cunning; *n* **subtlety.**
subtract *v* take away, deduct; *n* **subtraction.**
sub-tropical *a* between temperate and tropical zones.
suburb *n* outlying part of town or city; *a* **suburban.**
subversive *a* attempting, tending to undermine authority, morale etc; *n* **subversion.**
subway *n* underground passage; (*U.S.*) underground railway.
succeed *v* follow, come after; follow (as heir); accomplish purpose; *n* **success** fortunate accomplishment, attainment of desired object, or result; triumph; *a* **successful;** *n* **succession** act or right of following in office, rank etc; series of things, events; *a* **successive** consecutive; *n* **successor** one who follows another in office etc; heir.
succinct *a* concisely expressed, terse.
succour *v* & *n* help, aid in difficulty or distress.
succulent *a* juicy; full of sap; *n* **succulence.**
succumb *v* yield, give way; cease to exist.
such *a* of that, or similar kind, degree, quality specified, implied; *a* **suchlike** similar.
suck *v* draw (liquid) into mouth; dissolve in mouth; *n* **sucker** organ, appliance adhering by suction; (*sl*) gullible person; (*bot*) shoot from subterranean stem.
suckle *v* feed (young) with milk from breast; *n* **suckling** unweaned baby or young animal.
suction *n* act of sucking; creation of partial vacuum causing body to adhere to, or enter, something under atmospheric pressure.
sudden *a* done, occurring unexpectedly; abrupt.
suds *npl* froth of soap and water, lather.
sue *v* bring, take legal action against; beg, plead.

suède *n* soft undressed kid-skin.

suet *n* solid fatty tissue round kidneys etc. of oxen, sheep etc.

suffer *v* undergo; tolerate, be injured; be punished; *ns* **sufferance** toleration; **sufferer**.

suffice *v* be enough, adequate; *a* **sufficient**; *n* **sufficiency** adequate supply.

suffix *n* letter or syllable added to end of word.

suffocate *v* deprive of air, stifle; kill by depriving of air; smother; *n* **suffocation**.

suffragan *n* & *a* (bishop) assisting another bishop.

suffrage *n* vote, right to vote *esp* at elections; *n* **suffragette** woman who compaigned for right of women to vote in elections.

suffuse *v* (of fluid, colour etc) spread over, flood, cover; *n* **suffusion**.

sugar *n* sweet, crystalline vegetable substance; (*sl*) money; *v* sweeten with sugar; (*fig*) flatter, disguise unpleasantness of; *n* **s.-beet** variety of beetroot yielding sugar; **s.-cane** tall grass from whose juice sugar is obtained; *a* **sugary**.

suggest *v* imply; put forward, present for consideration; *a* **suggestive** evoking association of ideas; provoking indecent thoughts; *n* **suggestion** proposal; something implied, hinted, called up in mind; (*psych*) process of inducing someone to accept idea or belief uncritically, *esp* under hypnosis.

suicide *n* act of killing oneself; one who intentionally kills himself; *a* **suicidal**.

suit *n* action at law; set of clothes worn together *esp* man's outer clothes; one of four sets in pack of cards; *v* satisfy; match; please; be convenient; *n* **suitcase** portable flat oblong travelling case.

suitable *a* convenient; proper; becoming; *n* **suitability**.

suite *n* band of retainers; group, set (as of rooms, furniture etc).

suitor *n* petitioner; wooer.

sulky *a* sullen; lowering; *n pl* **sulks**, sulky mood; *v* **sulk** be sulky.

sullen *a* ill-tempered, morose, surly.

sully *v* stain, defile; tarnish.

sulphate *n* salt of sulphuric acid.
sulphonamide *n* one of group of organic compounds used in treating many bacterial diseases.
sulphur *n* pale yellow, inflammable, non-metallic element; *n* **s. dioxide** colourless gas with choking smell; *as* **sulphurous**; **sulphuric.**
sultan *n* Mohammedan prince or king; *n* **sultana** sultan's wife; kind of raisin.
sultry *a* hot, damp, close; (*fig*) having strong sexual allure.
sum *n* amount, total; *v* **s. up** summarize; (of judge) review and comment on evidence.
summary *a* affected, carried out, without delay; brief statement or abridgement of chief points (of document, speech etc); *v* **summarize** present briefly and concisely; *n* **summation** reckoning up.
summer *n* second, warmest season of year; *v* spend summer; *a* **summery**; *n* **summer time** period when clocks are put one hour ahead in summer.
summit *n* top, peak; (*coll*) political conference between heads of States.
summon *v* call, send for; demand attendance of (in court); *n* **summons** call; notice to appear before judge or magistrate.
sump *n* pool or pit in which water collects; well in crankcase for lubricating oil.
sumptuous *a* lavish, splendid, costly; *n* **sumptuousness.**
sun *n* luminous heavenly body round which earth and other planets rotate; chief source of light and heat in solar system; direct rays of sun; *v* exposed to, bask in, sun's rays; *n* **sunbathing** exposure of body to direct rays of sun; **sunburn** darkening of skin through exposure to sun; *as* **sunny, sunlit** lit by sun; *n* **sunflower** plant with large golden flowers; *a* **sunless.**
sundae *n* ice-cream with crushed fruit and nuts.
Sunday *n* first day of week.
sunder *v* put apart, sever.
sundry *a* several, of indefinite number; *n pl* **sundries** unspecified odds and ends.
sup *v* take by sips; take supper.

super- *prefix; forms compounds with meaning of* above, in excess. *Such words are not given when the meaning may be deduced from the simple word.*
super *a* (*coll*) marvellous; superb.
superannuate *v* pension off; dismiss on account of old age; *n* **superannuation** payment, pension given on retirement.
superb *a* splendid, magnificent.
supercharge *v* charge, fill to excess; *n* **supercharger** device to increase petrol mixture in cylinders of motor engine; *a* **-ed.**
supercilious *a* disdainful, haughty; *n* **-ness.**
superficial *a* of, on surface; shallow.
superfluous *a* more than necessary; redundant.
superhuman *a* of more than can be expected of ordinary man.
superintend *v* direct, control; oversee, supervise; *ns* **-ent** manager; police officer above inspector; **-ence.**
superior *a* higher in position, rank, grade; upper; not affected or biassed by; *ns* **superiority; s. complex** (*psych*) aggressively self-satisfied attitude.
superlative *a* of, in highest degree of excellence, or quality; *n* (*gram*) superlative degree of adjective or adverb.
superman *n* hypothetical being possessing supreme physical and mental powers.
supermarket *n* large self-service store.
supernatural *a* not explicable by known laws of nature.
supernumerary *n* & *a* (person, thing) in excess of normal number; extra.
superphosphate *n* acid phosphate; fertilizer.
supersede *v* replace; supplant.
supersonic *a* moving faster than speed of sound; of sound-waves of too high frequency to be audible to human ear.
superstition *n* irrational belief in charms, omens, etc; dread of supernatural; *a* **superstitious.**
supervene *v* happen as consequence, or in addition; *n* **supervention.**
supervise *v* oversee; inspect, control; direct; *n* **supervisor.**

supine *a* lying on back, face upwards; inactive; *n* (Latin) verbal noun.
supper *n* last meal of day; *a* **supperless.**
supplant *v* take place of, oust, *esp* by fraud, craft etc.
supple *a* pliant, flexible; docile, amenable.
supplement *n* something added to fill need; separable part of newspaper etc; *v* add to; supply deficiency; *a* **supplementary** extra; additional.
supplicate *v* pray for; ask for humbly; *ns* **-ation** entreaty; **suppliant** petitioner; *a* beseeching.
supply *n* provide for; produce; *n* something supplied; amount available; substitute; *pl* necessary stores, equipment etc.
support *v* hold, prop up; maintain; assist; *n* act, state of being supported; that which helps, supports; *n* **supporter** partisan, adherent.
suppose *v* assume, surmise; believe to be; *n* **supposition** assumption; hypothesis; *as* **supposable** conceivable; **supposed** assumed.
suppress *v* subdue, crush by force; prevent publication of; ban; *n* **-ion.**
suppurate *v* produce pus; *n* **suppuration.**
supra- *prefix* above, higher than; beyond.
supreme *a* highest, superior in rank, power, jurisdiction etc; utmost; *n* **supremacy.**
surcharge *n* extra charge; *v* demand extra payment.
surd *n* & *a* (*math*) irrational (quantity).
sure *a* certain; reliable; undoubted; *adv* & *interj* (*coll*) certainly, willingly; *n* **surety** one who makes himself responsible for another's good conduct; money laid down as pledge of person's good behaviour.
surf *n* foam of breaking waves; *n* **surfboard** board used in sport of surf-riding.
surface *n* exterior, outside; top, visible side; *a* superficially; *v* polish, dress surface; come up to surface of water.
surfeit *n* excess *esp* in feeding; satiety, repletion; *v* over-indulge.
surge *v* (of waves, water) swell; rise powerfully; *n* act of singing; sudden rush of electric current in circuit.
surgeon *n* medical practitioner who performs operations; *n* **surgery** treatment of disease and injuries

by operation or manipulation; doctor's consulting room; *a* **surgical.**

surly *a* sullen, gloomy, churlish; *n* **surliness.**

surmise *v* guess, conclude, infer; *n* conjecture, inference.

surmount *v* overcome (difficulty); be placed over top of; *a* **surmountable.**

surname *n* hereditary family name transmitted in male line.

surpass *v* go beyond, excel in degree, quality etc; *a* **surpassing** excelling all others; matchless.

surplice *n* loose white vestment worn by clergy and choristers.

surplus *n* excess quantity; *a* forming amount over and above what is required.

surprise *v* come upon unexpectedly; shock, startle; astonish; *n* astonishment; something unexpected.

surrealism *n* movement in art or literature that believes in expressing dream-like effects and irrational fantasies; *n* & *a* **surrealist.**

surrender *v* give up under pressure or voluntarily; hand over; submit; *n* act of surrendering.

surreptitious *a* stealthy, clandestine, furtive.

surrogate *n* substitute; deputy *esp* of bishop.

surround *v* encircle; be, come all round; *n pl* **surroundings** material environment; circumstances.

surtax *n* additional tax on high incomes.

surveillance *n* constant watch, observation.

survey *v* look over; review; inspect and assess value of (house etc); measure, map (area of land); *n* record of result of surveying; *n* **surveyor.**

survive *v* outlive; continue to live or exist; *n* **survivor** one left alive when others are dead.

susceptible *a* highly sensitive; accessible; *n* **susceptibility.**

suspect *v* believe or imagine to be true; doubt; mistrust; believe guilty; *a* rousing suspicion; *n* suspected person.

suspend *v* hang up; postpone, defer; debar, prohibit temporarily; *n pl* **suspenders** device for holding up stockings or socks.

suspense *n* state of anxious uncertainty; *n* **suspen-**

sion state of being suspended (in various senses); **s. bridge** bridge hung from cables supported by towers or piers.

suspicion *n* act of suspecting; feeling of doubt, mistrust; slight trace; *a* **suspicious.**

sustain *v* support, hold up; undergo; maintain; *ns* **sustenance** nourishment, sustenation, maintenance.

suture *n* act, process of sewing up wound; thread, wire used for this; (*anat*) articulation of bones of skull; *v* join with suture.

suzerain *n* feudal law; State with sovereignty over another; *n* **suzerainty.**

svelte *a* slender, graceful, willowy.

swab *n* mop; (*med*) absorbent pad; *v* clean, wash out, with swab.

swaddle *v* swathe, bundle up; *n pl* **swaddling-clothes, -bands** strip of cloth formerly wrapped round baby.

swag *n* (*sl*) booty, plunder; hanging wreath or festoon.

swagger *v* strut; show off; bear oneself jauntily; *n* such gait or manner.

swain *n* (*poet*) country lad; lover, admirer.

swallow *n* migratory bird with long, pointed wings and forked tail; *n* **swallow-tail** kind of butterfly or humming bird; dress-coat.

swallow *v* make (food, drink etc) pass down gullet; put up with (insult); believe implicitly; overwhelm; *n* act of swallowing food etc.

swamp *n* marsh, bog; *v* cover with water; (*fig*) overwhelm; *a* **swampy.**

swan *n* large, long-necked aquatic bird; *n* **swan-song** fabled song of dying swan; (*fig*) last work, utterance of actor, writer etc; *n* **swannery** place where swans are kept.

swank *v* (*coll*) swagger; show off; boast; *n* showing off; conceit.

swap, swop *v* exchange, barter.

sward *n* expanse of turf.

swarm *n* large mass of insects, *esp* cluster of bees with queen; crowd; *v* (of bees) leave hive with queen; gather in large numbers.

swarm *v* climb (rope etc) by clasping with hands and legs.
swarthy *a* dark-complexioned; sunburnt.
swashbuckler *n* swaggering boaster; braggart.
swastika *n* hooked cross, used as badge by Nazi Party; primitive sun-symbol, fylfot.
swat *v* crush, squash (insect etc).
swath *n* mark made or space cleared by scythe or mower in single course or sweep.
swathe *v* cover, wrap with bandage or cloth.
sway *v* swing, cause to swing unsteadily; move, influence; *n* swaying motion; influence; power.
swear *v* promise on oath; cause to take an oath; curse; *pt* **swore**; *pp* **sworn.**
sweat *n* moisture exuded by pores of skin; *v* exude sweat; work, cause to work hard for low wages; *n* **sweater** thick woollen jersey.
Swede *n* native of Sweden; kind of turnip.
sweep *v* clean with brush, broom; move in stately manner; form wide curve; drive, move violently away; *pt* & *pp* **swept**; *n* act of sweeping; long oar; wide curve; man who sweeps chimneys; *n* **sweep, sweepstake** gamble in which winner takes stakes contributed by all.
sweet *a* tasting like sugar; pure; fragrant; melodious; agreeable; gentle; *n* dessert; sweetmeat; *v* **sweeten**; *ns* **sweetbread** pancreas *esp* of calf, used as food; **sweetbriar** wild rose; **sweetheart** lover; **sweetmeat** piece of confectionery; **sweet pea** cultivated annual with brightly coloured, fragrant flowers.
swell *v* expand; be elated; increase in size; *pt* **swelled**; *pp* **swelled** or **swollen**; *n* act of swelling; succession of unbroken waves; (*coll*) smartly-dressed person; *a* (*coll*) excellent, fine.
swelter *v* be, feel extremely hot.
swerve *v* swing round, deviate from course; deflect; *n*.
swift *a* rapid, quick, speedy; *n* bird like swallow.
swill *v* rinse, wash out, with water; drink greedily; *n* liquid pig food.
swim *v* move through water by movement of limbs, fins etc; feel dizzy; be flooded; *pt* **swam**; *pp* **swum**; *n* spell of swimming; *n* **swimmer.**

swindle *v* cheat, defraud; *ns* **swindler; swindling.**
swine *n* pig; (*coll*) unpleasant person; *pl* **swine.**
swing *v* move to and fro, *esp* as suspended body; turn on hinge or pivot; (*coll*) be hanged; *pt* & *pp* **swung;** *n* act of swinging; seat suspended by ropes, to swing on; type of jazz music.
swipe *v* strike with powerful blow; (*coll*) steal.
swirl *v* whirl about; form eddies; *n* such motion.
swish *v* pass, cut through air with hissing sound; move with such sound; *n* swishing sound, or movement.
Swiss *n* native of Switzerland.
switch *n* slender, flexible rod; device for making, breaking electric circuit; movable rail at junction; *v* strike with switch; turn (electric apparatus) on or off; transfer, divert; *ns* **switchback** zig-zag railway with steep slopes, in fair ground etc; **switchboard** board with many switches controlling circuits; *esp* of telephone.
swivel *n* link consisting of ring and shank, allowing two parts to revolve independently; *v* turn on swivel.
swoon *v* & *n* (have) fainting fit.
swoop *v* descend steeply through air like hawk; *n* act of swooping; sudden attack.
sword *n* weapon with long sharp blade fixed in hilt; *n* **sword-fish** fish with long, sharp upper jaw.
swot *v* (*coll*) study hard; *n* one who studies hard.
sybarite *n* one who is fond of luxurious comfort; *a* **sybaritic.**
sycamore *n* tree allied to maple.
sycophant *n* servile flatterer; *a* **-tic;** *n* **sycophancy.**
syllable *n* division of word, as unit of pronunciation; *a* **syllabic.**
syllabus *n* programme; list of subjects.
sylph *n* sprite.
sylvan *a* of, in woods; rustic.
symbol *n* sign; anything representing or typifying something; *a* **symbolic;** *v* **symbolize;** *n* **symbolism** represented by symbols.
symmetry *n* balance of arrangement between two sides; *a* **symmetrical** duly proportioned; harmonious.

sympathy *n* fellow-feeling; sharing of emotion, interest etc; compassion; *a* **sympathetic**; *v* **sympathize.**
symphony *n* harmony of sounds; (*mus*) sonata or composition for full orchestra; *a* **symphonic.**
symptom *n* outward sign; change in body indicating presence or development of disease; *a* **symptomatic.**
synagogue *n* religious congregation of Jews; Jewish place of worship.
synchronize *v* make agree in time; happen at same time; *n* **synchronization.**
syncopate *v* shorten word by omitting medial sound; (*mus*) begin (note) on normally unaccented beat; *n* **syncopation.**
syncope *n* fainting fit.
syndicate *n* body of persons, combining for some enterprise.
syndrome *n* combination of various symptoms of disease.
synod *n* Church council; convention.
synonym *n* word with same meaning as another.
synopsis *n* summary, outline.
syntax *n* (*gram*) sentence construction.
synthesis *n* combination, putting together; *a* **synthetic** artificial.
syphilis *n* contagious venereal disease; *a* **syphilitic.**
syphon see **siphon.**
syringe *n* instrument for drawing in liquid by piston and ejecting it in jet; *v* spray, cleanse with syringe.
syrup *n* thick solution obtained in refining of sugar; *a* **syrupy.**
system *n* plan, scheme for organizing, classifying objects; complex whole; *a* **systematic.**
systole *n* shortening of long syllable; contraction of heart; *a* **systolic.**

tab *n* small flap, strap, strip of cloth; *v* fix tab on to.
tabard *n* herald's coat.
tabby *n* striped, brindled cat; female cat.
tabernacle *n* tent of Israelites; dissenting place of worship; small chest on altar to contain Host.

table *n* piece of furniture consisting of flat board supported by legs; set of facts, figures etc. arranged in lines, or columns; *v* enter into list etc; submit for discussion etc; *a* **tabular** arranged as table; *v* **tabulate** set out systematically; *ns* **tabulation**; **tabulator.**

tableau *n* group of motionless, costumed persons posed to represent well-known picture, scene etc; *pl* **tableaux.**

tablet *n* small flat slab; small flat medicinal pill or sweet.

tabloid *n* [P] medicinal tablet; *n* (*fig*) small, condensed, sensational newspaper; *a* concentrated, brief.

taboo *n* setting apart as sacred, certain persons or things; ban; restraint; *v* prohibit, forbid by taboo.

tabor *n* small drum.

tacit *a* implied, inferred by silence; *a* **taciturn** speaking little; *n* **taciturnity.**

tack *n* small broad-headed nail; long temporary stitch; rope fastening corner of sail; ship's course; (*fig*) course of action; (*sl*) food; *v* fasten with tacks; sew loosely; change course obliquely.

tackle *n* equipment; apparatus for moving; *esp* raising weights; *v* grip; grapple with.

tacky *a* sticky.

tact *n* skill in dealing with people, situations; natural perception of what is right and fitting; *as* **tactful**; **tactless** accidentally offensive.

tactics *n pl* art of handling troops, ships in action; adroit method of dealing with difficult situation; *n* **tactician**; *a* **tactical.**

tactile *a* of, relating to sense of touch; tangible.

tadpole *n* young frog or toad, having gills and tail.

taffeta *n* stiff fabric or silk, or wool.

taffrail *n* rail round stern of ship.

tag *n* projecting flap, end; metal point of boot lace; hanging label; cliché; *v* add on; append; (*coll*) follow closely.

tail *n* prolonged extension of animal's spine; anything resembling this; hindmost, rear part of anything; (*coll*) follower, pursuer; *pl* tail-coat; reverse side of coin; *v* follow (person) closely; **t. away, t. off**

dwindle; straggle; *as* **-tailed** (*suffix*) having particular kind of tail; **tailless**; *ns* **tail-coat** formal evening dress jacket; **tail-light** red light at rear of car etc; **tail-end** last part.

tailor *n* one who makes or sells outer clothing, *esp* men's; *v* work as tailor; (*fig*) adapt for special purpose; *a* **tailor-made** individually made; precisely made for specific need.

taint *n* stain; trace of decay; disgrace; *v* stain slightly; become infected.

take *v* seize, grasp; accept; receive into; rent, hire; consider; carry; *pt* **took**; *pp* **taken**; **t. aback** disconcert; **t. after** resemble; **t. place** happen; *n* **t. off** (aircraft) place, act of leaving ground; *a* **taking** attractive.

talc *n* magnesium silicate; *n* **talcum** powdered talc; toilet powder.

tale *n* story, account; rumour; narrative.

talent *n* marked aptitude; special faculty; *a* **talented** gifted.

talisman *n* charm, amulet; object regarded as having magic powers.

talk *v* speak; utter in speech; converse; discuss; *n* speech; conversation; *a* **talkative** given to talking.

tall *a* above average in stature; lofty; (*sl*) difficult to believe; untrue.

tallboy *n* high chest of drawers.

tallow *n* melted-down animal fat.

tally *n* notched rod to count by; *v* account by tally; agree, correspond exactly.

tally-ho *interj* & *n* huntsman's cry to hounds when fox is seen.

talon *n* claw.

tamarisk *n* genus of evergreen shrubs.

tambour *n* bass-drum; embroidery frame; *n* **tambourine** small shallow drum fitted with tinkling discs.

tame *a* not wild; subdued; dull; *v* make tame; *n* **tamer.**

tam-o-shanter *n* round woollen cap or bonnet.

tamper *v* interfere, meddle with; alter fraudulently, harmfully.

tampon *n* blood-absorbing plug of lint etc.
tan *n* bark of oak bruised to extract tannic acid; *a* of yellowish-brown; *v* make into leather; make become brown *esp* by sunburn; (*sl*) flog; *n* **tanner** one who tans; *n* **tannery** place where hides are tanned.
tandem *n* bicycle for two riders, one behind other; vehicle with two horses harnessed one behind the other; *adv*.
tang *n* projecting spike; strong flavour or smell; kind of seaweed.
tangent *a* touching, but not cutting; *n* line touching curve at one point; **go off at a t.** pass suddenly to different line of thought etc.
tangerine *n* small, sweet, thin-skinned orange.
tangible *a* capable of being touched; (*fig*) clearly defined in mind, practical.
tangle *v* form confused mass, intertwine; **t. with** (*sl*) come into conflict with; *n* intricate knot; disorder.
tango *n* type of S. American dance; music for this; *v* dance tango.
tank *n* receptacle for storing liquids, oil or gas; heavy armoured vehicle with tracked wheels and guns; *ns* **tanker** ship, lorry carrying oil, liquid fuel in bulk; **tank-engine** locomotive carrying its own water and fuel.
tankard *n* large drinking-vessel of metal, porcelain etc.
tannic *a* of, obtained from tan; *n* **t. acid**; *n* **tannin** astringent substance; tannic acid.
tantalize *v* torment by repeated renewal of hope and disappointment; tease; *n* **tantalus** stand for decanters, with locking device.
tantamount *a* equal in value or effect; equivalent.
tantrum *n* fit, outburst of violent temper.
tap *n* device with turning valve or screw for controlling flow of liquid from pipe, cask etc; instrument for cutting internal screw-threads; *v* fit tap in; draw off (liquid); listen in deliberately (to telephone conversation); *ns* **tap-root** long tapering root of plant; **tapster** one who draws beer.
tap *v* strike lightly; *n* light blow; sound of this.

tape *n* long narrow strip of woven fabric, or paper; *ns* **tape-machine** receiving part of telegraph recording system; **t.-recorder** apparatus for recording and reproducing sound; **tapeworm** parasitic intestinal worm; **red t.** pedantic insistence on formalities; *v* record on tape; **have** (something) **taped,** (*coll*) understand thoroughly.

taper *n* thin candle; *v* narrow gradually to point at one end.

tapestry *n* fabric on which designs are worked in wool by hand; *a* **tapestried** hung with tapestry.

tapioca *n* starchy food obtained from dried manioc.

tapir *n* pig-like mammal with flexible proboscis.

tappet *n* short rod transmitting motion intermittently.

tar *n* thick black viscous liquid distilled from coal etc; *v* cover, treat with tar.

tar *n* (*coll*) sailor.

tarantella *n* lively Italian dance.

tarantula *n* large venomous spider.

tardy *n* slow; late; reluctant; *n* **tardiness.**

tare *n* common vetch; weed.

tare *n* weight of unladen goods vehicle; allowance made for this.

target *n* object of attack (military, verbal etc.); round board marked in circles, to be shot at; butt.

tariff *n* list of duties on imports and exports; list of charges.

tarmac *n* mixture of tar and macadam used as road-surfacing material.

tarn *n* small moorland or mountain lake.

tarnish *v* spoil brightness of by exposure to air etc; (*fig*) stain, sully; *n* loss of lustre (*lit* & *fig*).

tarpaulin *n* water-proof canvas treated with tar.

tarragon *n* aromatic herb used for flavouring.

tarry *v* linger; stay in a place.

tart *a* sour; sharp; acid.

tart *n* open, or covered fruit pie; *sl* prostitute.

tartan *n* woollen fabric woven in various coloured checks, each pattern belonging to a Highland clan; this pattern.

tartar *n* incrustation forming on teeth; deposit

formed in wine vats; (*cap*) native of Tartary; (*fig*) violent person.

task *n* piece, amount of work imposed or undertaken; **take to t.** reprove; *ns* **task-force** military, police unit detailed for specific operation; **task-master** exacting master; overseer.

tassel *n* knotted bunch of silk or other threads, used as ornament.

taste *v* test, perceive flavour of; have particular flavour of; *n* faculty of experiencing flavours on tongue; small portion of food or drink; discernment, tact; tendency; liking; *as* **tasteful** showing refinement; in good taste; **tasteless** insipid; tactless; **tasty** pleasant to taste; savoury.

tatting *n* lace-like trimming of looped and knotted threads; *v* **tat** make tatting.

tatter *n* rag, torn fragment.

tattle *v* gossip, indiscreet talk.

tattoo *n* military pageant or spectacle; drum-beat or bugle-call of recall; knocking.

tattoo *v* mark (skin) by pricking and inserting indelible pigments; *n* mark so made.

taunt *v* reproach sarcastically, contemptuously; *n* jeer, gibe.

taut *a* stretched tightly, tense; *v* **tauten** make tight.

tautology *n* unnecessary repetition of same idea in different words; *a* **tautological**.

tavern *n* inn, public house.

tawdry *a* showy, flashy, gaudy; *n* **tawdriness.**

tawny *a* of light, brownish yellow colour.

tax *n* compulsory duty or levy imposed on income, goods etc; strain; *v* impose tax on; lay heavy burden on; *n* **taxation** act of levying tax; *a* **taxable**; *n* **taxpayer.**

taxi *n* taxi-cab, car for public hire; *v* (of aircraft) run along ground under own power before take-off, or after landing; *n* **taxi-meter** instrument recording fare due for mileage covered.

taxidermy *n* art of preparing and stuffing animal skins; *n* **taxidermist.**

tea *n* dried leaves of tea-plant, infused to make drink; light afternoon meal; *n* **tea-rose** scented China rose.

teach *v* instruct, train; impart knowledge; *pt* & *pp* **taught**; *n* **teacher** one who instructs; schoolmaster, -mistress.

teak *n* East Indian tree with very hard wood.

teal *n* kind of small wild duck.

team *n* number of animals harnessed together; number of persons working, acting, playing together; *n* **t.-work** co-operation; *v* **t. up with** (*coll*) work in harmony; match.

tear *n* single drop of saline fluid coming from eye; *as* **tearful** shedding tears; sad; **tearless**; *ns* **teardrop; tear-gas** irritant poison-gas, causing abnormal watering of eyes.

tear *v* pull apart; be torn; rend; rush; *pt* **tore**; *pp* **torn**; *n* rent, torn hole.

tease *v* tear apart fibres of; worry, bait; poke fun at; *n* one who torments; *a* **teasing** harassing.

teasel, teazle *n* plant with large burrs, formerly used to raise nap on cloth.

teat *n* nipple of female mammal's breast; nipple of feeding bottle.

technical *a* pertaining to industrial or mechanical arts; peculiar to some specific branch of science or art; not understandable by laymen; *ns* **technicality** state of being technical; technical term; detail of procedure; **technique** method of execution or performance; skill in methods of special art etc; **technician** one skilled in mechanical art; **technology** science of industrial and mechanical arts; **technologist.**

tectonic *a* pertaining to art of building; relating to structure of earth; *n pl* art of functional designing combined with artistic merit.

tedium *n* weariness; boredom; *a* **tedious** dull, long and boring; *n* **tediousness.**

tee *n* small peg off which golf ball is first played at each hole; (quoits) mark aimed at; *v* place ball on tee.

teem *v* abound with; be prolific; rain heavily.

teens *n pl* age between 13–20; *n* **teenager** adolescent between 13–20.

teethe *v* develop or cut teeth.

teetotal *a* of, observing total abstinence from intoxicants; *n* **teetotal(l)er.**
tegument *n* membraneous covering of animal body or organ; *a* **tegumental.**
tele- *prefix* at or over a distance; from far off.
telegraph *n* electrical apparatus for transmitting messages to a distance; *v* communicate by telegraph; *ns* **telegrapher, telegraphist;** *a* **telegraphic;** *ns* **telegraphy** art, process of communicating by telegraph; **telegram** message sent by telegraph.
telemark *n* swinging turn in skiing.
telepathy *n* thought transference; *a* **telepathic.**
telephone *n* instrument for transmitting conversation over a distance; *v* use, communicate by, telephone; *ns* **telephony** telephonic communication; **telephonist** one who work a telephone; *a* **telephonic.**
telephoto *n abbrev* **telephotography** photograph(ing) of distant objects through magnifying **t. lens.**
teleprinter *n* electric typewriter by which messages sent by telegraph are reproduced; *n* **telex** system of communication using teleprinters.
telescope *n* optical instrument for viewing magnified images of distant objects; *v* close, slide together as parts of telescope; compress forcibly; *a* **telescopic.**
television *n* transmission of visible moving images by electro-magnetic waves; viewing of such; *v* **televise** transmit by television.
tell *v* narrate; divulge; order, command; be of importance; inform; *pt* & *pp* **told;** *n* **teller** narrator; bank-clerk who pays out money; *a* **telling** impressive; *n* **tell-tale** sneak; *a* revealing.
tellurian *a* pertaining to Earth; *n* **tellurium** rare, brittle, non-metallic element; *a* **telluric.**
temerity *n* rashness; audacity; great boldness.
temper *v* harden (metal, glass etc.); moderate; knead and moisten clay; *n* degree of hardness (of steel etc.); frame of mind; angry mood.
tempera *n* distemper used in fresco painting.
temperament *n* natural disposition; emotional

mood; *a* **temperamental** unreliable; unstable; liable to strong changes of mood.

temperate *a* moderate and restrained; (of climate) not extreme; *n* **temperance** abstinence, *esp* from alcohol; moderation.

temperature *n* degree of heat or cold in atmosphere or body; (*coll*) **have a t.** be feverish.

tempest *n* violent storm; (*fig*) violent emotion; *a* **tempestuous** stormy; violently excited.

temple *n* building, place of worship.

temple *n* flat part of head on either side of forehead.

templet, template *n* mould, pattern, used as guide in shaping.

tempo *n* degree of speed, rate, pace.

temporal *a* pertaining to, limited by time; secular; *a* **temporary** lasting, short time; not permanent.

temporize *v* try to avoid making decision; be evasive.

tempt *v* try to persuade *esp* to evil; excite desire in; *ns* **tempter**; **temptation** act of tempting; attraction, inducement.

ten *n* cardinal number next after nine; *a* **tenth** ordinal number.

tenable *a* capable of being held, defended; (of opinions etc.) logical.

tenacious *a* holding fast; unyielding; retentive; *n* **tenacity**.

tenant *n* one who holds land or house etc. on rent or lease; *ns* **tenancy**; **tenantry** body of tenants.

tench *n* fresh-water fish.

tend *v* take care of; watch over; *n* **tender** one who tends; small ship in attendance on larger one; fuel and water carrier attached to locomotive.

tend *v* have inclination, move in certain direction; *n* **tendency** inclination, bent; trend; *a* **tendentious** not impartial.

tender *v* offer; make estimate; *n* offer made to carry out work etc. at fixed price; money offered in settlement of claim etc.

tender *a* delicate; sensitive to pain; easily injured; kind, loving; *ns* **tenderness**; **tenderfoot** newcomer; novice.

tendon *n* sinew attaching muscle to bone.

tendril *n* slender coiling stem in climbing plants; curl of hair.
tenement *n* house, dwelling divided into separate apartments.
tenet *n* opinion, belief held as true.
tennis *n* game for two or four players, in which ball is struck over net with rackets.
tenon *n* tongue cut on end of piece of wood to fit into mortise; *n* **tenon-saw**.
tenor *n* male voice between bass and alto; singer with this range; general direction or meaning.
tense *n* modification of verb to show time of action.
tense *a* taut; stretched tight; *a* **tensile** capable of being stretched; *n* **tension** act, process of stretching, tightening; emotional strain, (*elect.*) voltage.
tent *n* portable canvas shelter supported by pole(s).
tentacle *n* long, slender, flexible organ of feeling; feeler.
tentative *a* experimental; provisional.
tenter *n* frame for stretching cloth; **t. hook** hooked nail used in stretching cloth; **on t. hooks** in state of anxiety, suspense.
tenuous *a* thin, fine, flimsy; too subtle; *n* **tenuity**.
tenure *n* act of, manner of holding land, office etc.
tepee, teepee *n* wigwam or tent of N. American Indians.
tepid *a* lukewarm; (*fig*) showing little interest etc.
tercentenary *n* three hundredth anniversary.
tergiversation *n* shuffling, evasive conduct; vacillation.
term *n* limit *esp* of time; fixed, limited period; period when courts sit, schools are open etc; word used in any special art, science etc; *pl* conditions (of contract etc.); *pl* personal relations; *v* designate, call.
termagant *n* quarrelsome, scolding woman.
terminal *n* end part, extremity; *a* of, near end; *v* **terminate** bring, come to an end; *n* **termination** conclusion, ending.
terminology *n* system of special, or technical terms; *a* **-ogical.**
terminus *n* station at end of railway line etc; final point reached.

termite *n* one of order of destructive insects; so-called white ant.
tern *n* one of various sea-birds of gull family.
terpsichorean *a* pertaining to dancing.
terrace *n* raised level platform of earth etc; row of end-to-end houses; *v* build up, cut, into form of terrace.
terra-cotta *n* hard unglazed reddish-brown pottery.
terrain *n* tract of land; *esp* as considered for use as battlefield.
terrapin *n* edible fresh-water turtle.
terrestrial *a* earthly; of, living on dry land.
terrible *a* fearful; (*coll*) very bad; *a* **terrific** awe-inspiring, by reason of size etc; (*coll*) amazing; *v* **terrify** fill with terror; frighten.
terrier *n* one of several breeds of dogs; document setting out extent, rights etc. in land.
territory *n* region; district ruled by State or ruler; *a* **territorial** of territory; *n* **Territorial Army** force of volunteers, serving for home defence.
terror *n* extreme fear; *v* **terrorize** intimidate; oppress by fear; *ns* **terrorism** policy of using violence to obtain political or other demands; **terrorist** one who practises terrorism.
terse *a* concise; curt, abrupt in speech; *n* **terseness.**
tertiary *a* of third rank or order; *n* geological era; *a* **tertian** (fever) recurring every third day.
terylene *n* brand of polyester fibre, yarn or fabric.
tessellate *v* pave by interlaying in mosaic form; *a* **tessellated**; *n pl* **tessera** small squares of stone, glass etc. used in mosaic work.
test *n* method adopted to try or prove knowledge of; critical, searching examination; *v* prove quality, extent, reliability of; try by examination; *ns* **test-case** lawsuit which establishes precedent; **test-match** one of series of international matches (*usu* cricket).
testament *n* one of two major divisions of Bible; (*leg*) will; *a* **testamentary.**
testate *a* having left a valid will; *ns* **testacy** state of being testate; **testator**; *fem* **testatrix.**
testicle *n* sperm-secreting gland in male animals.

testify *v* bear witness; give evidence; *ns* **testimony** solemn statement; evidence; **testimonial** document setting forth person's character, ability etc; tribute given in token of esteem.
testy *a* irritable, irascible.
tetanus *n* lock-jaw; violent muscular contraction.
tête-a-tête *n* private talk, meeting; *a* confidential.
tether *v* fasten, tie up with rope; *n* rope, chain for fastening grazing animal.
tetragon *n* figure with four sides and four angles.
text *n* original words of author; verse, short-passage of Scriptures; main part of book etc; *n* **text-book** instruction manual; *a* **textual** of, based on, text; literal.
textile *a* woven; *n* woven fabric.
texture *n* quality, structure of fabric; degree of coarseness, fineness etc. as felt by touch.
than *conj* used in comparison of inequality.
thane *n* member of class of Anglo-Saxon land-owning nobles.
thank *v* express gratitude to; *n pl* **thanks** words of gratitude; *as* **thankful** grateful; **thankless** not appreciated; ungrateful.
that *dem pron* thing, person just mentioned, or pointed out; more remote thing or person; *pl* **those**; *rel pron* person who, thing which; *dem a* of person, thing just mentioned etc; *conj* introduces noun, or adverbial clause.
thatch *v* cover (roof, rick etc.) with reeds, straw etc; *n* **thatch, thatching** straw, reeds etc. used to cover roof etc.
thaw *v* (of snow etc.) melt; (*fig*) become more friendly or genial; *n* melting; (*fig*) detente.
the *def art* indicating particular person or thing.
theatre *n* place where plays are performed; scene of important events or actions; room in hospital where operations are performed; drama, dramatic works collectively; *a* **theatrical** pertaining to theatre; showy; affected, insincere.
thee *pron* objective case of THOU.
theft *n* act of stealing.
their *poss a* of THEM; *poss pron* belonging to them.

theism *n* belief in personal God, capable of revealing Himself; *n* **theist.**
them *pron* objective case of THEY; those persons or things; *pron* **themselves** emphatic and reflexive form.
theme *n* recurrent or important idea in talk or writing; (music) brief recurring melody.
then *adv* at that time; next; that being so; *conj* therefore; *n* that time.
thence *adv* from that place; for that reason; therefore.
theodolite *n* surveying instrument for measuring angles.
theology *n* systematic study of religion and foundations of belief; *a* **theological**; *n* **theologian** student, authority on theology.
theorem *n* proposition to be established by reasoning.
theory *n* supposition to explain group of phenomena; underlying principles of body of facts; (*coll*) opinion; *a* **theoretical** based on theory; speculative, hypothetical; *v* **theorize** form, put forward theories; *n* **theorist** unpractical person.
theosophy *n* mystic form of religious thought aiming at direct contact between individual soul and divine principle; *n* **theosophist.**
therapeutic *a* of, for healing.
therapy *n* curative treatment, *suffix* as psychotherapy.
there *adv* in that place; *advs* **therefore** for this, that reason; in consequence; **thereabouts** near that place; approximately.
therm *n* unit of heat; *a* **thermal** of, by heat; *n* vertical rising hot-air current; *a* **thermic.**
thermion *n* ion emitted by incandescent body; *a* **thermionic**; *n* **t. valve** system of electrodes in glass vacuum.
thermo- *prefix* of, by heat.
thermodynamics *n* branch of science dealing with relation between thermal and mechanical energy.
thermometer *n* instrument for measuring temperature; *a* **thermometric.**
thermoplastic *n* & *a* (substance) which becomes soft and plastic when heated.

thermos *n* [P] vacuum flask.
thermostat *n* device for regulating temperature automatically.
thesaurus *n* treasury, *esp* lexicon of words grouped by meaning, not alphabetically.
these *pron pl* of THIS.
thesis *n* proposition; essay, treatise written for purposes of university degree; *pl* **theses.**
thespian *a* of acting; *n* actor.
thews *n pl* sinews, muscles.
they *pron* third pers. pl. nom.
thick *a* of great depth laterally; (of intelectl) obtuse; crowded; foggy; *v* **thicken** make, become thick; *ns* **thickness** measurement other than length or breadth; **thicket** dense growth of shrubs, trees; *a* **thickset** short, broadly-built.
thief *n* one who steals; *pl* **thieves**; *v* **thieve** steal; *a* **thievish.**
thigh *n* thick upper part of leg.
thimble *n* small cap for protecting finger when sewing.
thin *a* reverse of thick; slender; sparse; loosely packed; *v* make, become thin; *n* **thinness.**
thine *poss pron* 2nd pers. sing. of THOU.
thing *n* any object, material or immaterial; *n pl* personal possessions, clothes etc; (*sl*) irrational feeling about.
think *v* use one's mind; ponder, reflect; believe imagine; deliberate; *pt* & *pp* **thought**; *a* **thinking**; capable of thought; rational; *n* **thought** act, result of thinking; idea; solicitude; *as* **thoughtful** considerate; **thoughtless** careless.
third *a* ordinal number of three; *n* third part.
thirst *n* craving for liquid; (*fig*) strong desire; *v* suffer thirst; *a* **thirsty.**
thirteen *n* & *a* cardinal number three and ten; *n* & *a* **thirty** three times ten.
this *dem a* & *pron* denotes thing, person near, just mentioned; *pl* **these.**
thistle *n* prickly-leaved flowering plant.
thither *adv* to, towards that direction, stage, result.
thole, thole-pin *n* pin of rowlock.

thong *n* narrow strip of leather, strap.
thorax *n* part of body between neck and abdomen; *a* **thoracic.**
thorn *n* prickle, spine on plant; (*fig*) annoyance; *a* **thorny.**
thorough *a* complete, absolute; *a* **thoroughbred** pure-bred; *n* pure-bred animal; *n* **thoroughfare** road for public traffic.
thorp(e) *n* hamlet village.
those *pron pl* of THAT.
thou *pron* (*poet, ar*) 2nd pers. sing. nom. cf YOU.
though *conj* in spite of; although.
thousand *a* & *n* cardinal number, ten hundreds; *a* **thousandth** ordinal number.
thrall *n* slave; *n* **thraldom** servitude.
thrash, thresh *v* beat out grains of; *v* **thrash** beat, flog; **t. out** (*fig*) clear up (problem etc.) by discussion.
thread *n* fine cord used for sewing; yarn; spiral groove cut in screw; *v* put thread into (needle etc.); pick out (one's way); *a* **threadbare** worn until nap is rubbed off.
threat *n* statement of intention to injure, punish etc; menace; *v* **threaten** utter threats; menace; *a* **threatening** foreshadowing disaster, etc.
three *n* & *a* cardinal number, one more than two; *a* **third** ordinal number; *adv* **thrice** three times.
threshold *n* stone or plank below door, at entrance to house etc; (*fig*) beginning.
thrift *n* frugality; economy; genus of plant, sea-pink; *a* **thrifty** frugal, careful in spending money.
thrill *v* stir emotions of; vibrate, tingle; *n* intense emotional stirring; exciting event; *a* **thrilling** exciting.
thrive *v* grow well; prosper; *pt* **thrived, throve**; *pp* **thriven, thrived.**
throat *n* front part of neck; gullet; wind pipe; *a* **throaty** hoarse, guttural.
throb *v* beat, pulsate strongly; *n* beat, palpitation (of heart etc.).
throe *n* pang; brief agony; **in the throes of** struggling with, coming to grips with (some difficulty).

thrombosis *n* clotting of blood in blood vessel.
throne *n* seat of state, *esp* of king; *v* enthrone.
throng *n* crowd, large number of people; *v* crowd.
throstle *n* song-thrush, mavis.
throttle *n* valve in engine regulating flow of steam, gas etc; (*coll*) throat; *v* reduce flow of steam etc; strangle.
through *prep* from end to end; by means of; across; *adv* from end to end; *a* unobstructed; (*sl*) finished; going all the way without changes; *adv* & *prep* **throughout** right through; in every particular; **t. and t.** completely; **be t. with** have done with.
throw *v* hurl, fling; dislodge (from saddle); form (pottery) on wheel; *pt* **threw**; *pp* **thrown**; act or distance of throwing; *n* **throw-back** one who, that which, reverts physically or mentally to ancestral type.
thrum *n* ends of thread of warp on loom after web is cut; loose thread; *pl* waste yarn.
thrush *n* one of varieties of song-birds.
thrush *n* inflammatory affection of mouth and throat, mostly occurring in children.
thrust *v* push; lunge, stab with violent action; (*fig*) obtrude oneself; *pt* & *pp* **thrust**; *n* onset with pointed weapon; lunge.
thud *n* dull, sound as of heavy body falling on ground; *v* make such sound.
thug *n* one of former fraternity of assassins, stranglers in N. India; murderous ruffian, robber; *n* **thuggery**.
thumb *n* short thick inner finger of hand; **rule of t.** rough and ready way of doing anything; *v* make dirty (pages of book etc.) by handling; (*sl*) **t. a lift** ask for lift by signalling with thumb.
thump *v* strike with heavy blow; *n* such blow, or sound of it.
thunder *n* loud rumbling sound following flash of lightning; any such noise (as of applause etc.); *v* emit thunder; utter with loud, powerful voice; *n* **thunderbolt** discharge of lightning accompanying thunder; any of certain stones etc. supposed to have fallen as result of lightning flash; (*fig*) unpleasant, overwhelming surprise; *a* **thundery** oppressive.

Thursday *n* fifth day of week.
thus *adv* in this way; accordingly.
thwack *v* & *n* whack.
thwart *v* oppose; hinder, obstruct; *n* seat for oarsman in boat.
thy *poss pron* (*poet*) of THEE; *pron* **thyself** emphatic form of THOU.
thyme *n* pungent, aromatic herb used in cooking.
thyroid *n* large endocrine gland in neck of vertebrates; *a* of thyroid; **t. cartilage** Adam's apple.
tiara *n* jewelled coronet worn by women; triple crown of Pope.
tibia *n* shin-bone; *pp* **-biae, -bias**; *a* **tibial.**
tic *n* convulsive twitching of facial muscles.
tick *n* any of various small blood-sucking parasites.
tick *n* outer covering of mattress, pillow etc; *n* **ticking** coarse strong material for this.
tick *n* slight clicking, tapping noise, as of watch etc; small mark (√) *v* mark with tick; make sound of tick; **t. off** reprimand.
tick *n* (*coll*) credit.
ticket *n* marked card or paper entitling holder to admission, travel, view etc; label; *v* mark with ticket; label.
tickle *v* itch, tingle; amuse, please; *n* irritation of superficial nerves; *a* **ticklish** sensitive to tickling; difficult to deal with.
tide *n* ebb and flow of surface of sea; (*fig*) trend, tendency; (*ar*) period, season; *v* **t. over** surmount; carry over; *a* **tidal** connected with tide, tides; *n* **t. wave** large ocean wave, *usu* caused by earthquake.
tidings *n pl* news.
tidy *a* trim, neat, orderly; (*coll*) fairly large; *v* put in order.
tie *v* fasten with rope etc. form into knot; (in games etc.) make equal score; *n* neck-tie; connecting piece; moral obligation; equality of scores in contest; *n* **t. up** close association or connection.
tier *n* row, rank; several rows placed one above the other.
tiff *n* trifling dispute; passing quarrel.

tiger *n* large, carnivorous Asiatic mammal, having tawny back with black stipes; *fem* **tigress.**

tight *a* firm compact; taut; cramped; (*coll*) stingy; (*sl*) drunk; *n pl* close fitting garment covering legs and lower part of body; *v* **tighten** make, become tighter.

tile *n* flat cake of baked clay used for roofing; one of finer clay, plastic etc. for inside use; *v* cover with tiles; *a* **tiled.**

till *prep* up to time of; *conj* to time that.

till *n* small drawer or box where cash is kept.

till *v* cultivate (ground).

tiller *n* lever to move rudder of boat.

tilt *v* slope, slant; tip up; *n* slope, slant.

tilt *v* take part in medieval contest with lances; (*fig*) **t. at** attack, criticize; *n* tournament; thrust in tilting; **at full t.** with great speed, or force.

tilth *n* tilled land.

timber *n* wood cut and prepared for building; trees; *v* furnish with timber; cover with trees; *a* **timbered** built of or with timber.

timbre *n* quality of sound of different musical instruments or voices.

time *n* concept of past, present and future; hour; duration; point in duration; period; opportunity; occasion; *v* do or say at right moment; calculate, note time of; *ns* **t.-bomb** one designed to explode at pre-arranged time; **t.-lag** delay between act and effect; **t.-piece** watch or clock; **t.-table** table showing hours of work, times of arrival and departure of trains etc; **Greenwich t.** time as settled by passage of sun over meridian at Greenwich; *a* **timely** opportune.

timid *a* shy, easily frightened; *n* **timidity** *a* **timorous** faint-hearted; apprehensive.

tin *n* white malleable metal; container made of tin or tinned iron; (*sl*) money; *v* coat with tin; preserve in tin container; *a* **tinny** (of sound) shrill; (of food) metallic tasting; *n* (*sl*) **tin-hat** shrapnel-proof steel helmet.

tincture *n* tinge, shade of colour; medicinal solution; *v* tinge; affect slightly.

tinder *n* inflammable material formerly used to catch spark from flint and steel.
tine *n* tooth; spike of fork; prong of antler.
tinge *v* colour, flavour slightly; *n* slight trace.
tingle *v* feel prickling or stinging sensation; smart; vibrate; *n* such sensation.
tinker *n* mender, *esp* itinerant, of pots and pans; *v* mend, patch *esp* clumsily.
tinkle *v* give out series of light sounds like small bell; cause to do this; *n* this action or sound.
tinsel *n* glittering material made of thin strips of metal, used for decoration; anything sham or showy.
tint *v* colour; tinge; *v* dye, give colour to.
tiny *a* very small; minute.
tip *n* slender or pointed end of anything; useful hint; small sum of money given to waiter etc. for service; private information; rubbish dump; *v* give tip to; tilt; be upset; pour out; **t. off** warn; *n* **tipster** one who gives information as to likely winners (of horse-races etc.).
tippet *n* covering for neck and shoulders.
tipple *v* take strong drink frequently; *n* **tippler**.
tipstaff *n* sheriff's officer.
tipsy *a* drunk; mildly intoxicated; *n* **tipsy-cake** sponge cake soaked in wine; trifle.
tiptoe *v* walk on toes; walk softly.
tiptop *a* highest point; (*coll*) first-rate.
tirade *n* long, vigorous, hostile speech.
tire, tyre *n* rim of metal, rubber etc. round wheel.
tire *v* become weary or fatigued; *v* weary; *a* **tiresome** annoying; tedious.
tiro, tyro *n* beginner, novice.
tissue *n* structural material of body of animals or plants; light woven fabric; *n* **tissue-paper** very thin wrapping paper.
tit *n* any of various small, brightly-coloured birds; (*sl*) breast, teat; **t. for tat** retaliation.
titanic *a* huge, gigantic; containing titanium.
titanium *n* rare, grey-coloured metallic element.
titbit *n* choice morsel; (*fig*) spicy item of news.
tithe *n* tenth part, *esp* of profit from land, produce etc. paid to church.

titillate *v* tickle, stimulate pleasurably; *n* **titillation.**
titivate *v* smarten up oneself; adorn; *n* **-ation.**
title *n* name, heading of book, picture etc; appellation of distinction or honour; name showing rank, occupation etc; admitted right or claim; *a* **titled** having title of nobility; *n* **title-deed** legal document establishing ownership, *esp* of land etc; *a* **titular** pertaining to title; nominal.
titmouse *n* small bird, allied to nuthatch.
titter *v* utter quiet laugh; giggle; *n* such laugh.
tittle-tattle *n* gossip; *v.*
to *prep* towards; as far as; expressing comparison, contrast; introducing infinitive mood of verb, indirect object; *adv* to, into normal, desired position etc.
toad *n* amphibian like large frog; *ns* **toadstool** any fleshy fungus other than mushroom; *esp* if poisonous; **toady** servile flatterer; *v* act thus; *n* **toad-in-the-hole** meat (*usu* sausage) baked in batter.
toast *v* make crisp and brown by heat; warm at fire; drink health of; *n* slice of bread browned by heat; proposal to drink health of; person toasted; *n* **toastmaster** announcer of toasts at banquet.
tobacco *n* plant whose leaves are used for smoking; its prepared and dried leaves; *n* **tobacconist** one who sells tobacco etc.
toboggan *n* sledge for sliding down snowy slopes; *v* use, slide on toboggan.
toby jug *n* mug shaped like man in tricorne.
toccata *n* musical composition for keyboard instrument.
tocsin *n* bell sounded to give alarm.
today *n* this day; *adv* on this day; at present time.
toddle *v* walk unsteadily, as small child; (*coll*) stroll; *n* **toddler** young child just starting to walk.
toddy *n* drink of spirits, lemon and hot water.
toe *n* one of five digits of foot; *v* touch with toes; **t. the line** (*fig*) obey orders.
toffee *n* sweetmeat made of boiled sugar with butter.
toga *n* loose flowing robe of ancient Romans.
together *adv* in company; as well as; happening at same time, place etc.

toggle *n* short metal or wooden pin fixed through loop (of rope etc.) to secure it; small wooden bar used instead of button.
togs *n* (*sl*) clothes, dress.
toil *n* severe labour; exacting work; *v* work hard, labour; *as* **toilsome** wearying; **toilworn** (of hands, face etc) hard and lined.
toilet *n* process, style of dressing; (*coll*) bathroom, lavatory.
toils *n pl* net, meshes, snare.
token *n* symbol; evidence; coin, disc or voucher.
tolerate *v* put up with; *n* **toleration**; *as* **tolerable** fairly good; bearable; **tolerant** forbearing; broad-minded; *n* **tolerance.**
toll *n* tax, duty paid for use of road etc.
toll *v* cause (bell) to ring slowly at regular intervals, *esp* at funeral.
tomahawk *n* light hatchet used by N. American Indians in war or hunting.
tomato *n* plant with bright red or yellow edible fruit.
tomb *n* grave, vault; *n* **tombstone** memorial stone on grave.
tombola *n* kind of lottery.
tomboy *n* romping boyish girl.
tomcat *n* male cat.
tome *n* volume, large book.
tomfoolery *n* foolish behaviour; silliness.
tommy *n* (*coll*) private soldier in British Army.
tommy-gun *n* short-barrelled sub-machine gun.
tomorrow *adv* on, during day after this; *n* day after today.
tom-tom *n* primitive African or Oriental drum.
ton *n* measure of weight, 2240 lbs.; unit of ship's carrying capacity; *n* **tonnage** freight-carrying capacity of ship; ships collectively.
tone *n* musical sound; pitch of voice; shade of colour; prevailing mood; vigour; *v* give tone to; *a* **tonic** of tones, sounds; invigorating; *n* invigorating medicine; (*mus*) keynote.
tongs *n pl* large pincers *esp* for lifting coal no to fire.
tongue *n* fleshy muscular organ in mouth; chief

organ of taste, speech, etc; language; speech; anything resembling tongue in shape.

to-night *n* this night; night after to-day; *adv* on, during this night.

tonsils *n pl* pair of masses of lymphoid tissue at back of throat; *n* **tonsillitis** inflammation of tonsils.

tonsure *n* act of shaving part of head as religious practice; part so shaved.

too *adv* in addition; excessively; as well as.

tool *n* implement, instrument, appliance used in mechanical operations: (*fig*) cats-paw, puppet; *v* shape, mark with tool.

toot *n* sound of horn or trumpet; *v* make this sound.

tooth *n* one of hard growths inside jaws of vertebrates; various pointed tooth-shaped objects; prong; cog; *pl* **teeth**; *v* furnish (wheel, comb etc.) with teeth; *a* **toothsome** agreeable to taste.

top *n* highest part, summit; highest rank, degree; highest in merit; *v* cut off, touch, reach, top; *as* **top-secret** of highest importance, to be kept very secret; *n* **top-hat** tall, silk hat; (*sl*) **topper.**

top *n* small spinning toy.

topaz *n* semi-precious stone usually yellowish.

tope *v* drink frequently and excessively; *n* **toper.**

topee, topi *n* pith sun-helmet.

topiary *n* art of cutting living shrubs, trees into shapes of animals, birds etc; *n* **topiarist.**

topic *n* subject of thought or discussion; *a* **-al** connected with subject of current interest.

topography *n* systematic description of place etc; detailed features of district; *n* **topographer.**

topple *v* fall over; overbalance.

topsy-turvy *a* upset, upside-down.

toque *n* brimless, close fitting hat.

tor *n* high rocky pointed hill.

torch *n* portable light or flame; *n* **torchlight** light shed by torches.

toreador *n* bull-fighter.

torment *n* suffering, anguish of mind or body; *v* torture; annoy, tease, harass; *n* **tormentor.**

tornado *n* violent, destructive localized storm; hurricane.

torpedo *n* self-propelled underwater missile used for destroying shipping; **t. fish** electric ray; *v* attack, destroy with torpedo.

torpid *a* sluggish, dull, apathetic; *ns* **torpidity** state of being torpid; **torpor** numbness; dullness, inactivity of mind.

torque *n* twisted necklace or chain; (*mech*) twisting force or movement.

torrent *n* violently rushing stream; (*fig*) rush of words; *a* **torrential** flowing, falling with great violence.

torrid *a* parched by sun; very hot; **t. zone** that between tropics.

torsion *n* act of twisting; state of being twisted.

torso *n* trunk of human body; limbless, headless statue.

tort *n* (*leg*) injurious, harmful act against which civil action can be brought.

tortoise *n* reptile with complete scaly covering for body; *n* **tortoise-shell** mottled brown shell of tortoise, polished and used commercially; *a.*

tortuous *a* twisting, winding; (of mind, aims etc.) devious.

torture *n* deliberate infliction of severe pain; great mental anguish; *v* subject to torture; *n* **torturer.**

Tory *n* & *a* (member) of British Conservative party.

toss *v* throw up; fling, pitch; be flung, thrown; **t. for** spin coin to decide (choice etc.); *n* act of tossing.

tot *n* tiny child; small quantity *esp* of drink, dram.

tot up *v* add up.

total *n* whole amount; complete number; *a* entire; complete; *v* add up; amount to as whole; *n* **totality** entirety; **totalizator** automatic betting machine on racecourse etc.

totalitarian *a* applied to State run by dictator or single political party, allowing no opposition or other political representation.

tote *n* abbreviation of TOTALIZATOR.

totem *n* tribal symbol or emblem; *n* **t. pole** post supporting this.

totter *v* walk unsteadily; (of building etc.) be about to fall.

toucan *n* large billed S. American bird.
touch *v* put hand on; make physical contact with; reach; move to pity etc; (*coll*) try to borrow money from; mention; *n* act; fact of touching; sense of feeling; characteristic method of technique; children's game; *a* **touching** emotionally moving; *prep* as regards, concerning; *ns* **touchline** side line of football field; **touch down** (of aircraft) landing; *v* (rugby football) score by touching ball to ground behind goalposts; *a* **touchy** easily offended.
tough *a* strong, firm; not brittle; sturdy; ruthless; needing effort to chew; *n* (*sl*) hooligan, criminal ruffianly man; *n* **toughness**; *v* **toughen**.
toupee *n* artificial tuft or front of hair; wig.
tour *n* journey round district; excursion; series of visits to different places; *v* make tour; travel; *ns* **tourist** one who travels for pleasure; **tourism** business of organizing, operating tours, and catering for tourists.
tournament *n* medieval contest between mounted knights; (games) contest of skill *usu* for championship.
tourniquet *n* device or bandage used to stop arterial bleeding.
tousle *v* make untidy; rumple, ruffl.
tout *v* importune, pester in order to sell; *n* one who acts thus; tipster.
tow *v* pull along (vehicle etc.) by rope; *n* act of towing or being towed.
tow *n* coarse fibre of hemp.
toward *a* imminent, at hand; *prep* **towards**, **toward** in direction of.
towel *n* cloth used for drying (skin, china etc.) after washing; *v* dry, rub with towel; *n* **towelling** absor bent cloth for making towels.
tower *n* tall strong structure often forming part of church or other building; fortress; *v* rise, stand very high.
town *n* group of houses and other buildings, larger than village; *n* **township** town and surrounding area forming municipality.
toxic *a* pertaining to, caused by, poison; *ns* **toxaemia**

blood-poisoning; **toxicology** study of poisons and their effects; **toxin** poisonous organic substance.

toxophily *n* archery; *n* **toxophilite** lover of archery.

toy *n* plaything; trifle, bauble; *v* trifle with.

trace *n* one of two straps by which vehicle is drawn by horse; visible signs left by anything; slight tinge; *v* follow course, track of; draw, copy exactly *esp* by use of tracing-paper; *ns* **tracer bullet (shell)** one which leaves visible trail; **tracery** intricate decorative pattern of lines; **tracing** traced copy of drawing; **t. paper** thin, transparent paper on which tracings are made.

trachea *n* wind-pipe.

track *n* mark, series of marks left by something passing; footprint; course; railway line; distance between two road wheels on one axle; metal belt surrounding wheels of tank or similar vehicle; *v* trail, trace, follow visible marks.

tract *n* expanse of country; (*anat*) system of related organs.

tract *n* pamphlet; treatise.

tractable *a* easily managed; docile; easily wrought.

traction *n* act, process of drawing along; *ns* **t. engine** steam engine for drawing loads along road; **tractor** motor vehicle for drawing plough etc.

trade *n* commerce; buying and selling; those engaged in trade; *v* traffic; buy and sell; barter; *ns* **trademark** manufacturers registered name or symbol; **trader, tradesman** retail shopkeeper; **trade-union** organized body of workmen of any trade representing their interests; **trade-wind** one that blows regularly towards equator from N or S.

tradition *n* belief, custom, law etc. handed down verbally from one generation to another; unwritten history; *a* **-al.**

traduce *v* slander.

traffic *n* passing to and fro of vehicles etc. in street; body of vehicles using street; trade; *v* trade; *pt* & *pp* **trafficked**; *pr p* **trafficking.**

tragedy *n* very sad event, calamity *esp* one causing death; drama dealing with human misfortunes and sorrows; *a* **tragic** of, like tragedy, fatal; disastrous;

ns **tragedian** tragic actor; *fem* **tragedienne; tragi-comedy** play with both tragic and comic scenes.
trail *v* drag along ground; follow track of; shadow; *n* track or trace; rough ill-defined road; *n* **trailer** expert in following trail; vehicle towed by another one; advertisement of forthcoming film etc.
train *v* educate, instruct; (of plants etc.) cause to grow in certain way; aim (gun); (*athletics*) follow course of physical exercise, dieting etc; *n* series of railway coaches etc. drawn by locomotive; trailing part of dress; retinue; line of gunpowder to mine etc; *ns* **trainee** one who is being trained in certain skill etc; **training** process of educating; art of preparing persons for athletic contests or horses for racing.
train-oil *n* oil obtained from blubber of whales.
traipse, trapse *v* walk around aimlessly.
trait *n* characteristic feature.
traitor *n* one who is guilty of treason; one who betrays a trust, *fem* **traitress**; *a* **traitorous** treacherous.
trajectory *n* path of missile fired or thrown through air.
tram *n* public vehicle running on rails in road; truck used in coal-mines; *n* **tram-car.**
trammel *n* kind of fish-net; shackle; anything which confines, hinders; *v* confine, restrict; hinder.
tramp *v* walk, tread heavily; travel as vagabond; travel on foot; *n* act of tramping; long walk; homeless vagrant; cargo vessel; *v* **trample** tread under foot.
trance *n* state of suspended consciousness; ecstasy, rapture.
tranquil *a* calm, serene; peaceful; unruffled; *n* **tranquility**; *v* **tranquilize** make calm; *n* **tranquilizer** sedative.
trans- *prefix* across, through, beyond. *Compounds, where the meaning is obvious, are not given here.*
transact *v* carry through (negotiations etc.); *n* **transaction** piece of business; *pl* proceedings.
transcend *v* go beyond; surpass; *a* **transcendent** surpassing.

transcribe *v* copy out; write out (notes) in full *n* **transcript.**
transept *n* part of cruciform church which crosses main nave.
transfer *v* move, convey from one person or place to another; *n* act of transferring; conveyance; design etc. transferred from one surface to another by heat pressure etc; *n* **transference.**
transfigure *v* alter appearance of; idealize; glorify, *n* **transfiguration.**
transfix *v* impale; (*fig*) root to the spot.
transform *v* change shape, character, nature of; *ns* **transformation**; **transformer** mechanical device in electricity for changing voltage of alternating current.
transfuse *v* transfer (blood) from veins of one person or animal to another; *n* **transfusion.**
transgress *v* exceed; violate (law); sin; *ns* **transgression; transgressor.**
transient *a* fleeting, brief, momentary; *n* **transcience.**
transistor *n* small electrical device used in place of thermionic valve; small portable radio containing this.
transit *n* passage, crossing; *n* **transition** change from one place to another; *as* **transitional; transitive** (of verb) requiring direct object; **transitory** not lasting.
translate *v* render into another language; transfer (bishop) from one see to another; *ns* **translator**; **translation.**
translucent *a* letting light pass through.
transmit *v* pass on; hand down (by heredity etc); communicate; *ns* **transmitter** one who transmits; apparatus for sending out radio waves; **transmission** act of transmitting; that which is transmitted.
transom *n* lintel; horizontal cross-bar.
transparent *a* permitting passage of light; (*fig*) clear, obvious; *ns* **transparence; transparency** quality of being transparent; picture on transparent material, visible when lit from behind.

transpire *v* exhale as vapour; become known; (*coll*) happen.
transplant *v* dig up (plant) and replant elsewhere; (*med*) remove (healthy organ, tissue) and graft elsewhere; *n* **transplantation.**
transport *v* carry, convey from one place to another; enrapture; *n* act, method of conveying persons, goods; vehicle, ship, etc. so used.
transpose *v* change order of; (*mus*) put into different key; *ns* **transposal; transposition.**
transubstantiation *n* change of substance or essence.
transverse *a* cross-wise; at right angles.
trap *n* device for catching, snaring animals etc; pitfall; two-wheeled carriage; device to prevent gas, foul air, etc. escaping; *v* snare; (*fig*) deceive by cunning; *ns* **trap-door** hinged door in floor, ceiling etc; **trapper** one who traps animals for their fur.
trappings *n pl* equipment; ornaments; one's belongings.
trapeze *n* swinging horizontal bar for gymnastic and acrobatic use.
trapezium *n* quadrilateral figure with only two sides parallel.
trash *n* rubbish; useless matter; worthless person; *a* **trashy** cheap, shoddy.
trauma *n* injury; emotional injury caused by shock etc; *a* **traumatic.**
travail *n* pains of childbirth; labour; *v* be in labour; toil painfully.
travel *v* move along; make journey; *n pl* journeys; tour *esp* abroad; *ns* **traveller** one who travels; one who travels to obtain business orders, often **commercial t.**; **traveller's joy** wild clematis; *a* **travelled** experienced in travelling; *n* **traveller's cheque** cheque issued by bank to client, for use abroad.
traverse *v* pass, lie across; swivel; *n* ledge etc. crossing rock-face horizontally; sideways movement (of gun).
travesty *n* parody; ridiculous distortion; *v* make, be travesty of.

trawl *n* open-mouthed fishing net drawn along sea-bottom; *v* fish with one; *n* **trawler** fishing vessel using trawl.

tray *n* flat board, slab of wood, metal etc, with rim, for carrying things.

treachery *n* betrayal; perfidy; breach of trust; *a* **treacherous** disloyal; unreliable; dangerous.

treacle *n* thick syrup obtained from unrefined sugar, molasses; *a* **treacly.**

tread *v* set foot on; trample; oppress; *pt* **trod**; *pp* **trodden** or **trod**; *n* manner, sound of walking; part of tyre in contact with ground; top surface of step; *ns* **treadle** lever worked by foot; **treadmill** cylinder turned by treading on steps fixed to rim; (*fig*) monotonous routine.

treason *n* violation by subject of allegiance to sovereign or state; *as* **treasonablc**; **treasonous.**

treasure *n* stored up valuables; money, riches; *v* store, regard, as valuable; cherish; *ns* **treasurer** person in charge of funds of club, society etc; **treasury** department of state, collecting and controlling public money and taxation; place for storing treasure; **treasure-trove** gold, silver articles found hidden, with no evidence of ownership.

treat *v* behave towards, use; seal with chemically; pay expenses of; negotiate; *n* pleasurable event; entertaining; *n* **treatment** act, mode of, treating, attempting to cure; manner of artistic handling.

treatise *n* systematic written account of something.

treaty *n* agreement, contract entered into between states etc.

treble *a* threefold; high pitched; *n* treble part or voice; *v* increase threefold.

tree *n* large perennial plant having woody trunk; cobbler's last; **family t.** diagram showing descent; from common ancestor.

trefoil *n* plant whose leaf has three lobes; clover (*archi*) carved three-lobed ornament.

trek *v* make journey, travel; migrate; *n.*

trellis *n* lattice, structure of crossed wooden strips.

tremble *v* shiver, quake; *n* tremor, quiver; involuntary shaking.

tremendous *a* vast; amazing; awe-inspiring; (*coll*) very exciting.
tremolo *n* quivering effect in playing or singing.
tremor *n* shaking; qualm; thrill.
tremulous *a* shaky, trembling; timid, fearful.
trench *n* long opening, furrow, cut or dug in earth; *v* cut trench or groove in.
trenchant *a* keen, incisive, biting.
trencher *n* wooden platter, formerly used as plate for food; *n* **good trencherman** one who has good appetite.
trend *n* course, direction; (*fig*) general tendency; fashion; *a* **trendy** in latest fashions.
trepan *v* remove portion of bone from skull; *n* small cylindrical saw for perforating skull; *n* **trephine** trepan.
trepidation *n* state of alarm; nervous fluster.
trespass *n* go unlawfully on another's land; commit an offence; *n* act of trespassing; offence, injury; *n* **trespasser**.
tress *n* lock of hair; *pl* hair of head.
trestle *n* framework of board supported by wooden legs.
trews *n* tartan trousers.
tri- *prefix* three.
triad *n* group of three.
trial *n* act of trying, testing; adversity; source of irritation; judicial inquiry.
triangle *n* figure with three angles; musical instrument; *a* **triangular**.
tribe *n* social unit; class, group; *a* **tribal**; *n* **tribesman** member of tribe.
tribulation *n* grief; affliction; mental distress.
tribunal *n* court of justice; special court of enquiry.
tribute *n* tax, payment made by one state to another; act performed, words uttered as sign of respect, esteem, affection for; *a* **tributary** paying tribute; auxiliary; *n* stream flowing into larger one.
trice *n* instant, brief space of time.
trick *n* deception; swindle; illusion; prank; mannerism; cards played in one round; *v* cheat; deceive; *n* **trickery, trickster**; *a* **tricky** shifty; ingenious.

trickle *v* flow slowly; *n* thin flow.
tricolour *n* national flag with three stripes of different colours, *esp* French.
tricycle *n* three-wheeled cycle.
trident *n* three-pronged fork.
triennial *a* happening every three years.
trifle *n* small, insignificant thing of no value; sweet dish of sponge-cake, wine and cream etc; *v* speak idly; behave insincerely; *a* **trifling** trivial.
trigger *n* catch which releases spring *esp* to fire gun; *c* **t. off** initiate large scale process by small act.
trigonometry *n* branch of mathematics dealing with relationship between sides and angles of triangles.
trilateral *a* having three sides.
trilby *n* soft felt hat.
trill *v* sing, with vibrating sound; warble; *n* such singing.
trilogy *n* series of three connected literary or musical works.
trim *v* prune; decorate (garment etc.); adjust balance of (ship, aircraft etc.); *a* neat, tidy, in good order; *n* state of being trimmed.
trinitrotoluene *n* high explosive; *abbrev* T.N.T.
trinity *n* the three divine persons of Godhead; state of being threefold.
trinket *n* bauble; worthless trifle.
trio *n* group of three; music for three voices or instruments.
trip *v* stumble, make false step; skip, dance; *n* stumble; journey, excursion; *n* **tripper** holiday-maker *esp* day excursionist.
tripartite *a* of, in three parts.
tripe *n* stomach of ruminant animal, prepared as food; (*coll*) nonsense, rubbish.
triple *a* threefold; *v* increase threefold; *n* **triplet** three of a kind; *as* **triplex** threefold; **triplicate** made in three identical copies; *n* one of three identical copies.
tripod *n* three-legged stand, support etc.
tripos *n* examination for Honours degree at Cambridge.

triptych *n* picture, carving on three hinged panels, *esp* altar-piece.
trireme *n* ancient Greek, Roman war-galley, with three rows of oars.
trite *a* banal; commonplace.
Triton *n* minor sea-god.
triturate *v* grind to powder, pulverize; *n* **trituration.**
triumph *n* victory; success; exultation; processional entry of victorious ancient Roman general; *v* achieve success; prevail; exult; *as* **triumphal**; **triumphant.**
triumvir *n* one of three men sharing supreme power in Rome; *n* **triumvirate** group of three such men.
trivet *n* three-legged stand for pot or kettle.
trivial *a* trifling; of little consequence; *n* **triviality.**
trochee *n* metrical foot of two syllables, one long, one short.
troglodyte *n* cave-dweller; common wren.
Trojan *n* inhabitant of Troy; person of courage and endurance.
troll *v* fish by trailing bait *esp* behind boat; sing cheerfully.
troll *n* fabulous Scandinavian goblin, giant or dwarf.
trolley *n* light low cart or wheeled table, pushed by hand; truck on rails; metal arm conveying current from overhead wires to tram-car; **t. bus** bus powered by overhead electric cable.
trollop *n* slovenly disreputable woman.
trombone *n* powerful brass wind-instrument with sliding tube; *n* **trombonist** trombone player.
troop *n* number of people; subdivision of cavalry squadron; *pl* soldiers; *v* move as troop; crowd; *n* **trooper** cavalry soldier.
trophy *n* token of victory; prize.
tropic *n* one of two parallels of latitude 23° 28° N & S of equator; *pl* hot regions of earth between these parallels; *a* **tropical** extremely hot; growing occurring in tropics.
trot *v* (of horse etc.) move rapidly but not at gallop; run easily with short steps; *n* rapid pace of horse etc; quick walk.
troth *n* fidelity, word of honour.

troubadour *n* medieval poet.
trouble *v* disturb, afflict; agitate; worry; *n* agitation; difficulty; disturbance; *as* **troublous** disturbed; **troublesome** annoying; unruly.
trough *n* long narrow container for food or water for animals; narrow channel between waves.
trounce *v* beat; defeat; censure.
troupe *n* band of actors; touring company; *n* **trouper.**
trousers *n pl* two-legged outer garment, enclosing legs from waist to ankles.
trousseau *n* bride's outfit.
trout *n* edible fresh-water fish.
trowel *n* small flat-bladed took for spreading mortar; small hollow-bladed tool for lifting, planting plants.
troy *n* system of weights used for gold, silver, etc.
truant *n* person who stays away from school, work etc. without permission; *a* shirking school or duty.
truce *n* temporary agreement to stop fighting; respite.
truck *n* open railway-wagon; lorry, barrow.
truckle *v* cringe; **t. to** fawn on, submit to.
truckle-bed *n* low bed, *esp* on wheels, which could be pushed beneath another one.
truculent *a* aggressive; fierce, violent; *n* **truculence.**
trudge *v* walk wearily, with effort; *n* long tedious walk.
trudgen *n* swimming stroke.
true *a* in accordance with fact; accurate; genuine; correct; *ns* **truth** quality, state of being true; honesty; sincerity; **truism** statement of something obviously true; *adv* **truly** really; loyally; sincerely; *a* **truthful** habitually speaking truth; *n* **true bill** bill of indictment endorsed by grand jury.
truffle *n* adible fungus, growing below ground.
trug *n* shallow wooden gardening basket.
trump *n* card of suit temporarily ranking above others; *v* take trick with trump.
trumpery *a* showy, rubbishy; worthless; *a* **trumped up** fabricated, concocted.
trumpet *n* metal wind instrument; funnel; *v* sound on trumpet; (*fig*) proclaim, announce widely.

truncate *v* cut off, lop.
truncheon *n* short thick staff or cudgel, baton of office.
trundle *v* cause to roll along; move on wheels.
trunk *n* stem of tree; person's body not including head or limbs; main body or line (of railways, telephones etc.); large suit-case; long flexible snout of elephant etc; *pl* tight-fitting drawers for swimming etc; *ns* **trunk line; trunk road.**
truss *v* bind, tie up, tie wings (of fowl etc.) before cooking; *n* bundle (of hay etc.) cluster of blossom; surgical support for ruptured organ; framework of beams etc. supporting roof etc.
trust *n* confidence, faith; group of persons administering fund; responsibility; property held for another; *v* have faith in; rely on; *n* **trustee** one legally holding property in trust for another; *as* **trustful** confiding; **trustworthy** reliable, dependable; **trusty** faithful, loyal.
try *v* test, attempt; conduct judicial inquiry into; purify, refine (metals); *n* attempt; (Rugby football) touch-down; *as* **tried** proved, reliable; **trying** provoking; painful; wearisome.
tryst *n* appointment, rendezvous.
tsar *n* formerly emperor of Russia; *fem* **tsarina.**
tsetse *n* African fly which conveys parasite of sleeping-sickness.
tub *n* wooden vessel, often shaped like half barrel; (*coll*) bath; boat used for rowing practice; *v* (*coll*) bathe, take bath.
tube *n* long, hollow cylinder; pipe; underground electric railway; *a* **tubular** shaped like tube; *n* **tubing** series of pipes; piece of tube.
tuber *n* swollen part of underground stem; containing buds, e.g. potato; *a* **tuberous** producing, growing from tubers.
tubercle *n* small swelling; small morbid growth on organ *esp* lungs; *a* **tubercular**; *n* **tuberculosis** infectious disease causing growth of small nodules at affected part, caused by tubercles.
tuberose *n* bulbous garden plant like lily, having spikes of fragrant flowers.

tuck *v* gather up; fold; be folded up; press together; **t. into** eat heartily; *ns* stitched fold; (*sl*) schoolboys' food, *esp* cakes, jam, etc; **t.-shop** school sweet shop; **tucker** (*Aust sl*) food; (*obs*) lace trimming on bodice; *v* **tucker out** exhaust, tire out.

Tudor *a* pertaining to, made in age of Tudors.

Tuesday *n* third day of week.

tuft *n* bunch, bundle *esp* of grass, hair etc.

tug *v* pull violently; *n* act of tugging, small steam boat used for towing; *n* **tug of war** contest of strength between two teams pulling in different directions on same rope.

tuition *n* teaching; instruction.

tulip *n* bulbous plant of lily family; *n* **tulip-tree** tree allied to magnolia.

tulle *n* soft fine silky material.

tumble *v* fall down; stumble; turn somersaults; upset; rumple; *n* fall; somersault; *n* **tumbler** acrobat; part of lock moved by key; drinking glass without stem or foot; *a* **tumbledown** falling into ruin.

tumbrel, tumbril *n* rubbish cart; ammunition cart; cart in which victims of French Revolution were taken to guillotine.

tumid *a* swollen, enlarged.

tumour *n* morbid swelling in some part of body.

tumult *n* uproar, disturbance; *a* **tumultuous** noisy, greatly agitated.

tumulus *n* ancient burial mound or barrow.

tun *n* large cask for storing, fermenting beer and wine; formerly measure of liquid 252 galls.

tuna, tunny *n* large edible sea-fish.

tundra *n* frozen desert of N. Russia and Siberia.

tune *n* air, melody; harmony; correctness of pitch; **change one's t.** (*fig*) speak, act very differently; *v* adjust to correct pitch; adjust radio etc. to receive programmes on certain wave length; *n* **tuner** one who, that which tunes; *as* **tuneful** melodious; **tuneless** out of tune.

tungsten *n* greyish white metallic element, wolfram.

tunic *n* military surcoat; loose belted knee length garment.

tunnel *n* underground passage *esp* one for railway;

burrow (of mole etc.); *v* make tunnel through.
turban *n* Oriental head-covering made by coiling long strip of cloth round head.
turbid *a* muddy, opaque; (*fig*) confused etc.
turbine *n* motor driven by jets of steam, water etc. playing on blades.
turbo-jet *n* & *a* (engine) using exhaust gas to drive turbine.
turbot *n* large edible flat sea-fish.
turbulent *a* riotous; unruly; disorderly; *n* **turbulence.**
tureen *n* deep, lidded dish for soup.
turf *n* area of earth covered by grass; sod; peat; **the t.** horse racing; **turf out** (*coll*) turn out roughly.
turgid *a* swollen; inflated, pompous; *n* **turgidity.**
turkey *n* large, domestic fowl of pheasant family, used as food.
Turkish *a* pertaining to Turkey, the Turks; *n* **T. bath** hot air or steam bath; **T. delight** sweetmeat of flavoured gelatine coated in sugar.
turmeric *n* aromatic plant of ginger family used as medicine, dye and condiment.
turmoil *n* agitation; uproar, confusion; tumult.
turn *v* shape, cut on lathe; spin, wind, cause change of direction; adapt; become sour; *n* act of turning; short walk; performance; opportunity which recurs at intervals; (*coll*) shock; *ns* **turncoat** renegade; **turner; turncock** valve regulating water flow; **turnkey** gaoler; **turn-out** gathering, meeting; dress, appearance; output; **turnover** folded over pie; amount of business done in given period; **turnpike** toll gate; **turnstile** revolving gate controlling admission to entertainment etc; **turn-table** revolving platform *esp* on record player; large revolving platform for turning engines etc. round; **turning point** crisis.
turnip *n* plant with large white globular edible root.
turpentine *n* liquid solvent, distilled from resin of pine trees.
turpitude *n* depravity, infamy.
turquoise *n* semi-precious greenish-blue stone; this colour.

turret *n* small tower; revolving armoured tower for guns in warship tank or aircraft.
turtle *n* marine tortoise; edible species of this.
turtle-dove *n* wild dove.
tusk *n* long pointed tooth in some animals, as elephants etc; *n* **tusker** animal with fully developed tusks.
tussle *n* scuffle, rough struggle; *v* engage in rough struggle.
tussock *n* clump of grass, tuft.
tussore *n* Indian silk worm; their coarse silk; fabric woven from this.
tutelage *n* state of acting as guardian, or being under guardianship.
tutor *n* teacher, private instructor; *a* **tutorial.**
twaddle *n* empty, foolish talk; nonsense.
twain *a* (*poet* & *ar*) two.
twang *n* nasal speech; vibrating metallic sound; *v* pluck strings of musical instrument.
tweak *n* & *v* nip, pinch.
tweed *a* & *n* (made from) Scottish woollen cloth.
tweet *v* & *n* chirp.
tweezers *n pl* small pair of pincers.
twelve *n* & *a* cardinal number one above eleven; *a* **twelfth** ordinal number; **T.-night** evening of 6th January.
twenty *n* & *a* cardinal number, twice ten; *a* **twentieth** ordinal number.
twice *adv* two times.
twiddle *v* twirl, twist.
twig *n* small branch, shoot.
twig *v* (*coll*) understand.
twilight *n* half-light after sunset and before dawn; **t. sleep** state of induced semi-unconsciousness, to lessen plains of childbirth.
twill *n* diagonally ribbed fabric; *a* **twilled.**
twin *n* one of two persons, animals born at one birth; *a* double; closely connected, resembling; *v* link, match closely; pair up.
twine *v* twist, coil round; *n* strong string.
twinge *n* sudden, sharp, shooting pain; pang.
twinkle *v* flash, sparkle intermittently; (of eyes)

show sudden gleam of mirth; *n* **twinkling** intermittent sparkle; brief moment.

twirl *v* turn or twist quickly; spin round.

twist *v* twine; wind round; act dishonestly; make. become spiral; *n* hank of thread etc; bend, coil; *n* **twister** one who, that which twists; (*coll*) dishonest person; *a* **twisty.**

twit *v* taunt.

twitch *v* pluck, pull jerkily; *n* spasmodic movement of body.

twitter *v* (of birds) chirp intermittently.

two *n* cardinal number next above one; pair; *as* **two-faced** deceitful; **twopenny-halfpenny** (*sl*) trivial; cheap; *n* **two-seater** motor car for two; *a* **two-way** moving, communicating in two directions.

tycoon *n* (*coll*) powerful business man.

tyke, tike *n* (*sl*) dog; ill-bred fellow.

tympanum *n* ear-drum.

type *n* class, group; kind, variety; example; (*print*) block of wood, metal with letter or symbol on surface; set of type; **in t.** set up ready for printing; *v* classify; print with typewriter; *ns* **typescript** typewritten draft of book etc; **typewriter** writing machine with keys tapped by fingers; **typist** one who uses typewriter.

typhoid *n* infectious enteric fever; *n* **typhus** contagious fever.

tyhhoon *n* violent whirlwind, hurricane.

typical *a* true to type; characteristic; *v* **typify** serve as type or model of.

typography *n* art of style of printing; *a* **typographical;** *n* **typographer.**

tyrant *n* despotic, harsh, unjust ruler; one who forces his will on others cruelly, oppressively; *a* **tyrannical** *v* **tyrannize** rule, exert authority harshly; *n* **tyranny** despotism.

ubiquitous *a* present, existing everywhere; *n* **ubiquity.**

udder *n* external milk gland of cow etc.

ugly *a* hideous; unpleasing to sight; (*fig*) offensive, menacing; *n* **ugliness.**

ukase *n* Russian decree; any arbitrary order.

ukulele *n* small four-stringed musical instrument, like guitar.

ulcer *n* open sore, discharging pus, on skin or mucous membrane; (*fig*) corrupting influence; *v* **ulcerate** (*usu* in *pp* as *a*) infect with ulcer; *n* **ulceration**; *a* **ulcerous.**

ullage *n* amount by which cask, bottle is short of being full.

ulna *n* inner bone of forearm; *pl* **ulnae**; *a* **ulnar.**

ulster *n* long, loose, belted overcoat.

ulterior *a* later in time; lying on farther side; (of motive etc.) undisclosed.

ultimate *a* furthest; final; last; fundamental; *n* **ultimatum** final demand, terms offered by person or power; *adv* **ultimo** (*abbrev* **ult**) in preceding month.

ultra- *prefix* beyond in space; beyond what is normal; excessively.

ultramarine *n* bright blue pigment; *a* of this colour; overseas.

ultramontane *n* & *a* (person) holding extreme views on Papal authority.

ultra-red *a* rays of spectrum below red; infra-red.

ultra-short *a* (radio) of waves below 10 metres.

ultra-violet *a* of electromagnetic waves between visible violet and X-rays.

ululate *v* howl; hoot, screech, wail; *n* **ululation.**

umbel *n* flower cluster with stalks radiating from central point; *a* **umbelliferous.**

umber *n* brown earthy pigment.

umbilicus *n* (*anat*) navel; *a* **umbilical** of, near naval; **u. cord** structure joining foetus to placenta; tube, cable linking spaceship with astronaut outside.

umbrage *n* feeling of resentment or injury; **take umbrage** be offended.

umbrella *n* folding circular shade or cover, for protection against rain or sun.

umpire *n* person chosen to judge, decide doubtful point, or enforce rules in game; *v* act as umpire.

umpteen *a* (*coll*) large number of.

un- *prefix* expressing negation before simple words or reversal of action before verbs. *Such words are not given when the meaning may be deduced easily.*
unaccountable *a* inexplicable; not responsible.
unanimous *a* being of one mind; agreeing; *n* **unanimity.**
unassuming *a* modest, unpresuming.
unavailing *a* ineffectual; useless.
unaware *n* ignorant, not noticing; *adv* **unawares** without warning; inadvertently.
uncanny *a* weird, mysterious.
uncate *a* hooked; *a* **unciform** hook-shaped.
uncle *n* brother of father or mother; husband of aunt; (*sl*) pawnbroker.
unconscionable *a* unscrupulous; excessive.
unconscious *a* not knowing; involuntary; insensible; *n* the subconscious; *n* **unconsciousness.**
uncouth *a* awkward; unrefined in manner.
unction *n* anointing with oil; (*fig*) fervour *esp* religious; suavity, gush; **Extreme U.** sacrament given to dying; *a* **unctuous** greasy, oily; (*fig*) smug gushing.
undaunted *a* bold, intrepid, not frightened.
under *prep* below, beneath; protected, ruled by; subjected to, undergoing; less than, inferior to *a* lower.
under- *prefix* lower; inferior; insufficiently; beneath. *Such words are not given when the meaning may be deduced easily.*
undercarriage *n* wheels on which aircraft lands; framework for these.
undercharge *v* charge too little.
undergraduate *n* member of university who has not yet taken first degree.
underground *a* below surface of earth; secret; *n* underground railway; secret resistance movement.
underhand *a* (of bowling, tennis) with arm lower than shoulder; sly.
underline *v* mark (word etc.) with line underneath; (*fig*) emphasize.
underling *n* subordinate.
undermine *v* wear away by erosion etc; (*fig*) weaken, injure by secret means.
underneath *adv* beneath, below.

underpass *n* tunnel or covered cutting taking one road under another.
understand *v* comprehend; assume, infer; learn, be informed of; *pt* & *pp* **-stood**; *n* **understanding** comprehension; sympathy.
understudy *v* learn part (of actor etc.) in order to deputize for him, if necessary; *n*.
undertake *v* enter upon; promise, pledge oneself; *pt* **-took**; *pp* **-taken**; *n* **undertaker** one who undertakes; one whose business is to arrange funerals; *n* **-taking** an enterprise; guarantee.
undertow *n* undercurrent of wave breaking on shore.
underwear *n* clothes worn beneath others; *n pl* (*coll*) **undies** underclothes.
underworld *n* criminals as social group; place of departed spirits.
underwrite *v* insure shipping; undertake to buy, take up shares not bought by public.
undo *v* reverse; ruin; cancel; unfasten; *pt* **undid**; *pp* **undone**; *n* **undoing** cause, source of ruin; unfastening; *a* **undone** untied; ruined; not done.
undue *a* excessive; improper.
undulate *v* rise and fall like waves; *n* **undulation**.
unearth *v* dig up; discover.
ungainly *a* awkward, clumsy.
ungrounded *a* false, unjustified.
unguent *n* ointment.
ungulate *n* & *a* (animal) which has hoofs.
uni- *prefix* one, single.
unicameral *a* with only one legislative chamber.
unicorn *n* fabulous animal like horse with one horn in middle of forehead.
uniform *a* not changing; similar in every way; *n* distinctive dress worn by members of organized body; *n* **uniformity** sameness.
unify *v* cause to be one, combine; *n* **unification**.
unilateral *a* one-sided.
union *n* act of uniting or being united; federation; trade union; *ns* **unionism, unionist; Union Jack** national flag of U.K.
unique *a* having no like or equal; unparalleled.
unison *n* harmony, concord; (*mus*) **identity of pitch.**

unit *n* single complete thing; group of people or things forming complete whole; least whole number.
unite *v* join into one; associate; combine; cause to adhere; *n* **unity** state of being unit; agreement of aims, interests etc.; harmony, amity; *a* **united** joined; in alliance.
universe *n* whole system of created things viewed as whole; the cosmos; *a* **universal** relating to all things or men.
university *n* institution for higher education, empowered to confer degrees; members collectively, governing body of such institution.
unkempt *a* of untidy appearance.
unless *conj* if not, except that.
unruly *a* disorderly, ungovernable.
until *prep* so far as, up to; *conj* up to time when.
unto *prep* (*poet* & *ar*) to.
untoward *a* inconvenient, unlucky, awkward.
up *adv* to higher or better position; before judge etc; (*fig*) expressing equality in merit, success etc.; *a* placed in, moving towards higher or better position; *comp* **upper**; *sup* **uppermost**; *prep* from lower to higher place, position etc.; *a* & *adv* **upward**; *adv* **upwards**.
up- *prefix*: *forms compounds with meaning of* upward, in higher position. *Such words are not given when the meaning may be deduced from the simple word.*
upbraid *v* censure, reproach, scold.
upgrade *v* raise status of; put higher price on.
uphill *a* ascending; (*fig*) difficult.
upholster *v* furnish (room) with carpets, curtains etc.; stuff and cover chairs etc.; *ns* **upholsterer** one who repairs, covers chairs etc. or who sells such goods; **upholstery** trade of upholsterer; goods supplied by him.
upland *n* (often *pl*) higher ground of region.
uplift *v* lift up, raise *esp* spiritually or culturally.
upon *prep* on.
upper-cut *n* upward blow to chin.
uppish *a* conceited; snobbish; imprudent.
upright *a* erect; (*fig*) honest, just; *n* upright post, beam, support etc.

uproar *n* noisy tumult; clamour; *a* **uproarious** noisy, rowdy.
upset *v* knock, turn over; distress, annoy; *n* state of disorder; cause of distress; (*coll*) quarrel.
upshot *n* final issue; conclusion.
upstart *n* one who has risen suddenly to high position or wealth etc.
uraemia *n* morbid condition of blood caused by presence of urine in it.
uranium *n* white metallic radioactive element.
urbane *a* courteous, affable, refined; *n* **urbanity**.
urban *a* pertaining to town; *v* **urbanize** change from rural to urban condition; *n* **urbanization**.
urchin *n* mischievous, roguish boy; (*dial*) hedgehog.
urge *v* drive, push forward; exhort insistently; *a* **urgent** requiring immediate attention; highly important; *n* **urgency**.
urine *n* fluid secreted by kidneys; *a* **uric** of urine; *v* **urinate** pass urine; *n* **urinal** place for urinating.
urn *n* large lidded, metal vessel with tap, in which tea etc. can be kept hot; rounded vase, often with handle, *esp* for ashes of dead.
us *pron* objective case of WE.
use *n* act of employing anything; advantage, purpose served; utility; habit, custom, usage; *v* employ; consume; behave toward; avail oneself of; *as* **usable** fit for use; **useful** serviceable; helpful; **useless**; *n* **usage** treatment; habitual practice.
usher *n* official in charge of entrance to court etc.; one showing people to seats, keeping order etc.; *v* act as usher; announce.
usual *a* commonplace; habitual; *adv* **usually** generally; as a rule.
usufruct *n* right to use & profits of another's property without damage to it or waste.
usurp *v* take possession of without right or by force; *n* **usurper**.
usury *n* lending of money at excessive interest; *n* **usurer** extortionate money-lender.
utensil *n* vessel, container for domestic use; any tool or implement for particular purpose.
uterus *n* womb

utility *n* usefulness; useful thing; *pl* **utilities** public services, as supplying of water, gas, electricity etc.; *v* **utilize** put to use, make profitable use of; *a* **utilitarian** serving material or practical ends; *n* **utilization.**

utmost *a* most extreme; to greatest, highest degree; *n* most possible.

Utopia *n* imaginary State with ideally perfect social and political system; *a* **utopian** ideally perfect but impracticable.

utter *a* complete, total; absolute; final.

utter *v* produce audibly with voice; say; express by word of mouth, or in writing; *n* **utterance** act of speaking; spoken words.

uttermost *a* farthest out; *n* **utmost.**

uvula *n* fleshy appendage hanging from back of soft palate; *a* **uvular.**

uxorious *a* excessively devoted to and fond of one's wife.

vacant *a* empty; unoccupied; (*fig*) empty-headed; *n* **vacancy** vacant post; gap.

vacate *v* leave empty; resign from; quit; *n* **vacation** act of vacating; fixed holiday period.

vaccinate *v* inoculate with vaccine; *ns* **vaccination;** **vaccine** preparation of virus (*esp* of cowpox) used as inoculation against disease.

vacillate *v* waver in mind; hesitate, be undecided; *n* **vacillation** indecision, hesitation.

vacuous *a* stupid; expressionless; *n* **vacuity** lack of ideas, interest etc.

vacuum *n* space empty or devoid of all matter or content; space from which air has been partially exhausted; *n* **v. cleaner** apparatus for removing dirt etc by suction; **v. flask** vessel with two walls separated by vacuum, used to keep liquids at constant temperature.

vagabond *a* wandering; having no fixed abode; *n* tramp, vagrant; (*coll*) rascal.

vagary *n* caprice, whim; freak.

vagina *n* female genital passage; *a* **vaginal.**

vagrant *a* wandering, nomadic; (*fig*) roving, wayward; *n* tramp; *n* **vagrancy**.
vague *a* indefinite; blurred; absent-minded; not clearly expressed.
vain *a* fruitless, futile; conceited, self-satisfied.
vainglorious *a* inordinately proud or boastful.
valance *n* short curtain above window or in space between bed and floor.
vale *n* valley.
valediction *n* farewell; *a* **valedictory**; *n* farewell oration.
valence, valency *n* (*chem*) combining power of atom or substance.
valentine *n* sweetheart chosen on 14 February; card or gift sent on that day.
valerian *n* perennial herb; its root as medicine.
valet *n* manservant who looks after his master's clothes etc.; *v* act as valet.
valetudinarian *n* & *a* (person) in poor health; (one) unduly engrossed by state of health.
Valhalla *n* (*myth*) feasting-place for souls of heroes killed in battle.
valiant *a* brave, courageous, heroic; *n* **valour**; *a* **valorous**.
valid *n* having legal force; well founded; *n* **validity** soundness; legal force; *v* **validate** make valid.
valise *n* small travelling-bag.
Valkyrie *n* (*myth*) one of twelve war-goddesses, who led the slain to Valhalla.
valley *n* tract of land lying between hills; large river-basin.
value *n* worth; purchasing power; precise meaning, force; relative proportion of light and shade in picture; duration of note in music; *v* estimate worth of; appraise; esteem, rate highly; *a* **valuable** costly of great worth; very useful; *n* (*usu pl*) valuable objects, goods etc.; *n* **valuation** estimated worth; *a* **valueless**; *n* **valuer**.
valve *n* device which regulates flow of air, liquid, gas etc. through opening, pipe etc.; *a* **valvular** of, like, affecting valves.
vamoose, vamose *v* (*sl*) go away quickly.

vamp *n* front upper part of footwear; improvised musical accompaniment; *v* (*mus*) improvise.

vampire *n* (*myth*) corpse that revives itself by sucking human blood; (*fig*) ruthless blackmailer or money-lender; *ns* **vampire bat** American blood-sucking bat; (*abbrev*) **vamp** woman who deliberately entices men; *v* allure (men).

van *n* covered goods vehicle.

van *n* leading part of army, fleet, procession; *n* **vanguard** van; (*fig*) leaders of intellectual, political movement.

vanadium *n* rare metallic element used in alloys.

vandal *n* one who wilfully or through lack of taste spoils beautiful things in art or nature; *n* **vandalism**.

vane *n* weathercock; blade of propellor; sight of quadrant or surveying instrument; web of feather.

vanilla *n* kind of orchid; its pods used for flavouring.

vanish *v* disappear; cease to exist; become invisible; *n* **vanishing point** point in perspective drawing where receding parallel lines appear to meet.

vanity *n* conceit; futility; worthlessness.

vanquish *v* conquer; subdue; be victorious; *n* **vanquisher**.

vantage *n* advantage; (tennis) first point after deuce; *v* **v. point** favourable position.

vapid *a* insipid; lifeless; *n* **vapidity**.

vapour *n* substance in gaseous state; steam, mist; (*fig*) freak of fancy; *v* **vaporize** convert into or pass off in vapour; *a* **vaporous**; *n* **vaporizer** atomizer.

varicose *a* (of veins) abnormally swollen.

variegate *v* mark with different colours; *a* **variegated** parti-coloured; streaked; *n* **variegation**.

variety *n* diversity; varied assortment; kind, type, group; *a* **various** of several different kinds; some; (*coll*) many.

varlet *n* groom, attendant; rogue, rascal.

varnish *n* gum or resin disolved in spirit, applied to surface to make it shiny; *v* apply varnish to.

vary *v* change; alter; modify; become different; *a* **variable**, *n* **variance** alteration; strife, dissension;

a **variant** different; *n* different form; *n* **variation** departure from standard, type etc.; extent of such departure or change.
vascular *a* containing, concerning vessels conveying fluid in plants and animals.
vase *n* ornamental container for flowers; similar ornament as architectural feature.
Vaseline *n* **(P)** soft petroleum jelly.
vassal *n* feudal tenant; dependant, bondsman.
vast *a* very extensive; huge; (*coll*) great; *n* **vastness**.
vat *n* large cask or tub.
Vatican *n* palace of Pope in Rome; (*fig*) papacy; Papal authority etc.
vaudeville *n* light theatrical entertainment.
vault *n* arched roof; arched cellar; strongroom.
vault *v* leap, spring over, *esp* with support of hands or pole; *n* such leap or jump.
vaunt *v* boast, brag about.
veal *n* flesh of calf, used for food.
vector *n* animal transmitting parasites; (maths) magnitude having direction; course of aircraft.
veer *v* shift, change in direction, position; (*fig*) change (opinion etc.)
vegetable *a* pertaining to, concerning, composed of plants or plant life; *n* plant, *esp* edible one; *n* **vegetarian** one who does not eat meat.
vegetate *v* live dull monotonous life; *n* **vegetation** plant growth and development; plants collectively.
vehement *a* passionate, impetuous; *n* **vehemence**.
vehicle *n* means of conveyance, *usu* on wheels; means, medium of expression etc.; *a* **vehicular**.
veil *n* covering for face or head; (*fig*) that which conceals; *v* cover with veil; conceal.
vein *n* blood-vessel conveying blood to heart; vein-like marking; crack; layer or fissure containing metallic ore; (*fig*) mood, disposition; *a* **venous** of veins.
veld(t) *n* open grass country of S. Africa.
vellum *n* parchment of calf-skin used for book-binding or manuscripts.
velocipede *n* early form of bicycle.
velocity *n* speed, rapidity of motion; rate of motion.

velours, velour *n* soft velvety material.
velvet *n* silk fabric with soft thick pile or nap on one side; (*fig*) soft downy surface; *a* **velvety** like velvet; *n* **velveteen** imitation velvet made of cotton.
venal *a* corruptible; mercenary; influenced by hope of reward; *n* **venality**.
vend *v* sell; *ns* **vendor**; **vending machine** automatic selling machine.
vendetta *n* hereditary blood-feud.
veneer *v* thin layer of fine wood laid over inferior kind; (*fig*) superficial polish concealing defects; *v* cover with veneer.
venerable *a* worthy of respect and veneration; *v* **venerate** revere, respect; worship; *n* **veneration**.
venereal *a* pertaining, due, to sexual intercourse.
Venetian blind *n* one made of horizontal movable slats.
vengeance *n* revenge; infliction of punishment for wrong done; *a* **vengeful**.
venial *a* pardonable; trivial.
venison *n* deer's flesh, as food.
venom *n* poison secreted by snake etc.; (*fig*) spite; bitter words; *a* **venomous** poisonous; spiteful.
vent *n* slit, hole, outlet; *v* pour forth; utter.
ventilate *v* supply with fresh air; aerate; (*fig*) discuss freely; *ns* **ventilator**; **ventilation**.
ventral *a* pertaining to abdominal region.
ventricle *n* cavity in organ of body, *esp* main pumping chamber of heart; *a* **ventricular**.
ventriloquist *n* one who can speak and throw his voice without apparent movement of lips; *a* **ventriloquial**; *n* **ventriloquism**.
venture *n* risky course of action; financial speculation; *v* expose to risk or danger; dare to go etc.; presume to put forward; *a* **venturesome**.
venue *n* (*leg*) place fixed for trial; (*fig*) meeting-place.
Venus *n* Roman goddess of beauty and love; planet second nearest to sun; beautiful woman.
veracious *a* truthful; true; *n* **veracity**.
veranda(h) *n* open portico outside house.
verb *n* part of speech expressing action, existence in present, past, or future; *a* **verbal** pertaining to

words; literal; spoken, not written; *advs* **verbally** by word of mouth; **verbatim** word for word.
verbena *n* genus of fragrant herbaceous plants.
verbiage *n* use of too many words; *a* **verbose** prolix; wordy; *n* **verbosity.**
verdant *a* green, as of fresh young grass, foliage etc.; (*fig*) youthful; *n* **verdure** green vegetation.
verdict *n* finding; decision of jury; opinion, judgement.
verdigris *n* greenish blue deposit formed on copper or brass.
verge *n* edge, brink; *v* **v. on** approach, border on.
verger *n* bearer of wand of office; church caretaker.
verify *v* prove; confirm; authenticate; *a* **verifiable;** *n* **verification.**
verily *adv* truly, in truth.
verisimilitude *n* appearance of truth; likelihood.
veritable *a* real, genuine, true, actual.
verity *n* truth, reality; established fact.
vermicelli *n* thin, worm-like kind of macaroni.
vermiform *a* worm-shaped; *n* **vermicide** preparation for killing worms.
vermilion *a* & *n* (of) brilliant red colour.
vermin *n* destructive, harmful animals (*usu* small) collectively; *a* **verminous** infested with vermin.
vermouth *n* fortified white wine flavoured with wormwood etc.
vernacular *a* of native, commonly spoken language; *n* native dialect; strong language.
vernal *a* of spring.
veronica *n* genus of flowering herbs.
versatile *a* adaptable; changeable; fickle; many-sided; *n* **versatility.**
verse *n* sub-division of poem or chapter of Bible; poetry; *v* **versify** tell in verse; compose verses; *n* **versification.**
version *n* translation; personal account, statement.
verso *n* left hand or reverse of page of book; reverse of coin, medal.
versus *prep* (*abbrev* **v.**) against.
vertebra *n* one of joints of spine; *a* **vertebrate**

having backbone; *n* vertebrate animal; *a* **vertebral** pertaining to vertebrae.

vertex *n* summit; zenith; *pl* **vertices**; *a* **vertical**; overhead; perpendicular.

vertigo *n* giddiness; *a* **vertiginous.**

verve *n* vigour, liveliness of spirit.

very *a* actual, real; *adv* exceedingly; absolutely.

Very light *n* coloured flare fired as distress signal or momentary lighting.

vesicle *n* blister; small sac, cavity filled with air or fluid; *a* **vesicular.**

vespers *n pl* evensong.

vessel *n* any hollow article or receptacle; ship; duct for blood, fluid, sap etc. of animal or plant body.

vest *n* undergarment worn on upper part of body; waistcoat; *v* endow; confer right, power etc.; *n* **vestment** ceremonial garment worn by clergy.

vestal *a* chaste, pure, virgin.

vestibule *n* ante-chamber, lobby.

vestige *n* visible trace, or mark; rudimentary survival (of organ, etc.); *a* **vestigial.**

vestry *n* room in church where vestments and Communion vessels are kept, and parish meetings are held.

vet *n* (*coll*) *abbrev* of **veterinary (surgeon)**; *v* (*coll*) examine critically.

vetch *n* plants of bean family.

veteran *n* one with long experience *esp* in fighting services.

veterinary *a* of, concerned with diseases of animals; *n* **v. surgeon** one trained to treat sick animals.

veto *n* constitutional right to reject an enactment, or act of administration; absolute prohibition; *v* forbid; excercise veto against.

vex *v* irritate, cause worry to; *n* **vexation** mental distress; worry; *as* **vexatious; vexed** angry, cross, much disputed.

via *adv* by way of, calling at.

viable *a* capable of maintaining separate existence; practicable; *n* **viability.**

viaduct *n* long, high bridge carrying railway, road etc. over valley.

vial, phial *n* small glass bottle.
viands *n pl* articles of food, provisions.
vibrate *v* move rapidly to and fro; quiver; oscillate; *n* **vibration**; *as* **vibratory**; **vibrant** throbbing; resonant.
vicar *n* clergyman in charge of parish; *n* **vicarage** house of vicar.
vicarious *a* acting as substitute; done, felt on behalf of another.
vice *n* defect, fault; wickedness; immoral conduct, depravity; *a* **vicious** lewd, grossly immoral, (of horse) badly trained, having bad tricks and habits; **v. circle** chain of events each of which aggravates the other detrimentally.
vice *n* device for holding, gripping an object in given position.
vice- *prefix forms compounds with meaning of* second to; in place of. *Such compounds are not given where the meaning may be deduced from the simple word.*
viceroy *n* one who rules as representative of sovereign; *fem* **vicereine** wife of viceroy; *a* **viceregal**; *n* **viceroyalty**.
vice-versa *adv* conversely.
vicinity *n* nearness; neighbourhood.
vicissitudes *n pl* ups-and-downs of life.
victim *n* human being or animal offered as sacrifice; one who suffers through no fault of his own; *v* **victimize** make to suffer; penalize *esp* unjustly; *n* **victimization**.
victor *n* conqueror; winner; *n* **victory** conquest; act of winning; *a* **victorious** triumphant; winning.
victual *n* (*usu pl*) food; *v* supply, take in stores, food; *n* **victualler** supplier of victuals; **licensed v.** publican licensed to sell alcoholic liquor.
vicuna *n* llama-like animal; fine cloth made from its wool (and cotton).
video *a* pertaining to television; *n* **videotape** recording of both sound & picture on magnetic tape.
vie *v* strive with; rival; content with.
view *n* act of seeing; sight, scene; picture, photograph of scenery etc.; opinion; plan, intention; *v* look at; consider; hold specified opinion; *ns* **viewer**

one who views, watches (*esp* TV); **view-finder** part of camera showing area to be photographed; **view-point** opinion; standpoint.

vigil *n* act of keeping watch (*esp* on sick-bed) or of praying all night; eve of feast-day; *a* **vigilant** watchful, alert; *n* **vigilance**.

vignette *n* small delicate illustration in book; (*fig*) short word-sketch.

vigour *n* strength, potency; vitality; *a* **vigorous** strong, active, forceful.

Viking *n* Scandinavian pirate or sea-rover.

vile *a* depraved; shameful; atrocious; *n* **vileness**; *v* **vilify** speak ill of; slander; *n* **vilification**.

villa *n* smallish suburban house; country house *esp*. in Italy or south of France.

village *n* small rural community with cottages, shops, church etc.; *n* **villager**.

villain *n* scoundrel; *a* **-ous** wicked, vile; *n* **villainy**.

villein *n* feudal serf.

vim *n* (*coll*) energy, vigour.

vinaceous *a* of grapes or wine.

vinaigrette *n* bottle for smelling-salts; salad dressing.

vindicate *v* establish truth or merit of; prove innocence of; *ns* **vindication**; **vindicator**.

vindictive *a* revengeful; punitive.

vine *n* climbing plant with tendrils, *esp* one bearing grapes; *ns* **vineyard** grape vine plantation; **vinery** hot-house for growing grapes.

vinous *a* of, like wine.

vintage *n* gathering of grapes for wine-making; yield of wine grapes in given year; (*fig*) date, as criterion of quality; *n* **vintner** wine merchant.

vinegar *n* acid liquid got from fermented wine, beer etc.; *a* **vinegary** very sour, acid; (*fig*) bitter, spiteful.

viola *n* genus of plants including pansy, violet etc.

violate *v* desecrate; rape; infringe; *ns* **violation** act of, thing which violates; **violator**.

violent *a* forcible; boisterous; passionate; using, showing great physical strength; *n* **violence**.

violet *n* plant of viola species; bluish-purple colour; *a* of this colour.

violin *n* fiddle; small four-stringed musical instru-

ment; *ns* **violinist** player of violin; **viol** medieval instrument like violin; **violon-cello** large bass violin.
viper *n* venomous snake, adder.
virago *n* loud-voiced, ill-tempered woman.
virgin *n* one who has never had sexual intercourse; *a* being a virgin; chaste; undefiled; (of land) never before cultivated; *a* **virginal** of, like virgin; pure, fresh unsullied; *n* kind of spinet; *n* **virginity** state of being a virgin; maidenhead.
viridescence *n* greenness, verdure; freshness, youthful vitality; *a* **viridescent**.
virile *a* manly; not impotent; *n* **virility** masculinity; sexual potency in men.
virtu *n* **object of v.** exquisite object of artistic merit.
virtual *a* in effect but not in name; *adv* **virtually** to all intent and purposes.
virtue *n* integrity; female chastity; moral excellence; merit; *a* **virtuous** morally good; chaste.
virtuoso *n* one with high degree of technical skill in one of fine arts *esp* in music; *n* **virtuosity**.
virus *n* one of small parasitic agents causing disease; *n* **virology** study of viruses and virus diseases; *a* **virulent** highly toxic; (*fig*) very bitter; *n* **virulence.**
visa *n* endorsement on passport; *v* endorse passport with visa.
visage *n* human face.
vis-a-vis *adv* & *prep* opposite, facing.
viscera *n pl* internal organs of animal body, *esp* heart, lungs, liver, bowels etc.; *a* **-eral.**
viscid *a* glutinous, sticky; *a* **viscous** sticky; semi-fluid; *n* **viscosity.**
viscose *n* form of cellulose used in making artificial silk.
viscount *n* rank of nobility immediately below earl; *fem* **-ess.**
visible *a* perceptible; apparent to the eye; *n* **visibility** state, quality of being visible; degree of atmospheric clarity *esp* in navigation.
vision *n* sight; intuition; something seen; apparition, phantom; *a* **visionary** impracticable; unreal; *n* impractical idealist.

visit *v* go to see, call upon socially; inspect; *n* temporary stay; social or professional call; *ns* **visitor**; **visitation** official, formal visit; calamity.
visor, vizor *n* movable front part of helmet.
vista *n* distant view *esp* if seen through avenue of trees etc.; mental prospect of past events etc.
visual *a* of sight; **v. aids** diagrams, pictures etc used in teaching; *v* **-ize** form mental picture of.
vital *a* essential to life; lively, animated; necessary to some object or purpose; *n* **vitality** capacity to live; vigour; *v* **vitalize** make alive; give animation to.
vitamin *n* one of organic substances present in food, essential for preventing deficiency diseases.
vitiate *v* destroy force of; taint; (*leg*) invalidate; *n* **vitiation**.
viticulture *n* cultivation of grape-vines.
vitreous *a* pertaining to glass; glassy, transparent; *v* **vitrify** convert, become converted, into glass; *n* **vitrifaction**; *a* **vitriform** glass like.
vitriol *n* sulphuric acid; (*fig*) biting sarcasm; *a* **vitriolic**.
vituperate *v* abuse loudly, scold violently; *n* **-ation**.
vivacity *n* liveliness, gaiety, sprightliness; *a* **vivacious**.
vivarium *n* place where living animals are kept in natural surroundings.
viva-voce *adv* by word of mouth; *n* oral examination.
vivid *a* (of colour) brilliant, intense; animated, graphic.
viviparous *a* bringing forth young alive and capable of independent life.
vivisection *n* operating or experimenting on living animals.
vixen *n* female fox; (*fig*) spiteful woman.
vizier *n* State Minister in Moslem countries.
vocabulary *n* stock of words used by person; alphabetical list of words, and their meanings.
vocal *a* of voice; uttered by voice; *n* **vocalist** singer.
vocation *n* profession, occupation; divine call to spiritual or religious life; *a* **vocational**.
vocative *n* (*gram*) case used in addressing or calling person or object.

vociferate *v* shout; bawl, utter loud cries; *a* **vociferous** noisy; *n* **vociferation.**
vodka *n* Russian spirit distilled from rye.
vogue *n* prevailing mode, custom etc.; popularity.
voice *n* sound produced by organs of speech; quality of such sound; wish, desire expressed as vote; *v* give utterance to, express; *a* **voiceless.**
void *a* empty; lacking; legally invalid; *n* empty space, vacuum; *v* excrete from body; nullify.
voile *n* thin cotton, woollen or silken material.
volatile *a* evaporating quickly; changeable; lively but unstable, *n* **volatility**; *v* **volatilize** render, become volatile; evaporate.
vol-au-vent *n* light raised pie of puff pastry.
volcano *n* mountain formed by eruption of molten lava, ashes etc. through opening in earth's crust; *a* **volcanic** of, like volcano; (*fig*) acting with sudden violence.
vole *n* mouse-like rodent.
volition *n* act or faculty of willing; choosing.
volley *n* number of missiles thrown or shot at once; (*fig*) torrent of words, etc.; (tennis etc.) striking of ball before it touches ground; *v* fire, hit volley; *n* **v. ball** hand ball game played over high net.
volt *n* unit of electromotive force; *ns* **voltage**; such force measured in units; **voltmeter** instrument for measuring electromotive force.
volte-face *n* reversal of opinion or direction.
voluble *a* fluent in speech; talkative; *n* **volubility.**
volume *n* book; mass, bulk, size in cubic units; intensity of sound; *a* **voluminous** bulky; abundant.
voluntary *a* acting without compulsion; done freely; (hospitals etc.) supported by private donations; *n* organ music before & after church service.
volunteer *n* one who offers services of own free will; *esp* in armed forces; *v* offer freely.
voluptuous *a* fond of, addicted to sensual pleasure; plump and sexually attractive; *n* **voluptuary** one addicted to luxurious sensual pleasures.
vomit *v* discharge from stomach through mouth; *n* that which has been vomited.

voodoo *n* form of witchcraft practised by W. Indian & U.S. negroes.
voracious *a* greedy ravenous; *n* **voracity**.
vortex *n* whirlpool; whirling mass; (*fig*) anything which engulfs; *pl* **vortices**; *a* **vortical**.
vote *n* formal expression of one's wish, opinion etc.; right to vote at elections etc.; *v* give vote; (*coll*) suggest; *n* **voter**.
votary *n* one vowed to service of a god, devotee of cause etc.; (*fem*) **votaress**; *a* **votive** given, offered to fulfil vow.
vouch *v* guarantee; assert, confirm; be responsible for; *n* **voucher** document confirming fact or authenticity of something; ticket acting as substitute for cash; *v* **vouchsafe** condescend to grant.
vow *n* solemn pledge, promise *esp* to God; *v* promise faithfully.
vowel *n* speech-sound produced by unhindered passage of breath through mouth; letter representing such sound.
voyage *n* journey, *esp* long one, by water; *v* travel, make a journey, by water; *n* **voyager**.
voyeur *n* one who enjoys seeing sexual objects or acts.
vulcanize *v* treat (rubber) by sulphur, under heat; *ns* **vulcanite** hard substance so made; **vulcanization**.
vulgar *a* unrefined, ill-bred; coarse, indelicate; **v. tongue** vernacular; **v. fraction** one with numerator above denominator; *ns* **vulgarian** flamboyant, vulgar person *esp* one newly enriched; **vulgarism** unrefined way of speech, **vulgarity** coarseness; rudeness; bad taste; *v* **vulgarize** make vulgar, unrefined, or too widely known etc.
Vulgate *n* 4th century Latin translation of Bible.
vulnerable *a* capable, of being, liable to be, wounded, attacked etc.; open to criticism; easily hurt; (bridge) having won one game towards rubber; *n* **vulnerability**.
vulpine *a* pertaining to foxes; sly, crafty.
vulture *n* large carrion-eating bird of prey; (*fig*) rapacious extortioner.

wad *n* small pad of fibrous material; compact bundle of paper *esp* bank notes; *v* pack, press, etc. with wad; *n* **wadding** soft material used for stuffing etc.
waddle *v* walk heavily with swaying motion, like duck; *n* this gait.
wade *v* walk through water, mud, etc.; (*fig*) work laboriously (through); *n* **wader** one that wades; *pl* long waterproof boots.
wadi, wady *n* dried-up desert watercourse.
wafer *n* thin sweet biscuit.
waffle *n* thin crisp cake of batter.
waft *v* carry lightly and smoothly through air or over water; *n* breath of wind; faint odour, whiff.
wag *v* move or shake up and down or from side to side; as of dog's tail; *n* humorous, joking person; *a* **waggish** comical, droll.
wage *n* payment for labour; *v* carry on (war).
wager *n* & *v* bet.
waggle *v* wag; *a* **waggly.**
wag(g)on *n* four-wheeled vehicle for heavy loads; railway truck; *ns* **wag(g)oner** driver of wagon; **wag(g)onette** four-wheeled open carriage with facing seats.
wagtail *n* small long-tailed bird.
waif *n* homeless, straying person or animal; (*fig*) neglected child.
wail *v* howl; lament; *n* cry of grief.
wain *n* (*poet*) wagon or cart; *n* **wainwright** builder of wagons.
wainscot *n* wooden panelling on walls of room.
waist *n* part of body between ribs and hip-bone; narrowed middle part of some objects; middle part of ship's upper deck; *n* **waistcoat** sleeveless garment worn under jacket.
wait *v* await; defer action; serve and hand dishes at table; *n* act of waiting; *pl* Christmas carol-singers; *n* **waiter** (*fem*) **waitress** servant in restaurant etc.
waive *v* relinquish (claim etc.); forgo; *n* **waiver** legal renunciation.
wake *v* rouse from sleep; stir up, excite; *pt* **woke, waked;** *pp* **waked, woke, woken;** *n* vigil beside corpse; lamentation, feasting during wake; *pl* annual

holiday in N. England; *v* **waken** wake up; rouse; *a* **wakeful** watchful, vigilant.
wake *n* track left in water by ship; **in the w. of** (*fig*) following as consequence of; close behind.
walk *v* move along on foot at moderate pace; cause to go at walk; *n* act of walking; gait; journey on foot *esp* for pleasure, exercise; **w. of,** or **in Life** position in society; occupation; *ns* **walker; walkie-talkie** (*coll*) portable two-way radio set; **walk-out** industrial strike; **walk-over** unopposed, or easy victory.
wall *n* upright structure of brick, stones etc. forming part of building or room, or as fence; (*fig*) barrier; *v* surround, defend with wall.
wallflower *n* perennial plant; (*coll*) girl who has no partners at dance.
wallaby *n* species of small kangaroo.
wallet *n* flat leather case or pocket book; small bag or case for tools.
wall-eyed *a* having eye(s) with whitish iris; squinting.
wallop *v* beat severely, thrash; *n* (*sl*) beer; *n* **walloping** thrashing, beating; *a* (*coll*) of large size.
wallow *v* roll about in water, mud etc.; (*fig*) revel in.
walnut *n* edible nut with crimpled surface; tree bearing this; decorative hardwood used in cabinet making.
walrus *n* large amphibious mammal.
waltz *n* dance in triple time, performed by couple; *v* dance waltz; whirl, twirl round.
wan *a* pale, sickly; livid.
wand *n* long, slender rod.
wander *v* roam, ramble; stray; be delirious; be absent-minded; *ns* **wanderer; wanderlust**; urge to travel.
wane *v* diminish in amount, itensity, power.
wangle *v* (*sl*) use irregular means to obtain something; *n* (*sl*) something obtained by guile or dishonesty.
want *v* lack; desire; *n* deficiency; need.
wanton *a* capricious; unchecked; purposeless; loose, dissolute; *v* frolic without restraint.
war *n* armed conflict between nations; hostility; *v* contend, fight; *ns* **warfare** act of waging war;

(*fig*) hostility; **warrior** fighter; **war-paint** paint applied to body by savages; (*sl*) ceremonial dress; **on the war-path** (*fig*) in fighting mood; *a* **warlike** martial; bellicose.

warble *v* sing with trills, as bird; *n* **warbler** genus of small wild singing birds.

ward *n* action of watching or guarding; minor under care of guardian; division of city; section of hopsital, prison etc.; *pl* ridges, notches in key or lock; *v* guard; *ns* **warder** (*fem*) **wardress** prison officer; **warden** governor; person having authority; **wardrobe** cupboard in which clothes are kept; stock of clothes; **wardroom** naval officers' mess-room.

ware *n* articles for sale, collectively; manufactured articles *esp* pottery; *pl* goods, merchandise; *n* **warehouse** storehouse for goods; *v* store, place in warehouse.

ware *v* (*coll*) guard against, avoid.

warlock *n* wizard, sorcerer.

warm *a* moderately hot; affectionate; ardent; (of colour) suggesting warmth; (*coll*) wealthy; *v* make, become warm; *n* **warmth** mild heat; (*fig*) cordiality; anger.

warn *v* caution; admonish; be a signal to; *n* **warning** notice, hint of possible danger, consequences etc.; premonition; notice to terminate employment.

warp *v* twist, distort; become twisted; *n* threads running lengthwise in fabric; rope; distortion in timber caused by contraction.

warrant *n* authority; document that authorizes; *v* justify; guarantee; *n* **warranty** justification; guarantee.

warren *n* ground honeycombed by rabbit-burrows.

wart *n* small hard growth on surface of skin.

wary *a* cautious, prudent, vigilant.

wash *v* cleanse with water or other liquid; flow past, lap; *n* act of washing; waves caused by ship's screws; application of thin paint; *ns* **washer** one who, that which washes; ring of metal, rubber etc., placed under nut or bolthead; **washing** clothes to be washed; **wash-out** (*coll*) failure; unsuccessful person; *a* **washy** watery; insipid.

wasp *n* stinging insect; *as* **waspish** spiteful; biting; **w.-waisted** having very slender waist.

wassail *n* drinking-bout; carousal.

waste *v* use extravagantly or uselessly; devastate; cause to shrink; lose strength, become emaciated; *a* desolate; useless; *n* desert; extravagant, unnecessary expenditure; refuse; *n* **wastage** amount lost by waste; loss; *a* **wasteful** extravagant; *ns* **waster** spendthrift; **wastrel** good-for-nothing; profligate.

watch *v* remain awake and alert; observe; guard; *n* alertness; vigilance; (*naut*) spell of duty; small portable clock for wrist or pocket; *a* **watchful** vigilant; observant; *ns* **watchman** man who guards premises at night.

water *n* transparent, tasteless liquid (oxide of hydrogen); body of water (sea, river, lake etc.); state of tide; any liquid secretion of animal body; quality, lustre (of diamond etc.); *v* sprinkle, moisten with water; dilute; cause (animals) to drink; supply with water; *a* **watery.**

water-closet *n* lavatory flushed by water.

water-colour *n* pigment diluted with water; picture painted with this medium.

watercourse *n* stream; channel for stream.

waterfall *n* cascade of water.

watermark *n* faint design in paper.

watershed *n* line dividing two river-basins.

waterlogged *a* saturated, soaked with water.

waterproof *a* & *n* (garment) proof against water.

watertight *a* tightly fitting to ensure exclusion of water; (*fig*) flawless, unassailable.

watt *n* unit of electrical power.

wattle *n* fencing of plaited twigs and wicker; fleshy lobe on neck of turkey; Australian acacia.

wave *v* move to and fro in air; undulate; greet by raising and moving hand; (of hair) arrange in undulations; *n* act, gesture of waving; swelling ridge on surface of water; (radio etc) vibration of electromagnetic forces alternating in direction; *a* **wavy**; *ns* **wavelength** distance between maximum positive points of two successive waves; **wavelet** ripple.

waver *v* flunctuate; hesitate; yield, give way.
wax *v* increase in size, (chiefly of moon).
wax *n* solid insoluble substance, non-greasy & melting at low temperature, used for candles, models, sealing etc.; secretion of ear, bees; *a* **waxy**; *n* **waxwork** wax effigy of human figure; *pl* exhibition of wax effigies of notabilities; **waxbill, waxwing** kinds of small birds.
way *n* track, path; direction; distance travelled; course of action; method; *pl* habits; *n* **wayfarer** traveller; *v* **waylay** ambush; lie in wait for; *pt* & *pp* **-laid**; *a* **wayward** perverse, wilful; *n* **way-bill** list of passengers and goods.
we *pron* (*1st pers pl nom* of I) ourselves.
weak *a* lacking strength; frail; irresolute; insipid; faint; *a* **weakly** not robust; *v* **weaken** make, become weaker; *ns* **weakling** person or animal lacking strength; **weakness.**
weal *n* mark left on flesh by blow from lash etc.
weal *n* well-being, welfare.
weald *n* open country once wooded.
wealth *n* abundance, profusion; riches; *a* **wealthy** rich; *n* **wealthiness.**
wean *v* accustom to food other than mother's milk; (*fig*) cause to break away from object of interest etc.
weapon *n* any object used for attack or defence.
wear *v* to be clothed, have upon body; bear; diminish, be reduced by use; withstand usage; (*sl*) tolerate; *pt* **wore;** *pp* **worn;** *n* act of wearing; clothes; damage from usage; lasting quality.
weary *a* tired; bored by; tedious; *v* tire; become bored by; *n* **weariness;** *a* **wearisome,** tiresome, tedious.
weasel *n* carnivorous animal resembling ferret.
weather *n* general atmospheric conditions; *v* expose to action of weather, season; show effect of such exposure; come safely through; *ns* **weathercock, -vane** pivoting device indicating wind-direction; *as* **weather-beaten** having rough, sunburnt skin; showing effects of exposure.
weave *v* form (threads) into web or fabric by intertwining; plait; wind in and out; *pt* **wove;** *pp* **woven;**

ns **weaver**; **weaving** act of doing this: fabric so made.

web *n* something woven; net; cobweb spun by spider; membrane between digits of aquatic bird, frog etc.; *n* **webbing** strong upholstery tape.

wed *v* marry; (*fig*) unite; *ns* **wedding** marriage ceremony; **wedlock** matrimony.

wedge *n* V-shaped piece of wood, metal etc.; *v* make, become firm with wedge; split with wedge; fix immovably; **thin end of the w.** slight, unimportant action having considerable results.

Wedgwood *n* (P) fine earthenware; **W. blue** soft powdery blue.

Wednesday *n* fourth day of week.

wee *a* very small, tiny; *n* & *v* (*sl*) urine, urinate.

weed *n* wild plant *esp* one which tends to choke cultivated ones; *v* free (ground) from weeds; *a* **weedy** full of weeds; lanky.

weeds *n pl* widow's mourning dress.

week *n* period of seven days *esp* from Sunday to Saturday; *ns* **weekday** any day except Sunday; **week-end** from Friday or Saturday until Monday; *a* & *adv* **weekly** once a week.

weep *v* shed tears; (of trees etc.) droop gracefully; *pt* & *pp* **wept**.

weevil *n* small beetle harmful to corn etc.

weft *n* threads woven into and crossing warp; woof.

weigh *v* test weight of by scales etc.; have specified weight; (*fig*) consider; raise (anchor) from water; *n* **weight**; heaviness of anything; one of standardized pieces of metal used to ascertain weight of mass of anything; (*fig*) value, significance; *v* burden, overload, *a* **weighty** heavy; important.

weir *n* river-dam.

weird *a* eerie, uncanny.

welcome *a* causing gladness; free to use or enjoy; *n* cordial greeting on arrival; *v* greet.

weld *v* unite (hot metal) by fusion or pressure; (*fig*) unite; *n* **welder**.

welfare *n* well-being; comfort, health, happiness.

welkin *n* (*poet*) sky.

well *a* in good health; suitable; favourable; *adv*

satisfactorily; skilfully; easily; *interj* expressing surprise, doubt etc.; *as* **well-done** thoroughly cooked; **well-off** rich, well-to-do.

well *n* shaft sunk to obtain water or oil; natural spring; liftshaft; deep enclosed space in building; *v* spring, gush.

wellingtons *n pl* waterproof boots up to knee.

Welsh *a* of Wales, its people or language; *n* **W. rabbit (rarebit)** toasted cheese.

welsh, welch *v* (of bookmaker) decamp without paying winners of bets; *n* **welsher, welcher.**

welt *n* strip fixed to shoe to strengthen join between sole and upper; ribbed edging to top of sock etc.; weal; *v* provide with welt; (*coll*) thrash.

welter *v* wallow, tumble; *n* tumult; disorder.

welter-weight *n* boxer weighing between 135 and 147 lbs.; extra weight carried by racehorse.

wen *n* sebaceous cyst on skin.

wench *n* young woman.

wend *v* **w. one's way** proceed slowly on journey.

werewolf *n* (myth) person changed into wolf.

Wesleyan *a* of John Wesley and Church founded by him.

west *n* direction of setting sun; one of four points of compass; (*usu cap*) capitalist as opposed to Communist countries; America & Europe as opposed to Asia; *a* pertaining to the west; situated in or facing west; *a* **westerly**; **western**; **westward**; *n* **western** film, story dealing with cowboy life in American West, *v* **go west** (*coll*) die.

wet *a* covered, saturated, moistened with liquid; rainy; *v* make wet; *n* moisture, rain; *n* **w. blanket** (*coll*) spoilsport; **w. nurse** woman who suckles another's child.

wether *n* castrated ram.

whack *v* hit, slap sharply, noisily *esp* with stick; *n* such blow; (*sl*) due share; *a* **whacking** (*coll*) huge; *n* beating.

whale *n* huge aquatic mammal; **w. of a** (*coll*) great; *ns* **whalebone** thin, horny substance growing in upper jaw of some whales; **whaler** man, ship engaged in hunting whales; *v* **whale** hunt whales.

wharf *n* berth where ships tie up, load & unload; *ns* **wharfage** dues for use of wharf; **wharfinger** wharf owner or manager.
what *pron* that, those which; which thing? how much? *a* which? of which kind? how much, how great.
what(so)ever *pron* & *a* anything at all; no matter which; emphatic form of WHAT.
whatnot *n* shelved display-case for ornaments etc.
wheat *n* cereal plant; edible grain, ground into flour; *a* **wheaten** made from wheat.
wheatear *n* small migratory bird, like thrush.
wheedle *v* coax, cajole.
wheel *n* circular frame with spokes or solid disc, revolving round axle; *v* move on wheels; cause (line of men) to turn as on pivot; *n* **wheelbarrow** barrow with one wheel; **wheelhouse** enclosed space on deck for housing helmsman, wheel, compass etc.; **wheelbase** distance between front and rear axles of vehicles; **wheelwright** one who makes and repairs wheels and wheeled vehicles.
wheeze *v* breathe with audible friction; *n* noisy breathing; (*coll*) trick, joke; *a* **wheezy**.
whelk *n* edible marine mollusc.
whelp *n* puppy; cub of lion, tiger etc.; ill-bred youth; *v* bring forth young.
when *adv* at what time? how soon? *conj* on occasion that, at time that; *adv* & *conj* **whenever** as soon as; as often as.
whence *adv* & *conj* from what place or source.
where *adv* & *conj* to, at, or in which place or part? *adv* **whereabouts** in what place? *n* locality, situation; *conj* **whereas** in view of fact that; but on contrary, while; *advs* **wherefore** why? for which reason; **wherever** in, to, at, any place.
wherry *n* light row-boat; broad heavy barge.
whet *v* sharpen; stimulate, excite (appetite, curiosity) *n* **whetstone** stone for sharpening knives etc.
whether *pron* (*ar*) which of two; *conj* expressing doubt, alternative possibility.
whey *n* watery part of milk separated from curd.
which *a* what person or thing? *pron* the thing(s) that; what person, thing? *pron* **which(so)ever** any that.

whiff *v* puff; emit slight unpleasant smell; *n* puff, breath, slight gust; small cigar.
while *n* space of time, period: *conj* as long as, during; *v* cause (time) to pass without boredom; *conj* **whilst** while.
whim(sy) *n* passing fancy, caprice; *a* **whimsical** capricious; quaint; *n* **whimsicality**.
whimbrel *n* kind of small curlew.
whimper *n* feeble, fretful cry; *v* cry thus.
whin *n* gorse, furze; *n* **whinchat** small bird.
whine *n* high-pitched noise (in motors) or long-drawn thin wail; *v* cry or emit this.
whinny *v* (of horse) neigh gently; *n* such a sound.
whip *v* strike with lash; whisk (eggs, cream); (*coll*) defeat, overcome; move fast and suddenly; *n* lash attached to handle; M.P. who ensures presence of his party members at voting time; hunt servant in charge of hounds; *ns* **whipcord** hard tough cord; ribbed fabric; **whipper-snapper** impudent person; small boy; **whipping boy** scapegoat.
whippet *n* small, cross-bred dog like greyhound.
whip-poor-will *n* small American bird.
whir(r) *v* revolve, move with rapid buzzing sound; *n* this sound.
whirl *v* rotate, spin rapidly on axis; *n* rapid rotation; bewilderment; *ns* **whirligig** spinning toy; merry-go-round; **whirlpool** rapid circular eddy; **whirlwind** column of rapidly rotating air.
whisk *v* sweep lightly, briskly; twitch, beat lightly; *n* light, stiff brush; instrument for beating eggs etc.
whisker *n* (*usu pl*) hair growing on sides of man's face; long bristles growing at side of animal's mouth.
whisky *n* alcoholic liquor distilled from malted grain *esp* barley; **whiskey** Irish whisky.
whisper *v* speak in low voice; (*fig*) tell as secret; *n* such speech.
whist *n* card game for two pairs of players.
whistle *v* produce shrill piping sound from wind instrument or through pursed-up lips; (of bird, missile etc.) make shrill sound; summon by whistle; *n* shrill, piercing sound; device, instrument producing such sound; *n* **whistler**.

white *a* colourless; of colour of unstained snow; of fair complexion, of Caucasian race; (*fig*) honourable, sincere; *n* white pigment; white of egg; white man; (*pl*) white sports clothes; *v* **whiten** make, become white; *n* **whiteness**; *a* **whitish**; *ns* **w. elephant** useless, unwanted possession; **w. ensign** flag of Royal Navy; **w. lie** harmless lie; **w. paper** government report on specific subject.

whitebait *n* young of various fishes eaten whole as delicacy.

whitethorn *n* hawthorn.

whitethroat *n* species of warbler bird.

whitewash *n* solution of lime in water; *v* coat, cover with whitewash; (*fig*) gloss over; clear of blame.

whiting *n* edible sea fish.

whither *adv* to what place? to any place that.

whitlow *n* inflamed tumour near finger nail.

Whitsun(tide) *n* weekend that includes Whit Sunday (seventh after Easter).

whittle *v* shape, pare (wood) with knife; (*fig*) reduce gradually.

whiz(z) *n* buzzing sound; *v* move very quickly; make buzzing sound.

who *pron* (*obj* **whom** *poss* **whose**) which or what person? that person who; *pron* **who(so)ever** anyone (at all) who.

whodunit *a* (*coll*) detective story.

whole *a* intact; entire, complete; *n* complete sum, amount; entirety; *adv* **wholly**; *a* **whole-hearted** sincere, single-minded; *n* & *a* **wholemeal** (flour) containing husk and grain of cereal; *n* **wholesale** sale of goods in bulk or quantity; *a* relating to bulk sale; (*fig*) unlimited, indiscriminate; *n* **wholesaler** trader in bulk; *a* **wholesome** healthful; (*fig*) salutary; morally sound.

whoop *n* loud cry or yell; noise peculiar to whooping-cough; *v* utter such sound; *ns* **whooping-cough** infectious respiratory disease; **whoopee** (*coll*) gay time.

whop *v* beat severely; *n* (*coll*) **whopper** anything especially large; *esp* lie.

whore *n* prostitute.

whorl *n* circular group of petals, leaves etc.; single coil of spiral.
whortleberry *n* bilberry.
why *adv* for what reason? because of which; *interj* expressing surprise; *n* cause of reason for something.
wick *n* length of thread in candle or oil lamp, which when lighted burns until wax or oil is consumed.
wicked *a* evil; vicious, depraved; (*coll*) mischievous; *n* **wickedness.**
wicker *n* & *a* (fabric) made of interwoven osiers etc.; *a* & *n* **wickerwork** (made of) plaited wickers.
wicket *n* small gate or door in larger one; set of three cricket stumps and bails; cricket pitch.
wide *a* broad; far-reaching; spacious, vast, of extensive scope, range; *n* ball bowled past wicket out of reach of batsman; *v* **widen**; *n* **width** breadth.
widgeon *n* migratory wild duck.
widow *n* woman who has not remarried after death of husband; *masc* **widower**; *v* make widow of.
wield *v* handle, make use of (implement, weapon etc.) control.
wife *n* married woman; *pl* **wives**; *a* **wifely.**
wig *n* artificial hair for head; *a* **wigged.**
wigging *n* (*sl*) severe scolding.
wiggle *v* move quickly from side to side; wriggle.
wigwam *n* N. American Indian's conical tent.
wild *a* not domesticated; uncultivated; savage; demented; disordered; reckless; *ns* **wildness**; **wildgoosechase** (*fig*) futile search; **wildcat** (*fig*) unofficial strike.
wilderness *a* desert; desolate expanse of land, water.
wildfire *n* phosphorescent light; **like w.** very rapidly.
wile *n* (*usu pl*) ruse, cunning sratagem; *a* **wily** crafty, artful.
wilful *a* stubborn; capricious; premeditated; *n* **wilfulness.**
will *v aux* forms moods & tenses expressing future, intention, resolve etc; *pt* **would.**
will *n* faculty of deciding what one will do; volition; wish; document making disposition of property

after death; *v* wish; leave as bequest; *a* **willing** ready, eager to help; *n* **willingness.**

will-o-the-wisp *n* phosphorescent light over marshy ground; (*fig*) elusive person or thing.

willow *n* genus of trees, yielding osiers; this wood; (*coll*) cricket bat; *a* **willowy** slender, graceful.

willy-nilly *adv* whether one will or not; inevitably.

wilt *v* (of plants) fade, droop; wither.

wimple *n* linen cloth covering head, sides of face and neck, worn by nuns.

win *v* gain, achieve by effort; obtain as prize; prevail; *pt* & *pp* **won**; *n* victory, success *esp* in contest.

wince *v* shrink away; flinch; *n* involuntary recoil.

wincey *n* strong cotton and wool fabric.

winch *n* machine for hoisting, windlass; crank used as handle.

wind *n* air in motion; breath; flatulence; (*fig*) rumour, hint; *v* cause to become breathless, *esp* by blow; *ns* **windfall** fruit blown down; (*fig*) unexpected good fortune; **windjammer** large sailing vessel; **windmill** mill, water-pump driven by force of wind; **windscreen** front window of vehicle; **windsock** canvas tube flown from mast to indicate wind direction; *a* **windy** exposed to wind; (*fig*) wordy; (*coll*) frightened, scared, *adv* **windward** towards wind.

wind *v* turn, meander; tighten (watch spring) by turning; make into ball; twine; *pt* & *pp* **wound**; *n* **windlass** apparatus for hoisting or hauling by rope or wire wound on drum etc.

window *n* opening in wall, roof, vehicle etc. to admit light, air etc *usu* filled by glass panes; *ns* **w.-dressing** art of arranging goods in shop window; (*fig*) attractive presentation; **w.-sill** ledge under window.

wine *n* fermented grape juice; *v* entertain (person) to wine; drink wine.

wing *n* limb by which bird, insect etc. flies; projecting part of aircraft's structure by which it is supported in air; side, flank; side projection from building etc.; group of three R.A.F. squadrons; *pl* pilot's badge; sides of stage; *v* fly (over or through); wound in wing; (*fig*) disable.

wink *v* open and close eye rapidly; blink; *n* act of winking.
winkle *n* edible shellfish, periwinkle.
winnow *v* separate grain from husks by fanning; (*fig*) sort out good from bad.
winsome *a* engaging. attractive, charming.
winter *n* coldest season of year; *v* spend winter in; tend animals, plants during winter. *a* **wintry** of, like winter; cold, snowy; (*fig*) frigid.
wipe *v* clean, dry by rubbing with cloth etc.; *n* **wiper** one who, that which, wipes; **w. out** (*fig*) erase; destroy utterly.
wire *n* fine-drawn slender flexible thread of metal; (*coll*) telegram; *v* fasten with wire; equip with electrical wiring system; telegraph; *as* **wiry** like wire (of persons) lean & tough; **wire-haired** having short stiff hair.
wireless *n* transmission of sound by electro-magnetic waves; (*coll*) radio set; *a* pertaining to radio or broadcasting.
wise *a* prudent, sagacious; having knowledge, intelligence; *ns* **wisdom** sagacity, sound judgement; **w. tooth** one cut during adult years.
wise *n* way manner, fashion.
wiseacre *n* person who assumes air of wisdom.
wisecrack *n* (*coll*) smart remark, witticism.
wish *v* have desire, long for; *n* desire; expression of desire, *esp* order, request; *a* **wishful** desirous; hoping.
wisp *n* small bunch of straw etc.; thin, straggly lock of hair.
wistaria *n* mauve flowered climbing plant.
wistful *a* yearning, sadly pensive.
wit *n* understanding, mental power; ability to perceive unexpected relations between incongruous ideas, and faculty of expressing them cleverly; humour; *as* **witless** foolish; **witty** cleverly amusing; *n* **witticism** witty remark; *adv* **wittingly** knowingly; deliberately.
witch *n* sorceress; hag, crone; *ns* **witchcraft** magical power *esp* for evil purposes; **witchery** fascination; **witch-doctor** magician, medicine-man in primitive tribes.

witch-elm, wych-elm *n* drooping variety of elm.
witch-hazel, wych-hazel *n* N. American shrub whose bark yields astringent medicinal substance.
with *prep* against; in company of; beside; possessed of; by means of; *adv* **withal** besides, moreover.
withdraw *v* draw, take back; retire; *pt* **-drew**; *pp* **-drawn**; *n* **withdrawal.**
wither *v* fade; decay; grow feebler; (*fig*) snub.
withers *n pl* ridge between shoulder-blades of horse.
withhold *v* keep back; refuse to bestow; *pt* & *pp* **-held.**
within *prep* & *adv* in, inside; *adv* **without** outside; *prep* lacking.
withstand *v* oppose; resist; *pt* & *pp* **-stood.**
withy, withe *n* flexible twig; osier.
witness *n* testimony, corroboration; one who gives evidence; person or thing furnishing proof; *v* see; attest; testify.
wizard *n* sorcerer, magician; (*fig*) expert; ingenious person; *a* (*sl*) marvellous.
wizened *a* shrivelled; dried up.
woad *n* herbaceous plant yielding blue dye.
wobble *v* move, sway unsteadily; *n* oscillation; unsteady movement.
woe *n* cause of sorrow; misfortune; *as* **woebegone** mournful, doleful; **woeful** sorrowful; pitiful.
wold *n* expanse of high open country.
wolf *n* savage, carnivorous animal of dog family; (*fig*) rapacious, greedy person; *pl* **wolves**; *v* eat greedily; *n* **wolf-cub** junior Boy Scout; young wolf.
wolfram *n* mineral ore yielding tungsten.
wolverine *n* small carnivrous animal; its fur.
woman *n* adult human female; female sex; *pl* **women**; *ns* **womanhood** condition of being a woman; **womankind** women in general; *as* **womanly** having good qualities of woman; **womanish** effeminate.
womb *n* female organ in which embryo develops.
wonder *n* prodigy, marvel; emotion, feeling of awe, excited by marvellous object, person etc.; *v* be amazed; be curious about; *as* **wonderful** amazing, marvellous; **wondrous** inspiring wonder; *n* **wonderment** astonishment.

wonky *a* (*sl*) wobbly; hesitant; not well.
wont *a* accustomed; *n* usual practice.
woo *v* court, seek to win love of; *n* **wooer** suitor.
wood *n* tract of tree-covered land; solid substance of trees; timber; *as* **wooden** made of wood; (*fig*) show-no emotion; **woody** covered with trees; like wood; *a* & *n* **woodland.**
woodcraft *n* knowledge of forestry & wood life.
woodcut *n* engraving on wood block; print from this.
woodlouse *n* small insect (*pl* **woodlice**).
woodman *n* forester.
woodpecker *n* bird that pecks holes in trees.
woodwind *n* musical instruments *usu* made of wood & played by being blown.
woodwork *n* carpentry; wooden part of structure.
woof *n* threads crossing warp in woven fabric.
wool *n* fleece, coat of sheep, angora goat, alpaca etc.; *n* & *a* **woollen** (cloth) made of wool; *n* & *a* **woolly** (garment, jersey) made of wool; (*fig*) not clear, woolly-headed; *n* **woolsack** bale of wool; Lord Chancellor's seat in House of Lords.
word *n* simplest element of speech; unit of language serving as name of object etc; brief speech; message; promise; *v* express in words; *a* **wordy** verbose.
word-blind *a* unable to spell; dyslectic.
work *n* bodily, intellectual labour; occupation; product of labour or artistic activity; *pl* factory; mechanism, engine etc.; *v* cause to function; toil; be employed; ferment; make, shape; *pt* & *pp* **worked, wrought**; *a* **workable**; *ns* **worker**; **workman** manual labourer; **workmanship** skill in making; product of this; **workshop** place where work is carried on.
workhouse *n* home for paupers.
working *n* functioning; way in which process works; worked area of mine; *a* of, at, for work; used at, spent in work; *ns* **w. class** proletariat; **w. load** safe load; **w. man** member of w. class, wage-earner; **w. party** committee of experts investigating project; group of people assigned to manual task.
world *n* universe; mankind as whole; particular range

of activities, interests; *a* **worldly** materialistic, earthly.

worm *n* long invertebrate; earthworm, grub, maggot; spiral thread of screw; (*fig*) weak, obsequious person; *v* insinuate (oneself into); wriggle, edge along slowly; *a* **wormeaten** full of worm-holes; old.

wormwood *n* aromatic bitter herb; (*fig*) bitterness.

worry *v* seize with teeth and shake; pester, harass; be anxious, troubled; *n* anxiety; cause of this.

worse *a comp* of BAD; *v* **worsen** make, grow worse; deteriorate.

worship *v* revere, adore as God; idolize; adore; *a* **worshipful**; *n* **worshipper.**

worst *a sup* of BAD.

worsted *a* & *n* (made of) woollen yarn.

worth *a* having specified value; deserving of; *n* merit; material value; *a* **worthy** virtuous; deserving; *n* eminent person; *n* **worthiness**; *a* **worthless.**

would *pt* of WILL; *a* **w.-be** aspiring (*usu* in vain).

wound *n* cut, hole or tear in skin or tissue of body; *v* inflict such injury on; hurt (feelings of).

wrack *n* sea-weed cast up on shore.

wraith *n* apparition, ghost, spectre.

wrangle *v* quarrel, dispute angrily; *n* noisy quarrel; *n* **wrangler** one who argues thus.

wrap *v* fold round; cover (person, thing) in (folding material or garment); *n* **wrap, wrapper** loose garment; covering.

wrath *n* anger; *a* **wrathful.**

wreak *v* give vent to (anger etc.); exact (vengeance).

wreath *n* circle of intertwined leaves or flowers; garland; wisp of smoke; *v* **wreathe** twist, wind into wreath; surround; wind round.

wreck *n* destruction *esp* of ship by wind and waves; ship fast on rocks; ruin; broken remains of structure; *v* cause wreck of; *ns* **wreckage; wrecker** one who engineers wreck.

wren *n* species of small song-bird.

wrench *n* violent twist; adjustable spanner to turn nuts; (*fig*) grief felt at separation; *v* twist; seize forcibly.

wrest *v* tear away, take by force.

wrestle *v* grapple with & try to throw opponent; (*fig*) strive with (difficulties etc.); *n* **wrestler.**
wretch *n* miserable unfortunate person; *a* **wretched** miserable, unhappy; squalid; *n* **wretchedness.**
wriggle *n* squirming, twisting movement; *v* move thus.
wring *v* twist; squeeze out moisture; *pt* & *pp* **wrung.**
wrinkle *n* small crease, fold *esp* of skin; (*coll*) useful hint; *v* make wrinkles in; pucker.
wrist *n* joint between forearm and hand.
writ *n* (*leg*) document issued in sovereign's name giving instructions to do or refrain from doing, something; **Holy W.** the Bible.
write *v* mark paper etc., with symbols representing words or sounds; compose, send letters; *pt* **wrote;** *pp* **written;** *n* **writer** person who writes *esp* author; *ns* & *vs* **write-off** complete loss *esp* of damaged vehicle; **write-up** flattering notice; praise in writing; bring diary etc. up to date.
writhe *v* twist, contort body about (in pain etc.); be distorted.
wrong *a* wicked; incorrect; mistaken in opinion etc.; unsuitable; *n* that which is wrong; harmful act; evil; *v* do wrong to; *a* **wrongful.**
wrought *a* worked; **w. iron** iron hammered, beaten into shape.
wry *a* twisted; (*fig*) ironical, expressing distaste; *n* **wryneck** bird related to woodpecker; *a* **wry-necked** with deformed, twisted neck.

X *n* (*math*) unknown quantity; (*fig*) any person, anything unknown.
xen-, xeno- *prefix* relating to hospitality; external, foreign.
xenon *n* inert, heavy gas present in air.
xenophobia *n* irrational hate or fear of foreigners, strangers.
xer(o)- *prefix* dry; dryness.
Xerography *n* [P] photo-copying process.
xerophilous *a* able to thrive in conditions of drought; *n* **xerophyte** drought-loving plant.

X-rays *n pl* electromagnetic short wave radiation capable of penetrating matter; photograph taken by x-ray; *v* take such photograph.
xyl(o)- *prefix* wood, pertaining to wood.
xylocarp *n* hard, woody fruit, or tree bearing it.
xylograph *n* wood-engraving; *n* **-grapher**; *a* **-graphic.**
xyloid *a* of, like wood.
xylophone *n* musical percussion instrument of graduated wooden bars, which vibrate when struck.

yacht *n* light sailing vessel used for racing or pleasure-cruising; *n* **yachtsman** owner or sailor of yacht.
yaffle *n* green woodpecker.
yahoo *n* ungainly, coarse, rude person.
yak *n* long-haired ox of Central Asia.
yam *n* fleshy edible root of tropical climbing plant; sweet potato.
yank *v* (*coll*) pull sharply, jerk; *n* sharp tug.
yankee *n* inhabitant of New England states; (*coll*) American.
yap *n* bark of small dog; *v* yelp, bark; (*coll*) chatter.
yarborough *n* hand at bridge or whist with no card higher than nine.
yard *n* unit of length, 36 ins; long spar supporting sail; *n* **yardstick** yard-measure; (*fig*) standard of comparison.
yard *n* enclosed space, often paved, adjoining building; enclosure for some specific purpose.
yarn *n* continuous thread of twisted fibres (of wool, cotton etc.); (*coll*) tale, chat; *v* tell a yarn; talk at length.
yarrow *n* white-flowered perennial herb.
yashmak *n* veil worn by Mohammedan women.
yaw *v* (of ship, aircraft) fall away from course; steer unsteadily.
yawl *n* small cutter-rigged boat; jolly-boat.
yawn *v* open mouth widely and breathe in involuntarily; (*fig*) open wide, gape; *n* act of yawning *esp* arising from boredom, sleepiness.
ye *pron* (*ar*) you.

yea *interj* & *n* yes; affirmative statement.

year *n* period of time taken by earth to revolve once round sun; unit of time, 365¼ days; *n* **yearling** animal one year old; *a* **yearly** every year; *adv* annually.

yearn *v* desire earnestly; feel tender longing towards; *n* **yearning**.

yeast *n* fungoid substance used as ferment in brewing, bread-making etc; *a* **yeasty** frothy, fermenting.

yell *v* cry loudly and sharply; *n* loud piercing cry.

yellow *a* of colour between green and orange in spectrum; similar to colour of gold, lemons etc; (*sl*) cowardly; *n* this colour; *n* **yellow-hammer** yellow feathered bird.

yelp *v* give short sharp bark of pain or anger; *n* such cry.

yen *n* Japanese dollar; (*sl*) intense desire, urge.

yeoman *n* (*hist*) small landowner cultivating his own land; **y. service** effective assistance; *n* (*hist*) **yeomanry** yeomen collectively; territorial volunteer cavalry force recruited mainly from country districts.

yes *interj* expressing affirmation, consent; is that so? *n* **yes-man** one who weakly agrees with his leader's opinions.

yesterday *n* day before today; (*pl*) past times, former days.

yet *adv* until now; now; besides; *conj* nevertheless, but still.

yew *n* evergreen coniferous tree; its wood.

Yiddish *n* mixed dialect of German, Hebrew and Slavonic, used by Jews in Europe and America.

yield *v* produce, return as food; bring in (as financial return); concede; give up; be amenable (to treatment); *n* amount produced; result, profit, return.

yodel *v* warble, changing rapidly from natural voice to falsetto; *n* wordless, song or cry in this style.

yoga *n* Hindu system of meditation, having as object union of human spirit with that of universe; *n* **yogi** one who practises yoga.

yoghurt, yogurt *n* thick milk preparation, fermented by bacterial action.

yoke *n* cross-piece shaped to fit necks of draught-animals, to which plough etc may be attached; part of garment cut to fit shoulders; (*fig*) authority, dominion; *v* harness with yoke; (*fig*) unite.
yokel *n* countryman, rustic.
yolk *n* yellow central part of egg.
yon *a* that, those over there; *a* **yonder** over there; *adv* in that direction.
yore *n* only in **of yore** formerly, long ago.
yorker *n* ball which pitches in batsman's block.
Yorkshire pudding *n* baked batter eaten with roast beef.
you *pron* (*2nd pers sing* & *pl*) person(s) lately spoken to; one, anyone.
young *a* in early stages of life; not yet old; immature; inexperienced; *n* offspring; *n* **-ster** child *esp* boy.
your *a* belonging to you; *pron* **yours** *poss* of YOU; *pron* **yourself** emphatic form of YOU; *pl* **yourselves**
youth *n* early life; state of being young; young man; young people; *a* **youthful**.
Yule *n* Christmas season or festival; **Yuletide** Christmas time.

zany *n* clown; idiot, fool.
zeal *n* ardour, fervour; intense enthusiasm; *a* **zealous** enthusiastic; earnest; *n* **zealot** fanatic.
zebra *n* striped African quadruped; *n* **zebra crossing** black and white pedestrian-crossing in street.
zenith *n* point of heavens directly overhead; (*fig*) highest point, climax; acme.
zephyr *n* West wind; (*poet*) gentle breeze; very thin fine woollen fabric.
zeppelin *n* German dirigible airship used in World War 1.
zero *n* figure 0; nought; starting point on scale of measurement; (*fig*) lowest point; **z. hour** (*mil*) precise time fixed for offensive to begin.
zest *n* keenness, gusto, ardour; relish, flavouring.
zigzag *n* line having repeated sharp bends in alternate directions; *a* forming zigzag; *adv* with such course; *v* move in such course.

zinc *n* bluish-white metallic element.
zinco, zincograph *n* design in relief on zinc plate; print made from this.
zingaro *n* gipsy.
zinnia *n* annual plant of aster family.
Zion *n* hill in Jerusalem; (*fig*) City of Jerusalem; religious system of Jews; Christianity; *n* **Zionism** political and military movement which established independent Jewish state of Israel.
zip *n* light whizzing sound; device for fastening with two rows of interlocking teeth, opened by sliding grip; (*coll*) energy, vigour; *v* whizz; fasten with zip-fastener.
zither *v* flat, stringed musical instrument.
zodiac *n* imaginary belt in heavens, divided into twelve sections or signs, within which moon, sun and chief planets have their paths; *a* **-al.**
zombie *n* corpse revived and controlled by witchcraft in W. Indian voodoo; (*coll*) one who acts mechanically, without feeling or intelligence.
zone *n* belt, band; one of five regions of earth differentiated by climate; specified area, region; *n* **zoning** designated areas of town etc.
zoolite *n* fossil animal.
zoology *n* scientific study of animals; *n* **zoologist**; *a* **zoological** of, for zoology; *n* **z.gardens** place where wild animals are kept for exhibition; *ns* **zoodynamics** animal physiology; **zoogeography** study of distribution of animals on surface of earth.
zoom *v* compel aircraft to ascend rapidly at sharp angle; (*fig*) rise sharply in price; *n* **zoom** zooming.
zoophyte *n* plant-like animal, *e.g.* sea-anemone.
Zouave *n* French infantryman, originally recruited from Algeria.
Zulu *n* member, language of Bantu or Kaffir people of S. Africa.
zygal *a* H-shaped; *n* **zygodactyl** bird with toes arranged in pairs, two pointing forwards and two backwards.
zygote *n* fertilized ovum.
zymotic *a* (of diseases) induced by propagation of living germs, introduced from without.

hugo

Pocket Dictionaries

French–English/English–French
German–English/English–German
Spanish–English/English–Spanish
Italian–English/English–Italian
Dutch–English/English–Dutch
Russian–English/English–Russian

all with Imitated Pronunciation

English Pocket Dictionary
(without pronunciation)

Tourist Phrasebooks

France, Germany, Spain, Italy, Greece, Holland, Portugal and Scandinavia.

Essential words and phrases for most holiday travel situations.

“Three Months” books

French, German, Spanish, Italian, Portuguese, Greek, Dutch, Norwegian, Danish, Swedish, Russian, Latin and English for foreign students.

Complete, concise courses which are essentially practical.

Audio Cassette Courses

French, German, Spanish, Italian, Dutch, Greek, Portuguese and Swedish.

The most up-to-date way of learning a language quickly and easily.
For details of these and other language-learning aids, write to:

Hugo’s Language Books Ltd
104 Judd Street, London WC1H 9NF